CHARLES R. RITCHESON received his B.A. from the University of Oklahoma in 1946, studied at Harvard and the University of Zurich, and received his PhD. from Oxford University in 1951. He has served as chairman of the department of history at Kenyon College, and since1966 has held the same position at Southern Methodist University. Professor Ritcheson is also the author of *British Politics and the American Revolution*.

Books That Live
The Norton imprint on a book means that in the publisher's
estimation it is a book not for a single season but for the years.
W. W. Norton & Company, Inc.

SBN 393 00553 4

PRINTED IN THE UNITED STATES OF AMERICA
1 2 3 4 5 6 7 8 9 0

AFTERMATH OF
REVOLUTION

British Policy Toward the United States

1783-1795

CHARLES R. RITCHESON

The Norton Library

W · W · NORTON & COMPANY · INC ·

NEW YORK

FOR ALICE

Post Tot Naufragia Portum

INTRODUCTION

IN THE September, 1827, issue of the *American Quarterly Review*, John Quincy Adams published an unsigned essay entitled "British Colonial and Navigation System." His object, he said, was "to illustrate the uniform policy and spirit of Great Britain and the United States respectively, and to teach our countrymen how they ought to feel, as well as reason."[1] He succeeded. The son of the second President of the United States and himself the incumbent of that high office, he proceeded to lay down an interpretation of British policy toward the United States which ultimately became a classic piece of national history.

With the War for Independence ended, the thesis ran, the first great problem confronting leaders of the two nations had been the commercial connection between the new republic and the remaining New World colonies, especially the islands in the West Indies. The Earl of Shelburne, "a man of enlarged views and of liberal principles," who made the Peace, and his chancellor of the exchequer, the younger Pitt—"in the dawn of manhood, and the meridian of intelligence, before the ingenuous candour of youth had been adulterated by the sordid passions of vindictive refugees and the selfish interests of the shipbuilders"—wished to continue treating American ships and goods very much as if they were still within the system of imperial preference. This had been the purpose of their American Intercourse Bill. It was a plan founded upon the "principle of equal and honest reciprocity." The fair prospect was blasted, however, by the coalition ministry of Charles James Fox and Lord North, who overturned Shelburne, defeated the American Intercourse Bill in Parliament, and in the regulation of America's trade with the Empire invoked (most unlike Fox) "the arbitrary will of the Crown." A series of Orders in Council beginning July 2, 1783, "interdicting all trade," severed the commercial connection between the United States and that country's natural market, the British West Indies.

The action had been "even more unreasonable and more unjust" than Britain's policy during the colonial period of American history. As long as Americans and West Indians possessed the same sovereign, there was some color of right in George III's attempts to give them both the law. In 1783, however, the tyrant sought to impose his will on a free and independent people! It was "rapaciousness," to be sure; but more, the "*pretension*" itself was "offensive and revolting." The king of Great Britain proposed, in effect, to tax American merchants and his own subjects in the West Indies for the benefit of British shipbuilders and seamen. The Adams temper gave way: there was "not upon the records of human legislation, an example more clearly marked with the violation of the laws of nature, and of the maxims of equal justice."

This was but the first item on a long list of British offenses, Adams claimed. From 1785 to 1788, the United States maintained a minister plenipotentiary (whom the writer had some cause to know more than casually) in London. Fully commissioned to negotiate a commercial treaty on terms of "fair and equal reciprocity," John Adams as minister found his overtures spurned and his country insulted by a refusal to send a British diplomatic representative to the United States. The final affront came in 1788 when a formal act of Parliament summed up and made permanent the provisions until then laid down in the temporary Orders in Council. John Adams went home.

Unwittingly, the son's theme continued, British harshness and injustice provided powerful encouragement for a reform of the impotent Confederation; and the new federal Congress, demonstrating a vigor and a vitality unknown to its predecessor, promptly imposed discriminating duties on imports and foreign tonnage. American views were, however, too enlarged to allow matters to rest there. Within three months, President Washington commissioned Gouverneur Morris to hold informal conferences with the ministry in London to learn, among other things, if Britain was disposed to make a commercial treaty on principles of "reciprocal advantage." The offer was "treated with as little attention as those that had preceded."

Delays and evasions finally gave way to the truth: the former mother country professed a wish for a commercial treaty, but there were strings. She would also have "a treaty of alliance, offensive and defensive," although the cabinet, according to Morris, was divided between servants of the Crown desiring good relations with the United States and those in the grip of "sour prejudices and hot resentments."

Secretary of State Jefferson's report on foreign discriminations against American trade and Congressman James Madison's proposed countermeasures might well have solved the country's problem, John Quincy Adams believed, had the war between Britain and revolutionary France not changed the entire complexion of international affairs. American hostility toward Britain deepened as outrage succeeded outrage: impressment of American seamen, "a prostration of all rights of neutral navigation," and new Orders in Council "utterly incompatible with the universally acknowledged laws of nations." To prevent war, Washington dispatched John Jay on a special mission to London.

Jay's Treaty saved the peace, rescued the country from French revolutionary "infection," and made certain commercial provisions advantageous to the United States. At this point, President John Quincy Adams seemed to say, "So much for dispassionate analysis!" He exploded in anger: "The character of all our negotiations with Great Britain, has borne the stamp of liberal concession on our part, and of reluctant, niggardly boon-peddling, on hers." Britain's was a "captious and unbending spirit."

Consciously or unconsciously, the great majority of American writers on British policy toward the United States during the period immediately after the Peace of 1783 have reflected John Quincy Adams' interpretation.[2] There are disagreements in plenty about domestic politics; but treatment of Anglo-American relations shows a high degree of unanimity. Beaten in war and vengeful, Britain spurned the wise policy of conciliation, preferring rather "the error of supercilious neglect." Early troubles besetting the United States called forth not sympathy and friendship, but "disgust and exultation."[3] Evincing "casual contempt,"[4] Britons developed a policy aimed at "humiliating the Americans";[5] and they plotted "how to punish their former colonies."[6] Great Britain callously and cynically broke the Treaty of Peace; and when, finally, she deigned to honor the United States with a diplomatic representative, he merely per-

formed "shadow motion," designed "to delay positive action" in settling dangerous issues threatening renewed war.[7] Individual Americans, among them Alexander Hamilton, John Jay, and John Adams,
bear harsh criticism for "anglophilia," a term which sometimes seems
to mean little more than a rejection of undying hatred for Britain as
the sole foundation of American foreign policy.[8]

These are salient points in the orthodox American treatment of
the subject. The vein is strongly and understandably nationalistic;[9]
but there are shortcomings common to all national histories. The
view is too confined. It is one-sided, usually based on the vast, monumental native sources and neglectful of those from "the other side."
At the worst, it posits the indefensible principle that the right lies
wholly with one party, the wrong with the other.

The first purpose of this book is to lay out the fundamentals of
British policy in the years immediately after the War for American
Independence, and to examine the interesting changes which developed in them. The second, implicitly, is to subject the Adams thesis
to critical scrutiny and to offer a new perspective on Anglo-American relations during a very critical period.

The list of persons and organizations who have made this book
possible would, if put into print, add materially to its bulk. The
omission of specific mention of some to whom I owe much diminishes
not an iota my gratitude to them. Others must be set down publicly
and openly by name, so great was their assistance to my work.

The Social Science Research Council provided a grant-in-aid of
research in 1955, and followed this with a three-year Faculty Research Fellowship. Without this important support, it would have
been difficult to begin my research or to carry it through to a conclusion. The Eli Lilly Foundation made possible a summer's research
at the Clements Library at the University of Michigan. The American Council of Learned Societies gave me a generous fellowship,
which facilitated the last stages of research and writing. To all these
organizations, and to the splendid and helpful people composing
them, I express deep gratitude.

Professor D. B. Horn, chairman of the Department of History
at Edinburgh University, has a double claim to my thanks. When I
was Fulbright Professor there in 1963-64, he kindly allowed me
time to pursue my own research and writing; and he interrupted his
busy schedule to give several chapters of the manuscript a crit-

ical reading, which both encouraged the author and improved his work. I owe much, too, to the late Professor Vincent Harlow, who more than a decade ago directed my attention to the importance of the problem treated here. His untimely death must ever remain a matter of profound regret to all who knew him and his superb scholarship. I recall also—with pleasure, gratitude, and, it must be admitted, awe—several conversations at the Institute of Historical Research in London with the late Sir Lewis Namier, whose brilliant insight inspired as it instructed.

How can I sufficiently thank friends and colleagues closer at hand? To a splendid host of them, some now beyond the reach of human voice, I say thanks and know the word grossly inadequate. Professor H. Landon Warner, former colleague at Kenyon College, deserves special mention for his helpful and illuminating reading of the manuscript virtually in its entirety.

During the course of my studies, I have worked in many libraries and archives. It was quite customary for the staff in each to be helpful and diligent; but one library and those who work there deserve special tribute. It is the Clements Library at Ann Arbor, whose director, Howard Peckham, and his colleagues have created a place and an atmosphere so finely suited to scholarly pursuits that the Clements is surely unique in this or in any other country.

I am indebted to George Grenville Fortescue, Boconnoc House, Lostwithiel, Cornwall, for extraordinary generosity in allowing me access to Lord Grenville's papers (not all of which were published in the *Dropmore Papers*) and for permission to quote them in my text. I acknowledge with thanks the permission of the trustees of the British Museum, of the officials of the Public Record Office, and of the Librarian of Congress to make use of the extensive manuscript sources listed in the bibliography.

Mrs. Celia King and Mrs. Eleanor Solon typed portions of the manuscript; and Howard Malchow and Mrs. Alice Cochran worked on the bibliography and index. They deserve both thanks and sympathy. On another page of this book, I have tried to make a small payment on the overwhelming debt I owe my wife.

CHARLES R. RITCHESON

Southern Methodist University
March 3, 1969

CONTENTS

PART I

*The Basic Assumptions
Of British Policy*

CHAPTER ONE

The Maritime Danger

IN ALL THE CONFUSION, heat, and clash of contending arguments among British politicians and public in 1782 and 1783, one preoccupation remained constant: how to secure Great Britain's primacy at sea.

Britain's inglorious performance at sea during the War for American Independence had led to a defeat both humiliating and costly. Obliged to supply, equip, and even feed royal forces in North America from bases in the Home Islands themselves, the British navy and merchant marine were faced with a logistical problem insoluble in the age of sail. The long American coastline defied systematic blockade; and at critical moments the presence of French naval forces in American waters was decisive. Rodney's great victory over the French in West Indian waters in 1782 was a unique exception, but it was unable to reverse the tide of defeat.

The merchant marine had suffered grievous losses, too, and this at a time—the colonies then in rebellion—when one of the major sources of ship timber and masts was inaccessible. Further, American shipping, until then part of the sinew and muscle of the Empire, was to become foreign—and thereby doubly dangerous, not merely representing a subtraction from imperial resources, but also becoming an active competitor with considerable advantages. Cheap and abundant materials, for example, meant prices lower for American vessels than for European, the former commanding $33.00 to $35.00 the ton, the latter $55.00 to $60.00. In happier days, colonial ships had been welcome remittances for British creditors. When the United States became an independent power, however, the matter appeared in another light altogether.[1]

Worse, there was the prospect that the former fellow subjects would continue their alliance with France, while geography itself seemed to favor any American design against the British West Indies. Even if Anglo-American peace were preserved, could the Sugar Islands be prevented from drifting irresistibly into the economic orbit of the northern neighbor? Potentially, the situation was as ugly as it was unprecedented. Little wonder that it sparked a tumultuous and bitter debate among Britons.[2]

The quarrel did not turn upon the urgent need to preserve and expand the national marine in face of the American secession, but upon how best to achieve this vital end. The Earl of Shelburne, the architect of the Peace of 1783, and his small band of liberal friends were as solicitous for the country's naval power as Lord Sheffield, Charles Jenkinson, and William Eden, Shelburne's implacable enemies. So were the West Indians and the "Americans," the merchants eager for a conciliatory settlement with America.

Shelburne, directing the peace negotiations in 1782, would solve the problem by retaining as much as possible of the old Anglo-American connection: if independence was necessary, then let it be followed by federal union, with economic and defense systems coordinated. Should Americans accept common naturalization, so much the better.[3]

Richard Oswald, friend of Henry Laurens, of Shelburne, and of Adam Smith and his doctrines, went to Paris at Shelburne's behest to negotiate such a peace with the American commissioners. He soon understood that Shelburne's dream was impracticable: the colonies, scorning even the loosest sort of union, were lost forever. It was a matter of little moment to the Scottish emissary, however,

provided they dont Seperate under the Idea of a perpetual Representation of political Union & Confederacy; & Such as to put it in the power of that Representation, or Congress, to direct & command the exertion of their Naval Power in any manner that may [be] Suteable to the views of that Assembly.

What troubled Oswald more was the Franco-American alliance, with the attendant possibility that

there might be issued from these Colonies, under the direction of [French] Influence, & the allurements of Depredations, Such force of Naval power, as in conjunction with that of France, might be fatal to every foreign possession belonging to Great Britain as well as to every concern we have afloat upon the Ocean in any quarter of the World.

Even if the Americans demanded British recognition of the principles of the Armed Neutrality, Britain should acquiesce gracefully, he advised, since they had it "so much in their power to extend their Enterprises of Navigation to every Quarter of the World, as Adventurers on their own account, or Carriers for other Nations." British opposition would be futile, Oswald told Shelburne, since the Americans were destined to become so powerful at sea that no European power with overseas colonies could safely pretend "to impose any limitations on their Navigation."[4]

Shelburne's emissary was arguing the necessity of a generous peace, but he was preaching to the converted. Determined to salvage what he could of the Anglo-American connection, Shelburne wished to pave the way for immediate economic co-operation and future union; hence, he agreed to a peace treaty which recognized independence and made a cession of territory so extravagant that Vergennes blinked and Britons growled. His settlement included, too, freedom for Americans to take fish off the Newfoundland Banks and in the mouth of the St. Lawrence, uninhibited navigation of the Mississippi (in so far as it was Britain's to bestow), and use of the carrying places between the United States and Canada. Generosity without precedent was but the first half of his grand design. The second, embodied in the American Intercourse Bill, aimed to keep the former rebels economically within the Empire by blending the interests of the two nations—the one, the manufacturer and carrier; the other, the customer and producer of raw materials, preoccupied (it was supposed) for centuries with the opening up of new lands.

The bill's fate was uncertain from the outset. By the time it came before Parliament in the spring of 1783, Shelburne had fallen from power; and the lukewarm support it received from the younger Pitt, caretaker chancellor of the exchequer, did nothing to recommend it to the House of Commons. Former friends of America, among them Edmund Burke and Charles James Fox, advised caution, while those less well disposed to the new republic rallied Parliament and public to a defense of the navigation system, imperiled, they said, by men who would sell out the country to aliens.

William Eden, who possessed much ability and experience in the lower purlieus of politics and who had taken the measure of the Americans at close range as a member of the Carlisle Peace Commission, raised the standard for opponents of Shelburne's bill. His arguments spoke to the hearts of a war-weary and exasperated people: the bill was an effectual repeal of the Navigation Act; American proximity would bring her domination of the economy and the carrying trade of the British West Indies; and Britain would lose a crucial nursery of seamen. In the end, the naval power of the former mother country would inevitably sink. It was a stark appeal to fear, but the response in Parliament and among the public indicated that Eden had touched upon a fundamental concern. The Fox-North coalition ministry, taking over in April, gave the death blow to the bill; and, at Eden's suggestion, an act was passed vesting in the King in Council temporary authority to regulate Anglo-American commerce.[5] A subsequent Order in Council, July 2, 1783, became a major cornerstone of Britain's policy toward the United States for more than a decade. Its principal provision was a rigid exclusion of American ships from the carrying trade to the British West Indies: American produce was to enter the islands in British or colonial bottoms only. Shelburne's dream was shattered.

The economic nationalism of the mercantile system was thus turned against Americans, now alien by choice; and Lord Sheffield, Eden's friend and colleague in the House of Commons, intended that the temporary regulation should become permanent. His celebrated *Observations on the Commerce of the American States* agreed powerfully and cogently with arguments against indulging the Americans in any way. With an eye on Secretary of State Charles James Fox, who at the very moment had an emissary in Paris engaged in commercial negotiations with the American commissioners, Sheffield used massive data drawn from official customs-house sources to prove to the satisfaction of the great majority of Britons that to allow American vessels to carry their own produce to Britain's Sugar Islands would be to invite the loss of the carrying trade and, inevitably, maritime decadence. The roar of approval which greeted his performance was the voice of the nation.[6]

In the end, Sheffield's and Eden's apprehensions about Secretary Fox were groundless. The former friend of American rebels could not—perhaps did not wish to—stand against the outpouring of public support evoked by Sheffield's pamphlet. Ignorant of economics—it was said that he had not even read *Wealth of Nations*—conscious of the increasing unpopularity of his political alliance with Lord North, his whipping boy during the American War, and disliked by the King, who treated him with cold forbearance, Fox was driven inexorably toward the position taken up by Eden and Sheffield. Apparently, it was an unconscious process; and even at the end, with the game lost, he could convince himself that the Order of July 2, 1783, left something for serious negotiation between his emissary and the American commissioners in Paris. If Shelburne's besetting sin was to overestimate remaining American affection for the mother country after the war, Fox's was to underestimate the determination of many of those about him to draw the line, once and for all, between the Empire and the United States. Of the two men, Fox was the weaker. Shelburne knew what he wanted in the way of an Anglo-American settlement, fought for it, and politically died for it. Fox never made a stand. Unfortunately, he was always a man to whom failure came more naturally than success; but on this occasion the Secretary seemed even unaware of the issues.[7]

In the spring of 1783, Fox sent his friend David Hartley to Paris, charged with concluding a definitive treaty of peace and negotiating a commercial arrangement with Benjamin Franklin and his colleagues. Warm-hearted and scholarly, long known to Franklin, Hartley was an eloquent apostle of Anglo-American reconciliation, believing, as he said, that Britain and America must become the closest of friends or the bitterest of enemies. His arrival in the French capital was reassuring to the American commissioners. Apparently inspired by Franklin's (insincere) suggestions that further British concessions would win American reconciliation, Hartley urged a bold course: American independence should be guaranteed by the Royal Navy and American goodwill won by granting the freedom to the former colonials to carry their own produce to the West Indies. American shipbuilding might be encouraged; but this would, as in colonial times, furnish a means for remitting to British merchants and creditors.[8]

The proposal was made before the appearance of the Order of July 2, 1783, and of Sheffield's pamphlet, events which shocked Hartley as much as they did the American commissioners. When the news arrived in Paris, Franklin and his colleagues knew that the game was over, that their concept of "reciprocity"—freedom of trade in their own vessels within the Empire—had been rejected. Hartley, however, striving desperately to keep negotiations alive, wrote frantic dispatches home. Respect for the navigation system, he told Fox, should not obscure the possibility that some "fundamental change of circumstances" might "reverse all its former operations if henceforward it should be turned to the exclusion of all Americans as aliens." Some system of "co-partnership with America" should be devised and Britain should be induced to open her ports to vessels jointly owned and navigated by nationals of the two countries. Only such novel and desperate measures would save the Royal Navy, itself the child of trade.[9]

In the end, Hartley's persistence won him only the humiliating rebuke of his own government and the contempt of the American commissioners, who knew he was powerless to implement his good intentions. Viewed from London, he and the small number of fellow subjects who agreed with him offended on two counts. First, they indulged in "this very absurd notion that a nation could be independent and not alien, enjoying all the privileges of subjects, owing no allegiance." Second, they assumed that naval power was a derivative of commerce. (It was an argument soon to be made systematically and as powerfully as possible by the West Indians.) Hartley and his friends also seemed not to attend to the fact that the Order of July 2 granted unprecedented favors to the alien ships and goods of the United States in British home ports. The Americans spoke of "reciprocity." Let them answer with terms as favorable![10]

Why did not the West Indians and the merchants in the American trade support the Hartley position, or at least oppose the Order of July 2, 1783? Their silence is indeed remarkable. They possessed a long tradition of power in British politics. The Molasses Act of 1733, the Sugar Act of 1764, the retention of Canada instead of Martinique and Guadaloupe at the end of the Seven Years' War, and a large number of seats in the House of Commons testified to the potency of the group.[11] In addition, they were skilfully led and well organized, with two major groups in London and a third in Bristol: in London the Society of West India Merchants and the Society of West Indian Planters and Merchants (with much overlapping of membership and leadership), and in Bristol the West India Club. Famous and substantial island names were involved. The Beeston Longs, junior and senior, were successively chairmen of the London Society of West

India Merchants from 1786 to 1820. Lord Penrhyn chaired the West Indian Planters and Merchants Society.[12] James Allen and Samuel Long were upon occasion secretary and treasurer of both London groups. Among the membership there were Beckfords, Fullers, Braithwaites, and others of power and standing. Their interests were directly involved. Why, then, did they not defend themselves by opposing the Order of 1783?

In the first place, the political scene was one of incredible confusion, with the war just ended and the Fox-North coalition locked in deadly conflict with the younger Pitt and his friends. The levers of power were difficult to find. More important, apparently the West Indians and American merchants had been taken completely by surprise by the Order—"thunderstruck," to use William Knox's word.[13] (Knox undoubtedly claimed an undue share of responsibility for the Order, but his description of the islanders' reaction has the ring of truth.) Finally, the Order was limited to six months' duration; and its expiry coincided roughly with the accession of the Pitt ministry, an event which must have heartened West Indians and Americans alike. The opponents of the July Order thus looked to the end of 1783 as the reckoning time; and after much consulting and planning, they launched a determined effort to win for American vessels admission to West Indian ports.

There was a barrage in the press. In column after column, the islanders and their friends asserted, with pathos and eloquence, that to interdict American vessels in the West Indian carrying trade would be to imperil a prime market for rum and the source of vital provisions. The West Indians could "no more be supported without a free intercourse with North America, than Great Britain can maintain her fleets and armies without taxes." Anticipating the deadly countercharge that they would sacrifice the imperial marine for their own sordid economic gain, they argued that fully 90 per cent of the prewar American trade had been carried in small, crude vessels, often no more than rafts built by groups of two or three neighboring farm families in the South who thus conveyed to the islands their own domestic produce.[14] Ingenious, ingenuous, and untrue! Blatantly ignored were the proud merchantmen of New England, competitors with British vessels in the island trade in rum, sugar, and slaves.

A more authoritative and systematic champion of the West Indian cause avoided such manifest untruth, but he accepted the basic as-

sumptions. Bryan Edwards, property-owner in and historian of the
West Indies, developed his position in a number of published works,
including at least one major reply to Lord Sheffield.[15] His notable
contribution to the controversy's literature paralleled his friends' letters to the press, but heightened the level of discourse immeasurably.
The admission of Americans into West Indian ports, he wrote, would
not give them a monopoly of the carrying trade, if their tonnage was
limited to vessels too small to make a trans-Atlantic crossing. This
simple restriction would secure Britain's maritime interests. Certainly,
the naval strength of the Empire was a vitally important consideration; and every encouragement should be given to home navigation
and shipbuilding. But the navigation system was not first and fore-
most a means to maritime power. It was an economic system. Grasping
the nettle firmly, Edwards declared:

in truth, the monopoly of our colonial products, and the advantages arising
from the supply of the wants of the colonists, might not only be supported,
even though foreign-built vessels were incorporated into the great body of
our shipping, but it may eventually happen, that both our trade and navigation would be greatly improved and extended by such a measure.

Merchants and manufacturers required, however, the cheapest possible freight: and their markets were expanding rapidly throughout
the world. Further, the need for ships to carry their goods was constantly growing. What was to happen if, as seemed very probable,
markets outran available shipping? Clearly, foreign ships should be
used, else trade, like the victims of Procrustes, must be "lopped and
shortened" to make it fit the measure of the British marine. Even if
foreign ships were used, the Royal Navy would ultimately benefit,
since "navigation and naval power are the *children*, not the *parents*,
of commerce."[16]

It was a *tour de force*, a bold attempt to turn the tables on those
who cried, "Care for the British navy!" To reverse the sense of Adam
Smith's pronouncement, if there was enough opulence, defense would
automatically be secured.

While it is possible that free traders of another century found
comfort in Edwards' thought, the immediate reaction was violent
condemnation by public and politicians alike.[17] The press was vitri-
olic. Moved by "unbounded avarice and unnatural attachments," the
West Indians were said to be willing to sacrifice the navy, the guardian

of their very existence.[18] Edwards found, too, an opponent more worthy of his steel: George Chalmers, a loyalist and formerly a resident of Maryland. Returning to London, the exile capitalized upon personal connections to become, in 1786, First Clerk in the Committee for Trade. Esteemed and trusted by Charles Jenkinson, who, as Lord Liverpool, was to chair the committee, Chalmers undoubtedly exercised the considerable influence always at the disposal of the assiduous and zealous civil servant at the subministerial level.

That Chalmers was a man of tough mind and considerable intellect is obvious from his reply to Edwards, a reasoned and devastating assault upon the West Indian position. Any American participation in the island carrying trade, he said, invited enervation of British naval power and the loss of the islands themselves to the aggressive new republic. Contradicting Edwards directly, Chalmers declared that colonies were valuable not for the profit which accrued to merchants and planters, but for the development of the country's navigation. The West Indians proposed to "sacrifice the *end* to the *means.*"[19]

Decisively defeated in the cockpit of public controversy, the West Indians appealed to the ministry early in 1784. Pitt himself received a delegation in late February. Apparently, he led his visitors to believe that he personally favored a direct American trade in vessels of eighty tons or less. The Prime Minister doubtless referred to the Committee for Trade's pending study of the whole matter, however, and he probably recommended that they make their representations in that quarter.[20] The West Indians lost no time. When the committee began its two and a half months' study in March, the first action was to consider a petition from Lord Penrhyn and his associates, strongly urging an amendment of the July Order in favor of American vessels.[21]

All in all, the West Indian performance before the committee was abysmal. It was asserted again that before the American War the great balance of island commerce—75 per cent, Penrhyn declared—was carried in small American ships, scarcely ever exceeding fifty tons and manifestly unfit for trans-Atlantic voyages. Yet in another passage of their presentation it was urged that the exclusion of American ships worked to deprive Britain herself of a profitable trade with the New Englanders who exchanged American cargoes for island produce, sailed to Britain, and there sold the whole, vessel included, as remittance for American debts. Perhaps the contradiction was not absolute; but it obviously involved an attempt to argue two fundamentally incompatible positions. The outcome could have surprised no one. The committee, noting the "indulgence" enjoyed by the Americans through the admission of their produce (in British bottoms) into the islands, pronounced in favor of renewing the Act of Parliament and the Order grounded upon it.

This was not, however, the end of the matter. Indeed, it was scarcely the beginning. The temporary nature of existing arrangements must have troubled the bureaucrats of the committee from the first. Should not a permanent solution be found? Were American supplies absolutely necessary to the islands? Was it possible to supply them from the remaining North American colonies? Now, as Lord Sheffield hoped? At some future date, as William Knox believed?

As the committee's inquiry deepened, so did the conviction that the West Indian request was utterly unreasonable and fraught with the most dangerous implications for the British Empire. Sir Guy Carleton, recently returned from the New World, warned equally against the peril of a strong American navy and the taint, already discernable in the West Indies, of American republicanism. More positively, William Knox quoted official figures to demonstrate the addition of a new dimension to British navigation, a direct result, he said, of the exclusion of the Americans. Corroboration on this point was forthcoming from a number of respected and experienced officials: Brook Watson, for example, Member of Parliament for London and sometime commissary-general for North America. Thomas Irving, the prickly but efficient inspector-general of the imports and exports at the Customs House, summed the matter up bluntly: "As a commercial object, I have never considered the Trade with the West Indies beneficial to the interest of this country, but in another Point of View advantageous, in so far as it promotes our Navigation, and of course strengthens our Marine."[22]

Had the West Indians anything to reply in rebuttal? The performance on May 17 was weak to the point of vapidity. Vague references to inevitable smuggling and to spiraling prices left intact the testimony of the experts.

The committee's report of May 31, 1784, rejected the West Indian argument completely and without qualification, and solidly ratified the policy of the Order of July, 1783. Some 60,000 British seamen,

it was noted, had recently been demobilized and required employment. Were more vessels needed? Then let British shipbuilders set
about it, as indeed, they appeared to be doing already. The West Indians "seem not to be aware that the consequences of success in their
present application must eventually be not beneficial but, on the contrary, even dangerous to themselves by diminishing these resources of
naval strength on which the safety of the British Islands particularly
depend." Asked to consider petitions from the Assembly of Jamaica
and the Council of Barbadoes some months later, the Committee for
Trade curtly rejected them. Since they contained no new information,
their lordships declined to "enter into a fuller Examination . . . than
they have already done."[23]

Whatever the cost in inconvenience to the West Indians, loss to
the Americans, and encouragement to smuggling, it cannot be denied
that a significant increase in British shipping occurred. In 1774, the
last full year of peace before the outbreak of revolution, 6,650 British vessels (including colonial American), totaling 699,818 tons, entered British ports in the Home Islands; in 1784, the first full year of
peace after the war, the numbers had risen to 6,839 vessels (now
excluding American), representing 869,081 tons.[24] Markets other than
American were involved too, but ample evidence points to the beneficial results of the reordering of the trade between the United States
and the British West Indies. Thomas Irving was something of a professional anti-American, or so he appeared to Gouverneur Morris,
who dined in his company in 1791; but there is no reason to doubt
the truth of his statement in 1787 praising the Order of July 2, 1783:
"Near four Years have now elapsed . . . and the experience of that
Period amply justifies the measure." The American demand for British West Indian rum was greater than ever, his official data indicated;
and the islands were adequately provisioned. In addition to the new
commercial acquisition of £250,000 a year in freights, Britain had
given employment to "upwards of 60,000 Tons of British shipping,"
the political advantages accruing therefrom to British naval forces
being "sufficiently obvious."[25] Irving's optimistic conclusion was fully
justified by the data carefully collected from consuls abroad, customs-
house records, and private sources, in the monumental Report of the
Committee for Trade of January 28, 1791.[26]

Newfoundland and the Maritimes were other areas of prime interest to the champions of Britain's navigation system against the

possibility of American encroachment. Newfoundland was especially highly prized as "the grand Nursery for raising seafaring Men." Prevented by law from settling permanently on the island, fishermen were expected to return to Britain at the end of each season. As early as 1765, however, twelve thousand persons had established themselves there; and obviously, in the postwar years, permanent settlement under the guise of serving the needs of the fishing fleets continued to grow on a rising scale.[27] British officials were concerned because men who should have been plying the Atlantic in ships were in fact landlubbers; and, worse still, they were dangerously close to sources of American foodstuffs and produce.

The question of supply became critical in the winter of 1784-85, when famine threatened the fishing settlements. On humanitarian grounds, Prime Minister Pitt moved in the House for a temporary bill to allow importation of American foodstuffs into Newfoundland. This should be done, it was stipulated, in British bottoms only; and even they were required to have cleared out from one of His Majesty's European ports no longer than seven months prior to calling at Newfoundland.[28]

The proposal was innocuous enough; but the merchants of Poole and Dartmouth, home ports for the fishing fleets, immediately took the alarm, and their parliamentary friend, William Eden, now moved to foil this newest attack upon Britain's maritime interests.

Replying to Pitt's motion, Eden treated the House to a waspish tirade. The bill condoned permanent settlement in Newfoundland, he charged, and the admission of American supplies compounded the error. The navigation system, the sole guard of the strength and wealth of the Empire, "however inapplicable to abstracted theories of free commerce," was violated twice over. If there must be settlers, however, they should certainly be supplied with imperial produce carried in imperial ships.

He did not dwell upon the physical hardships Pitt's bill meant to alleviate; and when the First Minister mildly protested that the temporary measure could hardly be construed as a danger to the established system, Eden snapped back that Pitt's argument was "enough to have provoked any man to the rudeness of telling the right hon. gentleman that he had never read the Navigation Act." Charles Jenkinson, whose devotion to mercantile dogma could scarcely be questioned, defended his chief, insisting that the bill was designed to meet an existing crisis and certainly did not preclude "subsequent, and more serious deliberation." Eden remained truculent: he could not sanction the introduction of "systems, by act of parliament, contrary to that monopolising system, which, however described by theoretical writers, must be considered as the rock of salvation and strength of this country." Pitt had his way, of course. There was not even a division. But the watchdog was awake and growling. Newfoundland was to be prevented from becoming another New England, always appropriating "every benefit to itself, without regarding the naval advantages of the Mother Country."[29]

The exclusion of American vessels—coupled with the act "for encouraging the Fisheries carried on at Newfoundland and Parts adjacent, from Great Britain, Island, and the British Dominions in Europe,"[30] with its system of bounties and measures to prevent desertions—contributed significantly to the growth of British shipping. By the end of the first season of the act's operations, there were some 450 ships and 10,000 seamen employed in the Newfoundland fisheries; and a new trade between that island and the British West Indies was flourishing.[31]

A similar problem affecting Nova Scotia and New Brunswick was solved in much the same way and with much the same results: exclusion of American vessels brought important accretions to the British merchant marine. The influx of loyalists at the end of the war quickly exhausted native sources of supply. Desperate governors threw their ports open to American vessels and American produce. By midsummer of 1784, however, the situation settled sufficiently to allow the trade to be confined to British bottoms. An Order in Council of June 18, 1784, was accordingly issued and in the spring of 1785 an omnibus act extended the regulation beyond Nova Scotia, New Brunswick, and Newfoundland to Prince Edward Island, Cape Breton, the coast of Labrador, and all the lands bordering the Gulf of St. Lawrence.[32] A flourishing shipbuilding industry developed in Nova Scotia and New Brunswick, and by 1791 the number of British vessels engaged in trade with British North America increased dramatically. A parallel development was to be observed in maritime commerce between the remaining North American colonies and the West Indies.[33]

A capstone was provided in Charles Jenkinson's monumental act "for the further Increase and Encouragement of Shipping and Navigation."[34] About to become Lord Liverpool and president of the

Board of Trade, he made a proud valedictory to the House of Commons.[35] Imperial ships entering home ports in 1774—including, of course, American vessels—totaled 701,452 tons, he said; as early as 1784, the total without the Americans had risen to 869,259 tons. The moral was clear: wartime losses had been overcome, and British shipping was undergoing a magnificent expansion. Final proof was abundantly documented in the great Report of January, 1791.

Americans at the time, and subsequently, interpreted Britain's policy not as a legitimate effort to build up her own navigation, but as a hostile design aimed at the United States. "There is too much attention to the Navy," Minister John Adams wrote to Jefferson from London in 1785. "The design of ruining if they can our carrying Trade, and annihilating all our Navigation and Seamen is too apparent." There was a deep-seated jealousy of American naval power, he told John Jay; and Britons grudging "a single Ship and a single Seamen" to any foreign nation seemed especially hateful toward an American marine.[36] Here was the classic American view of the Order of July 2, 1783, and of the policy it initiated.

John Adams, America's first minister plenipotentiary to London, saw William Pitt on August 24, 1785.[37] In their "sprightly conversation," Adams expressed alarm at British exclusiveness and, making use of reports from Boston that Massachusetts was about to adopt a navigation act of her own, threatened that the United States as a whole would soon develop a general measure retaliating against Britain. Pitt responded that the American trade was important to Britain, but the kingdom was also "much attached" to her own navigation. The American took up the point and attempted to read the British minister a lecture on the true purpose of the navigation system, which was, he said, "to confine the commerce of the Colonies to the mother country." Sound British policy would entice American trade to confine itself to Britain. Instead of this, he continued, British policy was founded on jealousy of the Republic's small marine and a determination to prevent its growth.

Here, in his reply to Adams, Pitt defined succinctly and clearly the very essence of the British position. "If we endeavored to lessen your shipping and seamen without benefiting or increasing our own," he said, "it would be hard and unreasonable, and would be a just ground of uneasiness; but when we only aim at making the most of our own means and nurseries, you cannot justly complain."

The Americans were learning the hard facts of life in the cold world of sovereign nations. Aliens by their own choice, they were face to face with Britain's vital dependence upon sea power—so much "an object of our dearest anxiety," wrote an anonymous pamphleteer in 1787, that even "a losing trade that promotes our navigation becomes reconcilable."[38]

To British minds, it was naïve for Adams and his countrymen to expect "commercial reciprocity" if by this they meant liberty to carry American produce in American bottoms to every port within the Empire. To Pitt and his colleagues, reciprocity existed when ports of the two home countries were opened to each other's vessels and goods. This Britain, for her part, had already granted. As for the wider liberty demanded by the Americans, Britain had been stung enough by the inveterate hostility of her former subjects. Was Britannia now to place the asp in her bosom?

In judging British policy and the hardheaded empirical men who made it, it seems clear that they served their nation well. Their path was the old and tried one, the safe one. Lord Shelburne and the apostles of Anglo-American reconciliation in 1782 and 1783 may have given voice to a magnificent dream and discerned the lineaments of the distant future. The grave crisis with revolutionary France was not distant, however, and within a decade of the Peace of 1783 Britain would be locked in a struggle of long duration and unprecedented ferocity. When the crisis arrived, British shipping and the numbers of its seamen were at unprecedented levels.[39] Introducing in 1786 his bill for the encouragement of shipping, Charles Jenkinson, proudly referring to the remarkable growth of the British marine, observed to the House that "though we have lost a dominion, we might almost be said to have gained an empire."[40] Had he been alive when the wars with France were finished, he could have added justly, "Aye, and saved one, too!"

CHAPTER TWO

The Regaining of Britain's Pre-eminence
In the American Trade

THE FIRST GREAT OBJECT of Britain's American policy was to secure the British marine in the face of an unprecedented threat. The second was to regain the pre-eminence in the American trade that she had enjoyed before the war. The first required that a line be drawn against the Americans; the second involved a rather different approach.

In the latter stages of the war, fear of losing the American trade became a nightmarish preoccupation with British statesmen and merchants. The result, it was somberly predicted, would assuredly be inevitable decline for Britain; and compounding these apprehensions was the conviction that what Britain lost, France surely gained.[1]

Merchants in the trade passed up no chance to express their alarm to Parliament. Even before the peace was concluded, they demanded "having their commerce restored and being reunited with their former connections"; and, in March, 1783, while Parliament debated the American Intercourse Bill, and again in the following July, addresses to the King prayed the removal of "every difficulty in the way of Great Britain being the medium thro' which the Produce of America is to be conveyed to foreign markets." The mayor, aldermen, and commons of London gave their solid support, announcing their "firm Persuasion, that the great Commercial Interests of this Country and of North America, are inseparably united."[2] The peace was not many months old before it appeared to all the world that while "the firm Persuasion" of the Londoners was well founded, the widespread fears and dire predictions were not.

Even while these gloomy prognostications were circulating, a respectable and growing body of literature was taking a contrary position. Whatever the outcome of the war, it was asserted by several writers, Britain would hold as much of the American trade as she wished. New European markets, in Adam Smith's words, "infinitely more advantageous than that of so distant a country as America," were bound to develop with the return of peace.[3] Another Hibernian, James Anderson, whose work was read by Lord Shelburne, put the matter clearly and succinctly: by ridding herself of the costs of imposing political and economic control over America, Britain might "lose a feather," but in exchange, "obtain a real treasure." The United States would certainly "carry on *from choice* with her a *free* trade as extensive as their circumstances would admit, to the mutual emolument of both parties." The original and polemical Dean of Gloucester, Josiah Tucker, holding that the political connection with the Americans should be "discarded" entirely, insisted that mutual interests must continue to tie the two nations together economically "till the end of Time."[4] It was Lord Sheffield's *Observations*, however, which seized upon this optimistic view and elevated it to the position of national dogma. Every dictate of reason and national interest required Britain to build anew a self-sufficient imperial system, he argued. Across the Atlantic, the Americans would soon learn that they themselves were best served by reviving prewar economic patterns. The Republic required an "inexhaustible supply" of British manufactures for eons to come, and only British markets had the capacity to absorb American produce.

Undoubtedly these arguments encouraged the nation's self-confidence at a critical moment; but the recovery of the role as European entrepôt for the American trade was a *desideratum* of such magnitude that it was not to be left to the operation of "inevitable principles" adduced by optimistic theoreticians. To encourage prewar channels of trade to fill again as rapidly as possible, the Fox-North ministry quickly repealed wartime prohibitions as well as the legal technicalities applicable to American colonial status. More important, even while moving to exclude Americans from the West Indies, the government decided to admit unmanufactured goods of American origin as if they were colonial. Summed up in an Order of May 14, 1783, the measure was followed on June 6 by an Order allowing free importation into Britain of indigo and of American naval stores—tar, pitch, turpentine, masts, and bowsprits. Tobacco, too, was allowed in upon payment only of the "Old Subsidy" of colonial days, 5 per cent ad valorem, and the giving of necessary bonds if re-export were projected. Two further Orders, of November 5 and 19, allowed the giving of bond for even the "Old Subsidy" and the securing of tobacco under the King's locks until required by the owner, either for domestic vending or for re-export—a measure operating to reduce considerably the merchant's committed capital. American tobacco was further favored by the continuation of the prohibition on domestic cultivation and of very high duties on Spanish and Portuguese weed. Further, a new Act of Parliament provided for a drawback on all duties upon the re-export from Britain of American rice.[5]

An omnibus Order of December 26, 1783, summed up these regulations, and although whale oil was excluded, the list of items admitted from the United States at a lower rate of duty than similar produce from other countries was impressive. In addition to those mentioned already, it included dyers' berries, beaver skins, cocoa nuts, coffee, pimento, pot and pearl ash, undressed calfskin, hemp, hides, bar iron, pig iron, raw silk, and timber.[6] George Chalmers roundly declared that in the whole of international trade "there is not to be found a traffick so liberal in its policy and so unrestricted in its vent."[7] In Paris, even the American commissioners accepted the Orders of May 14 and June 6 as evidence of Britain's liberal and friendly disposition; while in London, Secretary Fox rightly described British policy as affording favors to American trade exceeding the treatment extended to any other "most favored nation." Britain knew that the United States was bound by her treaties with France and Holland not to afford unique commercial privileges to any other power; but, it was asserted, the former mother country was content to be treated equally with her competitors. Hence, in the British view, the country clearly exceeded "reciprocity" toward the former colonies; and the rising threat of West Indians and Americans reacting angrily to the Order of July 2 to retaliate against Britain made little sense logically and none commercially.[8]

Senseless, perhaps, but nonetheless worthy of consideration, the possibility of an American embargo upon trade with the British West Indies and the Empire was duly examined by the Committee for Trade in the spring of 1784. It was quickly established that a flood of British goods had already poured into the parched American market, thereby demonstrating the force of both economic interests and necessity, which would operate, be the American reaction what it might.

If it came to an attempt to cut off commercial relations with Britain, British goods were sure to find their way circuitously to the new republic through France and Holland. British credit, especially, was irreplaceable, a fact underscored by French and Dutch efforts to vend goods in New York, but only for immediate cash payment—a condition arising from the many bankruptcies suffered by continental traders in the United States. "So far from attempting to shake off their commercial connection with us," Thomas Irving concluded about the Americans in his testimony before the committee, "they, within their present situation and for many Years, [will] be under the necessity of courting our Credit more than at any former period." In truth, William Knox assured their lordships, American orders for British goods were greater than ever before in history.

The committee rendered its judgment in the Report of May 31, 1784.[9] All available information indicated a flourishing state of affairs for British interests—in the United States, in the West Indies, in the remaining North American colonies, and at home. American trade (in British bottoms) to the West Indies took off annually seven million gallons of rum, a necessary item in the American economy, and gave the United States a favorable balance of £345,000 a year. It was highly unlikely that the Americans would interrupt so profitable a trade. Although detailed figures were not yet available, British exports to America were obviously greater in volume than ever before. The inference was clear: "The Americans would never have given Orders for so large a Quantity of Goods if they had really meant to prohibit or obstruct the Commerce of this Country." Having bought British goods even during the war, were they likely to forego them during a time of peace? The committee was confident that the quality of British produce and the availability of British credit were sufficient inducements to secure the patronage of American consumers against any possible obstacle interposed by the authorities in the former colonies. Only one amendment in the present happy state of affairs suggested itself to the committee: it appeared that some British merchants "have given credit beyond all bounds of mercantile Judgement and Discretion."[10]

Considerable economic distress arose. from the massive exportations of 1783. With the American market glutted, and lacking many of the old means of remitting to Britain, American merchants found debts mounting rapidly and alarmingly. A sharp recession attended by speculation and shortage of specie developed; and as numerous debtors in the former colonies defaulted, British merchants took a sharp second look at the American trade, the loss of which they had so greatly feared only a short time before. One, whose bitterness obviously arose from experience, declared it was strange indeed "to view all Europe shuffling and bustling about who shall first clothe and equip the bankrupt States of America." If they had money or goods to pay for European products, he continued, Americans were bound to deal with Britain, the source of the best and cheapest products they required. If they wanted credit, they would come to Britain too because "in no part of the world will they find so many fools to trust them." The harsh judgment was echoed time after time in the British press; and by the summer of 1786, the widely-read and respected *Morning Chronicle* soberly recommended that "the less our commercial interests are interwoven with theirs the better."[11]

There were Americans, too, who were aware of their country's growing reputation for commercial irresponsibility—and even dishonesty. "It has been the fashion," wrote New Yorker Rufus King to a friend in 1785, "to suppose all grievances originated with the British nation; but in this instance much of the pressing difficulty ... is to be carried to the account of the execessive importations made on credit, and the mismanagement of the importers in the sale of their merchandise."[12] Abigail Adams, in London with her diplomatist husband, agreed. Writing to her son, John Quincy, she said:

Our countrymen have most essentially injured themselves by running here in shoals after the peace, and obtaining a credit which they cannot support. They have so shackled and hampered themselves, that they cannot extricate themselves. Merchants, who have given credit, are now suffering, and that naturally creates ill-will and hard words.

An austere New Englander, she was harsh upon Americans who "thoughtlessly rioted upon the property of others."[13] Her ministerial husband, who felt the ground cut from under him by the conduct of his fellow citizens, wrote in anguish of their abuse of credit, lack of confidence in each other, and "the trifling with public Faith," which had brought the United States to the brink of disaster. Under such circumstances, he wrote home, to expect Britain to change her policy toward America was to be deluded. Let Americans open their eyes and regard "their true situation and real danger."[14]

When the recession immediately following the war abated, Anglo-American trade entered another period of notable expansion; but once-burned Britons never again bestowed the old confidence, fearing unscrupulous "Yankee" exploitation.

In view of official statistics proving a growing trade with the United States, and of continuing suspicion and mistrust of American mercantile practices, what leverage did John Adams believe he could derive from threats to divert his country's trade away from Britain? Once, stung to fury by British coolness to his efforts to gain admission for American vessels to the West Indian carrying trade, he burst out, bidding Secretary of State Carmarthen to consider

whether the United States, if they found themselves excluded from the English [West Indian] islands, would not think it necessary to purchase a free admission of their flour and ships, as well as fish and other things, to perpetuity, by stipulating with the French Court some perpetual advantage, in some particulars, over the English commerce.[15]

The noble lord was unmoved. Adams was bluffing. Both men knew it. No such thing would happen, although some Britons wished it would.

Implicit in the newly regained British pre-eminence was the failure of France to capitalize on her friendship and alliance with the United States to become the European entrepôt of the American trade. During the war, it was widely assumed both in France and in the United States (and feared in Britain) that peace would see American trade naturally centered in France. For its part, the French government—particularly Vergennes, his successor (in 1786), the Comte de Montmorin, and the Comptroller Calonne—also looked to the closest economic relations between the two allies. At war's end, a series of *arrêts* favored American trade. In 1784, free ports in the French West Indies were opened to American vessels; and the use of Mauritius (Ile de France) was granted as an entrepôt for the developing American trade in the Far East. The latter liberty was extended by Calonne in 1787 throughout all French possessions in the vast area.[16] With goodwill in high places both in France and in the United States, what is the explanation for the utter failure of France to win even a respectable—let alone dominant—place in America's foreign trade?

First, official relations were not always smooth. With the battle won, there came quite naturally a cooling of relations. Misunderstandings occurred during the negotiation of the Treaty of Peace. Vergennes was angered by America's success in her virtually unilateral dealings with the British. The consular convention, negotiated by Benjamin Franklin and signed on July 29, 1784, roused hot criticism in Congress, which objected to extraterritoriality for French consuls in the United States. When Massachusetts and New Hampshire, attempting to retaliate against Britain for the Order of July 2, 1783, passed navigation acts of their own favoring American vessels at the expense of all foreign ones, even French, the French were, in their turn, offended. Deeming the acts violations of the "most favored nation" provisions of the commercial treaty of 1778, Vergennes used stern and formal language in his protest to Thomas Jefferson, then minister in Paris: he had been ordered by the king "de vous observer combien peu on a égard en Amérique à la régle de la réciprocité et combien on y est disposé à écarter des principes qui ont servi de baze aux liens qui subsistent entr'Elle [France] et les Etats-unis." The French minister ended with an undisguised threat: "le Roi se trouvera Forcé, malgré lui, de chercher des expédients propre à mettre les choses dans une parfaite égalité." Amendments were forthcoming, but confidence and harmony were not restored.

A few months later, Jefferson, whose commitment to Franco-American co-operation was absolute, sought to make some use of an unpleasant and obvious fact. Pressing Vergennes to facilitate further trade and remittances between these two nations, he mentioned that he had heard frequent complaints "that little of our Commerce came to it [France], that while our Flag covered the Thames it was rarely to be seen in a Port of France, and that this proceeded from national prejudices." The charge was true, but the cause mistaken. The remedy, he suggested, lay with France. There followed a *mauvais quart d'heure* for Jefferson. Vergennes flared out at his visitor that the French "did not find a sufficient Dependence on Arrangements taken with us"; administration of justice was so tardy that their creditors "considered it as desperate"; American commercial regulations were in general "disgusting." Vergennes spoke in French; and Jefferson, taken aback and inept in the language, made no answer. In the privacy of his study, however, and to a fellow American, he admitted that Vergennes had raised problems, "new, serious, and delicate."[17] They were never to be solved.

An important reason lay in the private sector. Let French official policy be ever so favorable to the United States, let Thomas Jefferson labor night and day in behalf of Franco-American trade, the merchants of the two nations did not draw well together. Differences in language, religion, and custom combined with the officiousness of bureaucracy and powerful vested interests—as for example, the Fermiers-Général—to revive old prejudices and animosities and to create new impediments to a flourishing trade. In the summer of 1784, the Duke of Dorset, British ambassador in Paris, reported with satisfaction that

the Americans are very much displeased with the reception their ships have hitherto met with in the French ports where they have been detained several weeks owing to disputes with the custom house officers and which have proved the more vexatious owing to the total ignorance of the Americans of the french language.[18]

Without doubt His Grace was showing a measure of *Schadenfreude*, but there is much reason to believe him right in his diagnosis of a deep-seated antipathy between French and American citizens. For example, consider the case of Colonel David Franks, American consul in France. With infinite patience and persistence, Jefferson succeeded in inducing the French to open a direct packet service from Europe to New York in competition with the long-established British service. Colonel Franks took passage on the first voyage. Upon his arrival in New York, he fired off to Jefferson a devastating description of his experience. Fatigued and seasick, he and his fellow passengers had found overbearing officers impossibly unpleasant, the provisions inadequate and—scarcely to be excused on a French ship— the wine execrable. The price of passage he thought outrageous; but any other vessel at *twice* the fare would have been preferable. "There are two English Packet Boats now in this Harbor," Franks concluded, "and sorry am I to say that they not only merit a Preference but that they will have it too."[19]

Merchants of the two countries distrusted each other. James Bowdoin of Boston, future governor of his state, used Yankee candor when he told Luzerne, the French minister, that Americans "imagine that there is always some Deceit in the qualities of french Merchandize." Wartime commerce had confirmed the suspicions, with French merchants selling their goods "extravagantly dear," even though they were "the Refuse of the shops in Nantes and Bordeaux," available at cheaper prices in Holland than in France.[20] The rice-exporting firm of Brailsford and Morris of Charleston, South Carolina, complained to Jefferson in 1787 that "since the Peace, we have never had a single French House, that commanded respect, or that has been entitled to it." At the moment, they observed, there was none in Charleston. It would have been altogether better for France if there never had been one, "as we have been only troubled with a set of needy Adventurers, without Fortune or Character, who by importing the refuse of the French Manufactures have effectually strengthened our prejudice in favor of the British."[21]

Frenchmen returned the compliment. Louis Guillaume Otto, going out to America as chargé d'affaires in the summer of 1785, heard from the chief merchants of Nantes and Bordeaux of their discouragement with the American trade. They had sustained repeated losses because of "peut être trop peu de bonne foi de la part des Americans." The Americans who had established trading houses at L'Orient, a major port for the Franco-American commerce, had uniformly failed, "et le nom Americain est devenu partout un signal de crainte et de mefiance." Cash, they told the envoy, was the only basis for selling to America; and this was admittedly an almost impossible condition.[22]

Jefferson characteristically blamed the British for slandering America with "tales of want of faith and bankruptcy," but even he admitted that the French were "too easily rebuffed by difficulties."[23] The case was more complicated, however. Even wartime co-operation was insufficient to erase a century and a half of mutual suspicion and distrust. In addition, there was another insurmountable difficulty helping to account for both French failure and British success in the American trade. French industry, producing great quantities of "modes and trifles," to use Jefferson's phrase, was simply unable to supply the economic needs of the new and developing republic across the Atlantic. Brandy, wine, cambric, and silk, major items of export from France to the United States, might add considerably to the "*agremens*" of life, but they were of limited utility in subduing a frontier.

In sum, by 1785 France had not gained an even moderately respectable portion of her wartime ally's commerce, which had already come to center once more in Britain. The fact furnishes a major part of the explanation for the failure of John Adams' mission to London. Speaking of "the most perfect equality and reciprocity," the American minister meant the admission of his countrymen's vessels into the British West Indies. Clashing headlong with one of Britain's prime national interests, her "nursery of seamen," he found in the threat to swerve his country's trade to Britain's enemy his only diplomatic stick. It was but a broken reed.

In his first interview with the Secretary of State, the Marquis of Carmarthen, on June 16, 1785, Adams took the position that Britain's commercial regulations were harmful to herself because they impeded the ability of American merchants to make remittances to correspondents in the kingdom. Great quantities of goods had been imported into the states, he said, in the expectation that the United States would continue to enjoy access to imperial markets. The result was widespread loss to both British and American merchants. Carmarthen did not meet Adams on this ground, mentioning rather the reports then current of efforts by Massachusetts to discriminate against British shipping. Adams then took a slightly stronger line, asserting the probability that the action of his native state would become general among her sisters. Britain would lose the American trade, "either by increasing manufactures in America, or opening new channels of commerce with other countries, which might easily be done, unless some arrangements were made which might facilitate remittances."

Carmarthen was unimpressed. It was not the part of the British government to protect imprudent merchants who extended credit to bad risks. Neither could he accept seriously the threat that America would turn to manufacturing for herself or transfer her trade to British competitors. Finally, the prospect of a policy of commercial retaliation common to all the states seemed too remote to merit serious discussion.

Adams was shaken, and already pessimistic. In frustration, he imagined a wry little dialogue between himself and the British.

"*Cui bono*?" they cry, "to what end a treaty of commerce, when we are sure of as much American trade as we have occasion for, without it? The experiment has been tried, and the Americans have found that they cannot supply themselves elsewhere; there must be *quid pro quo*; and what have the United States to give in exchange for the liberty of going in their own ships to our sugar colonies and our colonies upon the continent?"

Adams' only answer to these "smart reasoners" was the reminder that Britons were allowed to come in their own vessels with their own produce to all the ports in the United States—"true reciprocity," which he made the central element in the draft treaty of commerce he forwarded to Carmarthen on July 29. If Britain continued to impede remittances from America with her trade policy, he argued, the result would probably be the loss of all American trade.

Privately and to his own countrymen, Adams admitted the fatal weakness in his position. In something like despair, he cast his mind back to 1783, before American trade had fully returned to the British entrepôt and before Britain had decided upon her policy toward America. In those days, he said, America was respected in the former mother country and highly regarded. How the situation had changed!

Now, the boast is, that our commerce has returned to its old channels, and that it can follow in no other; now, the utmost contempt of our commerce is freely expressed in pamphlets, gazettes, coffee-houses, and in common street talk. I wish I could not add to this the discourses of cabinet counsellors and ministers of states, as well as members of both houses of parliament.

The whole nation, he continued, was united in support of the Navigation Acts, a "decided cast" of opinion resting comfortably upon the conviction "that in all events this country is sure of the American commerce."[24]

Unwilling to rest his case with Carmarthen, whom he detested, Adams sought out Prime Minister Pitt himself; and in a long review of common problems on August 24, he once more introduced the idea of a commercial treaty.[25] What, Pitt inquired, were the lowest terms which would satisfy America? Adams answered with a reference to his project then in Carmarthen's possession. He brandished once again the Massachusetts act aiming at discrimination against British merchants and vessels, and threatened anew that the policy would become general in the United States if Britain did not mend her ways.

Presently, Pitt asked the American if his country could grant Britain by treaty any trading advantage which would not (in virtue of the Franco-American Commercial Treaty of 1778) immediately become the right of France. Adams replied in the negative, but added, "If the advantage was stipulated to England, without a compensation, France would be entitled to it without a compensation; but, if it was stipulated for an equivalent or reciprocal privilege, France must allow us the same equivalent or reciprocal privilege." If only British policy were placed upon "so free a footing as that of the mutual liberty of natural-born subjects and citizens," Britain need not fear French competition. If it came to mutual navigation acts, however, France was assuredly destined to win more of America's commerce than Britain. "In short," Adams told the Prime Minister, "Britain would lose and France gain, not only in our commerce, but our affections, in proportion as Britain departed from the most liberal system." Pitt could have deduced no great attachment here to America's French connection; and Adams' concluding advice must have strengthened the impression: Britain should

take from America every thing she can send as a remittance; nay, to take off every duty, and give every bounty that should be necessary to enable her to send any thing as a remittance. In this case, America would prescribe to herself no other rule than to take of British productions as much as she could pay for.

It was deadlock. Adams made a flaming speech to the phlegmatic Carmarthen in October; but he adduced no new argument except, perhaps, to weaken further his unenviable position by revealing on more than one occasion willingness to favor Britain over France if suitable terms could be arranged.[26] In November, Adams, in desperation, drew Carmarthen's attention to a new French *arrêt* discriminating against all foreign fishermen (including American). Here, surely, Adams pressed Carmarthen, was a deliberate and dangerous menace to the British fisheries. It was to be countered, in his opinion, "only by the freest communication of supplies from the United States." Carmarthen was offhanded: the idea "deserved consideration." "And that," growled Adams, "was all the oracle would deliver."[27] The British Secretary's *sangfroid* is not difficult to comprehend. Carmarthen knew the disposition of his neighbors across the Channel better than the American.

Any force Adams might have derived from the French bogey— minor at best—was about to be dissipated completely and publicly, much to American chagrin and humiliation. Britain and France were on the verge of negotiating a commercial agreement of their own. Hard diplomatic bargaining between the two powers occupied the remainder of 1786; and it was not until autumn that a discouraged and morose Adams sent home the substance of the accord negotiated for Britain by William Eden, sometime peace commissioner to the rebellious American colonies. Undoubtedly the most liberal commercial agreement between major powers in the eighteenth century, the Eden Treaty sought to establish an unprecedented freedom of trade between the two nations, until then traditional enemies. Its operation ruined by the outbreak of the French Revolution, it nonetheless stands as a monument to economic liberalism and the rejection of the traditional view that in trade, what one nation gained, another lost.[28] Cold comfort for John Adams! France and Britain, he told Secretary Jay, aimed "to impose upon the United States," adding in somber gloom that the time was not distant when the two powers might well unite against the Republic.[29]

Parliamentary debate on the treaty in February, 1787, was vicious; and it touched on Anglo-American relations in an interesting, if minor, way.[30] Charles James Fox and his Whig friends objected vehemently to the agreement with the "natural enemy"; they argued that France, enjoying unrestricted access to British manufactures and credit, would soon dominate the American market as she had never been able to do with her own resources. Young Charles Grey, in his maiden speech, developed the theme to its ultimate, alleging a deep-laid plot to harm Britain by depriving her of the trade to the former colonies. With something of a theatrical flourish, he produced to the House of Commons a copy of a letter from Calonne, the French comptroller-general, to Minister Thomas Jefferson.[31] Dated October 22, 1786, less than a month after the signature of the Eden Treaty, the letter announced several mercantile concessions to the Americans. These included additional free ports in France, the suppression of duties on the export of brandy to the United States, favorable treatment of American fish oil, the removal of duties on books and certain wines, and other minor concessions. To Grey, the import was sinister. Britain could escape the prepared trap only by negotiating a commercial treaty with America. Why, indeed, he asked—and vague echoes of Whig sympathy with rebellious Americans were to be heard —had not a treaty already been formed? There was no connection capable of producing more good to the kingdom. Were Americans adverse to the treaty? Certainly not. A representative from the United States was in London, willing and eager to negotiate on fair and equitable terms; but clever and insidious France, strengthened by the new treaty, was well on her way to the fulfilment of her abiding ambition—to isolate Britain in Europe and from America, "with whom, upon every principle of mutual interest, we ought to be connected."

Maiden speeches are rarely occasions notable for displays of profound political sagacity; and so it was with the efforts of the young Whig. Edmund Burke held out a helping hand to the neophyte, condemning the treaty as portending irretrievable ruin; but Pitt's friends, Matthew Montagu and William Wyndham Grenville, slapped down the rickety opposition with brief, deadly effectiveness. Old prejudice and animosity in America made negotiations difficult, they said, but even so, "the silent operation of convenience" insured American recourse to the British market. As for the Eden Treaty, Britain gained every advantage, including the supply of America indirectly through France, should the new republic ever decide against her interests to cut off trade with the former mother country.

It was the effective conclusion of the Adams mission. Borrowing an expression from his old enemy, Sir Francis Bernard, the Yankee emissary described himself as "at the end of my tether." No step that he could take and no statement he could make would affect the situation for good or for ill.[32] Soon, the regulations excluding American vessels from the colonial carrying trade, until then promulgated in the form of temporary Orders in Council, were summed up in a new Act of Parliament, no longer subject to periodic renewals. Adams looked on helplessly, dreaming of an America isolated from Europe and passionately desiring to go home.

In the summer of 1789, Lord Hawkesbury's Committee for Trade began the long and painstaking study which culminated in the Report of January, 1791. The massive data proved how successful British policy had been in outstripping the competitors for America's foreign trade.[33] About 75 per cent of the foreign shipping clearing outward from Charleston, South Carolina, in the two-year period beginning November, 1785, was British; and roughly the same figure held good for inbound vessels. For the two-year period beginning September 5, 1787, Britain held 80 per cent of the foreign shipping entering Philadelphia, and stood within 20 per cent of the total American tonnage. In 1789, Britain held 98 per cent of the foreign tonnage entering New York, amounting to 40 per cent of the total tonnage, with the United States herself possessing 56 per cent. In 1788, imports entering Great Britain from the United States amounted to £1,024,000; exports from Great Britain to the United States (representing chiefly domestic consumption, since there was no longer re-exportation to the British West Indies), to £2,106,000, a balance favorable to Britain of over £1,180,000.

So overwhelming was the British mercantile presence in America that a Charleston trader noted, "In walking our streets, whether convinced by the Dialect, or the Names of those who supply our wants . . . we should rather conceive ourselves in the Highlands of Scotland than in an American State."[34] Thomas Jefferson (who, it is sometimes forgotten, did not always speak for all Americans) complained that his country had yet to free itself from British "vassalage"; but British traders had a complaint of a different kind—"not that they have too few orders from America," Lord Hawkesbury remarked in 1789, "but too many."[35]

The reasons for the Briton's complacency are clear: a burgeoning marine and the lion's share of the American trade. Foreign competitors had been overwhelmed. But what of the possibility that an irate Congress might retaliate against Britain for her failure to accept the American view of "true reciprocity"?

CHAPTER THREE

The Question of American Retaliation

UNTIL THE END of the 1780's, when the newly constituted federal government under President Washington found itself able to function effectively and efficiently, the makers of British policy had constantly to take into account the political impotence of the Confederation. American weakness and disorganization both helped and hindered British interests. *Taking the near view*, however, benefits outweighed detriments.

That the American Union would fall apart with the end of the war was an assumption general throughout Europe. Frederick the Great predicted collapse. Closer and friendlier observers shared his opinion. Barbé de Marbois, French envoy to the United States in 1782, referred to the new nation as "ce Tableau continuellement mobile." Attached to independence as its citizens were, the Republic left "encore beaucoup à desirer." There was "bien peu de Patriotisme, et il N'y a plus d'Enthousiasme. Sept Années de Guerre l'ont entierement etaint." Barbé's compatriot, the Marquis de Chastellux, who knew America well, expressed to Gouverneur Morris his pain at the lack of harmony and union in the new republic, adding, "I should say your *republics*; and in employing this expression, I have perhaps explained all." He refused to conceal from his friend that America's reputation was at a very low ebb in Europe. It would remain thus "till you order your confederation better, till you take measures in common to pay debts, which you contracted in common, till you have a form of government and a political influence."[1]

If these were the opinions of allies and neutral observers, it is scarcely surprising that recent enemies entertained doubts of their own. Dean Tucker, James Anderson, and Lord Sheffield all wrote about the inevitable dissolution of the Confederation, the latter fore-seeing in American independence the first stage of a whole epoch of revolution in the New World calling forth a succession of independ-ent states in the backcountry. Even British friends of America were deeply disturbed. Dissenting cleric Richard Price, for example, told Jefferson of his concern for the reputation of the "new governments." His use of the plural was again significant. Shelburne, recently cre-ated Marquis of Lansdowne, wrote to Jay of his deep anxiety—shared by many in Britain, he said—for American prosperity, reputation, and "interior tranquillity." Empirical evidence of approaching col-lapse of the Confederation government was garnered in America by astute and influential British observers on the scene. Shelburne's for-mer confidential secretary, Maurice Morgann, wrote from occupied New York that while hostilities raged, Congress had "obtained Credit for Wisdom," but it was "Wisdom Upon Compulsion." With the cessation of the fighting, however, Congress, acting now "on choice and design," faced the more complicated problems of governing in peacetime. The results would assuredly be civil strife and anarchy. Sir Guy Carleton, commanding the British evacuation at New York, bluntly predicted the speedy overthrow of Congress by Americans themselves. Barbé's unfavorable opinions, too, were fully known to the British ministry from his intercepted dispatches.[2]

Ironically, on two important occasions during the negotiations of the peace preliminaries in 1782, American negotiators based argu-ments upon the exact premise adduced by European observers: the inability of the American Confederation to make its writ run in its own land. In the early exchanges with Richard Oswald, Benjamin Franklin, the senior American commissioner, told the Briton that the recovery of prewar debts owed by Americans to British creditors was no proper object of treaty by representatives of the Congress. It was rather a matter for the individual states. Although blunt John Adams, to the honor of his country, gave away the game, declaring he had "no notion of cheating any Body," the exchange caused a twofold injury to the American cause. The object of Franklin's maneuver eluded him; and while the treaty in final form spoke in firm language about the debts, the fact remained that Franklin's statement con-firmed doubts in British minds about the ability of the United States government to function efficiently and effectively.[3]

A similar but more serious incident occurred during the negotiations about the loyalists. Adamant against territorial concessions for settling loyalists in the backcountry, or for compensating them for their losses, Franklin, Adams, and Jay found themselves pressed to guarantee no further persecution or confiscation of loyalist estates and to restore properties seized during the war. Because of the prevailing hatred against the "tories" in the United States and of the equally emotional insistence in Britain that "loyalists" be shielded from their sworn enemies, this was a critical and delicate point in the negotiations. In early November, 1782, Adams and Jay admitted to their opposite numbers, Oswald and Strachey, that certain states had indeed stopped payment to British creditors and confiscated loyalists' lands during the war, but argued that they had been "excited thereto by the unnecessary Destruction of private Property" by the British armed forces. The two Americans, holding that it was "*just* that private Contracts made between Individuals of the two Countries before the war, should be faithfully executed," proposed to incorporate in the treaty guarantees that British creditors would meet with no further lawful impediment in the recovery of their debts. Possibly, too, the wartime seizure of loyalist estates may have had "a latitude not justifiable by the Law of Nations." Hence, the commissioners would have Congress "recommend" to the states "to correct, if necessary, the said Acts respecting the Confiscation of Lands in America belonging to real british Subjects as to render their said Acts consistent with perfect Justice and Equity."[4]

Next day, on November 5, Strachey left for consultations in London, while Oswald, remaining behind, sought to win further concessions for the loyalists from the Americans. Calling on Adams on Sunday, November 17, he urged the Bostonian to consider that the loyalists had merely responded to the call of duty, even as Americans themselves had done. Were he a member of Congress, "he would shew a Magnanimity upon this Occasion, and would say to the Refugees, 'take your Property. We scorn to make any Use of it, in building up our System.'" Adams' reply invoked the weakness of the central government of the United States. "We had no Power," he declared, "and Congress had no Power, and therefore we must consider how it would be reasoned upon in the several Legislatures of the separate States."[5] There was real danger that the British ministry, agonizing over the plight of their persecuted fellow subjects in America, might take the emissaries from Congress at their word. If the commissioners persisted in denying they possessed authority to bind their government, Secretary of State Townshend told Strachey, "they are driving us to a necessity of applying directly to those who are allowed to have the Power of Negotiating on them."[6]

With the fate of the treaty hanging delicately in the balance, a compromise of sorts was struck; and peace preliminaries were signed, sealed, and delivered on November 30. Article V bound Congress to "earnestly recommend" to the states restitution of certain classes of loyalist property seized during the war; and refugees were to be allowed to return peaceably to the United States, remaining unmolested for as much as a year while they wound up their affairs and pursued restitution of sequestered estates. Article VI promised cessation of further prosecutions and confiscations.[7]

Compromise or not, the Americans had clearly carried their point about the loyalists; and it was a bitter draft for the British nation. Shelburne himself pleaded in justification that it was necessary to sacrifice a part to save greater injury to the whole. Making his political swan song in the House of Lords, the falling minister somberly told the peers that he had fought for the loyalists until the entire treaty was at stake and the question quite literally was peace or renewed war. In his opinion, the nation was unable to take the field again. At any event, he continued, the American commissioners were disabled from making further concessions, as was Congress itself, "for, by the Constitution of America, every State was Supreme." If the states refused to accept the recommendations of Congress, Shelburne glumly conceded, there was no option but for Britain herself to indemnify the loyalists.

Shelburne's line of reasoning was scarcely calculated to restore confidence in, let alone amity with, the new republic. To British minds, the Americans were certainly vindictive; but even more important in the long run was the fact that they had won their point by insisting upon the inability of their own government to govern. The public's contempt and condemnation were voiced by "A Briton" in the *Morning Chronicle* of February 17, 1783: "The Commissioners of Congress have not presumed to do *more*," wrote the outraged author, "because they knew that neither themselves nor the Congress had authority to do so much."[8]

Britons found many portions of the treaty exceptionable, but the abandonment of the loyalists seemed the ultimate degradation. Their peacemakers were held responsible, of course; but equally reprehensible was a government which rested an important part of its case on the inability to command obedience from its own citizens.

When loyalists, acting under the treaty, sought to return to the United States to salvage what they could of confiscated rights and property, their worst apprehensions became reality. Violence and persecution greeted many of the wretched men, while wartime discriminatory laws remained in force in many states and new ones were actually passed. Some Americans sought to defend their country from charges of bad faith and treaty-breaking by taking refuge in the "recommend" clause; but many citizens of power and influence in the Republic expressed dismay and disapproval.[9] The conclusion drawn on the eastern side of the Atlantic was direct and blunt: the new nation was "without energy and government . . . consequently, no dependence or faith can be put in a government so subject to revolution—no treaties can bind it." To evade a clear treaty obligation by asserting that the Confederation was bound only to "recommend" to the several states relief for the loyalists was despicable. "A quibbling sophist might be expected to make the above disgraceful distinction without the loss of character," wrote an outraged correspondent to the *Morning Chronicle*, "*but a nation ought to be ashamed of it.*"[10]

The events of the summer of 1783 did nothing to refurbish the American image. Revolt suddenly boiled up within the ranks of the unpaid and neglected Continental Army. Congress, confused and humiliated, fled precipatately from Philadelphia to Princeton. Order was soon restored by a tactful General Washington; but even to his own countrymen, the United States seemed a mere fiction.[11] Collapse of the Confederation was imminent, the *Morning Chronicle* believed; and its sentiment coincided with the view of the nation as a whole. As for a union of sentiments and interests in the former colonies, the editorial added, "an expectation of it would disgrace Bedlam at the full of the moon."[12]

The source of suffering for the loyalists—the weakness of the Confederation government—had a brighter implication for ministers in Whitehall. It virtually ruled out the possibility of retaliation against Britain for the Order of July 2, 1783, and the exclusion of American vessels from British West Indian ports. The point was put most clearly by Dr. Edward Bancroft, in the United States as agent for several British creditors when news of the Order arrived: American merchants and leaders, he reported home, were "very much surprised and alarmed" at the measure. There was bold talk about tonnage duties discriminating against British vessels, but it was vain rhetoric—what Americans said and what they did were two very separate matters. In fact, Bancroft assured the ministry, they would do nothing. Lacking both unity and effective government, the erstwhile rebels were unable even to raise a revenue sufficient to pay the interest on the public debt or to defray the expenses of Congress, let alone engage Britain in a trade war.[13] He was not alone in these opinions, he declared; they were shared by "the wisest and most respectable People" in the country—and Bancroft knew many of them.

Congress presently gave the Britons pause. In April, 1784, a resolution was adopted calling for additional powers to regulate the commercial affairs of the Republic. An obvious response to the Order of the preceding July, it clearly pointed toward a unified, retaliatory policy. Bancroft, observing developments closely, was anxious, but only briefly. Within a month he reported to Whitehall that America was as disunited as ever, and that there was no real prospect of effective national discrimination against British shipping. Returning to London in June—a guest aboard the vessel assigned to carry back the French envoy!—the British agent composed for the ministry a lengthy memorandum about the United States. In brief, it held that if Congress should gain the powers it wished, a retaliatory policy might well result. There was, however, no need to worry. The condition was clearly impossible. Indeed, if Britain but persisted, a dissolution of the Confederation itself was a distinct possibility.

Bancroft's memorandum merely confirmed the reasoning developed in the Report of May 31, 1784. Any retaliation would be completely unjust, of course, the committee reasoned. The United States was not entitled to the privilege of independence and the benefits of colonial status simultaneously. The "General Law of Nations" gave no nation the right to trade with the colonies of another. Casting theory aside, the committee moved to the realm of fact. The committee was well aware of the efforts going forward in certain states to punish Britain for the Order of July, 1783. Maryland, for example, was experimenting with a tonnage act, laying a discriminatory tax on both vessels and goods of British origin. South Carolina was threatening to subject produce from the British West Indies to duties ranging some 50 to 100 per cent higher than those levied on similar items from other West Indian islands. Georgia was toying with the idea of prohibiting all intercourse with the British islands in the Caribbean until the offending Order was withdrawn. New York's legislature was debating a duties and tonnage bill. Virginia, too, it was reported, was looking favorably upon such a measure; and North Carolina was bound to follow her lead.

Effective American opposition to British policy was impossible, the committee concluded. Whatever the efforts of certain individual states, they were bound to be short-lived and ineffectual. Riven by deep sectional differences, they would devise no common course of action. Could southerners, for example, agree to exclude British vessels and thereby to confer a monopoly of their carrying trade upon the New Englanders? Certainly not! The "general Ferment" affecting several states was evident, but it was assuredly transient and innocuous, a fact aptly demonstrated by America's burgeoning trade with Britain and (in British bottoms) with the Sugar Islands. Even if the impossible came to pass, however, and Congress by some miracle adopted a common policy, there was no need to fear, because

the nature of their Country, full of Ports and Creeks, the feebleness of their Government, the Interests of Individuals and the contradictory views, in this respect, of their Planters and Merchants, will not allow them to enforce the Execution of any restrictive Measures They may adopt.[14]

A third effect of American political disunion was to put out of court once and for all the idea of a commercial treaty between Britain and the Confederation, the prime goal of American foreign policy. William Eden, for example, in a characteristic piece of backstairs intrigue, warned Charles James Fox, whose earlier predilection for the rebels could not be forgotten, against such an accord with the Americans. "Unless you can make a much better Treaty than I believe possible," he told Fox, "I venture to foretell that you will *repent* of making any." The Articles of Confederation, he explained, "expressly reserve the Power of making Commercial Treaties to the Separate States!"[15] Even Jefferson attributed Britain's lack of interest in a commercial treaty to the certainty that America was incapable of united retaliatory action. Respect in Britain for the American government, he told a friend, was "annihilated . . . from an idea of its want of tone and energy."[16] By far the bleakest monument to American political impotence, therefore, was John Adams' mission to London, the overriding purpose of which was to win admission for American vessels and goods into the British West Indies.[17]

Following the collapse of the Hartley negotiations in Paris in 1783, the American commissioners, Franklin and Adams, were joined by Thomas Jefferson, who replaced John Jay, newly appointed his country's foreign secretary. Fresh instructions from Congress duly authorized treaties of amity and commerce with some sixteen nations, among them Britain. Hartley was approached, but his return to London followed almost at once. When the Duke of Dorset, the new British ambassador to France, appeared in Paris, the commissioners formally renewed their effort, notifying His Grace that they were empowered to conclude a treaty of amity and commerce with his country and to settle certain matters arising from the treaty of peace.

Dorset naturally referred the communication to London. In November, a month after the American approach, acting on instructions from the Pitt ministry, the Duke suggested that the United States send a representative to the British capital, a location "more suitable to the dignity of either Power than would be the carrying on at any third Place a negotiation of so great importance." His government, he added, stood ready to consider any American proposals "that can tend to the establishing a system of mutual and permanent advantage to the two Countries."[18] It was not a surprising response. Fox had made a similar suggestion months before and, in any event, Dorset had no power to negotiate with American agents. Despite Jefferson's suspicion that the British were merely playing for time "to see how their schemes will work without a treaty," the commissioners responded that although they could not send a "public minister" to London, they would be willing to go there themselves for the purpose of negotiation.[19]

There the matter rested, the British apparently expecting the momentary arrival of the commissioners in London, the Americans evidently desiring some further invitation, and both parties standing to an excessive degree on dignity and protocol. Then, in the spring of 1785, there came news that His Majesty's government was dispatching a consul-general to the United States. Franklin and Jefferson, disagreeing with Adams, saw the measure as a deliberate attempt to seize a right which could legitimately arise only from a concluded treaty of commerce or consular convention, and as a slight to themselves. Bypassing in their turn the Duke of Dorset, the commissioners, angry and uneasy, undertook to probe, indirectly, the intentions of the British ministry. A member of the London Committee of American Merchants, obviously acting in response to the commissioners' initiative, called on Carmarthen in London. From the account which reached the Americans in Paris, the Secretary of State's response was blunt: an invitation to London had been extended by the Duke of Dorset; but the Americans had not appeared. Why? He "really wished you would come." The sting was in the tail. Did Congress, Carmarthen wished to know, really have power to treat in behalf of the individual states? Adams lost his temper. What more could he and his colleagues have done unless they had "flown over in an Air Baloon, alighted at Lord Carmarthen's House *Pour demander a diner of his Lordship?*"[20]

Whatever the reason, the delay was unfortunate. The Americans were angry; and British confidence in Congress, in the commissioners, and in the powers of both was seriously diminished. At the same time, new and dangerous issues were arising between the two nations. One of these Dorset, following official instructions, made the subject of a formal representation: a complaint to the British secretary of state from the Committee of North American Merchants in London alleged that they were suffering great losses in America because many of the states placed legal impediments in the way of British creditors pursuing their debts. Although the treaty of peace was explicit, British merchants in particular and the public at large had learned from painful experience, Dorset told the commissioners,

how little the authority of Congress could avail in any respect, where the Interests of any one individual State was even concern'd and particularly so where the concerns of that particular State might be suppos'd to militate against such resolutions as Congress might think proper to adopt.

The Duke drove home the point, inquiring "what is the real nature of the Powers with which you are invested; whether you are merely commision'd by Congress, or whether you have receiv'd separate Powers from the respective States?"

It was a cutting question—but, under the circumstances, not an unreasonable one. Dorset rubbed salt in the wound, informing the Americans:

The apparent determination of the respective States to regulate their own separate interests renders it absolutely necessary towards forming a permanent system of commerce, that my Court should be inform'd how far the Commissioners can be duly authorized to enter into any engagements with Great Britain which it may not be in the power of any one of the States to render totally fruitless and ineffectual.

The commissioners were deeply offended, Dorset noted with some amusement; but, he advised Carmarthen, there need be no "hurry to form any Commercial treaty with America."[21]

In April, news arrived that in the preceding February Congress had made new diplomatic arrangements. Franklin was given leave to return home in honor; Jefferson was named to succeed him at Versailles; and Adams was appointed minister plenipotentiary to London. The two latter were given a joint commission to negotiate treaties of commerce. Dorset's awkward question about powers was sidestepped. Adams' imminent departure for London made "a more particular answer" unnecessary.[22]

What Adams evaded in Paris he could not escape in London. In the very first audience with Secretary Carmarthen, on June 17, 1785, the Briton repeated to Adams the complaint made earlier by Dorset that some states were impeding the collection of debts owing to British creditors. The Secretary was polite, somewhat vague, and obviously more interested in obtaining justice for the creditors than in discussing Adams' list of matters outstanding between the two countries. Adams sought to turn the conversation to the subject of a commercial treaty; but before the conference ended, feeling himself on the defensive, he was driven to blurt out a threat. If an understanding were not reached with Britain, his fellow countrymen were confident that "they had the power in their own hands to do themselves justice, as soon as they should find it denied them here."[23] In the diplomatic game in which he was engaged, he played thus early the highest card in his hand.

Adams was not long in learning the limited extent of his powers. There would be no commercial treaty, he reported to Secretary Jay, until Britain was "made to feel the necessity of it." To Jefferson, however, he confided that he was convinced of "what I did not believe before"—that Congress was generally thought to lack power to negotiate commercial treaties, and that the United States could never unite sufficiently to retaliate against Britain.[24] Worried and in growing disillusionment, the Bostonian continued his efforts to make bricks without straw. Encouraged momentarily by reports of a Massachusetts navigation act, he returned to the charge in August, telling Pitt that the United States was moving rapidly toward a truly national policy directed against Great Britain. Warming to his theme, he told the Prime Minister that every nation possessed the right to regulate its own commerce, exports and imports. (Apparently the double-edged nature of the statement eluded him.) Presently, after a discussion of other matters, Pitt asked Adams if he allowed Britain the same right he claimed for the United States. Certainly, Adams responded; but if both nations exercised their rights, there would be no trade between them at all. It was a weak argument and Pitt's answer contained high irony: "To be sure, we should well consider the advantages and disadvantages in such a case." Let America get her national policy first, Pitt was saying; then Britain would appraise the situation anew. A month later, a desperate Adams tried to meet the critical issue head-on. Writing to Carmarthen ostensibly in answer to Dorset's letter, which first questioned the powers of the commissioners and of their principals, he cited Articles VI and IX of the Confederation, forbidding any state from sending or receiving embassies or treating with foreign powers. Congress reserved to itself alone the field of foreign policy. He was forced to admit, however, that the power of the several states to levy imports and duties on foreign trade, or to prohibit the export and import of any kind of goods, was not to be diminished by any treaty.[25]

The American's démarche could have done nothing to remove the British doubts, and news from the United States soon weakened Adams' position even further. Connecticut responded to the Massachusetts navigation act not with parallel legislation of her own, but with a declaration opening her ports. It was not to be disguised that New Jersey was prepared to serve New York in the same manner; and Delaware aimed to do the same to Pennsylvania if that state followed the Massachusetts precedent. Further, rising sectional differences and interests were making an unmistakable appearance, dividing the eastern and middle states from the southern states.[26] In the Virginia Assembly, for example, a member told his colleagues that it was "problematical, whether it would not be better to encourage the British than the eastern marine."[27] Foreign Secretary Jay's dealings with the Spanish further poisoned the atmosphere in America, Madison concluding that his well-meaning and temporary renunciation of

the right to navigate the Mississippi was "fatal . . . to an augmenta-
tion of the federal authority if not to the little now existing."[28]

In Paris, Jefferson had to bear the mock solicitude of Dr. Bancroft, concerned, he said, for the "general discredit" attending "every
thing and every body" connected with America.[29]

This was the gloomy state of American affairs when Thomas Jefferson arrived in London in March, 1786, called there by Adams to
assist in commercial negotiations with Portugal and Tripoli. It was
only natural that the two ministers should make a last effort with the
British ministry as well. Adams duly informed Carmarthen of Jefferson's arrival and requested an interview with the British Secretary. In
the meeting which followed, the Americans presented their joint commission, due to expire on May 12, to negotiate a commercial treaty
with Great Britain. Carmarthen's response was a brush-off: "After
harping a little on the old String, the insufficiency of the Powers in
Congress to treat and to compell compliance with Treaties," he promised, *pro forma*, to lay the matter before the king.

A few days later, the two Americans accidentally met the British
Secretary. His manner was desultory and vague, but he suggested that
the earlier draft treaty submitted by Adams be purged of all "political
Regulations" and transmitted to the ministry again as a purely commercial proposal. Despite the obscurity of the "oracle," the two envoys immediately fell to work, soon producing a document effectually
reversing the policy of American exclusion from the British West
Indies. It was a futile gesture. The final American proposal went un-
answered and even unacknowledged.[30]

As the weeks passed, Thomas Jefferson's outrage grew. "That nation hates us," he wrote of Britain; "the ministers hate us, and their
king more than all other men." It was wild talk. Adams was closer to
the truth. British policy was not undergirded by hatred, but by a cool
assessment of the political situation in the United States. "If an angel
from heaven," wrote Adams, "should declare to this nation that our
States will unite, retaliate, prohibit, or trade with France, they would
not believe it."[31] John Pownall, commissioner of the customs, who had
drafted Shelburne's American Intercourse Bill in 1782, expressed the
British view crisply and succinctly. Examining the Newfoundland
fishery bill in the spring of 1786, he noted the discriminations it proposed against foreigners—virtual invitations to American fishermen
to migrate to His Majesty's dominions. The measure might invite re-

taliation from other European powers, he told Charles Jenkinson, but the United States could be offended with impunity, "for in their present State at least, that is a circumstance not of much moment."[32] Even so, the American nadir remained to be reached. The capture and plunder of ten to twelve American vessels by the Barbary pirates showed the American government unable to raise revenue either to punish the pirates or to ransom the enslaved American citizens. Funds were lacking indeed for the most necessary and elementary functions of governing. "Their requisitions produce little," Jay wrote of Congress to Jefferson; "and Government (if it may be called a Government) is so inadequate to its object that essential alterations or essential Evils must take place." In the autumn of 1786, Shays's Rebellion stripped the last shred of respectability from the Confederation government.[33]

In the new year, Phineas Bond, former loyalist, went out to Philadelphia as British consul for the Middle States. Unlike Sir John Temple, consul-general at Boston, Bond was also styled "Commissary for Commercial Affairs." The seemingly innocuous title suggested by British merchants trading to America implied that Bond was expected to enter direct relations with the governments of the several states. It was in fact a flagrant attempt to bypass the Confederation government; and although Congress declined to receive Bond in his commissary capacity, his acute and voluminously documented observations of the American scene confirmed his home government in its low opinion of the Confederation. Congress was only "nominally the great executive Body," he told the ministry, each state claiming and exercising its own sovereignty and adopting or rejecting measures of the central government as they promoted or conflicted with local objects. Indeed, foreign powers could have "no reliance upon the Engagements of the federal Government, nor can the Confederation exist."[34]

The United States clearly stood at a crisis point. Remedial measures were urgently necessary to save the precarious union. The central government was "at an end, and unless a remedy is soon applied, anarchy and confusion will inevitably ensue." The opinion was expressed not by Sir John Temple, Phineas Bond, or indeed, any other Briton. It was voiced by George Washington.[35] British observers were only a little less concerned.

PART II

The Broken Treaty of Peace

CHAPTER FOUR

The Gordian Knot: Loyalists and Debts

THE WEAKNESS and disorganization of America's central government secured Britain against commercial retaliation; but there was a more somber implication: the Confederation was unable to compel obedience to important portions of the treaty of peace. The Americans spoke incessantly of a new commercial accord with Britain. This was nonsense, the British held. If only the ministers would "see that the Treaty of Peace, bad as it is, was complied with," wrote a correspondent to the *Morning Chronicle*, "the country would readily excuse them from entering upon any new stipulations."[1] Accompanying the disinclination to make additional treaties with America, therefore, was a rising sense of grievance against the Republic because she was unable and her constituent states refused to abide by the solemn agreements which she had undertaken.

Britain's first complaint against the United States was the mistreatment of loyalists contrary to explicit treaty stipulations. American hatred for the "tories," traitors within the gates, exceeded the feeling against even the British. Henry Laurens, but recently out of the Tower of London in 1782, expressed the general attitude. "How are the Refugees to be provided for? They are yours," he told British questioners; "maintain them—had they honestly remain'd with us, they would not have been Beggars." Harsh, but worse was to come as he warmed to his theme. "With what face can any Man say either by himself or his Council [*sic*] to Congress, 'I am a Loyalist, I used my utmost Endeavors to get you all hanged and to confiscate your Estates and beggar your Wives and Children: Pray make a Provision for me or let me enjoy my Estate.' " The British principle of war had been "to pay the Charges out of forfeited Estates, deducting the Expence of Halters." The tories had acted in aid of that principle. Now, let them suffer![2]

The passions of war are never pretty and rarely lend themselves to the making of fine distinctions. Laurens' terrible anger took no account of the thousands of decent, honorable, and conscientious men whose sense of duty, deeply and honestly held, required them to support the old order. Some Americans were more moderate than the outraged and irascible Laurens; but for the first few years of restored peace the issue remained a highly emotional one, charged with great bitterness and wounded sensibilities on both sides of the Atlantic.[3]

As we have seen, British and American negotiators in Paris in 1782, after very hard bargaining, finally wrote into the peace preliminaries two articles dealing with loyalists. One (Article V) promised that Congress would "earnestly recommend" to the individual states the restoration of property and rights confiscated from "real British subjects" during the war. The same benefit would be extended to residents in areas held by British forces, if they had not borne arms against the United States. For a year, loyalists would be permitted free entry and peaceable residence within the territories of the United States while they sought restitution of their losses. (Wartime purchasers of loyalist property would be entitled to a return of their money.) Congress would also recommend a "reconsideration and revision" of all laws touching the loyalists passed by the states. The object would be to render these laws consistent with justice, equity, and conciliation. Returning refugees would not meet with legal impediment in the pursuit of their rights.

The second article (Article VI) provided an amnesty; forbade further confiscations, persecutions, or arrests; and promised the cessation of prosecutions in progress. It should be noted that the "recommend" provision in Article V, so important a feature of the future American defense against British charges of treaty-breaking, made no part of Article VI.[4] The preliminary treaty was signed on November 30, 1782, and was followed by an armistice dated January 20, 1783, the day preliminaries were concluded between Britain, on the one hand, and France and Spain on the other. Subsequently, the definitive treaty (identical to preliminaries) between Britain and America was signed on September 3, 1783, and was ratified and proclaimed in the United States in January, 1784. The dates are important in weighing charges and countercharges of "prior infraction."

The loyalist provisions were minimal in view of the exiles' miserable situation; and they were seized upon by Shelburne's enemies in Parliament to help in overturning the ministry.[5] North's friends, out of office since the end of the war, were especially violent. Alexander Wedderburn, Lord Loughborough, for example, even on his honeymoon found his "repose" destroyed by news of the unsatisfactory terms for the loyalists. The old ministry to which he had belonged had seen losses, to be sure, he fulminated to his friend William Eden; but they were "only such as the fortune of war may produce in spite of Valor or of Wisdom." (Apparently he had forgotten his recent savage criticisms of Lords North and George Germain.) "But," he continued, striking a rare note of righteous indignation, "to make a gratuitous sacrifice of the rights of the State and of the national faith, to proclaim ourselves beaten Cowards incapable of protecting the Adherents to our wretched fortune, is such a Loss of Credit as no Calamity of War should have made a People submit to."[6] Lord North, his own distaste for politics overcome by a period in the wilderness, summoned his followers to the opening of the parliamentary session to do battle against "this base Treatment of the Loyalists."[7] Despite the unconscious irony in their hot espousal of the loyalists' cause—no one had done more to bring the refugees to their sorry state than those who had mismanaged the American War—the issue was critical, indeed fatal, for the Shelburne ministry. The Earl's own apologia, noted earlier, that a part would have to suffer to prevent the destruction of the whole, was scarcely designed to rally the nation to his side; and the hapless First Minister departed with the triumph of his enemies and the maledictions of the loyalists ringing in his ears.[8] For his successors, the coalition ministry, there was reserved the cold comfort of accepting the provisional treaty unchanged as the definitive settlement.

That the loyalist issue played a major part in overthrowing Shelburne is clear. But what of the assertion, frequently made, that the exiles exercised a determining or important influence in the formulation of British policy toward the United States? John Adams, for example, faced with the ruin of his British diplomacy, attributed many of his troubles to the refugees. Even Shelburne, not to mention the coalition and Pitt ministries, he believed to possess an "immoderate attachment" for the exiles, who, he thought, were themselves scheming to persuade the British government to a "new system": fortification of the Canadian border, construction of a Great Lakes fleet, intrigue among the Indians, and the retention of the posts in the Old Northwest ceded to the Republic by the treaty of peace. Adams' conviction that tory malice and intrigue were working steadily and effectively against the interests of the United States was shared by many of his fellow citizens, among them Jefferson and Jay. As late as 1790, Gouverneur Morris, President Washington's unofficial envoy to London, accounted for Britain's American policy by blaming the "tories" in Britain, who, he believed, urged on commercial hostilities between the two countries because of "losses and disappointments" during the war.[9]

The West Indians, agreeing with the Americans, also detected loyalist plots, responsible, they concluded, especially for the failure of their efforts to win American admission to their ports. Bryan Edwards, for example, declared that the Report of May 31, 1784, bore the imprint of the refugees, men who possessed "a lurking taint of resentment and malignity" and a desire "to wound the new republic through the sides of the West Indies."[10]

The problem of loyalist influence on British policy is far from simple. Although it would be helpful to know precisely how many refugees there were, data are far from complete. Statements which sound authoritative—like John Adams' famous generalization dividing the American population into thirds—are at best the roughest approximations. One does not stand on much firmer ground, unfortunately, in estimating that loyalists constituted one-third and revolutionists two-thirds of the "politically active population."[11] The number who bore arms for the royal cause may be estimated with greater accuracy, but the margin of error remains large;[12] and the number who stood silent, choosing to submit to a new order they detested or accepted reluctantly or passively, can never be even reasonably approximated.

Further, the term "loyalist" embraced equally the subject who had fought for the royal cause, hazarding life, limb, and worldly possessions—often to the loss of all—and the merchant or his agent, temporarily resident in the colonies. In between, there were other gradations: absentee property owners—William Knox, for example—and professional men, like the lawyer George Chalmers, who came out to the colonies intending to live there a few years at most, to gain experience and a stake before returning "home." Some statistically-minded civil servant in the years immediately after the war might have differentiated at least between the native-born loyalist and the recently-arrived or temporary immigrant; but that chance has gone forever. Only the educated guess remains: migration of the loyalist began even before the end of the war, and it ultimately involved from 60,000 to 100,000 persons.[13] Of these, perhaps one-half settled in Nova Scotia and in what would become New Brunswick. Some 10,000 supplied the flesh and bones for Governor Simcoe's "Upper Canada." A part of the remainder found new lives in the British West Indies. But by far the largest portion went to the British Isles.

Despite these strictures on evidence about number, it is true beyond doubt or qualification that the refugees returned fully the backbiting and hatred of their former compatriots. As they carved out new homes in the remaining colonies or sought to adapt themselves to life in Britain, their daily lives were standing reminders of past misfortunes and their causes. Given the opportunity to exercise an anti-American influence on British policy, they would assuredly take it.

Those who went "home" were dangerously close to the center of power. Several among them were experienced in the possession and exercise of political authority as governors, customs officers, or magistrates.[14] Among these, Thomas Hutchinson, formerly governor of Massachusetts, was the most illustrious. Received at court and made something of a celebrity upon arrival, he might well have been influential in ministerial circles (although he himself doubted it); but he died in 1780. John Tabor Kempe, late attorney-general of New York; William Smith, chief justice of the same province; Joseph Galloway of Pennsylvania; and Harrison Gray of Boston were all prominent members of the former colonial "establishment." There were younger, less well-known, but talented and ambitious men with careers to make, too. Some climbed several rungs of the ladder. George Chalmers, erstwhile resident of Maryland, won the notice of Charles Jenkinson, who in 1786 made him First Clerk of the reorganized Committee for Trade and Plantations. He has been correctly called Jenkinson's right-hand man and a principal agent in the execution of British policy toward the United States;[15] but it is also evident from a study of Jenkinson's voluminous papers that whatever influence Chalmers enjoyed he derived from his role as a hard-working assistant, not as an *éminence grise*.

Further, by the time of Chalmers' appointment in 1786, the fundamentals of British policy had been laid down. Brook Watson, wartime commissary-general of the troops in North America, and William Knox, who never forgot the loss of his property in Georgia, were Members of Parliament and active in subministerial levels of government. Knox claimed chief responsibility for the Order of July 2, 1783; but in reality his function was essentially that of the clerk—to incorporate in written form decisions already made by his superiors. In any event, to classify either Knox or Watson as a "loyalist sufferer" is surely to stretch the meaning of the term to the breaking point.[16] William Smith—the Adamses called him by his nickname—wielded considerable influence as a trusted adviser of Sir Guy Carleton, who went out as Lord Dorchester to govern Canada. It was with Smith's advice, however, that Dorchester opened the overland trade routes with the southern neighbor. Lieutenant General John Simcoe, an energetic, feared, and effective adversary in war, became governor of the new province of Upper Canada when it was created in 1791. The outbreak of war in Europe and the mutual suspicion of Canadians (among them many refugees) and Americans very nearly brought an extension of hostilities to the New World; and Simcoe's initiative must be reckoned an important element in the near collision. Yet (while he somewhat inconsistently dreamed of an Anglo-American family compact), his greatest exertion could not persuade the government to treat with Vermont at a time when it appeared altogether possible that the province might be induced to return to its allegiance to the crown.[17]

Other loyalists found places in the new British consular service in the United States. Sir John Temple, self-styled baronet, became first consul-general at New York. Related distantly by blood to the Marquis of Buckingham and by marriage to Governor Bowdoin of Massachusetts, he devoted what zeal he possessed to making the best of both worlds. Pompous, vain, and jealous, Temple wrote dispatches which were superficial, hopelessly incomplete, and generally incompetent. They influenced his government, however; Phineas Bond, himself a loyalist, was sent out to be consul, and later consul-general for the Middle States, thereby limiting severely Temple's area of responsibility. Bond was the perfect consular official. Prompt and painstaking in executing orders from home, he was indefatigable in collecting and reporting mercantile data as well as in the guarding of British commercial and maritime interests within his province. Esteemed and respected by his superiors, Bond supplied much valuable information; but the formulation of policy he left to others. Colonel John Hamilton became consul in Virginia and George Miller in South Carolina and Georgia. Both men acquitted themselves well in the discharge of their duties.

The list of loyalists in office could doubtless be extended, but a single observation applies to them all. There was no effective loyalist organization influencing the formulation of high policy. The pursuit of pensions and compensation for wartime losses engrossed the loyalists virtually to the exclusion of all else. Even the relatively few who found places in government were the tools, not the makers of policy; and the great majority of their fellows lacked even this limited influence. Some made attempts, but ministerial doors did not open easily. Joseph Galloway, for example, holding no official position, tried very hard to establish himself as the government's resident expert on American affairs. Long, rambling, and finally bitter letters were addressed to the Earl of Hardwicke, the only friend he had who could pretend to an entrée among the political mighty. The noble lord's pipeline to the higher reaches of government, however, was limited, perhaps by design, to Undersecretary of State George Aust, who read the letters passed on to him by Hardwicke and forgot them.[18] Thomas Hutchinson, shortly before his death, summed up the plight of his wretched companions. "We Americans are plenty here, and very cheap," he wrote. "Some of us at first coming, are apt to think ourselves of importance, but other people do not think so, and few, if any of us are much consulted, or enquired after."[19]

Politically innocuous they may have been; but they were objects of public sympathy and compassion, and the first important irritants in Anglo-American relations after the war. Indignantly, Britons likened the exiles to the royalists who fled the tyranny of Cromwell. "Persecuted without intermission, by a cruel, relentless, bigotted, consequential, in their own opinions, deluded and infatuate race of men," they and their posterity would "remember to the latest ages, the unjust and inhuman acts of the lawless banditti."[20]

With no material assistance to be expected from the United States, the British government undertook the expensive task of compensating the sufferers and affording them a measure of financial relief. By 1782, something in excess of £40,000 was being paid each

year, and in addition there were occasional grants totaling £17,000-
£18,000 a year.[21] The end of the war brought an enormous increase.
Under an act of Parliament passed in the summer of 1783, a commission was created to investigate and validate loyalist claims;[22] and in
1785 the chairman, John Anstey, and two of his fellow commissioners, Thomas Dundas and J. Pemberton, went out to the New World
to collect information on the spot. Before the commission could report, however, the government paid out about £3 million to loyalists.
The refugees in Canada also received about £2 million, including the
cost of provisions (for two years), tools, lumber, surveying fees, and
other similar items. In 1788, an additional £1⅓ million was paid out;
and by 1789 pensions totaled more than £1 million. By that time, the
loyalists had cost Britain about £7,500,000, roughly twice the interest on the national debt in 1763.[23] This was a gauge of Christian charity, however, not of influence in the formation of grand policy.

Loyalists who elected to make new homes in the remaining colonies—rebuilding the strength of the shattered empire—rarely found
the bounty and gratitude of the mother country flagging. The Report
of May 31, 1784, stated as one reason for discriminating against
American vessels the desire to open for the overseas loyalists an opportunity to move into the maritime vacuum created by the departing former brethren. The refugees at "home" in Britain, however,
were another matter. More and more disillusioned with life about
them, they indulged in impossible dreams of returning to the native
land and drew together in their clubs and committees, a group apart.
Ever more isolated from the mainstream of British life, the exiles
spent time, thought, and energy not on questions of high policy but
on schemes to obtain or increase pensions and compensation. Some
proved grasping and thus gave a bad name to all. Living reminders of
of a lost war and a continuing drain on the taxpayer, the loyalists in
Britain, brooding on the past and indulging in self-pity, found their
position deteriorating very soon indeed. Within a year of the peace,
charity itself was begrudged; and while the desire to forget the unpleasant past was natural, the speed with which the refugees in the
mother country found sympathy turning to cynicism and even harsh
criticism was surprising. If ever there had been an opportunity for the
emergence of a well-organized and powerful loyalist "lobby," it disappeared very quickly.

Reaction began even while public declarations of support for the exiles were at their warmest. Unfortunate they were, wrote "Impartial Reason" in the *Morning Chronicle*; but in every "state commotion" a few must suffer, and in the present instance numbers had been greatly exaggerated.[24] Charges of greed and self-serving followed. During the evacuation of Charleston, the British commander exclaimed in exasperation to his superior that although he had given a plentiful supply of provisions—sufficient for three to six months—to every loyalist leaving the place, there were no "bounds to the unreasonable demands of all sorts of People."[25] Benjamin Vaughan, on the periphery of the peace negotiations in Paris in 1782, urged Shelburne—doubtless at the prompting of Franklin—to ignore "the noisy clamors" of the refugees and to remember that he could "*judge* more truly than they can *relate*." From New York, Maurice Morgann, Shelburne's confidential secretary (who was involved in his chief's ill-fated and ill-judged attempt to hasten Anglo-American reconciliation by a direct approach to Congress), warned that loyalists were not to be trusted: their advice was based solely on self-interest. An American visitor in London, admittedly not the most objective agent, informed Alexander Hamilton that "the Loyalists here are a great burden to the Government, and they know not how to ascertain the real losses they have suffer'd, for the Estimates presented to the Commissioners are swell'd to a most enormous Sum." The soul of moderation, John Jay considered the claims to "afford conclusive evidence of their inattention to truth and common decency."[26]

The charges received documentary support from the commissioners of loyalist claims. In their first report, dated August 10, 1784, in which they dealt with the claims of 2,063 loyalists for compensation amounting to about £7,050,000, Anstey and his colleagues bluntly stated that the figure was grossly inflated. In a subsequent report in 1790, the commissioners showed that 216 persons had claimed £306,000. After close examination of evidence, only £66,125 was allowed.[27] Exaggeration had clearly passed into attempted fraud; and there was fastened upon the loyalists, no doubt unjustly in the majority of cases, a reputation for persistent, unscrupulous, and dishonest pursuit of private enrichment at the public charge.

A true measure of loyalist influence in Britain was provided in 1787. In April, Earl Bathurst, whose career as lord chancellor during much of the American War cast no luster on that high office, introduced a bill into the House of Lords. Entitled "An Act for the better preventing vexatious Suits being brought for the Recovery of Debts contracted in America previous to the Treaty of Peace," it was seconded by the cantankerous and incorrigible Lord Chancellor Thurlow. Aiming to screen loyalist debtors from American creditors suing for recovery in British courts—in obvious retaliation for protection enjoyed by American debtors from British creditors—it was supported enthusiastically by the refugees,[28] who thereby collided headlong with the important and well-organized Committee of Merchants trading to North America. In a resolution of April 13, 1787, the merchants declared that the bill

has a very dangerous Tendency, that its Principle is repugnant to the 4th Article of the Treaty of Peace . . . that it may in its Consequence operate to increase the Difficulty of recovering Debts due from America to this Country, and therefore calls for the immediate Exertions of the Committee to prevent its passing into a Law.[29]

It was a very effective quietus, and the proposed legislation was quickly withdrawn; but the affair sparked a violent controversy in the press, casting in the process much light on the position of the exiles in British politics.

Soon after the bill had been thrown out, a loyalist signing himself "Plain Truth" published a letter in the *Morning Chronicle*, bitterly castigating the merchants who had opposed it. They had, it was charged, procured assignments of debts due American creditors by loyalists, as payment of debts due themselves by those same Americans. The merchants, "actuated by a strange enthusiastick predilection for the Americans," found themselves swindled out of millions in goods by former rebels; and, "Plain Truth" concluded, they aimed now to recoup their losses from the loyalists.[30]

A week later, there came a savage rejoinder. How long would "Plain Truth" and his brethren "abuse the patience of the people of England?" How long would they "violate decency, humanity, and truth?" Would they not be content with "daily vomiting forth . . . froth and venom against the Citizens of the United States" without continually libeling fellow subjects and "even an higher character" —a reference to the King—who thought them "a mischievous and troublesome set of people?" The merchants had not caused the war— a vicious thrust—but they bore the burden of it. Meantime, the loyalists "move heaven and earth to secure and put yourselves in *status quo* by the impoverishment and ruin of others." What meant the welfare of commerce or the sanctity of treaties to such people? "Go on, Sirs," they were admonished, "until you have made yourselves as thoroughly odious to all ranks in this kingdom, as you are in America."[31] When the wretched loyalist returned to the attack, he drew upon himself additional condemnations, including that of the powerful Committee of Merchants trading to North America.

The manifest contempt and brutality of "Plain Truth's" enemies and the absence of a single voice raised in defense of the refugees militate powerfully, to say the least, against allegations of loyalist influence on British policy. The exchange was a commentary on the melancholy fate of those who eat the bread of exile. John Adams' fears and suspicions of loyalist influence, shared by so many of his fellow citizens, and to a lesser extent by West Indians, reflected frustration and disappointment and the need for a face-saving rationalization of failure.

To rule out significant loyalist influence in the active shaping of British policy is not, however, to state that the refugees were without a considerable importance in Anglo-American diplomacy. American mistreatment of them furnished ground for a British complaint that the United States was guilty of the first breach of the treaty of peace.

In America, war-born rancor and hatred made a mock of the loyalist articles in the treaty of peace. Mild as they were, Abigail Adams wrote from Massachusetts to her husband, they "raised the old spirit against the Tories to such a height that it would be at the risk of their lives, should they venture here. It may subside after a while, but I question whether any State in the Union will admit them, even for twelve months."[32] Reaction in the southern states was especially violent. Ravaged by the war and owing vast sums to British merchants, an irate citizenry used every means—physical assault, intimidation, threats, riots, tar and feathers—to prevent the return of the exiles. In South Carolina, the arrival of the peace preliminaries was the signal for riotous demonstrations and loud and unruly demands that all loyalists be banished whatever the treaty might say. In Virginia, Joseph Williamson, a loyalist, returned to Essex County in the autumn of 1782, carrying with him the written permission of the Council and of Governor Benjamin Harrison. The gubernatorial script notwithstanding, Williamson was attacked by a mob and tarred and feathered. The ringleader, one William Gatewood, as a reward

for his performance, was elected to the legislature and relieved of all
fear of judicial proceedings by a bill of indemnity passed by his fellow
solons in May, 1784. In July, 1783, Governor Harrison proclaimed
that no loyalist departing the state in 1777 might return. Many falling under the new ban were already in the state, protected, they believed, by the treaty of peace; but they promptly became objects of
riots and mob violence. Even the intervention of the legislature with
an act of December, 1783, declaring that only those who had actively
opposed the United States should be denied entry, failed to calm public turbulence. In some states, new acts of banishment, some of which
survived the War of 1812, closed the borders to large numbers of
loyalists.[33]

In New York, where public opinion was inflamed by a prolonged
British occupation (until November, 1783), Governor George Clinton—wishing to perpetuate his own power by disfranchising as many
opponents as possible—and the state legislature attempted to disfran-
chise all who had remained voluntarily within British lines and to
make the "offence" misprision of treason. When the bill was thrown
out by the Council, it was immediately replaced with a test act, disfranchising all who would not swear they had never abetted the
enemy. More flagrant yet was the state's Trespass Act, allowing Americans who had evacuated homes and business premises in New York
City and its environs in the face of the enemy's advance to sue and
recover damages and accrued rent from those who might have taken
possession. Defendants were expressly barred from pleading a British
civil or military order as justification. Because of the long British occupation of New York, few buildings in the entire metropolis were
unaffected. It was an invitation to a "carnival of spoliation," and a
"Tory witch-hunt" ensued.[34]

Even loyalists who did not attempt to return to America, but
sought through agents to retrieve something from shattered estates,
found the treaty's stipulations ignored. Venerable Harrison Gray, for
example, sometime of Boston and a veteran in the "establishment" of
the royal province of Massachusetts, was attainted and exiled by the
revolutionary state government and his property confiscated. "Patriot" debtors, to whom he had extended credit in happier days, immediately refused him payment. Subsisting on a British pension of
£200 a year, he looked to Article V of the treaty of peace as his recourse in the recovery of his American debts. Pursuing his cause in

the courts of Massachusetts, he found the defendants immediately relieved on the plea that he was an "outlawed Tory." There the matter
could easily have rested, had not his grandson, Harrison Gray Otis,
whose loyalty to the new regime was unimpeachable, put family above
politics. Receiving assignments of the debts, he proceeded to sue successfully in his own name. The collusion ultimately recovered much
of the £8,000 due; but the process was long, arduous, and embitter-
ing.[35] Few refugees could have matched the relatively happy issue of
Gray's troubles. Judicial discrimination, tar and feathers, the whip's
thirteen stripes across the bare back, mob assaults, and even lynch-
ings were not uncommon forms of treatment for loyalists seeking
restitution of their losses.

Many responsible Americans stood aghast at the scene. Alexander
Hamilton, whose "Phocian" essays of May, 1784, blasted the Disfranchising Act in New York, took his future in his hands even earlier.
Appearing before the Mayor's Court of New York City in February
in behalf of a loyalist defendant, he argued powerfully in the case
of *Rutgers vs. Waddington* that the Trespass Act, the basis for the
action, was in violation of established international law, the rights
of conquest, and the treaty of peace. Although he won the point,
Hamilton took little joy from his victory. "Instead of wholesome regulations for the improvement of our polity and commerce," he wrote
to Gouverneur Morris, "we are labouring to contrive methods to
mortify and punish tories and to explain away treaties." His father-
in-law, General Schuyler, bitterly anti-Clinton, inveighed, too, against
the actions of people who had "hardly been emancipated from a
threatened tyranny, forgetting how odious oppression appeared to
them," before they began "to play the tyrant, and give a melancholy
evidence, that however capable we were of bearing adversity with
magnanimity, we are too weak to support, with propriety, the prosperity we have so happily experienced."[36] Hamilton's victory notwithstanding, suits continued to be brought under the Trespass Act. In
1785, for example, British General Tryon was sued successfully for
£5,000 damages to a New York patriot's farm, although the land in
question was worth less than the award. Verdicts for exorbitant rents
continued; and the act was not repealed until 1788, when the legislature of New York at long last repealed all earlier legislation contravening the peace.[37]

American representatives abroad were hard put to it to defend or palliate their countrymen's treatment of the loyalists, and they were painfully aware of the condemnation general throughout Europe. John Jay in Paris wrote home in alarm, advising the Republic to act with greater humanity. Excepting only "the faithless and the cruel," he would pardon all who had fought openly and honorably, or who had fled timidly before the storm.[38] Exerting himself to minimize the violence and his country's responsibility for it, Franklin assured "My dear Friend" David Hartley of the "moderate disposition" entertained by Congress toward the loyalists. The persecutions were not due to the central government, President Boudinot informed Franklin in a letter which the American passed on to Hartley, but to Britain's prolonged occupation of New York and to the "Cruelties, Ravages, and Barbarities" committed by the loyalists themselves during the war. Newly arrived from Europe, Jay wasted little time in assuring British correspondents that he had "met with whigs and tories at the same table."[39]

The grim truth, however, could not be hidden. There remained the flood of reports both from eyewitnesses and from the sufferers themselves: in virtually every state of the Union, the loyalist provisions of the treaty were flagrantly ignored and local authorities in many states were complacently acquiescing in continuing persecutions. In Britain, it was clear that the United States government was unable to impose its will on its constituents, a fact which might explain but did not excuse the breach of the treaty of peace from its inception.

The loyalist issue furnished the substance of the first official British complaint against American infraction of the treaty. On August 17, 1783, Sir Guy Carleton, commanding the evacuation of New York, wrote to President Boudinot protesting American abuse of the loyalists contrary to the treaty. A second and more portentious episode unfolded over the several months following. In November, General Steuben, envoy from Congress, inquired of General Haldimand, commander in chief in Canada, when the United States might expect him to deliver up the ceded posts in the Old Northwest. Haldimand, lacking both orders and authentic news of a definitive settlement, brushed Steuben's query aside. In May, 1784, however, a representative of Governor Clinton of New York called on the British general and posed the same question Steuben had asked earlier. Again, Haldimand said he had no orders, but added that in his private opinion, the posts would not be given up until America honored her treaty obligations toward the loyalists. In his report home, the General—convinced on additional grounds of the need to retain the posts—suggested that the Republic might be compelled to extend the period of one year allowed by the treaty for the return of the loyalists. Until then, he added, "the want of government and good order in the different states" had rendered it unsafe for the exiles to return. Secretary of State Lord Sydney, in his reply of April 8, 1784, to Haldimand's first dispatch, commended the General for his handling of the congressional envoy. Sydney also observed that while Britain was bound to hand over the posts with all convenient speed, America had yet to comply "with even one article of the treaty." A delay in delivering the posts to the Americans could thus be justified.[40]

A second and related British grievance now emerged, ultimately outstripping the loyalist issue in importance. Many states refused to remove legal impediments to the collection of prewar debts owed to British creditors as the treaty of peace enjoined.

The outbreak of the American War had come so suddenly that few British merchants or their agents had time to settle their accounts in the colonies before they found themselves exiled or fleeing for their lives, and their property seized by rebels. Termed "loyalists" or "American sufferers," they differed from others in the same category in one extremely important way: the British government absolutely declined to assume responsibility for compensating them for American debts. Despite Benjamin Franklin's maneuver during the peace negotiations, Article IV stood in the treaty explicitly forbidding legal impediment in the pursuit and recovery in full of all bona fide prewar debts. There was no "recommend" provision. The burden of undiluted responsibility lay with the government of the United States.

The solemn stipulation to the contrary notwithstanding, many of the individual states retained and even reinforced their laws discriminating against British creditors. Some states made provisions for payment by instalments but delayed the last payment until distant dates, meantime forbidding suits for recovery. Executions against American property by alien creditors were forbidden until the lapse of a certain number of years, a practice applying in some instances not merely to prewar debts, but also to debts contracted since the peace. Other states made worthless land legal tender, and it passed at

once to the state when assigned to British creditors because of a declaration by the courts forbidding aliens to hold land. Some states required that no suit begin until a demand for payment had been made
in writing, a manifest attempt to delay justice. In another, British
factors and agents aiming at the collection of debts were ordered to
depart immediately. Virtually all states outlawed interest during the
war; and in one, no interest was allowed until after May 1, 1786.[41]
There was, in addition, the question of wartime laws, particularly flagrant in Virginia and Maryland, allowing Americans to discharge
British debts by paying amounts due into the state treasuries in vastly
depreciated state and continental paper currency. Marylanders, who
could at one time pay a debt of $5,000 for only $10, rid themselves
of £144,574 in debts for paper money worth £86,744 sterling; Virginians paid off £273,554 for only £12,035 sterling.[42]

By 1790, unfriendly judges and juries notwithstanding, British
creditors in the northern states were moderately satisfied. In the South,
however, appalling abuses continued. In Georgia and the Carolinas,
legal actions for the recovery of British debts were either prohibited
outright by law or discontinued at the order of the bench. Even if a
judgment were gained against a defendant, he evaded its execution
very simply—by making over property to a friendly agent, spending
a few days in jail, and emerging purged of the debt. Virginia and
Maryland were the most incorrigible of all.[43]

Shortly after the adoption of the federal Constitution, the debts
amounted to about £5 million sterling, including fourteen years' interest, reckoned at five per cent per annum. Some 194 creditor houses
were involved, with 95 and 67 from Glasgow and London respectively. Of this huge sum, the southern states, Virginia, North and South
Carolina, Maryland, and Georgia, owed a staggering £4,190,000. The
remaining states accounted for only £795,000.[44]

The Glasgow merchants, the largest single group of creditors and
second only to the Londoners in the amount of debts held, were behind no one in persistent agitation for official intervention in their
behalf. Sixty-six of them joined to memorialize Shelburne on the subject of their debts even before he took office in 1782.[45] Presently an
effective organization emerged, devoted to forwarding their cause at
every opportunity. John Adams had scarcely arrived in London to
begin his mission before the Glasgow creditors put a mass of data into
the hands of Henry Dundas, treasurer of the navy, member of the

Committee for Trade, and guardian in chief of Scottish interests at Whitehall. Intended to serve as the basis for an official representation to the American envoy, the material revealed that the great balance of the Glasgow debts were owing in Virginia, Maryland, and North Carolina, with the first two states responsible for most of the sum outstanding. Including real property seized by the Americans but excluding all debts which seemed bad and one-half those regarded as doubtful, the sum claimed by the Glasgow merchants was £1,336,000. Twenty-five per cent was due from retailers in America and seventy-five per cent from planters there.[46]

The debt-ridden planter is a stereotype in eighteenth-century American history. The organization of the tobacco trade and the way of life adopted by Tidewater grandees served to make the debtor status almost hereditary. They were men rich in lands and slaves, but poor in money; and a roll call of planter debtors would include many high and mighty names, Madison, Randolph, Mercer, Washington, and Jefferson among them.[47] Federalists, in the 1790's and subsequently, blamed them as a group for refusing to pay their just debts to British creditors and contributing thereby to the perpetuation of Anglo-American discord. In 1791, Fisher Ames of Massachusetts delivered a stinging indictment of the southern planters, contrasting their attitude with that of his own friends in New England dedicated to the defense of property by steady laws and a strong government. In the South, political power was held by a few gentlemen, Ames charged, who found in the law "their coat of mail," which warded off "the weapons of the foreigners, their creditors, and at the same time . . . governs the multitude." It was, he concluded, a compound of "both government and anarchy"; and to such men, possessing "land and negroes, and debts and luxury, but neither trade nor credit, nor cash, nor the habits of industry, nor of submission to a rigid execution of law," a strong central government able to compel payment of debts was unwelcome.

In a similar vein, Oliver Elsworth denounced the southern debts as a cause both of the American Revolution and of the anti-federalism he found so detestable. Oliver Walcott, writing after the turn of the century, charged that "the *whiggism* of Virginia was chiefly owing to the *debts of the planters*," and that "the severe and impolitic hostility shown toward British creditors "occasioned great dissatisfaction among reflecting men in this country and deeply injured the popularity of the American cause in Great Britain." The climax of Tory John Adolphus' panegyric on General Washington (in the *History of England from the Accession to the Decease of George III*) declared that although a rebel, Washington, unlike many of his fellows, "had no debts in England to extinguish or delay by a revolution in America."[48]

Resistance to the debt provisions of the treaty of peace did not, however, arise from or flourish among the Tidewater magnates who bore the brunt of federalist wrath. Generally, they accepted the treaty, lukewarmly in some instances perhaps, although Madison called it "glorious" and Jefferson expressed great delight—sentiments, he told Jay, shared by all Americans, "a few ill-designing debtors excepted." Edmund Randolph, whose own debts played a sinister role in the strange end to his career as secretary of state in 1795, was highly critical a decade earlier of Virginians who worked to frustrate the debt provisions of the treaty and who committed violence against returning loyalist creditors.[49]

Planters who had long subsisted on credit—from British merchants and from each other—would surely hesitate to disrupt established modes of commercial intercourse and thus to sacrifice both good name and credit rating. The resumption of economic relations with Britain at war's end meant that British credit was again required. Was it to be hazarded by irresponsible, not to say dishonorable, abuse of creditors? From both interest and principle, the great planters would favor the protection of private property, uninterrupted dispensation of justice, and unimpeded borrowing and payment of debts. A delay in payment of prewar debts or settlement by instalments might be welcomed; but repudiation of debts would appear an altogether unacceptable solution.[50]

It was not the "land and slave rich" planters who refused to pay the prewar debts. It was the small farmers and poor westerners—in Virginia, the "popular party," dominant in the legislature and led by Patrick Henry, whom Randolph identified as "indefatigable in his endeavours to suppress the payment of british debts."[51] The reason for this is clear: they, not the wealthy magnates of the Tidewater, owed the great balance of the debts in question.

Consider the case of the large Glasgow firm of Cunningham, Findlay & Co. Before the war, they operated five stores in the South at Port Tobacco, Chaptico, Leonard Town, Blandensburgh, and

Georgetown. In the closing years of the century, with debt collection still impeded in many places, the company indicated that 180 debtors had paid a total of about £7,000 and 90,500 pounds of tobacco. (The payments included no interest for the war years—a loss reckoned by the company at about £3,000 and 5,000 pounds of tobacco per debtor.) In fact, only fifteen persons owed more than £100, and no one owed more than £500.

The Virginia stores in Blandensburgh and Georgetown showed outstanding debts amounting to just under £3,000, excluding interest, owed by 177 debtors. For these debts, the company had found no legal remedy, although "from the personal Knowledge and best information the Agents could get," the debtors were solvent in 1783. Many had since migrated into "the back parts of Virginia." Sixty-eight owed £5 or under; seventy-seven, between £5 and £20; twenty-five, between £20 and £50; four, £50 to £100; and only three, over £100. The company likewise noted that debts (not included in the figures immediately above) amounting to about £6,000 had been "paid" with paper money possessing true value of less than £1,500.

A second Glasgow firm, Alexander Donald & Co., revealed a similar pattern. With one store in Mecklenburg County, they held debts, exclusive of interest, totaling about £5,600, "which cannot be recovered in the Courts of Virginia," because the debtors' residence and circumstances were unknown. There were 306 debtors involved. Of these, 134 owed £5 or under; 109, £5 to £20; 39, £20 to £50; 11, £50 to £100; eight, £100 to £200; and only five over £200.[52]

The general picture remains the same in claims submitted by other trading houses in Glasgow and London: the great majority of debts were owed in small sums by poor men—farmers and frontiersmen traditionally favoring paper money, suspension of taxes, and relief from debts however obtained. How many slaves, it may fairly be asked, did these persons, subsisting marginally and by the sweat of their own brows, possess? It may fairly be answered, very few.

Twice in 1784, the popular party in the Virginia legislature swamped efforts by James Madison to remove legal impediments to the payment of the prewar debts. On a critical vote, a majority of representatives from Virginia's Northern Neck—where only 30 per cent of the adult males owned land, with those owning 1,000 acres or more controlling 45 per cent of the land and slaves—supported Madison. Delegates from Southside, an area of small farmers and a center of agitation for paper money and suspension of debts and taxes, opposed the motion by 5½ to 1.[53]

Madison's well-meant efforts had a single concrete result: to tie the issue of debts to the slaves alleged to have been "abducted" by the retiring British forces in 1783 in violation of the treaty of peace. On June 22, 1784, following the overwhelming defeat of Madison's first motion, the Virginia legislature formally resolved that payment of British debts should be suspended until Congress made an effective remonstrance to Britain for carrying off Virginians' slaves. The basis for the action was an "investigation" by Patrick Henry, whose phenomenal speed in rendering a report was greatly facilitated by his limiting his inquiry to a single person, a legislative colleague who had recently returned from an unsuccessful attempt to locate lost slaves in New York.[54] Three years later, a bill was passed in response to a congressional request repealing all Virginia laws contravening the peace; but a rider, suspending its operation until Britain herself complied with the treaty, rendered it a travesty.

The situation was not without a certain humor: the humbler elements in southern society extending their protecting cloak to the grandees of the Tidewater, who quietly acquiesced, pleased, no doubt, at the postponement of payment of debts without their having to bear responsibility for the manner in which it was secured. On the eastern side of the Atlantic, the joke was not apparent. Southern actions were interpreted rather as affording another, unfortunately typical, example of American faithlessness and sharp practice.

Comments in the press, both in editorials and in letters to the editors, showed that for the British public the question of their country's "prior infraction" of the treaty of peace did not exist. The Americans were clearly guilty. Reared on Locke and the sanctity of private property, Britons could boast that "during the bloodiest wars their most inveterate foes trust large sums in their funds and in the hands of their merchants, perfectly secure." The use of public authority to the detriment of private rights was especially offensive; America was "only steadfast in refusing to pay her just debts," and her citizens were "contemners of public faith." Until justice was done to British creditors, citizens of the new republic would continue to appear a "pack of pitiful, unprincipled scoundrels to all Europe."[55] The ministry at home was castigated for "passive behaviour" in response to America's first breach of the treaty with regard to the loyalists.

The lesson was clear: if the Confederation government could not of its own motion secure justice within its territories for British subjects, the former mother country would have to secure it herself. Means lay ready to hand: there were the several forts in the Old Northwest ceded to America under the treaty of peace, but still held by the British. While the continuing occupation doubtless was displeasing to the Americans, the *Morning Chronicle* declared on January 17, 1787, Britain should retain them "to see justice done by the various British creditors of the Americans."[56]

CHAPTER FIVE

The Gordian Knot: Slaves and Posts

ARTICLE VII of the treaty of peace provided for a cessation of hostilities, liberation of captives, and the evacuation of American territory "with all convenient speed." An additional stipulation enjoined that the withdrawal was to be accomplished "without causing any destruction, or carrying away any negroes or other property of the American inhabitants." Britain violated these stipulations on two capital points: after the signing of the peace preliminaries, certain of her subjects "abducted" slaves, the property of Americans, and her forces continued to occupy the ceded forts in the Old Northwest.

From the outset, the slave issue was complex, and probably insoluble on any reasonably accurate statistical basis. During the war, many slaves had fallen into British hands. Some had been legitimate prizes of war, liberated by advancing royal forces and, for the most part, continuing as free men their menial roles as servants and domestics. Others, attracted by proclamations aimed at weakening the American war effort, deserted their masters and sought promised freedom behind British lines. Some took up arms against the rebels. Loyalists moving to a refuge behind the protecting shield of the British army brought numbers of their own slaves with them. Also, American and French soldiers had an unfortunate propensity for looting slaves within the territory under their control.[1] The British argued that Article VII did not apply to Negroes in their hands before the signing of the peace preliminaries. Even so, British garrisons undoubtedly became magnets for runaway slaves and concentration points for slaves seized after Article VII was in full force. To sort out these uprooted blacks, however, was for all practical purposes impossible.

The loss of slaves was understandably a matter of considerable im-

portance to southern planters; and soon after the war ended, it began
to figure in American diplomacy. In September, 1782, James Madison offered a resolution, immediately adopted by Congress, directing
the foreign secretary to instruct the peace commissioners in Paris to
offset claims in behalf of the loyalists with counterclaims for slaves
and other property carried off or destroyed during the war. A detailed
statement of the number and value of slaves and other property was
promised.[2] It was never prepared; but Benjamin Franklin made good
use of the threat to compel British negotiators to accept the loyalist
provisions of the treaty of peace. There the matter might have rested
but for the fortuitous presence in Paris of Henry Laurens, himself
nominally a peace commissioner. Apparently at his suggestion, Article
VII of the preliminaries incorporated the specific prohibition against
carrying away Negroes and other property.

Surviving data are inadequate, unreliable, and fragmentary. It is
known, for example, that the British removed 5,000 Negroes from
the Yorktown area before the final catastrophe; but these could not
have been "abducted" in violation of a treaty not yet negotiated. At
Savannah, evacuated in July, 1782, well before the signing of preliminaries, 1,900 Negroes withdrew with the royal forces. The peace
preliminaries could have applied to none of these. By the end of the
year, 3,524 more blacks had emigrated from the Georgia capital, and
many of these probably came into British hands after the preliminary
treaty was in force.[3] The same is true for the 5,327 Negroes evacuated from Charleston late in 1782. Approximately 3,000 Negroes
were removed from New York after the cessation of hostilities, and
perhaps another thousand left the city "informally." Doubtless many
were "abducted" in the meaning of Article VII. The cities mentioned
were, of course, major staging areas; but Negroes continued to con-
gregate in all places still in British hands until the very end of the
withdrawal, and an undetermined number ultimately left the United
States under circumstances now impossible to ascertain.

To their credit, senior British commanders, plagued by the countless details of military evacuation, tried to separate Negroes legally
and morally entitled to their protection from those who remained
bona fide American property. In May, 1782, General Leslie, commanding the evacuation of Charleston, South Carolina, ordered his
officers to remove Negro servants, legal American property, from the
vessels of the withdrawing fleet. The General readily accepted, too,

the idea of a joint commission to oversee the embarkation of Negroes and permitted American members of the commission to reside within his lines. Slaves who had not been promised their freedom under military proclamation or who had not rendered themselves "obnoxious" to the Americans by overt co-operation with the British, it was agreed, would be returned. Even though the arrangement broke down because of mutual ill will and suspicion, Leslie's intention and good faith were evident.

Sir Guy Carleton, in New York until it was abandoned toward the end of 1783, also showed himself eager to co-operate with the American authorities. In April he ordered the masters of British vessels to abide by the treaty by refraining from carrying off Negroes. At his instigation, too, the New York "Inspection Roll of Negroes," the best and most trustworthy evidence available, was compiled. An American commission—including Colonel William S. Smith, John Adams' future son-in-law and secretary of legation in London—was admitted to inspect British vessels leaving New York. Although it proved impossible for the Americans to perform their duty in the turmoil prevailing in the city, Carleton's intentions were as clear and honorable as Leslie's. Indeed, in a personal interview with Washington in May, the British commander informed the American that although the promise to slaves who had sought the protection of British wartime proclamations would have to be honored, compensation would be given for those carried away after November 30, 1782, the day the peace preliminaries were signed.[4]

Such efforts notwithstanding, the unquestionable fact remains that slaves were removed from the United States in violation of Article VII. The problems are: How many? How much were they worth? Who owned them and deserved restitution? There are no answers. The source from which they should have come stood silent. The American government unfortunately failed to gather authoritative data on the subject. (At a critical point in his mission, John Adams appealed to *British* evidence.) It was an omission the more glaring when compared with the systematic and painstaking efforts of the British government to collect data about the prewar debts.

In May, 1783, Congress instructed the commissioners in Paris on several important points. One was to require firmly and decisively full satisfaction for slaves and other property carried away in violation of the preliminaries. When the matter was raised with Hartley, the coalition ministry had already determined to transform the preliminary treaty into a definitive one and to reserve the discussion of other issues, including a commercial treaty, to negotiations not under the eye of France. The demand concerning the slaves, however, struck fire, Fox bluntly telling Hartley that to have returned Negroes "whom we had invited, seduced if you will, under a promise of liberty, to the tyranny and possibly Vengeance of their former Masters, would have been an act as scarce any orders from his Employers (and no such orders exist) could have induced a Man of Honour to execute."[5] Fox was speaking generally, however, and did not rule out the possibility of "abductions." As Hartley told Franklin, "ulterior points" would constitute part of future negotiations.[6]

Some months intervened, during which Hartley was recalled and the American commission reorganized, Thomas Jefferson replacing John Jay, the new foreign secretary, as the colleague of Dr. Franklin and John Adams. It was not until the autumn of 1784 that conditions seemed favorable for a resumption of diplomatic contact with the British. In October the Americans informed the Duke of Dorset, Britain's ambassador to Paris, of their desire, first, to negotiate a commercial accord with Great Britain, and second, to clarify certain points arising from the treaty of peace. There was especially the question of the prewar debts and "some unusual circumstances . . . that seem to merit consideration." Proposals to modify Article IV were promised. Further, it was suggested that satisfaction should be made speedily for the slaves carried away, with other property, contrary to Article VII.[7] Dorset, of course, was not authorized to enter ministerial discussions with the Americans; but their effort to connect the debt and the slave issues was evident. When John Adams was appointed to London, the new minister tried the same tactic. During Dorset's courtesy call in Paris, in May, 1785, Adams declared that by carrying off the slaves the British had made it harder for debtors to pay their creditors. It was therefore "perfectly just" for the latter to withhold payment. Dorset was polite but noncommittal.[8]

Adams' assumption, of course, was that the loss of the slaves had been sustained by those who owed the greater part of the prewar debts. In London he was quickly disabused of the notion. Conferring with two representatives of interested Glasgow merchants—Alexander Brown and Patrick Colquhoun, sometime provost of the northern metropolis and a friend of Colonel William Smith—he won acceptance of the principle of instalment payment. Colquhoun expressed fear, general among his associates, "at the spirit of migration into the wilderness of America." The merchants "thought it wrong to be restrained from arresting the person or attaching property of a debtor whom they saw about to remove to Kentucky and other places, where they could never be come at." Clearly, the creditors' chief concern was not the great plantation owner; and Adams was candid enough to admit that "this was new to me."[9]

Unsure of his ground and lacking information, Adams was prepared to turn to other matters. When he met William Pitt on August 24, he mentioned the slaves in an almost offhand manner, giving priority to the posts and a new commercial accord. The American must have been surprised, therefore, when Pitt turned at once to the slaves. In what was obviously an attempt to clear away less important differences before meeting the larger problems, Pitt admitted that the British had clearly violated the treaty and promised satisfaction. How many Negroes were involved? The question was fundamental, but Adams was unable to answer it. The flustered Bostonian could refer only to the very incomplete data possessed by Sir Guy Carleton and by his own secretary, Colonel William Smith—who, it will be remembered, had been a member of the inspection commission at the time of the evacuation of New York.[10] Altogether, it was not a happy performance—an American minister appealing to British evidence for substantiation of a complaint against the British government. Worse, it was a missed opportunity. If Adams had been able to take advantage of Pitt's opening, it is altogether possible that a settlement of the slave issue might have been achieved at the very outset of the mission. Had this been the case, the reassuring and friendly influence of the development might well have changed dramatically the subsequent course of Anglo-American negotiations.

For a time the American minister was optimistic. Mrs. Adams wrote to her son in September that Pitt and Carmarthen appeared generally to possess "the most liberal ideas with respect to us." As for the Negroes, specifically, the two ministers were "full and clear that they ought to be paid for." In May, 1786, Adams reported home that although he was concentrating attention on the posts, the British continued to admit in conversation that recompense for the Negroes must be made. He would defer further action, however, until Secretary Jay transmitted "the whole amount and evidence of the claim."

Would Congress, he asked, give explicit instructions "to demand payment for the negroes in money, and especially at what prices they should be stated?"[11] Congress did not respond; and the issue rested on dead center while more serious differences arose to plague Anglo-American relations.

The end of the war found Britain in possession of nine forts in the Old Northwest. Two were at the head of Lake Champlain; Oswegatchie (Ogdensburg, New York) controlled the Upper St. Lawrence and Oswego the route from Lake Ontario to the Mohawk; Niagara, Presqu'isle (Erie, Pennsylvania), and Sandusky dominated routes from Lake Erie to the Ohio. Detroit and Machilimackinac shielded the mouth of Lake Michigan. These places the British were bound under Article VII to hand over to the Americans "with all convenient speed."[12]

From the first, the cession, part of Shelburne's calculated generosity to the Americans in the interest of reconciliation and close economic partnership, caused considerable indignation in Britain. The fur traders of Quebec, too, were outraged at the abandonment of hunting areas and centers of supply and transportation—hence their staunch support of Sheffield and Eden in the campaign of 1782 to destroy the American Intercourse Bill and to draw the strict line of economic nationalism against the former subjects. The coalition ministry, critical of Shelburne's peace and pressed by the fur traders, tried to retrieve the situation by instructing David Hartley to propose to the American commissioners free and equal rights on the waterways of "Quebec" for both parties. Posts and forts contiguous to these avenues, the proposition continued, would be held by Britain for three years to safeguard the evacuation of her nationals and their property. Here was the first indication of a desire to delay evacuation of the posts, and the validity of the reason cannot be gainsaid.

In June, 1783, Hartley reported home from Paris that the Americans were willing to let a limited number of British troops remain in the posts, but only until Congress called upon them to withdraw. At that time, the new sovereign would provide garrisons sufficient to protect the inhabitants of the surrounding country.[13]

The preoccupation now shared by both sides at the negotiating table was no longer with the fur trade, but with the fear of hostilities in the backcountry waged by savages "enraged to find themselves betrayed into the hands of those people against whom they have been excited to war."[14] As we have seen, Hartley's negotiations with the Americans were broken off; but fears for peace with the Indians continued to grow more intense.

The specter of an Indian uprising figured, too, in General Haldimand's encounter, noted above, with General Steuben. Telling the American agent that he continued to hold (temporary) possession of the posts because the definitive treaty had not yet come to hand, Haldimand justified himself to the home government by pleading the imminent danger of an Indian attack upon British subjects in the area of the posts.[15]

By the time the dispatch reached London, the Fox-North coalition had fallen, Pitt had taken office, and the political world was in confusion for several months as the new government fought to establish itself. It was not until April, 1784, that the Pitt ministry, with a triumph in the general election behind them, took up Haldimand's report. Secretary of State Lord Sydney, formerly Thomas Townshend, conveyed to the commander in Canada the official sanction for his action, and himself contributed another reason for delaying delivery of the posts: retaliation for breaches of the treaty by the United States, which had not complied with "even one article of the treaty." Britain, therefore, could surely "reconcile it in the present instance to delay the evacuation of these posts." Still, Sydney clearly intended the measure to be temporary—"at least until we are enabled to secure the traders in the interior of the country and withdraw their property."[16] He noted that the treaty had, after all, set no fixed date for the transfer of the posts.

In May, 1784, before Sydney's approving dispatch could have arrived in Canada, Haldimand again anticipated his government. In a statement noted earlier, he informed Lieutenant Colonel Fish, envoy from Governor Clinton of New York, that while he lacked official instructions, he privately believed the posts would be retained until the United States honored its commitments toward the loyalists. In July, Haldimand administered another polite but firm rebuff to Colonel Hull, a new representative from Congress.[17] The commander in chief in Canada and the secretary of state in London thus concluded almost simultaneously and independently that the posts should be retained temporarily. Their reasons now were: first, to secure British lives and property in the backcountry; and second, to force American compliance with the treaty of peace. Quite obviously, consideration for the fur trade had ceased to play an important role in British thinking, and Britain was founding basic justification for the decision to retain the posts on the "all convenient speed" clause of Article VII.

By the autumn of 1784, the Americans knew the British game: to keep the posts until the Republic repaired her own breaches of the treaty, above all the debt stipulations. Inexorably, then, two dominant issues, debts and posts, had come to face each other in maddening equilibrium—the United States demanding delivery of the posts, but unable to compel obedience to the debt stipulation; Britain clinging to the posts, "a rod over our heads," as Abigail Adams rightly diagnosed, to force payment of debts to her subjects.[18]

Adams was fully aware of the importance of the debt issue. He worked hard in London to achieve an understanding with the creditor merchants, and particularly to win their agreement to payments both delayed and by instalment. After a trial run with Dorset in Paris— to let loose the law in the present circumstances, he argued, would ruin debtor and, consequently, creditor—the American minister presented a more elaborate brief to the British creditors themselves.[19] On June 4—very soon after his arrival in London—he received the visit from Glasgow merchants Colquhoun and Brown mentioned earlier in this chapter. The visitors expressed delight that Congress had sent a minister and, pointedly, declared their hope that the debt question could be settled without their having to make application to the government for its intervention. Apparently some specific reference was made to delinquencies in New York and Virginia.

Adams' defense was good-humored and moderate: America had just emerged from an impoverishing war; agriculture and commerce had suffered; much property had been destroyed. All this "rendered it difficult for any debtor, and impossible for many" to pay their debts immediately. There was "a general disposition" to pay as fast as possible, but "time and patience" were necessary. Glossing over actions of the southern states, and especially those of Virginia, Adams continued that "if there had been any interposition of the governments in America, it had been, as I presumed, solely with a view of giving time to negotiate an explication of the article of the treaty, and to prevent the imprudence of hasty creditors from hurting themselves as well as the debtors, to no good end." A principal object of his mission, he said, was "to negotiate this affair with the ministry," but he would always be ready to hear proposals, explanations, or arguments from individual Britons. He was optimistic. If only the merchants could be brought to forego wartime interest and to consent to "a reasonable time" for payment, he thought "the whole might be arranged to mutual benefit and satisfaction."

Adams found the response gratifying. Avoiding a specific reply on the subject of interest, Colquhoun assured him that the Glasgow merchants were fully aware of the American situation. They were willing to wait, but they wished to be specific about the number of instalments—five were acceptable. Here, too, the Scot expressed the general alarm among his friends at "the spirit of migration."

Adams, admitting that the point was new to him, replied that even Kentucky and other frontier settlements were under the legal jurisdiction of some state. Suits could thus go forward; and, indeed, he added, warming to his subject, "as those removals commonly advanced the fortune of the emigrant, it might be rather a benefit to his creditors." (As it turned out, the merchants obviously apprehended the realities of frontier life more clearly than the gentleman from Braintree.) Virginia particularly, Adams maintained, had suffered heavily in its ability to pay its debts by the loss of its slaves. New York was hurt by the loss of a lucrative fur trade, the result of the British retention of the Northwestern posts. It was an ingenious attempt to connect slaves and posts on the one hand with debts on the other.

The interview broke up with satisfaction on both sides, however; and the Glaswegians believed they were on the verge of an understanding about the debts. Hence, they promised they would return to Scotland without seeking a parliamentary intervention which, they said, would doubtless cause great "clamor." Congratulating himself for having avoided so noisy a business as a "petition to parliament," Adams was evidently within reach of a magnificent success.

He bungled the next step, however, and the splendid opportunity disappeared. Instead of working carefully and patiently to settle the debt issue, he sought to use it to force a comprehensive settlement—on American terms—of Anglo-American differences, including the much-desired relaxation of British commercial restrictions. By grasping at too much, he destroyed the fragile web of merchant confidence, roughly touched Britain's maritime interests, and roused official suspicion of American motives and good faith.

Because Secretary of State Carmarthen was ill, Adams was unable to see the minister until June 17. It was a critical interview.[20] The envoy began with a *tour d'horizon*, listing American grievances against Britain: the posts, the Negroes, and the "losses of our merchants as well as theirs if we were unseasonably pressed for the payment" of the prewar debts. There were several minor points and a final major one: British commercial restrictions upon American commerce. Taking the bull firmly by the horns, he admitted that the debts appeared to be the most important issue between the two countries. American debtors were eager to pay the British creditors, Adams declared; nothing had higher priority with them: "they thought their moral characters and their reputations as men, as well as their credit as merchants, concerned in it." In his view, however, the salient features of British policy—retention of the posts, the abduction of slaves, the trade restrictions, and even the post-armistice captures of American vessels and the slowness in liquidating the accounts of prisoners of war—were much to blame, contributing "very much to obstruct our merchants in their honest exertions to discharge their debts to the merchants of Great Britain."

After hearing Adams out, Carmarthen read aloud a petition from several merchants (all "clamor" had not been avoided, then), complaining specifically of the failure in the Virginia legislature of Madison's bill repealing legal impediments to the recovery of debts. Other more general grievances were also listed: the loss of interest during the war and the inability to restrain debtors from alienating property or from escaping legal process by disappearing into the wilderness. Carmarthen added, however, that he was not without hope that in time and with patience all differences could be extinguished. Private passions might sometimes get in the way; but "while the ministers on both sides could keep right," he was sanguine about success. Let Adams put something in writing "to begin upon"; and since the posts seemed most pressing to the Americans, they would furnish the appropriate first entry in the list. So far so good.

At this point, Adams, lulled by the tone of the interview, was indiscreet. He told the Secretary, "between him and me," that he was instructed by Congress "to require" (a strong word) evacuation of the posts. He wished, however, to be as delicate as possible. Would Carmarthen indicate the ministry's intentions? Had orders perhaps already gone out for the evacuation of the posts?

Carmarthen must have been surprised by a query which, at best, could only have appeared ingenuous. The Secretary, now obviously on the reserve, made a curious request: would Adams put his question in writing to give Carmarthen himself ground for taking up the matter with his colleagues? The matter was so serious that the Briton was apparently unwilling to make a Cabinet issue of a subject presented in a *viva voce* exchange.

Three days after the meeting, on June 20, Adams sent Carmarthen a memorial upon the posts.[21] Recalling Article VII of the treaty of peace, he noted that two years had elapsed, and American posts and territory were still held by British forces. He was particularly instructed by Congress to ask if orders had gone out to the governor of Canada or commanders in chief in America for the withdrawal of the garrisons, or whether His Majesty's ministers had fixed upon a date for the evacuation of them. The word "require" was not used. A lengthy silence followed. Pitt and his colleagues were deeply engaged in urgent Irish business, and the collection of data on the prewar debts was also proving a time-consuming task.

As the weeks passed, Adams' early optimism began to fade. In July some minor matters were discussed, but the envoy had ample time to draft his project for a commercial treaty.[22] It was late August, after the controversial Irish resolutions had been rejected and Parliament had risen, that negotiations were seriously resumed.

Pitt himself met with Adams on August 24. He was obviously ready to give satisfaction for the slaves and the less important issue of post-armistice maritime captures. As for the posts, however, they were "a point connected with some others, that I think must be settled at the same time." He meant the debts. The issue was thus fully and unequivocally joined: the posts for the debts. No other peripheral matters—of wartime interest or the alleged difficulty of paying debts because of British trade restrictions—could obscure that fundamental fact.[23]

The British position was simply reaffirmed when Adams saw Carmarthen in October. When the American sought to argue that Britain's retention of the posts was encouraging the Indians to rise against the American frontier, Carmarthen was obviously preoccupied, replying "in broken sentences" that he wished "the ministry would answer everybody" and "conveyed a hint that it did not depend upon him." Whatever Carmarthen's meaning might have been, it certainly did not extend to a retreat about the debts: " 'To be sure, nothing could be done until the debts were paid,' " Adams quoted the minister as declaring. " 'Paid! my Lord!' " the angry Adams ejaculated, " 'that is more than ever was stipulated.' " According to his own account, he then charged Britain with the first breaches of the treaty, specifying the Negroes and the posts. They were infractions without which he "did believe that the debtors would not have had influence enough in any assembly to have procured an act or vote to impede the course of the law." Adams may have spoken more obliquely to Carmarthen, however, than the blunt statement reported to Jay. The American recorded no response from the Briton, and Carmarthen's account made no mention of Adams' declaration.[24]

For several weeks, contact between Adams and the ministry was limited to relatively minor matters. The American was invariably treated with courtesy; and officials were obliging—even conciliatory. When Adams protested against the insulting behavior of a British naval captain at Boston, for example, full satisfaction was immediately forthcoming. Complaints at the impressment of American seamen were given sympathetic attention.[25] But on the subject of his memorial, Adams met only silence.

The British government was, however, far from inactive. Preparing to place posts against debts, it was heavily engaged with the creditors, collecting massive information and receiving voluminous advice and encouragement from them. Soon after Adams' interview with Carmarthen, the Glasgow group memorialized Home Secretary Henry Dundas. Fearing—rightly—that the American envoy intended to use the unpaid debts to force a more favorable commercial agreement from Britain, they urged that the two matters be kept quite distinct unless, it was innocently suggested, the government itself should grant compensation from the public coffers.[26] The Committee of Merchants of London, Bristol, Whitehaven, and Glasgow trading to Virginia, Maryland, and North Carolina before 1776 supplied similar counsel—"A Few Hints"—to the Foreign Secretary. An equitable adjustment of the debt issue, they said, should precede any new commercial negotiation. Complaining bitterly that in Virginia and Maryland there was "more Ability than Inclination" to pay debts, they would willingly accept payment in instalments in order to avoid further losses through deaths, bankruptcies, and migrations. In a second memorial, they demanded the decisive interposition of government to compel American observance of the treaty.[27]

Simultaneously, Adams, impatient and weary, prepared to bring matters to an issue. About November 30, he finished drafting a formal demand requiring Britain to evacuate the posts. For more than a week, he kept the document by him. Chancing to meet Carmarthen at court on December 8, he asked the Foreign Secretary if the ministry had reached a decision on the major points of difference between the two countries. The answer was negative: "Nothing was yet determined," Adams quoted Carmarthen to Jay; "Mr. Pitt had all my papers under consideration, and he had not yet determined any thing." Adams thereupon presented the requisition prepared days before.[28]

Carmarthen duly forwarded the document to Pitt; and on December 16 the First Minister gave his opinion. It was "very material" to settle differences with America, and he saw many reasons "to make dispatch very important." He insisted, however, that this should be done independently of any new commercial negotiations. The American demand was firmly founded upon the treaty, to be sure; but the Prime Minister wrote, "there are Articles to be performed on their Part which we must equally insist upon." He left no doubt of his meaning. Carmarthen was asked "to collect the several applications which have been made by the American Creditors for the Interposition of Government." The answer to Adams' memorial was "to state that, and every other Point in which We have any Claim on them as necessary to go Hand in Hand with what they ask."[29]

Pitt's desire for speed notwithstanding, six weeks passed before Adams had his answer. There were further consultations with the American merchants involving both Carmarthen and Pitt, and the collection of data about the debts continued with great thoroughness. A spate of newspaper paragraphs quite unjustifiably predicted an Anglo-American commercial treaty. Adams himself began to entertain a flicker of hope. "I have only time to acquaint you," Adams wrote to Jay in early January, 1786, "that, since my last, there have been some appearances of an intention in ministry to take up American affairs." Quickly, he supplied the British merchants with confidential information (transmitted through Smith, his secretary, and probably Duncan Campbell, chairman of one of the merchant committees) about the American position. Rumors soon reached him that the merchants' representation to their own government was in strong language, presumably sympathetic to America. He had not, he admitted, been able to get a copy; but he had heard that the merchants "pretend to say that Mr. Pitt assured them their report had given him new light, and they think America may have whatever she desires, except a free trade with the West India Islands."[30] It was well that he had not lost all sense of caution.

The fantasy was rapidly coming to an end. Denouement was at hand. In mid-January, Adams learned from Carmarthen that he was "labouring at an Answer" to the November memorial. The American minister was relieved that the period of waiting was almost over. "For whatever Conditions they may tack to the Surrender of the Posts," he wrote to Jefferson, "We shall find out what is broiling in their Hearts, and by degrees come together." He did not expect a rough answer. "They will smooth it as much as they can and I shall transmit it to Congress who may again pass the smoothing plain over it." The end would be, he confidently predicted, an accommodation, even though he thought it might take another year and a half to finish the business.[31]

On February 27, Carmarthen apologized to Adams again for the continuing delay, but explained that the collection of all available information on the debts—to allow him to "state in one view, all acts of the assemblies which had imposed impediments"—had been a lengthy affair, indeed.[32] The very next day, however, Adams had his answer. It was a shower of ice water. The King's fixed determination was always to act in conformity with principles of justice and good faith; the Americans, by contrast, had flagrantly violated the treaty of peace. Already many British subjects had been reduced to the gravest degree of distress. Treaty stipulations were mutually and equally binding on the contracting parties. It was folly and injustice to think Britain alone was obliged to a strict observance of the treaty while America was "free to deviate from its own engagements as often as convenience might render such deviation necessary though at the expense of its own National Credit and Importance." When justice was done to British creditors and America manifested a "real determination to fulfil her part of the Treaty," then Britain would quickly prove her sincere desire to co-operate in putting the treaty of peace "into real and compleat Effect." Accompanying the formal answer was a "State of the Grievances" indicating that every state in the American Union had violated Article IV, although it was obvious that the vast majority of offenses had occurred in the southern states.[33]

The cold formality of the communication deserves some measure of explanation. Earlier contacts between Adams and the ministry had been civil enough, if not cordial; and the American envoy had been generally pleased at his reception, public and private, in Britain. There was public indignation, of course, at mistreatment of loyalists, but this had been present since the end of the war. To be sure, pressure from creditors was mounting steadily in 1785 and 1786, but this cannot account for the tone of Carmarthen's reply to Adams. The explanation must lie rather in Adams' maladroit use of the debt issue and, even more rankling, in his "requirement." Here was the envoy of a government unable to make its writ run in its own land, lacking information on a point of fundamental importance to his mission, paying no attention at all to serious British grievances, yet "requiring" Britain to act at America's good pleasure, and demanding in the bargain a new commercial accord directly conflicting with British maritime interests. It was impudent and absurd, and, Pitt and his colleagues must have concluded, fully deserving Carmarthen's tough answer.

The traditional interpretation of these events has been that of Thomas Jefferson, who visited Adams in London in the spring of 1786, well after Adams had played—and lost—the game. The principal purpose of the trip to the British capital was to lend a hand with certain negotiations not involving Britain; but it was also the occasion for the celebrated confrontation at George III's levée, as well as abortive attempts to reopen commercial negotiations with the ministry and to reach a conclusive understanding with the creditors.[34] It was a traversing of old ground, and the outcome was predictable, particularly since the two Americans tried once more to tie the debts to a new commercial treaty.

In a meeting with Duncan Campbell, chairman of the Committee of Merchant Creditors, the envoys suggested a settlement based on immediate legal judgments, payment in five annual instalments, and interest before and after, but not during, the war. Campbell termed the proposal about interest "a bitter pill," but he did not reject the proposition as a whole. At this point history repeated itself: the Americans told their visitor that a necessary prerequisite to a settlement of the debt issue was a commercial treaty, "were it only as a means of enabling our country to pay its debts." Campbell quite properly replied that he was not authorized "to speak on the subject

of the future commerce," and withdrew, promising to consult Carmarthen about the Americans' proposal for the payment of the debts
and to communicate again with the Americans.[35] It was a promise he
never kept. In truth, there was nothing further to say until the
Gordian knot was sundered.

Jefferson, again in Paris and full of bitterness against the un-
forgiven enemy, probed the French minister Vergennes on his government's view of Britain's continued occupation of the posts. Proceeding delicately, since he feared Vergennes might respond with a query
about an American guarantee for the French West Indies, Jefferson
charged Britain with the initial breach of the treaty of peace and
added that the merchants in London had wished to compromise the
debt issue. An accommodation would have been reached, he believed,
but for Carmarthen, who showed "no disposition to have these matters arranged." Here for the Virginian was "a sufficient proof" that
the debt issue "was not the true cause of their retaining the posts."[36]
Jefferson's version was in embryo the venerable and widely accepted
myth of devious, intriguing, and vengeful Britain ardently persecut-
ing virtuous and long-suffering America.

Jefferson was, however, involved in Adams' negotiations only in
the most peripheral manner. British and American positions had been
laid down well before he appeared, so briefly, upon the London
scene. Further, his disposition to put the most unfavorable interpretation possible upon British motive and policy is well known. In
short, Jefferson's view of Adams' mission and of his own small contribution to it was based on partial evidence, interpreted by a prejudiced agent. The dispassionate observer must reject it as a basis for
his own conclusions. Adams, who *knew* the facts, was well aware of
the underlying reasons for his diplomatic failure—and his account
jibes very little with Jefferson's. "There is a subject so closely connected with the business of my mission to this court," he wrote to a
relative in the Massachusetts Assembly, "that I can no longer be silent
upon it with honor. The most insuperable bar to all my negotiations
here has been laid by those states which have made laws against the
treaty." His countrymen had "too long trifled with public and private faith, public and private credit." America herself should comply with the treaty, he recommended. Having put herself in the
right, she should then demand that Britain do the same. If the latter
failed to evacuate the posts immediately, he "would not go to attack

them, but declare war directly, and march one army to Quebec and another to Nova Scotia."[37] What a pity that his country failed to accept this manly and honorable advice!

There were Americans who agreed with Adams, and some were high in the councils of the Confederation government. "They who ask Equity, should do it," Foreign Secretary Jay told his friends, and he incorporated the principle in his secret report on Carmarthen's answer to Adams, which he presented to Congress on October 13, 1786. There had not been "a single day since it [the treaty] took effect, on which it has not been violated in America, by one or other of the States," he told Adams. If only his country could be brought to admit her infractions with candor and goodwill, he believed the way would be opened to a comprehensive and amicable settlement with Britain.[38] In an extraordinary and desperate effort to keep the Adams mission afloat, Jay even informed British Consul-General Temple of the nature of the secret report, asking only that the information not be repeated in the United States. The document was, Temple immediately (and accurately though ungrammatically) reported to Carmarthen, "a full acknowledgment that many of the most important Articles in your Lordship's statement were just—Must be admitted as fact— and consequently a violation of the Subsisting Treaty."[39]

Congress, stirred by the communications from Jay and Adams, duly called upon the states in the spring of 1787 to repair their infractions of the treaty. Massachusetts complied almost at once; Connecticut and Maryland followed. New Hampshire, Rhode Island, New Jersey, and New York then acted. North Carolina complied before the end of the year. John Adams was encouraged, and proudly informed the British government that Congress was indeed fulfilling the treaty. Suggesting a joint commission to settle the slave issue, he declared that his country was ready "fairly to discuss and accommodate every difference or Complaint that may arise relative to the Construction, or to the Performance of the Treaty—that they are determined to execute it with good Faith."[40]

Brave words and a gallant effort—but Consul Phineas Bond, at his post in Philadelphia, saw the fatal weakness. There was indeed a disposition in Congress "to remove every Cause of Complaint on the Part of Great Britain," he wrote home; but the Congress lacked "means to enforce their regulations." A single state, he noted, was able to nullify the most urgent congressional recommendation.[41]

The single state he had in mind was Virginia. Duly repealing her laws impeding the recovery of British debts in her courts, the legislature of the state went on to mock both British and Confederation governments: the action was suspended until the former mother country made amends for her prior infraction of the treaty.

PART III

*Federal Measures
And British Policy*

CHAPTER SIX

"Unofficial" Diplomacy

ON SEPTEMBER 20, 1787, Consul Phineas Bond dispatched to Carmarthen a copy of the new American Constitution, the crowning achievement of the convention which had completed its work only three days before. The plan of government "when due Consideration is paid to the democratic Temper of the Times" was, in Bond's opinion, "perhaps the best Shape in which it could have been handed forth to the People."[1] Carmarthen himself congratulated a defeated and disgruntled John Adams on the eve of his return to the United States. "I presume, Mr. Adams, that the States will all immediately adopt the new constitution," the Briton told the envoy. "I have read it with pleasure; it is very well drawn up." Adams, scornful of this "oracular utterance," read Carmarthen's meaning correctly: it was "what has all along been insinuated, that there is not as yet any national government; but that, as soon as there shall be one, the British Court will vouchsafe to treat with it."[2]

Carmarthen was, in fact, expressing the prevailing British opinion that the new political arrangement in the United States heralded an altogether more promising and respectable stage in the life of the Republic. The press followed the convention's work closely; and when the new instrument of government was handed to the world, it was published in full for the scrutiny and edification of the newspaper readers of the kingdom. The battle over its adoption aroused the keenest interest. The Constitution was a "work of inspiration," the more praiseworthy because it included "something like King, Lords, and Commons, though under different names." It recalled "the wisdom of Greece and Rome." When Washington assumed the presidency, he was saluted as "that illustrious character who has shewn himself superior in war, and equally serviceable to his country in peace."[3] Much of the British enthusiasm focused upon the Constitution's explicit language about the sanctity of treaties and the system of federal courts. Straitened merchants with prewar debts and the ministers who received their complaints believed they could finally look forward to a speedy settlement of the troublesome issue.[4]

The new political arrangements in America did not, however, produce an immediate solution for Anglo-American discord. Instead, the acquisition of strength by the central government sparked something very like a crisis in Anglo-American relations, producing a flurry of "unofficial" diplomatic activity, a thoroughgoing re-examination of British policy toward the Republic, and, finally, the appointment of Britain's first minister plenipotentiary to the new nation.

On April 8, 1789, during the very first session of the First Congress, Representative James Madison, whose ardent support of the Constitution in Virginia had cost him a seat in the Senate, brought forward proposals which promised a heavy blow to British interests. The Virginian would have American vessels pay a duty of 9¢ the ton; those belonging to foreign powers in commercial treaty with the United States, 30¢; and all others (principally, of course, Britain), 50¢. Import duties would favor French brandies over West Indian rums.[5]

Any pretense that Madison's aim was not specifically anti-British was cast aside in debate, the Virginian contrasting British discrimination with French efforts to relax trade regulations. While the United States opened every one of her ports to Britain, Madison argued, the latter excluded American vessels from the rich trade with her sugar islands and allowed them to carry only their own native produce to the British Isles. To force Britain to accept the American version of reciprocity, discrimination against her vessels and her goods was necessary. At the same time, by judicious encouragement, the country would gain ships sufficient for its own purposes, seamen to man them, and, thus, the basis of a naval power to protect her trade and territory. Knowing his proposals would be opposed by many of his fellow southerners, fearful that freight prices would rise at the hands of greedy and favored New England shipowners, Madison was willing to discriminate in favor of American vessels but slightly at the outset. Higher levels would come later, after the country had provided herself with vessels enough to accommodate American needs.

On three separate occasions, the House of Representatives declared in favor of Madison's proposals; but in June they were rejected by the Senate. Southerners, including the senators from Virginia, were, indeed, apprehensive that discrimination against British shipping would ultimately cost their constituents increased freight charges. New Englanders and New Yorkers—profiting from trade with Britain, the exclusion from the West Indian ports notwithstanding, and objecting to the duties on rum—opposed as well. Subsequently, the Senate action was upheld by the House; and the first attempt to discriminate against British vessels and produce failed.[6]

British observers took some comfort from the rejection of Madison's proposals; but they remained surprised and perturbed, uneasy that the attempt had come at all and had so nearly succeeded. Phineas Bond lamented that Madison was "ill informed as to the permanent System of commercial Intercourse between Great Britain and these states—and loses Sight of the great and equitable Principle of Reciprocity."[7] His colleague Temple expressed alarm, too; and George Miller, in Charleston, deduced that the Virginian aimed at forcing Britain into a trade treaty "by waging a kind of commercial war" to compel "some relaxation in her Navigation laws." There was no panic, however, no suggestion that Britain hastily modify her policy. If America insisted on a trial of strength, Britain must spurn any thought of changing her navigation system. She would surely find "methods to counteract this policy without such a sacrifice; and congress being the Aggressor, cannot be surprized with retaliation."[8]

Refusing Madison's discriminatory resolutions, the new Congress nonetheless passed two other acts, one levying import duties and the other a tax on ship tonnage. The line was drawn between favored American ships and goods on the one hand, and all foreigners on the other. Even without overt discrimination against Britain, they furnished much food for thought in political and commercial ranks of the kingdom; and at the end of September the two acts were referred for study to Charles Jenkinson, new Lord Hawkesbury and president of the Board of Trade.[9]

When, the following year, the Tonnage Act came up for renewal, the indefatigable Madison—encouraged by the arrival in New York of Thomas Jefferson, the new secretary of state—again attempted to induce Congress to adopt commercial discriminations against Britain. A press campaign in which both Jefferson and Madison were active underscored the latter's indictment in Congress of British policy.[10] Despite early signs that success was within his grasp, Madison failed once more to carry his program of strong measures; and on June 24 the Tonnage Act was adopted without change. Left behind, however, were much anti-British sentiment and a rising indignation, shared by both Federalists and their enemies, at Britain's exclusion of American vessels from her West Indian islands.

The new vigor and initiative—unknown in the days of the Confederation—were presently translated to the diplomatic scene. In October, 1789, President Washington—accepting the advice of Secretary of the Treasury Alexander Hamilton and Chief Justice John Jay, who themselves may have been reacting to a *sub rosa* approach from the British ministry—set in motion a plan to probe British intentions.[11] As Britain had never appointed an official minister to the United States, John Adams' mission to London nothwithstanding, it was deemed more dignified to give the new American agent an unofficial character. Washington settled on Gouverneur Morris of New York, then in Paris on private business. On October 13, the President, enclosing a letter of credence in his own hand, asked Morris to undertake the assignment. He was instructed to inform the British ministry that the new Constitution and system of federal courts removed the ground for British retention of the northwestern posts; and that the country looked to their speedy evacuation. Inquiry should likewise be made about the expected compensation for the slaves.

The question of a commercial treaty was to be raised as well. Reminding Morris of Madison's recent efforts to induce discrimination against British trade and nagivation, the President asserted that only "conciliatory considerations, and the probability that the late change in our government and circumstances would lead to more satisfactory arrangements" had prevented the success of the proposed measures. Morris should learn, therefore, what terms the British required for a treaty of commerce. There was a single American *sine qua non*: "the privilege of carrying our productions in our vessels to their islands, and of bringing in return the productions of those islands to our own ports and markets." Without an assurance on this vital point, commercial negotiations should not even be allowed to begin.

Finally, Morris was to ascertain British intentions about sending a diplomatic representative to the United States. Washington's instructions were moderate—tacitly acknowledging American breaches of the peace by contending that the new Constitution answered British complaints against the United States in this regard—and included at least a degree of flexibility. The two areas of negotiation, the unfulfilled peace and commercial relations, were not made contingent upon each other (as Jefferson and Adams had intimated they were in their conversations with representatives of the British merchants in 1786). Even if the subject should arise at the outset of Morris' *pourparlers*, however, and the British ministry should indicate an adherence to established policy, the American might still succeed in clearing the air about the unfulfilled treaty of peace and in establishing an atmosphere of cordiality looking to a subsequent settlement by official representatives of the two countries.[12] Unfortunately, Gouverneur Morris failed in these modest but important tasks; and it is to be feared that the reasons cannot be divorced from his own shortcomings.

Morris received Washington's commission on January 21, 1790, immediately accepted it, and expressed optimism about the British disposition to form a "connexion"—a word which recurred frequently in the subsequent proceedings—with the United States. He would, he promised the President, proceed immediately to London.[13] It was not until the middle of February, however, that Paris was put behind him. After wending his way through the Low Countries at a leisurely pace, Morris finally arrived in London on March 27. Unknown to him and to the public, Britain, incensed by the seizure of certain vessels in Nootka Sound off the northwestern coast of North America, stood on the verge of war with Spain. Had he tried, the new envoy could scarcely have arranged a more awkward moment to begin his mission.

Gouverneur Morris shared much with John Adams, his official predecessor. Both served their states and the nation with ability and dedication during the American Revolution; the sunshine patriot was not their *genre*. Each exhibited, withal, a conservatism which made the French Revolution, less than a decade after the successful conclusion of their own struggle, detestable. Talent was mixed inextricably with vanity; and contempt for "popularity" masked deep concern for one's public image. They shared, too, the same gnawing sense of insecurity, which led each to conclude that he was undervalued by his fellows.

Even greater, however, were the differences which separated the two men. Adams' intellectual depth was matched by Morris' super-ficiality; his solemn and moral rectitude, by dashing and successful raids upon the boudoirs of Paris. Common sense and industry marked one mission to London; misjudgment and supercilious trifling, the other. Years later, after a hot political argument with French radicals, Morris wrote in his diary, "I had better have let this alone; but zeal always gets the better of prudence." He could well have made the same judgment on his dealings with the British ministry in 1790.[14]

Morris conferred with Carmarthen, recently transformed by the death of his father into the Duke of Leeds, for the first time on March 29.[15] The beginning was auspicious enough. The Briton expressed "much warmth and gladness" at Washington's letter and gave general assurances of his government's readiness "to cultivate a friendly and commercial intercourse" with the United States. Almost at once, Morris proceeded to specifics. The adoption of the Constitution and the organization of the federal courts, he told Leeds in accordance with Washington's instructions, effectively removed all obstacles to the recovery of the prewar debts. America, therefore, stood acquitted of her treaty obligations. In response, Leeds was polite, but was far from accepting Morris' proposition. Let the unsatisfied conditions of the peace, he urged, be performed in the order they held in the treaty itself—a suggestion which would clearly leave the evacuation of the posts contingent on American satisfaction on debts and loyal-ists.

For a second time, Morris asserted that the new order in the United States was in itself a sufficient performance. Rather inconsis-tently, however, he then shifted ground, explaining the non-payment of debts as an "overruling necessity," the result of the abduction of slaves. Payment for the Negroes, he added, interpreting the treaty in a manner which may have shocked Leeds, was stipulated in the peace; and American debtors—the old story again—"had formed a reliance on such payment for the discharge of debts contracted with British merchants, both previously and subsequently to the war."

Mentally, Leeds must have thrown up his hands. The "little em-barrassment" Morris thought he detected in the Duke was, doubtless, surprise and annoyance that Morris—who had evidently not been briefed on the course of the Adams mission—had resurrected the posi-tion which Adams himself had learned long ago was untenable. The Secretary replied shortly that he wished the slave issue had already been settled, obliquely implying that the failure was none of his doing. Probably concluding that Morris intended to justify a continuing refusal to give justice to British creditors, Leeds deliberately steered the conversation into another channel. Expressing regret that Britain had not sent a diplomatic representative to America already (a regret doubly felt, no doubt, since he might then have been spared the present interview), Carmarthen attributed the delay to the desire "to have a man every way equal to the task, a man of abilities and one agreeable to the people of America." This was difficult, he continued, since the Republic was "a great way off and many object on that score." Morris was skeptical and broke off abruptly, if not rudely. It was not "worth while to discuss the winds and weather"; Leeds would probably choose to consider the matter a little, and to read again the treaty and compare it with the American Constitution." He expected a speedy reply. None came.

Morris' brusque behavior aside, there were other reasons for ministerial distance. Even before he called on Leeds, the American visited La Luzerne, the French ambassador in London, and communicated to him "*in confidence*," as he subsequently reported to Washington, "that you had directed me to call for a performance of the treaty." His explanation for what must have appeared to the British to be a gratuitous and studied affront was that "the thing itself cannot remain a secret"; and he wished his country to be able to say "that in every step relating to the treaty of peace we have acted confidentially in regard to our ally." It was a sense of delicacy which did not always mark Morris' action.

A second indiscretion soon followed. On April 17, about three weeks after he met with Leeds, Morris dined in company with Charles James Fox. He took the occasion to question the inveterate enemy of the ministry about its plans for American affairs. Fox, scarcely a great authority on the formulation of the government's policy, spoke critically of the Prime Minister: Pitt "would not trouble his head about the matter, but would probably leave it to Lord Hawkesbury and Mr. Grenville, who are both of them indisposed" to America. This idle and partisan remark thrown off at the dinner table became evidence for Morris' conclusion that "there is but little disposition for treating with us at present," and was duly reported home to the President of the United States.[16]

Subsequently, Major George Beckwith explained to Alexander

Hamilton that much of the British "backwardness" in dealing with
Morris was due to his undiplomatic associations in London and to his
curiously angular deportment toward the ministers—reasons in plenty
for the early decision by Pitt and his colleagues to limit their contact
with Morris and to depend rather on Beckwith in New York as a
channel of communication with the United States government. After
the initial encounter, Leeds was silent toward Morris until April 28,
and then he replied to him only after two needling letters from the
American. The Duke's tone was friendly. The delay was due, he said,
to illness and to the (erroneous) report that Morris was in Holland.
Further, there had been "a multiplicity of engagements" (scarcely to
be doubted in view of the still secret Nootka crisis). The burden of
his reply, however, was a full and categorical rejection of Morris' position. The matters raised in President Washington's letter Leeds deemed
"of the highest importance," and the delays by both parties in performing the treaty of peace were regrettable. Perhaps, the Duke continued, introducing a new and worrisome note, the long-continuing
noncompliance on the part of the States may have rendered complete
American performance "impracticable." Britain would necessarily retard her own performance "until Redress is granted to our Subjects
upon the specific Points of the Treaty itself, or a fair and just Compensation obtained for the non-performance of those Engagements"
by the United States. As for a treaty of commerce, Britain sincerely
wished "to cultivate a real and *bona fide* system of friendly intercourse."[17]

The "Redress" Leeds had in mind was compensation for the growing number of prewar debts irrecoverable because of death, bankruptcy, and migration. It was a somber sign that Anglo-American
problems, far from disappearing with the passage of time, were becoming more complex and increasingly difficult to solve. Leeds's position implied, too, a complete rejection of Morris' argument that the
creation of the federal government was in itself adequate fulfilment
of the treaty: new systems of government might promise much; but
promises, as British creditors well knew, paid no debts.

Morris asked Leeds for clarification of the point concerning redress for British subjects and of the ambiguous statement about a
commercial treaty, but he had already concluded that the ministry
had no intention of treating with America. The British would keep
the posts, he reported to Washington, withhold compensation for

slaves, and avoid a negotiation of commercial matters, but without appearing to do so, counting on American economic dependence and sectional differences to prevent retaliation against them. At the least, Morris' analysis was premature, resting upon little more substantial than inference. Yet it was duly passed on by Washington to Secretary of State Jefferson, who accepted it as conclusive proof of Britain's sinister intentions toward the United States.[18]

Suddenly Morris was presented with an altogether unexpected and magnificent opportunity. On April 30, Pitt's cabinet resolved to demand full satisfaction from Spain for the ship seizures at Nootka Sound. Preparation for war was begun at once; and a press of seamen, the first public intimation of the grave crisis, took place on May 4. Several American sailors, mistaken for British, were taken up. On May 20, Morris called on Leeds in their behalf. The Foreign Secretary, admitting the justice of the complaint, apologized and promised to confer with the Admiralty. In passing, he told Morris that he had apparently misunderstood the British attitude toward a commercial treaty, since the Duke had meant to convey a willingness to enter one. (Evidently, the cabinet had had time to reflect on the value of American benevolence in an Anglo-Spanish war.) Morris, perhaps sensing improved prospects and not intending to be bought cheaply, abruptly dismissed the subject, turning again to the impressments, "the only instance in which we are not treated as aliens." Leeds invited him to return next day.

When the American arrived at Leeds's office on the twenty-first, he found not only the Secretary of State, but Pitt himself. Obviously, the British ministers intended a far-reaching and important exploration of the differences between the two countries. Facing a war with Spain—and back of Spain stood France—Britain doubtless wished to clear the score with America and, if possible, to achieve an understanding about the backcountry, where Britons, Americans, and Spaniards stood in uneasy confrontation.

There was an initial discussion of the impressment and related issues. Then came an abrupt change of subject. Both ministers told Morris he had misunderstood British intentions about a treaty of commerce with the United States. Morris, aware of the full magnitude of the Anglo-Spanish crisis and determined to exploit it to the full, answered coolly that "it was very easy to rectify the mistake, but it appeared idle to form a new treaty until the parties should be thoroughly satisfied with that already existing." Rebuffed, Pitt turned accordingly to the peace treaty. The American delay over the debts, he asserted, following Leeds's earlier line, rendered future compliance "less effectual." Morris replied that he knew the ministry had been "annoyed" with applications for redress from many creditors "who had, and those who pretended to have suffered." Their injuries, he told ministers who had full evidence in their offices, were "much smaller than imagined." Only debtors "who had the ability, and not the will, to pay at the peace, and were not deprived of the ability" could justly be held violators of the peace. These he could not suppose to be numerous. In all other cases, he continued, interest would furnish proper compensation for delayed payment. It was "impossible to go into an examination of all the incidental evils."

With this airy dismissal of "incidental evils," Morris turned to the slave issue, demanding in his turn compensation not merely for abducted blacks, but also for those who had taken advantage of British wartime proclamations. Next, he repeated the old argument that the planters could easily show that the loss of their slaves had produced the inability to pay the debts. Pitt's reaction was immediate and unmistakable: he "exclaimed at this, as if it were an exaggerated statement." (If the planters could produce proof, the first minister must have thought, why had they not done so long since?) Morris surprisingly gave ground, admitting that the slave issue was exaggerated, but maintaining in addition that British complaints against America were unrealistic. This merely tended to show, he told Pitt, "that these complaints and inquiries are excellent, if the parties mean to keep asunder; if they wish to come together, all such matter should be kept out of sight, and each side perform now, as well as the actual situation of things will permit." It was a clumsy attempt to meet the suggestion of redress or compensation for the withheld debts; and in making it, Morris gravely weakened his demand for slave compensation. Further, it was surely odd doctrine to argue that the true way to Anglo-American reconciliation lay in avoiding discussion of the very problems which produced the tensions. Odder still was the general proposition that Britain should evacuate the posts and pay for the slaves, leaving American debtors to reimburse British creditors when and if they could—"as well as the actual situation of things will permit."

Pitt, trying to establish common ground, spoke in generalities for a moment, mentioning the "earnest desire to cultivate the best understanding, &c. &c." He then produced the most interesting and potentially valuable suggestion made by anyone in authority since the days of the Adams mission. Let them consider, the Prime Minister urged, "if, on general ground, some compensation would not be mutually made." If the Americans insisted on connecting slaves and debts, he reasoned, the Gordian knot might be cut by settling both issues simultaneously. Again, Morris rebuffed the Prime Minister: "If I understand you, Mr. Pitt," he said, "you wish to make a new treaty, instead of complying with the old one." According to the American, Pitt replied that this was "*in some sort*" his idea. Morris cut him off: "even on that ground I did not see what better could be done, than to perform the old one." (The British ministers might have murmured, "No more do we.")

Turning to British infractions, Morris argued that compensation for the slaves was "too trifling an object for you to dispute." The only serious issue between the two countries was accordingly the posts; Morris supposed the British wished to retain them. ("Why, perhaps we may," interjected Pitt.) Yet the posts were not worth Britain's keeping. The cost was great and the fur trade, the only possible benefit to be derived from them, would center in Britain, no matter who held the posts. If they were so trivial, Pitt interrupted with a "well turned" answer, there was the less reason for the American preoccupation with them. They touched the safety and honor of his country, replied Morris, while Britain held them only to force America "to comply with such conditions as you may impose." British honor was concerned, too, asserted Pitt, in securing justice for Britons injured by the delay in American performance.

In the heat of charge and countercharge, the wheel turned full circle. The tantalizing glimmer of a new approach contained in Pitt's suggestion disappeared; and the British reverted to the earlier position: the posts for the debts. Morris thereupon read Pitt a lecture. Rather than to have retained the posts, the "natural and proper course" for Britain would have been "to comply fully on your part, and if then we had refused compliance you might rightfully have issued letters of marque and reprisal to such of your subjects as were injured by our refusal. But the conduct you have pursued naturally excites resentment in every American bosom." (Pitt may well have wondered how great would have been the resentment had he accepted the invitation to wage maritime war, particularly as the burden would have fallen upon the northern states, whose debts had been largely paid.) As matters stood, Morris continued, America knew her rights and—a pointed reference to Nootka—would assert them *"when time and circumstances may suit."*

Pitt's question about Morris' powers produced an admission that the envoy could not treat, and a reproach for the British failure to send a minister to the United States. The Prime Minister asked whether the United States would reciprocate, if Britain should name a a minister. Morris "could almost promise that we should, but was not authorized to give any positive assurance." When the Prime Minister said "they might communicate" to Washington their intention to appoint, there followed an ill-tempered dialogue sparked by Morris' punctilious and unnecessarily harsh strictures on improper communications to the President of the United States.

Finally, there was a concluding exchange between Pitt and Morris on commercial relations, the latter citing the failure of the attempt in the House of Representatives to lay discriminations upon British vessels as proof of American disposition toward a good understanding. Pitt answered that instead of restrictions, the Americans should consider giving "particular privileges" in exchange for those enjoyed by American vessels in British ports. Since British interests were served thereby, riposted Morris, "we felt no favor, we owned no obligation." The subjects, as well as the participants, were "now pretty well exhausted." The Britons told Morris they would confer and communicate with him again.[19]

It had been a thoroughly unproductive and exasperating encounter. Morris spurned advances from Pitt himself because he hoped to capitalize on the Nootka crisis; but, too stiff and unbending, he overplayed his hand and ruined his usefulness in London. He charged that the ministry was unwilling to negotiate with America. Pitt and his colleagues were not unwilling to negotiate; they were now merely unwilling to negotiate with Gouverneur Morris.

Ten days after the unsuccessful meeting with Morris, Home Secretary William Wyndham Grenville requested information of General Haldimand, now back in England: whether "by giving over the posts in Canada, the trade with the Indians would lose much, and if by fortifying posts opposite them that trade might be secured?" Obviously, the ministry was considering the implications of ceding the posts, although it is clear that Grenville hoped to win American agreement to a line of communication between Canada and the Mississippi.[20] Learning of Grenville's inquiries about the posts, Morris surmised that "they are nearly determined to give them up." He had even heard rumors that Grenville had spoken of a possible commercial treaty in response to American overtures and hence wished to be prepared, although the matter appeared far from certain. For Morris, the ruling consideration remained Britain's relations with Spain. If war came, the Pitt government would be glad to form—in the American's words —"a friendly connexion" with the United States.[21]

The idea of "friendly connexion" was soon to undergo an interesting metamorphosis and to figure significantly in American interpretation of British policy. On August 12, Secretary Jefferson acknowledged Morris' dispatch of May 29 and commended him for his treatment of the British proposal to exchange ministers. He also informed the envoy of the presence in New York of Major George Beckwith. The Briton's conversations there with Alexander Hamilton were so informal, he wrote with suspicion, that the British could disavow them whenever they pleased: "Through him," Jefferson continued, "they talk of a minister, a treaty of commerce, *and alliance*. If the object of the latter be honorable, it is useless; if dishonorable, inadmissible. These tamperings prove, that they view a war as very possible."[22]

In fact, the word "alliance" was Hamilton's—did the wish father the thought?—used in his undated memorandum composed for the President to inform him about his meeting with Beckwith on July 8; it does not appear in Beckwith's own account to Grenville. Even if the word were used by one or the other of the men, however, it was clearly intended to apply to an understanding directed against Spain in the event of war over Nootka. Later, Hamilton's most energetic efforts to elicit something from the Major on the subject of an alliance failed completely. Doubtless, Jefferson was briefed on the Hamilton-Beckwith meeting and learned of the alleged proposal of an Anglo-American alliance. His dispatch thus confirmed Morris' original reading of British intention to effect a "friendly connexion" with America. Furthermore, the "alliance" idea furnished Morris a very welcome explanation for his failure in the British capital. It was then but a short distance to the unequivocal and unqualified assertion, in his dispatch of September 18, 1790, that the British ministers "will not treat with us at present, unless they can see their way to an offensive and defensive alliance, which we shall be in no hurry to contract."[23] When President Washington referred Morris' correspondence to Jefferson, the dispatch of September 18 was included, and the assertion about an "alliance" duly figured in the Secretary of State's Report of December 15, 1790, and in Washington's message to Congress the following February. In reality, the major thrust of British policy remained precisely as defined by Pitt and Carmarthen: to win payment of prewar debts in exchange for the posts and compensation for slaves.

Throughout the long summer, Washington's envoy, in virtual isolation from the ministry, cooled his heels in London, writing home gossip about "the poor King of Hungary" and the designs of Prussia upon the Polish ports of Thorn and Danzig. Somewhat forlornly, he told Washington that his personal inclination was to depart, but he remained, hoping for "a favorable occasion"—that is, for the Anglo-Spanish war which stubbornly refused to break out.

On July 24, Spain and Britain exchanged declarations which, in effect, ended the Nootka crisis, although the formal convention was not signed until late in the following October. Still, Morris remained in London, whiling away his empty hours with speculations about the Turk, the Empress of Russia, the Swede, Finland, Austria, Prussia, Flanders, France. "In a day or two," he wrote Washington on August 30, "I expect to learn something here respecting us." Finally, on September 10, Morris wrote to Leeds: he had waited since May; and his departure could be postponed no longer. Led to believe that a "friendly connexion"—a familiar phrase—might have taken place between the United States and Britain, Morris admitted that it would have been "of great consequence" to his country. Disappointment had been his portion, however, much to his concern. The response to his request for clarification of the nature and extent of the redress Britain expected for American noncompliance with the treaty of peace had been Leeds's "pointed avowal" of the British intention to withhold performance until the United States acted—and, then, prolonged silence. The Duke's failure to communicate might well be construed by Americans as an "unconditional refusal" to fulfil the treaty. Such a conclusion, he warned, "may lead to Measures which in their Consequences shall eventually induce the two Nations to seek rather the means of reciprocal Injury than of mutual advantage."[24]

Leeds's reply on the same day was as polite as ever; but it was general and noncommittal.[25] He remembered well what had passed between them. Each party had reason for complaint about breaches of the treaty of peace. He lamented it. He forebore, however, "entering a ministerial discussion" about the reasons for "not being already further advanced" toward an object of mutual interest—"a real *bona fide* intercourse of friendship." He spoke "confidentially, my own private opinion," about differences which have "not been hitherto in my power to remedy." He hoped "very soon to address myself upon a new subject to Genl. Washington." Thus signifying an intention to send a minister to the United States, Leeds gave Morris his dismissal. The word "alliance" had never fallen from the ministerial pen.

Morris called again on Leeds on September 15, ostensibly to take leave; but he could not resist the temptation to turn his visit of courtesy into a lengthy (and coolly regarded) fishing expedition. Leeds, Morris subsequently reported, showed in his countenance that he "felt obliged to act an awkward part." (There is a more probable explanation for the ducal expression!) Renewed assurances about a British diplomatic appointment to America were given; there was a person in contemplation, but he had not been "absolutely agreed on." Fair words were spoken, too, by both men about "a real *bona fide* connexion, not merely by the words of a treaty, but in reality." (Morris guarded himself against the bogey of a proposal for an alliance by conscientiously confining his remarks to "a commercial intercourse for mutual benefit on liberal terms.") The British Secretary expressed the wish that the difficulties stemming from the broken treaty of peace "could be got out of the way."

Morris broke new ground, however, with a lengthy exposition of the dangers to Britain of continued retention of the backcountry posts. She was, for example, held immediately responsible in the United States for Indian unrest. Britain could never act freely with her European neighbors as long as America was a doubtful quantity. In case of a British war with the House of Bourbon, Morris continued, America could give the West Indies to whom she pleased. Leeds reportedly "acknowledged that this was naturally to be expected, and it seemed from his manner, that the same thing had been represented before, but not in such strong colors." After threatening an American navigation act to match that of Britain, Morris referred again to the Nootka crisis, during which he had "supposed *they would naturally square their conduct towards us by their position in respect to other nations.*" The observation was made "in a careless manner, as a thing of course; but immediately fixing my eye upon him, he showed that it was exactly the circumstance they had wished to conceal." With affairs in Europe to her satisfaction, Morris presumed Britain was prepared to "speak definitely" to America. Here he paused, waiting for an answer which, he said, he did not expect to receive. Leeds was "sufficiently embarrassed," however, and "from his look and manner I collected quite as much as he was willing to communicate." Morris' psychoanalytical diplomacy culminated in his bald, surprising, and from all evidence, altogether unwarranted conclusion that Britain aimed at an offensive and defensive alliance with America.[26]

In December, Morris returned to London on private business. His persistent efforts to see Leeds were unsuccessful, the Duke fobbing him off on Under-Secretary James Bland Burgess, whose warm and loquacious courtesy was repaid with a cool hauteur Morris could have wished to display toward the inaccessible Foreign Secretary. On one occasion, Burgess expressed his joy that Anglo-American difficulties over impressment had been settled, and continued with assurances that the

Administration had every desire I could wish for a treaty. Many cabinet councils had been held upon it. A great many difficulties had arisen in fixing on the persons to whom the management should be committed. This matter, however, was adjusted. A reference had been made above three months since to Lord Hawkesbury. His Lordship very diligent, but his report not yet made. When received, no time would be lost in setting all the different engines at work. Hoped we should soon have residents with each other, &c. &c. &c.

It was to Morris "a deal of civil nothingness."[27]

Civil, but not nothingness: Burgess' statement stood in palpable contradiction to Morris' conclusions about British policy, to Jefferson's report upon his dispatches, and to Washington's message to Congress on the mission.

Jefferson reported to the President on December 15, 1790. With Morris' dispatches to September 18 before him, he concluded that Britain was unwilling to hazard existing advantages in the American trade by accepting "reciprocity," unless the United States would "agree to make it a treaty of *alliance* as well *as commerce.*" Any further propositions for a treaty of commerce or an exchange of ministers would accordingly be "dishonorable . . . useless and even injurious." It was obvious, too, Jefferson maintained, that Britain intended to keep the posts. The suggestion of redress or compensation from America, where performance of the treaty stipulations had become impracticable, proved the design. Should America admit it, the President was told, Britain would set the price of any indemnification so high that it would be unacceptable, thereby insuring a continuation of the disagreement. As to the slaves, the British had so successfully concealed the evidence of their misdeeds that little direct proof could be found to support the American claim. (Had they also, one might legitimately ask, suborned the former owners of the slaves?) Let diplomacy rest until the country was prepared to do herself justice. Morris should be ordered to break off his talks with the London ministry.[28]

In his message to Congress of February 14, 1791, President Washington with his own authority stamped as fact the inferences and surmises of his secretary of state and unofficial representative in London. It was evident, he told the legislators, that Britain intended to decline fulfilling the treaty of peace until the United States performed her obligations, including compensation where delay now made performance impracticable. Nor did the former mother country show any disposition to enter a merely commercial treaty—information which might some time "have influence on matters under your consideration." Britain, Morris was satisfied, would tie a commercial treaty to an alliance offensive and defensive, or to an understanding in the event of an Anglo-Spanish war. The position in London on sending a minister he described as ambiguous.

The presidential message was little less than a recommendation to pass discriminatory legislation against British commerce and to begin commercial warfare. What would have been the most portentous step in the foreign policy of the United States since the achievement of independence would thus have been based on a fundamentally incorrect reading of British policy toward the United States.

That it made a "War of Duties, Tonnage and Restrictions" a serious probability was evident even to Sir John Temple. Widespread new demands for anti-British discriminations, signs of a rising American nationalism, were immediately heard; and the consul discerned "a vast alteration in the minds and sentiments of the People in general." Singling out Jefferson especially as Britain's enemy, Temple warned his government that "the Secretary of State's Party and Politicks gains ground here, and . . . will have influence enough to cause Acts and

Resolves which may be disagreeable to Great Britain, to be passed early in the next session of Congress!" At that very moment, Jefferson and his friend Madison were on a tour of the eastern states, "there to Proselyte as far as they may be able, to a Commercial War with Great Britain."[29]

That Gouverneur Morris' mission and the report and message founded upon it did not produce an Anglo-American economic war—and once begun, as a British agent observed to Chief Justice Jay in the summer of 1791, "there is no saying where it may end"[30]—was due in no small part to two other sets of unofficial conversations between Britons and Americans. The first involved British Major George Beckwith and the secretary of the treasury, Alexander Hamilton; the second, American Colonel William S. Smith and the new foreign secretary, William Wyndham Grenville, now Lord Grenville. Both helped to counteract Morris' faulty inferences and conclusions, and consequently to damp down the threatened crisis in Anglo-American relations.

The Morris mission, Jefferson's report on his correspondence, Washington's message, and the consequent renewal of efforts to pass anti-British legislation in Congress constitute an important episode in the history of domestic political parties in the United States. Fundamental divisions had appeared earlier during the battle over the Constitution. They were elaborated and solidified by the titanic program of federal finance associated with the name of Alexander Hamilton. These matters, important as they were in the development of the new nation, cannot receive full and systematic treatment within the context of the present study. Still, questions of American foreign policy, particularly as they concerned Britain and France, injected a dangerous and bitter element into America's domestic politics; and this, in turn, affected British policy toward the United States.

At bottom, American political development turned on two irreconcilable and hostile views of man and his government, as old as society itself. On the one hand, looking more and more to Thomas Jefferson and James Madison for leadership, were men deeply mistrustful of centralized governments, striving to create in America a new and purified political order, and despising Britain as the corrupt tyrant who would have made them slaves and who aimed to keep them in thrall if at all posible. These were the Jeffersonian Republicans. Commonly, they were debtors—viewing as inimical men like Alexander Hamilton, the proponents of strong government and vested financial interests, whom they believed intent upon undoing the work of their own revolution. They saw France, not England, as the natural ally; and often, their gratitude for wartime aid turned into anxious adulation, as the cleansing fire of revolution mounted ever higher on the eastern side of the Atlantic.

On the other hand, there were the Federalists: men who believed that the history of the Confederation was ample proof of the necessity for a strong central government. The contemptible posture of a nation unable to compel obedience to obligations undertaken in the name of its constituents was to them intolerable. The new federal authority would have to possess resources, fiscal resources above all, to make itself respectable at home and abroad; and it would have to be based solidly on the propertied class—those who owned the country were meant to run it. Hamilton intended to create such a government when he built his great edifice of federal finance. It was not Anglophilia or "monarchomania"—to use Jefferson's epithet—which caused Hamilton and his friends to struggle so desperately to preserve amity with Britain; it was the acknowledgment of Britain's preponderant role in America's trade and, hence, in furnishing the federal government with the revenues which were the means of life.

There is much of the epic in the struggle between the Federalists and the Jeffersonians, and, especially, in the duel between the two leaders. Jefferson—deeply emotional, forever engaged in a dialogue between head and heart, and possessed of a subtle and far-ranging intellect—was profoundly moved by a fundamental concern for the mass of the people and was able to lead in the creation of a political party dedicated to their service. This is no mean claim to greatness. It does not follow, however, as some have assumed, that Jefferson and his associates were infallibly correct in the policies they espoused.

As President of the United States, Thomas Jefferson accumulated a treasury of grace upon which the politically needy have drawn ever since; but to justify Jefferson, the secretary of state in Washington's cabinet, by the merits of Jefferson, the third President of the United States, is worse than unscientific. It is wrong. If Jefferson had died in 1795, his position among the founders of the Republic would have been little better than that of, say, Gouverneur Morris or James Dulaney—honorable, but scarcely stellar. If he had carried his point as secretary of state, if his pro-French policies had not been checked by Hamilton and, to a lesser extent, by Washington, there might well have been no Republic to survive to perpetuate its founders' names.

Alexander Hamilton sought power, not as an end, but as a means of creation. Lacking to a certain degree virtue in the Puritan sense, he possessed it in full measure in the Roman. He had the will, the capacity, the splendid opportunity to bring order out of chaos, to found lasting institutions, to lay the basis of a nation upon which his enemies and those who claimed descent from them would later build. He could be ruthless: he manipulated Washington, domineered weaker colleagues, usurped business from other offices, and flayed opponents vindictively and virulently in the press.

Unlike his enemies, Hamilton was no great politician: the task of government was to govern, even though it occasionally contravened for their own good the wishes of the mass of the governed. Recognizing the limiting realities, the circumscribing practicalities of politcal action, he detested the "speculative." He would not indulge a "womanish" resentment against Britain, whose measures against American vessels in the West Indies he balanced against the favors conferred in other areas, and whose commerce furnished the federal treasury so much revenue: hence, in 1789, his emphatic disavowal to a British agent of Madison's discriminatory resolutions; hence, his similar determination in 1791.[31]

For Hamilton and Jefferson, and also for their partisans, the Morris mission and its aftermath intensified a deadly, bitter, and desperate political struggle. The significance was great in the development of domestic parties; but it also contained profound implications for Anglo-American relations.

Hamilton began to doubt Morris' diplomatic talents soon after the envoy's initial contacts with the British ministry. When David Humphreys, sometime aide to General Washington, was dispatched to Europe in 1790, carrying instructions from Thomas Jefferson to American envoys in Paris and Madrid to cover the contingency of an Anglo-Spanish war, Hamilton confessed to him that he was "not perfectly satisfied with the manner in which Mr. G.M. had conducted the business entrusted to him with the Duke of Leeds." Would Humphreys investigate the "temper of the British Administration with regard to the points in agitation between the United States and Great Britain" and report either to the President or to Hamilton himself?

Humphreys declined the invidious assignment, pleading Jefferson's instructions to "avoid all suspicion of being on any public business."[32] As it fell out, however, Hamilton achieved his purpose, through another agent.

A second channel of communication with the British authorities was supplied by Major George Beckwith, himself an "unofficial" agent sent to the United States by Lord Dorchester, the governor of Canada.

George Beckwith was a veteran of the American War, successively aide-de-camp to the Hessian Generals Knyphausen and Losberg and to Sir Guy Carleton, the commander in chief. Promoted from captain to major in 1781 for gallantry in action, he returned to England with the personal commendation of Sir Henry Clinton. When Carleton, created Lord Dorchester, went out to the government of Canada in 1786, the young officer accompanied him as a member of his personal staff.

Dorchester, naturally interested in conditions prevailing within his country's southern neighbor, sent Beckwith to the United States for three months in the spring of 1787, and again for two months in 1788. When he returned to Britain in the autumn, he found himself accepted as something of an expert on American affairs. Important and influential people, among them Home Secretary Lord Sydney and the Duke of Richmond, conversed with him; he conferred frequently with Charles Jenkinson, Lord Hawkesbury. In the summer of 1789, the Major met William Wyndham Grenville, Pitt's cousin, who supplanted Sydney at the Home Office and as Lord Grenville was soon to move to the Foreign Office. Again, Beckwith underwent a thorough questioning about American affairs. In August, he returned to the United States carrying from Grenville to the American authorities a message undoubtedly designed to conciliate and thus to discourage retaliatory commercial measures like those proposed by Madison in the First Congress.

According to Beckwith, the delivery of the message, probably to Alexander Hamilton at New York (Jefferson, presently to become secretary of state, was still in France), produced "certain overtures" to Britain from the United States—an obvious reference to the mission of Gouverneur Morris. His work done, the Major proceeded to Canada to join Dorchester once more.

Early in 1790, Dorchester dispatched Beckwith southward once again to report on American military preparations, ostensibly against the hostile Indians, but possibly, he feared, against the northwestern posts. As war with Spain over Nootka loomed, it became an additional object to gauge the role the United States might elect to play, particularly in the backcountry. After briefly returning to Canada, Beckwith was settled in the United States by July, 1790. He remained there for twenty-one months, until he was superseded by the arrival of George Hammond, Britain's first minister plenipotentiary. Technically unaccredited, he was nonetheless instructed to report not only to Dorchester but to Grenville himself.[33]

As Beckwith's communication with Hamilton, instead of Secretary of State Jefferson, has occasioned critical comment, it should be observed that the Major undoubtedly met Hamilton well before Jefferson arrived from Europe in March, 1790, to take up his post in the new government. Secondly, Beckwith held no formal diplomatic appointment which would require *pro forma* correspondence with the secretary of state. Thirdly, Washington himself, who was ultimately responsible for the foreign policy of the United States, was informed about the course of Hamilton's dealings with the Briton, corresponded with Hamilton about them, and interposed no objection to the Treasury Secretary's active role. Finally, Hamilton and Beckwith obviously got on well together and spoke the same language; in strong contrast to the *pourparlers* between Morris and the British ministers, their efforts produced a clarification of issues between the two countries at a critical moment in their mutual affairs.[34]

Beckwith's first object in the United States was quickly achieved after his arrival in 1790. Undoubtedly drawing on information derived from Alexander Hamilton, "the gentleman high in office with whom I am in the regular habit of intercourse," he reported home that the American military preparations which had alarmed Dorchester were indeed directed against the Indians and did not portend an attack upon the northwestern posts.[35] The Nootka crisis, news of which arrived in the States in midsummer, provided a second object: to learn what position America would take in case of hostilities, to give assurances of Britain's pacific and benevolent intentions toward the United States, and to counter Morris' unfriendly reports from London.

Beckwith saw Hamilton for a lengthy conversation on July 8.[36] As the Treasury Secretary reported to the President, the Major spoke with Dorchester's authority only. Even so, he was knowledgable about the prospective war with Spain, observing that "it was one in which all commercial nations must be supposed to favor the views of Great Britain." He presumed the United States would "take part" with Britain instead of Spain if war came.

About Morris, the Briton declared that Lord Dorchester had been informed of the negotiations in London. He was at pains to explain that any appearance of delay in the proceedings was "partly on account of Mr. Morris's absence on a trip to Holland, as was understood." The delay "and some other circumstances" may have led Morris to conclude that there was "an idea of backwardness on the part of the British ministry," but Dorchester had directed Beckwith to declare explicitly that such an inference was not well founded. The Governor "had reason to believe" that Pitt's cabinet "entertained a disposition not only towards a friendly intercourse, but towards an alliance with the United States," particularly in the case of war with Spain. (It should be recalled that "alliance" was Hamilton's word.)

To support his assertions, Beckwith actually produced a letter signed by Dorchester, although it was "in more guarded terms, and without any allusion to instructions from the British cabinet." It contained also "hints at the non-execution of the treaty of peace" by the United States. Hamilton observed that the letter seemed to express only the private sentiments of Lord Dorchester; but Beckwith replied that "whatever reasons there might be for that course of proceeding in the present stage of the business, it was to be presumed that his lordship knew too well the consequence of such a step, to have taken it without a previous knowledge of the intentions of the cabinet."

Finally, Beckwith gave assurances in Dorchester's name that recent Indian depredations along the American frontier, obviously an increasing problem, had neither his support nor his countenance. Indeed, he had taken every opportunity to encourage a pacific disposition in the Indians and had actually sent a message to them in an unsuccessful attempt to prevent recent outbreaks.

Hamilton immediately informed the President of the conversation; and a few days later, a second meeting occurred.[37] According to the Treasury Secretary's own testimony, Secretary Jefferson was "privy to the transaction."

Assuring his visitor that he had made proper use of Beckwith's declarations at the last interview, Hamilton observed that the conversations were "wholly without formality," although it was accepted that Dorchester was informed of the course of the Morris negotiations and that his dispatch of Beckwith was sanctioned by the London authorities. He noted, however, that there was a material difference between Morris and Beckwith: the credentials of the former—from Washington himself—were not formal, but proceeded "from the proper source." Beckwith's were "neither formal nor authoritative."

Having established the private, unofficial nature of his conversations with Beckwith, Hamilton met the Briton's earlier assurances of goodwill. There was in the United States government a sincere disposition to remove all misunderstandings arising from the incomplete execution of the treaty of peace and to lay the foundation of future amity "by establishing liberal terms of commercial intercourse."

Hamilton then took up the idea of "alliance." It "opens a wide field," Hamilton told the Briton; and it was "susceptible to a vast variety of forms." Hamilton was fishing. " 'Tis not possible," he told the Major, "to judge what would be proper or what could be done, unless *points* were brought into view. If you are in condition to mention particulars, it may afford better ground of conversation."

Hamilton paused for a reply. Beckwith was unable to say anything "more precise"; but the American did not let go, repeating that "the thing is in too general a form to admit of a judgment of what may be eventually admissible or practicable." If the subject were to be raised "in an authentic and proper shape," he had no doubt "we shall be ready to converse freely upon it." The United States would naturally pursue her own interests "as far as may consist with our honor"—an obvious allusion to the treaty with France. He would not at the present juncture "raise or repress expectation." It was a bold invitation to the British ministry to make concrete proposals. Beckwith, uninstructed on the subject, could say "nothing explicit," although he took the opportunity to sound Hamilton on any "connection" between Spain and the United States.

Hamilton eschewed "mystery," declaring without hesitation that there was "no particular connection" with Spain. It was notorious, he continued, that the question of the Mississippi was still outstanding. Hinting cautiously at the American dislike for any move against New Orleans, the Treasury Secretary again invited Beckwith to explore the possibility of an Anglo-American arrangement against Spain. The United States, he declared, was ready "to go into the consideration of the question."

Hamilton had grasped clearly the implications of an Anglo-Spanish war for the United States. He would have had Anglo-American co-operation, perhaps even military, in the American hinterland, against a power inimical to them both. The traditional pattern of partnership against at least one Bourbon power would have been revived and differences extinguished, or at least ameliorated, in the prosecution of a common cause. From the standpoint of Anglo-American relations, it was unfortunate that Britain and Spain did not go to war in 1790, or, in any event, that Beckwith was not empowered to meet Hamilton's persistent initiative on the subject of an alliance.

Still, much good might be done. Toward the end of September, with the peaceful settlement of the Nootka crisis a fact, Beckwith offered his explanation for the reluctance of the London ministry to negotiate with Morris; and early the next month, he saw Hamilton for a very far-reaching conversation.[38] The prewar debts were discussed, the Major expressing hope that the judicial branch of the federal government would give rapid and effective relief to the creditors and Hamilton professing the "most perfect confidence" that this would be the case. Although he believed the losses claimed by the British agents to be exaggerated, he admitted the American actions toward them had been indefensible.

A second subject, portentous for the future, made its initial appearance: Beckwith, undoubtedly following instructions from Dorchester, suggested to Hamilton that a just and honorable peace with the Indians would serve the interests of the United States well—a clear hint at British mediation with the savages.

The remainder of the conversation was devoted to American foreign policy, and it was notable for Hamilton's recurrence to the idea of an alliance between Britain and the United States. Certain matters had occurred since the peace, he told the Briton, which left America "altogether free with respect to France, even if she should *go to war as a principal.*" Would it not be an "act of wisdom" for Britain to "attach and connect the States upon political as well as commercial considerations"? He proceeded to specifics: Let Britain open her West Indian ports to American vessels "under certain limitations," gaining thereby secure and plentiful supplies for the islands, both in peace and in war, and, by implication, "the political weight of America in the British scale."

Beckwith, uninstructed and unauthorized to discuss political arrangements or Hamilton's interesting anticipation of Article XII in the Anglo-American treaty of 1794, was able only to transmit his account of the conversation to London and, meantime, to keep open the channel of communication with the Secretary of the Treasury.

It is tempting to consider what might have been the response of the British ministry to Hamilton's suggestion had relations between the two countries remained stable for a short time longer. As it transpired, however, Jefferson's Report of December 15, 1790, and Washington's message in the following February, both based upon the Morris correspondence, produced an element of crisis in Anglo-American relations; and Beckwith suddenly found himself precipitated into a struggle to combat the rising tide of anti-British sentiment in the United States.

Immediately to be feared was something like Madison's discriminatory resolutions so very nearly adopted in 1789.[39] Anxiously, the Major sought out Hamilton on both January 19 and January 20. The Treasury Secretary was calm, candid, and reassuring about Jefferson's report. The Briton knew, he was told, that there were serious differences of opinion in America about Britain and France. One party, remembering the bloody revolutionary struggle, thinks "nothing good can come from Great Britain, and that our obligations to France are never to be forgotten." Co-operating with that party were "worthy individuals" who believed that commercial discrimination against Britain would induce her to enter a more favorable trade treaty with the United States. At the same time, there were men who, "from every circumstance, are convinced that you are the nation with whom we can trade to the greatest advantage." Probably Congress would soon adopt "something similar to the British Navigation Act." This would not be catastrophic, however, Hamilton told Beckwith. There would be no prohibited articles, and the new act would be of no consequence to British shipping. Britain should really send a minister to the United States. He had heard rumors that a mission was intended; and he was glad, since, he hoped, it would produce "a future good understanding, and put an end to the suggestions of that party with us, who wishing well to a French interest, take every occasion to insinuate that we are held in no consideration by the English Government."[40]

Beckwith's uneasiness mounted, Hamilton's comforting words notwithstanding. He was troubled at the news—given him by a

friendly senator—that the French *chargé*, Guillaume Otto, had made
a formal representation to the American government against the Tonnage Act of 1789, which discriminated equally against all foreign
vessels in favor of native American ones. The claim that the provision violated the Franco-American treaty of commerce of 1778,
guaranteeing French preferential treatment, was apparently supported by the "French interest here," Beckwith reported to London.
The worry soon proved groundless; but the Briton found more alarming corroboration of a deep-laid Jeffersonian plot in Washington's
message of February 14.

Beckwith learned the import of the message on the fifteenth, although it was not yet public; and the next day he called on Hamilton
for another lengthy conversation. Hamilton's earlier ebullience was
missing. Obviously unsympathetic to the tenor of the presidential
message and mildly critical of Morris, he rather somberly repeated his
former assurances that there was no secret understanding with France;
nor did his government consider itself obliged to give France unique
commercial privileges, he added, the French protest to the contrary
notwithstanding. The President himself was no Anglophobe, Hamilton said; but there were "certain persons" in the country who were.
This made it difficult to predict what Congress might do, although the
Treasury Secretary was "strongly inclined to think, no immediate
warmth will arise from the House of Representatives," while he was
certain the Senate would remain cool.

Recalling to Hamilton his instructions from Dorchester empow-
ering him "to think and to say that we have the most friendly dispositions towards the States," Beckwith declared that the recent train
of events in America tended to "check the growing friendship, evidently likely to take place between us, to prevent possibly a mutual
appointment [of resident ministers], and to give a bias to a French
interest." In some agitation, he declared to Hamilton that he had
studiously refrained from public controversy during his stay in
America and had "shunned explanations, even to gentlemen in your
legislature." The present moment was so critical, however, that he
was forced to "speak out," and he wished to have his sentiments
known "where they ought to be." Hamilton would soon receive a
letter from him, and was free "to make what use you please of it"—
obviously an invitation to lay it before the President.

The very next day Beckwith wrote the letter; the day after that he placed it personally in Hamilton's hands. Thence it went immediately to the President, who read a respectful and firm assertion that Britain possessed a most sincere and favorable disposition toward the United States. Mutual need and ancient friendship called for "an improvement of this disposition to its utmost extent, and the giving it a permanent effect." Even the distance between the two countries was advantageous, and the "immense commercial capital of the one country feeds the enterprise of the other." Thus Beckwith labored to clear away the false assumptions incorporated in Jefferson's report and the President's message.

To Hamilton, the Briton's language was more explicit. If the "violent party" were misled into believing America's trade so indispensable to Britain that they could with impunity load her with discriminations, they should realize that it was of merely "relative importance." Should Congress adopt discriminations, it might well be that the measure would finally prevent an "amicable arrangement" of outstanding differences. In short, Beckwith was saying to the President that Morris had misinformed his government, and to the Secretary of the Treasury that America's discriminatory measures would be repaid in kind.

On tenterhooks for weeks, as he followed the crucial debates in the House of Representatives, Beckwith breathed a sigh of relief when it was finally determined that the whole question of commercial discrimination by foreign powers should be referred to Thomas Jefferson, the secretary of state. (The intention was clearly to postpone further action until autumn.) A breathing space had been vouchsafed —little more—and in the American view, the next move was clearly up to Britain. "I am very explicit with You on this Subject," a Federalist senator told Beckwith, "and I wish to impress you with its being my conviction, that there is an absolute necessity of following up this Business during the summer; a delay I do assure you will at least be dangerous, and may throw us into a French interest."

It was accordingly with a sense of alarm and rising crisis that Beckwith wrote hastily to London of the recent events in America which required, in his opinion, the ministry's "immediate notice." American self-esteem was rising, he told his principals; and the accession of Vermont and Kentucky to the Union, revenues from imports and tonnage, Hamilton's far-reaching fiscal plan, and rapidly growing population and trade were all reasons, especially for a people naturally inclined to "over-rate their own consequence." There remained in the public mind an attachment to British manners and "every thing that is English." There was, in addition, a "wish to be connected with us." When the latter desire was rebuffed, disappointment was so much the stronger, furnishing a fair field for those Americans partial to France. Let there be a treaty of commerce, he urged. With almost Shelburnian enthusiasm, he wrote that he had long considered the "birth of every child from New Hampshire to the river Mississippi, as the production of a being destined to extend the manufactures of the Empire." The need for action was urgent. If a negotiation did not begin during the summer, he predicted, "our commerce will not remain on its present footing beyond the month of November next." A few days later, the British agent wrote again identifying Jefferson as the leader of the pro-French party. Beckwith underlined his earlier call for immediate negotiations and added that the site should be Philadelphia. There he believed Hamilton's influence could counter Jefferson's control of an official American negotiator in London: "A measure which may fail in London may succeed in Philadelphia."[41] It was a major miscalculation.

A third channel of communication, this time running from London to Philadelphia, was provided by Colonel William S. Smith, John Adams' son-in-law and formerly his secretary of legation in London. Compared with Morris and Beckwith, Smith was relatively unimportant; but nonetheless, at a critical time in Anglo-American relations, he and his friends helped damp down a rising crisis.[42]

In the British capital on private business for several months in 1790 and 1791, Smith re-established contact with former acquaintances, among them the Glasgow merchant, Patrick Colquhoun, who had discussed the prewar debts with Adams in 1786. The Scot was not without a certain influence; lord provost of his city in 1782 and 1783 and founder of the Chamber of Commerce, he was a close friend of Henry Dundas, home secretary after Grenville moved to the Foreign Office, and confidant of the younger Pitt. Smith and Colquhoun conversed at length about Anglo-American affairs, agreeing particularly upon the desirability of a commercial treaty and the urgent need for a British minister to the United States—preferably Colquhoun himself.[43] Presently the two embodied their thoughts in a memorandum which was duly forwarded to Lord Grenville.

The date was March, 1791; and Washington's chilly message to Congress of the previous month was still unknown. Smith and Colquhoun stated little new in the way of argument; but there was an oblique suggestion that in return for the entry of American vessels of limited tonnage into British West Indian ports (the idea was apparently in the air in the United States), an appropriate *quid pro quo* would be an American undertaking never to impede the loading of grain by British vessels bound for the West Indies. A second novel suggestion called for joint efforts to protect the citizens of both powers from the Indians and to co-operate in pacifying and civilizing them. Consideration of a defensive treaty was said not to be impossible.

Grenville received Smith several times, and the whole range of Anglo-American problems was discussed. The Foreign Secretary was at pains to stress Britain's benevolent disposition toward America and his intention to send a minister in the near future. Hamilton, informed of the conversations, took exception to an ambiguous remark by Grenville about Indian affairs, but generally pronounced the talks "pleasing and promising." Beckwith, too, expressed satisfaction, especially since his own conversations with the American Secretary of the Treasury "accorded perfectly with the assurances recently given to Colonel Smith in London," and directly contradicted Morris' interpretation of British policy.[44] His final memorandum on domestic American politics drove home once more to the British ministry that only urgent steps could prevent the triumph of the pro-French party in the United States.

On the eve of his departure for America, Smith, expressing astonishment at the "favourable sentiments that are nourished in England relative to my country," enjoyed a last honor when Grenville ordered the Falmouth packet to delay its departure until the Colonel could arrive. While it is undoubtedly true that Smith and Colquhoun subsequently exaggerated their importance almost scandalously, it is not without significance that Grenville took the trouble to extend extraordinary courtesies to Smith. Quite obviously, the British Foreign Secretary was deeply intent on relaying a message through Smith to the United States government. Upon his arrival in New York, Colquhoun later told Grenville, Smith rushed nonstop to the new capital city, Philadelphia, to announce Grenville's promise that "*England would speedily manifest her good disposition to cultivate a friendly*

Intercourse with America by the appointment of a Minister, he hoped would arrive, (if possible) before the next meeting of Congress in October."

Secretary of State Jefferson attempted to minimize the importance of Grenville's message; but Smith's efforts coincided far too directly with Beckwith's to be altogether ignored.[45] Contradicting the reports of Morris, both men reinforced and strengthened each other's assurances that Britain wished an amicable settlement with America and intended to send a minister at an early date.

Serious anti-British sentiment remained, however, in America. Only time had been won for the settlement of the old and persistent problems; and they were emerging in new and even more sinister forms. The British might claim the possession of the northwestern posts was just retaliation for the prewar debts; but the frontier forts had suddenly appeared in an altogether different light when a war in the backcountry between Spain and Britain appeared probable. Further, could they be much longer regarded as diplomatic gambits when westward-moving American frontiersmen met hostile Indians, British clients, in savage combat not far away? Foreign policy in the United States, especially as it touched upon the Anglo-American relationship, was indeed becoming the sport of domestic political strife; but there was a rising sense of grievance against Britain common to all Americans. Beckwith, preceding Jefferson and Madison on their celebrated "proselytising" tour of Pennsylvania, New York, and New England in the summer of 1791, could try to nullify the impact of the Virginians by making "declarations to different individuals with whom I thought it necessary to converse freely"; but he was a Canute figure, in the presence of national forces not to be deflected by the best-intentioned of unofficial agents. John Jay touched a deeper truth when he reminded the Major, not without pathos, of the year 1782. Then, an Anglo-American agreement "that trade and navigation should go on precisely as if the separation had not taken place" had seemed almost settled. Sheffield and his friends had ruined the plan. Now, almost a decade later, the Chief Justice warned, Britain should be aware of a somber fact: America was at the turn of a generation. Mortality was daily taking its toll of Americans who remembered the old Empire after the French and Indian War, standing at a peak of grandeur, the object of a proud loyalty and deep affection. This sense of "an internal participation in its glory" was disappearing, as young men, "educated in a period of passion and prejudice," took the seats of power. America thus stood at a crossroads. For Britain's own sake, there should be "an immediate settlement between the two Countries."[46] A worried Phineas Bond, too, noted and reported home with serious concern the fiery and emotional outbursts from press and public at the time of Washington's message. Britain's "refusal" to give up the posts or pay for the slaves and the widely accepted allegations that she was supplying the hostile Indians with arms and ammunition from Detroit all portended a growing popular clamor for harsh measures against Britain. Within the Executive itself, Bond asserted, "some Branches" would give encouragement.[47] All signs pointed to the urgent need for fundamental readjustments in British policy toward the United States.

CHAPTER SEVEN

Britain Reappraises Her Policy

BEFORE THE FEDERAL GOVERNMENT began its operation, British policy toward the United States aimed to protect and extend the imperial marine by excluding American vessels from the West Indies and circumscribing their participation in the trade with the remaining colonies in North America. The Republic's economic necessity nonetheless guaranteed to Britain a major portion of its market, a situation made doubly secure by the inability of the weak Confederation government to retaliate effectively. These assumptions of British policy proved correct. Opulence and strength rose in tandem. The only regrettable feature—admittedly a major one—was the inability of the weak American government to compel obedience to the debt and loyalist provisions of the treaty of peace.

The adoption of the Constitution and the creation of a strong central government portended for Britons the rapid settlement of the troublesome issues. They were deceived. In reality, the new political arrangements in America overturned major assumptions of British thinking about the United States and brought on something like a crisis in Anglo-American relations. Madison's discriminatory resolutions failed, but the debate and hostility they sparked toward Britain produced a thorough reappraisal of British policy toward the United States and a headlong clash of two very different views within Pitt's ministry about America and her position vis-à-vis the British Empire.

One view was identified with Lord Hawkesbury, president of the committee which was soon to become the Board of Trade. The news of Madison's efforts in Congress affected the noble lord in a predictable way. On June 9, 1789, a letter was dispatched to His Grace of

Leeds: Would the Foreign Secretary ask all British consuls and other appropriate persons resident in the United States to make the fullest inquiries into and to report at the earliest possible date upon a number of important points? What was the tonnage imposed by Congress or by individual states? Were there discriminations against British or imperial shipping and goods? What was the state of American agriculture, shipping, manufacturing? How important was foreign shipping to the United States? How much immigration and emigration were there?[1] It was obvious that a minute and thorough inquiry was in the making. Hawkesbury, the master bureaucrat, fond of careful deliberation and thorough investigation, nonetheless knew that some haste was in order. He would "lose no Time in paying Attention to this Business," he told Henry Wilckens, a merchant friend of Liverpool; and, perhaps ill-advisedly in light of subsequent developments, he suggested that a representation against the American threat of discrimination from the merchants of the city might be appropriate.[2]

The technique of stirring up petitions and memorials to win or to give the appearance of possessing popular support for a certain policy was in common use in British politics. A representation from the merchants of Liverpool, Hawkesbury must have reasoned, would strengthen the hand of government in whatever measures it might decide to adopt in answer to the American action. It is possible, too, that by hurrying the Liverpool merchants on, Hawkesbury sought to forestall a craven relapse into the heresy of Shelburne's American Intercourse Bill. Before the end of September, however, Hawkesbury knew that Madison's resolutions had failed. When Wilckens wrote rather proudly that the merchants of Liverpool planned to petition Parliament for counterrestrictions against the Americans, the President of the Committee for Trade cautioned his friend to "wait some little time longer." He was rather apologetic. The merchants of other cities would have to be consulted, too, before the government "came to any Determination on the Measures which it may be proper to take." Wilckens would "not be surprised that some Delay has occurred in this Business."[3] The failure of Madison's proposals removed the immediate threat. There was time for a good, old-fashioned inquiry.

Fresh material requiring scrutiny was already at hand. Two new acts of Congress, one on duties and another on tonnage, were passed in July. Next month, Bond transmitted them to Hawkesbury. Generally favoring Americans over all foreigners, they did not, indeed, specifically discriminate against Britain. British interests were, however, involved; and the circumstances described in detail by Bond were worrying, especially in view of Madison's near success.[4] The consul at Philadelphia informed Hawkesbury that even though southerners generally opposed discrimination against Britain because of their need for vents and carriage for their produce, it was nonetheless widely expected that "some Relaxation of the Navigation Laws of England may take Place." Indeed, the consul continued, the suspension of Madison's resolutions was ostensibly due to anticipation of a commercial treaty. There followed a sermon to the converted: even though the new American government was "efficient," hence able to perform treaty obligations, the United States could give nothing in treaty sufficient to purchase her way into the British sugar islands. The concession would be a "general and extensive Loss" incurred unnecessarily. The logic of economic necessity still operated: the country was debt-ridden, in need of credit, capital, manufactures, vents. The moral was as obvious under the new federal government as it had been earlier. Discrimination against Britain remained unlikely. It was true that there was "a very formidable French Interest at work" in the United States, but against that Bond balanced his belief that there was "a majority in the different Departments of the new government favorable to a close Connexion with Great Britain, and who will strive to promote it." In a sense, however, these were secondary considerations. Even American threats to assist British enemies or promises of neutrality during wars should not shake the British determination to guard inviolate the true bastion of her existence—her naval power. Exclusion of Americans from the "nursery of seamen" must be continued, and the system adopted with such good effect at the end of the war maintained.

At the end of September, the two American acts were formally referred to Hawkesbury's committee for examination.[5] Much data was still expected from consuls and other British subjects in America; and in October, more was requested from likely sources in Britain. The Committee for Trade sent a circular letter to the Committee of Merchants trading to America, the shipowners of Bristol, Liverpool, and Glasgow, officers of the customs, and others, asking their appraisals of the acts and recommendations on how to meet them.

Despite frequent prodding letters, reminding recipients that the committee's inquiry was of "great importance," it was not until February, 1790, that systematic study of the evidence began. Meanwhile, much had happened. Beckwith, charged with a message to the American authorities from a government worried by Madison's actions, was in America; and Morris, carrying Washington's letter of credence, would shortly arrive in London. Discrimination against Britain remained the talk of many in Congress, while the merchants of Liverpool, doubtless stirred up by Henry Wilckens, continued to complain against the American acts. They were "every Day more anxious and pressing about this Business," determined to petition Parliament for action against the Americans, and "heavily aggrieved by the Consequences arising from these Laws." Their special worry was "how the Encouragement held forth to the Americans tends to induce them to build ships."[6]

In May and June, 1790, Madison, as we have seen, renewed his efforts to persuade Congress to discriminate against the shipping of nations who did not have commercial treaties with the United States.[7] The course of the debates was not altogether clear even to Americans; and it was especially obscure to Hawkesbury, whose agent—charged with recording the proceedings in shorthand—collapsed "from his drunkenness and other Vices."[8] On June 24, however, the former Tonnage Act, making no distinction between foreign vessels, was reenacted. The new defeat for discriminatory measures may have had Madison's acquiescence, in view of the compromise negotiated at about this time by southerners and northerners over the assumption of state debts and place of residence for the federal government. Left behind in Britain, however, was much uneasiness—intensified by the concurrent Nootka crisis.

In the autumn of 1790, with massive evidence at hand, Hawkesbury, aided by his First Clerk, George Chalmers, began to draft a report; but suddenly, a completely new direction was given to their proceedings. About the middle of November, Foreign Secretary Leeds wrote signifying the royal pleasure that the committee consider "what proposals of a Commercial Nature it might be proper to make to the United States of America."[9] The matter was clearly urgent. The recent Nootka crisis, the repeated American efforts to discriminate against Britain, the departure of the disgruntled Morris, and the accounts from Beckwith and Bond of mounting hostility in America meant that a diplomatic representative had to be dispatched across the Atlantic as soon as possible. Using his accumulated data, Hawkesbury now bent his efforts to the answering of Leeds's query, and in the process produced one of the last great defenses of pure mercantilism. Read and approved on January 28, 1791, the report was printed and transmitted to Leeds on March 31.[10] Adam Smith might never have lived.

At the outset, the tone was faintly aggrieved: the subject of its consideration was very difficult, demanding more time than had been allowed. The merchants examined had been hesitant and uncertain; and some of the evidence was contradictory. There were "other circumstances," obviously a reference to the Nootka crisis, which had caused a temporary suspension in the committee's work. Then, without warning, Leeds's letter had come, saying that it was intended "forthwith to send to America a Person . . . to treat with the Government of the United States on commercial, as well as other matters," and requesting the committee's recommendations. The delay explained, the committee turned to a review of Anglo-American relations since the war.

American independence had dissolved the colonial connection; and the two powers confronted each other as sovereigns. The weakness of the Confederation, however, and the authority of the individual states in regulating their own commercial affairs had caused Britain "to suspend the Consideration of a Compleat Commercial arrangement . . . and to make only Provisional Regulations." The new Constitution and the creation of a respectable central government now made it necessary "to determine, by what principles the Commerce between the said States and the different Parts of your Majesty's dominions should in future be regulated."

Past policy was described in detail. Emphasis was laid on the favors to American commerce in British ports; some were in direct contradiction to the principles of the Acts of Trade and Navigation, and had never before been granted to any foreign power. American goods in American ships were free from Alien's Duty, a concession so unique that it had been the object of complaint from supposedly "most favored nations." On much produce, American merchants enjoyed the status of native Britons; and all unenumerated goods or manufactures had "most favored nation" treatment, saving only where Britain was bound to the contrary by treaties of commerce with other powers. American produce, excepting salted provisions and the products of the fisheries, was allowed into British colonies in North America or the

West Indies as before 1776, except, of course, that the sea carriage was confined to British and colonial vessels. Americans, the report continued, complained more of this last regulation, now set out in an act of Parliament, than of any other item in Britain's commercial policy toward the United States; but it was not new, having been "founded in the Ancient Law of this Country." The principle had the general acceptance of all colonial powers who "have ever claimed a Right of restraining the Trade and Navigation of their Colonies, in such manner as in their Judgment will be most conducive to their respective Interests." British policy, more liberal by far than French or Spanish, thus granted a considerable body of advantages and favors to the Americans.

American conduct toward Britain was in the strongest contrast. Under the Confederation, several states individually attempted to discriminate against British goods and shipping. British vessels on the average paid 2/3d. more per ton than Americans, a charge amounting to £22-10 for a 200-ton vessel. British goods, if carried in British bottoms, cost about two per cent more than similar goods imported in American ships, a difference of about £40 on a cargo worth £2,000. These arrangements were "certainly unfriendly" and gave just cause for complaint.

These were mere pinpricks, however, when the laws impeding the collection of the prewar debts were considered. Listed by individual states, they were denounced as flagrant violations of the treaty of peace, and as "destructive of all Mercantile Confidence and Credit . . . contrary to every Principle of Honor and Justice."

In general, the new order in North America had witnessed a diminution in Britain's American trade; but this had been more than offset by increases in the remaining North American colonies and the British West Indies. Britain had more than recovered from the disruption of trade caused by the American Revolution and, by cutting America out of the carrying trade to the sugar islands, had acquired a new source of profit and power for herself. A sizable decrease in the value of American exports to Britain, chiefly rice and tobacco, was noted. It was evident, however, that since the war the value of exports to the United States so far exceeded the value of the imports from that country, that the balance of trade was "now much more in favor of Great Britain than it was before the War"—proof, the committee believed, of the success of British policy.

In navigation, too, dramatic gains were registered. Despite a decrease in shipping engaged in the direct trade between Great Britain and the United States, a notable increase was seen in that between Britain and the remaining North American colonies, about 50 per cent in the number of ships and 400 per cent in tonnage. A similar improvement marked the navigation between Britain and her West Indies. Traffic between the remaining North American colonies and the United States had also climbed, an important development because it was confined to imperial vessels; before the war, the Americans had held a virtual monopoly.

It could not be denied that a great decrease had occurred in the shipping between the British West Indies and the United States. The loss was not, however, as great as might appear at first glance. Before the war, approximately 63 per cent of the total was American; the whole was now imperial. Many vessels now engaged in a new and profitable circuitous trade: manufactured goods were taken from Britain to the United States to be traded for provisions and lumber for the West Indies; in the islands, a second exchange was made, the merchantman then making for Europe or, perhaps, the United States. The trade was doubly valuable since it had "taken from the Navigation of the United States even more than it had added to that of Great Britain."

The largest increase was in the shipping between the remaining North American colonies and the British West Indies, the direct result of the exclusion of American vessels from the carrying trade, and especially from the fish trade between Newfoundland and the sugar islands, which had been almost wholly dominated by the Americans before the war. The imperial growth was the more significant when compared with the American decline in shipbuilding.

Britain had clearly retained possession of the lion's share of the Confederation's foreign trade. On the basis of the voluminous data supplied by the consuls in the United States, the committee concluded that by 1789 Britain held 60 per cent of all foreign shipping trading to America, a total which was especially gratifying to the British in light of the efforts made by foreign competitors immediately after the war to break into the American carrying trade. It was, therefore, evident that the measures of the Confederation government of the United States had been ineffectual in countering British policy.

A new era had begun with the founding of the federal government. Possessed of the authority to lay and collect taxes, duties, imposts, and excises, this government was, unlike its predecessors, able to form a single, uniform commercial system. Treaties were reckoned the law of the land; and there was other evidence of "principles of Justice . . . certainly favourable to commerce in general"—coinage and legal tender, a federal judiciary, salutary regulations dealing with *ex post facto* laws. The unjust and onerous measures adopted during the Confederation thus stood "condemned by the united voice of the people of America assembled in convention." It was reasonable to expect that the Congress, "composed of a Body of men assembled from every part of the United States, and, who act upon a larger scale, and in support of a more extensive general interest," would avoid "like acts of Injustice to which the Legislatures of particular states are too frequently liable, in favour of the immediate and pressing Interests of the persons by whom they were elected, and sometimes even to relieve the Distresses of the very Individuals who composed Provincial Legislatures."

In the committee's opinion, therefore, the general outlook was reassuring. Optimism was not, however, unqualified. Certain acts of Congress required close scrutiny. An act of the first session of Congress imposed duties which discriminated against foreigners in favor of American importers using American vessels. It was scarcely serious, however, the advantage given to American citizens amounting to a mere 7½ per cent. A Tonnage Act, passed in the same session, discriminated equally against all foreign shipping. In the second session, higher duties were levied on all but a few goods imported in any but American vessels; even so, the total duty came to only 8½ per cent to 9 per cent *ad valorem*. The new Tonnage Act was preceded by a sustained and very nearly successful effort in the House of Representatives to discriminate against shipping of nations not in commercial treaty with the United States. As finally passed, however, it was but a repetition of the first act.

All things considered, the report concluded, Britain had no cause for complaint against the Duties Act. No distinction was made in favor of other foreign powers; and the duties levied were but little more than those of individual states under the Confederation and much less than those levied by most European powers, even by France and Holland under their new and liberal commercial treaties with Britain.

Britain's manufactures and credit would continue to secure her competitive position in the American market; and there was no fear of American domestic manufacturing, "at least for a long course of years": agriculture was more convenient for a nation rich in land but lacking cheap labor, capital, and surplus manpower.

The committee then deduced two propositions relating to trade between Great Britain and the United States which might be made to the Americans in any commercial negotiation. First, duties on British exports to America should not rise above the existing level. If this were unattainable, it should be insisted that duties on British goods should not rise above those paid under Britain's treaties with France and Holland. Second, American duties on British goods should never exceed those on similar articles from any other foreign power. It was true that Britain stood upon such a footing at the moment; but, in view of the past conduct of the individual states, it would be wise to bind the federal government to such a regulation.

For her part, Britain might agree to forego imposing duties on American produce higher than were levied upon similar articles from most favored European nations. The American trade, consisting chiefly of an exchange of British manufactures for naval stores and raw materials, was entitled to "some Distinctions, (though not perhaps to the present Extent)." Britain could not bind herself, however, to continue even temporarily the present favors given to American goods, since she might thereby put herself at a disadvantage in future commercial negotiations with other powers. On the whole, it would be better to reduce duties payable by other countries instead of increasing those applying to the Americans. Any change should be gradual, however, because of the enormous amounts of British capital involved.

The report dealt summarily with American hopes to gain entry into the West Indian ports: It would be proper to agree to continue present regulations governing trade between the United States and both the sugar islands and British North America for a limited time only, not indefinitely. As British continental colonies increased their agricultural production, the islanders' need for American provisions would decrease annually. Eventually, it was held, the Empire would become self-sufficient. (The committee did not undertake to explain why Lord Sheffield's similar prediction of seven years before remained glaringly unrealized.)

While Britain received American vessels in the Home Islands on the pre-1776 footing and made distinctions against them only in the West Indian and British North American trade, where they were treated exactly as other foreign shipping, America discriminated against British shipping generally. Britain was not without certain advantages to offset the disadvantages, which were at any event less onerous than under the Confederation. Lower insurance premiums and port charges in British ports and a better competitive position based on a large and experienced merchant marine would put down any threat from the small, inexperienced American marine, suffering depredations from the Barbary pirates and discrimination at the hands of European colonial powers. There was, thus, no serious threat from the former subjects; but as a question of policy, was it prudent for Britain to allow the American Tonnage and Duties Acts to go unremarked? Discrimination to answer discrimination was the traditional British practice. Parliament should therefore seriously consider whether or not acquiescence to the present American system might encourage an extension of discriminations against Britain until they, in fact, became effective. The Liverpool merchants favored immediate retaliation; but those of London, Bristol, and Glasgow wished for negotiation before proceeding to the extreme position advocated by their brethren of Liverpool. (Did Hawkesbury have a twinge of conscience?) All accepted the possibility of retaliation, however, either immediate or eventual. If it became expedient, the committee would recommend an impost on tobacco and rice imported from the United States in American vessels higher than if they were carried in British vessels or those from other foreign countries, as well as certain other discriminations designed to favor the British importer and vendor. Southerners thus reminded of their true economic interests would oppose anti-British policies.

Retaliation for the moment quite aside, in any negotiation with the Americans touching navigation, it would be proper for Britain to propose only that her ships should be treated in American ports, with respect to tonnage and other duties, as American ships were treated in British ports. (This would incidentally bring the alien's duty into operation upon American vessels.) Congress would certainly propose an extension of this principle of reciprocity to colonial ports. Only one answer could be returned: "this Demand cannot be admitted, even as a Subject of Negociation." Just as Congress regulated interstate commerce, so Britain dealt with colonial trade. Her right to do so was derived from the "public law" of Europe, which gave every nation jurisdiction over the commerce of its colonies. No foreign government had the shadow of a right to interfere. Now independent by her own choice, the United States enjoyed the rights and advantages of her condition; the former subjects could "now have no Pretence to claim the Privileges, which they once enjoyed as British Colonies."

Britain could, the report continued, reasonably consent to all articles of maritime law recently included in her treaties with other powers, with one very important exception: she must never allow American vessels the right to protect the property of enemies of Great Britain in time of war. Such a concession to the United States would be more dangerous than the same concession made to any other foreign power. Geography would put it in the power of the United States to cover the whole trade of the Bourbon powers with their islands and colonies in America. The British navy must never be deprived of so important a means of harming the enemy.

It was right that Britain should hesitate before proceeding to the retaliation justified by American legislation. She should seek to persuade the former subjects "to consent to some fair and equitable plan of Accommodation, and to a liberal system of Commerce and Navigation, founded on reciprocal Advantages." (Americans would use almost the same words but mean something very different.) British subjects had suffered oppression and injustice at American hands; but a measure of understanding and forbearance was possible. Wartime bitterness in the United States would eventually evaporate. Time would heal the wounds of war, rancor subside. Then, "ancient Habits, and the recollection of former Connections might bring back the people of those States to a more favourable Disposition to Great Britain." Events might even "detach them from their new Connections" and make Americans and Britons, "tho' no longer fellow Subjects, friends at least, as they were before the War." There were certain promising signs already discernable. The new system adopted by Congress was more favorable than the measures of the several states during the Confederation. There was in Congress, especially in the Senate, "a party . . . already formed in favour of a Connection with Great Britain, which, by moderation on our part, may perhaps be strengthened and increased, so as to bring about, in a friendly way, all the Objects we have in view." Retaliation by Britain, therefore, was not to be considered at the moment, "just at the time that those who govern the United States appear to be more favourably disposed to this Country." Let negotiations commence, by all means, the report concluded, always supposing that early in the proceedings it should be made clear that Britain could "never submit even to treat on what appears to be the favourite Object of the People of these States, That is, the Admission of the Ships of the United States into the Ports of Your Majesty's Colonies and Islands." It would be wise to inform the Americans that Britain possessed sufficient means to protect and support her commerce and navigation in case Congress refused "a fair and equitable plan of Accomodation" and proceeded to further discrimination. Anglo-American trade benefited both parties; yet the United States had more to fear from an interruption than did Britain, whose trading interests extended throughout the world.

The report, save for the exhaustive data marshaled to support its contentions, might almost have been written in 1784, so completely did it mirror and vindicate the principles of the report of that year. There was a difference, of course: a thorough complacency marked the second report. The hypotheses of 1784 had been proved. In comparison, American actions in and out of Congress were minor considerations, requiring attention to be sure, but no fundamental readjustment of policy—hence the terms, which Americans would have thought ludicrously inadequate, deemed proper for a commercial treaty with the United States. A growl from the lion would suffice to prevent further and unacceptable legislation by the United States government.

Hawkesbury was the specialist par excellence, possessing a tough and well-stocked mind. He was at his best in grappling with the myriad deaails of trade, in meticulously marshaling them to demonstrate the validity of traditional and established mercantilistic doctrine. His strength, however, was also his weakness. Broader considerations eluded him. He refused to believe that economics was but a single branch of statecraft; and he forgot, if ever he knew, that in relations between nations, as between individuals, the decisions of the heart could prevail over the most rational expostulations of the head. The signs were there to be read—Madison's proposals, the Morris mission, the reports from Beckwith and the British consuls, all promising a rising storm in Anglo-American relations—but they meant little to Lord Hawkesbury. The existence of the Empire, he believed, depended

upon unswerving adherence to the Acts of Navigation: and he distrusted and feared the "fashionable language" of liberal commercial
treaties. He remembered Pitt's connection with the American Intercourse Bill in 1783, saw around him younger men in government to
whom the name of Adam Smith was not an epithet. The Report of
January, 1791, was to be a bulwark against the Shelburne heresy. Its
author said in effect: "Regard the success of the present policy. To
change it will hazard both strength and opulence. Hold to the
course!"

The report was officially transmitted to Leeds on March 31. By
then, the Duke was on the point of retiring from the Foreign Office,
making way for William Wyndham Grenville, newly created Lord
Grenville. The ministerial reshuffle coincided with Hawkesbury's personal desire to produce a delay in dealing with American business, a
capital misfortune since the presence of a British minister in America
could have done much to damp down the rising crisis. Furthermore,
the contents of the report became known in America, and disaster
was averted only because this occurred after Congress had adjourned
in the summer of 1791. Had it happened earlier, perhaps during the
debates on Madison's resolutions, it is difficult to see how discrimination against British trade and navigation could have been avoided and
a trade war averted.

In April, 1791, William Temple Franklin, grandson of Benjamin,
was in London arranging for the publication of his illustrious grand-
father's works. Having many friends in the capital, he soon learned
that "a very considerable Report" had been made by the Committee
for Trade to the Privy Council, and that it dealt with Anglo-American commercial relations. This information he transmitted immediately to Jefferson, adding that although he had not yet seen the document, he understood it evinced a disposition "more favorable than
formerly" toward the United States. He would, he promised the Secretary of State, get access to the document, and transmit its contents.

In the Jefferson papers, there is an "Abstract of a report . . .
made to the Privy Council, and handed to the King, (a few copies
of which were printed off for the members of the Cabinet, and called
in again by a sudden Order of Council)."[11] The recall must have been
a belated attempt to keep the document confidential; but Jefferson's
abstract, in all probability sent to him by Franklin, testified to its
failure. A full and accurate précis of the original report in Jefferson's

hands provided grist for the mill of those who wished anti-British discrimination and wounded the Federalist party, which, though devoted to the course of friendly negotiation, was now branded as virtual agent of a foreign and hostile power. Robert Morris, himself no friend to anti-British measures, wrote in alarm to Patrick Colquhoun. He had learned, he said, some of the particulars in the report. There was a well-founded sentiment abroad in the United States, he confided rather wryly, that "your Government want better Information from this Country than they possess. Let a Minister therefore be sent but as soon as possible."[12]

A fuller, and thus more alarming, dispatch came to Grenville from Beckwith.[13] With some anguish, he revealed the nature of the deep offense given to Britain's American friends. Reminding the British Secretary of earlier warnings on the same subject, Beckwith wrote of "the peculiar delicacy necessary to be observed with respect to this country, in whatever might have a tendency to mark, if any, even the most remote degree, an increasing or even existing cordiality on the part of any description of persons here towards Great Britain." Certain gentlemen—obviously Hamiltonians—had recently called on him, expressing themselves concerned "to find that their motives are misunderstood and that their views for the best interests of their own Country have been ascribed to an undue preference for another." The agitated Americans were referring, of course, to the report's bald statement that British retaliation against the United States ought to be avoided " 'as there was a growing English interest in that Country' or words to that effect." With great concern, Beckwith told Grenville of "the very bad consequences" such a statement would have in the country, "where it might be made such a use of by another description of persons, as would infallibly prevent all future confidence." He had soothed his irate visitors as much as possible, assuring them of his own acceptance of the purity of their motives. "I hope the alarm is over," he concluded his dispatch. "The principles which actuate this party, are founded unquestionably in an American interest, but the operation of those principles is important, and if prudently cherished, may have a weighty influence in the concerns of this Country." The implication was clear: if the principles were not "cherished," if they were treated complacently, as the report had treated them, they would cease to operate to Britain's advantage.

Initially, outraged Hamiltonians were chiefly concerned with clearing themselves of the charge of constituting an "English interest." Later, however, the report's suggestions for a commercial treaty came under scrutiny. Early in October, Phineas Bond wrote hastily and in some alarm to Grenville.[14] While news of the appointment of a minister to the United States was "received very joyfully by those who wish well to an Intercourse of strict Amity between the two Countries," some members of the American administration believed the British attitude toward a commercial treaty was "not very favorable," an opinion founded on knowledge of the report. (It was "fit your Lordship should be informed that the Tendency of this Report is fully *understood* by the Ministers of the United States.") Bond himself had done good work during the last session of Congress, "inspiring" certain members of both houses with a sense of the commercial advantages Americans enjoyed in their trade with Britain. It was obvious, however, that even the most moderate men considered "some sort of participation in the carrying Trade to our Islands as the indispensible Basis" for an Anglo-American commercial treaty. Perhaps an alternative, designed to captivate the New Englanders, would be "legitimating" American vessels of a certain size sold to British subjects or remitted in payment of debts. Bond was undecided personally; but he knew that no commercial treaty with the United States was possible if the restrictions laid down in the Report of January, 1791, were adhered to rigidly.

Even before the appointment, let alone the arrival, of a British minister to the United States, the disturbance thus caused by the report muddied the prospects of an Anglo-American settlement. Jefferson and his friends were confirmed in their suspicions and hostility; Hamilton and his followers in Congress were discomfited, saddled with the epithet "Anglophile," from which even yet they have not been rescued. The position laid down by Hawkesbury and his committee did not, in fact, become the negotiating position of the British minister to the United States; but the bad impression created by the report was never overcome.

A measure of Hawkesbury's comfortable assurance disappeared with the news of Washington's Message of February 14, 1791, and of the alarming interpretations put upon it by British agents. He knew, too, perhaps, that at Jefferson's instructions the American chargé at Paris, William Short, was seeking to induce Spain, France, and Portugal to join the United States in a navigation act directed against

Britain.[15] On May 24, Hawkesbury's committee wrote to Foreign Secretary Grenville, telling him something which he must have surmised already: it appeared "that in the next Session of Congress, Measures are again likely to be proposed for imposing new Burtherns" upon British ships and goods. The American Executive was "likely to give their whole weight" to such measures and to attempts to return members who would support them in the congressional elections. After months of delay, the committee now stated its conclusion that "as little time as possible should be lost in taking proper Measures for counteracting the Intentions of those Members of Congress whose Interest or Inclination it may be to support any Proposition unfriendly to the Commerce and Navigation of this Country." A new sense of urgency was in evidence, but there was no shift from the advice laid down in the report, "in which . . . will be found the Sentiments of the Committee upon every part of this important subject."[16] Whatever reservations he may have held, Hawkesbury realized that the dispatch of a British minister was a matter of pressing importance, if only to prevent harmful American actions.

The Pitt ministry had long intended to send a minister to the United States. Settled in power at the head of his new government in 1783, the Prime Minister had fully expected an early establishment of normal diplomatic relations between the two countries. Replying to his father's old colleague, the Duke of Grafton, who with Lord Camden had recommended that merchant Thomas Walpole succeed David Hartley to negotiate with the American commissioners in Paris, Pitt explained his position. He doubted "whether much can be hoped from a negotiation with America conducted under the Eye of France," and was "inclined to think our best Chance of cultivating a good Correspondence would be that of a direct Intercourse thro' Ministers sent from Hence to America and from America hither."[17] There was considerable difficulty, however, in finding a man willing to go out to America. The distance was great and the post minor.[18] Indeed the appointment, though desirable from the government's point of view, was held to be of so little significance by prospective incumbents that Leeds could make a jocular, malicious suggestion to Pitt that William Eden be given the mission. A leader of opposition and detested by Leeds and his friends, Eden, in the Duke's opinion, "would be as well *out* of England as in it." Eden also possessed abilities, Leeds added, "just of the nature I think fit for the business of that appointment, consisting chiefly of narrow and illiberal Intrigues."[19]

As relations between the two nations settled down, at least to British satisfaction, the intention to send a minister seemed less and less pressing. Continental problems were closer at hand and more important in terms of the balance of power and international prestige. When Americans complained of the neglect, apologies were invariably made; and there is no reason to doubt their sincerity. John Adams was assured, soon after he arrived in London, that the government wished to send a minister; the failure to do so was not due to coldness or want of respect toward the United States, it was said, but to the difficulty of finding a suitable candidate for the post.[20] Other matters preempted the ministry's attention, however, and again the appointment was not made. A well-organized and efficient consular service (excepting only Sir John Temple) was established in America, despite the lack of a consular convention between the two powers. Americans grumbled at the omission, but reciprocated with the appointment of consuls to Britain.[21] Although consular officials were not, technically, empowered to act in a diplomatic capacity, there was on both sides a certain informality. Bond could remonstrate with state authorities over laws pertaining to the British debts; Joshua Johnson, American consul at London, could make representations about impressments. The tendency, therefore, was for British ministers to let things rub along as they were. Relations with America were chiefly of a commercial kind anyway. Consuls could guard essential British interests, and the expense of a new diplomatic establishment be avoided.

With the establishment of the federal government, second thoughts became urgently necessary. Even before the new political arrangement began functioning in the United States, young Robert Liston, chargé in Madrid, hinted to William Carmichael, the deplorable American minister there, that Pitt might be about to name him representative to America.[22] However, matters moved slowly. It would be nearly a decade before Liston and his charming wife graced the scene at the new capital city of Washington. Meanwhile, his services were thought to be required more urgently in Stockholm and Constantinople than at Philadelphia. Washington's instructions to Gouverneur Morris in 1789 bade the envoy take up in pointed terms the British failure to dispatch a minister. Leeds subsequently renewed the plea of difficulty in finding the right man equal to the task and acceptable to the American people for the distant post.[23] Early in

September, 1790, however, he told Morris that he actually had a prospective minister under consideration. It was probably Hugh Elliot,
formerly at Berlin, then at Copenhagen. Elliot was about to be recalled from the latter court, and hence was available for reassign-
ment. An offer was made, but declined, although Morris suspected
(incorrectly) that the plan had been suspended because the resolution
of the Nootka crisis freed Britain of fear about American opinion.[24]
As we have seen, Jefferson deduced from Morris' correspondence that
Leeds favored an exchange of ministers, but that opposition within
the cabinet made the issue uncertain. Washington accordingly told
Congress that the British position was equivocal. The British ministry was, in fact, at that very moment scanning the lists for a likely
man, but in vain. Patrick Colquhoun would have gone in a moment;
but he was both by training and temperament unfit for a diplomatic
assignment. A more interesting, if even less acceptable, candidate for
the post was General John Graves Simcoe. In March, 1791, about to
depart for his government of Upper Canada, he suggested that he
combine that office with the American appointment, "the original
object of my wishes."[25] It does not require much speculation to arrive at the probable reception the former commander of Simcoe's
Rangers would have had in the United States. While the post was being declined by the right men and sought after by the wrong ones,
there continued to arrive from every quarter—from Beckwith, Smith,
Colquhoun, Bond—increasingly urgent advice to send out a minister, lest the "French" party triumph through Britain's default.

The man finally fixed upon was George Hammond. Secretary to
David Hartley during the negotiations with the Republic's commissioners in Paris—an association which must have been pleasing to
Americans—he subsequently served as chargé at Vienna; and in 1790
he went to Copenhagen. Shortly thereafter, he became minister plenipotentiary at Madrid, serving under Ambassador Alyne Fitzherbert,
Lord St. Helens. Leeds may have had him in mind for the American
appointment at the time he was assigned to Madrid; in mid-Septem-
ber, 1790, the Foreign Secretary summoned him to London from
Copenhagen "in order to settle several Points with you previous to
your setting out for Madrid, or any other Mission you may perhaps
be entrusted with."[26] If there was a plan, it was put aside; Spanish
affairs were more important than American. By May, 1791, however,
America seemed intent on precipitating a crisis. The appointment

could be put off no longer. Hammond was recalled from Madrid; and at the age of twenty-eight he was appointed minister plenipotentiary from His Britannic Majesty to the United States of America.[27]

The instructions given the new envoy were of great significance in themselves and, additionally, because they proved the existence of a major difference about American policy within the British cabinet. It was the first since 1783. On the surface, it seemed mild; but the fact remained that Foreign Secretary Grenville and Committee President Hawkesbury possessed quite divergent ideas about the Hammond mission. Their disagreement grew until, in the critical negotiations with John Jay in 1794, it became open and bitter, with Hawkesbury overruled on a critical point—the admission of American vessels of limited tonnage into British West Indian ports.

At Grenville's request, Hawkesbury composed a draft of instructions for Hammond in early July. Confining himself to commercial questions, the president of the Committee for Trade took his guidelines from the Report of January 28, 1791. As a secondary matter, Hawkesbury wished to instruct Hammond to point out to Americans how their actions toward British subjects differed from the treatment they received from Britons, an invidious comparison designed to prove the essential injustice of the one and the rectitude of the other. Again, the report was invoked: it held "many Arguments in defence of the conduct of Great Britain, in retaining the posts and Forts on the Western Frontier of the United States." Even on this most political of points, however, Hawkesbury saw as the dominant concerns the fur trade, the navigation of the Great Lakes, and communication between the Lakes and the St. Lawrence. The posts were to remain British, the argument ran, as long as American conduct should "continue to justify this measure."[28]

In a proposed set of particular instructions, Hawkesbury extended and developed his advice for the commercial negotiations he assumed were about to begin. The spirit and occasionally even the wording came from the Report of January 28, 1791. He stated explicitly that American entry into the British West Indies could not be admitted even as a subject of negotiation, and called for threats of retaliation in the event of further American discrimination.[29]

The instructions finally given to Hammond were written by Lord Grenville, and they differed from Hawkesbury's draft very greatly in both scope and detail. The chief difference, however, was the priority

Grenville assigned to extinguishing the problems arising from the broken treaty of peace and to a certain flexibility, compared with Hawkesbury's stern rigidity and preoccupation with commercial questions.[30] A stern line of argument was laid out for Hammond. His Majesty held in his hands the northwestern forts as retaliation for American breaches of the peace; yet these could not be considered adequate compensation for the losses sustained by loyalists and merchants through American injustice. Even if the United States should now desire to remove the causes of British complaints, they would not automatically acquire thereby the right to claim the cession of the forts. One party to a treaty could not withhold performance of her obligations as long as it pleased her, and, then, at a moment of her own choosing, perform the stipulations and claim reciprocal action from the other contracting party. Furthermore, nothing could now place many loyalists and creditors in the situation to which they were entitled at the signing of the peace; since that time records of debts had been lost or destroyed, witnesses had died, families dispersed. In consequence, many Britons had "suffered great and irreparable Losses, and this Country has been subjected to a heavy Expence." The King would, therefore, be justified in declining any negotiation at all upon the subject of the posts. The royal and sincere desire, however, to "remove every occasion of misunderstanding" induced the King to "direct that you should express His readiness to enter into Negotiation upon the Subject, and to consent to such Arrangements as may be found to be of mutual convenience, and not inconsistent with the just claims and Rights of His Subjects." It was "an essential and sine qua non condition" that "every practicable Measure should be adopted by the States for the execution of the Fourth, Fifth, and Sixth Articles . . . as far as the circumstances of the length of time which has elapsed, render it possible that effect should now be given to those Stipulations." This, Hammond was specifically enjoined, was to be considered "the first and leading Object of your Mission." From recent communications on the subject, Grenville continued, there was hope that "there exists among those who have the greatest Influence in the Government of America, a real disposition to meet the just Expectations of this Country in that respect." Hammond should, therefore, give assurances that Britain was disposed to contribute toward "removing the Grounds of future difficulties by some practicable and reasonable Arrangement on the Subject of the Posts."[31] He was to proceed immediately to discuss measures for the full execution of the peace or arrangements founded upon it "as the circumstances of the present moment will admit, and to receive and transmit for consideration, any reasonable Proposals which may be made to you on those Subjects." In the interim, the status quo would be maintained in the backcountry; and American settlers within the limits of the territory occupied by the British should be given "every degree of discouragement" by both governments.

Two other points of a "political" nature remained to be treated. The first was the chronic Indian war along the frontier, a subject which would naturally arise in every discussion of the posts. Hammond, with full knowledge of Lord Dorchester's dispatches to the home government, would be able "to disclaim in the most unequivocal manner" any notion that Dorchester was encouraging the Indians. On the contrary, the British government had a "strong commercial and political interest in the restoration of Peace; and nothing would be more satisfactory to His Majesty than to find himself enabled to contribute his good Offices for that Object, thro' the medium of His Government in America." Even before the defeat of the American General St. Clair at the hands of the Indians, it occurred to Grenville that an American disaster might well present a favorable opportunity for an offer of British mediation. Secondly, Hammond was told to inform himself of the American relations with other foreign powers, particularly with France and Spain. If American differences with the latter should lead to a war, as appeared likely, Hammond should be careful to preserve neutrality, aiming at interposing good offices and preserving the friendship of both parties.

In a set of additional instructions, Grenville turned to the problem of commercial negotiations. Referring to the recent debates in Congress and what was manifestly an intention to resume discussion of Anglo-American trade at the coming session, Hammond was told to regard this as "a principal object" of his attention. The language he was to use on the point was to be general and in harmony with Hawkesbury's report. Indeed, he was advised to draw directly from the report supporting material on existing British favors to American trade and on the relative importance to Britain and America of the commerce between them. If the Americans should propose a commercial treaty—the initiative was to be left with them—Hammond was to express his willingness to enter negotiation and "to consent to stipulations for the benefit of commerce and navigation, on terms of reciprocal advantage." This he was to understand to mean "the placing the commerce of each country with the other reciprocally, on the terms of the most favored nation." Trade between the United States and Britain's colonies would also be placed on the basis of most favored nation. He should bring to the Americans' attention the fact that they enjoyed under present arrangements favors transcending such a status, "the strongest proof of the friendly disposition towards the American Commerce which is entertained here." Continuance, however, could be secured only by reciprocal benefits given to British subjects.

As for navigation, the "most natural and convenient principle" would be equivalent treatment of the two countries' vessels. If America persisted in her discrimination, however, Britain was prepared to do the same, although at the higher levels imposed by the American Tonnage Act. Hammond would "let it be understood that a plan of this nature has already been formed, tho' it will be with the greatest reluctance that His Majesty's Servants will find themselves obliged to bring it forward." Any other proposals from the Americans, including the inevitable request for admission to the West Indian ports, were not to be rejected out of hand as Hawkesbury had advised, but to be taken *ad referendum* and transmitted to London. The instructions closed with the usual stipulation that no treaty was to be concluded without prior and express directions from the ministry.

Hammond was charged with negotiations in the same two major areas which had confronted Americans and Britons ever since the end of the war: breaches of the treaty of peace and commercial relations. Priority was given to the first, and neither was to be contingent upon the other. The circumstances prevailing in 1791 were, however, very different from those in 1785. Old problems had become more difficult of solution; and grave new ones, threatening direct consequences to amity and even peace between the two nations, had emerged.

PART IV

British Interest in
An American Settlement 1789-1791

CHAPTER EIGHT

The Debts, Vermont, and the American West

AT THE END of the summer of 1791, Thomas Jefferson told a friend that, the many reports to the contrary notwithstanding, he doubted the intention of the British to send a minister to the United States. Even if they did, he added, he was certain "they have no serious view of treating or fulfilling treaties."[1] The Secretary of State was wrong. Persistently underestimating British good faith and desire to negotiate differences, Jefferson clung to his view with a tenacity and single-mindedness which would have done credit to his old enemy George III.

There were good and pressing reasons why Britain wished to treat with the United States. One, as we have seen, was the desire to avoid further commercial discrimination; another, the "first and leading Object" of Hammond's mission, was the old, familiar intention to secure justice for the prewar creditors.

The adoption of the Constitution brought fair hopes and high expectations among the interested merchants in Britain. A flood of new legal actions rolled in on the federal, district, and circuit courts; and optimism soared when Chief Justice Jay sternly admonished those in New York, Connecticut, Massachusetts, and New Hampshire to observe treaties as the law of the land.[2] From the outset, however, the behavior of the courts in Virginia was the critical question.

Between 1790 and 1795, virtually no British trading house active in Virginia at the outbreak of the war failed to bring at least one suit to recover debts. It was clear within months of the adoption of the Constitution by the state, however, that satisfaction was not to flow automatically from her courts—state or federal—to British creditors. First, many debts did not come within the purview of the federal courts at all; and there was a complicated system of state courts able and willing to hamper British creditors pursuing their debtors. The county courts had jurisdiction of civil cases not involving more than £10. Even if some long-suffering British trading house should conclude that it would be financially worthwhile to pursue hundreds of small debtors owing £10 or less, it would have to face decisions rendered by local courts extremely unlikely to lend a sympathetic ear to the alien.[3] Above the state courts were the new federal courts; but even in the higher ones, it soon became evident that justice was not to descend like the gentle dew of heaven. The first debt case, Jones (representing the Bristol house of Jones and Farrel) *vs.* Walker (a citizen of Albemarle County), was called on November 23, 1791, in Richmond's circuit court. The eloquence of the defense counsel, Patrick Henry, combined with new attempts of the state assembly to resolve that British debts should be suspended until Great Britain performed her treaty obligations, made the outcome doubtful from the first. Early in the new year, the court adjourned without rendering a decision, much to the disgust of the creditors.

Maryland, too, was of great importance to British creditors because of the total amount owed there. They were encouraged when the Superior Court of the state ruled in the autumn of 1790 that the treaty of peace restored to British creditors the right to recover, even in the face of the "discharge" of debts by payment into the state treasury (in depreciated paper currency) during the war.[4] It quickly became apparent, however, that, in fact, little relief was to be forthcoming from the lower courts in Maryland. Indeed, throughout most of the southern states, years would pass before the prewar debts were extinguished; and then, it was the work not of the several states— or even of the individual American debtors—but of the government of the United States.

There had been no ministerial discussion of the debts since John Adams' residence in London. As Hammond prepared for his new post, the creditors bombarded the government with new statements of their claims and urged the greatest exertion in their behalf. Home Secretary Henry Dundas, ever mindful of the stake of the Glasgow merchants in the debts, invited full communication, including new substantiating data; and he gave welcome assurances that the government intended to continue its efforts in their behalf.

The Committee of British Merchants trading to North America immediately informed Dundas that in the eastern states "the Amount

[due] is now considerably reduced, by payments which some of the Individuals have been fortunate enough to receive." The "greatest part," however, "namely those connected with the Southern provinces have received little or nothing." There remained some thirty thousand debtors to settle their accounts. It was impossible in the majority of cases to state "the present Situation of such Debtors, by reason of Deaths, Emigrations, alteration and alienation of property and Insolvencies occasioned by the long delay." In these southern areas, it was evident that the brave words of the new Constitution were still but words; "the original obstructions were by the last Advice still in force."[5]

The case of William Cunningham of Glasgow and his partners was typical of the plight of British creditors.[6] Cunningham, speaking for two companies in which he was a senior partner, described to Dundas the debts incurred by Americans before the war at his several stores in Virginia and Maryland. The principal due at the beginning of the war or at the date of expulsion from the states "for not taking a part against Britain in the revolt," he stated to be:

In Virginia, to William Cunningham & Co.	£ 95,200
to Cunningham personally	520
In Maryland, to Cunningham, Findlay & Co.	16,308-2-3d.
to Cunningham, Browne & Co.	1,454-0-9d.
Total (excluding interest)	£113,482-3-0d.

It was a very large sum—equivalent, for example, to half a year's profit in the Canadian fur trade. The creditors had employed "every prudent method that occurred to them" to recover it. Very soon after the war, agents had been sent out "on the Faith of the Fourth Article of the provisional Treaty, with Instructions to prosecute the Collection with as much Lenity as possible." The expense to the firm was enormous, the return trifling. Now, even with the new Constitution in force, Cunningham and his partners had "yet to learn that it has hitherto produced any beneficial Consequences," particularly in Virginia. Suits in district and local courts were dismissed in as cavalier a manner as in the days of the Confederation, "on the plea of their being british Debts, uniformly pleaded by the Defendants." Even if a federal court should hand down a verdict for the plaintiff (and Cunningham duly noted the adjournment of the Circuit Court at Richmond without acting), it was still "exceeding problematical" that the state courts would abide by it.

That, however, was only a part of Cunningham's problem. As irksome as waiting might be, if the creditor could only look forward to certain, eventual recovery, he might reconcile himself to the situation; but the amount of recoverable debt was decreasing daily. In 1791, it was already "too evident" that even if legal impediments should be removed at once, the action would "at this late Day . . . be of little Avail to the Creditors," and certainly "not place them on the footing they were entitled to by the Treaty at the Termination of the War."

The argument had already been made by Leeds to Morris, but the Committee of British Merchants, in their memorial of November 30, gave it a point which must have concerned and even nettled His Majesty's government: failing satisfaction from the Americans, the British authorities should make restitution to the creditors. The Prohibitory Act of 1775, the merchants said, had first interdicted commercial transactions with the rebels. (The implication—that without the Act, Americans in arms would have hastened to discharge their debts to Britons—seems, at the least, doubtful.) Secondly, the merchant committee maintained, the Americans alleged that Britain's failure to deliver the northwestern forts and to pay for the slaves caused the delay in settling the prewar debts. The merchants did not presume to judge in the matter; they could only observe that they had suffered from it. The country presumably derived some benefit from the retention of the forts. The merchants therefore believed that they had a valid claim upon the government for compensation.

It was small reward to the ministry to have the American contention flung in their faces by the very men whose interests they had sought to protect. The position was as unacceptable from Britons as from Americans, but it underscored a troubling fact: justice for the creditors had become more complicated than simple repayment. Some debts were already irretrievably lost; more were disappearing daily. Pressures from the despairing merchants, arguing that the government should make good their losses as it had done for the loyalists, were mounting. Their agitation emphasized the urgent need for negotiations with the United States.

Concern for the creditors and the threat of hostile American legislation against British ships and goods were but two of the reasons for a British diplomatic initiative. A third was the increasingly complex and potentially explosive situation in the American backcountry, where Britain, for a number of important reasons—the retention of the posts among them—was deeply involved. First, the new settlements in the American backcountry promised an expanding market beyond the wildest dreams of British merchants. Second, Britain claimed, with the United States, freedom of navigation on the Mississippi; and Spain remained adamant in refusing it to both. Might not ground be found here for a common cause? There were darker, more ominous considerations, too: the new order clearly necessitated vigilance along the Canadian-American frontier. Numerous tribes of Indians roamed the woods, regarding national boundaries but little, clinging to traditional friendships with the British, and fighting to hold off Americans, covetous of their hunting grounds. In addition, the separatist tendencies in Vermont and Kentucky, the founding of new communities in the West, and the near collision of Britain and Spain over Nootka added to the unstable and dangerous situation in the backcountry.

By 1790, however, the dominant concern, touching every other aspect of British policy in the area, was the retention of the posts—no longer a retaliatory tit-for-tat, but a growing challenge to the sensitive, proud, and energetically governed Republic. Until the posts were finally evacuated following the Jay-Grenville treaty in 1794, British troops occupying the northwestern posts had to live with the constant possibility of "incidents" precipitated by American regular or irregular forces. Were the posts worth a war with the United States? Haldimand thought not in 1790 and the British government agreed with him; but the problem facing Pitt and his colleagues was far from simple. To give up the posts involved the creditors, the client Indians, and the safety of Canada. To continue to hold them offended the Americans, invited the intrigues of separatist elements in the backcountry, and encouraged Indian depredations against the encroaching Americans. The implication was plain: both wisdom and self-interest indicated the desirability of a general settlement with America.[7]

It has been asserted that Britain was disinclined to treat with America and to give up the posts because she wished to retrieve her lost influence and territory in the American backcountry. Had this been the case, she could not have hoped for fairer opportunities than arose in Vermont and the West.

Lying between New York and New Hampshire, the little province of Vermont looked mainly northward, geographically and economically, to the St. Lawrence. Politically, the dominant power—at least until the "revolution" of 1790 carried the state in favor of joining the Union—was the Allen family: Ethan, whose exploits at Ticonderoga and Crown Point in 1775 gave him a place in schoolboy history out of all proportion to his just deserts; Ira, a colonel during the American War; and Levi, whose commercial and political schemes came to richly deserved grief. Brothers all, coarse and crude, they shared a vulpine quality repugnant to better men. "Ethan Allen died this day and went to Hell," wrote President Stiles of Yale on February 12, 1789.[8] Few doubted the location of the eventual family reunion.

The Allens' wartime efforts were exerted not to secure American independence, but to seize for themselves lands disputed by New Hampshire and New York. In 1777, Vermont claimed sovereign status, independent equally of the British Parliament and of the American Congress. Soon, the Allens were negotiating with Canadian officials for recognition of the state's independence and neutrality.[9] Although the treaty of peace, by drawing the Canadian-American boundary at the 45th parallel, recognized the territory of Vermont as within the jurisdiction of the United States, the Allens, their creature Governor Chittenden, and their friends did not give up their plan. The attitude of Britain was crucial.

Early in 1783, it appeared that Congress might move against Vermont with an armed force, thus establishing American authority within the province. Agents of Vermont promptly informed General Haldimand in Canada that they lacked ammunition and wished Britain to provide a supply. The worried governor requested instructions from home. If the Americans attacked Vermont, he feared, the assault might well be extended to the northwestern posts. The coalition ministry refused to fall in with the Allens' design for Vermont. Lord North, secretary of state for home and colonial affairs, gave a succinct and plain response to Haldimand: "No assistance can be given to the inhabitants of that State, to enable them to act against the Americans."[10] The anticipated clash did not occur; and Britain remained in unmolested possession of the posts. The exchange was, however, revealing. The former mother country had shown no disposition, even in a moment of threatened crisis, to intervene in an area she had recognized as American. That American authority was not established within the province was not due to British intrigue.

The Allens, unchecked by the United States, continued their machinations. Controlling the governor and council, they obtained a semblance of legal authority to negotiate with the British in Canada; and from 1783, they worked persistently to win a treaty of commerce, establishing free trade between Vermont and Canada. Britain had an opportunity, Ira told the Council of Quebec during one of his visits there in 1785, to cement "a friendship which no vicissitudes of time will be able to alter."[11] He scarcely needed to explain that, for her part, Vermont would win in return recognition of her independence; and the Allens, the dominant influence in a British client state, would be forever secure from their enemies, foreign and domestic. Lieutenant-Governor Hamilton of Quebec immediately recognized the political implication of the Allens' request. It reflected, he told London, "a jealous apprehension of their neighbors and . . . the difficulty of procuring warlike supplies except by the channel of the St. Laurence."[12]

Although they won some support from mercantile circles in Quebec and London for freeing trade between Canada and Vermont, the Allens never persuaded the British government to go beyond the limits Dorchester and his council established for inland trade with the United States. Disappointed Vermonters might wheedle the former mother country for "a few particular indulgencies" and advise her "to retain the forts at this time and to be strong in Canada," but the British government studiously avoided granting unique distinctions.[13]

The adoption of the Constitution in the United States and the creation of an efficient government clearly spelled danger for the Allens and their friends. Engaged in a "large plan" to sell naval timber directly to the British Admiralty, a project which involved long and tortuous negotiations by all three brothers in Quebec, they feared Vermont's entry into the Union would mean the end of all their hopes and schemes. It was during a visit to Canada in July, 1788, that Ethan Allen made his (though not his brothers') last bid to win for Vermont the protection of Great Britain. In a long analysis of American politics, Ethan recounted to Dorchester the many reasons for his state's inclination to "the British interest" and suspicions of the United States.[14] The Republic was heavily burdened with debt, strife-ridden, and suffering from "the licentious notions of liberty taught and imbibed in the course of the late revolution." Vermont, he told the Governor, was well able to fend off any American aggression. Indeed, with a potential force of fifteen thousand men, probably more than the United States could find, she might well join with friendly frontiersmen and anti-federalists within the Republic itself "to crush the premised federal government" if circumstances warranted. The state appeared small at first sight, he continued, but she possessed "a heavy influence in the American politicks, and may turn the scale," a fact "well worth the attention of Great Britain." He was not suggesting an open alliance, but an informal understanding to guarantee Vermont's neutrality. In times to come, he hinted, other arrangements might be made.

Dorchester immediately forwarded this undisguised invitation to Lord Sidney in London. No official action was taken. In January, 1789, a month before Ethan died, Levi Allen embarked for the British capital. Carrying a letter of introduction to Evan Nepean, Sidney's under-secretary, he was in hot pursuit of the "large plan." Arriving after the Admiralty contract for naval timbers had been closed, however, the disappointed and disgruntled merchant promptly improvised a new role. Lacking any shadow of authority, he announced to the ministry in June, 1789, that he was duly commissioned agent for his native state to negotiate "a commercial and friendly intercourse" with Great Britain.[15] In a memorial to the Foreign Secretary, he described Vermont's 160,000 inhabitants, many of them loyalist refugees, 75 per cent of whom he maintained were staunch friends of the former mother country.[16] They wished even to return to British allegiance, although "being in doubt with respect to its practicability, this part of their wish is not comprehended in the Commission." (There was a limit even to Allen's daring.) Levi lamented that the boundary line drawn in 1783 cut Vermont off from Canada, but he urged that what politics had put asunder, economics could join. An extensive list of Vermont produce—lumber, naval stores, grain, pot and pearl ash, pig and bar iron, livestock, provisions, flax, hemp, tallow, beeswax, honey—would be exchanged gladly for quantities of British manufactures, if only the trade were established "in the same manner and Subject to the same Duties, Imposts and Drawbacks as if said District of Vermont had been part and parcel of His Majesty's Province of Quebec." A second and similar memorial addressed to the Lords of Trade followed a few days later.[17]

The list of articles was little, if any, more extensive than that comprehended in the ordinances governing Canada's trade with the United States, including Vermont. Britain's signature to a treaty was, however, a prospect far more brilliant than any paltry trade concessions. No matter how innocuous an agreement might appear, it would have constituted recognition of the state's independence, and this was the Allen dream.

Foreign Secretary Grenville, himself deeply suspicious of the "agent" from Vermont, referred the whole affair to the Committee for Trade.[18] In view of the delicate implications of Allen's proposition, it was scarcely surprising that the committee under President Hawkesbury proceeded with something more than its habitual deliberation. Months passed, and Levi's impatience grew. He would have left England before the end of the year, had it not been for the intervention of John Graves Simcoe. The future governor of Upper Canada, who had met the Vermonter and made his cause his own, persuaded Levi to postpone his departure; rushed up to London from his country retreat in Devon; and bearded Grenville in behalf of "an Object which seemed to have been hitherto unattended to . . . but which I had always considered of the greatest Consequence to this Country." The former colonel of the Rangers now set himself the task of convincing the government that a unique opportunity had presented itself. Vermont, inhabited by "a brave, virtuous, and English race of People," could become "another Switzerland" between Canada and the United States. With a defensive alliance and treaty of commerce, Britain could win vital assistance in the protection of Canada and of the northwestern posts, which he viewed as the necessary outworks of Canadian defenses.[19] Allen sent another memorial to the government in early March, 1790. Though the voice was that of Levi, the substance belonged to Simcoe.

The future governor of Upper Canada was tireless, pleading powerfully, both in personal interview and in writing, for an understanding with Vermont. "My mind is so fully occupied with the absolute *necessity* of an alliance with Vermont, if this country means to preserve Canada," he told Grenville,

that I hope [you] will pardon my seizing every opportunity of expressing my sentiments upon that Subject. I consider it as a great Operation of State, as an Alliance which will at once prevent War, give permanency to all future Settlements, and to the necessary but inferior considerations of Commercial Policy. Without Vermont, Canada is untenable.

If it were gained, Canada would be held; and similar republics in Kentucky and other areas west of the Alleghenies would rise "probably forever."[20]

Simcoe's argument appealed to both national fear and ambition; and it was stated with the authority of a man who knew America at first hand. His devotion to the Empire had been tested in the crucible of war; and, very shortly, he was to go out to serve in a new and sensitive post as governor of the province of Upper Canada. What he thought and wrote necessarily commanded attention. His thesis—that Canada, Vermont, and the retained posts were parts of the same defense complex—had to be examined carefully, especially since an important implication stood at its center: that the northwestern posts should be made permanently British for the sake of the safety of Canada.

It seems possible that Simcoe's suggestion made an impression of sorts on the Committee for Trade, whose conclusions were embodied in a letter, dated April 17, 1790, from the committee's secretary, Stephen Cottrell, to Foreign Secretary Grenville.[21] The committee's first assumption, that Vermont was not federated with the American Union, was correct. It followed, therefore, that a British treaty with Vermont was not a legal impossibility. It was noted, however, that Dorchester, responding to the Allens' original application to him, had already extended to Vermont and the United States important and favorable trade negotiations. Short shrift was given to the proposal of a specific treaty with Vermont. In the first place, offense would be given to the United States; and, secondly, British policy required something more than an arrangement with a single, petty province. The British gaze should include Vermont, but should go farther to embrace the great American backcountry, a step especially necessary "at a time when there is reason to suppose that a Commercial Treaty may soon be negotiated with the Congress." Britain's interest was simply expressed: "the Manufactures of this Country are improving and progressively increasing in so great a Degree that it is necessary to seek for new Markets in every part of the World." The significance of the American hinterland for British policy makers—as Shelburne, in his day, well knew—lay precisely in the fact

that it offered a market potentially rich beyond avarice. Rapidly filling with settlers who would be engaged for centuries in clearing the
land and farming it, the Cottrell letter assumed, the great transmontane region would require endless quantities of British manufactures.

Shelburne had dreamed of a grand Anglo-American economic
partnership based on renewed amity and eventual alliance. Cottrell
and the committee wished to secure Britain's commercial position in a
very different way: the carrying trade on the Great Lakes and adjacent rivers should be confined to British vessels, and "the Posts which
command the Entrance of those Lakes, and which are best situated
for securing the Navigation of these Rivers" should be retained "(*if
other important Considerations will so permit*)" and be garrisoned for
defense—thus securing British access across the Lakes to the tribu-
taries of the Mississippi and down the great river itself, to the new
and endless markets in the American West.[22] Pursuing these commercial ends, Britain woud find it beneficial, too, if Vermont, Kentucky, and all the new settlements in the interior remained independent of the United States or any other foreign power. Perhaps a
whole series of "Treaties of Commerce and Friendship with Great
Britain" might be formed. In a passage evidently written before the
Nootka crisis, the committee secretary predicted that the United
States would soon quarrel with Spain about the navigation of the
Mississippi. Britain had an interest in the question, too, but she should
watch carefully and avoid formulating a policy until the event came
to pass. It was observed, however, that "there will be less Danger in
encouraging the Navigation of Spain in those Seas than that of the
United States and that the Ships of the United States are more to be
apprehended as commercial Rivals, than those belonging to the Subjects of the Spanish Monarchy." From a commercial point of view,
the advice was not without wisdom: the proximity of the United
States would certainly make her a more dangerous competitor than
Spain.

Cottrell's long letter has been held to indicate the British government's intentions to intrigue against the Americans in their own hinterland and to retain the posts. The argument fails on three fundamental points. First, the committee, through its secretary, deliberately
confined its view to commerce, making no pretense at a comprehensive treatment of Anglo-American relations. The committee was not
advocating a policy of massive intervention in the affairs of the

American West, but one of seizing opportunities to forward British commercial interests whenever they arose. Hawkesbury and his colleagues wanted, to use Shelburne's words, trade not dominion. Second, the suggested retention of the posts was a highly conditional one: "if other important Considerations will so permit." Finally, it has occasionally been forgotten that not even a report of the Committee for Trade, let alone a communication from its secretary, although either might carry great weight, was a pronouncement of policy. The Cottrell letter was merely advisory and not by any means binding upon the government.

The cabinet's decision was to keep the Vermonters at a distance without alienating them. If war with Spain broke out, they had it in their power to facilitate a Canadian thrust against the enemy along the Mississippi. Further, the "friendship of the Inhabitants of Vermont," Secretary Grenville wrote to Dorchester in secret dispatches of May 6, 1790, "would, under the circumstances of any alarm from the side of the United States, be of the greatest import." The Governor's attention could not be "too much directed to this object," and he was ordered to delay his return to Britain pending resolution of the crisis, standing until then strictly upon his guard against a possible American attack upon the posts. Grenville informed Dorchester of Levi Allen's presence in the country. Although his powers were taken to extend only to commercial negotiations, the Vermonter had been given enough encouragement to "dispose him to exert any influence which he or his connections may possess in whatever manner your Lordship may think proper to direct it."

The tenor of Grenville's instructions about the United States was defensive. Far from instigating aggression against the Republic to the south, he suggested that, if war came, America might be brought to favor Britain by playing on her desire to have Spain ejected from New Orleans. Grenville plainly hoped to win American co-operation by appealing to common interest, not to incur hostility by riding roughshod over republican aspirations and sensitivity.[23]

Vermont was not the only opportunity in North America which could have encouraged a bold and aggressive Britain. A confusing, even sinister game was afoot in Kentucky and other parts of the American West. Unscrupulous men, greedy for wealth and power, maneuvering for position, showed themselves willing to embark on desperate adventures with whatever aid they might find ready at

hand. As early as 1788, Britons heard reports that the idea of independence from the United States found much favor in Kentucky,
that men there looked to the seizure of New Orleans, and that the aid
of the former mother country was considered highly desirable.[24] At
about the same time, Dorchester received the "Desultory Reflections
by a Gentleman of Kentucky"; and a copy was handed to Grenville
himself by Brooks Watson in August, 1789.[25] The "Gentleman of
Kentucky" was presumably James Wilkinson, a veteran of the American Revolution who was determined to seize what he could for himself in the West, come what might; his "Reflections" were an open
appeal for Britain's intervention. The new settlements would, his argument ran, inevitably and rapidly outstrip the American states. The
East was destined to sink as the West rose to independence and a prosperity based, for generations to come, on agriculture. Foreign protection would be required, since the United States, riven by deep sectionalism, was incapable of giving it because of the vast distance from
the Atlantic seaboard. By holding out her hand, Britain might gain
control of the Mississippi and dominate its basin "as the key does the
lock." A crisis was already at hand. The settlers were bound to appeal
soon either to Britain or to Spain. Let Britain prepare for the day.

The temptation to imperialistic adventure quite aside, there was a
second reason why British attention would fasten on the West: the
fear—not unjustified—that France, the ancient enemy, might suddenly thrust herself into a contest for the American backcountry. As
parallel reading for Wilkinson's "Reflections," Grenville also had a
copy of a memorial from a former French subject living in the American West. Addressed to the government of the old fatherland, the
document spoke of the "Republiques naissantes" in the West, and
called on France to enter the race for their control. With a magnificent
disregard for grammar and diacritical markings, the Bourbon power
was asked to suppose "qu'un jour, l'harmonie qui subsiste entre la
France et les Etats Unis, veut a etre troublee par des evenemens." The
eastern seaboard was forever separated from the West: "Elles seront
habitée par des hommes qui parlent la meme langue, mais ce ne sera
pas long tems le meme peuple." The vast Mississippi basin invited the
ambitious foreign power. The first to open its arms would "fait la
plus grande acquisition que l'on puisse ambitionner dans le noveau
monde." France should not let the moment pass, "un de ceux, qui
ne se presentent pas deux fois." Let her seize New Orleans, "la Clé de

l'Occident"; negotiate with Spain a settlement by which she would establish herself east of the Mississippi; and guarantee the western side to the despoiled ally. A rupture with the United States would of course be inevitable, but the memorialist showed no disposition to consider the prospect alarming.[26]

The sentiments of a French immigrant homesick for *la patrie* were not in themselves very important; but they were shared by a more important Frenchman, the Comte de Moustier, minister pleni-potentiary to the United States. Indeed, the similarity between the anonymous memorial and Moustier's longer report to his home authorities suggests that the minister was in direct touch with Frenchmen living in the American backcountry.[27] Moustier's vision—a revived French Empire in the New World based on New Orleans, instead of Quebec, and extending into the West Indies—was passed on to his government at a moment of great convulsion in the life of the French nation; but his grand design was to be revived one day by republican France and her stormy emissary Edmond Charles Genêt.

Compared with such grandiose dreams of ambitious and intriguing Frenchmen and American westerners, British policy was simple. There was no plan for the forcible acquisition of American territory. Secure in her ability to outproduce and undersell all competitors for American trade, seaboard and transmontane, Britain's interests in the region were chiefly economic. Only two conditions were necessary: the federal government must not cripple Britain's commerce by hostile legislation, and the backcountry was not to pass under the control of rival European powers.

As early as 1787, Consul George Miller at Charleston saw a great possibility. Britain, he advised Foreign Secretary Carmarthen at that time, ought to prepare for a clash between Spain and the United States over the Mississippi. When that inevitability occurred, he continued, the Americans would look "with an eye of hope to a future connexion of a different kind, with Great Britain, which might afford them assistance and protection."[28] As it happened, the clash came between Britain and Spain; but Miller's logic remained valid: the Anglo-Saxons possessed a community of interests in the American backcountry against the Spaniard, and the United States government could be expected at least to stand neutral, while thousands of her western citizens would join the enterprise to force open the Mississippi.

As Britain prepared to hit Spain in 1790, she moved to exploit the common ground with the United States which Miller had noted. Foreign Secretary Grenville asked General Simcoe to submit his thoughts on "our present Situation in the Back Settlements of America and how the force of the Empire may be diverted in that Quarter to an attack on the Spanish Territory." After consulting hurriedly with Levi Allen, Simcoe transmitted to the Foreign Secretary his "Suggestions for an Expedition from Vermont."[29] Vermont, he repeated his old theme, must be secured; and the United States must be deflected by adroit diplomacy from any attack, financed by Spain, upon the province, or from "a more popular Attempt" upon the posts. Then, Simcoe recommended, the Allens were to raise a force of Green Mountain Rangers. A corps was to be raised at Detroit. Simcoe himself was to undertake to find a similar number among the American westerners, "Kentucky people" to be won by titles and half pay. He would buy off the southern Indians and would proceed to fall upon "the upper Parts of Mexico," New Orleans, and the Floridas. An ambitious, even impracticable scheme, it rested on the assumption of America's neutrality and acquiescence in the passage of British troops through her territory. Simcoe, far from projecting aggressive designs upon the United States, clearly depended on a high degree of American co-operation.

A similar view was taken by an obscure British agent, M. T. Young, who was engaged in the 1780's in founding new settlements along the Mississippi. In London during the war scare of 1790, he composed a memorandum for Pitt, who passed it along to Grenville for study.[30] Dwelling upon the riches to be derived from trade if the Mississippi were opened to Britain, he, too, predicted that thousands of western Americans would join in a British project to establish free navigation of the river. Again, there was the unspoken but vital assumption that the United States government would at least not impede the plan, which involved to a considerable extent the participation of her own nationals.

From the redoubtable Phineas Bond came similar counsel. The American government, he argued to the home authorities, was indeed "strongly inclined to favor the Interests of France"; but it would not join Spain against Britain, even though France should enter the war as a Bourbon ally.[31] Britain should therefore launch an attack upon Spain's Mississippi positions. Forces could be collected near the Ohio (in American territory) and proceed down that river (through

American territory) to engage the enemy. Some might think it "hazardous" to undertake the expedition without American concurrence; in his opinion, however, the Republic could be persuaded to acquiescence. It was true beyond question, however, that the westerners themselves, "a hardy Race of Men, Adventurers by Profession and ready to seize every opportunity of Profit or Employment," would readily join with Britons against the Spanish, who had shut the Mississippi to them.

This body of exhortation and advice gave depth and substance to the points raised in the Beckwith-Hamilton conversations. The idea of an understanding directed against Spain in the West was far from being the invention of an Anglophile American secretary of the treasury. It was in the air, a natural and obvious coincidence of national interests. Even Jefferson appreciated this. Fearful of British conquest of Spanish possessions in North America, he would have wished strict neutrality; but he would not forbid Dorchester's passage across American territory, preferring to avoid committing the country until circumstances should indicate the best course of action. He hoped to barter American neutrality for a commercial treaty with Britain; and he advised informing that power that the United States would view with "extreme uneasiness" any upset to the balance of power along the frontier.[32] To Madrid, however, he proposed to be brutal, requiring that court's recognition of the American right to port facilities and free navigation of the Mississippi. He would use the language of ultimatum:

even the unavoidable delay of sending a negotiator here, may render the mission too late for the preservation of peace. It is impossible to answer for the forbearance of our western citizens. We endeavor to quiet them with the expectation of attainment of their rights by peaceable means. But should they, in a moment of impatience, hazard others, there is no saying how far we may be led; for neither themselves nor their rights will ever be abandoned by us.

Even France, Jefferson believed, should be informed of the American position if war between Britain and Spain broke out. It was high language, to be sure, but even so, not as high as Jefferson's first draft of the instructions to Carmichael in Madrid: he would have had the minister threaten open alliance with Britain to win the navigation of the great river, reserving New Orleans for the United States and western Louisiana for the British.[33]

The Nootka crisis subsided. The heady and tantalizing possibility of a triumphant Anglo-American partnership, of a joining of hands, even if under the table, for the spoliation of Spain's North American possessions remained unrealized. It was a misfortune for relations between the two powers that the war stubbornly refused to develop. By the time the crisis was past, however, some salient features of Britain's policy toward the American backcountry were illuminated. Whether European peace were maintained or not, British interests there required friendly relations with the United States. If, on the one hand, there continued to be peace, she could penetrate the markets in the West, but only if her efforts were not disrupted by hostile American legislation. (To what end, then, retain the posts permanently? The prewar debts would certainly be forfeit and American hostility rendered permanent.) If, on the other hand, war came with Spain, a considerable measure of American co-operation, tacit or explicit, would be necessary. The way had been pointed out by Beckwith, Bond, and Young; but, indeed, it required no great acumen to fix upon it: Britain must use adroit diplomacy and negotiate with the United States before the relationship disintegrated beyond rescue.

CHAPTER NINE

The Indians

THE PRESENCE of the red man along the western frontier is one of the constants in the American experience from the first coming of the colonists in the seventeenth century to the miserable "final solution" of the nineteenth. Almost from the first, hostility between restless, westward-moving, land-hungry Americans and Indians jealous for their forest hunting lands was deep and unrelenting. In the long and savage strife, barbarism was monopolized by neither the one side nor the other.

With the expulsion of the French from Canada in 1763, Britain was faced with the delicate problem of pacifying Indian allies of the defeated enemy. It was the necessary first step toward exploiting the magnificent territorial acquisition in the North American hinterland, and it was made even more urgent in the very year of the Peace by Pontiac's outburst. For a time, success seemed within the grasp of the London government. The Grenville ministry saw the magnitude of the imperial problem and formulated a comprehensive solution which called for troops in the backcountry to guard against Indian attack or French reconquest; a temporary halt to westward expansion from the Atlantic seaboard; an imperial office of Indian affairs with agents in the field to negotiate peaceable acquisition of territory claimed by the natives; and then, systematic settlement, the establishment of government and social institutions in new inland colonies. It is not the least tragic element in Anglo-American history that this sensible, humane, practical plan became hopelessly entangled in the rising constitutional crisis over the question of imperial taxation of the colonies.

While the American government formulated a magnificent plan, in the Northwest Ordinance of 1787, for the exploitation of the backcountry, it never developed an Indian policy beyond the law of the knife. This lamentable failure was due chiefly to the needs, rarely comprehended within the limits of morality, of an expanding population and to the Confederation's weakness—the simple inability to establish effective authority in the West. By the time the United States acquired a reasonably competent federal government, too much blood had flowed, too many wounds had been sustained, too many fundamental challenges had been given and received to permit any solution but the appeal to arms.

There were other contributory factors, however: for example, the absence of any central Indian authority able to negotiate for, and to bind, all—or even a major portion—of the tribes. It may be argued, too, that by 1783 hostility between Indian and American had become so deep and implacable, particularly in view of the Indian participation in the war just concluded, that it was no longer possible to envisage a peaceable settlement. Further, the interests of Spain worked against peace as she intrigued persistently and effectively among the southern Indians, seeking in them a buffer to keep the ever advancing frontiersmen from the Mississippi. The presence of British troops on the soil of the United States also undoubtedly gave encouragement to Indian truculence and hostility in the Old Northwest, as did more active agitations, shadowy and difficult of substantiation, ignited on a considerable scale by private agents, merchants and traders from Canada. It must finally be stated, however, that primary responsibility for the Hobbesian state of nature along the American frontier rested with the government and people of the United States. Putting aside moral considerations, it is obvious that American citizens aggressively seized Indian lands. Their government should have been equally forward in making a decent, humane, and comprehensive settlement. Unfortunately, the Confederation was weak; and by the time a remedy had been found, patterns of conduct, attitudes, immigration, and policy had hardened beyond change.

The Peace of 1783 brought no tranquillity to the frontier. The authority of Congress was legally extended to the Northwest Territory, but establishing it in reality was a very different affair. Several agreements, scarcely important enough to be called treaties, were concluded with the Iroquois and certain other tribes in the southern portion of the trans-Ohio country. The Treaty of Fort Stanwix was made in 1784, and the following year the Treaty of Fort McIntosh, named for a small post, some miles down the Ohio from Pittsburgh, commanded by Lieutenant Colonel Josiah Harmar. Both involved limited cessions of Indian lands, promises to respect Indian rights, and the establishment of a few small posts along the Ohio.

In 1787 efforts were actually made to clear out frontiersmen who had settled along the right bank of the river in defiance of the government's promises to the Indians, but it was a sweeping back of the sea. Newly breveted Brigadier General Harmar went on to occupy Vincennes on the Wabash and points in the Illinois country; attempts to subordinate the Indians in the area overturned the beehive. Race war spread along the frontier, into Kentucky and even Virginia.[1] Could the savages fight so viciously and destructively without encouragement and assistance from outside? Americans, at the time and subsequently, seeking to explain their country's difficulty in establishing its authority in the western regions, answered the question with an indignant negative and pointed the finger at the British in the Old Northwest. Harmar himself complained in 1787 that the road westward would be blocked until the posts were delivered up: "Villainous emissaries have been continually sallying from thence," he wrote, "poisoning the minds of the Savages & depreciating the character of the Americans." A single treaty at Detroit "would give Dignity & Consequence to the United States and answer every purpose. . . . Elsewhere it would be of little or no effect."[2] The "villains" Harmar had in mind were traders and trappers down from Canada; but those suffering from Indian depredations were not likely to make fine distinctions between private subjects and public authority. In American minds, the Indian troubles were inevitably attributed to British intrigue among the savages.

In reality, British policy and interests called for peace and stability along the frontier with America. This had been true for Shelburne's ministry and for the coalition which succeeded it, and it was true for the Pitt government, too. Shelburne's plan for an Anglo-American economic union—blurring national boundaries, with Canadians and Americans traversing the great forests and trapping and trading with equal freedom—envisaged a "commercial empire of the St. Lawrence." But his successors and the Americans themselves sharply underlined the political reality of the Canadian-American boundary: and the attempt to tie up British, American, and Indian interests in one package failed.

The question inevitably arose of Britain's responsibility to her wartime Indian allies inhabiting the territory of the United States, and with it a dilemma of a powerful and dangerous kind. A withdrawal behind the Canadian frontier, as defined by the Peace of 1783, would clear the arena for a desperate American-Indian struggle, lay the British themselves open to charges of ingratitude to those who had rendered them assistance at a moment of peril, perhaps cause a savage assault upon the Canadian hinterland, and sacrifice the fur-traders and the profits they derived from the area. The early suggestions from Haldimand, noted above—that, for American and British benefit alike, Britain might retain the northwestern posts "for some time" while Indian affairs were placed on a stable basis—coincided with the lobbying of the fur-traders in London and Quebec. A third and more pressing concern—securing justice for British loyalists and creditors—also supported the wisdom of retaining the American posts temporarily. But the constants, the Birtish and Indians, faced a variable: the American advance westward, bringing pressures which were bound to mount steadily and rapidly. Far from courting hostilities, the London government accepted as fundamental the premise that some kind of settlement, peaceably reconciling the interests of all parties, must be achieved lest the balance be overturned.[3] It was a position of the greatest delicacy. If the Americans were allowed to carry their point and to gain possession of the posts unconditionally, Indians and prewar creditors would consider themselves abandoned by the home government: the former would look to British scalps for revenge, the latter to the British treasury for proper indemnities. If the posts were retained too long, however, the consequences would be equally disagreeable: the hostility, open or covert, of the Americans; and, as their people migrated into the disputed territory, an inevitable clash with the Indians, and probably with the British themselves. Timing was vital if the edge of the knife were to be walked to safety. It is not surprising, therefore, that to some British policy should have appeared hesitant and indecisive. But bold decisions and brilliant strokes are not always appropriate; there are times to stand vigilantly on the defensive, to observe the momentum of events, to deflect danger by the timely parry. This was the informing spirit of British policy in the Old Northwest.

In June, 1783, Joseph Brant and John the Mohawk, paramount chiefs of the Six Nations, met General Haldimand in Quebec. Suspicious that Britain had indeed given their hunting lands away to the Americans, they sought from him reassurances he could not give. Embarrassed and apprehensive, the Commander in Chief feared imminent war between the Indians and their new sovereigns. Intending to preserve peace if at all possible, he knew by the end of 1783 that the Indians would insist upon the boundary fixed not by the Anglo-American treaty of peace, but by the Treaty of 1768. As the Americans could not be expected to accept the Ohio River line without a fight, Haldimand's peaceable intentions appeared doomed to failure. His famous recommendation that the forts be retained for a limited time followed. Though based on reasons more complicated than Haldimand knew, the British government's decision to hold the forts calmed the Indians and probably prevented the outbreak of a full-scale frontier war with the Americans.

In spite of this, the Indians remained suspicious of British intentions; and their volatile discontent made the course of events unpredictable and a source of constant worry to the London authorities. In the winter of 1785, Chief Joseph Brant journeyed to England to ask support for the Six Nations if war should come between his people and their enemies to the south. He received assurances of gratitude for past support, compensation for losses suffered during the American war, and advice to remain at peace.[4] Simultaneously, instructions went out to Lieutenant-Governor Hope in Canada: open and avowed assistance to the Indians, in case they went to war with the Americans, "must at all events in the present state of this country be avoided." The balance was, however, to be maintained; it would comport neither with justice nor with good policy "entirely to abandon" the savages, who would inevitably turn against Britain. Within these general limits, the Lieutenant-Governor, on the scene and possessing firsthand knowledge of events, would have to exercise his own judgment and discretion in "a business so delicate and interesting."[5] In short, Hope should assure the Indians of Britain's abiding benevolence, which would involve the continuation of traditional gifts, among them rifles and ammunition for hunting and self-defense; but he should not provide them with the means of making offensive war against the Americans. Indeed, he was ordered to avoid offending the southern neighbor in his dealings with the red men. Here was the very essence of the British dilemma. As long as the two combatants stood beyond arm's length of each other, Britain had room for maneuver;

but the distance between them was steadily diminishing, as Americans moved ever farther westward. Little wonder that British leaders began to dream of an Indian buffer zone between Canada and the United States, closed to white settlement, though open equally to traders from both countries.

The dilemma sharpened after Dorchester arrived in Quebec in 1786. The new governor of Canada intended to cling to the middle course, as his predecessors had done; and he promptly instructed the imperial Indian agent, Sir John Johnson, to make it clear to the Indians that he had not come to start a war with the United States, and that he lacked power to do so. Instead, every effort was to be made to persuade them to make peace with their new sovereigns. Clearly hinting at a possible cession, Dorchester also told Johnson to inquire into the attitude of the Six Nations toward continued occupation of the posts by Britain. The same logic which bade Britain hold the Indians in check, however, forbade her passive acceptance of an American assault upon the posts. If, Johnson was told, the former rebels attempted to overturn the delicate balance, "war must be repelled by war."[6]

The British posture was defensive; but if attack from the south were not to be invited, Dorchester reasoned, Britain would have to put her ability to defend herself beyond question. Cession of the posts, he believed, would deliver the Indians into the hands of the Americans; and the savages would seek revenge along the Canadian frontier. Abandonment and destruction of the posts would only retard the evil. It was obvious to the military mind that Britain had to stand firm where she was. More men and money, Dorchester warned London, were necessary to put the posts in a proper state of preparation. What, he pointedly asked, should be his course of action in case the Americans attacked and captured the posts?[7]

It is easy to understand Dorchester's growing preoccupation with the preparedness of his forces. At the same time, there was the danger that each side, American and British, might misunderstand the intentions of the other and construe defense measures as preparations for an attack. Mutual suspicion and apprehension might well escalate into an Anglo-American clash in the backcountry before the government in London even knew what was afoot. The delicate balance would go by the board; and the interests of Indians, Americans, and Britons would be cast into the crucible of war. The London gov-

ernment, with a view broader than Dorchester's, accordingly told the
General that he might disburse funds to put the posts in a "temporary
state of defence." The Indians were to be supplied, according to past
practice, with the means of defending themselves; but this was to be
accomplished in the manner least likely to alarm the Americans or to
incite the Indians to an attack. (Dorchester was, thus, being asked to
judge the point at which British assistance transcended the capacity
for self-defense and became the ability to wage offensive war against
the Americans.) As for Dorchester's question, if the Americans
should seize the posts and if the Governor believed himself strong
enough to recover them, then his duty was clear. If hostilities were
confined to the Americans and the Indians, however, it would be imprudent for him to be drawn into rendering active assistance to the
savages.

Under the Confederation, the Indian issue was a relatively minor
concern in Anglo-American diplomacy. When Minister John Adams
saw Foreign Secretary Carmarthen on October 20, 1785, for example,
he mentioned that an Indian war was in prospct; but he carefully
avoided any charge of official British encouragement of Indian outrages along the frontier. They constituted, he said, only one of the
evils occasioned by Britain's retention of the posts. There were more
important things on his mind than Indian affairs, and the threatened
frontier war was merely a subordinate point in his pursuit of the
posts.[8] Even Gouverneur Morris, as late as 1790, used the issue as a
subordinate supporting argument in favor of a cession of the posts.
Like Adams, he made no charge of complicity against the British
government, although he pointed, as Adams had done, at the connection in the minds of the American public between Britain's retention of the posts and Indian hostilities. Every murder committed
by the Indians was "attributed to British intrigue; and although some
men of liberal minds might judge differently, their arguments would
have little weight with the many, who felt themselves aggrieved."
According to Morris, Carmarthen admitted the force of his argument; but, even so, it was evident that the subject was secondary to
more important matters.[9]

The force of the westward movement and the vigor of the federal government brought the matter to a head. The great western
legacy was not to be enjoyed until Indian affairs were settled, and
by 1790 the only means to this end appeared to be war. As Americans

set about organizing and equipping a sizable expedition, Dorchester took the alarm, fearful that the true object of the attack might be the northwestern posts. As we have seen, Beckwith was accordingly dispatched to the south to observe and report. Presently, the reassurances given by Alexander Hamilton were speeding northward. The Nootka crisis, however, with the possibility of an Anglo-Spanish clash along the Mississippi, added a new dimension to Beckwith's mission. Aware of the importance of the attitude of the United States in the event of hostilities, the British emissary hurried to give Hamilton Dorchester's categorical denial that the British were implicated to the slightest degree in the depredations along the American frontier. Indeed, Beckwith said, the governor of Canada had "taken every proper opportunity of inculcating upon the Indians a pacific disposition" toward the United States. Dorchester was reported to believe that the guilty savages did not belong to the northern Indian tribes, but were "a banditti, composed chiefly or in a great part of Creeks or Cherokees," over whom he had no influence, intimating at the same time that "these tribes were supposed to be in connection with the Spaniards." With the British position clarified in this explicit fashion, Beckwith told Hamilton that there were doubts about American intentions. Reports received in Canada stated that certain Americans at Fort Harmar "had thrown out menaces with regard to the posts on the frontier, and had otherwise held very intemperate language." Dorchester believed these to be "effusions of individual feelings" rather than official statements; but Beckwith was eager to know Hamilton's thoughts about them.[10]

The Secretary of the Treasury informed Beckwith, some days later, that "the menaces which had been mentioned" were unauthorized, "proceeding probably from a degree of irritation which the detention of the posts had produced in the minds of many." On his side, Beckwith once again affirmed his earlier statement to the effect that Dorchester had given the Indians no encouragement in their attacks.[11]

The circumspection preceded a severe disappointment for the government of the United States. Having carried out a small and inconclusive foray against the Shawnees on the Scioto River, General Harmar left his base at Fort Washington (Cincinnati) in September, 1790. He had under his command an ill-disciplined, badly equipped force of 1400 to 1500 men, all but 320 of whom were raw militia, with which he proposed to attack the redoubts of the Indians in the Maumee Valley. Several villages and considerable quantities of corn were destroyed; but he was far from delivering the chastisement he intended. On the return march, a detachment of 400 of Harmar's men encountered a party of Indians on October 22; and, again, the issue left Indian power intact and American military reputation blemished. Harmar's expedition was by no means the desperate defeat suffered a year later by St. Clair, but nothing could disguise the fact that it was a failure. A sizable expenditure in money and effort had produced nothing, except to arouse the savages further. War parties followed closely upon the heels of the retreating Americans, visiting all the horrors of Indian war upon the small settlements along the Ohio.

Wounded American pride demanded two things: an ego-salving explanation for the fiasco and a renewed effort to retrieve the situation. The latter would become the concern of General Arthur St. Clair; the former was provided by the British. All the assurances in the world could not quiet the deep suspicions of British complicity. Even Alexander Hamilton took pointed notice of the report that Grenville had expressed to William S. Smith the hope that the United States did not aim at an extirpation of the Indians, since Britain could not remain indifferent to the event. Secretary of State Jefferson was much more suspicious of British actions. Declining to deal directly with Beckwith, he raised the subject of British assistance to the Indians through his friend and Beckwith's fellow boarder, James Madison. The Major asserted once more, as he had to Hamilton earlier, that his country was opposed to Indian hostilities against the Americans; he suggested that supplies, including firearms, had come into their possession through the regular course of trade. The Virginian told him bluntly that since the hostiles traded with British subjects only, "their being able to carry on hostilities was of itself sufficient evidence in the case." Madison did not suggest the British government itself was involved; but Jefferson was less cautious.[12] In an official memorandum on the question of the expedience of informing Dorchester about St. Clair's objective in 1791, he assumed that the Canadian governor had the Indians at his disposal, could direct them as he wished, and supplied them, albeit secretly, with aid. For his part, the Secretary of State favored recommending that St. Clair be instructed to pursue the Indians until too late in the season to allow

Dorchester to move against the Spaniards along the Mississippi in the event of the expected Anglo-Spanish war.[13]

Jefferson's rising suspicions were unfortunately matched in Canada, where it was observed that St. Clair's preparations were proceeding amidst the gusty ill-temper occasioned in America by the failure of the Morris mission and by Washington's message to Congress. Even Phineas Bond, on the scene in Philadelphia, felt it all too possible that the new American effort against the Indians would endanger the posts, "a Matter which there is too much Reason to apprehend will rather be encouraged than checked." Although "no Man of Information and Candour" could suppose that the Indians were encouraged by the British goverment to make war, Bond wrote to Grenville, the idea was put about by "Persons high in Office here and fallacious Representations very injurious to the humane Character of the British Government, have been disseminated, to increase the prejudices of the People and aggravate Resentments already too prevalent."[14]

Dorchester interpreted the reports from British agents in the United States and warnings from Canadians to indicate that a threat to his military position along the Canadian-American border might well be in the making. Common prudence demanded vigilance. To the commanders of the "upper posts," he wrote from Quebec that he deplored the hostilities between the Americans and the Indians, adding that if only he could be "instrumental in putting an end to these calamities it would give me great satisfaction." Britain was at peace with the United States, he continued; she wished to remain so. Indeed, "there is no power in this Country to begin a war." She could not, however, passively accept an American assault:

Should the assertions ascribed to some of the prisoners lately taken by the Indians, that the States mean to attack the Post of Detroit in the Spring prove true, I can only repeat that such a step must be considered as a commencement of hostilities on their part. And war must be repelled by war.

He could not believe the United States would precipitate a conflict; but not to guard against the possibility would be an inexcusable violation of the soldier's duty.[15]

The situation was more serious than even Dorchester knew. The British government itself had begun to suspect American intentions, fearing that the United States aimed at an offensive alliance with the southern Indians in order to offset British influence with those of the

Northwest and to attack the posts. Further, if Britain engaged with
Spain over Nootka, who was to say with certainty what the American
course would be, Hamilton's assurances to Beckwith notwithstanding?
British and American interests might appear to coincide to an amaz-
ing degree in the backcountry, but who would be bold enough to assert that it was impossible that the United States, already angered by
the failure of the Morris mission and by the continued British retention of the posts, would embark on a dangerous game in the backcountry? The rules of logic might indicate the wisdom of Anglo-
American co-operation along the Mississippi; but wounded national
pride and expanding ambition could conceivably produce a very
different American policy. It was the more worthy of consideration
because the Spanish territories in North and South America furnished prime targets for British arms if war came.[16]

At the moment the Nootka crisis began—the Spanish complaint
against the British interlopers was made on February 10, 1790—
there was present in London a flamboyant adventurer, the self-styled
Venezuelan Count de Miranda. Obviously possessing great personal
charm, he systematically scraped up acquaintances with prominent
persons, in both the New World and the Old. William Duer, the
American speculator and financier, introduced him to George Rose,
Pitt's secretary to the treasury; and he was on letter-writing terms
with many prominent Britons and Americans, including Washington's secretary of war, General Knox, Colonel William S. Smith, and
the former colonial governor, Thomas Pownall. Pownall talked privately and confidentially with the "Count" about the possibility of
a revolt against Spain in the South American colonies; and when the
Nootka crisis broke, he sent the visitor to see Pitt himself. Several
meetings followed, during which the possibility of co-operation between British and insurgent forces for the "liberation" of Spanish
America was thoroughly canvassed.[17] In such an eventuality, it would
be necessary to take into account not only the Americans, but also
the southern Indians, athwart a British invasion route to the south.

Miranda's schemes were to prove as insubstantial as a sand castle,
but under the circumstances of a possible war with Spain, they accomplished something: the American backcountry was brought under
the close scrutiny of the British ministry.

To the south were the Cherokees, Choctaws, Chickasaws, and,
most important of all, the Creeks, who, under a capable half-breed

chief, McGillivray, occupied territory between the Spaniards in Florida and Louisiana and the Americans in the Carolinas and Georgia. Here would be potent instruments in the hands of powers hostile to the United States. Bitterly anti-American because of the constant encroachments of the frontiersmen, McGillivray angrily avoided even commercial contacts with them and almost single-handedly engineered trading arrangements through the commercial house of the Scot, William Panton, operating in Spanish-occupied Florida.[18] Political arrangements—involving supplies of military stores beyond those commonly furnished for hunting and, in addition, open assistance in case of a defensive war—were made with the Spanish governors Zéspedes of St. Augustine, O'Neil of Pensacola, and Miro of New Orleans. Thus secured, McGillivray felt able in 1786 to scorn the efforts of commissioners from Georgia to negotiate a settlement of disputes about lands along the Oconee River. By 1787, the Creeks were waging a bloody and effective war against the Georgians and the Cumberland settlers; indeed, it was clear that they held the offensive. In January, 1788, Miro, who had no desire to embroil his nation in a struggle with the United States, informed McGillivray that Spanish aid would be decreased. It was at this moment, marked by warfare along the southern boundaries of the United States and by rising Indian-Spanish suspicions, that there appeared upon the scene a bold and opportunistic young man, William Augustus Bowles, ready to capitalize upon events to the benefit of his own fortune. Dispatched as a commercial agent to the Floridas by Lord Dunmore, who was then governor of the Bahamas, and his associates in the trading house of Miller and Bonamy of Nassau, Bowles's object was to break the virtual monopoly of the Indian trade held by Panton. The adventures which followed his arrival were half charade, half drama—all based on a monumental imposture.[19]

Drummed out of a loyalist regiment at Pensacola during the American War, Bowles, erstwhile soldier, painter, actor, and gambler, retired to enjoy life among the Lower Creeks and Seminoles, acquiring a knowledge of language and geography which stood him in good stead in 1788. An initial welcome from McGillivray turned to cold hostility, however, as his promises of lavish presents went unfulfilled. Panton undermined him further by denouncing him to the Spanish governor of New Orleans as a "British agent," urging the official to "give pointed orders to have him knocked in the Head."[20]

Bowles accordingly took a prudent leave early in 1789 in company with a half-dozen Indian confederates; but the Creek country would see them again.

With Bowles out of the way, McGillivray and the Cumberland settlers reached a truce; and commissioners from the new federal government made approaches for a negotiated settlement with the chieftain. They were rendered fruitless for a time by American maladroitness and promises of aid from the Spaniards, whose interests would not be served by too great a degree of American-Indian peace. In the spring of 1790, however, McGillivray suddenly accepted an invitation to New York to treat with the United States government. One reason for the apparent *volte face* was the increasing activity of land speculators along the Georgia border, which promised further trouble for the Indians. More important was the threat that the impending Anglo-Spanish war would ruin Panton's supply trade to the Creeks. Short of ammunition and manufactured goods, they would be put at a serious disadvantage in their dealings, hostile or diplomatic, with the Americans.[21] For its part, the United States government naturally desired to establish a stable peace along the southern frontier. It wished, too, to assert its own authority against that of Georgia both in Indian affairs and in the granting of lands.

The Treaty of New York, signed on August 7, 1791, was a moderate compromise, although McGillivray successfully insisted upon allowing Panton to continue in his virtual monopoly of the southern Indian trade. The chieftain was at the height of his power and prestige, honored by high officials of the United States, courted by agents of Britain and Spain, and speaking with almost sovereign authority.[22] In the autumn of 1791, however, his self-esteem was rudely shocked: William Bowles arrived again in Creek country. The comic opera character of some of the events which followed concealed deeper, more important ramifications of high policy.

Since his departure in 1789, Bowles had traveled widely. To Governor Parr of Nova Scotia he presented himself and his companions, dressed in elaborate and bizarre costumes found in a wrecked schooner on the Florida coast. That puzzled official, showing the flair of the true bureaucrat, quickly passed them on to his superior, Dorchester, at Quebec. The Earl's reaction was similar; and in January, 1791, the whole motley band arrived in London. There they caused something of a sensation, parading the streets in "native" dress and titil-

lating a gaping public at the Covent Garden performance of the
new pantomime, *The Death of Captain Cook.*

Bowles, whatever his shortcomings, possessed the address and
plausibility of a genuine confidence man. Posing as the chieftain of a
mighty Indian confederacy in the South, he represented to the British ministry in a formal memorial that the Creeks and Cherokees
stood united; that the Chickasaws and Choctaws had formed an offensive and defensive league with them; and that the four tribes commanded a combined military potential of forty thousand warriors.[23]
Adroitly taking advantage of a British preoccupation, he complained
that the Indians felt abandoned by Britain. In a fairly successful imi-
tation of stately Indian prose, Bowles wrote to His Majesty's government that his people feared the Americans and, in spite of the treaty
of peace of 1783, they "still looked towards Great Britain; They still
considered the King of G. Britain as their father, who had left them
for a while, but who, after a time, would return."

In a private and secret communication to Lord Grenville, Bowles
revealed the true measure of his impudence: his project to seize for
his *soi-disant* people two supply ports in Spanish Florida by treaty or,
if necessary, by force. This done, he would drive the Spaniards from
Florida, lower Louisiana, and Mexico, where, echoing Miranda, he asserted that discontent was smoldering. Of Britain, he would ask free
intercourse between the Florida ports and the West Indies and an alliance, even though a secret one. Cleverly drawing to his use reasoning
he must have known had been put to the ministry already, he asserted that he could count on the support not merely of "his" Indians,
but also of discontented and disaffected Americans along the southern
frontier. Already these latter had suggested to him a joint attack
upon the Spaniards, and had promised six thousand troops.[24]

The sweep of the man's imagination staggers. Unaware of the
magnitude of the fraud, however, the British government would undoubtedly have found Bowles's project intriguing. Certainly, the allegations of sinister American designs in the backcountry required consideration. In April, 1788 (before he had even arrived among the
Creeks), the Americans, Bowles told Grenville, had made secret offers of an offensive-defensive alliance. Their object—and again adroit
use was made of Britain's growing fear—was to attack the northern
Indians and to overrun the northwestern posts. Bowles virtuously
declared that the insidious approaches had been rejected; but, he ad-

monished, the British government should be aware of continuing determination in the United States to seize the remaining portions of the British Empire in North America. His deduction was simple: Britain should ally herself forthwith with Bowles's Indians as a matter of self-defense.

A tender spot had been touched. American military preparations were afoot. Dorchester and the new governor of Upper Canada, General Simcoe, were convinced that a crisis in the backcountry, endangering vital British interests, was in the making. Congress seemed on the verge of declaring commercial war. Bowles, with his great lie, seemed to confirm that the American thrust westward had British forces, as well as Indians, as its object. Hawkesbury already had under his consideration the earlier memorial. Grenville promptly dispatched Bowles's secret letter.

The "chief," Grenville told the president of the Committee for Trade, was "unfortunately for our purpose by what I hear of him, rather of a questionable character." Hawkesbury would know, however, "that the utility of things of this sort very often stands on very different grounds from that of the honesty of the persons employed in them."[25] It was possible, the Foreign Secretary believed, that Bowles exaggerated a little—"(tho' perhaps not much)"—the ability of the Indians and American back settlers, "who nearly resemble them in character," to hurt the Spanish colonies. In any event, it was certain that "no encouragement of that sort will be given him here." It was rather Bowles's remarks about American intentions which troubled the Secretary. "It is unquestionably true that the Americans have, for these last two or three years, been meditating Attempts against our Posts," he told Hawkesbury, "and that nothing could be so effectual for opposing them, in case of an attack, as a general confederacy of those Indians and Back Settlers." Altogether, Grenville concluded, it would be unwise to send Bowles away completely empty-handed. While his credentials at the very least left much to be desired, it was just conceivable that Bowles was not a complete rogue, and that he might be useful under certain circumstances. It would not do to commit Britain too greatly. The answer was a compromise: something to indicate British goodwill but without making a protégé of the "chief."

Grenville's proposed solution was finely calculated to this end. He would grant the request for admission into Britain's West Indian free ports (if Bowles could make good his own boast to seize the two Florida ports), but the favor would be given discreetly, wrapped in the tortuous and legalistic language of statute. Hawkesbury was accordingly asked to consider whether the Free Port Act (27 George III) could be changed, "not ostensibly pointing at the object." The whole scheme might, he conceded, prove impracticable; but it was at least worth some thought, "as I am really much impressed with the importance of the ultimate object of attaching these people."

Subsequently, the Free Port Act was amended (under 31 George III, c. 38). Under the same legislation, changes were also made in the act regulating the trade carried on between the United States and British colonies in North America and the West Indies, and between the two sets of British colonies and the foreign West Indies (28 George III). Certain provisions, superficially innocuous, incorporated Grenville's suggestions. Under them it would have been hypothetically possible for Bowles and his Indians, having taken possession of the Florida posts, to avail themselves of free port privileges in the British West Indies; but the wording of the statute made the favor covert and carefully avoided officially committing the British government to open recognition of the rebels.

Grenville soon had reason to be relieved that the encouragement to Bowles had been so guarded. Major Beckwith managed, surreptitiously and probably through the influence of Alexander Hamilton, to see McGillivray of the Creeks, then a guest of the American government at Philadelphia. The Briton asked the chief if Bowles was in fact what he appeared to be. McGillivray's response does not demand great imagination.[26] Bowles's luck held, however. Returning to Creek country in the autumn of 1791, perhaps hoping to capitalize on an Anglo-Spanish war, he found McGillivray ill of a fatal disease—the chief died in 1793—and unable to counter his fantastic projects. Presently, he created himself "Director of Affairs" of the Creek nation and, to the Spaniards at New Orleans, denounced the declining McGillivray as an American puppet. His own staunch anti-Americanism he proved by interfering with attempts to run a boundary between Georgia and the Creeks. The "Director" then promoted himself to "General" and—more dangerous to Anglo-American relations— "agent" from Great Britain to the Creeks; and he courted support among the Indians by distributing what was said to be £50,000 in presents. Popularly believed to have come from the British government, the gifts were probably furnished by Governor Dunmore and his merchant associates. The value was a gross exaggeration, and the role of the British government a crass falsehood. Working to stir up a Creek attack along the Georgia frontier, Bowles announced, with a straight face, the imminent arrival of British troops to help the Indian cause. Little wonder that George Hammond, in Philadelphia, reported home that accounts of Bowles's activities were causing "some little alarm" among the Americans. Fearful that the bold adventurer's assertions of British support would gain credence, he made every effort to deny British complicity in the most categorical manner.[27] From his side of the Atlantic, Foreign Secretary Grenville hastily wrote, too, ordering Hammond to issue the strictest disavowals of Bowles and his claims of authority and support from the British Crown.[28]

The charade was about to end. The Spaniards, who had never been taken in by Bowles, saved the British government further and potentially dangerous embarrassment. In mid-January, 1792, they enticed the "Director" aboard a vessel on the pretext of carrying him to a conference with the governor of New Orleans. He was shanghaied and sent to Havana, and thence to Madrid. The Creeks had not seen the last of him; but his reappearance among them toward the end of the century has no bearing on our present subject.

The importance of the Bowles episode lay in the light it threw on the unstable situation along the frontier, a fertile field for international suspicion and misunderstanding, and the increasing preoccupation with military preparedness. A glib and plausible impostor built upon British apprehensions by alleging as fact what many Britons believed all too possible: namely, that the United States aimed to win the southern Indians over as allies for a grand offensive against the Six Nations and the posts in the Old Northwest. For a time, the British were tempted by the Nootka crisis to use Bowles for purposes of their own; but every shred of evidence indicated their intention to keep their stakes small and concealed. The impostor's blandishments notwithstanding, Britain embarked upon no grand aggressive design, seeking only security for Canada and the northwestern posts. She intended to maintain peace if at all possible; although if the Americans attacked she would feel compelled to defend what she had. Simcoe, who met Bowles in London, exemplified this defensive psychology on the eve of his departure for the government of Upper Canada: believing that an American attack was altogether possible, he termed the posts "what Calais formerly was to Great Britain," centers for trade and peace and "outlets into the Enemy's Country" in wartime. Neither Simcoe nor Dorchester was a saber-rattling warlord bent on predatory conquest. They were rather relatively simple, honest, and patriotic soldiers, committed to doing their duty as they saw it. Possessing the soldierly virtues, they had also the shortcomings of the military mind. Preoccupied with questions of defense, they did not sufficiently understand that the Americans, determined to crush the Indians and convinced of British assistance to the savages, might see defensive preparations in Canada as something of a very different nature. Here precisely was the danger: that Britain and America might interpret each other's motions in the backcountry as a gathering of strength for attack.

Nerves tautened in the summer of 1791, as General Arthur St. Clair, governor of the Northwest Territory, began to organize his forces to accomplish what General Harmar had so signally failed to do—to chastise and subject the northwestern Indians. Once again, the British government had to face the possibility, even the probability, of a triumphant surge of American power into the vicinity of the posts. Surely Harmar's experience had taught the Americans how to deal with the enemy. Britons could not count upon a second inconclusive performance. If the republicans overturned the delicate balance by beating the Indians, would they stand at ease while Britain continued to occupy their posts? What of defeated and disgruntled Indians? Would they forego revenge upon false friends who had not extended a hand in the moment of supreme peril? The sharpening dilemma harshly reminded the British ministers that there was much business to be done at Philadelphia.

From the British point of view, the solution was obvious: mediation between the belligerents to produce a negotiated peace, as part of a general settlement which would see all interests—British, American, and Indian—harmonized. Early in September, 1791, Foreign Secretary Grenville, in his first set of additional instructions to George Hammond, told the envoy to draw the Americans into "some practicable and reasonable Arrangement on the Subject of the Posts."[29] Until they agreed to do justice to Britain, however, it was absolutely necessary to preserve the status quo in the Old Northwest. Yet it was vital to avoid misunderstanding on the point; Hammond should, therefore, disclaim, as Beckwith had done before him, "in the most unequivocal manner" any idea of Dorchester's aid to the Indians. Indeed, the American government should be made to realize that Britain had "a strong commercial and political Interest" in the restoration of peace between the Indians and Americans. Nothing could give more satisfaction to His Majesty than to contribute his good offices to such an object. If a suitable opportunity occurred, Hammond, taking care to concert his measures with Dorchester, should interpose with offers of good offices.

Even while Grenville wrote, St. Clair was leading his army (two months late) against the Indians. Ordered to establish a chain of posts stretching from Fort Washington on the Ohio to the rapids of the Maumee, in the heart of the powerful Miami Indian Confederacy, St. Clair represented danger to the Canadian commander. Uncertain of the American's true intentions, a worried Dorchester alerted his officers and urgently reported the beginning of the American offensive to the London government.

Home Secretary Henry Dundas, speaking for the cabinet, laid down the official line of conduct.[30] Commending Dorchester for his prudent preparations, Dundas earnestly trusted nonetheless that "whatever may have happened between the contending Parties, His [Majesty's] Officers have constantly observed the strictest system of neutrality, and have in no degree involved this country in these unfortunate disputes." This was the more necessary because of "the suspicions entertained and the Language held by persons in the service of the United States," the countering of which was assigned to the new envoy to the United States. Dundas then turned to British mediation. For the sake of both belligerents it was "indispensably necessary" to adjust the matters at issue; but a solution was equally necessary to Britain herself. It was "but too evident" that if it were not found, "this country must sooner or later be placed in a very unpleasant & embarrassing situation." Dorchester should take every practicable measure "for healing the differences that at present exist, and for effecting if possible, a speedy termination of the War." No sacrifice of the Indians to their enemies was proposed, however. Minister Hammond, it was hoped, would induce the American government to request British mediation. Apparently echoing General Haldimand's suggestion of 1783, Dundas declared that a chief object of the British envoy was to secure for the Indians the quiet possession of their hunting lands. The interests of the British traders in the area would be safeguarded as well.[31]

It was unfortunate, the Home Secretary continued, that the northwestern posts were deeply involved in the whole affair. Measures designed to secure the posts and contiguous areas against attack were only prudent; Hammond's negotiations in Philadelphia would naturally extend to possession of the posts, however, and Dorchester was instructed to keep the envoy informed about his measures relating to them. It might logically be expected that the reasons already exhibited to the Americans for British retention of the posts would dissuade them from "any Step which may reduce Your Lordship to the necessity of adopting measures of force for putting a stop to their proceedings." Dundas did not need to state the clear implications: if the United States was not dissuaded by reason, if she attacked the posts, Dorchester would have to fight. It would be a defensive measure, however—the *dernier resort*. Meantime, Dorchester should be alert, avoid provocation, work to preserve the status quo, and await the outcome of negotiations, which, with luck, would relieve Britain from the terrible dilemma in which she found herself in the Old Northwest.

On November 9, 1791, the *Public Advertiser* in its "Weekly Review of Politics" reported the latest news from America: some weeks earlier, St. Clair had been on the point of departure to the west. The Americans had "a fair prospect of obtaining a permanent peace with the Indians"; and every man, from "motives of humanity," would rejoice at it. Peace was particularly desirable for Britain, as it would bring a growing population in America—"and the greater that population shall be, the increasing connexion between America and Great Britain will render our commerce more extensive." The account would appear naïve, perhaps, to British commanders along the Canadian frontier, especially in its bland assumption that victorious Americans would be content to leave British forces on American territory undisturbed. Even so, it was an interesting reflection of official policy: not an aggressive, truculent, provocative design to wound, either directly or indirectly through the Indians, but rather a search for a negotiated peace by every means which honor could sanction, protecting all parties in their vital interests and, most especially, letting Britain retire with honor, justice secured to allies and subjects, from American territory in the Old Northwest.

Suddenly, almost inexplicably, an opportunity seemed granted by the god of battles. On November 4, 1791, five days before the *Public Advertiser* published its encomium on approaching peace in the backcountry, St. Clair's army met an Indian force about a day's march from the present Fort Wayne, Indiana. The issue made Harmar's humiliation appear an accolade of triumph. Although the Americans outnumbered the Indians, St. Clair's army was cut to pieces and routed. In this unexpected disaster lay yet another urgent reason for British diplomatic initiative at Philadelphia. The situation in the backcountry, always unstable, was now in wild flux. If ever America was to heed British offers of good offices with the Indians, it would surely be now, in the hour of her chastening defeat and bitter humiliation.

CHAPTER TEN

The Anglo-American Community: Trade and Grain

ANGLO-AMERICAN RELATIONS during the fifteen years after the end of the American War are commonly described in terms of mutual antagonism and hostility, mounting crisis and imminent war. A détente of sorts in 1794 is conceded, but considered a mere prelude to 1812. The story involves much more than a gigantic *tu quoque*, however, much more than reciprocal insults and injuries, much more than festering suspicions flaring finally in new and preordained military conflict. These elements figure in the truth, but they are only a part of it—and not even the most important part. Certainly, they should not be allowed to determine the limits of a discussion of British policy toward the United States, or of Anglo-American relations generally. A broader view is required; and when it is taken, one of the most intriguing features of the period stands revealed: a new Anglo-American community was emerging, not as closely knit nor as far-reaching and institutionalized as Shelburne and Hartley would have wished, but considerable and important. Here, in the proliferation of mutual interests and reconciliation, lies the mainstream of Anglo-American history, not in the perpetuation of national animosities and the inevitable drift toward a new war.

Well before the outbreak of hostilities against revolutionary France in 1793, both the British government and the public had become accustomed once more to thinking quite naturally in terms of an Anglo-American community. As early as 1785, amidst much criticism and invective directed at the United States, sentiments of a different kind were to be found in British newspapers. An Anglo-American union, based on "mutual advantage and perfect equality of freedom," would naturally develop, it was predicted, "when irritation is thoroughly forgot and the comparatively languid attachment and *selfish* assistance of their *new* friends cooly weighed. Then their own interest, with the *ancient* ties of consanguinity will probably do the rest." During the Shays Rebellion—perhaps the nadir for the American image abroad—Americans were told that Britons were far from rejoicing at their country's troubles. In the former mother country, the bitter past had been forgotten. Let Americans do likewise; and "let the connection which may hereafter arise between us, be formed from the similarity of religion and language." Ultimately "a foedereal amity" would surely develop.

Public opinion as expressed in the London press became even more friendly when Americans formulated and adopted the federal Constitution. Promising a respectable government and due regard for international obligations, the new scheme of government received highest praise because of its "approach to the English constitution." Washington, who had presided over the convention and was the obvious choice for the first President, was hailed with enthusiasm as the "great and wise leader" of his country. Hamilton's plans for national finance fired the British public's admiration as well, and congratulations were forthcoming for the revival of America's public faith and credit, "the best and most sure criterion of the progress also of private punctuality and credit."[1] Miranda, the Venezuelan adventurer then in London, testified also to the impact of the new scheme for federal finance, writing to Hamilton in quaint French:

vos *Plans* des finances; de Banc-nationalle; des colection des Taxes etc., non seulement ont merite l'admiration des gens de la plus grande consideration ici; mais ills ont donne aussi la plus haute idee du nouveaux Gouvernement, que se conduit a cet egard, par des principles d'*honeur*, et de *dignite* tres peu connus dans les gouvernmens modernes.[2]

Soon, a correspondent to the press found it impossible to imagine "two countries better calculated to engage in a commercial treaty." During the parliamentary recess late in 1789, it was rumored, without foundation but with widespread approbation, that the ministry was preparing to make a commercial treaty with America, "a connexion that will be equally advantageous to both." Somewhat later, with the Nootka crisis just past and crisis threatening in the Baltic, Britain was urged in a letter to the editor of a newspaper to seek her naval stores from America. It would be a natural arrangement since "every Englishman, from the similarity of manners, the same language, and the same habits with his brethren of America would prefer a trade with them to any other people under the Sun." Another writer extended the subject: if Britain took her naval stores from America, as she had done during colonial days, a "reciprocal treaty of commerce" would be in order. It could "not fail of being a permanent one"; and the "closest connexion" would ultimately develop, making both countries "equally strong, rich, and happy, as if under one head, and probably more so than if they had remained dependent on Great Britain. Jealousies ought and are now done away."[3]

When George Hammond went out to America as minister plenipotentiary, the *Public Advertiser*, in an editorial, welcomed the mission as presaging an alliance "long wished for" and "pointed out by mutual interests, by similar habits, and by every circumstance that is likely to unite two great nations." (Public opinion was running ahead of officialdom.) When war with revolutionary France threatened, America was immediately cast in the role of benevolent neutral. She would supply Britain, according to "A Ship Owner," with "an inexhaustible resource for mariners." When men-of-war of the Royal Navy visited American ports, he reasoned, they could fill up their crews with sailors pressed from British merchant vessels in the vicinity. Deprived merchant captains could quickly find American replacements, "who might reasonably be expected when once in our service, to have no particular desire to leave it." The argument was naïve, certainly, ignoring the accepted criteria of neutral conduct and grossly overrating the amenities of life aboard British vessels; it is significant for its basic assumption that, in time of need, Anglo-American co-operation could be expected as a matter of course. Americans themselves, citizens of "a rapidly rising Power," were described as changed: "insolent and indifferent to consequences whilst Great Britain was to back and defend them, but prudent and infinitely cautious now they know they must trust to themselves; it is this consideration which has improved their ideas of National faith, and given a new turn to National manners."[4]

By the eve of war with France, therefore, a dramatic shift in British public opinion had taken place. Differences between the two nations were recognized, but minimized. Wartime bitterness had dissipated, and, with it, the deep sense of betrayal by fellow subjects in

league with the House of Bourbon. The government's suspicions of
American motives in the Old Northwest were not even reflected in
the press. From a country of rebels, competitors, and potential enemies, the United States was transformed, in the public eye, into
friend and natural ally, whose complementary interests and historical
development bound her in a close and unique manner to the former
mother country. There were several important developments but-
tressing this conclusion.

There was, in the first place, a rapidly expanding trade between
the two countries, welcomed by public and government alike. The
report of the Committee for Trade of January 28, 1790, showed that
direct Anglo-American trade had yet to achieve the prewar level;
but encouraged by the political and fiscal stability of the new federal
government, commercial activity in the United States was increasing
in quickening tempo.[5] Sir John Temple noted the advance and, ever
inclined to the superficial, attributed the new "Spirit of Temperance
and Industry" to a decline in the consumption of rum: "It seems almost supernatural!"[6] In any event, Britons were enthusiastic at a
trade which "fortunately for England, is every day rapidly increasing."[7] American customs data for the period from August, 1789, to
September, 1790, were proudly published. Total exports from the
United States amounted to $20,415,965; tobacco accounted for $4,-
349,567; wheat for $2,510,232; wood for $1,263,334; provisions for
$5,757,482; fish products for $1,263,334; cattle for $486,105; rice
for $1,753,796; poultry for $60,000; and indigo for $537,379.
Britain took off $9,363,416 worth. The nearest competitor was
France, with $4,698,735. Spain took $2,005,907; Portugal, $1,283,-
462; Holland, $1,963,880. Smaller portions went to the German
states, Denmark, Sweden, Flanders, the East Indies, the Mediterranean, Africa, and the northwest coast of America. The total value of
imports into the United States, paying *ad valorem*, in 1790 stood at
$15,388,409, from which the United States government derived a
customs revenue of about $2,320,000. Of the total value of imports,
$13,797,168 came from Britain.[8]

The figures indicated a flourishing state of affairs, greatly benefiting both nations. With Britain receiving almost half of America's
exports and the United States taking something more than four-
fifths of her imports from Britain, there was obvious reason to rejoice, as the *Public Advertiser* did, that the "connection and trade

between this country and America has been rapidly on the encrease, for nearly the whole time of the establishment of their independence." Remittances were regular and punctual, "every difficulty thrown in the way of commerce of the two countries, being now nearly removed." There could be no doubt that the trade was "speedily becoming an inexhaustible source of riches and strength to both Empires." A glancing blow at an old enemy could not be foregone: "While England and America are thus rapidly healing the wound, and recovering from the burdens incurred by the late war, France is borne down by an accumulation of evils."[9] So rich a trade was worth some care by both parties; and the days had passed when Britain could depend on mere economic necessity to guarantee her position. Hence, the urgency of Hammond's mission to counter American threats to discriminate against British trade. Hence, too, the efforts of Hamilton and his Federalist friends to come to some understanding with the country which bestowed so much wealth on Americans and revenues on their government.

Direct trade between the two countries was only one way in which an Anglo-American community of economic interests was developing. In the years after the Revolution, the United States assumed the role of granary for the "North Atlantic triangle." Hopes of achieving imperial self-sufficiency after the American secession were long-lived among orthodox mercantilists in Britain. Lord Sheffield in 1783 argued (incorrectly) that the goal was immediately within reach. The Committee for Trade in its report of 1784 concluded that it would take some time to achieve the goal and that, in the interim, the importation of American produce in British bottoms into the sugar islands was to be tolerated. Assuming from testimony heard at its board that Canadian self-sufficiency was established, the committee recommended that in the following year importation of any American produce whatsoever into that colony by sea should be prohibited. An appropriate Order in Council was issued on April 8, 1785; and in March, 1786, a second order specifically closed the ports of the province of Quebec to American goods and commodities.[10]

Canadian merchants, not to mention the Allens of Vermont, chafed at the restrictions which they believed to extend to all trade with the United States. Under pressure from these quarters and correctly doubting the adequacy of domestic sources of supply, the new governor, Lord Dorchester, took the opinion of his chief justice,

William Smith. As a result, the orders were interpreted as applying solely to seaborne commerce. Exercising his own discretion, Dorchester promulgated the proclamation of April 18, 1787, which created "in some degree a commercial intercourse" overland and via Lake Champlain. It was an experiment, he explained to the home authorities, "the effects of which we shall soon perceive on the minds of our neighbours and on our trade and navigation."[11] American produce—masts, yards, bowsprits, lumber, naval stores, hemp, flax, all cereals, cattle, sheep, hogs, poultry, provisions, and "whatsoever else is of the growth of the said States"—would be accepted, much for re-export. Dorchester professed himself unable to "think it possible that British ships were forbid to carry from the river St. Lawrence, what is permitted to be imported into Great Britain by ships of the United States, from their own ports." On April 27, Dorchester's council acted to extend the list of permissible imports from the United States to include leaf tobacco and pot and pearl ash for re-export to Great Britain. In turn, Canada would send south all articles grown or manufactured in Great Britain, furs and pelts alone excepted.

Any uneasiness which Dorchester may have felt at his unilateral creation of a virtually free trade in the interior was dissipated by the response of the Committee for Trade. In a dispatch of August 24, 1787, Hawkesbury himself transmitted to the Governor an Order in Council of the preceding July. Dorchester and his counsel were empowered thereby to regulate overland trade with the United States as they should think proper, always with the reservation that any action they might take would not be inconsistent with the mercantile system as established by law. Under no circumstances, for example, were foreign European manufactures or spirits to be admitted, nor peltry exported.[12] Dorchester's original proclamation was quickly transformed into an ordinance by his council, and a second from that body ordered that the carrying trade on Lake Champlain be confined to British vessels.

The logic of the new arrangement was not difficult to fathom. The prohibition of sea trade was preserved, protecting British navigation. With that essential secured, the overland trade held certain advantages—both political and commercial—for Britain, as Stephen Cottrell, writing from the office of the Committee for Trade, told Grenville in April, 1790. Re-exportation of American produce down the St. Lawrence, on the same footing as Canadian, would increase British navigation; and the country would be in a magnificent position to take advantage of the trade in the growing American back-country—if only, of course, peace with the Indians could be maintained and the post issue settled amicably. The prospect was dazzling: an expanding (and friendly) United States; and, thus, increasing consumption of British manufactures.[13] Shelburne would have approved.

There was, however, a deeper, more immediate concern. From the mercantile point of view, it was vital that no dependence for the necessities of life be placed on foreign powers. If ever the Empire was to become self-sufficient again, Canada would have to become a great and productive agricultural land. There were grounds for some optimism. From 1763 to 1768, for example, considerable quantities of grain were available for export from the northern province. The crop of 1768 was very deficient, however, and a period of dearth and high prices ensued. But Canadian farmers moved successfully to meet the challenge by bringing more land under cultivation. Until 1775, there was a steady rise in production of grain and flour and in the quantities exported. The year 1774 was a peak, with an unprecedented 450,000 barrels of flour leaving the colony. In the year or two after the war, the great influx of loyalists into Canada disoriented the economy of the province, and crops were poor. The Maritime Provinces and Newfoundland, especially, suffered badly in the winter of 1784-85.

Early in 1785, the Committee for Trade began a study of Canadian commerce generally, with great weight given to the Canadian merchants and factors, who testified, the recent deficiencies notwithstanding, that the attempt ought to be made to create a self-sustaining Canada. Orders in Council of April 8, 1785, and March 24, 1786, were accordingly issued.

The sensitive point was Newfoundland. The important "nursery of seamen" was bound to suffer more, in any dearth, than the "colonies of settlement." The supply of the island, which lacked any significant agricultural resource of its own, was therefore of major concern. The merchants of Poole and Dartmouth trading to Newfoundland raised the question with the Committee for Trade early in 1785, even while the shortage prevailed, and asked for the exclusion of both American ships and American produce from the fisheries, alleging that the necessary foodstuffs would more properly come from Britain, Ireland, and Canada. The committee, having the good sense to look beyond this patently self-interested suggestion, called before it the governor of Newfoundland, Vice-Admiral John Campbell, the naval officer, Archibald Buchanan, and the collector of the customs there, Richard Routh. All three officials did much to counter the merchants' testimony. The exclusion of American vessels was acceptable, they asserted; but an embargo on American foodstuffs was not wise: prices would soar and profits for shippers engaged in the fisheries would diminish.

The committee reported early in February, 1785, and the merchants' request was rejected, albeit somewhat regretfully.[14] The lords knew that "in a general View of Policy" it would be best to confine the supply of "every article necessary" for the Newfoundland fisheries to imperial sources. Desirable in theory, it was, however, impracticable under the circumstances "without incurring the Inconveniences and Dangers so forcibly pointed out" by the island's officials. The solution proposed was an experiment for one year, during which Newfoundland would receive American provisions—bread, flour, and livestock—in the least exceptionable manner: in British vessels, navigated according to law and strictly licensed.

Within a matter of days, Parliament had before it a bill (subsequently 25 George III, c. 1) embodying the committee's recommendations. Several days of sharp debate, occasioned chiefly by the violent and eloquent opposition of William Eden, followed. Two points were significant. One, Eden's attempt to portray the act as a threat to British shipping, has already been examined;[15] the second concerned Canada's ability to supply the fisheries.

Pitt declined to grant Eden's request that testimony be heard at the bar of the House, observing that Newfoundland's need was so notorious that additional proof was unnecessary. An Eden supporter, the former commissary-general of North America, Brook Watson, managed, however, to introduce the substance of the Canadian and London merchants' views in his speech. His informants, Watson told the House, were confident that, in spite of the recent crop failure, Britain and Canada were perfectly capable of supplying Newfoundland. There was consequently no reason "why the trade of Great Britain and her colonies should be delivered over to a foreign power." The assertion brought to his feet Henry Cruger, sometime of New

York, who had only recently returned from a visit to the United States. Blunt about merchants and their "interest or prejudice, or that worse impulse, an inveterate attachment to the spirit of monopoly, for which some of the Canadian merchants [are] remarkable," he gave the House the benefit of his personal observations in Philadelphia the preceding August. Two British vessels had been loading flour, selling at thirteen shillings the hundredweight in the Pennsylvania port. They were bound for Canada, where a price of twenty-two shillings prevailed. How could it be seriously asserted, then, that the province, needy herself, could supply Newfoundland?

Jenkinson intervened with the soothing observation that the bill was after all only temporary, gauged to prevent Newfoundland's existing distress. Surprisingly for one of the strictest of mercantilists, he then went beyond even Cruger's expressions of doubt about Canada's ability to supply the fisheries. By choosing exceptional years, he said, a case might be made out in favor of Canada; on the whole, however, it was apparent to him that the province had to be supplied from the United States. "In fact," he concluded "Quebec [is] not a flour country." Jenkinson was always preoccupied with navigation rather than trade. (On one occasion during the American War, he confided to Lord North that he revered the acts of navigation, but considered those of trade of little worth.) With the British naval monopoly secured, he could now afford to take a broader view. Not so William Eden, who was outraged.

If Jenkinson were correct, Eden declared, the prospects for Canada were melancholy indeed. Deprived of the fur trade by a disgraceful treaty of peace, she had no other recourse but to make herself the granary of the Empire. What, he seemed to say, would some inconvenience, even suffering, in Newfoundland matter if Canada were thereby established as she ought to be, and a closed and self-sufficient imperial system achieved? When a Pitt supporter reminded Eden that Newfoundland could be supplied more cheaply and easily from the United States, that Canada's ability to produce the necessities was at best sporadic, that even Britain herself was subject to frequent deficiencies and was forbidden by the Corn Laws to export grain when prices attained a pre-determined level, the angry man flung back that the bill was not "favourable to any interests but those of the United States."

Lashing out at Cruger, he called upon the former New Yorker

to state whether he had also seen in the United States "the singular benevolence with which British subjects were treated by the New States, . . . the sanctimonious attention to the faith of the treaties." Indeed, was he aware of the "peculiar duties and restraints" put by some of the states upon British ships and cargoes, even though in Britain American imports were placed on a footing beyond that of the most friendly powers of Europe? Eden was trying to raise the anti-American whirlwind, to repeat his masterly performance at the time of the American Intercourse Bill. He failed. Maritime interests were not at issue. An important portion of the Empire required sustenance; and the most splendid hopes for Canada's future could not feed a hungry man. The bill passed without a division. The meaning was plain: Canada was not to be relied upon as a source of necessities; the United States was.

Then, for a time, nature seemed to make sport of Eden's opponents. Canadian grain was plentiful in the 1785 harvest, and there was a surplus for export. Next year, there was even more—some 113,000 bushels of wheat, 11,000 barrels of flour, and 11,000 quintals of biscuit going to supply the needs of the other New World colonies. A third bountiful year followed, the export of wheat reaching almost 230,000 bushels, in addition to some 6,000 bushels of peas.[16] Mercantilist hopes rose to dizzy heights. If Canada continued her prodigious development, American produce might be foregone at least partially and perhaps altogether.

In view of the 1785 harvest, the committee, faced with the expiration of the year's limit, was uncertain whether or not to recommend renewal. Witnesses were called once more. In contrast to the previous inquiry, it was established that while some grain recently consumed in Newfoundland had come from the United States, "much the largest quantity" had come from Canada. The tone was generally optimistic. A considerable trade in lumber was developing between Newfoundland and Canada and the Maritimes; the West Indies were sending increasing quantities of rum in exchange for fish. Nevertheless, caution again prevailed. The principle of the Report of February, 1785, was reaffirmed, and the act of the preceding year renewed. Canada's ability to serve as a stable source of supply remained to be demonstrated conclusively.

When 1786 proved a good year, the Committee for Trade reviewed the matter again. They may have been tempted to alter the act, but in November they heard the new governor of Newfoundland, Rear Admiral Andrew Elliot, urge perseverance in the existing policy. In his judgment, the act had lowered the cost of provisions in the island by one-third; encouraged participation in the fisheries; and thus contributed to an increase in the naval resources of the Empire.

The third good year in a row was too much, however. The committee learned that some ten thousand loyalists were beginning to make their contribution to the colony's total production; and a systematic effort was under way to teach the old French *habitants* more modern and productive methods of cultivation. It was an exhilarating prospect; and the Lords of Trade were swept off their feet, recommending that the Newfoundland Act be changed to prohibit American produce. But to be on the safe side they also advised giving the King in Council authority to grant governors and commissioners of the customs emergency discretion to license British ships for the importation of American produce. The new provision was duly accepted, and the amended act was distributed to officers of the customs in the spring of 1788.

The committee's precautionary measure was wise. Fate suddenly redressed the balance. On December 8, 1788, Dorchester wrote almost casually to the London government, enclosing a memorial from certain grain merchants, millers, and biscuit makers of Quebec, stating that the recent harvest had been scanty and there would be little, if any, wheat and wheat products for export. The Governor was not worried about the supply of his own province and the fisheries in the Gulf of St. Lawrence; but other colonies should make their own preparations. The Lords of Trade, in some consternation, immediately procured necessary authority to allow Newfoundland to import American bread, flour, and Indian corn in British vessels for the coming season. An extraordinary provision was added. Whereas previously British vessels carrying American produce to the fisheries were bound to clear out of some British European port no longer than seven months prior to calling at Newfoundland, they could now be legally cleared for a voyage to the United States from a Newfoundland port. Similar permission was extended to Nova Scotia, New Brunswick, Cape Breton, and St. John's Island, where the authorities were empowered to exercise discretion in allowing importation of American foodstuffs for the coming season. No license for that purpose was to be issued after June 30, 1789. In view of Dorchester's reassurances, no steps were taken with regard to the province of Quebec or the St. Lawrence fisheries.

The omission immediately brought a request from John Fiott, a London merchant trading with his partners to Canada, that a license be granted for one or two vessels to load provisions in the United States for the fisheries at Chaleur Bay. The committee replied that the new act did not allow the importation of any American goods or commodities into the province of Quebec by sea or coastwise, or up the St. Lawrence River from the sea; it had, therefore, no authority to comply with Fiott's request. After a second communication from the merchant, urging similar treatment for the Quebec fisheries and requesting permission to import American provisions under license, the committee acquiesced, agreeing to prepare the necessary legislation. The trade would be limited to licensed vessels sailing first from Britain's European dominions to the fisheries in question, afterward proceeding to an American port to take on supplies for a return voyage to the fisheries in the Gulf of St. Lawrence and on the islands and coasts adjacent, as well as Labrador. Permission, it was assumed, would last only for the coming season.[17] The committee, still under the impression that Dorchester's description was accurate, must have seen their action as probably unnecessary, but prudent. In May the necessary legislation was passed and an order issued; merchants in Britain, Newfoundland, and Quebec were enthusiastic in their reception of the new system.[18] As yet there was no suspicion that all was not well in Canada.

In reality, the crops there had failed disastrously. Unaware of the catastrophe, the Committee for Trade sedately turned to a study of Canadian-American commercial relations in general, secure in the belief that all contingencies had been provided for. In March, they heard Thomas Ainslie, collector of the customs at Quebec, give a confident and optimistic account of the province's economy. The fur trade, still supplying the largest single Canadian export, amounted to about £260,000 in 1788; and great quantities of manufactures were going south to Vermont and the United States. Lumber, pot and pearl ash, and grain (an additional comfort for the committee) were finding their way overland to the north in exchange. Some rum, sugar, molasses, and beaver pelts were being smuggled, as well as East Indian articles like tea and piece goods, brought up the Hudson and across Lake Champlain; but even this was no cause for worry. The smuggling was "not very considerable," although, conscientious official that he was, Ainslie admitted "it is an object."[19]

The air of unhurried consideration suddenly vanished. The truth had finally broken upon Dorchester; and at a meeting of June 12, 1789, the lords of the committee had before them two new letters from a very worried governor. One of February 14 informed the committee that conditions had made it advisable to open the port of St. John for the free importation of provisions, bread, biscuit, wheat and rye flour, Indian corn, oats, barley, and other grains for the supply of Canada. Lake Champlain and the River Sorel had been opened for traffic for the same purpose. The measure was temporary, the terminal date having been set for the following August 1.

The second letter, dated March 4, announced the opening until August 1 of St. John for the free importation of beef, pork, and all other kinds of meat, salted, cured, or smoked. To guard against future crises, the governor of Canada also requested discretionary authority to permit free importation of wheat and flour from the United States by sea in case of emergency or distress.

The committee was aghast. In a dispatch prepared for Hawkesbury's signature, the chairman clearly showed his anger with the governor of Canada.[20] He outlined the actions already taken for the relief of the fisheries. They had proceeded no further, it was pointedly stated, because of the assurance contained in Dorchester's dispatch of the preceding December. A copy was enclosed to refresh His Lordship's memory. It was now too late in the parliamentary session, Hawkesbury continued, to pass an act giving the Governor the discretionary power he wished, or, for that matter, to effect the relief of the inhabitants (that is, to give legality to measures already taken by Dorchester). Even though Dorchester's measures were not sanctioned by existing statute, Hawkesbury accepted their necessity; but he obviously took a dim view of the Governor's lack of foresight. Dorchester was told curtly that if "upon further consideration" he should continue to believe that "the scarcity to which the inhabitants of the province are now exposed is likely to occur again and that in order to prevent the same it may be expedient to lodge a discretionary power in the Governor and His Council," he should recommend the measure again. Let his new dispatch arrive before the next session of Parliament. The committee would be happy to consider it and to offer His Majesty appropriate advice.

It was brusque treatment, but merited. Dorchester was clearly at fault in not learning of the prospects of a dearth months earlier and informing the government in London of it. Indeed, the plight of Canada was even worse than the committee believed at the time of Hawkesbury's crisp communication. Another dispatch, dated April 11, 1789, arrived from Dorchester. Necessity had required him to take matters further into his own hands. Because of the distressed state of the settlements north of Montreal, he had allowed free admission of flour and other provisions. The magnitude of the province's need was drawn further to the committee's attention when, inquiring into Britain's own meager corn supply, they heard two factors report that very little grain was to be found in the entire state of New York, so great had been the quantity of the exportations northward.

Dorchester's permission for "free importation" by sea—even though it was confined to imperial vessels—made chaos of the system established in 1785 and 1786; and it was finally decided that his actions were so flagrantly contrary to law that they required special parliamentary sanction. Despite the lateness of the season, therefore, clauses were inserted into a new corn bill, giving grudging approval, although it was strictly limited to one year's duration.[21]

It was not until 1792 that Canadians began to speak again about supplying Newfoundland. On January 25 of that year, a group of merchants and traders in London sent a memorial to the Committee for Trade. The prices of bread and flour were so low both in Britain and in Canada, they said, that there would be no need, at least for the present year, to supply the Newfoundland fisheries from the United States. Would the committee kindly withhold the "customary" orders on the subject?[22] Again, the times were out of joint. The committee replied at once that only on the twentieth of January they had advised a continuation of the existing regulation allowing importation into Newfoundland of bread, flour, and Indian corn from the United States for the coming season. The Order in Council had actually been issued on the very morning the merchants' representation had been received. It was therefore too late to act on their memorial. The committee would, however, be eager to have more timely information in the future.

In the year or two before the outbreak of Britain's war with France, there were signs that the mercantilists' hopes for Canada were, once again, brightening and that grain production was on the increase.[23] Even so, the base remained unstable and untrustworthy as long as peace lasted. Within a few weeks of the merchants' memorial, for example, the Committee for Trade had before it a dispatch from Thomas Carleton, lieutenant-governor of New Brunswick. Their lordships were informed that the continuance of permission to import grain and other provisions from the United States by sea was indispensably necessary. Indeed, after repeated applications from his people and at the advice of the council, he had added lumber to the enumerated list of American products.

No amount of wishful thinking or propaganda from interested merchants could alter the essential fact that Canada had failed to become a dependable source of supply for the Empire, or even for herself, before the outbreak of the French war. Unable to build a sound and self-sufficient system upon that wintry, northern province, British statesmen could place ultimate reliance only on the American granary. Only the United States could dependably supply the staff of life for the sugar islands, the Newfoundland and St. Lawrence fisheries, the Maritimes, Canada, and Great Britain herself. This fact helped to a certain degree to balance American economic dependence on Great Britain, encouraging a spirit of interdependence to replace the earlier "patron-client" relationship.

The years 1788-89 mark a watershed in British economic history. Britain herself had very scanty harvests, while wide-scale crop failures occurred in France and over much of the continent. Under the Corn Laws, a considerable export from Britain's meager supply had occurred before prices rose to the level at which exportation was legally forbidden. But then, famine was a distinct possibility. Urgent examination of Britain's situation in 1788 produced two important conclusions. First, she was no longer able to depend upon her own capacity to feed her people. Second, a secure and adequate outside source of supply would have to be found. Almost automatically, Britain looked to the United States.

As the Committee for Trade began its study, it discovered that a significant change had occurred in Britain's economy during the period from 1770 to 1788. Imports of grain had risen so steadily that it was obvious that the country was no longer self-sufficient. Britain had become dependent upon foreign sources for a sufficiency of cereals, save only barley; and for these important grains the coun-

try paid out about £291,000 annually. The committee's report was
not gloomy, however.[24] The new state of affairs arose from no general decline in agriculture, but rather from an increase in human
population, cattle, and horses. These, in turn, indicated remarkable
advances in trade, industry, and national opulence.

Even the opulent must be fed, however, and how this was to be
done was a problem of the greatest importance. Continental sources
were inadequate; even in ordinary years, the report maintained, "the
Produce of Grain in Europe is not more than equal to the Consumption of the Inhabitants." There was, in fact, only one source available; and the committee did not hesitate to name it. Whenever crops
should fail in Britain, "the Deficiency can only be supplied from the
Harvest of America."[25]

The truth of the committee's conclusion was suddenly and harshly
demonstrated. In 1788 spring harvest in the United States was badly
infected with the "hessian fly," a weevil popularly believed to have
been introduced in the straw bedding of the mercenaries during the
war. Warnings were soon forthcoming from Phineas Bond in Philadelphia: the ravages of the insect were fatally destructive to the
crops; Britain must avoid infection of her own grain at all costs. On
June 25, 1788, therefore, an Order in Council temporarily prohibited
the entry of American wheat into the kingdom. Notice was immediately sent to consular officials in the United States, while Sir Joseph
Banks, president of the Royal Society, was asked to study and report
upon the insect and its infestation. The British envoy to Portugal,
Robert Walpole, was also ordered to communicate to the Portuguese
government the news of the weevil depredations, without however
revealing his source. He was instructed, too, to find out if the insect
had appeared in Portugal, where recent large importations of American wheat had been made.[26]

Thomas Jefferson, in Paris, was, rather typically, convinced that
the British embargo signified a deep-laid plot "to do us injury by
spreading a groundless alarm in those countries of Europe where our
wheat is constantly and kindly received." It was "a mere assassina-
tion," the future secretary of state believed. Thomas Paine, in his
own right an expert in detecting British villainy, agreed.[27] So did
many Americans at home. "Very severe strictures have been made
here," Bond told Leeds, "upon the regulations applied to the Importation of American Wheat into Great Britain, and very unjust and

acrimonious Censures have been thereupon thrown out against the officers of the Crown residing here."[28]

American suspicions and charges were completely unfounded. The prohibition was a painful necessity, undertaken to protect British agriculture. The home country's need for American wheat was, in fact, great and growing. Further, the Canadian dearth was about to declare itself, with all its somber implications for the province's sister colonies. Bond, anxiously watching the northward surge of the weevil in the autumn of 1788, described the destruction it wreaked as "beyond all conception"; and almost in desperation, he made the unpalatable suggestion that Britain's prohibition of American wheat need not automatically exclude American flour.[29]

By February, 1789, the ports of Bristol and Poole were open for the importation of foreign grain (excluding the infected American grain, of course). The price of wheat in London climbed to the critical 44/- to 48/- range. Predictions were freely made that it would continue to advance, automatically ending all export of grain from the kingdom. The most recent harvest had been small; and profiteering factors were shipping out great quantities to the continent to take advantage of the high prices there. If the government suddenly acted to prohibit exportation, the potential crisis might well blossom into full-blown reality, as panic buying and hoarding by the public would inevitably follow.

It was a wracking situation for the ministry. If Britain's next harvest were short and if American wheat remained prohibited, famine would be at hand. A government which remained inactive under such circumstances would not be forgiven. But what action was indicated? The predicament was not rendered any less uncomfortable by the knowledge that great quantities of American wheat (selling at the fantastic bargain price of 3/6d. to 4/- the bushel) were being shipped to southern Europe and to France.[30] If the weevil should establish itself on the continent, the ministry must have asked itself, would Britain be long spared? The painful abstention from American grain might well go for nought. In July, 1789, the Committee for Trade began battening down the hatches, launching an inquiry into the stores of wheat and flour within the kingdom. It was soon apparent that additional supplies were required; but where were they to be found? France had engrossed anything available on the continent; the northern countries were carefully holding supplies at home, and prices there had advanced 100 per cent in three months. Surely the time had arrived to accept the advice of the factors to suspend exportation from Britain as the first step to meet the threatening crisis, let the public alarm rise as it would.

It was with something like desperation, therefore, that William Fawkener, writing for the Privy Council to the Duke of Leeds on November 23, 1789, asked the Foreign Secretary to instruct the consuls in America to procure and transmit at the earliest possible moment information about the most recent harvest in the United States.[31] How bad was weevil damage? What prices prevailed? What quantity was available for export? How great was the demand from other European countries? Leeds immediately complied with the Privy Council's request, hastily sending out a circular letter the very next day.[32]

There remained a winter to be got through. It promised to be a grim one. Deeply perturbed, the ministry decided upon a gamble: they would act at once, even before official information in response to Leeds's letter could be received. The spring harvest in the United States had been reasonably good; but the supply in the northern states had been exhausted by the Canadian factors, the weevil notwithstanding. Little had been exported from the southern states, however, "for want of Ships . . ., the Measures of this Country having diminished their quantity of Shipping," the factors explained to the committee. Early reports stated, too, that the autumn harvest had also been plentiful. Further, unofficial and private sources said there was a chance that the weevil had subsided. Still, the news was undependable; and a premature end to the embargo meant danger of importing weevil-infested wheat to the permanent damage of British agriculture, which would heighten dependence on foreign sources of supply. Conscious of the stakes, the Committee for Trade nonetheless resolved on November 27, 1789, only three days after Leeds's circular letter, to advise lifting the prohibition on American wheat forthwith. Urgency was so great that a sloop-of-war sailed especially to carry out to the United States the subsequent Order in Council of December 4. News was hurried, also, to the merchants trading to the Republic.[33]

British good luck held. In the spring of 1790, Phineas Bond sent welcome confirmation that the most recent crop was bountiful, and, equally important, the infestation by the hessian fly had greatly abated. Pennsylvania, an important producer, was almost entirely free of it. Enormous orders for American produce were pouring in, not only from Britain, but also from France, Spain, and Portugal. Bond noted with satisfaction that most of the cargoes, even those destined for other European powers, were under the care or guarantee of British commercial houses.[34] For the impartial observer, the truth of the report of 1788 was evident: deficiencies in grain in Britain could be filled only from the harvests of America.

Following the brush with famine, the British ministry attempted to pass legislation designed to forestall a repetition. In a new corn bill, introduced in the spring of 1791, it was proposed, among other things, to build official warehouses for the free storage of foreign grain. The country would thus prepare in times of plenty for the lean years. For once, Thomas Jefferson and Lord Sheffield agreed: both opposed the measure. The one saw it as an insidious maneuver to rob America of her carrying trade and continental grain markets; the other castigated it as detrimental to British agriculture.[35] The clause was defeated by a small margin of 56-70 after a brief debate in the House of Commons on April 11, 1791.[36] Before the division, however, Pitt's friend and sometime joint under-secretary at the Foreign Office, Dudley Ryder, the future Lord Harroby, spoke in support of the measure. His statement underscored the importance of America in supplying Britain. In times of need, he told the House, it was the United States "to which we must naturally look for a supply when wanted."

CHAPTER ELEVEN

The Anglo-American Community:
Areas of Private Interest

THE BRITISH GOVERNMENT's desire for an amicable settlement of differences with the United States was more than seconded by vast numbers of private citizens who were busily working out with like-minded Americans their own individual areas of co-operation, not always with the blessings of their government. Taken together, they provide important evidence of friendship for America and of a new Anglo-American community.

The public optimism in Britain which greeted the Hammond mission ran well ahead of the British government's response, but it was no less significant for that fact. Indeed, in a free society with a parliamentary system, it might be argued that the voice of the people was calling the government to follow. "The prejudices against Britain, on account of the war, are daily wearing off," the *Morning Chronicle* declared about America in October, 1791. Nature herself, the editorial continued, had decreed a great Anglo-American community of complementary interests: were "100 weavers, or any other tradesmen, to emigrate from Europe, there would be 99 of them farmers in the course of three years." The Republic, "we are happy in being enabled to state," wrote the editor of the *Public Advertiser* on October 24, 1791,

is rapidly advancing in national prosperity and importance. Her credit has astonishingly increased, her population, her manufactures, her commerce, and her wealth all are immensely advancing; but above all gratifying to Englishmen, and advantageous to the British Empire, the connexion and commerce between the United States and Great Britain is every day becoming of more importance and value.

At the end of the year, the same newspaper could claim the prospect of an American alliance, which it wrongly thought it saw in the offing, as a crowning triumph for the Pitt administration.[1] The prospect "must afford satisfaction to the patriots of both countries," the editorial declared. "The connexion is pointed out by mutual interests, by similar habits, and by every circumstance that is likely to unite two great nations."

This shift in British public opinion, in such strong contrast to the ill will and bitter condemnations just a few years earlier, was not mere sentimentalizing. Many Britons let their money speak for them, investing their private means in the United States. Above and beyond financial commitments in the ordinary course of trade, there was an important and significant portion of the American national debt funded by British capital. Alexander Hamilton's great structure of federal finance may have occasioned harsh debate and eternal cleavage between the Treasury Secretary and his followers and Thomas Jefferson and his supporters; but the British public registered nothing but admiration and enthusiasm. Agents in America saluted Hamilton's "genius and judgement" and the fair prospects he was opening for his country.[2] Even the "desperate and ruinous speculation," which Sir John Temple reported to be accompanying the new developments, did nothing to tarnish the bright confidence in the new system, which "serves to shew the rising credit of the States, their wealth, and the high opinion they entertain of the benefits likely to result from their National Bank."[3]

The federal debt consisted of some $12 million owed to France, Holland, and Spain; $42.5 million owed domestically; and $25 million in debts owed by the several states and now assumed by the central government. In May, 1791, full details were published by the British press. For about two-thirds of the total amount, Congress would issue certificates, transferable at the Treasury of the United States, bearing six per cent interest from April 1, 1792. The remaining one-third, Congress proposed to fund with "6% Deferred" certificates, bearing interest payable on January 1, 1801. A third type of certificate, the "3%," was issued to take up three years' arrears of interest on the national debt due on January 1, 1791. British private investment began at once. In May, 1791, the "6%'s" were selling at 17/6d. in the pound sterling; the "Deferreds" and "3%'s" at 9/- to 10/-. Purchases were registered at one of fourteen loan offices founded in the United States, one for each of the states and an extra one for the federal treasury itself. The New York Loan Office was the most important because of the city's standing as a commercial center and port.[4]

Analysis of the transactions registered at the New York office reveals a significant amount of British capital involved, with the inflow far overbalancing the outflow.[5]

British Investments in the American National Debt
New York Loan Office

	6%	6% Deferred	3%
1790	$ 10,000	$ 7,783	$ 39,280
1791	409,696	333,341	403,090
1792	297,565	454,753	1,885,345
1793	407,182	392,665	1,069,943
1794	434,811	409,572	774,360
1795	447,682	505,742	521,053
Totals:	$2,006,936	$2,103,856	$4,693,071

Certificates could be sold, of course. Against these totals, therefore, there must be placed the outflow of British capital during the same period.

Sale of Certificates held by British Investors

	6%	6% Deferred	3%
1791	$ 12,896	$ 16,000	$ 69,200
1792	166,811	70,534	328,359
1793	346,054	161,844	661,620
1794	163,225	238,766	496,720
1795	215,965	312,470	470,816
Totals:	$904,951	$799,614	$2,026,715

It is clear that well over half of the British capital finding its way into the funding of the American national debt, at the New York office, remained there during the period under discussion.

The totals of all transactions, regardless of nationality, at the Federal Treasury Loan Office at Philadelphia were much smaller (and so, it may be assumed, were the totals at the remaining dozen offices). Between 1791 and 1795, inclusive, some $908,000 in 6% Certificates was issued at the seat of government, $888,000 in the 6% Deferreds, and $512,000 in the 3%'s; British holdings accounted for about 17 per cent, 12 per cent, and 12 per cent, respectively.

The data presented here are by no means a complete analysis of British holdings in the national debt. A dozen loan offices remain to be investigated. Studies of the transactions at New York and Philadelphia are more than random samplings, however, and can well furnish adequate basis for generalization about the scope of private British activity and the Britons who engaged in it.

Investment by the large banking and trading houses was enormous. The house of Henry M. Bird of London, for example, bought a grand total (in face value) of $715,421 in American securities between 1791 and 1796, although between 1792 and 1796 it sold or transferred some $637,047. Similarly, the London merchants Lane, Son, & Fraser bought about $395,000 in certificates in 1792; by 1796, they had sold enough to withdraw their original investments, presumably leaving the profit invested. John Henry Cozenone and Nephew of London bought some $315,000 between 1792 and 1795, and sold only $137,000. Samuel and Henry Waddington of London bought $235,000 and sold only $70,000. Hodgson Atkinson, London merchant, bought about $190,000 and sold $138,000. Other large investors at the New York Office included John Walker and Thomas Mullet, William Leatham, and Miller, Hart & Co., all merchants of London, and Waldo, Francis, and Waldo, merchants of Bristol. At the Philadelphia office, sizable investors included Donald and Burton, London merchants; Robert Smith, Lord Carrington, Westminster banker; John Waring & Co. and Benjamin Savage of London. Not the least investor, although he may have been acting as agent for other parties, was Consul-General Phineas Bond, who in 1791 bought $52,000 in the 6%'s, $16,000 in the 6% Deferreds, and $29,000 in the 3%'s; in any case, he sold out after having held the securities for about a year.

In 1795, with much of the country disputing violently over Jay's Treaty, the United States government sent $1,460,000 in 6% Certificates to England for sale; the purpose was to meet payments due on the Dutch debt and to prepare to deal with the Barbary pirates. Details of sales to individual investors, particularly the smaller ones, are obscure. On the face of it, it would appear, however, that the great trading and banking houses of the kingdom snapped up most of the certificates, although it is possible that they, in turn, sold to smaller investors.

That so many "hard-headed" British businessmen, commanding great financial resources, found the American national debt a good investment testifies dramatically to the shift in opinion about the United States since the days of the Confederation. Against the background of the unpaid prewar debts, it is astounding. Of equal interest, however, in gauging the sweep of the change is the great number of small British investments in the American debt. There was Robert Abrahams, "gentleman" of Taunton, who bought $4,000 in 6% Deferreds from the New York office. The Reverend Henry C. Adams of Shrewsbury invested the same amount in September, 1792; the following February and March, he bought $8,275 more. John Aiken, M.D., Mordecai Andrew, clerk, and Margaret Atkinson, widow, invested small sums in the American debt. Was Samuel Boddington of London following a "tip" when he invested $930 in 6% Deferreds registered at the Philadelphia office in 1794? How many strokes upon the anvil accounted for the $692 in 6%'s, the $346 in Deferreds, and the $187 in 3%'s bought in 1791 by Peter Browne, Kensington blacksmith? Did he perhaps talk American affairs with Samuel Brustar, shipwright, also of Kensington, who regularly invested small sums between 1791 and 1794? Did Jane Capper of Martin Lane, Cannon Street, London, use pin money from her merchant husband to build up a small nest egg for herself? Could not a bereaved Mary Knowles, widow, and John Owen, clergyman, find investments closer at hand than the former's $12,000 in 6%'s and the latter's $1,000 in Deferreds? Why did Catherine Smyth, spinster of Norfolk, buy $123 in Deferreds? John Willday, the Warwickshire hatmaker, clearly had a going concern when he could invest, as he did in 1792, more than $13,000 in 6%'s, almost $7,000 in Deferreds, and $5,500 in 3%'s. He was far richer, certainly, than Abraham Goldsmid of London who invested $90 in 3%'s in 1791, and cautiously matched it in 1792. What visions of independent means did Hieronymus Geyer of Northhamptonshire entertain, that he bought $24 in 6%'s and $12 in Deferreds every year from 1791 to 1795? Who was Henry Houston of London who bought $11 in Deferreds and $20 in 3%'s in 1794, and who followed it with another $11 in Deferreds the next year? Was one Samuel Engles, a carpenter of Southwark, abiding by some "puritan ethic" as he systematically invested, every year from

1791 through 1795, $3 in 6%'s, $3 in 3%'s, and $2 in Deferreds?

Revenue derived from duties on imports into the United States, the great balance of which came from Britain, was of fundamental importance to Hamilton's plan of federal finance. So, however, was British capital invested in the national debt. Little wonder that Washington's secretary of the treasury and his friends strove mightily to stave off attempts by their political enemies to destroy the very basis upon which the political system ultimately depended! Considered from the British view, the very act of investing, the large amounts committed, and the character of the individual investors served first as a testimonial of faith in the government of the United States, and second as an additional motive for an amicable settlement of differences between the two countries.

A certain degree of co-operation, considerable enough to cause anguish to British consular officials in the United States, developed, too, between Britons and Americans trading to the Far East. American voyages to the Orient began soon after the war, encouraged by the natural adventurousness of American seamen and the exclusion of their vessels from the British West Indian carrying trade. As early as 1783, Robert Morris of Philadelphia sent out ships to China, seeking a trade unhampered by British and French restrictions. From this beginning, the traffic increased rapidly. In 1785, the very first report from Consul-General Temple in New York mentioned a 400-ton vessel fitting out there for the China trade. The Briton took some comfort from the scarcity of specie in the country, which he believed would make the voyage unprofitable; but less than a month later he reported two more merchantmen fitting out at Philadelphia. Trouble was clearly ahead, he predicted, for the British East India Company. A year later, another agent sent word of the arrival of the American *Empress of China* in New York from Canton; her cargo was so rich that Boston and New York merchants were immediately inspired to send out three more vessels.[6]

By the time Phineas Bond arrived at Philadelphia, the trade was flourishing and growing daily. The new consul was worried from the outset, and over the next few years' he repeatedly expressed to his home government a deeply-held fear: the United States would find herself capable, if Britain did not take preventative measures, of successful competition for the European market in Far Eastern produce. It was natural, he held, that the Americans would seek to replace trade lost in the West Indies; but there was danger in this for the former mother country, her revenue, and her commerce, and it was growing in direct proportion to the former colonists' penetration of the Far Eastern market. From his personal knowledge, he wrote in July, 1787, he could list some twenty American merchantmen from Salem, Boston, New York, and Philadelphia, plying the trade and bringing back to the States cargoes of tea, cassia, silk, pepper, china, and similar items. It was but little consolation that the margin of their profit was very small. (The quality of the imports, especially tea, was as yet too low to command a respectable market.) Efforts were going forward despite the many difficulties of distance, capital, and poor return. A new 300-400-ton vessel was on the stocks at Philadelphia at that very moment; and a newly completed one, the largest ever built in North America, comparable in size to a 50-gun ship-of-the-line, had just sailed. A spate of recent arrivals was spurring further American initiative.

What gave the greatest alarm, however, was the role of British merchants, agents, and factors who habitually provided "considerable Credit, and made great Advances" to men who should have been viewed as dangerous competitors. Ships were purchased and outfitted, cargoes supplied, "the means of Remittance" furnished, in what were to all intents and purposes partnerships between profit-hungry Britons and American adventurers. At the end of 1787, the new 320-ton *Asia* (Captain Barry) and two other American merchantmen sailed for the Far East, laden with ginsing, rum and other spirits, and British goods suitable for the Chinese market, all supplied by "the too liberal Faith of British Merchants" who gave the Americans the chance of "speculating and sporting with the Property of their Creditors and screening themselves under a most relaxed System of Laws." Even from India, the strict preserve of the East India Company, came news that American vessels found a friendly reception there. An indignant Bond told London in the summer of 1789 that the *Chesapeake* arrived at Amboy with a cargo from Madras and Bombay, and that its Captain O'Donnell reportedly spoke "in Terms of high respect of the civil Treatment he received while he lay in the Ganges." Somewhat later, the *Morning Chronicle* of July 29, 1791, expressed its fear that within a few more years the Americans would "materially affect the interests of the India Company." Their merchants could already, it was said, undersell British tea by 20 per cent.

The danger of open competition in purveying Far Eastern goods to the European market was compounded with the known propensity of the Americans for smuggling. Some illicit trade went north to Canada, but the major markets for American smugglers were the British West Indies and the Home Islands themselves. Late in the autumn of 1787, Bond raised the alarm. American tea was being smuggled into the West Indies in great quantity and, disguised as grain, would certainly appear shortly in Ireland and Britain. Several tea vessels were even then on the verge of sailing from Philadelphia. From the "complexion" of their owners, it was certain that their destination would be the British and Channel Isles. Sir John Temple talked in April, 1788, with a New York merchant engaged in the Far Eastern trade. The latter scouted the suggestion that American merchants would soon find their markets saturated with tea and other Eastern items; there were always England and Ireland, the New Yorker said, with what must have been viewed as great impudence. Only the previous October, he confided to His Majesty's consul-general, he had sent 250 chests of tea to Britain, where "they sold very well." In July, 1789, two merchantmen arrived in the United States from India. Despite great efforts to keep the nature of their cargoes secret, a furious British consul managed to discover that they consisted of Indian goods in such quantity that it "far surpasses the ordinary Consumption of the Inhabitants." It was "very clear that a Vent is found to Europe, as well as to the West India Islands, for whatever articles do not command a ready sale here."

Bond repeatedly pled for government action against the American participants in the trade and the British capitalists who aided them: there should be an "early check or Restraint" administered, "either by thwarting their Credit, or by withholding the Articles suited to their Commerce." Britain had, he argued, the means at her disposal to achieve the purpose; and if employed, the Americans "would never rally." Returning to the attack at a later date, he called again for a "very little matter of check," which was all that was required to disorganize and destroy a trade which, though not yet fully established, was full of the most pernicious implications for Great Britain.[8]

Bond's advice went unheeded. Carmarthen ordered consular officials in the United States to observe and report upon American participation in the Far Eastern trade; but beyond that, the British government declined to act.[9] The "very little matter of check," so urgently requested, was not administered. Several reasons may be adduced to explain the apparently passive official acquiescence. The French had granted the Americans freedom of the Ile de France (Mauritius), a factor which might well have made the island an entrepôt of American trade to the Far East, had British policy borne too harshly. Secondly, the area involved was so vast that Britain, even if she desired, could not exclude determined Americans from it. In any event, American profits would tend to center in Britain in the form of remittances. Further, ambitious Yankee merchantmen engaged in the Far East would be less inclined to agitate incessantly for a portion of the West Indian carrying trade. After the official attitude is explained, however, the fact remains that British merchants were co-operating with Americans in a remote but growing and mutually profitable trade, and that this was happening with the knowledge of the British government.

Fear that the Americans would engage in smuggling Far Eastern produce was but a small part of a vaster concern. A great, subterranean network of smuggling, collusion, clandestine partnerships, and other illicit practices developed, infuriating the British government, but constituting a source of mutual profit to many Britons and Americans. Despite frequent countermeasures by the London authorities, the network remained intact, complacently regarded by the American government, and even flourished until the outbreak of the French revolutionary wars. It would be wrong to conclude, as some have done, that the British system by law established was a failure; the data presented in the great Report of January, 1791, is sufficient to prove the contrary. Furthermore, hard facts, particularly quantitative ones, about illegal transactions are understandably difficult to come by. It is beyond question, however, that illicit practices, involving a high degree of private Anglo-American co-operation, were widespread. Their ultimate importance lies not so much in the light they shed on the inefficiency of British law as in the development of a pattern of commercial intercourse, which survived even the outbreak of the Anglo-French war in 1793.

There were two general types of illegal activities involving American and British participants: the first consisted of offenses against the Navigation Act; the second, of smuggling and related practices. The first task for imperial administrators at the end of the

American War was simply to find some means to distinguish American vessels from British. The former still possessed their old, prewar registers, and could therefore enter imperial ports with a pretense of legality. It was doubly easy if the customs officer was compliant. Some enterprising captains, taking advantage of the administrative confusion prevailing in the months after the war, were actually allowed by friendly officials in imperial ports to trade their old registers for new British ones. Early in 1785, Home Secretary Sydney instructed the governors in the West Indies, where the offense was flagrant, to inquire into the matter and to give orders to their revenue officers to prevent such gross irregularities.[10] At best, success was limited. In April of the next year, Admiral Hughes, commanding in West Indian waters, reported from Barbadoes that the use of old, irregular, and false registers and papers was still very much in evidence. At the very moment of writing, he had two American vessels under seizure, each possessing two complete sets of documents, British and American. Two other American brigs were likewise clearly guilty of the same offense, but, although Hughes had reported them to the attorney-general of Grenada, that civil official, clearly unwilling to enforce the law, had declined to proceed in the matter. The Admiral's report was referred to Thomas Irving for his opinion. It was not long in coming. His shock was obvious: "The Subjects of the new States are become our Rivals not only in the Foreign European Settlements, but also in the Markets of our own Islands."[11]

When William Eden, preparing himself for commercial negotiations with France, ran across official data on the growth of British shipping in the West Indian carrying trade, he transmitted it jubilantly to Lord Sheffield as proof of the wisdom of excluding American vessels. "You must not be too much flattered by the appearance of so many British ships," the noble lord replied. "A great part of them are American with false Registers. The abuse in this respect is extreme."[12]

In due course, the Committee for Trade took up the question; the commissioners of the customs, when asked for their recommendations, called for a sweeping inspection of all vessels claiming the right to British registry and the issuing of new and fuller documents of identification. Administration should be tightened and a thorough study made of frauds practiced by foreign (i.e., American) ships.[13]

The Committee for Trade plunged further into its inquiry, but as it accumulated evidence, the problem broadened. Frauds in ships' papers there were in plenty; but equally if not more worrisome were illegalities in the building of British ships. Merchant James Anderson, resident of Boston from 1753 to 1775 and then of New York until the British evacuation, pointed urgently to the need for regulations to prevent Americans from "Building Vessels in the British Colonies for the purpose expressly of enjoying the Privileges of British Vessels." He himself favored prohibiting the importation of lumber and timber of any kind from the States into any British colony— an extreme measure—and preventing merchants of the kingdom from owning colonial-built ships beyond a certain low displacement. Lord Sheffield added his warning that Americans and colonials in the New World enjoyed certain advantages over Britain in the building of ships; among these were lower costs of materials, the profit from a first cargo brought from the West Indies to Europe, and credit from British merchants for outfitting. The moment had come "for checking the mischief." Charles Jenkinson agreed. An effort to meet both problems—the use of fraudulent papers and violations of "British built" qualifications—was made in the Act for the Encouragement of Shipping and Navigation. While the balance of Jenkinson's speech introducing the bill to the House of Commons was couched in the highest optimism about British navigation generally, he took the occasion to warn that illicit practices had grown so great that they demanded stricter attention. Vessels as small as fifteen tons, for example, would from then on be required to carry a full set of documents; and new ones were to be issued to all British ships forthwith.[14]

British consular officials greeted the stricter regulations with enthusiasm. "There can be no better Test, my Lord," Bond wrote to Carmarthen from the United States early in 1787, "of the Importance of the new Act, and its Tendency to increase the carrying Trade of Great Britain, as far as it respects this Country, than the alarm and Perplexity it has occasioned here." The practice of providing double papers to American ships, "an ingenious Collusion between Partners in Trade, residing in different Countries," whereby ships enjoyed the advantages both of British bottoms in British ports and of American bottoms in American ones, had been "very successfully managed" hitherto. Now, he expected, the iniquity would be checked. In fact, Bond was disappointed. Months later, the new legislation notwithstanding, the Philadelphia consul was still complaining of "the Stratagems used by the Inhabitants of the United States" to elude it. He was especially perturbed at "the prevailing Practice of joint Concerns in Vessels entitled to the Privileges of British Bottoms, which, by the Connivance of British Houses, affords American Traders the Benefit of participating in those Advantages, which the Act of Navigation means to confine to British subjects alone." Wrathful against the "many cases" of joint ownership, he was apprehensive that "as long as oaths are treated with so much Levity, it may be difficult to contrive a Remedy to meet the Mischief."[15] From the anonymous British agent, "P. Allaire," or "P. Arlington," as he sometimes signed himself, also came confirmation of continuing infractions. "We are the Compleatest and most Enterprising Merchants this side the Equator," he wrote to Sir George Yonge from New York.

No Laws you can pass, or the severest restrictions you can Establish, can restrain us. We have now British Ships, British Registers, British Certificates, British oaths authenticated with British Seals, British Subjects with Certificates of their Births, British Mediterranean Passes, and Names on their Sterns, and Neither Vessell or Crew was ever to the northward of Nantucket.

He admitted himself to be part-owner of two such vessels trading from New York to the British West Indies.[16]

To forged and fraudulent ship papers, false claims to British registry, and joint ownerships must be added a further ingenious practice. British and colonial vessels were allowed under British law to receive minor emergency repairs in American ports. By 1789, a fully developed system was in evidence: British vessels, by receiving carefully planned "repairs" on consecutive voyages, were being virtually rebuilt in a relatively short time with cheap American parts. An enterprising owner of a vessel needing extensive repairs might send her to an American port with instructions to the master to declare her in a state of distress. Complete overhaul or extensive rebuilding would follow, with no law broken. The arrangement could be adapted in an infinite variety of ways, as harassed British officials knew to their chagrin and frustration. In April, 1789, for example, Lieutenant-Governor Parr of Nova Scotia informed Secretary Sydney that a merchant of the province had asked to register a brigantine; Parr knew that the vessel was built largely with timber taken from a ship owned by a citizen of the United States. The particular instance was, perhaps, not of signal importance, but the Governor feared encouraging another, more serious evil: he was "well aware that Frames of Vessels may easily be transported into the said Province from any of the neighbouring States, and that thereby they may in a great measure become our Ship Builders." He took the opinion of his law officers, who reported in favor of issuing the certificate of registry. Parr did so; but he was clearly uneasy. Anticipating similar cases, he requested specific instructions from the home government.

The Committee for Trade referred Parr's communication to the commissioners of the customs. A report was forthcoming on July 7, 1789; and, as a result, the Act for the Increase and Encouragement of Shipping was amended to specify that British ships be built of "legal" parts, produced in British dominions or imported legally in a raw and unmanufactured state from foreign countries.[17] Parr himself, however, had put his finger on the fatal flaw in the plan. Geographical proximity made it far too easy for parts to be carried into his and other provinces, where they were, of course, received and put to use by subjects of His Majesty interested more in turning a profit than in abiding passively by the Act of Navigation.

When Congress passed the Tonnage Act, discriminating against not merely British but all foreign vessels, certain British shipbuilders and merchants, wishing to cirmcumvent the new tax, began to build vessels in the United States. For once, the cold, impersonal façade of Hawkesbury, the bureaucrat, gave way. He expressed his rage to his Liverpool friend, Wilckens: any measure should be adopted, he fumed, "to prevent this Mischief and to punish severely those who have so little sense of the Duty they Owe to their Country." Part of Hawkesbury's anger came, however, from a sense of impotence. It would be, he admitted, "very difficult to apply any adequate Remedy to it."[18]

Another matter of great concern to the British government was the informality with which American vessels in British ports observed the Navigation Act's stipulation that ships be legally navigated. The law required that the master and three-quarters of his crew be of the nationality of the vessel; but violations were so frequent that a special Order in Council of March 19, 1788, pointedly applied the provision to American vessels. A flood of evidence indicated, however, that to speak the law and to enforce it were two widely separated functions. In 1788, for example, Edward Burrow, the customs officer at Glasgow, reported to Hawkesbury that he had seized the American ship *Jenney*, guilty of a sensational list of infractions, including the composition of her crew: seven Americans and four Britons. The laws of mathematics proved the delinquency. The master had pled ignorance, but this was an untenable defense. Burrow's brother, collector at Liverpool, made similar seizures; and Henry Wilckens, of that city, told Hawkesbury early in 1790, from his personal knowledge, that four American vessels had recently called at London and had remained unmolested there although the master and "every man on board" was British. Nor did the evil exist merely in London, he said: it was also "every where else." Phineas Bond, conscientious in this as in every duty, confirmed from America that vast numbers of British subjects had become mariners aboard American vessels—a fact not altogether irrelevant to the vexing impressment issue which arose after the outbreak of the Anglo-French wars.[19]

Ministerial annoyance in Britain was intensified by the knowledge that Americans regularly enticed British seamen to desert to their service. Hawkesbury was furious about the "Methods which the Americans pursue" in filling their rising need for trained seamen as their foreign trade expanded. To protect and foster "nurseries of seamen" was all very well, good, and necessary, but to what purpose, Lord Hawkesbury must have asked himself, if the children supported a wicked foster-mother? A strict implementation of the law was ordered. Collectors at all British ports were bound, he said, to "be very vigilant" in discharging their duty in this respect. Tightening regulations caused some discomfort. The Americans complained, Wilckens proudly told Hawkesbury, that they were "no where so scrutinized upon" as at Liverpool. At home, they delivered "very severe strictures" upon the treatment meted out to them by examining British customs officers. Try as he would, however, Hawkesbury could but admit his fear that "this Evil is also without remedy."[20] The attempt to find one was destined to contribute to the outbreak of the War of 1812.

In the great debate of 1783 and 1784 over the exclusion of American vessels from the sugar islands, West Indians warned that the measure would produce large-scale smuggling. Hints were even dropped that they themselves would actively co-operate with illicit traders. Events proved their candor.

The execution of the Order in Council of July 2, 1783, did not follow immediately upon its promulgation. The distances were great and the opportunities for misunderstanding, wilful or otherwise, even greater. The trade the order intended to stop was ancient, firmly established, and enormous. The sheer physical problem of enforcement was difficult under the best of circumstances. Under the worst, such as prevailed in the islands, it proved impossible to destroy effectively American trade to the British West Indies.

An example is furnished by young Horatio Nelson, captain of His Majesty's Ship *Boreas*, who arrived in West Indian waters in June, 1784, to join the squadron of Admiral Sir Richard Hughes. His experiences on that station were so shocking and personally infuriating that he made them the subject of a narrative account, a formal memorial to the King, and repeated remonstrances, written and verbal, which approached insubordination to his commanding officer. At Barbadoes almost a year after the Order in Council of July, 1783, he "very soon found that the Bay was full of Americans, who were lading and unlading without molestation."[21] It was too much for the future victor at Trafalgar. Eloquent in support of the navigation system, the source of his country's wealth and safety, he harangued his fellow captains in favor of stricter measures against the erstwhile rebels. The answer which was returned—that the Admiral had given no orders to prevent the entry of American vessels—might have stopped a lesser man. Not Nelson. In an interview with the Admiral himself, the young officer reported the frequent irregularities he had witnessed. Hughes, dashing youthful heat with cold water, "seemed not to take any notice of it other than saying, he believed it was the case in all the islands."

Sir Richard himself was without orders on the subject, a point he made to Nelson's brother captains, who were also troubled by the Admiral's inactivity in defending the navigation system. To one of them, Captain (and future Admiral) Collingwood, Hughes repeated what he had said earlier: the reception of American vessels was common throughout the West Indies, and he did not choose to interfere with it since he lacked instructions from the Admiralty.

When Hughes issued orders to his captains in November, 1784, nothing was said about the American foreigners trading to the islands. The omission led Nelson and Collingwood to pay a call on the Admiral. With difficulty—the two captains had to find and present to Hughes a copy of the Navigation Act, which he said he had "never seen or noticed before"—Hughes was persuaded finally to issue orders, dated November 12, to prevent illicit American trade; American vessels seeking to enter British West Indian ports were to be turned back.

The young captains immediately fell to work with a will, turning back American vessels at Barbadoes, Montserrat, Nevis, and St. Kitt's; but they could not be at all times in all places. Collingwood admitted to Nelson that the minute after he left a port, "the Customs-house allowed them to fill again . . . and the Americans were always very compliant in furnishing whatever the rules of office required at the expense of any number and sort of oaths that were wished for." Here was the telling weakness of the system: no manner of strict enforcement by naval authorities could prevail in the face of collusion between the islanders and the Americans. Hughes, probably again under pressure from his zealous subordinate, issued additional orders on December 29, 1784. American ships illegally present in West Indian ports were to be detained, unless in genuine distress, until the local governor could be informed. If that official or his representative should think it proper to allow the entry, however, the Royal Navy was not to interfere. Young Nelson was furious. Early in the new year, he wrote—"lectured" may be a better word— the Admiral. Dependence could not be put in the governors, he said; they would be imposed upon by Americans willing to swear "through everything (even, as the sea-phrase is, 'through a nine-inch plank')." According to his own testimony, he went on to say that so long as he had the honor to command an English man-of-war, he would never be subservient to any governor nor co-operate with him in illegal proceedings: supremely confident, he told Hughes, "I know the Navigation Laws." Any response the Admiral may have made has not survived; but neither were stronger measures forthcoming. Presently, Nelson, sailing very close to the wind, took matters into his own hands, issuing a declaration that after May 1, 1785, he would seize law-breaking Americans. On May 2, against the warnings of customs officials in the islands, he made his first capture, the American schooner *Eclipse*, fraudulently registered at St. Kitt's, although built and owned in Philadelphia and crewed by Americans only. Two weeks later, Nelson found himself explaining to an island judge the basis for his action. The proceedings were annoying and time-consuming, but the ruling was in his favor. His right as a Royal Navy captain to make legal seizures was affirmed in the face of contradictory assertions by the officers of the customs, who claimed it pertained only to themselves to order seizures.

Nelson continued his captures, much to the irritation of the Admiral, who told him bluntly that he would "get into a scrape." In fact, at the end of May, the zealous captain found himself sued at Nevis for £4,000 damages; and a subscription was set on foot throughout the islands to defray the cost of prosecuting him. For several weeks he kept to his ship, knowing full well that he would be arrested the minute he set foot ashore. In the autumn, Secretary Sydney finally sent out instructions—but only that Nelson should be defended by Crown lawyers if he were indeed prosecuted at Nevis. An additional humiliation was reserved for the Captain. When praise —for the "very commendable zeal in endeavouring to put a stop to the illicit practices which were carrying on in the islands, in open violation of the law, and to the great detriment of the navigation and trade of his Majesty's dominions"—was finally handed out by the Treasury Board in London, it went to Hughes!

It was the widespread collusion between interloper and islander which put it quite beyond the British Navy's power to exclude the Americans as the order of July 2, 1783, required. American vessels would not have been in West Indian ports had not the authorities there allowed them to enter and do business. Hence Nelson's contemptuous criticism of Hughes's ineffectual orders of December 29, 1784. "The Custom-houses seemed to glory in the ruin they were heaping upon Great Britain," he wrote of this time at a later date, "and seemed to think they were beyond the reach of power, for they minded nothing if the [American] men would but swear official oaths." Failing to find satisfaction with the easygoing Admiral, he wrote to Sydney himself, telling the Home Secretary that the law was "most shamefully evaded, by connivance in some and indisposition in others, of the officers of the customs; so that nearly the whole trade, between the British Colonies and the United States of America, was carried on in American bottoms."

Hughes, too, in his dispatch from Barbadoes on April 2, 1786, reported the existence of collusion. The attorney-general of Granada had been told about two American brigs clearly in possession of irregular papers; but the civil official had declined to proceed in the matter. The Admiral mentioned also the case of an American vessel illegally admitted to entry at Antigua by the customs officer there. The vessel had been seized by one of his captains, and the proceedings which followed brought to light iniquity in plenty: American vessels were commonly allowed to enter port, but not to deliver their cargoes there. They were free, however, to find a purchaser and to arrange a rendezvous with him, usually at St. Eustatia, the Dutch island not far away. A transfer of cargo took place there, and the produce entered duty-free, "legally" imported in British bottoms. In case of seizures by naval officers, Hughes also confirmed, the law officers in the islands harassed and impeded them in every way possible; and if a legal opinion was requested, outrageous fees were charged. Thomas Irving, to whom Hughes's dispatch had been referred, was bitter against "the want of energy in the executive Government, and a general disposition of all Classes in the West Indies to favour an illegal intercourse with the American States."

Even conscientious customs officials could not, however, insure due observance of the law. Gilbert Franklyn, collector at Jamaica, and his subordinate, the comptroller, Jonathan Dawson, found themselves the objects of the Assembly's wrath because of their efforts to enforce the navigation system. By an act of 1725, foreign vessels in distress were allowed to enter Jamaican ports for repairs and to pay with a portion of their cargo. It was, of course, a standing invitation to American ships "in distress."[22] When Franklyn and Dawson tried to interfere by boarding, searching, and seizing, they found that "those on board have only to state that they came in for water, or any frivolous pretence, and the goods will be deemed not Imported, and acquitted by a Jury." The unhappy pair presently found the fees of their office diminished by the Assembly and a sizable tax levied upon them—£50 for the Collector and £20 for the Comptroller. Dawson and his son were even set upon and injured in the line of duty by an irate mob. The triumph of the unjust was complete: the assailants were acquitted by a Kingston jury, and the chief justice himself declared that officers of the customs had no right to enter houses or warehouses or to seize and carry away goods. Seizures virtually ceased in the island. Dawson, nursing his wounds and grimly reflecting upon the depravity of man, reported home: his well-meaning efforts had raised

much Clamor . . . amongst the advocates for an open and unlimited intercourse with America, who I am sorry to say are very numerous, and many of them of the first distinction here. A combination has been enter'd into, and a subscription raised for the purpose of supporting suits at Law, against any officer who shall dare in future to make such seizures.[23]

These several specific episodes point to the development and growth of a formidable indirect trade between the United States and the British islands via the foreign West Indies. Jenkinson's Act of 1786, which ended, or should have ended, all confusion about registry, ships' papers, and penalties for vessels trading illicitly in imperial waters, actually encouraged the traffic. Governor Lincoln of St. Vincents described it in its early stages of development: American vessels brought their produce to the foreign islands, exchanging it there for British island produce, which had been legally transported to that point by the British planters themselves in small ships navigated according to law. American produce was thus imported into the British islands quite legally.

From many other sources, including Admiral Hughes's dispatch of April 2, 1786, similar information poured in. By July, 1786, Grey Elliot, solicitor to the customs in London, had studied the evidence in detail and was alarmed. "I am concerned to find," he wrote to Hawkesbury, "that the Illicit Trade thru St. Eustatius is carried on to an extent, which I could not have conceived." British vessels, possessing the right to import the "growth and produce" of foreign plantations, were bringing in flour, bread, lumber, horses, oxen, corn, and peas, articles which quite plainly could "never be allowed the Growth and produce of Saint Eustatius." A "Vile Practice" was afoot, and it called for remedy.[24] The long-suffering Jonathan Dawson in Jamaica added his account. By introducing their produce into the British islands through foreign possessions, the Americans were "becoming nearly as much our carriers, to all intents and purposes, as they were before their separation from the British Empire." The Leeward Islands, in particular, he said, were "supplied almost entirely" from Martinique, Curaçao, and St. Eustatia. Until his own timely arrival, British officials in Jamaica had connived at such villainy, but, he fancied, he had put a stop to it—a claim which may explain much about the mob assault upon him. Dawson identified another center of illicit trade with the Americans: Turks Island in the Bahamas. The barren rock produced only salt, much of which was sold to the American fishing vessels, a traffic in itself illegal. It was a minor transgression, however, compared with the heavy traffic of British vessels clearing from Jamaica for Turks Island and returning laden with American goods duly certified by the superintendent of the customs at Turks Island as legally imported![25]

The Committee for Trade decided that action was necessary. Early in 1787, about to advise renewal of the act authorizing the King in Council to regulate trade with the United States, they asked the law officers of the Crown to recommend "what measure it may be proper to adopt to prevent the Importation of any Articles from the Foreign West India Islands into the British Islands, which are not the produce of such Foreign Islands."

Even as they awaited the report, however, the committee received new evidence of the iniquitous trade. There was, in fact, no law to prevent it. Subsequently, when the regulatory act was renewed, it included certain alterations. Henceforth, the importation of flour, bread, and provisions from foreign islands into the British West Indies was to be forbidden.[26]

The West Indians in London and the merchants trading to the islands presented an interesting argument against the immediate implementation of the new prohibition. A sudden enforcement, they said, would create widespread suffering in the British islands—surely an admission of the importance of American foodstuffs received in the circuitous trade. British officials were not unsympathetic: governors were to be reminded of their discretionary authority to open their ports, if the need arose, until the following October.[27]

The tightening of regulations notwithstanding, hurricanes still occurred, island assemblies and juries remained disdainful of the finer points of British navigation regulations, and collusive officers in the customs and civil administrations continued to hold their posts. Illicit American trade to the British West Indies flourished—to the vexation of the London authorities. In 1788, the Foreign Secretary asked Phineas Bond to concert measures with the West India governors to put it down; but the object was never accomplished.[28]

Illicit American trade was not vital to the British sugar islands; they had access, after all, to American produce carried in British bottoms. Nevertheless, a considerable portion of the old pattern of commerce was kept alive by administrative confusion, clashing claims to authority, and collusion involving populace, civil officials, and assemblies in the islands on the one hand and, on the other, American interlopers. While it would be incorrect to conclude that the navigation system as by law established had failed—appeal may be made once more to the Report of January, 1791, as proof of its essential success—still, the evidence points to more than casual violations. At the least, one may speak of a community of interests in the area surviving the disruption of the first British Empire and binding many Americans and Britons, often in direct conflict with official policy, in covert alliance.

In British North America illicit commerce never achieved the volume which characterized it in the sugar islands, for several reasons: the relative freedom of overland trade between the United States and Canada; the massive, convenient, and perfectly legal importations of American produce; and the smaller population in the northern colonies. Nevertheless, in 1786 Thomas Irving, as might have been predicted, saw it as an enormity which demanded extraordinary measures to suppress; and he demanded of the Committee for Trade the strictest implementation of laws against illegal fishing and trading by the Americans at Nova Scotia.[29] Lieutenant-Governor Parr of Nova Scotia had fears about the importation from the United States of frames for the construction of "British" vessels, a point duly settled in an amendment of Jenkinson's Act; and Collector Ainslie, at Quebec, mentioned in 1789 a certain trivial contraband trade from America in East India produce, which he believed could be readily put down with the appointment of a few more customs officers. When specific cases of illegal trading arose, speedy action was usually forthcoming. In August, 1787, for example, the Committee for Trade crisply rejected the petition from one Patrick McMaster and his brothers for permission to import into Nova Scotia goods from the United States taken in payment for prewar debts. There is, too, some evidence of collusion: for example, the judge of vice admiralty at Newfoundland in 1786 was found to be too free with issuing licenses for importing American provisions. Some years later, with crops better in Canada, a group of Newfoundland merchants petitioned the governor, Sir Richard King, to take action against the merchants of Nova Scotia and New Brunswick who were obtaining illegal entry into the provisions trade to the United States. Someone was supplying fraudulent clearances.[30] In general, however, these were trivial concerns for the London government.

A much greater worry was the smuggling of tobacco into the

British Isles themselves, in spite of the relatively favorable treatment given the American weed (an attempt, of course, to keep the entrepôt in Britain). Foreign tobacco paid 3/6d. the pound upon entry; American, 1/3d. Even so, the duty paid on the latter was still about five times the cost. With a tax so great—as Minister John Adams wrote to Jefferson from London—smuggling was bound to occur. If only one pound in five got safely past the vigilance of the customs officers, the smugglers broke even; two pounds in five would yield a handsome profit. Fully two-thirds of the tobacco consumed in England, Adams believed, was smuggled. His estimate did not differ too greatly from Hawkesbury's own a few years later. Sometime early in 1790, the president of the Committee for Trade jotted down a memorandum for himself: "It appears that only 6,000,000 lbs. of Tobacco pay Duty and that the consumption is between 14,000,000 lbs. and 16,000,000." Well might he add a reminder "To get the more recent American Dispatches that are in curculation." Phineas Bond, who made it a special object to scrutinize tobacco exports from Philadelphia, estimated that in 1784 some 5,200 hogsheads had gone illegally from that single port to Ireland alone; and in 1785, 4,700. The duty which should have come to the British Treasury amounted, for the two years, to about £550,000. The fraud was, as Bond exclaimed to Under-Secretary Fraser, enormous.[31]

Watchful British customs officials have provided much information about the organization of the trade and, with it, voluminous evidence that not every smuggler made the handsome profit Adams mentioned. Until 1787, when the Irish Parliament passed a Navigation Act essentially the same as the British (to the jubilation and relief of Lord Hawkesbury), Ireland was the smuggler's chief terminal on the eastern side of the Atlantic.[32] Afterward, the Channel Islands came into their own. Illicit and clandestine traders preferred the winter, when days were short, the weather bad, the ocean gray and forbidding, while revenue officers chose the comforts of hearth and kettle over their duty on sea and shore. What Bond called the "old trick of double papers" was used by the master of the vessel carrying illegal tobacco. One set, for use in clearing out from American ports, showed the real cargo; the other, for use as required, recorded a small amount of tobacco aboard or even none at all. During the voyage, the hogsheads were cut into quarters and bound up by ropes, to be slung over the backs of horses and quickly carried away upon the surreptitious landing. Tobacco smuggling was so "reduced to a system," Bond reported, that it was common to insure the safe landing of the illicit cargo duty free.

Bond, who urged the government to appoint special agents in American ports to watch tobacco shipments, kept a close and constant watch himself. In June, 1787, for example, he reported to Under-Secretary Fraser the case of the American ship *Ann*, which had sailed from New York the preceding winter for Londonderry. On her departure she had, to his knowledge, 150 hogsheads of tobacco aboard. When she arrived at her destination, however, "she appeared to have nothing on board but a freight of Staves." It was a warning to be vigilant in case the vessel reappeared. Another ship, the *Penelope*, was even then en route to Londonderry, also bent on nefarious proceedings.[33]

In due course, customs officials caught up with the *Penelope*. Consigned to McLaughlin and Co. of Londonderry, she arrived on July 1, 1787. Upon inspection, her cargo was discovered to contain 132 hogsheads of tobacco not listed on the manifest; the master declared they were destined for Ostend. Despite the highly suspicious circumstance that twelve hogsheads were already cut in quarters and bound with ropes, the customs officials allowed the vessel to depart. Perhaps they were hoping to catch her red-handed, for she was kept under close surveillance. Nine days after she cleared Londonderry, she was finally arrested, hovering off the Irish coast obviously seeking an opportunity to land her illegal tobacco.[34]

Other smugglers met similar fates. Edward Burrow, the Glasgow collector, seizing the *Jenney* because she was improperly navigated, was shocked to find aboard thirty North Carolina hogsheads for which there was not a shred of a manifest. The tobacco was accordingly subjected to penalty. Burrow's zealous brother at Liverpool took more drastic measures with the weed taken from two American ships in his port: he burned it.[35]

Despite sporadic—even frequent—seizures, however, an enormous quantity of smuggled tobacco got through, as Hawkesbury's own estimate indicates. In 1792, the British government attempted to act. In January of that year, Foreign Secretary Grenville advised British representatives abroad that, "Considerable Inconvenience having arisen from the Importation of Tobacco in Foreign Vessels into the Ports of his Majesty's Dominions contrary to . . . the Navigation Act," the Act would be strictly enforced in the future.[36] He was referring to smuggling, not legitimate trade; but the circular letter was badly drafted and ambiguous, making possible an alarming construction—that the whole system of Anglo-American trade, regulated by Act of Parliament and Order in Council, was overturned and that United States produce, including tobacco, was placed forthwith on a footing with less favored nations.

George Hammond, in Philadelphia, saw at once what interpretation was likely to be put upon Grenville's letter by Americans, especially those already disposed to discriminate against British commerce. Not without a qualm, he decided to withhold the contents of the circular from the American government, pending clarification from London. But Sir John Temple forced his hand. The Consul-General at New York, to whom a copy of the letter had been sent, officiously and without prior consultation published the document in the newspapers of the city. Hammond, furious, wrote home of the "universal alarm and commotion" in the United States, far exceeding "all the apprehensions I had formed." Further delay impossible, the British envoy sought out Jefferson on April 11, 1792. The Secretary of State was gruff and menacing; Hammond, soothing. It was his private opinion that no general change of policy was intended; only tobacco was mentioned, and even in this single item the object was only to end the countless frauds practiced by American vessels. His explanation was accepted, and the tempest subsided. A rather embarrassed Grenville sent Hammond his approbation,[37] and the tobacco smuggler and his British correspondent continued their activities, exploiting for mutual profit their own form of the community of interests.

PART V

The Hammond Mission

CHAPTER TWELVE

Collision with Secretary Jefferson

WHEN GEORGE HAMMOND, minister plenipotentiary from George III, arrived in Philadelphia in October, 1791, chances for the success of his mission seemed fair. The near brush with commercial retaliation in Congress and the considerable anti-British sentiment among the Jeffersonians were troubling; but the mutual interests calling for a settlement of differences between the two countries were numerous and, in the eyes of many important Britons and Americans, compelling. Further, a new spirit of conciliation was in evidence. American complaints at the impressment of seamen during the Nootka crisis met with speedy satisfaction; and Secretary Hamilton showed "Candor and Liberality" by mitigating or even remitting penalties incurred by British vessels violating the American Tonnage Act.[1] George Hammond's mere presence in the American capital exercised a calming influence. Awaiting the formal presentation of his credentials, he expressed gratitude for his friendly reception in the United States: "As far as I have hitherto been able to learn," he wrote home, "a majority of the leading characters in the country is not only well inclined, but solicitous, to promote a good understanding between Great Britain and America." Secretary Jefferson himself gave assurances that the British ministerial appointment would be reciprocated; and when Hammond had his "audience" with President Washington on November 11, he was treated with the "utmost politeness and respect."[2]

Blossoming optimism was presently blasted by Jeffersonian frost. The Secretary's doubts and suspicions about Hammond and his government soon became all too obvious. His decision to confine communication with the envoy to the written word seemed at the least to court protracted and laborious negotiations—at the worst, to cast serious aspersions on British motives and good faith. The implications of this altogether unusual method of diplomacy were not lost on George Hammond.[3]

Jefferson quickly seized the initiative. Writing to the envoy on November 29, he acknowledged Hammond's appointment as a "friendly movement" of the British government, but he went on to demand immediately "explanations of the intentions of your court" toward the northwestern posts. The conclusion contained an oblique threat and a leading question: "With respect to the Commerce of the two Countries, we have supposed that we saw in several instances, regulations on the part of your government, which if reciprocally adopted, would naturally injure the interests of both nations." He would beg to be informed "whether you are authorized to conclude, or to negotiate arrangements with us, which may fix the Commerce of the two Countries on principles of reciprocal advantage."[4]

Hammond replied the very next day. In courteous and conciliatory language, he set out his country's general position: the retention of the posts was a consequence of American violations of the peace. "These two objects," he wrote, "are, therefore, so materially connected with each other, as not to admit of separation, either in the mode of discussing them, or in any subsequent arrangements, which may result from the discussion." Confident of meeting a similar disposition in the United States, he and his government desired to remove "every ground and occasion of misunderstanding." Hammond himself stood ready to discuss measures to implement the peace fully. As for commercial questions, George III was well disposed "to promote and facilitate" trade between the two nations, and his minister was authorized to negotiate an arrangement upon "principles of reciprocal benefit."[5]

Did Hammond mean, Jefferson asked in return, that he was not furnished with "any commission or express powers to arrange a treaty with us, or to make any specific propositions on the subject of commerce; but only to assure us that his Brittanic majesty is ready to concur with us in appointing persons, times and places for commencing such a negotiation?" If this were the case, Jefferson added with an air of innocence, "some steps on our part may be necessary in consequence of it."[6]

Hammond answered at once that he was fully authorized to negotiate a commercial accord, although he naturally could not himself conclude one.[7] Jefferson professed to be unsatisfied: Would the envoy please communicate his full powers to negotiate a commercial treaty as a preliminary to proceeding to that object?[8] Puzzled, Hammond appealed to his earlier statement and general plenipotentiary character; to Foreign Secretary Grenville, he expressed apprehension at Jefferson's "anxiety in urging this matter at the present juncture, and in proposing to me questions so pointed and categorical."[9]

Clearly, Jefferson intended to force the earliest possible discussion of the commercial issue. He had no faith in British intentions to negotiate seriously; and he was well aware of the contents of Hawkesbury's Committee for Trade Report made in January, 1791, with its apparent veto on American admission to the British West Indies. Besides, the Secretary of State was eagerly awaiting new and liberal trade proposals from a France just beginning to find her soul in revolution. What a splendid opportunity, he must have reasoned, to confront French friendship for his country with British hostility, if only he could smoke out the fatal admission from Hammond.[10]

Hammond, however, refused to be drawn. Jefferson perforce shifted his ground; but the initial encounter and the method in which it was conducted had already inflicted irreparable damage to the personal relationship between the two men. Hammond henceforth gravitated toward Alexander Hamilton, Jefferson's political enemy, whom he had met before and had come to like.[11]

On December 15, Jefferson gave up the futile wrangle over Hammond's commercial powers, setting out instead a systematic indictment of Britain for her infractions of the peace treaty: the retention of the posts, the consequent exclusion of Americans from the fur trade, and the abduction of the slaves.[12] Hammond had been preparing for the event ever since his arrival in Philadelphia, and both he and Phineas Bond had worked hard to collect the fullest and most recent information available.[13] It was a lengthy process, however, and the British rejoinder—citing ninety-four specific acts of state legislatures and courts in violation of the peace—was not ready until early March, 1792.[14]

In the interim, Hammond sought Hamilton out for "a loose and general discussion." The Treasury Secretary, commenting freely on his cabinet colleague's bill of particulars against Britain, was obvious ly sanguine about a settlement. He foresaw difficulties only over the posts. When Hammond described the nature of the countercharges he had leveled at Jefferson, Hamilton readily "admitted their magnitude," excusing them only on the ground of the inefficiency of the former Confederation government. The new federal courts, he promised, would soon see to the performance of American obligations under the treaty. When the Briton asked about "equivalent Compensation" in cases of irrecoverable debts, the American stated his belief that his government would agree to any reasonable proposal on the subject, but said he frankly doubted one could be devised.

Hamilton then turned to the sensitive commercial question. Well aware of the near success of Madison's discriminatory propositions during the last session of Congress and anticipating renewed efforts failing a settlement with Britain, he urged Hammond to consider the benefits which a new and sound commercial agreement would bestow on both countries. Let Britain, he argued "with much force and emphasis," admit America to "a small participation in the carrying trade with the West Indies." Restrictions on size and tonnage of vessels would be both understandable and acceptable. Hammond listened carefully, but "studiously avoided dropping any hint" which might lead Hamilton to conclude that Great Britain "would ever consent to any modification" of her system.[15] There the commercial question was to rest, critically suspended, while Hammond's mission turned to other grave matters.

George Hammond's negotiations with Thomas Jefferson have been widely criticized to the former's disadvantage. His age—only twenty-eight when he began his mission—has been taken to prove the callowness and immaturity of his efforts against the American master diplomatist. Hammond's subsequent career has been held to show his essential mediocrity: he became a mere undersecretary of state. Twenty-eight is admittedly some little time from three score and ten; but Alexander Hamilton and James Madison, not to mention the prime minister of Great Britain, could scarcely be described as full of years and gray hairs. Hammond never became foreign secretary, to be sure, but this cannot derogate from his worth as a sound, hardworking, and accomplished sub-minister. Although after many months of great pressure and provocation the young man's temper slipped its leash and he lost his usefulness as an implement of British diplomacy in Philadelphia, on balance he acquitted himself well under exceedingly difficult circumstances. The envoy's communication to Jefferson of March 5, 1792, has been especially harshly treated; yet it must be objectively judged a carefully constructed, voluminously substantiated, well-reasoned document.[16] The language was modest and conciliatory, courting compromise: every effort had been made to secure accurate information, Hammond said, but possibly relevant material had been inadvertently overlooked or omitted. He knew of no errors or misrepresentations; but if any existed in his paper, they were totally unintended, and he would be eager to have them explained and corrected.

The argument was developed forcefully: contrasting American actions with British, Hammond pointed out that Parliament had never enacted regulations invalidating a national compact or interfering with "the sacred tenor" of engagements between individuals. Courts of law in Britain stood freely open to American citizens, and they dispensed equal protection and impartial justice to all who had recourse to them. It was only in consequence of American violations of the treaty that Britain had declined to fulfil Article VII completely. This, however, was "a mere suspension"; whereas the United States had "withheld from subjects of the crown that redress to which they were entitled, under the terms of the treaty," and in addition, even after the Peace, many states had passed new acts in violation of the treaty, imposing additional hardships on persons insured against and protected from future injury by the national faith of the United States "pledged under precise and solemn stipulations." Prewar debts and legal impediments, moreover, were not subject to the "recommend" provision in the treaty. Congress itself, in official pronouncements, had on more than one occasion admitted American infractions, the cause of irreparable injury and heavy expense to many British subjects.

While suspension of Article VII was therefore perfectly justifiable, Britain did not seek mere justification. She desired "to remove every occasion of misunderstanding"; and Hammond was ready "to enter into negotiation with respect to those articles of the treaty which have not been executed by the two countries, respectively." He was prepared "to consent to such arrangements upon the subject, as, after due examination, may now be found to be of mutual convenience, and not inconsistent with the just claims and rights" of British subjects.

A clearer, less contentious, more authoritative statement of the British position is impossible to imagine. Differences arising from the treaty of peace were grave and important, Hammond admitted; but all were negotiable, if only British desire for a settlement were met with a similar American disposition. Jefferson's reply, dated May 29, 1792, completely demolished such a possibility.

The American's tone was sharp, dogmatic, and uncompromising.[17] Wartime bitterness was recalled. Britain was guilty of prior infraction of the Peace, thus providing full justification for American breaches. If a settlement of differences were truly desired, Britain would have to accept American terms. The reply came close to being an ultimatum.

More specifically, Jefferson defined the exile of loyalists and confiscation of their property as legitimate acts of war; Article V was, in any event, merely recommendatory. Congress, therefore, stood discharged of its obligation, which the states "refused or complied, in a greater or less degree, according to circumstances, but more of them, and in a greater degree, than was expected." As for the debts, a discussion of them required, first, explanations of the earlier British offenses. The carrying away of the Negroes injured the United States by "withdrawing the cultivators of the soil, the produce of which was to pay the debts." The retention of the posts interfered with the establishment of peaceable relations with the Indians and deprived the country of its share in the fur trade. Britain's violations preceded and "*produced* the acts on our part complained of."

When one party broke a treaty, Jefferson continued, the other was then free to break it, either in whole or in part. Congress chose to make no use of its option. Certain individual states, however, decided to modify the provisions for recovering prewar debts. In 1787, Congress, "induced, at length, by assurances from the British court, that they would concur in a fulfilment of the treaty," required of all states formal repeal of any acts touching the debt issue. Compliance was so full "that no such laws remained in any State of the Union, except one." Even that one—Virginia—would have complied, Jefferson argued, "if any symptom of compliance from the opposite party had rendered a reiterated requisition from Congress important." Congress' original requirement was in fact "only to take away pretext: For, that it was at all times perfectly understood, that treaties controlled the laws of the States." Courts of law stood open to British creditors; and the latter had "for some time, been in the habit and course of recovering their debts at law." Remaining pre-war debts were "but a small proportion of the original amount." Hammond complained that the "few attempts to recover British debts, in the county courts of Virginia, have universally failed, and these are the courts wherein, from the smallness of the sum, a considerable number of debts can only be recovered." The county courts did, indeed, have cognizance of debts below £10, and a recent law had even raised the limit to £30; but, Jefferson explained, it was known "that a very inconsiderable proportion of the British debt consists in demands below that sum." Some "accidental checks" may have been given to the course of justice in some subordinate courts because of error or chicanery; but these were "immediately rectified, either in the same or the superior court, while the great mass of suits for the recovery of sums due to the subjects of the crown of Great Britain, have been uniformly sustained to judgment and execution." Although no ministerial demand had ever been made on the subject, Jefferson devoted a lengthy passage to refusing wartime interest on the debts.

Summarizing, Jefferson concluded with an assertion that the United States was not bound to restore confiscations of loyalist property made before the Peace; and none subsequently took place. Recovery of debts was "obstructed *validly* in none of our States, *invalidly* only in a few, and that not till long after the infractions committed on the other side." There could be no question of paying wartime interest. "These things being evident," the Secretary of State wrote with apparent self-assurance, "I cannot but flatter myself . . . that an end will now be put to the disquieting situation of the two countries, by as complete execution of the treaty as circumstances render practicable at this late date." Claiming for his country a constant "desire of friendly accomodation," he continued to insist that Britain had no just grievances. There was no "*lawful impediment*" to the pursuit of their rights by British subjects. If there were "unlawful ones," aggrieved persons had only to appeal from inferior to superior courts. Until legal remedy was exhausted, there was no ground for complaint, let alone for refusing to comply with "solemn stipulations, the execution of which is too important for us ever to be dispensed with."

Hammond politely acknowledged receipt of Jefferson's communication on June 2; and, as so little scope for his own negotiation remained, he promised to send it to London without delay. Pending additional instructions, he planned to gather fresh evidence supporting his own position; but, he told Jefferson, he feared answering the Secretary's "various and extensive" paper would be a lengthy affair. He would observe at once, however, that "some of the principles, which you have advanced, do not appear to me, at the present moment, to be entirely relevant to the subjects actually under discussion."[18] To Foreign Secretary Grenville, he wrote of the

> great quantity of irrelevant matter . . . the positive denial of many facts, which I had advanced upon the authority of the British agents and of other respectable persons in this country, the unjustifiable insinuations thrown out with respect to the mode of prosecuting the war, and to the conduct of his Majesty's ministers subsequent to the peace, and the general acrimonious stile and manner of this letter.

All these, he concluded with something of an understatement, "contributed to excite in me considerable surprize." It was, as he told Hamilton, "an extraordinary performance."[19]

Jefferson's paper has been judged by many authorities the greatest he ever wrote as secretary of state.[20] If this were true, little luster would attach to his other briefs. Once again, he brought out the old, discredited connection between slaves and debts. Even more surprising, however, was his assertion that the treaty had been fully observed by the United States under the Confederation.[21] Further, it was altogether false that "a very inconsiderable proportion" of the British debts was below £30, or even £10—and Jefferson should have known it. To state that "the great mass of suits" by British creditors had been "uniformly sustained to judgement and execution" and that only a small proportion remained unpaid was a palpable mockery of British creditors and their widows and heirs, who had been so long deprived of their property. To argue that there were no legal impediments to the recovery of debts because the treaty of peace made them illegal made sport of both logic and candor. His implication that the British government prevented his and Adams' agreement in 1786 with representatives of the creditors in London for the payment of debts by instalments flatly contradicted the facts. The charge of prior British infraction was vital to America's case; but the tedious whirl of the squirrel cage could—and did—run in both directions.

It has been claimed that Jefferson's paper had "full official sanction."[22] This is true in a technical sense only. Exhibited in draft to Madison, who made minor corrections, it was also read by Attorney-General John Randolph and Alexander Hamilton. Washington, it is said, approved the document as it stood.

The President returned from Virginia the very morning Jefferson delivered his document to Hammond. It is altogether unlikely, therefore, that Washington read it closely or followed its involved reasoning in any detail. Hamilton's statement to Hammond—that the President "relied upon Mr. Jefferson's assurance, that it was conformable to the opinions of the other members of the executive governments" —probably describes the situation more accurately.[23] Hamilton himself certainly never gave his assent to the paper. He sought to tone down his colleague's rancorous references to the war, but found his suggestions overruled. Faintly praising Jefferson's use of the "recommend" provision in the treaty and of the slave and post issues, he unsuccessfully urged extenuation, rather than vindication, of the states' violations of the treaty. Indeed, to Hammond himself, Hamilton lamented Jefferson's "intemperate violence," and told him that the State Secretary's opinions were "very far from meeting his approbation" and were not, moreover, "a faithful exposition of the sentiments of his government." To Jefferson, Hamilton stated with masterful simplicity the fatal weakness in the brief: it was "an obvious truth . . . that Congress alone has the right to pronounce a breach of the treaty, and to fix the measure of retaliation. Not having done it, the States which undertook the task for them, contravened both their federal duty and the treaty." Jefferson's reasoning, he suggested, adversely affected the character of the federal government itself.[24]

Possibly, Jefferson realized he had overplayed his hand. On June 3, 1792, the day after Hammond had formally and noncommittally acknowledged receipt of his letter, the Secretary of State dropped his insistence on written negotiation and suddenly invited Hammond to dine "solo" with him that very evening, "that we might consider the matter together in a familiar way."[25] Subsequently, Jefferson told his close friend, James Madison, that the conversation had been "full, unreserved & of a nature to inspire mutual confidence." Hammond, it would seem,

acknowledged explicitly that his court had hitherto heard one side of the question only, & that from prejudiced persons, that it was now for the first time discussed, that it was placed on entirely new ground, his court having no idea of a charge of first infraction on them, and a justification on that ground of what had been done by our states, that this made it quite a new case to which no instructions he had could apply.

Jefferson's report cannot be accurate. An experienced diplomatist —and, for all his youth, Hammond was that—could not have been brought to make the admissions put into his mouth by the Secretary of State. It would have been a capitulation both personal and professional. Psychologically, it was impossible; further, Hammond's testimony directly contradicts Jefferson's.[26] Reporting the incident to Grenville, the envoy said the American began by asking "in what light I considered the present state of the negotiations." As the United States had already fulfilled the treaty, he continued, was Hammond "empowered to shorten the discussion by consenting to the execution of it on the part of my sovereign?" Then, in complete disagreement with Jefferson's account, Hammond, in his own words, replied that he and the Secretary of State were "completely at issue upon one point, viz., the specific nature of the infractions mutually complained of." There were, perhaps, some errors in his own information, he admitted; but, certainly, they were not sufficiently important to overturn his position, or even to damage it materially.[27] He renewed his promises given earlier in writing that the London authorities would consider the situation and that he himself would spend the summer gathering more evidence to support his memorial.

A satisfactory explanation for this extraordinary conflict is difficult to come by. Perhaps Jefferson, in the heat of battle, allowed his enthusiasm to carry him away. If so, he was indulging in self-deception—not a practice greatly to be recommended for secretaries of state.

The arrival of Jefferson's paper in Britain, delivered by Phineas Bond, threw the creditor merchants, already uneasy and nervous, into despair. "It is evident," wrote one of them, "that they mean to evade the 4th Article of the Treaty of Peace, or at least to procrastinate complying with it as long as possible, which is Ruin to us." An agent in Virginia declared that he had "come to a determination of relinquishing this Business for the present"; there was so little likelihood of collecting debts in the state that to take money from British employers would be "next to picking their pockets." William Molleson, a leading Glasgow creditor, bemoaned the somber "situation of Men deprived of the fruits of many Years industry, which they, with reason, hoped to enjoy in the decline of Life, and to leave as a provision for their families." A fellow sufferer announced his determination to withdraw his agents from Virginia and "thereby put an end to a very heavy expence we have been incurring there from Year to Year since the Peace." What use to "continue to subject ourselves to this ruinous expence searching after a shadow in Virginia?" Consul John Hamilton, himself a creditor, wrote home of "the impracticability of a Recovery of British Debts, particularly in the States of Virginia and North Carolina," and added his voice to those begging the government "to take our Case into Consideration, and either to oblige the Citizens of America to comply with the 4th Article . . . or to let us have our redress from the Government."[28]

The ministry accepted Jefferson's response to Hammond as an effectual suspension of negotiations. Grenville promptly referred the document to Phineas Bond, recently arrived in London, for study. Bond soon concluded that Jefferson's argument was

evasive &, in many Instances, unfounded—nor does it by any means agree with the Sense & opinion of the ingenious & discreet Part of the Government of the United States, who do not hesitate to declare the Pretensions of the British Creditors cannot be resisted upon any Principles of Justice, which govern the Conduct of Nations toward each other.[29]

To George Hammond went the King's "gracious and entire Approbation of the prudent Conduct you have held upon this Occasion." Under existing circumstances, the envoy could but pursue "by every means in your Power the obtaining from the States the Justice due to the British creditors."[30] After a summer's researches, the envoy found his original conclusion merely strengthened—that Jefferson had been grossly misinformed or had wilfully deceived himself.[31] Further evidence of Jefferson's sophistry, had it been required, arrived in Hammond's report on New Year's Day, 1793: the Federal Circuit Court in Virginia had just ended another sitting without rendering its long-promised decision on British debts. Virginia was virtually alone, Hammond admitted, in denying justice to the creditors; but the sum which was involved came to well above £2 million sterling.[32]

For his part, the American Secretary of State was in a fury with both Hamilton and the British, flaming out to Washington that the Treasury Secretary's policies, domestic and foreign, were "adverse to liberty" and "calculated to undermine and demolish the republic." Hamilton's "cabals," "high-toned declamation," and conferences "of his own authority" with foreign envoys had overturned his own efforts "to give some satisfactory distinctions" to France and to place "some restrictions" on Britain to "induce them to abate their severities against our commerce."

A distressed Washington sought to reconcile his two bitterly quarreling cabinet members, but to little avail. Intending a devastating attack upon the British, Jefferson was nearing completion of his long-delayed report on the foreign commerce of the United States.[33] Hammond—invited, in common with the representatives of France, Holland, and Spain, to comment on abstracts from Jefferson's draft —was deeply suspicious, sensing an attempt to entrap him into admissions of facts and deductions hostile to his country, or to provoke him into unguarded asperities. He declined the Secretary of State's invitation; but, fearing misrepresentation, he took the precaution of communicating under the seal of confidence the whole of his correspondence with Jefferson to two members of the House of Representatives committee assigned to receive Jefferson's report.[34] Even the House's decision not to call for the report did not allay Hammond's deep distrust of Jefferson: the Secretary of State, he believed, merely wished to gain time to allow Monsieur Genêt, newly appointed minister from republican France to the United States, to arrive and to present the favorable new commercial propositions he was believed to carry. It was all a plot, Hammond was convinced, to forward French interests at the expense of Britain.

To such an end had come the last chance to settle the festering disputes arising from the unfulfilled treaty of peace before the outbreak of the wars of the French Revolution.[35]

CHAPTER THIRTEEN

Developing Crisis in the Old Northwest

IN THE YEARS immediately preceding the Anglo-American treaty of 1794, Britain wished desperately to preserve a delicate counterpoise of forces in the Old Northwest while she fashioned a settlement acceptable to all parties—Britons, Americans, and Indians. Failure on either count promised unpleasant, even dreadful penalties: the disruption and loss of trade with the Indians or the Americans, perhaps both; an open break, possibly war, with the United States, already roused to overt hostility by the continued retention of the posts and by the aid rendered to its savage enemy; claims by loyalists and creditors despairing of compensation from the former rebels; and, finally, an Indian assault upon Britons who "deserted" the allies. The grim variable, no longer in Britain's power to control, was the sporadic but intensifying warfare between the Americans—the new sovereigns in the backcountry—and the Indians.

The dangers were clearly understood, but the British response was curiously disjointed. Distance added immeasurably to the problem, of course; messages did not pass quickly along the legs of the North Atlantic triangle defined by London, Quebec and Toronto, and Philadelphia. A second reason was the growing preoccupation of British leaders at home with the alarming events across the Channel in France. In August, 1792—within a few days of the arrival of Jefferson's brief of May 29—London recalled the ambassador at Paris, an event marking the beginning of a rising crisis which culminated the following year in war. Inevitably, American affairs diminished in relative importance and were left more and more to officials in the field: George Hammond in Philadelphia, for example, and John Graves Simcoe in Upper Canada. There lay the danger:

that as the London ministry fixed anxious eyes on France, subordinate officials in North America, nominally the executors of policy, would, by default and on the spur of the moment of sudden crisis, become the makers of it. Aware of the magnitude of the stakes to be won or lost, suspicious of American intentions, and receiving only minimal direction from home, they might well initiate decisions and embark upon actions precipitating a final explosion.

London's initial, and much favored, solution for the complex and potentially disastrous situation in the Old Northwest was British mediation between the Americans and the Indians. A prudent regard for imperial interests and common humanity recommended the idea; and it figured first, apparently at Lord Dorchester's suggestion, in Beckwith's conversations with Hamilton. The American's response was not encouraging. While he would welcome the unofficial exertions of the Canadian governor to influence the red man to the ways of peace, Hamilton would not consider a formal mediation.[1]

George Hammond was instructed at the very beginning of his mission to make an official offer of good offices if he found a likely opportunity. Late in 1791, the time seemed at hand. On December 10, Hammond sent Grenville news of St. Clair's defeat. A week later he revealed to Major General Alured Clarke, lieutenant-governor of Lower Canada and acting commander in chief during Dorchester's absence in England, that he had had a conversation with "a person of the first weight and distinction in the administration here," obviously a circumlocution for Hamilton. The envoy mentioned the King's sincere desire to see the Americans at peace with the Indians; and, intimating that Britain stood ready to mediate, he said he had "some reason" to think that an American request "would not be ineffectual."[2]

Hamilton again rejected the idea of a formal request, but reiterated, too, American interest in an informal interposition. His government was determined, he told Hammond, "to prosecute the War with the Indians with vigor"; but, desiring a just and permanent peace, the United States would show "every proper degree of gratitude" if His Majesty's government in Canada chose to make a "*voluntary* interference" with the Indians. Hamilton was not indulging in polite generalities. He passed at once to specifics. When the United States regained the posts, he told his visitor, he would favor giving British subjects "such privileges and immunities" as would "secure them in the undisturbed prosecution of the Fur Trade."[3] The door was not shut. It was left at least a bit ajar.

The Indian victory over St. Clair knocked the door from its hinges, the British government concluded; and a splendid opportunity was at hand. For the first time, that government showed itself willing to subordinate the immediate interests of the prewar creditors to what it believed to be larger and more compelling considerations: peace and disengagement in the Old Northwest, with all the resultant blessings—both political and economic. The great *sine qua non* was, of course, American acceptance of the mediating role played by Britain.

Consulting closely with Dorchester, the ministry in London hammered out new instructions embodying a bold plan.[4] Hammond was to enter "more directly and particularly" into the subject of the Indian war and to connect it with a settlement of the dispute over the northwestern posts, that "long depending Business." If Hammond should judge that "the then existing circumstances" afforded a prospect of success, he was authorized to make a ministerial offer of good offices for the restoration of peace.

The first step successfully accomplished, the envoy was then to reveal the "general Grounds" of an accommodation. The lands and hunting grounds of the Indians were to be secured "as an independent Country." Both Britain and the United States would abandon all claims or possessions, abstain from building any forts, and bind themselves and their peoples not to acquire any land within the agreed area. The advantages were sufficiently obvious to overpower any opposition to the plan, it was fondly believed: the cause of "difficult and hazardous Discussions" between Britain and America would be removed; and the Indians, secured in their possessions, would be pacified. Hammond was, therefore, authorized to offer an abandonment of the posts, "supposing the Americans should consent, on their Part, to renounce all claims of theirs to those Posts, and to leave them, in common with the rest of that Country, in the undisturbed and independent Possession of the Indians." He was, however, to use his own judgment in choosing the time and mode of bringing forward the proposition. To insure full co-ordination, Grenville continued, Home Secretary Dundas was dispatching parallel instructions to the Canadian authorities. They, in turn, would send to Hammond a person "more particularly versed in the detail of Indian Affairs" to assist in the negotiations assumed to be in the offing. A map, based on suggestions made by a deputation of Indian leaders to Dorchester before his departure from Canada, was also enclosed.[5] Finally, Grenville concluded the lengthy dispatch, "it may also be thought right to insert in any Agreement of this Nature with the United States, an Article for securing to the British Creditors, Justice and Protection in the Recovery of their Debts as to the utmost Extent which may be found practicable, after the long Delay which has taken place in this respect." It was almost an afterthought. The posts, held so long as "rods" over the American heads to compel payment of the pre-war debts, were now to purchase a permanent peace in the Old Northwest.

Several excellent reasons deprived the grandiose scheme of the slightest chance of success. Hammond knew them all and duly reported them home. First, the British government quite obviously misjudged the nature of American reaction to St. Clair's defeat. Humiliation ran deep, but the response was not despair: it was, rather, a heightened determination to subject the Indians. Their confidence and friendship might be courted through American (not British) diplomacy; but, failing the ways of peace, the Indians would have to learn a new lesson—the terror of American arms. Foreign mediation, especially British, would degrade the United States in the eyes of the Indians and thus encourage war instead of the reverse.[6]

Second, while the nature of the relationship between the United States government and the Indians inhabiting its territories remained undefined in many aspects, it was fundamental to American thinking that the savages did not possess sovereignty in the accepted sense of the term. They were not, to use Hamilton's words to Beckwith, "a great or respectable nation," but "vagrant Indian tribes," subjects of the United States and not proper parties for mediation among sovereigns.[7] Jefferson, too, in discussions with Hammond, remarked on the "sort of right and jurisdiction" his government claimed: the relationship was not fully formulated, he admitted; but it included, at the least, the right of the federal government to pre-empt the soil. Indians could not dispose of land without the consent of the United States.[8]

The United States government was gradually feeling its way toward the principle inherited from the British and openly adopted in the summer of 1793, when the American commissioners treating with the Indians admitted—too late to save the peace—that the United States held not an absolute ownership or outright title to Indian lands, but the sole right to acquire them by treaty.[9] Even then, however, the clear implication remained that the government of the United States was sovereign; the Indian, subject.

The British themselves seemed to recognize and accept the American view. Dorchester, speaking to a delegation of western chiefs in 1791, sought to define the nature of the Indians' relation to their new sovereign. The treaty of peace of 1783 had not infringed upon their rights, he assured them. Even supposing the posts in the Old Northwest had been given up—and he left his visitors in no doubt that they would have been surrendered long since, had America fulfilled her part of the treaty—the Indians would have been placed in precisely the same position in relation to the United States government as they had been earlier under George III. The governor of Canada wished, of course, to shield his country from charges that she had abandoned her Indian allies. He accordingly stressed that the king's rights over Indian lands, made over to the newly independent Republic in 1783, consisted in acquiring "such parts of the country as had been fairly ceded by you yourselves with your own free consent by public convention and sale."[10] The unstated premise of his argument, however, was that the Indians were subjects—formerly, of the king of Great Britain; now, of the United States of America.

British mediation was unacceptable to the Americans for another important reason: Britain was, after all, an interested party. She held the forts. A claim to the role of impartial arbiter was inadmissible on the face of it. Even before the instructions of March 17, projecting the creation of an Indian barrier state, were written, Hammond reported to the home government—and subsequently, he repeated the message to Simcoe—that he had heard from "pretty good authority" that the United States government was determined to reject mediation from anybody, especially from Britain, as long as the posts were occupied. The "anxiety" to gain possession of them, he added, had not abated because of St. Clair's defeat. It was, in fact, "not a little augmented" by it.[11]

Hammond knew that a British offer to mediate was bound to be interpreted in Philadelphia as an effort to serve ulterior motives. Why this was not equally clear to the ministry in London is difficult to fathom, although Dorchester may well have been responsible for keeping alive groundless hopes and false illusions. An honorable and upright soldier, the General was on balance an ineffectual and undistinguished governor, dependent upon aides and advisers. Without their assistance while in London on leave, he apparently convinced himself and the ministry, which quite naturally valued him as an expert, that the Americans would accept British mediation and an Indian barrier state.[12]

There was still another reason why British hopes to mediate were unrealistic: the Americans were convinced of British complicity in the Indian war. Some might distinguish between official and private aid to the savages, but all agreed that when an Indian fired a shot at an American in the Old Northwest, both bullet and rifle came from British sources. In the aftermath of St. Clair's defeat, criticism became so severe in Congress and in the press that Hammond made an official denial of his government's guilt, incorporating in passing an oblique reference to Jefferson's own anti-British journalistic activities.[13] The American Secretary expressed gratitude for the statement, adding some tongue-in-cheek advice: Mr. Hammond should really pay no attention to effusions in the public press. How could the United States government suspect the British government of supporting the Indian war?[14]

Hammond was bitterly aware that his repeated denials that Britain had aided the Indians were ineffectual. Soon after his visit to Jefferson, he learned from an influential member of the government, probably Hamilton, that while he himself was not suspected of lying, it was believed that he was simply uninformed. The American authorities knew positively that "means had been found to supply the hostile Indians from the forts on the lakes, with a much greater quantity of arms and ammunition than any amount that might be stipulated in the treaties with those nations." (This information came, Hammond believed, from "interested traders" and American agents within the forts themselves. He urged Lieutenant-Governor Clarke to uncover these ill-disposed persons and put an end to their damaging lies.)[15]

Finally, mediation between Americans and Indians was impossible because territorial claims overlapped and clashed absolutely. There was no room for negotiation or compromise. In July, 1791, Dorchester—believing, from Beckwith's account of his conversations

with Hamilton six months previously, that he was about to be invited to mediate—convoked a council of western chiefs. As the first
step, the Canadian governor wished to learn the terms upon which
the Indians would make peace with the Americans. Alexander Mc-
Kee, the experienced and effective agent of Sir John Johnson's Department of Indian Affairs, was present at the meeting near the
rapids of the Maumee River. His report to Dorchester, subsequently
confirmed by a delegation of chiefs who sought the Governor out in
his capital, indicated claims which no American government could
have found acceptable. The Indians demanded a boundary which
went eastward along the Ohio River as far as the mouth of the Mus-
kingum, and northward up that river to the portage connecting with
the line furnished by the Cuyahoga and Venango Rivers and farther
up to Lake Erie.[16] The area thus included portions of the modern
states of Pennsylvania and Illinois and all of Ohio, Indiana, and
Michigan.

The tide of white settlement, however, was already moving along
the coastline of Lake Erie and pushing across the Ohio; and the rate
of migration was, as Hammond informed his government, accelerat-
ing rapidly.[17] The Six Nations in western New York and Pennsylvania had been cut off from the western Indians. The Genesee country, a forty-two-mile strip of the southern shore of Lake Ontario,
consisting of about a million acres, was already divided into town-
ships and had a population of well over four thousand, with more
arriving every day. Land speculation was active even farther to the
west. Along the shore of Lake Erie, some land east of the mouth of
the Cuyahoga, claimed by Pennsylvania, had already passed to Revolutionary War veterans of the Pennsylvania Line, as well as to casual
purchasers.[18] Both British barrier proposal and Indian claims were
open to the same American objection: they required of the United
States the dereliction of a vast tract of territory and the forcible ejec-
tion of countless frontiersmen, many holding titles under legal
American authority.[19] The United States could never agree; and
Hammond said so to the home government.

Convincing London was another matter.[20] Even with his dispatch
of February 2—expressing the belief that there could be no British
mediation as long as the posts were withheld—in hand, the ministry
could not bring itself to give up or even modify a scheme which
promised so much. Hammond's "full and able Statement" on Ameri-

can breaches of the treaty of peace, Grenville wrote to the envoy, would surely make

a very considerable Impression on the Minds of all those to whom it may have been communicated, and must have disposed them to the Acceptance of some Proposition grounded on the Basis explained in my last Dispatch to you; and combining the re-establishment of Peace with the Mutual Dereliction of that Territory, which this Country cannot continue to hold without exciting Jealousy on the Part of America, and which the King cannot, on the other Hand, be expected to give up to the United States, without receiving Compensation for the non-execution of the Articles of the Treaty, and for the great Expense incurred by the Public on that Account.

In addition, the increasing difficulties of the Indian war would doubtless aid in inducing the Americans to accept the great plan. Hammond's instructions on the subject were, therefore, unchanged, although he was again granted the power of discretion in choosing a time to bring it forward.[21]

The plan was so perfect, its beauties so obvious to the members of the British government, that they deceived themselves into thinking that all who beheld it would marvel and accept. This was a major miscalculation, based on two mistaken premises: that the defeat of St. Clair had impaired the American will to subdue the Indians, and that Hammond's diplomacy had successfully and persuasively asserted the British position in the controversy over the unfulfilled treaty of peace. The blame cannot be laid at Hammond's door. It belongs to the government, which chose to disregard his accurate appraisal of circumstances. At the same time—given Jefferson's intransigence toward Hammond and the determination of the Americans to achieve their goals in the Old Northwest—it is difficult to imagine an alternative short of Britain's withdrawal from the area, a course inviting Indian attack, loss of prewar debts, and the other unpleasant possibilities mentioned above.

Both Britain's proposed mediation and Indian barrier state were, in fact, dead issues by the time Grenville's new instructions reached Philadelphia. Responding to the dispatch of March 17, Hammond reported that his earlier opinion was confirmed by much new evidence.[22] A delegation representing the Six Nations was in Philadelphia, and members of the American government were searching for the basis of a negotiated peace both with them and with their brothers farther to the west. If diplomacy failed, however, new measures of military force were in preparation under Anthony Wayne, a vigorous general and veteran of the Revolutionary War, recently appointed to command a new expedition against the Indians. Popular approval for the appointment and the project was obvious.

In addition, considerations of a "more general tendency" indicated the American indisposition to admit British mediation (let alone a barrier state):

the knowledge of the general politics of the government and the country with respect to any foreign interposition in dispute with the Indians, the nature of the rights asserted by the United States over the Indians occupying territory within their limits, and above all the complicated and intricate claims to be investigated and arranged previously . . . to such a cession of territory.

All these were "difficulties almost insurmountable."

Hammond decided to "risque an experiment." Approaching Hamilton informally, he mentioned the conference then in progress between the delegation from the Six Nations and the American administration, and expressed the private opinion that the Indians wished not only an end to the existing war, but also the establishment of a system of permanent tranquillity. Surely, he continued, a solution could be devised to conciliate all interests—American, Indian, and British. He then suggested the buffer state idea as laid down in Grenville's instructions. Hamilton's reaction was chilling. He listened carefully, declined a discussion, and replied "briefly and coldly" that he wished Hammond to understand that any project comprehending "anything like a cession of territory or right" or interference from any foreign power would be considered by the government of the United States as "absolutely impracticable and inadmissible."

Hamilton's rejection could not have been stronger or more categorical, and Hammond considered himself precluded from raising the matter with him again. To remove the last shred of doubt, however, he threw out similar suggestions to Jefferson and to the secretary of war, General Knox. Both agreed that no solution involving a loss of American territory was possible.

The Americans were unanimous in their reaction. They might be brought to consent to conditions necessary for British security, commercial as well as political: American troops at the posts could probably be limited in number; fortifications might even be pulled down altogether; naval forces on the Lakes could be kept within agreed bounds; British persons and property involved in the fur trade, traversing the Lakes or traveling between them, could be guaranteed. Even free access to the Mississippi might be arranged. Such terms, Hammond believed, the Americans would accept "with alacrity"; but they were absolute and unchanging in their demands for the posts.[23] There was no alternative. In July, he gave up his attempts to follow Grenville's impossible instructions.[24]

As Hammond paused to reflect upon his situation, his thoughts were bleak; his early hopes, ashes. True, his arrival in Philadelphia probably influenced Jefferson to postpone his hostile report on America's foreign commerce, and Congress to put aside Madison's efforts to discriminate against British commerce; but even these small successes would disappear if Jefferson and his friends had their way. Overshadowing the successes were two monumental failures: the settlement of differences arising from the unfulfilled treaty of peace had proved impossible; and he had wasted time, effort, and goodwill pursuing the ministry's impracticable plan for the backcountry.

Having cut free from Grenville's instructions, Hammond knew that danger lay in inaction. He could not abandon the field, leaving the United States to settle with the Indians, by peace or war, without the slightest reference to Great Britain. What, then, he worriedly asked Clarke and Simcoe, would be the fate of Canada? "I am led to this inquiry," he wrote, "by the knowledge, that at this instant this government, notwithstanding its preparations for another campaign, is using, and will continue to use every effort (and through every channel except ours) to procure peace by negotiation, either with the whole confederacy of hostile Indians, or by partial treaties with the separate nations."[25] But if negotiations failed, there were the ominous preparations already being made by General Wayne.

Not until Grenville sent his dispatch of August 4, 1792, did the British government give its approval to Hammond's suspension of obedience, because, the envoy was told, Jefferson's communication of May 29 required detailed study.[26] By that time, however, Hammond had set in train a plan of his own, which had a small chance to snatch a measure of success from total failure. Two possible courses of events could conceivably cause the American administration to change its attitude toward British mediation, he reasoned. One lay quite without his power to influence: a third disaster to American arms. If Wayne were overwhelmed as St. Clair had been, American hauteur might give way to a meek acceptance of British good offices. The trial of arms would, however, necessarily be many months in the future. American preparations would require time; in any event, Wayne was, in Hammond's estimation, "unquestionably the most active, vigilant, and enterprizing officer in the American service."[27] The likelihood of another American defeat was not to be built upon.

The second possibility held somewhat more promise. The Americans refused mediation; but what would they do if the Indians requested it? Britain could then argue that she was obliged to act in response to the expressed wishes of allies "in whose existence and preservation we have a clear, decided and permanent interest." Delicacy was, however, an absolute requirement, Hammond told Clarke and Simcoe. Any request would have to appear unsolicited and spontaneous. If collusion were suspected, the Americans would never fall in with the plan.[28]

The Canadian commanders responded enthusiastically; and in August, 1792, a suitable opportunity for the new initiative seemed at hand: a great council of the confederated western Indians was gathering at the Maumee Rapids to hear from Joseph Brant and his brothers of the Six Nations an account of their talks with Washington in Philadelphia. Clarke immediately consulted with Simcoe on how best to bring about "the *spontaneous* wish of the Indians for the King's mediation." If Simcoe was agreeable, let him confer with Colonel McKee and Lieutenant Colonel John Butler, deputy superintendents of Indian affairs at Detroit and Niagara, respectively, and "give such directions respecting it as you may think most likely to accomplish the object Mr. Hammond had in view." Clarke, however, was frankly dubious—not at the prospect of obtaining a "spontaneous" request from the Indians, which he thought might be accomplished easily, but at the worth of the whole maneuver. "I wish the liberality and honor he possesses himself," Clarke wrote of Hammond, "may not induce him to overrate those qualities in, and the consequence of, the people he has to deal with."[29]

Simcoe, ever fearful of British involvement in the Indian war, fell to work at once. To McKee, who was already in the vicinity of the Maumee Rapids awaiting the gathering of the Indians, he wrote urging a "consolidation of the Indian territorial claims, and Rights," the first step, he conceived, toward creating a barrier territory. Aid for an offensive war was not to be expected from Britain, he added, but the Indians might be given copies of pertinent treaties, deeds, and the like from the official archives to support their land claims against the Americans. McKee was also to bring about the "spontaneous" request for British mediation.[30]

In mid-October, Hammond sent Simcoe his congratulations. The letter to McKee was "admirably calculated to obviate the appearance of too active an interference on our part in influencing the Indians to solicit His Majesty's mediation." He knew that the Indian council was under way, if not already concluded; and he was eager to be informed of the results, "not only on account of the discussion to which it may eventually give birth, but also as it will in some measure affect the negotiations actually existing between the Americans and myself."[31]

The council at "the Glaize," the confluence of that river with the Maumee, lasted from September 30 to October 9. Acrimonious exchanges occurred between the warlike western chiefs and the warriors of the Six Nations, whose talks with the American authorities rendered them suspect in the eyes of the former. They finally resolved, however, to meet American commissioners at Sandusky the following year—a decision rendered futile from the outset by the western Indians' determination (unknown to the American authorities) to demand the Ohio as a boundary. Finally, a formal invitation for Britain's mediation at Sandusky was sent to the governor of Upper Canada.[32]

The message traveled north slowly, and it was not until mid-November that Simcoe wrote to Hammond in some jubilation. He had received "the United Requisition of the Indians that I should be present at Sandusky, & bring with me the Antient Treaties, &c., which were held with them before the King had declared the Independency of the United States."[33] Simcoe was worried, however: what answer should he return to "these people, our Ancient Allies & True Friends?" They would construe a refusal as "Evidence that the British do not wish for Peace; a doctrine that in direct contradiction to the Servants of Government, self-interested Traders may have taught them." At the end of the month, Hammond replied to Simcoe both officially and privately.[34] First, he stated that the request of the Indians seemed so important that he would have to inform the American government of it. He told Simcoe unofficially, however, that he was hesitating to communicate the Indian request to the Americans "in any shape," as they showed not the slightest sign of changing their sentiments about British interposition. He would use his familiar tactics with them: to make an "informal" approach, taking care not to commit himself and his government and to avoid even the suspicion of a ministerial offer to mediate. He expected a refusal, which, he feared might well be "highly disrespecting" to the King and "*ultimately* tend to necessitate the adoption of measures, which I have the strongest reason to conclude are not in the remotest contemplation of his Majesty's Ministers at this juncture." His misgivings were well founded. A few days later, he reported to Grenville that both Hamilton and Jefferson had categorically refused the "informal" suggestion, although the Secretary of State agreed to lay the matter before President Washington.[35]

Even the reaffirmation of the Indians' request by a second, smaller council at Buffalo, this time in the presence of Lieutenant Colonel Butler, brought no softening of the American refusal. About the middle of December, Jefferson told Hammond that the President had authorized him to state "informally" that no British mediation could be allowed. A precedent for American mediation in the event of British troubles with the Indians would thus be set as well, the Secretary pointed out. Far better, he believed, for both powers to regard the Indians as not possessing the sovereignty necessary to permit an appeal for mediation by a third party. Should Governor Simcoe present himself at Sandusky in the spring, it would have to be as a mere spectator; and even so, the United States government would regret his presence there in any capacity. Furthermore, if the conference failed to bring peace with the Indians, it might be impossible for the government, itself without suspicion, to convince the mass of American citizens, too disposed already to blame Britain for the Indian war, that British intrigue was not responsible.

Hammond retrieved what little he could. Simcoe, of course, he told Jefferson, would not think of going to Sandusky under the circumstances. The Indians would have to be told, however, that their application was impracticable because the Americans opposed it. He suggested that some subordinate British officer—a colonel, perhaps, who enjoyed the confidence of the Indians and could explain the American offers—might be at the council. Jefferson seemed at least not to oppose the idea, although he observed to the envoy that the

American position would be so obviously just that there would be little need for explanations. Some small additional comfort may have been afforded by General Knox's confidential assurance that the American representatives at Sandusky would be unexceptionable in character and would entertain no "disposition unfavorable to Great Britain."[36]

Hammond expressed both his bitterness and his hope to Simcoe. After his experiences with the government of the United States, he could only hope that Britain would not sacrifice the Indians to American "arrogance or caprice"; and Simcoe was to give appropriate assurances to the Indians when he replied to their request. At the same time, the Governor was told to make it equally plain that no formal offer of mediation had ever been made to them. The intention had been merely to convey an expression of certainty that the King *would* mediate, if the United States was agreeable. He, himself, had tried, Hammond wrote, "to *extort*" American acceptance of McKee's or Butler's presence at the coming American-Indian conference at Sandusky; and this small concession had, in fact, been secured. British representatives at the council had to be both extremely cautious and vigilant, however: under the closest American scrutiny, they would be perfect scapegoats if negotiations failed. Silence, not open opposition to American offers, was the proper form of showing disapproval.[37]

Hammond's game was profoundly defensive: no longer the grand plan of mediation or barrier, but a desperate attempt to prevent what he feared would be complete and total overthrow of British interests in the Old Northwest. Simcoe, whose motives have been especially questioned and misunderstood, agreed. Instructed by Dundas in May to furnish Hammond "such arguments as may admit of being officially stated" proving the great hardship and suffering the continuation of the Indian war would inflict upon his province, the governor of Upper Canada responded, writing of "the most serious and alarming situation" which might develop from a resumption of hostilities.[38] The fur trade had declined greatly, he noted, but worse by far were rising Indian suspicions of British intentions, intensified especially by Simcoe's refusal to go to Sandusky. His dilemma was ominous: if the Indians defeated the Americans, they would fall upon the British, seeking revenge for their abandonment; if the Americans won, the Indians would flee to British territory, and "from thence continue a perpetual Warfare, that in either case sooner or later must involve this Government with the United States." If refuge were refused to the beaten savages, they would also attack Canada, doubtlessly spurred on by the triumphant Americans. Every consideration led to one conclusion: a renewal of hostilities would be a "calamity"; Britain's interest was "an immediate Pacification."[39]

How was this pacification to be achieved? The British solution to the vexatious problem demanded two prerequisites: a degree of Indian unity in the coming negotiations with the Americans; and, paradoxically, successful persuasion of the red men to hold their demands within the limits of the practicable. Hammond, Simcoe, their subordinates, and the Mohawk chieftain Joseph Brant, who was eager for peace and anxious for the preservation of his people, strove mightily to achieve these goals. They deserve credit; but gracious acknowledgment of considerable and not uninspired effort cannot disguise the magnitude of their failure. The council at the Glaize in 1792 discarded the Venango-Muskingum line and required the Ohio. When the American commissioners made their way westward in the spring of 1793, however, they carried instructions to demand the former, the "line of 1789," which had been established by the Treaty of Fort Harmar with some of the western tribes. Ready to pay an unprecedented compensation for the confirmation of titles disputed by the Indians, the American government was adamant in its determination not to give up lands already bought and granted to its citizens.[40]

Much was unclear early in 1793. The western Indians, believing that American willingness to come to a council indicated a disposition to accept the Ohio line, did not know the relatively narrow confines planned for them by the government at Philadelphia. The chieftains of the Six Nations did not know the determination of their western brothers. The Americans did not know that the Ohio line was expected. The British did not know the details of the coming American proposition—but both they and Joseph Brant did know that a demand for the Ohio line was unacceptable to the Americans. Their first task became, therefore, to induce the western Indians to modify their expectations.

The game began when Hammond "extorted" agreement from Jefferson to allow British officials to be present at Sandusky. Ham-

mond was the "captain," if the figure does not imply too great a
degree of direction; and his assumption of general authority was
blessed by the London ministry.[41] Simcoe's orders to Colonels McKee
and Butler to attend the council were couched in Hammond's language: the officers were not to consider themselves mediators. They
were only to explain the American offers and the relevant documents
made available by Canadian officials.[42] They received, too, the warning given earlier by the envoy in Philadelphia that they would be
closely watched by American commissioners ready to seize the slightest excuse to blame them if the conference failed. But Philadelphia
proved too far from Toronto—or even Niagara, Simcoe's temporary
headquarters—for Hammond to assume direction of field operations.
The task necessarily devolved upon Simcoe and his subordinates,
above all Deputy Indian Superintendent Alexander McKee.

The three American commissioners, General Benjamin Lincoln,
Timothy Pickering, and Beverly Randolph, arrived at Niagara on May
17. Carrying letters of introduction from Hammond, they accepted
Simcoe's hospitality, living under his roof—reluctantly, it is said—
for almost two months.[43] Toward the end of June, they made their
way from Niagara to Fort Erie to embark for Detroit and Sandusky,
their eventual destination. Windbound for several days, their vessel
did not sail until July 11. In the interim, the commissioners received
Joseph Brant and a large delegation of native chiefs.

Since April, a critical meeting between representatives of the Six
Nations and of the western tribes had been under way at the Maumee Rapids. McKee was present but, true to his orders, took no part
in the debate. The great burden of persuading the western Indians
to moderate their demands lay rather upon Brant, the cleverest and
most capable of all the chiefs of the Six Nations.[44] He had been to
Philadelphia, had talked to Washington, and knew, perhaps better
than any of his people, the determination of the Americans to win
or impose a settlement with the Indians. His own people, separated
already from their western brethren by broad areas of white settlement, had nothing to gain from renewed hostilities and much, perhaps all, to lose. Knowing that the Americans would never accept the
Ohio line, Brant fought powerfully, with craft and cunning, to
unite the Indians in support of the "line of 1791." His own eloquence and McKee's sympathy were unavailing. The western Indians
were unmoved. A desperate strategem seemed the only answer. Brant

set it in motion when he and his party found the American commissioners at Fort Erie on July 5.

Proceeding together to Niagara, Americans and Indians conferred for three days in Simcoe's presence. Trying to win time and to avoid an immediate and complete rupture of negotiations, Brant, whose domination of his party was remarkable, was less than candid. Were the Americans prepared to negotiate a new boundary? he asked. Their affirmative answer, he allowed his companions to believe, indicated a willingness to accept the Ohio line. Having, in addition, secured the restraint of Wayne during the duration of the treaty season, Brant and his fellows withdrew. The Mohawk had deceived both parties; but he had at least won time for a last attempt to carry his point with the western Indians.

His effort was futile. On July 28, another party of chiefs, Brant conspicuous by his absence, left the Rapids to seek the commissioners. Two days later, they found the Americans, who had "allowed" themselves to be entertained by another British official, encamped near the mouth of the Detroit River. The interview was brief and decisive. Would the Americans accept the Ohio as a boundary? the Indians asked bluntly. On the next day, July 31, the commissioners explained why they could not. A large compensation was promised, and the claim of absolute ownership of Indian lands was repudiated; but the "Sandusky council" was over, although the final word was not said until mid-August. It came from the Indians: let the Americans give their money to white settlers on Indian lands and remove them. They must have the Ohio boundary.

It has been said that only the United States profited from the breakdown of negotiations. On balance, this is true. Wayne gained an extra year for his military preparations, while his enemies were weakened.[45] The British, however, gained one small advantage worth mentioning: they made some progress in divesting themselves of their earlier responsibility toward their Indian allies, now subjects of the United States, and in rendering the American assumption of that responsibility at least a degree more palatable to the red men. McKee summarized this in his report to Simcoe after the collapse of the council:

The acknowledgement which the United States have at length made that the Indian nations possess the property or right of the soil of all Indian lands, has convinced them of the falsities, long propagated, that Great Britain has given away their country at the Treaty of Peace, and left them in a much worse condition than they were before the war.[46]

It was cold comfort for the moment, however, bringing little relief to worried officials apprehensive at being drawn, one way or another, into a savage backwoods struggle.

Why were the western Indians so unyielding? The British were not to blame; the achievement of a peaceful settlement was far too obviously in their interest.[47] Certainly, the victory over St. Clair gave the hostile confederacy a confidence in its ability to deal with the Americans in the field. Further, Brant's deliberate confusion of the boundary issue engendered a belief that the Americans would accept the Ohio line. The disappointment and anger of the western Indians when the deception suddenly came to light made for a spirit of determined defiance, not a disposition to modify their demand. More important still, however, was the expectation of aid from the southern Indians. Indeed, for a time, there loomed the terrible possibility of a general and united Indian assault along the entire American frontier.

While the council at the Glaize was deciding in 1792 to require the Ohio line, war parties of Creeks and Cherokees were embarked on a series of well-planned raids and massacres along the southern frontier. Hammond, reporting the development to London, mentioned the widespread rumor that the Spaniards were behind the attacks.[48] American suspicions were actually greater than he imagined. Washington diagnosed "a very clear understanding in all this business between the Courts of London and Madrid," with each of the European powers wishing to confine the growth and check the rising importance of the United States.[49] There was, in fact, a budding understanding between powers in the north and south; but it was of Indian inspiration, not European. Simcoe provided explicit information in a letter to his old friend Sir Henry Clinton.[50] Commending Brant for his unsuccessful efforts to bring about a peace, the governor of Upper Canada revealed that in 1792 the western Indians had sent messengers southward to invite the Creeks and Cherokees to join their alliance. They promised that "G. Britain would help them." It was, the Governor roundly declared, "a natural stroke of Lying and Policy." The southern Indians had responded, however, by immediately taking up arms, he wrote; and the Spaniards had urged the

Choctaws to do the same. The Chickasaws hesitated on the brink. The Creeks actually sent a message to Simcoe, saying that " 'they acknowledge no alliance but that of their father the King of England.' " Far from welcoming the declaration, however, Simcoe believed that "this untoward Event," which implied support for the hostile Indians to the north, prevented the acceptance of "Brant's boundary." A continuation of the Indian war was to be expected, Simcoe wrote glumly, "and nothing but great attention, and a good force can sooner or later prevent hostilities between *us* and the *Indians*."

The prospect of Indians warring against his frontier was dread enough; but it was only one horn of Simcoe's dilemma. A threat of equal or greater magnitude was posed by the presence of American military forces in the vicinity of the occupied posts. For a time— roughly from Jefferson's brutal rebuff to Hammond in late May, 1792, until the outbreak of war between Britain and France made American relations with belligerent powers the paramount issue— the dominant theme in Anglo-American affairs was the danger of an armed clash in the Old Northwest. The collapse of Hammond's diplomacy left military strength the sole safeguard for British interests in the backcountry. At the same time, Americans were determined to crush the Indian menace in the area. Aside from increasing American belligerence, there was an additional complication. With Britain increasingly engrossed in continental affairs, the London ministry's policy was reduced to a single maxim: restrain provocative actions and avoid war if at all possible. While the posture was clearly defensive, it gave great opportunity for nervous or trigger-happy military men to produce the kind of accidental incident which could rapidly become a *causus belli*.

Serious apprehension of an American military threat to Britain's position in the Old Northwest dated from St. Clair's defeat in 1791. The instructions to the hapless general from Secretary of War Knox were captured by the victorious Indians and turned over to the British in Canada. While there were certain ambiguities, they provided food enough for a growing suspicion that the United States aimed to precipitate a challenge at some future date.[51] George Hammond himself believed it "highly probable" that St. Clair's true objective was the establishment of a post at Sandusky, which would be a dagger pointed at Detroit.[52]

The appointment of Anthony Wayne to command a new American expeditionary force against the Indians—coming at the very time when the federal government was rejecting any thought of British mediation—intensified concern. It was not yet thought that America courted war with Britain, Hammond wrote to Clarke; but her anxiety to gain the posts was very great. There was little prospect of settling the issue amicably before another trial of arms with the Indians; and if the Americans were successful then, he would not be greatly surprised "if a desire of gaining possession of those posts by force should be either artfully inspired into the troops, or spontaneously conceived by them." The American government would undoubtedly be extremely cautious in ordering an attack on the posts; but if it were successfully undertaken without their knowledge, Hammond could "readily conceive that they would then join their sanction to it to the popular approbation which would infallibly ensue."[53] The character of the American general was the decisive element, the envoy concluded, and the reputation of "Mad Anthony" Wayne for rash and precipitate action made the course of the future appear perilous indeed.

If such thoughts troubled the civilian mind of George Hammond, the tenor of Lieutenant-Governor Simcoe's thinking can easily be imagined. If, as he sincerely believed would be the case after the Americans refused his mediation, Britain were pulled into the Indian war, the brunt of it, whether delivered by red men or white, would fall on him and his new province. From the middle of June, 1792, he requested reinforcements to prepare for "any sinister events." Not a warmonger bent on revenge, as he is commonly depicted, Simcoe believed himself weak militarily, and thus an easy prey for attack. He was dominated by nagging anxieties. Conceiving the American leaders to be men "totally destitute of Public or Private Morality," he feared they planned to force his country into the "greatest of all calamities, a War." He disowned, he wrote to an official in London, all personal fears or views except "Peace, Peace, Peace";

and as I know the Military Contempt in which I hold Washington and such like cattle may induce people to suppose I should not dislike war, I beg my friends to understand I think worse of his heart than his understanding, and fear he will urge us into war to support his power. I have now done with the subject, which, I own, oppresses me, but be assured, if we are forced into war while I govern Upper Canada, it shall not be the wisest sort, preventitive war, but absolutely and entirely defensive.[54]

Unfortunately, preparations for either type of war, defensive or offensive, have much in common; and two can chop the logic of "preventitive" war. A real possibility existed that Simcoe's zeal for putting himself in a respectable posture of defense—understandable, even commendable, as the desire might be—would invite the very attack he sought to avoid. Among his friends were men who, for one reason or another, were not beyond twisting fraying nerves a turn or two. One subordinate, for example, the young, meddling, rash, and presumptuous Captain Charles Stevenson, sent to New York with dispatches for England, wrote back to his chief warning that the Americans were "too restless a neighbour," and insisting that the Indian war "not be allowed to subside." In effect, counseling his superior to disregard the plain meaning of standing instructions, he suggested a covert and subterranean encouragement of Indian hostilities: "opinions without council," he stated in somewhat enigmatic language, although his intention was clear enough, could be circulated among the savages. In any event, the tempter whispered, England was too distant to override any action Simcoe might care to take at a critical moment. Stevenson sought also to open a surprising and entirely unsolicited correspondence—events would prove he had characteristically little regard for "channels"—with George Hammond. Would it be "contrary to policy and justice," he asked, for some suitable person, a "creditable merchant or others not in a public situation," to instruct the Indians in the rudiments of military science and thereby enable them to improve their performance against the Americans on "any future occasion?" Hammond's brusque rejection of the idea did not invite further exchanges: "merchants were not to be trusted," and public characters were bound by the declaration he himself had made to the American government. However, Stevenson's meddling was by no means ended. As he himself candidly and enthusiastically admitted, "I should like a little mischief amazingly."[55] No evidence indicates that the upstart actually convinced Simcoe to adopt one course of action over another; but he had Simcoe's friendship, perhaps even confidence (which he was to abuse sadly in 1793), and he undoubtedly influenced the climate of opinion around the Lieutenant-Governor, heightening the sense of impending storm whipping up from the south.

Youthful impetuosity and aged bitterness led to the same foolishness. Simcoe's old friend and sometime companion-in-arms, Sir Henry Clinton, sending through Simcoe a rifle to Joseph Brant, advised the Mohawk to "make proper use of it against all invaders of your property whether from the West or South." To Simcoe himself, he inveighed against American aggression against the Indians and preached the gospel of preventive war: "Let loose the whole tribe of Indians, offer terms to Vermont and Kentucky. Try to tempt (if these last decline connection with you) some of the Eastern Provinces, at least to give you their ports."[56] Again, it is impossible to demonstrate a direct influence, but Clinton's neurotic preoccupations must have added weight to Simcoe's own anxieties. It could have been no mere coincidence that he presently began to urge the home government to allow the fortification of new posts to screen his province from the south.

Simcoe's request, sent directly to Home Secretary Dundas, demonstrated another complicating factor which both encouraged confusion and made the possibility of a chance explosion in the Old Northwest even greater: Lord Dorchester's prolonged leave of absence, nearly two years in all, at this important juncture removed from the scene the only Canadian official with sufficient power, authority, and seniority to exercise a general and unquestioned supreme command. The governor of Upper Canada—"lieutenant governor," Dorchester would insist—was indubitably junior to the governor of Lower Canada at Quebec. His presence at his post would have relieved Simcoe of much of his anxiety. He could have passed the buck. It may, of course, be argued that, in view of the subsequent tension and ill-tempered bickering between Dorchester and Simcoe, the former was scarcely the man to answer the purpose. However that may be, it is beyond dispute that Dorchester's deputy, Major General Alured Clarke, so near Simcoe in rank and seniority, was unequal to the demand. The new dispensation in Canada, wrought by Grenville's Canada Act of 1791, the areas of responsibilities pertaining to the two governors' offices, and the administrative relations between the two officials were still too new, undefined, and inchoate for a clear and unhampered flow of business. In any event, Clarke himself came to share his colleague's misgivings and apprehensions, and the inevitable temptation was to refer everything to London. With the lines of administrative authority and responsibility seriously impaired, the burden fell directly upon the British ministry, an arrangement the dangers of which (though he would have used another word) were apparent even to Charles Stevenson.

The goal was peace, but not peace at any price. Dorchester's orders, issued shortly before he returned to England, that force must be repelled by force, were resolutely sustained. The ministry invariably insisted, however, that if war came, it would be because the United States demanded it. This was virtually the constant burden of Dundas' dispatches to Canadian officials, and especially to Simcoe. Answering his request for permission to take post farther south, Dundas reminded Simcoe of stated policy. Some form of British mediation in the Indian war might well restore peace, thereby obviating the necessity for considering the Lieutenant-Governor's suggestion in any detail.[57] It was a call for caution.

Simcoe's reaction casts light on all aspects of the problem: the intentions of American leaders, their deep suspicions, his own perturbation, and the difficulty in administering from London at a time of growing crisis. The government of the United States intended to have the posts, come what may, he wrote to Clarke. Uniformly hostile to Britain—Jefferson openly so and Hamilton covertly—they would never admit a negotiated solution. Congress was "laying in wait till some fortunate occurrences shall enable it to seize by fraud or other violence what is so justly and reasonably withheld." The ministers in London were obviously in urgent need of information from the officers of the Crown in Canada; and he was, therefore, taking the liberty of forwarding to Dundas a copy of his dispatch. His own solution would be to aim "at once to dissolve the Confederacy" to the south by driving a wedge between the wicked administration at Philadelphia and the people, who possessed a "morality . . . by no means so defective." Curiously anticipating the technique of Charles Edmond Genêt, Simcoe went on to recommend that Britain state her case to the American public, asking " 'whether the United States having failed on their part in doing Great Britain justice in most essential points of the Treaty of Peace, has not Great Britain a right to withhold the evacuation of certain posts till the stipulation on which they were to be evacuated shall be complied with?' "[58]

He extended his warning more specifically in his correspondence with George Hammond. The very minute the United States gained the posts, he declared, "there would be nothing to prevent the Indians from attacking our Settlements"; and an even more pressing danger, the reverse of the same coin, was at hand: "at present it is to be feared lest the Army of the United States should beat the Indians and follow the fugitives into Detroit." To agree with the Americans to limit the garrisons in the posts or naval forces on the Lakes would be "highly impolitic."[59] While Hammond concluded in November, 1792, that prospective American-Indian negotiations meant Wayne's military offensive was "entirely abandoned for the present," Simcoe remained convinced that hostilities would continue and intensify.[60] What course of action should he adopt in that case, he asked acting Commander in Chief Clarke? What should he do if the Americans tried to place gunboats in Lake Erie? Would it not be a hostile action, regardless of trumped-up excuses? Possession of the posts, he reminded Clarke, rested upon naval command of the Lakes.

While Simcoe's imagination raced ahead to encounter dangers, real and anticipated, the home government gave a firm tug at the reins. Secretary Dundas, having read Simcoe's earlier dispatch to Clarke, informed the lieutenant-governor of Upper Canada that the ministry was well aware of the importance of securing the boundary with the United States. A settlement should be sought at every opportunity. Meantime, it was "almost unnecessary" to say that "too much care cannot be taken (consistently with the Protection of His Majesty's Subjects and the Security of the Posts in our Possession), that in all matters of dispute between His Majesty's Subjects and those of the American States," the government of Canada should act "to preclude the Possibility of ill humour and discontent."[61]

War between Britain and France further alarmed the nervous Simcoe. Would not the Americans soon rally to the support of their French republican brethren? In that event, he would not decline the chance to restore to Britain "the power, honor, and dominion" lost during the American Revolution.[62] It was heated and emotional talk, and again it elicited from Clarke a call for caution. The Americans, he told Simcoe, knew too well their own interest to allow Jefferson and his party to lead them into "the wild and violent projects" of France; and he took special satisfaction in the recent proclamation of American neutrality.[63] The gravity of the new developments was not, however, to be minimized. The fundamental problems remained unremedied: Dorchester was still on leave—he would not return until the winter of 1793—and the home government was preoccupied almost exclusively by the European scene. A chance shove to the tiller might well swing policy to a new and stormy course in the northwestern backwater; and there was in London a man very ready to indulge his taste for mischief. Captain Charles Stevenson was home on leave.[64]

Enjoying at least a measure of Simcoe's confidence and friendship—he carried the Lieutenant-Governor's dispatches to London—Stevenson obviously possessed that kind of address and glib social ease which could gain him an entrée into the world of fashion in the British capital. He was "much with the Marquis of Bucks," he wrote to his chief, "to whom I was referred by the Duke of Gloucester." Neither Gloucester nor Buckingham was noted for intellectual prowess; but the former was the son of George III and the latter the brother of Lord Grenville, the foreign secretary, and the cousin of Pitt, the prime minister. The Marquis described Stevenson to his highly-placed brother as Simcoe's "right hand man" and as "particularly well informed." Presently, this junior officer, exhibiting an almost unendurable effrontery, was swaggering about London, posing as an authority on Canadian-American affairs and courting the notice of important cabinet ministers. In April, with the country in turmoil at the outbreak of war, Stevenson wrote to Simcoe that Home Secretary Dundas had "commissioned" the Speaker of the House of Commons to apologize in his behalf for not having conferred with him; he would, he promised, soon repair the omission.

The assurance notwithstanding, three months more elapsed before Dundas allowed himself the long-deferred pleasure of receiving Stevenson. In the interim, the insufferable meddler bustled about, intriguing (unsuccessfully) for new instructions to Hammond "to bring the Indian war to a conclusion by Great Britain taking a decided part." To Simcoe, he sent word that Pitt, Grenville, and Dundas wished he would take more responsibility in his province, a report scarcely calculated to win the Lieutenant-Governor over to the ways of caution. "They request you to act more from yourself," he wrote, quoting Buckingham, "and that you will meet with every support from them." He concluded with a flourish: Simcoe should be aware of the extent of his own power and the public's expectations of him.

The height of folly remained to be reached. It came toward the end of July, 1793, when Dundas finally saw Stevenson. What passed is not known in detail; but afterward, on August 1, the young officer wrote jubilantly to Simcoe: "At last there are hopes that I may get my requisitions and statements attended to." (The possessive pronoun absolves Simcoe from any direct responsibility for subsequent events.) He had had a long conversation with Dundas, he continued, and upon taking leave, the Home Secretary had asked him to "write down my requisitions and observations." He would "give me another interview and an answer" as soon as he conveniently could.

Stevenson described his paper as a recommendation that Britain act as "an armed mediator" in case the Americans declined to make peace with the Indians. In reality, the "Requisitions and statements for the Province of Upper Canada" were more detailed and more pernicious than his brief account to Simcoe indicated. First, he stated baldly, falsely, and without qualification that the document was submitted "by desire of Colo. Simcoe." Clothing himself in this spurious authority, he demanded artillery reinforcements for Upper Canada as "absolutely necessary," and the rank of brigadier for his chief as "necessary." A number of almost random points followed. French emigrés were to be settled at Detroit to "cover our right flank" and to "oppose their Aristocratical Principles against the Republick Ideas of the Americans." The northwestern posts must be retained, lest Canada be opened to invasion. An arrangement with Spain might secure the navigation of the Mississippi and perhaps of Pensacola, vantage places which, with the St. Lawrence line of communication, "must ever keep the Americans in subjection." Kentucky was soon to join Britain, thereby removing the only barrier to British power and commerce between Hudson's Bay and the Gulf of Mexico.[65]

Perhaps some of the "requisitions" reflected dinner-table conversations with Simcoe; but casual and idle chitchat does not furnish the stuff of a formal requisition to a minister of the Crown. The paper was, in fact, a farrago of nonsense, a fantasia of club politics, acutely embarrassing to Simcoe, who was thought by the ministry to be responsible for the effusion. Rather paradoxically, it indirectly served to dampen the sparks flying about the woods in the Old Northwest, giving the British government a pointed reminder of the risk of allowing events there to go unchecked.

The warning was certainly needed. In Canada, Simcoe saw the Americans around the posts, especially at Oswego, "ripening into a temper which may be productive of the most serious disputes"; and he anticipated incidents requiring the use of force.[66] Considering himself virtually in a state of siege, he wrote from "York, late Toronto," describing to Sir Henry Clinton his "little citadel," with the blockhouse named "Gibraltar, because I wish to inculcate its impregnable Idea." Plans were under way to find and fortify alternates to the retained posts: "neither Niagara or Detroit," he declared, "are worth preserving in respect to the States, and an Officer and fifty Taylors to strike the British flag would be the best Garrison in case of apprehension from a *Sudden* Irruption of these Gentry." Conceiving it all too possible that the "anti-federalists," favoring "war and no *payment of Debts*, and French alliance," might precipitate hostilities, the lieutenant-governor of Upper Canada was as fearful as ever of his second nightmare, an Indian assault. If Britain hastily gave up the American posts, he warned, without occupying new and better positions of strength, the Indians would attack. British influence with them was already "almost gone, from our necessary Neutrality."[67]

Before Henry Dundas addressed himself to the task of dealing with the "Requisitions," he reminded Simcoe once more, gently but firmly, that while vigilance was necessary, it was "equally so, that nothing should arise within either of the Canadas, of which any advantage can be taken" by Americans who might wish to stir up public opinion against Britain. He could not persuade himself that the Americans aimed at war; and it was certain that "no proposition can be more clear than that nothing should be done by Great Britain or any of its dependencies either to provoke or to justify Hostilities on their part."[68]

The "Requisitions" precipitated monumental rebukes. Dorchester's opinion of the document, requested by Dundas, was acid: the chain of command was violated; Simcoe was improperly styled "governor" instead of "lieutenant governor," an especially tender point with Dorchester; Pensacola would be difficult to get and impossible to hold; measures hostile to the United States were "highly inexpedient."[69] The blow direct came from the Home Secretary personally. His dispatch of October 2, 1793, impaled the hapless Simcoe: his communication was irregular; there could be no thought of establishing "strangers" at Detroit or anywhere else along the American boundary because of the embarrassment it would give to "Our future Proceedings" with the States. Other points were rejected curtly as impractical or immature. Express disapprobation was stated for any measure tending to encourage hostilities with the United States, and earlier advice was repeated: stand vigilant, but "studiously avoid whatever may give a pretence for urging on and inflaming the popular Prejudices now existing there against this Country."[70] An appalled and chastened lieutenant-governor of Upper Canada wrote home in alarm of his "great astonishment and Anxiety" at Dundas' stern language, and altogether disavowed Stevenson and the misuse of his name.[71]

Peace in the Old Northwest did not, however, depend solely on leashing Simcoe and his incorrigible subordinate. By the time Dundas' rebuke arrived in Toronto, the American Wayne had commenced his advance northward. By February, 1794, the newly returned Dorchester was himself afire with apprehensions that the intention was "to close us up at Detroit." Orders, solicited by Simcoe earlier but refused, were soon speeding from Quebec to Toronto. For the security of Detroit, Simcoe was to take post on the Maumee River at the site of the former British fortifications demolished at the peace. Armed ships and vessels were to preserve the British command of the Lakes.[72] Despite the unchanging tenor of British official pronouncements, a confrontation of the most ominous kind was apparently in the making. Britain—in admitted (though she would have it, justified) possession of American territory, bearing at least a remnant of the responsibility for the welfare of former Indian subjects, committed to the defensive principle and the search for a diplomatic settlement with the Republic to the south of Canada—had now to face an approaching military force commanded by a vigorous and aggressive general whose intentions were unknown and who represented a nation, the ally of an open and declared enemy, which evidently spurned a settlement of differences by negotiations in good faith.

PART VI

The Anglo-French War:
The Changing Context of Policy

CHAPTER FOURTEEN

The New Problems

THE OUTBREAK of war between Britain and France in 1793 provided a new and ominous context for Anglo-American relations. Old problems did not disappear. True, they were superseded, but they lost little of their urgency.

Above all, Britain desired neutrality from the United States; but certain provisions in the Franco-American accords of 1778 gave cause for worry. Article XI of the treaty of alliance, termed "eventual and defensive," bound the United States to guarantee French possessions in the New World. Article XVII of the commercial agreement granted reciprocal freedom for ships of war or privateers to carry the prizes made against an enemy power into the ports of the neutral ally, and there to dispose of them. Refuge was denied to foreigners preying on the marine of either contractor. Article XXII forbade any foreign privateer, hostile to one of the two powers, to fit out, victual, or sell prizes in ports of the other. The exact meaning of these general propositions, especially Article XVII of the commercial agreement, remained unclear, and troubled British diplomatists rarely missed an opportunity to probe America's interpretation of her obligation to France.[1]

When France declared war, speculation about America's role became widespread and anxious. Rumors, apparently emanating from Carmichael in Madrid and circulating in London political circles, had the American government declaring to the Spanish authorities that it would support France if that power were attacked. John Hamilton, consul at Norfolk, Virginia, clearly expected a renewal of Anglo-American hostilities, and said so to his government. In London, the anti-Pitt press used the probability of American inter-

vention as at least a secondary argument against war with France.[2]
The French National Convention's appointment of Edmond Charles
Genêt to succeed Ternant at Philadelphia caused great official concern, Grenville instructing Hammond to be especially vigilant in
discovering the nature of any Franco-American negotiations. A little
later, the British Secretary told the envoy to stand ready to counter
any French attempt to invoke the treaty of alliance with the United
States, since the war was an "unjust and unprovoked Aggression of
France." An appeal to the "defensive" treaty and the guarantee of
the French West Indies was unlikely, Grenville thought; but the
minister at Philadelphia was to watch diligently "everything that
can have the smallest relation with that subject" and to thwart any
possible French effort in every practicable way.[3]

Hammond wasted no time. Acting on instructions of January,
1793, he sought and received from Alexander Hamilton explicit assurances that no secret understanding bound the United States and
the "pretended" government of France. This was ground for some
comfort; but beyond that point, the uneasy Briton could only observe, surmise, and conjecture. A majority of Americans seemed to
him to prefer neutrality and even abrogation of the treaty with
France to participation in the war. He was nervously aware, however, that he could be wrong. The French Revolution was certainly
popular in some quarters. There was, furthermore, a party in the
country—pro-French, anti-Federal, many of them debtors and southerners—ready to capitalize upon it in any way likely to help them
achieve a double object: to weaken the federal government and to
hurt Great Britain. Led by Jefferson—himself a debtor, Hammond
remarked, "blinded by his attachment to France, and his hatred of
Great Britain"—they might conceivably swing the balance to war.
Hamilton would oppose this, knowing that "any event which en-
dangers the *external* tranquility of the United States, would be as
fatal to the systems he has formed for the benefit of his country, as
to his present personal reputation and to his future projects of ambition." The American Secretary of the Treasury had his supporters,
too, friends of the Constitution and of a determined neutrality; and
he dominated the cabinet. It was evident to Hammond, however,
that the men of Washington's administration were not "objects of
popular favor." Public opinion in the country was extremely vocal—
and volatile. Party strife, blazing out in a savage newspaper warfare,

was so bitter and deep that internal peace, if not national existence itself, was at issue. The United States was "in a moment of crisis," and a resolution was not long to be delayed. Conceivably, the forces favoring neutrality might be overborne; and Britain would have to face attempts against her possessions in the New World, annoyance of her shipping, a "partial" interruption of commerce, and sequestration of debts and of the unfortunately "lavish amount" of British capital invested in the country. Pushing his speculations further, Hammond noted that the means of defense were ready at hand. Unwise private investors would suffer, but they had only themselves to thank for their losses. Other inconveniences would be only temporary. America, however, would suffer "immeasurably" from a rupture, Hammond grimly concluded: trade destroyed, revenue blasted, her national ruin would inevitably follow. Surely, the facts were as obvious to Americans themselves as they were to Britain's minister at Philadelphia.[4]

Or were they? American neutrality was "necessary for the Success of his [Majesty's] Arms," Grenville wrote to Hammond in March. The envoy could not banish immediately the nightmare of triumphant and bellicose Jeffersonians, already dominant in the House of Representatives, sweeping the nation into war. On several occasions, he sought out Hamilton. By early April, he felt the ground somewhat firmer: the Secretary of the Treasury showed no signs of retreating from his earlier position. He would have "as strict a neutrality as may not be directly contrary" to his country's public engagements. Furthermore, he told his visitor, Washington himself "perfectly concurs . . . not only on the propriety, but on the indispensible necessity" of holding aloof from the struggle. Even though the government intended to recognize Genêt, who had not yet arrived, as minister *de facto* and to accept the treaties of 1778 as still binding, the execution of Louis XVI notwithstanding, Hammond was encouraged by Hamilton to believe that the wisdom of "prudence" was becoming plain to the nation as a whole.[5]

When Washington formally proclaimed American neutrality on April 22, 1793, Hammond's newfound optimism seemed justified. Citizens of the Republic were told by their President that the country required a "friendly and impartial" conduct toward all belligerents. They were not, on pain of prosecution, to commit, aid, or abet hostilities. Nor were they to carry to any belligerent articles deemed contraband "by the *modern* usage of nations."[6] It was, on balance, a gratifying statement for British leaders. (They worried not a whit about the omission of the word "neutrality.") Proclamations are one thing, however, actions another; and neutrality can be benevolent or the reverse. Washington's statement did contain at least one ambiguity—the definition of contraband, which had been introduced deliberately by Jefferson; and France, it was to be expected, would strive to capitalize to the maximum upon American friendship. The proclamation notwithstanding, therefore, it was plain that Britain continued to have "the utmost occasion" for watchfulness if American neutrality were not to be allowed to become as inimical to her interests as open hostility.[7]

Care was particularly required if Britain were to exploit to the maximum an obvious French weakness: shortage of provisions, especially grain and flour. Crop failures had been common for several years preceding the war. France suffered especially in 1792; and Britain saw a chance to reduce her enemy by shutting off supplies from the outside world. Co-operation was promised by Britain's continental allies, and the military logic of the plan seemed sound. Further, France had opened herself to such an attack by what Grenville was subsequently to call her "unusual mode of war," the unprecedented, systematic mobilization of the entire nation—civilian as well as military—for the prosecution of the struggle.

On January 21, 1793, Pitt, Hawkesbury, and Dundas, believing war imminent, met as the Committee of Trade and reached three important decisions. First, British vessels in home ports laden with grain and flour destined for France were prohibited from proceeding; some other destination might be chosen, although a security was required. Second—approaching the delicate question of neutral rights very carefully—any foreign vessel in a British port so laden and bound was to be informed, without any hint of coercion, that the British government was prepared to purchase its cargo, making fair allowance for a reasonable profit and for freight and other charges. Finally, all vessels with war stores bound for France were forbidden to proceed; His Majesty's government would buy the cargo or allow the vessel to sail to any non-French destination.[8]

With war a declared reality, the problem became more complicated, especially as it bore on neutral suppliers of grain and related products—chiefly the United States. The British government was well aware of a principal and urgent object of French diplomacy: to acquire massive supplies of American grain and provisions, for which they would pay by inducing the United States to liquidate completely and immediately her debt contracted with the Bourbon monarchy in earlier revolutionary days. The measure would have set aside established arrangements for discharging the debt—a long series of quarterly instalments—and would have been of very great help to Britain's enemy. Indeed, Washington's cabinet decided, when the French request was made by Minister Ternant in February, 1793, that it could not legitimately accede to it within the limits of bona fide neutrality. A certain amount of arrearage—about $200,000— was paid over to Colonel William Smith, the "confidential agent" for France in the purchasing of wheat and flour from the United States; but Hammond, who had had informal communication from Hamilton on the subject, told the British government there need be no fear that the French revolutionaries would persuade the American government to extinguish the entire debt immediately.

There was, however, a deeper consideration. It was the status of grain and flour purchased in the United States by France and shipped to its destination in American bottoms. On this fundamentally important issue, the British government showed not a moment's hesitation: Hammond was told to inform the United States government quite explicitly that enemy property was liable to capture, even aboard American vessels. Free ships did not make free goods. Britain had always maintained the principle, Grenville wrote; and to give it up in the present case would give France means of prolonging the war. If Hammond learned that the enemy was in fact buying grain and flour in the United States and preparing to ship them aboard any vessel at all, he was to make appropriate protests to the federal government. The matter was not to rest there, however. At the same time, the envoy was also to alert the commanders of His Majesty's ships cruising off the American coast. If diplomacy failed, force would be used.

The restrictions were not mere exercises in academic theory. At that very moment, Colonel Smith was negotiating in the United States for private credit to make purchases for France, and another shipment was in preparation: eight vessels were involved, Hammond reported, some seven of which were American.[9] The British envoy's report raised another, far more complex question. To adduce as a

general principle the right to seize enemy property even aboard neutral vessels was inadequate, if the plan to starve France into submission was to succeed. She must not even be allowed to receive grain
and flour owned by neutrals and shipped to France aboard neutral
vessels. Such traffic would make the British system an open sieve and
invite massive Franco-American collusion, as well as provide the enemy with necessary supplies.

Only one solution would answer: to extend contraband to include grain and flour. Precedents existed from the reign of Anne,
and urgent need provided additional justification.[10] Extremes were
to be avoided, however, the British government hoped; and much
was left unsaid in the hope that the end could be achieved without
an explicit assertion of the principle. Hammond was accordingly
instructed to warn the Americans in general terms that even their
bona fide property, if contraband, would be seized en route to France;
the term was obviously intended to mean any article sustaining life,
and hence contributing to the capacity to wage war. Grain and flour
were not explicitly mentioned, but the implication was so broad
that no doubt was possible. Although the ultimate disposition of
American produce forcibly diverted was left unstated, Britain was
clearly determined to deprive France of outside sustenance, enemy or
neutral.[11]

On April 21, a British cutter brought into Guernsey the American
brig *Sally*, bound for Le Havre and laden with 2,109 barrels of flour.
The goods were claimed as American, but it quickly came to light
that they were part of Ternant's purchases in the United States. The
case involved collusion, not the seizure of neutral property. A precedent was in the making; and the British ministry proceeded with a
nice regard for legal form.[12] Obviously, it was only a matter of time
before the question of neutral grain in a neutral vessel bound for
France would be raised. The British government moved to provide
the appropriate legal base for its system. On June 8, 1793, an Order
in Council was issued: ships laden wholly or in part with wheat,
flour, or meal, bound for enemy ports, were to be intercepted and
detained. In the case of neutrals, a fair purchase price and freight
charges would be allowed; or a master might, upon the giving of a
security, choose to dispose of his cargo in the port of any power
friendly to Great Britain. Copies of the order and appropriate additional instructions for commanding officers of the Royal Navy were

transmitted to Hammond on July 5. The dispatch also contained Britain's official justification, a guide for Hammond in his dealings with the American government.

Grenville's position was powerfully expressed. Drawing support from respected authorities on international law, especially Vattel, he argued compellingly that provisions could justly be regarded as contraband when there was a reasonable expectation of reducing the enemy to peace by cutting him off from outside sources of supply. France, he maintained, was notoriously in such a condition. Furthermore, the British measure was justified because France was a nation in arms, with resources of the entire nation, civilian and military, mobilized to an unprecedented degree. Trade itself was no longer "a mercantile speculation of individuals," but an operation of "the pretended Government of France itself," merely one weapon of many. Indeed, Britain would have been well within her rights if she had prohibited all provisions instead of only wheat and flour. She had not done so, however, exempting particularly rice, "an article so material in the scale of the commerce of America."[13]

The argument outlined in detail in Hammond's instructions was made by Grenville himself to Pinckney in London. The American minister, acting at his own initiative, protested to Grenville immediately upon learning of the order, but, perhaps fearing to go too far without official sanction, questioned the order chiefly because he doubted there was a reasonable prospect of reducing France by famine. Grenville's response also avoided principle: there was every well-founded expectation that France could be starved into peace, he told his visitor; and Britain was fully supported in the enterprise by her allies.[14] This sparring, however, was only preliminary.

Rumors of Britain's intentions toward neutral carriers circulated in the United States in the spring of 1793. Jefferson's immediate, though private, reaction was to consider the "idea," if true, a *casus belli*; but his second thought was more moderate.[15] The Secretary of State by May had formulated the official American position. Feigning disbelief that Britain aimed to commit "so unequivocal an infringement of the neutral rights," Jefferson instructed Pinckney to represent to the British authorities that, in the American view, free ships indubitably made free goods. Treaties with France and Holland incorporated the principle; and the accord with Prussia was even more liberal, abandoning the idea of contraband altogether. Britain

herself accepted the protective power of the neutral flag in her own
commercial treaty with France in 1786. Here was clearly an international consensus, Jefferson argued; and the principle was consequently a part of the law of nations. It should accordingly "form the
line of conduct for us all."[16]

At the end of August, with authenticated copies of the order before it, the President's cabinet decided to instruct Pinckney "provi-
sionally." If the order was an established fact, the American was to
denounce it to the London government as a violation of neutral
rights, to demand its revocation, and to claim full indemnity for
losses to citizens of the United States. Two restrictions only were
to be admitted binding upon neutral commerce: in the furnishing of
implements of war to any belligerent, and in trading to blockaded
ports. A warning of counteraction was also given: to preserve her
impartial neutrality, the United States might well find it necessary
to lay an embargo on all foreign trade. Should Britain persist in her
habitual inattention to American representations, silence itself would
be sufficient answer. Pinckney was to report home no later than December 1, to permit time for congressional consideration during the
current session—an undisguised reminder that Madison's retaliatory
resolutions could easily be resurrected.[17] Hammond approached Jefferson in September, but he met with a cold rebuff. He was crisply
informed that the United States government was offended by the
order, that the American minister in London was instructed to raise
the subject, and that the Secretary of State declined to discuss it with
him. Even Hamilton, Hammond wrote home, regarded the order as
"very harsh and unprecedented," militating against "the principal
branch of the present American exports." The Briton defended the
order "as well as I was able," but he had no illusions about his effectiveness. Hamilton continued to think it both inexpedient and unjust,
and considerable numbers of merchants and members of Congress
agreed. A second attempt to argue the point with Jefferson proved
unavailing. In that quarter, a lofty silence prevailed, while among
the public at large, "a state of agitation" grew over the entire question of neutrality.[18]

Within a matter of days after the promulgation of the order,
British cruisers began bringing in American vessels in considerable
numbers. Pinckney's first memorial, dated July 22, dealt with three
specific vessels, "only a small part" of the total. Grenville's response

was bland and amicable, but adamantine: the cases mentioned were under adjudication, hence beyond the interference of the British Executive. Inconvenience to American citizens would be kept at a minimum, Grenville wrote; but so far was Britain from violating neutral rights, that she had actually waived the full exercise of those rights pertaining to her belligerent status by not issuing a blanket prohibition of all provisions. Pinckney returned to the attack several times, notably on August 9; drawing his argument directly from Jefferson's dispatch of the preceding May, he asserted categorically that free ships made free goods, a principle supported by the "sense of a considerable majority of the Maritime Powers of Europe" and, hence, binding upon all.[19]

To every American protest, Grenville was polite but unshakable: the British government guaranteed complete and impartial justice to any person suffering in body or property from illegal acts, and completely disapproved of acts of violence and severity. In the course of a worldwide naval war, however, occasional inconvenience to neutrals was unfortunately unavoidable. He could only promise that every effort would be made to keep these inconveniences at the absolute minimum. In the event of "irregularities," the Foreign Secretary welcomed full communication of the facts; and the law officers of the Crown stood ready to assist in prosecution of British malefactors. His position notwithstanding, Grenville's manner was so conciliatory that Pinckney was convinced that the British government and public truly desired to preserve not merely correct, but cordial relations with the United States.[20]

The Opposition in Parliament and in the press had a quite different view, however; and, for the first time since the defeat of the American Intercourse Bill in 1783, American affairs emerged briefly as a party issue in British politics. Bitterly opposed to the war with France, Charles James Fox and his supporters grasped at the straw afforded by the Order of June 8, 1793, thinking it a cudgel with which to belabor Pitt and the ministry. British conduct toward the United States, Fox told his nephew Lord Holland, was truly "insufferable, both for arrogance and injustice." Prior commitments to France scarcely left the United States in the position of a neutral; but if Pitt chose to precipitate a quarrel with the Americans, "our commerce would suffer more in this war than any other preceding one."[21] The *Morning Chronicle*, Fox's prime newspaper supporter since the time of the regency crisis in 1789, predicted an American declaration of war and published, with glum satisfaction, premature reports of an embargo on British shipping and even the outbreak of hostilities.

By raising the issue, which was but a relatively minor aspect of its attack upon the Pitt ministry, the Opposition merely increased its own unpopularity, already great because of its affinity, more than suspected, for the French Revolution. *"Jacobinical"* in politics and principles, Fox and his friends strained to invent "every malicious rumour that may damp the spirit of Englishmen," exclaimed the *Public Advertiser*, firm friend of the ministry. Far from underrating the United States, however, the newspaper asserted that America possessed powers "of whose present resources no judgment can be formed, till some country has the misfortune to try them"; but surely she was too well aware of her own interests, commercial and political, to be misled by British jacobins or to plunge into a struggle at the side of "usurping miscreants who are at war with all Europe."[22]

Jefferson's basic argument against the order—an international consensus binding upon all nations, even upon those whose interests it fundamentally violated—became untenable not because of British argument, but as a result of French action. Even before the Order in Council of June 8, 1793, the French National Convention decreed the seizure of neutral vessels carrying provisions to enemy ports. The excuse given was Britain's own treatment of neutral carriers; but the action was, nonetheless, a direct violation of the Treaty of Amity and Commerce with the United States. Strong American protests brought only a momentary recantation. Before the summer was out, French policy was as fixed as British. By 1794, all belligerents were taking enemy property regardless of the nationality of the carrier.[23] Consensus, it would seem, came to operate on Britain's side.

The United States could bind herself in any way she pleased to observe the rights of the neutral flag, but the unalterable fact remained that the principle contradicted directly a point of British maritime policy which had been cherished for more than a hundred years.[24] To grant to Americans the right to cover with their neutral flag the goods of an enemy would be an act of peculiar folly, the makers of British policy reasoned. They would render the enemy's trade to and from the West Indies impervious to attack and vitiate the naval might of the Empire.[25] National survival was at stake;

and this was Britain's ultimate justification for her position, against which no plea could be allowed. "Each man hath a right to perform certain actions," wrote Charles Jenkinson in 1757: "but if the destruction of another should follow from them, would not this be a just reason of restraint? The rights of mankind admit of different degrees, and whenever two of these come into competition, the lowest in the scale must always give place to the higher."[26] Later, as a noble lord, he threw aside finespun theorizing, stating fundamentals with characteristic, blunt economy: "in time of War," he told Pitt, "the conduct of belligerent, as well as of neutral Powers, has been governed in these Respects, and probably will always be, by the Occasions and Circumstances, which the Necessities of War produce."[27] Jefferson, Pinckney, Fox, and, indeed, all the world might talk grandly about rights of varying descriptions; but before the right to survive, all others gave way.

By early autumn, American reaction appeared to the London government to have changed to grumbling acquiescence. Pinckney wrote to Philadelphia, advising abandonment of any hope that Britain would change the policy laid down in the order of June 8. If the country cared to pursue the matter beyond mere remonstrance, commerical retaliation, he told his government, was to be preferred to more bellicose counterstrokes. More surprising, Jefferson himself was "so moderate and lukewarm" in a conversation with Hammond about contraband, that the envoy advised London to disregard any threats of an alarming nature from Pinckney; they were "not meant to be seriously enforced."[28]

The new American mildness was in part deceptive. Secretary Jefferson had no intention of dropping the issue raised by the June order; but Hammond was right, too: after the first angry outburst, the American reaction had moderated. There were three major reasons for this: first and most dramatic was the disastrous diplomacy —if the word may be used—of Edmond Charles Genêt. His brazen attempt to turn the American Republic into a base for French aggression against Spanish and British possessions and maritime commerce in the New World dissipated much goodwill in the United States toward France, discredited the Jeffersonian Republicans, and committed the United States to a far stricter neutrality than would probably have been the case had the Frenchman's conduct been more discreet.[29]

Article XVII of the Franco-American Treaty of Amity and Commerce, as previously noted, allowed warships and privateers belonging to either power, if engaged separately in a war, to bring in and dispose of prizes in the ports of the neutral ally. Article XXII prohibited the enemies of the one country from fitting out privateers in the ports of the other. Genêt insisted that the clear implication of Article XXII bestowed on France the right specifically denied to her enemies. Without even waiting to discuss the matter with the federal authorities, he proceeded to act upon his assumption as soon as he landed on American soil. Arriving at Charleston, South Carolina, in April, 1793, he promptly commissioned several privateers in the name of the French Republic. Two were fitted out at Charleston; others were brought into service as the envoy progressed northward to Philadelphia. By the end of July, some thirteen American vessels, comprising a total force of 146 cannon and 920 men, were cruising off the American coast under the authority of France. Nine of these were the direct results of Genêt's activities in the United States. By year's end, the merchants, shipowners, and insurers of London were complaining mightily to the government of the many captures made by the Frenchmen off the American coast and disposed of by sale in ports of the United States. The crowning outrage, they said, was the condemnation of prizes by "courts" sitting under the presidency of French consuls in the United States, a monstrous violation of American neutrality and sovereignty.

Even before Genêt's arrival in the United States, Grenville alerted Hammond to the possibility of a French attempt to fit out privateers in American ports. The British envoy was told to stand ready to deliver "the strongest Representations" should the situation require them.[30] Hammond's efforts were, in fact, unnecessary. Washington's administration was already united in its uncompromising condemnation of Genêt's actions. The privateers were peremptorily ordered out of American ports. The impudent and insolent Genêt was not, however, so easily checked. Treating the American government with studied discourtesy and contempt, he denounced the proclamation of neutrality as both unconstitutional and, worse, disrespectful to himself. Appealing his cause directly to the American people over the head of the Executive, he embarked, Hammond gleefully reported home, upon "a most serious misunderstanding" with the federal government.[31] The Frenchman's every action made matters worse, hurting Franco-American friendship and weakening Jefferson's diplomacy with the British. Refusing to restore a cargo of American grain which had been seized by a French privateer while it was being carried by a British vessel, Genêt simultaneously argued that French property aboard American ships deserved the protection of the neutral flag.

There was a single alternative to acquiescence; and an appalled but irate Jefferson took it: there could be no doubt, he told Genêt, that under "the general law of nations," the goods of a friend found in the vessel of an enemy were free, while enemy goods found aboard a friend's vessel were lawful prize. To argue that goods "*follow the vessel*" was to insist upon "an exception depending on special conventions only." The abandonment of the "free ships, free goods" doctrine might have been written by Lord Hawkesbury himself.[32]

The fantastic drama—tragedy to Jeffersonian Republicans—continued to unfold: more privateers were commissioned in defiance of the strictest orders from the American authorities; the two Charleston privateers returned to American ports with new prizes; and the ultimate defiance was dealt to the federal government in the case of *Le Petit Democrat*, before her capture the British brig *Sarah*. Printed invitations appeared daily in Philadelphia newspapers exhorting all "*friends of liberty*," regardless of nationality, to seek service aboard French vessels of war in American ports. Abuse of the President, Hamilton, and Secretary of War Knox was scandalous and virulent; and it was public knowledge that Genêt and his secretary were deeply involved in the press campaign to discredit the American Executive.

Hammond watched at first incredulously, then with growing satisfaction. The rising indignation of the responsible, respectable, and propertied elements of the country was expressed in resolutions applauding neutrality and the federal government's efforts to maintain it. The cabinet reached a decision, described to Hammond by Hamilton himself as "final and *unanimous*," to deal sternly and effectively with Genêt's outrageous conduct. The privateers fitted out in American ports would be ordered to depart forthwith and forever; any attempt to return would be repelled with force. Captures made after June 7, the date the Charleston cruisers were originally ordered to leave American waters, would be restored or compensation would be made by the United States government from sums due France;

Genêt's recall would be demanded. By early autumn, five out of nine privateers were lost, dismantled, or·captured. Any remaining threat was dissipated by the arrival of a British squadron under Admiral Murray, for whom Hammond obtained "the *right* . . . under every possible situation (except that, which is prohibited by the treaty with France, of coming in with their prizes) freely to resort to, and to indefinitely remain in, the American ports." The American central government seemed fully committed to the enforcement of a true neutrality, and the clash with Genêt was absolute, leaving no room for compromise. If the National Convention of France were disposed to support its minister, Hammond told Grenville, war would certainly follow with the United States, an event "to which I know this government looks forward, as neither improbable nor distant." Indeed, Hammond had "every reason to be satisfied with the conduct of the *federal government*."[33]

A second reason worked to soften American resentment of the Order of June 8, 1793: the impact of the order upon American shipping proved to be an inconvenience, but not a disaster; and it affected primarily merchants and shippers, the very men most committed to friendly relations with Britain. Prohibited provisions which were bona fide American property were not confiscated, but purchased; and reasonable allowances were even made for freight and demurrage.[34] Condemnation itself, according to the first decision handed down in a case involving an American vessel, did not deprive the owners of freight, demurrage, and expenses.

The principal American complaint was the lengthy nature of the judicial proceedings; delays were the habit in the admiralty courts. Pinckney protested repeatedly, and with reason, that tardy justice was, under the circumstances, injustice. In the summer of 1794, the American envoy told Grenville that there were then in British ports fourteen American merchantmen—their cargoes pre-empted by the government's purchase, and, in addition, their freight and expenses awarded. Legally free, they were unable to proceed, since their masters lacked funds to pay the port charges they had incurred, first, while under detention and, subsequently, while awaiting payment by His Majesty's Treasury. Relief, due to the leisurely manner in which the British government did business, was not expected for some weeks. Pinckney therefore asked immediate payment of "such a portion of what is due them as will enable them to defray their Expences and proceed to Sea."[35] A response was forthcoming immediately: even though the admiralty court's decrees were not final, sums were advanced from payments due to allow outfitting and putting to sea.[36] Masters of detained vessels were also perfectly free to appeal judgments from the Admiralty to the High Court; but the gentle treatment and circumspection of British authorities and all the expenses involved in an appeal made American owners and masters "rather inclined to submit . . . than risk the event of a law suit."[37]

Finally, American wrath at the Order of June 8, 1793, abated because of some serious second thoughts within the administration. In the spring of 1794—after Thomas Jefferson, disgruntled and disillusioned, had resigned his cabinet post—Edmund Randolph, the new secretary of state, prepared an official communication to Hammond about the order. The Treasury Secretary, to whom he exhibited his draft, took note of Randolph's original assertion that Britain had not regarded provisions as contraband for a century past: "I fear examples may be cited upon you," he told his colleague, "which will include the point, and more." (The "more" was a similar declaration of Louis XIV's France to Holland.) Hamilton suspected, "from some later lights which I have received," that the Order of June 8 was more justified by the practice of nations than he had originally thought. He therefore advised Randolph to deliver a general statement, declaring that "the doctrines advanced in support of the instructions of the 8th of June do not appear to us well-founded."[38]

However confident Hammond might feel about the intentions of the federal government, he could not conceal from himself the somber fact that a dangerous polarization of American public opinion was under way. Clashing sectional interests and contrary notions about the relative strength of federal and state governments produced, he observed to London, corresponding differences in foreign policy. The Federalists, led by Hamilton, supported a strong central government and peace and conciliation with Britain; they were opposed by "Democratic" or "Republican" societies, with centers of strength in the southern states, which looked to Jefferson and his friends for leadership. Favoring Genêt and his countrymen, the Republicans—wedded to "lax notions" of government, Hammond noted, and including many indebted to British merchants—aimed domestically at using France "to increase the ascendency of the de-

mocracy, both in the federal government and in the separate states."
They would not hesitate, Hammond warned his government, to
drag their country into the war. The mob was their instrument; and
they lost few chances to use it against Britons within their reach—
merchants, sailors, agents, officers, and even American friends of
Britain. Indeed, violence against his countrymen was so common that
Hammond began a systematic collection of evidence upon which to
found an official protest. Late in 1794 he suspended his efforts, however, fascinated at the approach of the final denouement in the
Genêt affair. The discomfiture of the King's enemies, American and
French, was at hand, he believed; and his secretary jubilantly echoed
the envoy's optimistic dispatches: while French influence was on the
decline, Hammond was "turning the current in another direction
with a sure and silent progress."[39] With Jefferson gone from the
cabinet, the friends of France in dismay, and the Order of June 8
only mildly enforced, British interests in the United States seemed
more secure than at any time since 1783.

This picture was but an illusion, however. In reality, the two
nations were on the verge of a most dangerous crisis, with peace or
war hanging upon the resolution.

CHAPTER FIFTEEN

The Rising Storm

BEGINNING IN DECEMBER, 1793, and for many months thereafter, the pattern of Anglo-American relations moved steadily, and apparently inevitably, toward a second war. The barest outline of events indicates the growing pressures and rising danger: Washington's message to Congress of December 5, accompanied by "certain correspondences" between Secretary of State Jefferson and the envoys from France and Britain, Genêt and Hammond; Jefferson's presentation to the House of Representatives on December 16 of the long-delayed report on foreign trade; the presidential message of the same date on the Barbary pirates; the resurrection of Madison's discriminatory resolutions in January, 1794, and the angry debates which followed in Congress; the promulgation of the British Orders in Council of November 6, 1793, and January 8, 1794; the bellicose speech by Governor Dorchester to the Indians in February, 1794; Simcoe's reoccupation soon thereafter of a post, abandoned in 1783, fifty miles south of Detroit; the advance of Wayne to the north; and the perilous confrontation of British and American forces after the Battle of Fallen Timbers.

There were two immediate, major causes of the crisis, although others, equally important, appeared subsequently and added both impetus and intensification. The first major cause was Britain's roughshod and inept treatment of American shipping. Had she held to the line laid down in the Order of June 8, 1793, much mischief might have been avoided without sacrificing any significant interest. Instead, the Pitt ministry adopted—temporarily, they said, although this qualification was long unknown to Americans—a harsher rule. The second cause was the design of Secretary Jefferson and the emerging Republican party to temper public indignation at the Genêt affair by drawing attention to the country's grievances against Britain. Striking harshly at the economic interests of the Federalists, the friends of Britain and of neutrality, the first of these causes sustained and encouraged the second. It is not the least significant condemnation of British policy that it gave the Republicans a magnificent opportunity, seized immediately and adroitly, to appear as champions of the nation against both an aggressive Britain and a subservient minority at home, grasping for profits and power while sacrificing its self-respect and the nation's true interest.

Material for a vicious Republican onslaught was ready at hand. Jefferson's report on foreign commerce—requested by the House of Representatives in 1791, but periodically delayed—would document Britain's commercial discrimination, emphasize her unwillingness to negotiate a commercial agreement, and provide a reminder of Britain's infractions of the peace to refresh the sense of injuries, past and present. Spoliations of American commerce under the Order of June 8, 1793, would provide fresh sustenance for the public ire. British dealings with Algiers, in behalf of the Portuguese ally, could be given a sinister interpretation. If all these matters were encompassed in a single barrage, the impact would be enormous: Britain revealed as a consistent, determined, and insidious enemy; France benefiting by the comparison. This was the Jeffersonian intention.

Toward the end of November, Washington's cabinet considered Attorney-General Randolph's draft of a presidential communication to Congress on the subject of relations not only with France, but also with Britain, Spain, and the Barbary powers. Secretary Hamilton made a mild effort to tone down the treatment of British spoliations; but, although supported by Randolph and Knox, he did not push his point. Offended by the June order, he seemed not unwilling to remind Britain of American sensibilities. Washington concurred with Jefferson, and Hamilton did not seriously attempt to impede the latter in his course. On December 5, 1793, therefore, the President gave to Congress papers relating to the country's dealings with both France and Britain.[1]

The message accompanying the documents spoke first of the differences with the French, pointing especially to the forcible diversion of American provisions vessels into their ports and to their making enemy goods lawful prize wherever found. Genêt was mentioned

next. The Frenchman's activities in the United States had promised
war abroad, discord and anarchy at home. The government had
counteracted them, however, and certainly the French authorities
"would not suffer us to remain long-exposed to the action of a person who has so little respected our mutual dispositions." It was a
round damnation of Citizen Genêt, to be sure; but Washington
clearly implied that the man was only a passing disturbance, already
relatively unimportant when judged on the larger scale of relations
between friendly nations. His recall would certainly re-establish
earlier amity and good understanding.

The complaints against Britain were of an entirely different magnitude. Vexations and spoliations of American vessels and commerce
were charged to "the cruisers and officers of some of the belligerent
powers," but the specific culprit was evident to all. Britain acted "to
restrain, generally, our commerce in corn and other provisions, to
their own ports, and those of their friends." Copies of the instructions to Pinckney and of the minister's dispatches describing earlier
conversations with Grenville were furnished; and the President hoped
that further news would arrive from London in time to receive the
consideration of Congress during the current session.

The tail of the message contained a final sting: soon after the arrival of the British minister in Philadelphia, the President stated,
"mutual explanations on the inexecution of the treaty of peace were
entered into"; and Congress was now presented with most of the letters and memorials which had passed between Jefferson and Hammond. That body and, inevitably, the public were, in effect, invited
to inspect the recent proceedings, and Britain's unsatisfactory conduct throughout: her refusal to establish a basis for friendship with
a commercial accord; her perpetuation of old animosities by ignoring
the peace treaty; her intransigence which it was inescapably inferred
had brought negotiations to an end; her measure of guilt for the
Indian war implied by Jefferson's prodding letter to Hammond of
June 19, 1793, and the sinister new note it injected—that the detention of the posts extracted a daily toll of American "blood and treasure"; Hammond's exception, weakened by his admission that London
had not replied to him, a response which the hapless Briton could but
repeat toward the end of the year; and, final proof of British ill will,
her systematic violation of America's neutral rights since the outbreak of war with France. The correspondence included Pinckney's

report of September 25, 1793, indicating that protests were unavailing and that the British line toward neutral powers was immutably fixed. In sum, a single impression was put forth, enforced, and reinforced: Britain was a malevolent and hostile power. By comparison, how transient and trivial were American troubles with France! It was a formidable and ominous presentation.[2]

Hammond, suddenly cast down from his optimism and delight at the Genêt affair, was shocked and then outraged. Officially silent, he poured out his bitterness in dispatches home, in correspondence with friends, and in conversations with sympathetic Americans. The unilateral publication of his official correspondence was particularly odious to him, a flagrant breach of diplomatic usage and of common courtesy. This violation of confidence was bad enough, Hammond believed; but Jefferson's editing, aimed at creating a false and misleading impression for the benefit of France, was even worse. The negotiations on the unfulfilled treaty of peace had not ended, he told his superiors; they were merely suspended. It was not only wrong, but deliberately dishonest to assert that Britain refused to negotiate a commercial understanding; but most reprehensible of all, perhaps, was the implication—so powerful that it stopped just short of positive statement—that Britain intrigued with the Indians. With wicked purpose, to Hammond's mind, Jefferson omitted in his selection of documents the acknowledgment, in his own hand, that he and his government accepted the protestations Britain had offered of her own innocence.[3]

The presidential message was but the first shot in a triple salvo. On December 16, the House of Representatives received Jefferson's long-pending Report on Commercial Privileges and Restrictions— "the last labor of Mr. Jefferson's political existence as Secretary of State," wrote a furious Hammond. It dealt with all countries holding a significant portion of the trade of the United States; but its chief purpose was, quite obviously, to cast into glaring comparison the friendly measures of France and the prohibitions, duties, and discriminatory regulations of Britain. Lauding the theory of free trade with all the world, Jefferson asserted the necessity of meeting discrimination with discrimination in order to protect American citizens, commerce, and navigation. If "particular nations" sought to engross navigation unduly, seizing on America as "aliment for their own strength," measures of self-defense were not only justified, but necessary. Abandoning general language, Jefferson pointed his shaft openly at the enemy: British policy had already cost the United States between eight hundred and nine hundred vessels—almost forty thousand tons—and, of course, a proportional number of seamen, shipwrights, and the like. The country could no longer avoid "some effectual remedy." Compare, Jefferson invited his readers, Britain with France. The latter, "of her own accord," proposed negotiations for a new commercial treaty on "fair and equal" principles. Admittedly, "internal disturbances" had as yet obstructed the fulfilment of French benevolence; but repeated reassurances testified to her continuing disposition. Britain, spurning proposals for a friendly arrangement from the United States, enjoyed "a footing in law, and a better in fact, than the most favored nation." Under existing circumstances, she saw no need to alter her policy. The circumstances, Jefferson argued, should be changed forthwith.[4]

The report twanged at Hammond's fraying nerves. The product of passion and prejudice, he told London, it was based on the "avowed, undisguised tendency" to create a closer connection with France and to declare commercial war on Britain. Holding to a studied indifference in public, the Briton abandoned sangfroid in private: his country, he took every opportunity to say, refused ever to be intimidated into a dereliction of her traditional policy. American discrimination would be answered in the same language.[5]

The drumfire attack suddenly developed in a new quarter. On December 16, Secretary Jefferson forwarded to Congress a second report, dealing with the Barbary powers, Morocco and Algiers.[6] The American problem arose indirectly from her new independence, he stated. When the country separated from Great Britain, she lost the benefit of the mother country's arrangements—compounded of adroit diplomacy, well-timed flattery, and open bribery—by which imperial shipping was exempted from Moslem maritime depredations. A treaty was negotiated by the new republic with the emperor of Morocco; but the succession of a new ruler there, the refusal of the Algerians to come to terms, and their search for new victims in lieu of the Spanish, who had bought peace in 1785, marked Americans as fair prey. Two ships, with their cargoes and crews of twenty-one persons, were taken and carried into Algiers. There the wretched captives remained—their number dwindling, until at the end of 1793, they were only thirteen—held for ransom while their luckless government sought to buy their release. Admiral John Paul Jones was named commissioner in June, 1792, to treat with the dey; but Jones's death and that of his successor, Thomas Barclay, delayed matters further. Finally in March, 1793, Colonel David Humphreys, the minister resident at Lisbon, was charged with responsibility for the Algerian mission.

Humphreys arrived at Gibraltar in late September. Plague was ravaging Algeria, and there was no news of the captives. Suddenly, he learned of an alarming development. On October 8, he wrote in consternation to the American Secretary of State. Portugal, whose navy had until then kept the "Algerines" bottled up in the Mediterranean, had concluded a year's truce with Algiers; and a fleet of hungry, piratical cruisers had already actually passed through the Straits of Gibraltar into the Atlantic. The threat to American shipping was great and immediate. In a private letter to the President, Humphreys declared himself convinced that Britain had engineered the treaty for her Portuguese ally.[7]

The onslaught was prodigious; and Algerian demands for tribute, described by the redoubtable Captain O'Brien of the *Dauphin*, which had been taken in 1785 and held captive ever since, were outrageous. By December, 1793, thirteen American vessels and 119 American seamen were in Algerian hands. A Treaty of Peace and Amity was not signed at Algiers until September 5, 1795. Its negotiation, involving American tribute and eventual relief for the captives, lies without the scope of the present work; what is of relevant importance, however, is the conviction—expressed privately by Humphreys to Washington and publicly in the dispatches of the American consul at Lisbon, Edward Church—that the Portuguese-Algerian truce was the result of a British arrangement aimed in large measure at hurting the United States. "The conduct of the British in this business," Church wrote to Secretary Jefferson on October 12—in a document which was then laid before Congress by President Washington on December 16—"leaves no room to doubt or mistake their object which was evidently aimed at us, and proves that their envy, jealousy, and hatred, will never be appeased, and that they will leave nothing unattempted to effect our ruin." There was confirmation of "the hellish plot," the consul continued, in a truce just procured by the British for their Dutch allies. Only American and Hanse vessels now remained objects of Barbary attack. "We are betrayed," Church moaned, "and many, many of our countrymen will fall into the cruel snare." Perfidy was further compounded, he continued: one of the Algerine cruisers then in the Atlantic was said (but on whose authority, it is not clear) to be "a *very late* present from the British King." Humphreys found the truce no less odious than did Church; but he was inclined to clear the British government of complicity in a plot, laying the blame at the door of the British consul at Algiers. The American Congress and public, increasingly angry with Britain, were unlikely to recognize the distinction.

The news of the Portuguese-Algerian truce caused what Pinckney, in masterly understatement, described to Grenville in an unofficial communication as "a disagreeable Sensation in America." It was accepted not as the effort of one ally to help another, but as "a Measure calculated to distress the American Commerce." Joel Barlow in Paris, Rufus King in New York, Christopher Gore in Boston, and Secretary Jefferson in Philadelphia differed greatly in many fundamental matters; in one, however, they were unanimous: the Lisbon agreement with the Moslem pirates was the product of British chicanery directed at the United States. "The letting loose the Algerines on us, which has been contrived by England," wrote Jefferson, "has produced peculiar irritation. I think Congress will indemnify themselves by high duties on all articles of British importation. If this should produce war, tho' not wished for, it seems not to be feared." This was, perhaps, a case of the wish fathering the thought; but, in the bitter debates which were waged in Congress in the new year, the truce took its place on the growing list of grievances that America held against Britain.[8]

On January 1, 1794, the House of Representatives, sitting as the committee of the whole, took up the commercial report. Two days later, Jefferson's intimate, James Madison, moved resolutions essentially the same as those he presented unsuccessfully in 1791. In addition, an extraordinary tonnage tax on British vessels trading between the sugar islands and the United States was proposed, both as retaliation for the exclusion of the country's merchantmen from British West Indian ports and as a source of revenue with which to compensate its sufferers at the hands of the ·British navy.

The House debated Madison's proposals and related matters throughout January and much of February, Federalists and Jeffersonian Republicans bitterly opposed in a struggle which set the seal of

permanence upon party distinction in American politics. On the offensive and apparently commanding a majority of the representatives,
Madison and his friends took their position solidly from Jefferson's
report. American commerce, they said with a "self-love" Hammond
found remarkable, was so important to Britain that a merely temporary interruption would frighten her merchants, manufacturers, and
government into speedy acceptance of American terms. The Federalists opposed ably, indeed, brilliantly. William C. Smith of South
Carolina was Hamilton's own mouthpiece, presenting to the House
the substance of the Treasury Secretary's answer, prepared two years
earlier, to Jefferson's report: British commercial policy did not single
out the United States for discrimination, and was, in fact, more
friendly than hostile. Many important items of American produce
enjoyed special favors not accorded the produce of any other country.
Fully 75 per cent of American foreign trade went to Britain, while
less than 15 per cent of Britain's came to the United States. The
prime importance of the former mother country to the economy of
the United States—especially as compared with France—was established beyond question. The danger to America from an interruption
of trade with Britain far outweighed any inconvenience the latter
might feel.

The cold, hard facts of commerce were strong in support of the
Federalist position so long as the argument centered on foreign trade.
The real object of the Republican attack, however, whatever its ostensible nature, was not commercial; it was political, aiming not so
much at the protection of American trade as at the assistance of
France and the injury of Britain. A very worried George Hammond
saw and wrote home about the speed with which abuse of Britain's
commercial policy gave way to other grievances: her infractions of
the treaty of peace, her alleged assistance to the Indians, the Algerian
truce, and maritime spoliations. In a masterly speech on January 27,
Fisher Ames, the Massachusetts Federalist, nailed down Republican
inconsistency.[9] Dealing first with the economic implications of Madison's propositions, he ridiculed them as measures calculated to destroy,
not protect and foster, the commercial prosperity of the United
States. True, British policy was "not as favourable for us as we
could make it, if we could legislate for both sides of the Atlantick,"
but the "extravagant despotism" the Republicans desired toward
Britain accorded but little with their affected zeal for a free trade or

with the realities of American power. One fact was better than two theories; and facts proved the soundness of Smith's argument. The laws of nature told merchants to seek the best markets. Americans found them in Britain, and "trade flourishes on our wharves, although it droops in speeches." Even American navigation, laboring under what Republicans called ill treatment, Ames continued, was strong and prosperous. Wages and freights high, the nation's ships were fully employed. That a great many British vessels profited from the American trade, too, was indisputable; but even this was advantageous to the United States, because it gave rise to greater capital investment in the country and to more reasonably priced ocean freight. A steady and moderate encouragement to American shipping, provided under the Tonnage Act, was prudent; but a sudden and violent exclusion of British shipping could only produce higher prices and diminution of mercantile capital. The result, Ames slyly remarked, would be "no little violence and injury, to our southern brethren especially."

Having demolished the Republicans' pretended object, the Federalist leader then fell upon their real one. His opponents, he declared, consulted not mercantile interests, but "visionary theories and capricious rashness of the legislators." Not a single merchant in the House supported Madison. Not one navigating or commercial state patronized his program. It was "wrong to make our trade wage war for our politicks." Britain and America possessed a great area of common mercantile interests. The Republicans planned to destroy it, sacrificing thereby the country's true welfare to their own prejudices and private interests.

Ames's powerful speech effected a calming influence both in Congress and outside, where public opinion, as an anonymous Federalist representative testified to a British correspondent, was shifting notably to support for the "Friends of Peace" against Genêt, the French, and the American Republicans. Indeed, the American added, Congress seemed on the verge of delivering "a decided Sentiment in favor of those measures which could insure Peace; and were disposed even to conform to the present state of things."[10] The pacific disposition was further encouraged by Pinckney's calm, common-sense dispatch of November 25, 1793, which was made available to Congress on February 24.[11] Containing important reassurances on Britain's friendly disposition, it showed Grenville's attitude to be studiedly courteous and conciliatory in his conversations with the envoy. Pinckney had complained to the Briton that his country's policy seemed inimical to American prosperity, citing three "particularly calamitous" circumstances which bore heavily on the United States: the Indian War, caused, it was asserted, by British retention of the border posts; "the letting loose the Algerines upon us"; and, finally, the vexatious interruption of America's commerce and the violation of her neutral rights by the Order of June 8, 1793. Since Jefferson's instructions of September 7 required him to present a written memorial on the order, he forebore pursuing the subject; but a discussion of the truce had taken place, and Grenville was conciliation itself, giving Pinckney an explanation which was subsequently furnished to Hammond for his use in a dispatch of January, 1794.[12] In procuring the truce, there was "not the least intention or a thought of injuring us," Pinckney paraphrased the Briton. The explanation was simple. The Portuguese court, a friend and ally, had requested British interposition with the pirates; Britain's response was nothing more than friendship required. Furthermore, the Portuguese fleet, freed from guarding the Straits against the Algerines, was now available for operations against France, the common enemy—a military consideration of prime magnitude to Britain herself. If, as Pinckney said, Portugal was willing to grant convoy privileges to American vessels, Britain had no objection whatsoever.

As for the posts, Grenville had reminded the envoy that the subject was actually under negotiation in Philadelphia. Both he and Pinckney agreed, "for obvious reasons," that the venue should not be changed. The business of the broken peace treaty was far from being terminated, Grenville admitted, perhaps dryly; he continued to receive "pressing applications" from British creditors. Even if the posts were relinquished under existing circumstances, British settlements in the backcountry would be ravaged, and his government would have to pay the same price the Americans now paid. The Foreign Secretary therefore believed that the "administration would not be justified in relinquishing the posts *at this time*."[13] It was a matter of regret, Pinckney reported Grenville as continuing, that Hammond had found it impossible to negotiate in Philadelphia "some arrangement relating particularly to the posts, and (as I apprehended him) Indian affairs." British mediation and the possibility of an Indian buffer state were, however, matters about which the Americans had, in Grenville's words, given Hammond "to understand (though in the most civil terms) that the less that was said . . . the better."[14]

Pinckney's dispatch did not minimize Anglo-American differences, but made it abundantly clear that both Grenville and Pinckney believed them amenable to calm, sensible diplomacy. The reassurance was important, encouraging the opinion of some, both in Congress and out, to turn against Madison's resolutions. As late as February 26, 1794, with vague and disquieting rumors of a new Order in Council already beginning to circulate, three hundred of the principal merchants of Boston signed a protest against legislative discrimination against Britain, although they were the very men, Consul Thomas MacDonogh observed, "who have been asserted to be most likely to be benefited" by the measure. Other important eastern and middle Atlantic commercial and shipping centers followed the Bostonians' lead.[15]

Anglo-American relations seemed headed for smoother sailing, when suddenly, with very little warning, around March 11, authentic news of an extraordinary seizure of American vessels by British cruisers in West Indian waters arrived in Philadelphia. A new Order in Council, dated November 6, 1793, was in force. Open declaration of war, a bitter Federalist lamented, would have been more magnanimous.[16]

The order—instructions to commanders of royal ships of war and privateers—directed the seizure of "all ships laden with goods the produce of any colony belonging to France or carrying provisions or other supplies for the use of any such colony."[17] Promulgated and executed with a secrecy rare in the eighteenth century, it came into force at a moment when there was an unusually large number of American vessels in West Indian waters. Britain herself was partly responsible for the influx, as she sought to secure adequate provisions for her own islands and conquests. When French Santo Domingo was occupied, for example, the capitulation stipulated that provisions, cattle, grain, and lumber might be imported in American bottoms. Commanders in chief at Jamaica and in the Leeward Islands were also told that, while technically illegal, arrangements for Martinique similar to those at Santo Domingo would be covered by an Act of Indemnity. Governor Home of Grenada notified the London authorities in May, 1793, that provisions and lumber were scarce, too, throughout the British islands and that it would be advisable to open ports to American vessels. Hawkesbury, to whose committee the Governor's letter was referred, was, not surprisingly, unfriendly to a change in the cherished existing system: the Governor's suggestion was flatly contrary to law, but emergency powers granted by 28 George III, ch. 6, allowed importation of provisions from any of the friendly foreign islands in British ships navigated according to law.[18] (How the produce came to be there in the moment of need was of little concern, even to Hawkesbury.) France issued an even more enticing invitation. Under a decree of February 19, 1793, she threw her sugar island ports open to American vessels on the same footing that French vessels enjoyed. French and British needs, therefore, combined to call an extraordinary number of American merchantmen into West Indian waters. All in all, Hammond estimated, fully one-half of the country's navigation was involved. When British men-of-war and privateers suddenly swooped down, the bag was enormous: some 250 American vessels seized, 150 of which were subsequently condemned.

The manner of capture, adjudication, and condemnation by British authorities in the islands was brutal. An American consul, Fulwar Skipwith, was aboard one of the seized vessels, the *Delaware*, bound for Philadelphia. His report to the secretary of state was graphic: he and the captain were forcibly deprived of their papers, and the ship was carried into Montserrat, stripped of her sails, and condemned in company with thirty-three others. Massive arrests occurred at St. Kitts and throughout the Windward Islands, too, the outraged consul wrote home in dispatches soon before Congress, all of the arrested victims of the "arbitrary and unauthorized" conduct of a nation filled with "avarice and ambitious views." Sitting in courts which were often irregularly constituted, in both British and Dutch islands, harsh and high-handed vice-admiralty judges viewed themselves as participants in a war against their country's enemies, not as dispensers of justice, declaring (on their own authority, since there was never such an instruction from London) that "the Powers combined against France mean to suppress every species of neutral commerce, with the people composing that nation, while at war." Numerous crews, destitute and stranded, Skipwith himself reported, could but look to the American consul for sustenance and a return passage to the United States.

From Martinique, where British forces were trying to reduce the island, came a representation from some forty American masters. Confined for three days, they were then treated to a public tongue-lashing by a high British naval officer. Personal property was withheld from the "damned rascals," and their effects were plundered. It took a month to establish (illegally) a vice-admiralty court to hear their cases, and another month to decide that a double security, forfeit in the event of condemnation, was a necessary preliminary to trial. Unable or unwilling to meet the condition, the Americans, whose vessels had been condemned in a blanket sentence, were told by a ruthless judge that they were "Bad men, supplying the wants of Bad men in a Bad Cause, and were and ought to be considered as Enemies to Great Britain."[19]

From the explanations subsequently offered by Lord Grenville, it is apparent that the naval and local island authorities, intentionally or not, very greatly misunderstood the scope and nature of the November order. The immediate occasion was the complex situation prevailing in the French West Indies in the summer of 1793. The tragic story of misguided French idealism and British military misadventures in the islands cannot be described here in detail. It is sufficient to say that by the summer of 1793, military logic and the internal state of the French islands—some already the scenes of desperate race war with anguished French settlers calling out for rescue by Britain—invited a British offensive in the area.[20] The situation on Haiti, the French portion of Santo Domingo, was particularly volatile. Enraged Negroes, intoxicated with the heady doctrines of the French Revolution, rose against their former masters. Thousands were massacred, and the colony dissolved into a grisly shambles. White refugees in great number fled the fury, carrying as much of their property as they could hastily assemble and remove from the island. A sizable fleet made for New York, while other vessels converged on the area. There was sympathy in Britain for the miserable refugees, but alarm, too, at the prospect of vast shipments of French West Indian property to Europe, providing desperately needed sustenance for France's economy and war effort. The United States was directly involved. George Hammond, reporting the arrival in American waters of the refugee fleet from Santo Domingo, warned London that collusive arrangements would undoubtedly be devised to send goods to Europe as American.[21] The *Morning Chronicle*, no friend to Pitt or to the war, expressed precisely the same fear. Hawkesbury, too, worried, especially that French vessels might acquire American nationality through purchase, real or collusive; the noble lord well knew the difficulty of detection and proof in such cases.[22]

The first—and, Grenville insisted, sole—object of the new order was to prevent the "larger and altogether unusual quantity of French property," the produce of Santo Domingo, from being carried to European markets. The "just and reasonable presumption," Grenville explained to Hammond for the American government's benefit, was that attempts would be made to utilize American shipping, thereby giving to France the benefit of the neutral flag and creating "a Speculation wholly out of the Course of the Usual Trade" of the United States. Consistently emphasizing the unique nature of the Santo Domingo case, Grenville instructed Hammond to counter American protests with the assurance that the measure was merely temporary and, in fact, had already been withdrawn by a new order, that of January 8, 1794; copies of both were enclosed in the same dispatch.[23] The later regulation implemented the "Rule of '56," allowing direct trade between the French islands and the United States in American bottoms except for contraband of war, but prohibiting neutral participation in the trade—closed to foreigners in peacetime—between the islands and the French mother country.

The plan was tidy enough: a temporary order to deal with an extraordinary situation, a lightning thrust, and a speedy return to "normal." It should have been obvious to Pitt and his colleagues from the first, however, that the impact of the November order could not be confined exclusively to Santo Domingo. France had opened all her possessions in the West Indies; and while in the summer of 1793 American vessels may have concentrated in greater numbers around the strife-torn island, they were by no means limited to it. Hundreds of vessels moved in as French planters and merchants throughout the area took alarm at threats of slave rebellion and British military operations. If the November Order was limited, as Grenville insisted, it covered only goods removed from Haiti; but the text did not focus on the island, and the distinction the Foreign Secretary suggested was so impracticable that it did not even occur to the commanders of His Majesty's vessels or judges of vice-admiralty courts. Clearly, the decree was an emergency measure, carelessly drafted, hastily adopted, and brutally executed as a blow against

France. To American sufferers, however, Grenville's explanations seemed blatantly hypocritical.

The British ministry may be arraigned on another count as well. It was expected that the Order of November 6 and its revocation by that of the following January 8 would arrive in the United States simultaneously, the latter countering the anger aroused by the former. The entire course of the recent American War proved the folly of London's trusting to fine timing in the New World; but the lesson was ignored. News of the seizure of American vessels under the November order was known in the United States a full month before it was learned, at the end of March, 1794, that the Order of January 8 had been issued. By then, the damage done to Anglo-American relations had reached very serious proportions, and the Republic was in an anti-British turmoil.[24]

The violent results of the November order have been allowed to obscure the more permanent aspect of British policy laid down in the succeeding decree: implementation of the "Rule of '56," a principle adduced by Britain a quarter of a century earlier. At the beginning of the Seven Years' War, France had declared her colonial trade open to neutral carriers. Britain had answered promptly with seizures and condemnations, justifying herself by arguing that the liberty granted by the enemy was in effect a design to increase her own maritime resources, and hence a measure of war. British courts subsequently declared that a neutral was not to enjoy wartime privileges in colonial trade which she had not possessed in peace. It was a logical deduction from the universally accepted mercantile system; and the underlying assumption—that extraordinary favors to neutrals during a war by a belligerent with inferior naval power were intended to increase her ability to sustain and wage war—is impossible to refute. It was a unilateral pronouncement, however, enforced solely by the might of the British navy.

Before she entered the War for American Independence in 1778, France thought to avoid the Rule of '56 by announcing the "permanent" opening of her colonial trade. Britain, with the great maritime powers of Europe as well as the thirteen American colonies ranged against her either as belligerents or as members of the League of Armed Neutrality, allowed the rule to sleep. The return of peace showed the true measure of the French maneuver: the old, exclusive, mercantile system was in large measure re-established. True, famine in the islands periodically opened ports to cargoes of supplies in American ships; but, despite sporadic efforts in the early stages of the French Revolution, the French government was unable to effect a permanent change.

The case in 1793, therefore, differed markedly from that in 1778. The opening of the French colonial trade came well after the declaration of war, from which timing it could be argued that this measure was indeed an act of war against Britain. Furthermore, the major maritime powers of Europe now tended to side against France, not with her, as in the American War. In fact, the League of Armed Neutrality was dead. Britain was able to invoke both principle and expedience to justify the implementation of the Rule of '56.

Unfavorable reaction to the new measures was to be expected in the United States. Rather more surprising was the sentiment expressed by the Opposition in Parliament and press at home. The *Morning Chronicle* branded the November order a "direct attack" on one of America's most important branches of trade and predicted war. American patience was already stretched to the breaking point, the paper warned. The retention of the posts, the abduction of Negroes, the conviction that Britain had stirred up the Indians, the "selfish" exclusion from the West Indies, Britain's seizure of French islands guaranteed by America under her treaty with France—all were making a breach irreparable. The forbearance of the United States proved her desire to live on an "Amical" footing with the former mother country; but persistent British aggression could have only one result.[25]

The newspaper attack was paralleled in Parliament by the argument of the Marquis of Lansdowne. On February 17, the former Earl of Shelburne moved in the upper house for peace with France.[26] Pursuing his general theme, he cited eloquently the dangers of expanding the war, the inevitable result, he foretold, of mistreating the neutrals. The ministry's policy toward the United States, "our natural child, our friend, who spoke the same language, tied to us by every affection," was especially deplorable, implying Britain's loss of something more valuable than life itself; "we have lost our honour." The list of American grievances against Britain was ticked off again; and, for good measure, the Algerine depredations were added. Paymaster of a motley and greedy coalition, Lansdowne scolded, the kingdom would soon find another war on her hands when there was

nothing at all to gain from the one then raging. At most, a few paltry West Indian islands might be won. Of some use with America in
the Empire, the Marquis concluded, they were now not worth the
trouble.

There is not the slightest indication, however, that the Opposition's attack was effective. Europe was exploding. American affairs
were not of comparable importance. Even Lansdowne and the anti-
Pitt press cast them within the broader framework of the war against
France.

Had news of the alarming turn of events in December, 1793, and
January, 1794, arrived from the United States in time to give immediate substantiation to Lansdowne's warnings, the case of the
critics of the ministry would have been much strengthened. As it
was, however, Grenville, possessing Hammond's jubilant accounts of
Genêt's offensive conduct, delivered a singularly optimistic (and
ill-founded) judgment to the Lords. Replying to Lansdowne, he declared that if America entered the war, there was reason to believe
"it would be on the side of the allies." When the true state of affairs
in America was finally revealed several weeks later, John Jay was in
London, living proof that his country wished peace, not war.

Much blame must attach to Lord Grenville for the stormy aftermath of the new Orders in Council. He misjudged the temper of
America and mishandled the explanation and justification of the
British position. Admitting that the November order might cause
"a considerable degree of dissatisfaction" in the United States and
knowing that Pinckney was "much agitated," he counted, nevertheless, on the milder January order, a demonstration of Britain's
"liberal and friendly consideration" for American trade to the West
Indies, to restore the Republic's equanimity.[27] In his interview with
Pinckney on January 9, 1794, Grenville labored hard to establish a
curious distinction between bringing in vessels and cargoes for adjudication and bring them in for condemnation, an altogether unsatisfactory and flimsy explication both for the envoy and for his
countrymen at home.

Certainly, Grenville's bland assumptions seemed strange, viewed
from the western side of the Atlantic. Public opinion was so inflamed
that Hammond found it prudent to avoid public engagements and
wrote in alarm to London of "the most universal fermentations" in
the country at large. Madison's resolutions were laid aside temporar-

ily in Congress, but only to make way for proposals calling for measures of an even more hostile nature: embodiment of a large force of militia, fortification of ports, an embargo, sequestration of British debts and investments. Even many Federalists, hoping to exercise a moderating influence and fearing to appear as British sycophants in the eyes of the public, joined in the clamor, demanding strong measures to secure the national defense. At the end of March, an embargo on all foreign trade was passed by Congress and proclaimed by the President. Just as the country was refusing "the honor and happiness of being a Satellite of France," an embittered Federalist told a British correspondent, the Pitt ministry adopted what seemed "a settled design to drive us into the Arms of France." The "Faction" in America, prosecuting its vendetta against Britain, found weapons supplied by Britain herself. Hammond, increasingly acid at the "preposterous" American reaction to "pretended aggressions" upon the Republic's commerce, believed the embargo was but preparation for open hostilities.[28]

George Hammond was, in fact, an early casualty in the developing crisis. Resentful at his personal isolation and at the insults heaped upon his country, he gave way to anger, thereby obscuring his judgment and destroying his usefulness as envoy to the United States. He was "not wanting in common abilities," a Federalist acquaintance stated; but he was unable to rise above the "sixpenny disputes" separating the two countries. With the crisis of the winter of 1793-94 afoot, it was evident to the Federalist writer that "the great, permanent interests" shared by Britain and America, two countries "useful to each other almost beyond calculation," were to be preserved only by "the right Sort of Men."[29] Thus was the Jay mission foreshadowed.

On March 12, Senator Oliver Ellsworth of Connecticut called on President Washington. Speaking for himself and three other Federalist senators, King of New York and George Cabot and Caleb Strong of Massachusetts, the New Englander urged upon the President a program of action: vigorous steps to secure the national defense and the taxes to pay for them, an agent dispatched to the West Indies to establish the extent of American grievances there, and the appointment of an envoy extraordinary to Britain "to require satisfaction for the loss of our Property and to adjust those points which menaced a war."[30] By the end of the month, Hammond had wind of the plan, writing home that certain senators and members of Washington's cabinet were "extremely solicitous" to avoid a war and intended to send a special envoy to ascertain "the real views of his Majesty's government towards this country" and to enter "friendly and amicable explanations upon the subject."[31]

A last Federalist effort was made, however, to elicit from Hammond some sort of conciliatory statement or satisfactory explanation. Senator Rufus King, second only to Hamilton as a power in his party, sought out the Briton on April 7. Grateful for the attention, Hammond expressed regret that "others whom he called his friends had forborn to visit him for some time past." King proceeded at once to business. The November order, he said, was especially unjust and destructive to important American interests. Hammond's reply was scarcely calculated to soothe: he reminded his visitor of "the unworthy and prevalent Practices" commonly employed by Americans to disguise French property as their own, and made the speech Grenville had written for him. The offensive order no longer existed, he declared, and seizures had been brought in merely for "*Adjudication.*" King pressed further, mentioning the "generality and peculiar nature" of the captures. Adjudication, there had been; but the result had been condemnations. The proceeds from the prizes had actually been distributed; and these were, therefore, irretrievable losses. To what purpose speak of "adjudication"? Of appeals in British courts? Of overturning irregular proceedings by illegally constituted courts? Compensation by Hammond's government was, he concluded, the only solution.[32]

The troubled British envoy sought out Secretary Hamilton, but he found little comfort. The American was completely preoccupied with the November order. Hammond conveyed Grenville's "very conciliatory explanations"; but an angry Hamilton "entered into a pretty copious recital of the injuries which the commerce of this country has suffered from British cruizers." The United States wished to avoid extremes, he said, at least until "every mode of amicable negociation" was exhausted; but, come what might, American citizens deserved (and would have) the protection and vindication of their rights by the United States government. Would the United States, Hammond asked, actually demand compensation for American vessels, as King had earlier suggested? Admitting at least implicitly that free ships did not make free goods, Hamilton answered, all cases of prize in which property was proved to be French would be abandoned. If the evidence was inconclusive, however, or if, for whatever reason, appeals were impossible, indemnification was certainly expected.

Hammond's reply was defensive and ill-judged. Referring again to the many frauds and subterfuges used by American shippers to conceal French property, he insisted that the mere absence of legal proof of French nationality did not in itself establish the innocence of suspect vessels. Having abandoned a famous first principle of British justice, he proceeded to give up Grenville's contention that the intent of the November order was to meet a single and unique situation in Santo Domingo: it was, he said, merely Britain's habitual policy during a war. A lecture followed. Neutrals had naturally to expect to suffer "some inconveniences." If ever there was a time when these should not be "too nicely scrutinized," he told the prime American critic of the French Revolution, surely, it was the present. Civilized society was faced with bloody anarchy and war "(as he had often agreed with me)," between government and disorder. He concluded with a threat. A united government and people in Britain would never be intimidated into allowing the United States to derive from the war a commerce of greater utility to France than profit to herself.

Not surprisingly, Hamilton interrupted with "some degree of heat." The British people and their government might be united against France, he exclaimed; but when the wrongs sustained by American commerce were known in England, a "very powerful party" would rise in support of the United States. The two men parted amicably, but Hammond was considerably shaken by opinions and language familiar enough among "the demagogues of the house of representatives, and . . . the uninformed mass of the American Community," but scarcely credible in Alexander Hamilton. A few days later, on April 16, the envoy arranged a second, "accidental conversation" with the Treasury Secretary, and repeated his question about the American intention to demand indemnification for losses under the November order. The answer was less heated, but firm: the matter had been assigned to Chief Justice John Jay, newly confirmed envoy extraordinary to Britain. His instructions, were, however, "couched in the most conciliatory language," Hamilton confided.[33] The Anglo-American crisis had passed beyond the purview of George

Hammond. To Jay, the choice of the Federalist inner circle, belonged the task of pursuing the ways of peace with "unremitted zeal, before the last resource."[34]

The "last resource" was nearer than even Jay and his friends suspected. Accounts, vague and insubstantial for a time, began to arrive from Canada, telling of a bellicose and provocative speech made by Governor Dorchester in early February, 1794, to the Indians of the Old Northwest. The restless expansion of the Americans convinced him that war was highly probable; in such an event, he told the red men, they would have to draw a boundary with their tomahawks. This imprudent effusion became the subject of an official (and crusty) exchange between Secretary of State Randolph and Hammond, but not until the latter part of May, when it was already subordinated to a more alarming event.[35] The importance of the speech alone is, therefore, difficult to gauge. Undoubtedly, it contributed to existing tensions; but had matters in Canada been allowed to rest where Dorchester's speech had left them, the Governor's imprudence would probably have been placed toward the bottom of the list of American grievances. Rufus King raised the subject with Hammond in his interview of April 7, suggesting that the speech, taken together with the November Order in Council, seemed to indicate Britain actually meditated war. Hammond was conciliatory. He had hoped that Dorchester's rough oration might have escaped public attention. As it was, he could only admit that the reports were authentic, although the speech was not authorized by superior authority.[36]

Hammond's assurances did little to restore calm. Even with the Jay mission in the offing, John Adams told his wife, a majority of the House of Representatives were "clearly for mischief." " 'Vox populi, vox Dei,' they say," was his saturnine observation; "and so it is sometimes. But it is sometimes the voice of Mahomet, of Caesar, of Catiline, the Pope, and the Devil."[37] Late in April, the Representatives' propensity for "mischief" expressed itself in a non-intercourse bill directed against Britain; but the Senate, rejecting the measure only by the vote cast by Adams himself, chose instead to renew the embargo for a second month. Less than a week before Jay departed for England on May 12, Senators Monroe and Taylor, instructed by the Virginia legislature, moved to suspend the debt article of the peace treaty until Britain made amends for posts, Negroes, and maritime spoliations. Their defeat was unequivocal: the vote stood at fourteen to two.

Nevertheless, feeling against Britain clearly remained high. Indeed, a perturbed Phineas Bond noted, Congress showed a "most decided Disposition to embroil the two Countries."[38] "Street politicians" were out in force, too. British consular officials at Norfolk, Baltimore, and Philadelphia, and even Hammond himself were treated to threats, insults, and menaces. Four British officers, trying to return home on parole after capture at sea by a French vessel, were mobbed in Philadelphia. At Baltimore and Norfolk, vengeance was taken upon suspected friends of Britain "for a supposed Want of attachment to the American cause." Two French privateers, having been fitted out in the Delaware and having wintered there undisturbed, were believed preparing to put to sea, Hammond's remonstrances notwithstanding. British observers asserted that the embargo, although strictly enforced for British vessels, was lifted from time to time for the convenience of Frenchmen. At Newport, Rhode Island, an ill-tempered fracas over impressment occurred between the state authorities and the officers of the British sloop *Nautilus*.[39] Under such circumstances, Hammond privately disclaimed responsibility for maintaining peace for "*any* definite period."[40]

At this critical juncture, two deeply worried officials in Canada took a step which would very probably have led to the cancellation of Jay's mission, had the Chief Justice not already departed. As it was, it brought war so close, late in 1794, that the preservation of peace involved acts of almost miraculous self-restraint on both sides. Under Dorchester's orders (dated a week after his speech to the Indians), Governor Simcoe moved southward with a small force of regular troops to a position at the foot of the Maumee River rapids. The post was not new; it had been established during the American War, although with the return of peace it had been "evacuated in some respect" as useless and expensive. Subsequently, it had been reoccupied from time to time "as circumstances directed," but primarily to prevent smuggling and to distribute Indian presents.

The purpose of the new move to the south was profoundly defensive. Both generals in Canada were nearly frantic with fear that the American Wayne intended to straiten Detroit and to "cut it off under the most plausible pretences from All intercourse with the Indian Nations, preparatory to those People being turned against us." Dorchester himself categorically stated to London that "Wayne intends to march to Detroit"; and all intelligence from the south convinced the Canadian commanders that the Americans meant to seize the posts by force. The only reasonable assumption was that the Americans' intentions were, in Simcoe's words, "systematically of an hostile nature."[41]

New tensions arose to the east, too, where restless Vermonters were pushing against the Canadian boundary. A settlement was made at Sodus, which was in a disputed area and was a threat to the near-by posts of Oswego and Niagara. British subjects and their goods were seized along the New York border. A project to build ships at Presqu'isle was afoot, preparatory, it was believed in Canada, to a challenge to British maritime control of the Lakes. From the back-woods of Kentucky came reports that a lawless frontier force, led by George Rogers Clark, planned to march against New Orleans, a possession of Spain, Britain's ally.[42] Letters passed between Simcoe and Carondelet, Spanish governor of Louisiana; and while Simcoe declined to send troops to strengthen the Spaniard's post at St. Louis, he clearly envisaged close co-operation between the two crowns "should they be compelled into a War by the United States."[43] The presence of a French fleet in American waters raised the specter of an attack up the St. Lawrence. Dorchester decided to recruit his regi-ments to full strength and to raise two new battalions.

On May 20, the very day news arrived in Philadelphia of Sim-coe's occupation of the Maumee post, Randolph, in the strongest language, made an official complaint to Hammond. Dorchester's speech, he said, "only forbodes hostility"; Simcoe's movement was "if true, hostility itself." At a time when negotiations were pend-ing, Britain acted "to support an enemy whom we are seeking to bring to peace." The Jay mission proved America's true disposition; but honor and safety required that "an invasion shall be repelled." The President himself charged Randolph "to request and urge you to take immediate and effectual measures, as far as in you lies, to sup-press these hostile movements." As the troops of the United States advanced northward, it was all too possible that they would be un-able to distinguish between Indians and "any other people, associa-ted in the war."

Hammond's rejoinder of May 22, soon laid before Congress, was the weakest performance of his Philadelphia mission. He began with

a reflection upon Randolph's style and manner and a reminder that
he could not be expected to furnish a categorical explanation of
actions taken by the two Canadian governors. He admitted the authenticity of Dorchester's speech, but claimed that it was justified by
the hostile American movements toward and along the Canadian
boundary. As for Simcoe's reoccupation of the Maumee post, Hammond, who had heard only of the Governor's *intention*, disclaimed
knowledge of the *event*. Even if it were a fact, however, much depended on "the *place* in which you assert that the fort is intended to
be erected" and on its purpose. If it was intended to provide protection for British subjects residing in districts dependent upon the
fort at Detroit or to screen Detroit itself from the approach of the
American army, he believed the principle of the status quo would
support Simcoe's action "until the final arrangement of the points
in discussion between the two countries shall be concluded." He
promised to communicate immediately with Canada and London.
Thence, Hammond passed to a brief but deliberately offensive recital of British grievances against America since the outbreak of war
with France—" 'an enemy whom we are seeking to bring to peace,' "
he said, sarcastically echoing Randolph's reference to the Indians.[44]

Attack was, perhaps, Hammond's best available defense; but it
was not calculated to calm perturbed spirits. "The general ferment of
this country and the spirit of hostility to Great Britain which for
the last three or four months have been perpetually increasing,"
Hammond reported to Grenville a few days later, "have now risen
to a much higher pitch than before."[45] The situation was "so fluctu-
ating," he remarked to Dorchester, "that it is impossible to offer even
a satisfactory conjecture, with regard to the future conduct of
this government—whether it will immediately employ energetic
means (to use Mr. Randolph's own words) 'to repel an invasion,' or
whether it will wait the result of Mr. Jay's negotiations."[46]

Randolph's answer to Hammond, one of his ablest state papers,
utterly demolished the Briton's position. Pointing out the absurdity
of his contention that the status quo was to be preserved only by a
violation of it, he ridiculed the idea that the rapids of the Maumee,
fifty miles from Detroit, could be considered an appendage of the
post. Wayne's army, in any event, had no instructions to straiten or
annoy Detroit. If Simcoe's movement was dictated by a contrary suspicion, "it ought to be discontinued, as being without cause."[47]

Empty words, the Canadian commanders apparently thought, when compared with Wayne's actions. In July, Dorchester ordered Simcoe to report "the extent of your combined power in Upper Canada, and what force you may be able to assemble for your own defence and preservation."[48] Out of the welter of hostility, suspicion, misunderstanding, and old grievances, there emerged one inescapable conclusion: the ultimate moment for a settlement had arrived. The alternatives had become, simply, peace or war.

PART VII

The Preservation of the Peace

CHAPTER SIXTEEN

The Preservation of the Peace

I

UNTIL MAY, 1794, there was little suspicion in Britain that Anglo-American relations were undergoing an ominous disintegration. Late in the summer of 1793, someone in Grenville's office, perhaps an under secretary, read the spring dispatches from Philadelphia and Norfolk and circulated a memorandum: "It may be right to put Lord Dorchester and the Lieutenant Governors in America on their guard."[1] Months later—around the turn of the year and, therefore, after the promulgation of the November Order—a secret circular letter was drafted, probably by the same official, warning authorities in His Majesty's North American provinces to observe the strictest vigilance in the face of a possible American attack. Two senior ministers, however, dismissed the proposal as unduly alarmist. Dundas scribbled on the document itself that the news from America indicated only that there was "a French Party . . . of which we always understood *Jefferson* to be the head." The United States was unlikely to "proceed to Extremities," the Home Secretary confidently predicted, especially in view of Britain's successes against France during the past summer. The circular could do no harm, he noted in a somewhat condescending manner, "except that perhaps it states the alarm too strongly." Hawkesbury agreed, writing succinctly, "I think . . . the draft states the alarm too strongly."[2] The communication was never sent.

In the months that followed, ministerial confidence eroded, at first slowly and then with mounting acceleration as authentic intelligence, interrupted until then by the embargo, poured in. Private reports of American anger began to filter into the kingdom as early as mid-February, and in Parliament the Foxites began to mumble about the mistreatment of neutrals. The Pitt ministry, diagnosing the Opposition's reaction as a political maneuver, was unruffled. Even news of Wayne's advance northward merely suggested to Dundas that an American defeat might open the way to peace based on an Indian buffer state.[3]

At the end of April, rumors and press reports became more circumstantial; letters from different parts of America, the *Morning Chronicle* declared, spoke of "immediate hostilities" against Britain. Early in May, the *Oracle and Public Advertiser* published accounts of the proceedings of Congress through the middle of March. A false but chillingly prescient account told of a bloody clash between Americans and Indians near Detroit and of an impending confrontation between the army of the United States and the British. Ministers were far from panic-stricken, but they did conclude that a word of caution might not be amiss. On May 11, Dundas accordingly wrote to Simcoe, commending him for his prudence in securing his defenses, but reminding him that his measures did not "render the pacifick conduct and Behaviour of His Majesty's Servants in those Provinces the less necessary or important."[4]

Suddenly, word arrived of the American embargo, although the source was unofficial and tantalizingly scant of detail—merely a copy of a New York newspaper reaching London indirectly by way of Amsterdam. It was enough, however, to cause Grenville to write urgently to Hammond, complaining at the lack of official information "for some time past" and asking for a report of the circumstances and the reasons for the American action. The embargo was "so important in itself" that it would assuredly make "a considerable impression here and . . . engage the serious attention of his Majesty's government."[5]

As it happened, intelligence from Hammond was closer at hand than the Foreign Secretary knew. The envoy's dispatches from February to May—accompanied by a mass of letters, both private and official, and reports from the Canadian governors—reached England in early June, simultaneously with the arrival of John Jay. Speculation and half-formed suspicion were swept aside by ugly facts: America, aroused by maritime spoliations, angered by Dorchester's speech to the Indians, and outraged by Simcoe's march to the Maumee, stood on the verge of war with Britain. John Jay's presence in London underlined the gravity of the crisis. The Committee of

American Merchants called on Pitt on Saturday, June 14, demanding to know "whether they might with confidence prepare their goods for the American markets, as usual, or whether, under the existing circumstances, the alarm of a rupture was sufficiently grounded to make them hesitate in executing the orders they had received." The Prime Minister was somber. The governments of the two countries, he reportedly told his visitors, were disposed to preserve a good understanding, but "Jacobin principles had made their way in America to such an extent as to make it doubtful what would be the issue of the differences now to be settled."[6]

Laid originally for a month and renewed for a second, the embargo seemed to give life to the bugbear that Sheffield and Eden had anticipated in the great debate of 1783: the sugar islands, regrettably needing American provisions, were now cut off from their primary source of supply. Fortunately for ministerial peace of mind, Pitt and his colleagues did not have to share the prolonged apprehensions of British agents in the New World. By early July, it was known in London that the embargo, which had been hurtful to France and American agricultural interests as well as to Britain, was ended. That it had been laid at all, however, was a matter of grave concern to the British ministers and dramatic proof of the need for a general settlement with the United States.[7]

The news from Canada confirmed British disposition to treat with Jay and underscored the dangers of procrastination. A dispatch from Randolph to the Chief Justice established the authenticity of Dorchester's speech and described Simcoe's provocation. It did not reach London until July 14; but private accounts, circumstantial enough to carry conviction, had again outdistanced official communication. Dundas wrote to Simcoe on the fourth, reminding him of the "actual necessity of avoiding, if possible, proceeding to extremities, at a moment when it is to be hoped, that the presence of Mr. Jay . . . may lead to a final termination of all disputes and a perfect good understanding between this Country and the States of America." The Home Secretary professed himself well aware that Detroit was vulnerable even without a direct assault, but Simcoe was always to bear in mind "that the *immediate* protection of the Post itself, is the only object to be attended to." The American forts were only "Temporary Objects; a final arrangement with the United States of America, in all probability, leading to their evacuation." Sterner words were reserved for Dorchester, Simcoe's senior: the move to the south would cause, not prevent, war. The Governor was to avoid antagonizing the United States, especially as negotiations which were expected to produce a general settlement were already underway.[8]

Jay himself believed the omens favorable for his mission. There was not, he wrote home with satisfaction, the slightest tendency in Britain to defend either Dorchester or Simcoe. Indeed, he neither heard nor saw "any thing that looks like a hostile disposition in the mass of this nation towards ours, but the contrary." Reassured, he returned the compliment. General Wayne held no orders, Jay told Grenville, to attack any post held by His Majesty's forces at the end of the war. In an atmosphere of friendly cordiality, the way was opened to the first agreement of substance: on July 11, the two negotiators accepted the principle of the status quo pending a general settlement. Encroachments by either party in the Old Northwest were to be abandoned. If hostilities had already occurred, they were to cease; prisoners were to be released, and property restored. As a mark of good faith, Grenville actually allowed Jay to read his dispatch to Hammond setting out their agreement, and asked the American to take charge of its transportation to the United States to insure the speediest possible delivery.[9]

The news of the agreement did not arrive in Canada until October, however, long after the great American victory over the Indians at Fallen Timbers on August 20, Wayne's subsequent advance within range of the British guns at the Maumee fort, and his parley with Colonel Campbell, which was construed by the garrison as a summons to surrender. The Canadian commanders believed the events portended war, and their movements in the critical days before and after Fallen Timbers were based on that assumption. Wayne did not again approach the Maumee fort; but British fears for the safety of Oswego and Niagara led to a second tense encounter at Sodus, a settlement lying between the two posts. The American settlers, for their part, reciprocated in full measure British suspicion and hostility.

Quite obviously an armed clash between British and American troops was avoided by a hairsbreadth;[10] but to dwell on the nearness of the miss is to obscure a more important consideration: peace was preserved. The limits placed upon Wayne and the Canadian commanders by the two governments held at the critical moment. Even if blood had flowed, it is by no means certain that a general war would have resulted. Neither Wayne's army, its supplies and energy expended at Fallen Timbers, nor Simcoe's forces, standing strictly on the defensive, possessed the military potential to engage in more than minor skirmishing. In any event, the Jay-Grenville agreement of July 11 clearly covered the possibility of overt hostilities. It may be argued, of course, that further loss of American life, at British hands, would have roused the nation to such fury that a full-scale war would have broken out; but it did not happen that way. The mainstream of events, despite deadly shoals and turbulence, was kept within reasonable bounds by friends of peace in both countries.

Their task was made easier by the shift of the diplomatic cockpit from Philadelphia to London. The relative tranquillity of the British view—based to a considerable degree on preoccupation with the menacing state of affairs on the European continent—contrasted sharply with flaring tempers across the Atlantic. In the London press, expressions of friendship for the United States and of hopes for the settlement of outstanding differences were frequent. Simcoe, Dorchester, and even Hammond were lashed for their bungling ineptitude. Opposition papers debated whether to blame more "the intemperance of our Officers in America" or "the indiscreet orders they have received from Ministers at home." Whatever the answer, the *Morning Chronicle* concluded that both had operated "to put us into a situation the most afflicting to all men of both countries who are the friends of peace." Until definitive news of the Battle of Fallen Timbers arrived—Wayne's dispatches were published on November 12—wild rumors flew the rounds: the Americans had attacked or, by variation, had been attacked by a joint force of Indians and Canadian militia near Detroit. Many were dead—three hundred Indians, one report said, and eighty Canadians, most of them in regimentals. Hostilities had been formally declared. The accounts were exaggerated, of course; but it is significant that, circulating widely and received as credible, they occasioned no patriotic outburst against the United States to match that directed at France early in 1793 or at Britain by outraged Americans in 1794. At least one newspaper expressed the public hope that Britain would put all right by "a seasonable apology."[11]

Personalities, too, made a change in venue fortunate. Convinced that war was inevitable, despising Randolph, and bitter at "the motley herd, stiling itself the American people," Hammond was worse than useless. Secretary Randolph, whose talent as a polemicist was fully displayed in his communications to the British envoy, was little better. The two men seemed to work upon each other, goading on the fruitless and dangerous game of charge, countercharge, and recrimination. Jay and Grenville, by contrast, brought cool rationality and a friendly disposition to negotiate to a situation rapidly passing beyond the control of lesser men.[12]

Critics of John Jay and the treaty which bears his name have adduced several reasons, separately, simultaneously, or in varying combinations, to explain what they take to be a humiliating diplomatic defeat for the United States: a native conservatism—the word may be made to ring harshly—submerged by the heroic struggle for American independence, reasserted itself in Jay when the war was over; he was always a Francophobe, and his aversion increased with the French Revolution; he was a tool of the Federalist inner circle, and the treaty was really Hamilton's; he viewed Britain, with whom America had shared the splendors of the Peace of 1763, as the natural ally; he had a nostalgic affection for the former mother country which made him temperamentally unfit for his mission in 1794; he was vain, and flattering and hypocritical British ministers took him in, bedazzling him with royal attention and lordly hospitality.[13]

In truth, John Jay was nobody's creature; and he was not a dupe. If one word alone could encompass his character, it is "integrity." Politics for him was not separated from morality. Trained to the law, he insisted that those who asked equity should do it; liberty, the supreme civil good, should be ordered under law. Deeply committed to Christian principles, he was unyielding in the defense of what he believed to be right. The battle done, he forgave his enemies. Upon occasion, he became self-righteous and indulged in pompous preachments and tedious moralizings, but his austerity made him despise ephemeral popularity and hold cheaply both the honors and the vicissitudes of life. In 1794, he was at the height of his powers, maturer and more seasoned by a decade's public service since he had helped negotiate the treaty of peace. He was not a man to be used, or to be swayed from his course by threats, deception, or the agreeable amenities of London high life.

William Wyndham, Lord Grenville, His Majesty's Secretary of State for Foreign Affairs, was the scion of a clan remarkable, not to say notorious upon occasion, in both British and American history.

The son of George Grenville and nephew of the elder Pitt, he had already at the age of thirty-five a dozen years of seasoning in politics and policy-making at the highest levels. Invariably compared with his illustrious cousin, the younger Pitt, he has been underestimated, much as his father suffered in the shadow of the Great Commoner. In fact, his influence in questions of foreign policy was usually of ruling importance. In 1787 and 1788, for example, he determined the British course in the negotiation of the Triple Alliance; and, even though Carmarthen (Leeds) did not retire as foreign secretary until 1791, Grenville's thinking in matters pertaining to that department was already decisive with his cousin. Stolid and hard-working, he, like his father, lacked brilliance but possessed rectitude and sound intelligence in abundance. Personal warmth he saved for a few close friends. His dispatches could make heavy reading: at their best, they were marked by plain, unadorned exposition; at their worst, they were hastily thrown together, ambiguous, and unclear. In 1791, American tobacco growers were needlessly alarmed by an instruction which seemed to restrict the importation of the weed into Britain. The Order in Council of November, 1793, and its explication gave ample ground for the widespread and brutal misinterpretation by the West Indian authorities. These were exceptions, however. Usually, Grenville was forthright and unequivocal, characteristics shared to a great degree with John Jay himself. When the two men met, like struck like; and the friendship formed in 1794 was to be a lasting one, a personal testimony to the abiding public good these two honorable and sensible men accomplished for their countries.[14]

II

Jay's instructions—signed by Secretary Randolph, but formulated substantially by Hamilton and his Federalist friends—made the first objects of the mission the assertion of the country's neutral rights and a claim for reparations. When the envoy delivered a copy of his commission to Grenville at their first meeting on June 18, the Briton was put on notice that Americans considered the spoliations of prime importance.

Grenville immediately consulted Hawkesbury, as he habitually did throughout the negotiations until toward the end, when their difference over American participation in the West Indian carrying trade became irreconcilible. Hawkesbury—the cabinet colleague most intimately concerned with any negotiations with the United States touching trade or maritime questions—believed the November Order placed Britain in an equivocal position, and, therefore, counseled conciliation. Writing from the country, he told Grenville: "With respect to the Captures made in consequence of the Instructions of the 6th November last, I think We may fairly maintain that no Court of Admiralty had a Right to condemn any Ship or Cargo brought in . . . if she was not otherwise liable to Condemnation." American sufferers, he held, should certainly be allowed to appeal, the lapse of time fixed by law notwithstanding. Characteristically, he then advised Grenville to set about collecting every available scrap of information. In the meantime, Hawkesbury concluded, "all that can be done . . . is in general to hold a Language friendly and conciliatory." Grenville was in complete accord; and Jay was soon writing home that although he could report no firm commitment from Grenville, he expected that "our mercantile injuries will be redressed."[15]

In a manner reminiscent of the discussion of the abducted-slave issue during the Adams mission, the negotiations were delayed, rather ironically, by the Americans. Jay's information on the spoliations, provided before he left the United States, proved insufficient for a ministerial representation. He had a list of captures, but no statement of reasons for the condemnations. Pinckney could not supply this information; and the American agent, H. C. Higginson, who had been dispatched by the Philadelphia authorities to the West Indies to collect relevant data, had yet to report. (The latter's death of yellow fever while in the islands meant, in fact, that Jay would not receive full and authoritative data on the West Indian depredations in time to use them during the negotiations.) Under the circumstances, Jay did what he could. Relying on the British Foreign Secretary's professions of goodwill, he admitted the scantiness of his evidence, but asked, even so, that Americans be allowed to appeal sentences of the admiralty courts despite the expiration of the time prescribed by British law. In addition—a gentle hint—royal officials might be instructed generally "to promote, by their conduct, that friendship and mutual good will which the Governments of both countries desire to establish and perpetuate." Finally, if, after due investigation, the captures should appear of "such extent and magnitude as to merit the attention and interposition of Government," Grenville might declare "that then, &c. &c."[16]

One could wish the "&c. &c." were more explicit. What precisely was Jay's position on neutral rights? The evidence does not always speak clearly; but he undoubtedly shared the view of his Federalist friends, who were affected most directly by Britain's maritime policy and who were prepared—reluctantly, perhaps—in exchange for certain other advantages, to accept unpleasant realities as the price of peace. "That Britain, at this period, and involved in war," wrote Jay in November after his treaty had been concluded, "should not admit principles which would impeach the propriety of her conduct in seizing provisions bound to France, and enemy's property on board of neutral vessels, does not appear to me extraordinary." Clearly, the envoy had come to Britain prepared to accept the principle of preemption, to leave unchallenged the Rule of '56, and to abandon the principle of "free ships, free goods," if Britain would only meet American expectations in other areas.[17]

Jay's instructions called attention to earlier American arguments: by Jefferson, against pre-emption; by Pinckney, in behalf of "free ships, free goods"; and by Randolph himself, in defense of unlimited freedom for neutral traders and of the narrowest definition of contraband (excluding foodstuffs). Undoubtedly the special envoy saw in London Pinckney's memorial of the preceding January questioning both the Rule of '56 and the seizure of enemy goods in neutral bottoms. It is commonly claimed, or implied, that these doctrines were prescribed for Jay, too. They were not. The arguments laid down by Jefferson, Pinckney, and Randolph, the envoy was told, developed "the source of our discontent." His instructions took exception to the Order of June 8, 1793, to be sure, on the ground that provisions were not contraband except under the most stringently limited circumstances: seige, blockade, or investment of the destination. This constituted no injunction, however, to combat the June Order to the end, or even to adduce it as a major basis for a demand for compensation. True, Jay was told that British acceptance of free provisions would be an "infinite advantage" for his country; but he was not required to demand it as a *sine qua non*. The favorite Jeffersonian argument of "free ships, free goods" was already a broken lance; and weakened earlier by the former Secretary of State himself in his tilt with Genêt, Jay was told to plead the case for "free ships, free goods" only after he had settled the spoliation and compensation issues, as well as the differences over the treaty of 1783. Furthermore, the objects of Jay's commercial negotiation, where the "free ships, free goods" issue would have figured, were described as merely "desirable." It was not expected that "so great a latitude of advantages" as those set out in the instructions would, in fact, be won. Finally, because public events were so unstable and communication between North America and Europe was so slow, Jay's instructions were "recommendations only, which in your discretion you may modify, as seems most beneficial to the United States." Only two absolute prohibitions were put upon him: the country's commitments to France were to be left intact; and no treaty of commerce was to be considered which did not at least permit American vessels of limited tonnage to carry to and from Britain's West Indian colonies.

Should Jay have broken off his negotiations, as his critics at the time and subsequently seem to urge, because he could not compel Grenville to accept a set of theoretical principles, chiefly "free ships, free goods," incorporated in American treaties with France, Sweden, Holland, and Prussia? Britain, too, could cite a respectable list of precedents to support her position, the restriction of neutral trade with the enemy: two treaties with Russia and Prussia, as well as works by distinguished authorities in international law.[18] Beyond precedent and legal argument lay, too, the cold reality of Britain's desperate struggle with revolutionary France. There is not the slightest doubt that Britain would have gone to war with the United States rather than acquiesce in the Jeffersonian view of neutral rights. Can it be seriously maintained that American welfare would have been served in 1794 by a war fought to defend a shadowy and insubstantial "consensus" about neutral rights, when the country's most important interests and even its existence would have been at stake? John Jay and the Federalists did not think so; and they were right.

Jay did not present a formal memorial on spoliations until the end of July. The delay was due to the inadequacy of his information, to the reorganization of the Pitt ministry to accommodate the Duke of Portland and his splinter of the Whig party, and to the preoccupation of the ministry with the catastrophe threatening British arms in Flanders. Grenville saw the American frequently, however, in keeping with the preference of both men for personal diplomacy —a glaring contrast to the relationship between Jefferson and Hammond. Secretaries were excluded as the two men talked calmly and candidly about the grave problems confronting their countries. Probably a certain meeting of the minds was achieved before Jay handed in his written statement; the speed with which Grenville responded would support the assumption. Considerable numbers of American vessels, Jay wrote, had been "irregularly captured and as improperly condemned," whereby "great and extensive injuries" had been sustained by his countrymen. Some owners, lacking the necessary securities or impeded by other obstacles, had been prevented from instituting appeals; the way to summary and inexpensive justice ought to be opened. The greater number of cases, however, were quite beyond the ordinary reaches of courts of law. Condemnations had been followed by rapid sale and distribution of proceeds to numerous recipients, many now dead or otherwise unable to make restitution.

In reply, Grenville wrote of the "alledged" irregularities raised by Jay, and affirmed the king's desire for complete and impartial justice. He stated again that in a worldwide naval war it was inevitable that neutral shippers would suffer occasionally; they deserved and would have ample opportunity, however, to seek redress and compensation "where they are due." He was convinced that established judicial process would provide sufficient remedy for "a very *considerable part* of the injuries alledged." For the rest, the king's ministers would readily discuss appropriate measures and principles whenever it should be established that they were, in fact, needed. It was the beginning of "business apparently in good earnest," Jay believed; and he wrote to Washington on August 6 that prospects were "more and more promising." The principle of compensation had been clearly established, and a joint commission was to be erected and charged with a speedy solution.[19]

While Jay was writing to Washington, Grenville composed a dispatch to Hammond: he was disturbed at the American version— *ex parte*, he carefully noted—of the Martinique condemnations. If it was true, the proceedings were "wholly Informal and void," since no legal court of vice admiralty sat on the island. A wholesale reorganization of prize courts throughout the West Indies was under consideration. On the very same day, August 6, 1794, a new Order in Council was issued. It admitted American vessels and cargoes condemned in the West Indies to appeal, even though the prescribed time limit might have expired. Here was a substantial initial success

for John Jay; but there was more. A second Order also issued on
the sixth superseded, in effect, the earlier Order of June, 1793,
which had sanctioned the capture and pre-emption of American
grain bound for France.[20]

This surprising and conciliatory gesture, obviously the result of
assurances exchanged in private conversations between Jay and Grenville, stood as an earnest of Britain's good faith in the negotiations
then underway. It involved a small but significant shift in the Pitt
ministry's position on neutral rights, although Grenville's "Projet
of Heads of Proposals"—probably formulated to answer Jay's "Outline of a Treaty" of August 6—showed not the slightest weakening
on the Rule of '56. There were interesting indications, however, that
Hawkesbury, the most respected authority within the cabinet on
mercantile questions, had begun to part company with Grenville at
this point.

The President of the Committee for Trade and the Foreign Secretary worked closely in drafting a "Neutral Code" at about this
time.[21] Both document and ministerial comments were explicit about
interception and detention of neutral vessels suspected of carrying
contraband or enemy property. Hawkesbury, agreeing with Grenville that the November Order had produced "unfortunate Disputes," clearly supported the first Order of August 6: the spoliations
deserved to be settled in "as speedy and even as liberal a way as possible." More broadly, however, neutral rights were always "full of
Difficulties" during a war, and had to be defined "according to the
general Principles of the Law of Nations, and according to the Circumstances of the existing War." Let treaties say what they would,
he told Grenville, no belligerent would be bound "if the Success of
the War will justify the Breach." Neutrals, too, the pragmatist continued, would always engage in contraband trade: the profits were
too great to resist. On the whole, Hawkesbury concluded, it would be
more politic to avoid a precise enumeration of articles deemed contraband; but if America insisted, the list would have to include provisions.[22] Here was the difference between the two ministers: Hawkesbury would harshly and explicitly make grain contraband; Grenville
courted a benevolent American neutrality with the second Order of
August 6, 1794. The shift in policy was not great; but it was more
than the anti-ministerial *Morning Chronicle*, which called it "a mockery" of American complaints, believed. Two senior members of Pitt's

cabinet were on a collision course over Anglo-American relations.[23]

At the end of August, Grenville made counterproposals to Jay.[24] Arranged in the form of two *projets*, they aimed to extinguish all points in dispute between the two countries and to reach a commercial accord. An article in the first accepted Jay's proposal that British courts be opened to American spoliation appeals or, where a remedy at law was no longer feasible, that compensation be set by a mixed commission. There was something new, however: reparation was to be made, too, for British ships captured, within the jurisdiction of the United States, by hostile vessels armed in her ports or by privateers commanded or owned by American citizens. Since the principle had already been accepted by Secretary Jefferson, its appearance in Grenville's draft and, subsequently, in Jay's Treaty marked no concession from the American side. It was, however, a nice point of balance; and Jay apparently accepted it without demur.

Grenville's proposals touched upon neutral rights in other ways: both parties should observe toward each other essentially the same conduct accorded the most favored neutral nation in Europe. (Eden's Treaty of 1786, the first casualty of the war, was no longer in force.) Speedy justice would be guaranteed for vessels detained on suspicion of carrying enemy property or (unspecified) contraband, legal prizes even in neutral bottoms. The possession of false papers was punishable by condemnation. Hawkesbury, pleased that Grenville had avoided a detailed list of contraband items, gave his unqualified approval. "I think the Plan wise and just," he informed Grenville, "and it has therefore my full assent."[25]

Jay was struck by "several parting Points," especially Grenville's proposal to close the "Northwest Boundary Gap" by a cession of American territory, a proposition which continued to alarm and preoccupy him throughout the negotiations. Responding to Grenville on September 1, however, he took no exception to the British position on spoliations or the neutral flag. Preparing on the fifth for a meeting with the Foreign Secretary next day, he sketched out some notes. Again, the boundary question dominated his thinking; but in a brief treatment of other parts of Grenville's proposed treaty, he indicated his wish for a specific enumeration of articles to be deemed contraband.[26] Grenville's effort to sidestep the issue had failed; and, undoubtedly, the subject must have been thoroughly ventilated at the September 6 meeting. Afterward, the Briton, proposing "to narrow as much as possible the objects of our discussion," suggested that the words of Vattel be incorporated into the treaty. The jurist's list included "all arms and implements serving for the purposes of war, by land or sea" and "corn, grain, or provisions" under certain circumstances, that is, when there was an expectation of starving the enemy into submission. Unlike other contraband, however, foodstuffs were not to be confiscated, but could be pre-empted for purchase, either by the captor or by the government under which he acted. Full value, together with a reasonable profit, freight charges, and demurrage, was reckoned a fair price. If Jay must have his list, there it was, even if it meant blighting the friendly gesture of August 6.[27]

At this point, Jay must have paused to consider the negotiations on neutral rights in their entirety. That the British ministry sincerely desired an honorable settlement of differences on the principle of compromise, he had no doubt. He had clearly won the first major objects of his mission: the right to appeal the maritime sentences given under the November Order, and the principle of compensation. In addition, the second Order of August 6 promised relief for American grain ships; and a new Order, dated September 6, restrained impressment of American seamen. There were, of course, important British claims to be set off against these advantages: compensation for British subjects' vessels which had been captured illegally, and the rights to capture enemy goods aboard neutral vessels, to regard grain as at least quasi-contraband, and to deny to neutrals trade with the enemy in wartime which they did not enjoy in peace. All things considered, Jay concluded, it was time to bring matters to an issue.

The American's counter-*projet* of September 30 merely drew into ordered, written form conflicting proposals made previously by both sides, and in addition, as Jay explained in his covering letter, incorporated articles borrowed from the now defunct Eden Treaty between Britain and France and from a source Jay did not identify, the Franco-American commercial accord of 1778.[28] Article XII of the counter-*projet* proposed that neutral goods be safe from seizure aboard enemy vessels. It was an ingenious variation on "free ships, free goods," but as unacceptable to Grenville in the new form as in the old. Article XVI took up the conflict between the American proposal for free provisions—the "infinite advantage" mentioned in his instructions—and Grenville's quotation from the doctrine of Vattel. In words taken directly from the American accord with France, the former defined contraband as instruments of war, and explicitly excluded from the prohibited category a long list of items, including cloth, wearing apparel, naval stores, various metals, coal, agricultural produce and provisions: wheat, flour, and "every kind of corn and Pulse." A few lines later came Grenville's proposal: "And whereas corn, grain, or other Provisions can only be considered as contraband on occasions and in Cases when a well-founded Expectation exists of reducing an Enemy by the want thereof, It is agreed that in all such Cases, the said articles shall not be confiscated." Instead, they would be bought by the captors or the government at a price including full value, reasonable profit, freight, and demurrage.

Grenville's opinion of Jay's definition of contraband was graphically expressed: by a broad stroke of a quill pen deleting it entirely. If Jay was serious, the negotiations were in trouble. On October 7, the Foreign Secretary wrote to Jay that he had found in his draft "so much new matter, and so much variation in the form and Substance of the Articles proposed . . . that I am very apprehensive the discussion of these points will of necessity consume more time than I had flatter'd myself might have been sufficient to bring our Negotiation to a satisfactory conclusion." If Mr. Jay would call on the eighth, the Foreign Secretary promised to "mention to you a few of the leading points which must if insisted upon on your part create as I fear insurmountable Obstacles."[29]

It is impossible to follow the subsequent negotiations in detail because evidence is scant. There was no sign, however, of a sharp clash between the two men; and the negotiations did not break down. By October 13, Jay, in a letter to Grenville about Simcoe's threatening actions toward the Sodus settlement, could refer to "the present promising State of the Negociations," and decline accordingly to make a formal representation on the frontier incident.[30] Obviously, a mutually satisfactory clarification of contraband had been reached, probably at the meeting on the eighth.

On November 19, after hesitating momentarily to consider the possibility of referring the instrument unsigned to Philadelphia and of asking additional instructions, Jay put his signature to the "Treaty of Amity, Commerce, and Navigation" which has subsequently borne his name. Article XVII recognized the legality of the capture of enemy goods in neutral bottoms and guaranteed speedy adjudication. Contraband was defined in Article XVIII. Arms and imple-

ments serving purposes of war at land and sea were naturally included; the stipulation about provisions merits direct quotation:

and whereas the difficulty of agreeing on the precise Cases in which alone
Provisions and other articles not generally contraband may be regarded as
such, renders it expedient to provide against the inconveniences and misunderstandings which might thence arise: It is further agreed that whenever
any such articles so becoming Contraband according to the existing Laws of
Nations, shall for that reason be seized, the same shall not be confiscated.

Instead, they were to be pre-empted for purchase. There was no
mention of the Rule of '56.

Did Jay, having presented an "avalanche" of demands on neutral
rights, thus make a craven retreat?[31] Jay had won, in fact, a considerable success: the revocation of the June, 1793, provisions Order;
Britain's admission that the definition of provisions as contraband
was difficult and, by extension, open to legitimate question; and the
declaration in Article XII that two years after the end of the existing
war, Britain and America intended to negotiate a new commercial
treaty, "according to the situation in which His Majesty may then
find Himself with respect to the West Indies." At that time, the two
parties would try to agree "whether in any and what cases Neutral
Vessels shall protect Enemy's property; and in what cases provisions
and other articles not generally Contraband may become such."

Neutral rights and contraband were matters which occasioned
"much trouble, and many fruitless discussions," Jay wrote home in
November.[32] By acquiescing for a limited time in practices which the
strongest efforts, even war, could not have overturned, Jay won his
own first object—justice for despoiled shipowners and merchants of
his country—and he neatly avoided creating a precedent by reserving
the right to raise the question of neutral rights at a more tranquil
future date. The questions of "free ships, free goods" and contraband grain also remained—quite explicitly—open.

III

The second purpose of Jay's mission, "not inferior in dignity . . .
though subsequent in order," was to settle the longstanding differences arising from the unfulfilled treaty of peace of 1783. Instructions on the subject referred first to the prewar debts, and the "wish"
was expressed that the British ministers might be convinced that the

debts were actually in process of settlement in the new federal courts. If they proved unreceptive, however, Jay was to "support the doctrines of Government with arguments proper for the occasion, and with that attention to your former public opinions, which self respect will justify, without relaxing the pretensions which have been hitherto maintained." There was no explicit reference to the abducted slaves, the burden of the American complaint falling on the retention of the posts and the consequent expense in blood and treasure occasioned by the Indian war. The British government itself was acquitted of complicity in stirring up the savages; but, it was asserted, there was proof that "British agents" had been active. Britain must restrain the *provocateurs* or assume responsibility for countenancing them. The United States was "nearly in a state of war" with the former mother country, and was "anxious to obviate absolute war by friendly advances," if only Britain would reciprocate. The passage thus recalled Jay's earlier report to Congress as foreign secretary (bluntly condemning American infractions of the peace), reminded him that his own country's grievances were great, and gave his discretion virtually free play.

The speed with which Jay and Grenville solved the vexing problem of the unfulfilled peace treaty was a commentary on their anxiety over the precarious state of Anglo-American relations; and it was, too, a reflection on the failures of Adams, Morris and Carmarthen, Hammond and Jefferson. In contrast to the earlier missions, short shrift was given to the argument of prior infraction. Jay passed on to Grenville the charge Jefferson had made to Hammond, that Britain's retention of the posts was the first breach of the treaty; and, probably in anticipation of a struggle, someone in Grenville's office prepared a "Precis of Correspondence relating to alleged breaches of the treaty of Peace." Grenville's rejection of Jefferson's argument was absolute, and he rebutted it with powerful logic; but he did it in a private and friendly communication to Jay. Believing that the area of agreement on other points was already sufficiently broad to render the question irrelevant, he was ready to drop it altogether. When Jay suggested in an "informal conversation" that Britain had broken the treaty first by carrying away Negroes contrary to Article VII of the peace, Grenville repelled the charge but referred once more to his opinion, "well known to Mr. Jay," about prior infractions and disclaimed any wish "to introduce into the proposed

Treaties any Discussion of that Point."[33] Jay acquiesced. His "Outline of a Treaty" of August 6, mentioned above, showed that he and
Grenville had already come to an understanding about prior infractions: although both parties had just complaints and claims, the
preface declared, it was impossible to reach an agreement on the extent of these "Obstacles to Concord and Agreement." They were
accordingly "forever merged and sunk" in the articles which followed. The final treaty incorporated the sense and even the termi-
nology of Jay's draft: differences were to be terminated without reference to the merits of respective complaints and pretensions. Here
was the clear, cool voice of reason, regrettable only because it had
been so long in coming.

The debt issue came forward immediately. Jay has been criticized
vigorously for mishandling it: enjoined by his instructions to insist
that American courts were already giving effective justice, it is said,
he weakly consented to remove cases of debt to the jurisdiction of a
mixed commission, thereby needlessly impugning his country's judicial processes. The slur on the federal courts, whose chief officer he
was, was especially great, the argument runs; a test case had already
been heard before a federal district court in Virginia by Chief Justice
Jay himself and two associates, whose decision had established the
precedent that British creditors might recover unless payment had
been made into the state treasury during the Revolution. While Jay
negotiated in London, therefore, it is asserted, debt cases were receiving adjudication "in a way consistent with the terms of the treaty of
peace."[34]

The reasoning resembles that of the Irishman who considered
himself half-married to a rich heiress because he had given his own
consent. Abundant evidence proves that British creditors were not, in
fact, receiving justice, especially in Virginia. Consul John Hamilton
at Norfolk wrote home in June, 1793, complaining that justice had
yet to be given in North Carolina as well. While in Georgia, he said,
a British plaintiff won a judgment, only to have the attorney-general
seize the recovered debt as confiscated property. The consul noted
glumly that in Virginia, the grand debtor, even after the celebrated
test case, it was "next to an impossibility ever to collect anything of
Consequence . . . for the excuses, delays, and procrastinations are so
numerous, that it is altogether impracticable ever to surmount
them."[35] At the end of 1793, the Richmond agent for the Scottish

house of Hamilton and Findlay told his employers that the courts' requirements for proof of debt were so stringent and wartime destruction of business records had been so complete that commencing suit was an "utter impossibility." As late as July, 1794, the firm made the same complaint to Pitt himself; and at the end of the year, Consul Hamilton, using almost identical language, unknowingly provided corroboration, writing again to his government of the "utter impossibility of ever Collecting the Debts," even when American courts were opened and judgments obtained.[36]

Federal justice appeared anemic in British eyes; but the mortal complaint was against the state courts. The federal courts may have begun to function, Henry Glassford, who was prominent among Glasgow creditors, told Henry Dundas in June, 1794,

yet the State courts have not, they governing themselves by an act of their own Legislature which has placed a Bar against the Recovery of all British Debts contracted previous to the war till congress shall announce to the Governor of Virginia that Great Britain has delivered up the Forts within the Territories of the United States.

It was precisely here, on the level of the state courts, that Glassford and his fellow creditors were most interested in obtaining remedy. The state courts of Virginia, reserving to themselves all cases involving amounts below a certain level, held jurisdiction over what Glassford called "the great Bulk . . . due to us." The Glaswegians were, therefore, desperate to have the ministry win from Jay "an Absolute Assurance that the Virginia Courts shall be regularly opened." Until that was done, "the federal Court will be of little service."[37]

The proposal would not have answered the purpose, however; and Hawkesbury, the cold realist, stated the reason. Commenting on the debt article in Grenville's "Projet of Heads of Proposals to be made to Mr. Jay," the President of the Committee for Trade rejected the idea that substantial justice could be gained in state courts. His reason was two-edged: neither jury nor judge—in many cases debtors themselves—could be expected to act impartially when their neighbors were being hauled into court by British creditors; and this was especially true in view of the inflated claims all too commonly made by merchants seeking to recoup losses as best they might.

There was a final reason why justice could not be left merely to the American courts, state or federal. "In Virginia," Glassford told

Dundas, "a very large proportion of the Debts have, by this delay become desperate from the Death, Insolvency or Removal of Debtors, many of whom had property at the conclusion of the war and might then have been compelled to pay had the courts of Justice been at that time open." By 1794 many debts were, practically speaking, no longer subject to litigation in the usual way.

Article VI of Jay's Treaty devised the only method for giving justice and equity to both creditor and debtor: the process was to be assigned to a mixed commission. Did Jay thereby impugn American justice? No more than it deserved, an exasperated creditor might growl; and it was certainly no more than Grenville had done to British justice by agreeing to the spoliations commission. In fact, the American envoy won notable vindication of his country's judicial processes, and this in the face of enormous pressure from British creditors upon a government "besieged" by their representatives.[38] Absolutely determined to force a settlement, the long-suffering merchants strongly pressed for payment of a lump sum by the United States government. So eager were they to avoid further delay and litigation in the American courts that they confidentially declared their willingness to compromise by reducing their bills by a third, bringing the total outstanding down from about £3 million to £2 million. In early September, the disappointed creditors were told that the proposal was impracticable.[39] The treaty signed in November provided that the debt commission should determine principal and interest in cases "where full Compensation . . . cannot, for whatever reason, be actually obtained and received . . . in the ordinary course of Justice."

Could Jay have made capital of the "abducted" slaves? The answer must be negative. Britain's moral and diplomatic position on the subject was impregnable. The American claim, an official précis stated, could only be understood to extend to "the price of such Negroes as were not emancipated by Proclamation in the course of the War, *if any such instances can be assigned*." Britain's title to slaves, fugitive or captured, was as clear as her title to any other "Acquisition or Article of Prize." Furthermore, the deepest dictates of honor forbade returning freed Negroes to their slave status. Jay learned the British position when he saw Grenville on August 5, and reported it to his government in a dispatch of September 13. There is no evidence that he tried to confute it. The American personally found slavery odious, and it is very likely that he felt reluctant to push the issue. Furthermore, he believed that satisfaction for the Negroes had been obtained, "though not in express words," when he gained the northwestern posts and won privileges for his country's vessels in the British West Indies. In any case, had he been seriously expected to make a stand, his instructions should have been quite specific, and he should have been supplied with detailed data; but aggrieved slave-owners did not "beseige" the American government with their complaints and claims, as British creditors served the ministry in London. While, in the final analysis, responsibility for Jay's failure to make use of the slave issue must rest with his principals, the issue was, in reality, a "bagatelle"—to use Jefferson's own word —and had been grossly exaggerated by anti-British elements in the United States. Jay quite rightly refused to allow it to impede his progress toward far more important considerations.

For a dozen years after the peace, the issues of the prewar debts and the northwestern posts had been inseparably joined. Had America agreed to a settlement of the debts or, somewhat later, to an Indian barrier state in the Old Northwest, they might have been separated; but by 1794 neither alternative had been adopted.[40] Objections to the cession of the posts had been raised from time to time, principally by fur traders and military men. Certainly, the fur trade was not inconsiderable. Imports into Britain for the five-year period preceding 1794 averaged £250,000 annually, received in exchange for British manufactures distributed to the Indians. It could hardly be thought important enough, however, to impede achievement of a comprehensive Anglo-American settlement, which would open the limitless markets destined to rise in the backcountry and lead to the collection of millions in prewar debts. Furthermore, less than a third of the income from the fur trade came from the American Northwest; and even this fraction was dwindling year by year as the country became settled. The trade was "a paltry object at best," an authoritative advisor told the ministry, much of which would, because of custom and ease of transportation, come to Canada even if the posts were ceded to the Americans. A simple safeguard was finally considered sufficient for British interests: the cession of the posts, Grenville was to propose to Jay, must not interrupt "the usual Course of Communication and Commerce between the Two Canadas and the Indian Nations who are to the Southward and Eastward of the Lakes." What if Americans demanded a reciprocal freedom north of the Lakes, Grenville asked

Hawkesbury? They should have it, was the response. Even though the fur trade was diminishing in the south, Britain need have no fear from American competitors as long as she held Canada and enjoyed a free and uninterrupted navigation on the Lakes and adjoining rivers. Actual possession of the posts was of little significance to the fur trade, and the British ministry knew it.[41]

The reaction of the Indians to British withdrawal was a larger, more portentous question, especially important to military commanders in the Old Northwest: and whoever wrote in the spring of 1794 the "Memorandum on the Canadian trade to the Indian country," probably to brief Grenville and Hawkesbury, "had it much in mind." Reiterating the fears of Haldimand a decade earlier, the author declared that the mere suspicion of a cession of the posts would bring on a massacre of all whites of whatever nationality, north or south of the boundary. Hence, he insisted, ample time—two or three years—should be allowed British traders to collect their property and to get out before the posts were turned over to the Americans. Better still, avoid the blood bath altogether, he counseled: let Britain and the United States unite to establish and guarantee a just and equitable peace with the Indians. The continuation of the bloody and disruptive war between Americans and Indians was contrary to Britain's interests, for both were good customers. The British should become "umpires," establishing "an equitable Line . . . over which the Americans are not to trespass without a regular Sale and agreement with the Indians and Congress."

Hawkesbury took both warning and recommendation to heart. It was "absolutely necessary," he told Grenville, that "We should preserve a Right to mediate for the Indians, so that we may not appear wholly to have abandoned them." Otherwise, Britain would be charged with treachery, her subjects would die under the tomahawk and knife, and the Indian war would continue, though with one momentous change: "the War which they now wage against the Americans, will be changed into an Indian War against Us." Grenville was convinced; and again, a British minister offered his country's good offices to the United States. Jay turned the well-meant but impracticable suggestion aside: he lacked power to accept the offer; and in any event, "in the present state of acrimony and Warmth which prevails in America, with respect to this Country, and particularly on the Subject of the Indian War, it might not perhaps be attended with the Success which might be looked for under more favourable circumstances."[42]

In its final form, Jay's Treaty secured for Britain's fur traders their competitive position north and south of the boundary. With evacuation of the posts set for June 1, 1796, Britons, Americans, and Indians were to be free "to pass and repass by Land, or Inland Navigation, into the respective Territories and Countries" of the two contracting powers, excepting only the northern regions under the monopoly of the Hudson's Bay Company.[43] Freedom to navigate the Mississippi, a provision of the treaty of peace, was reaffirmed, and all ports and places on the eastern bank, "to whichsoever of the parties belonging," were declared open to both. Unprohibited goods might be carried (by land or inland navigation) by merchants of either party, paying only the duties of natives.

Of Britain's mediation, there was not a hint; but London had not abandoned hope. As soon as the treaty was concluded on November 19, Home Secretary Portland sent orders to Dorchester: the Governor was to exert himself to the utmost to persuade the Indians that ample provision had been made "not merely for continuing as heretofore, but for increasing, without the possibility of interruption our present Commercial Intercourse with them to the utmost extent to which it may be capable of being carried." Reassurance was also to be given more concrete form: "Our usual Attention to their wants, and our liberality in supplying them should for the present be increased." These, however, were but preliminary matters. The heart of Portland's instructions was concerned with ending the Indian war; and for this purpose, Britain intended once more to offer mediation. Nothing, Dorchester was told, could so facilitate the execution of the new treaty or materially enlarge the advantages for all parties; and the Canadian governor was ordered to co-operate in the attainment of "an Object so advantageous to all."[44]

A copy of the parallel dispatch from Grenville to Hammond was also enclosed with the instructions. The plan was designed to achieve a safe exit from the American Northwest, Grenville told Hammond, while preserving "harmony and union" with the United States. Britain's weary envoy in Philadelphia was even told to approach Hamilton confidentially and to enter into a secret understanding with the Treasury Secretary, if he should dislike a public transaction.[45]

The dispatches to Dorchester, Hammond, and Simcoe, Jay's original copy of his treaty, and, indeed, all of the November and December mail from Britain to North America were lost when the packet carrying them was taken by the French. Duplicates of the instructions to British representatives in Canada and the United States did not arrive until July, 1795. In truth, the delay, great as it was, did not matter much. British mediation would never have been acceptable to the United States; and the American General Wayne had already opened the way to a solution with his victory at Fallen Timbers. A preliminary peace between Americans and Indians followed the battle; and, somewhat later, the Treaty of Greenville opened most of Ohio to white settlement.[46]

Relief in Whitehall must have matched that at Philadelphia. In the light of day, the nightmare was over. British statesmen thought they saw all come right: fur trade, open; Indians, broken and unlikely to seek revenge upon Britons, who provided, after all, their sole refuge from the triumphant Americans; and, the intoxicating dream, first seen by the Earl of Shelburne, of a swelling stream of British manufactures pouring through the Canadian funnel into the unending markets of new American settlements in the Midwest, realized. Hawkesbury himself spoke eloquently of the prospect in his comments on Grenville's "Projet"; and the author of the "Considerations on the propriety of Great Britain abandoning the Indian Posts" spoke exuberantly of the future. "One Inhabitant that cultivates his Farm," he wrote, "is of more real Service to Great Britain than twenty Hunters." Let uncounted millions pour into the vast region: take their wheat and provisions in exchange for manufactured goods, and create the "foundation of future happiness and prosperity between the two Countries"! The future was not to work out that way, of course; but in 1794, and for many years thereafter, the vision proved an important ingredient in the creation of the first great Anglo-American rapprochement.[47]

IV

One of the most beguiling New World prospects to present itself to the British gaze after the American Revolution was the vast inland market destined, it was assumed, to arise in the American hinterland. A vast, circular trade was imagined, moving up the St. Lawrence, across the Great Lakes, and down the Mississippi, with British manufactures traded for native produce throughout the whole magnificent course. Access to the Mississippi was as vital, therefore, as freedom to pass and repass the northern boundary of the United States. The treaty of peace had, in fact, given both Britain and the United States freedom to navigate the river; but the agreement was rather cavalier, as it virtually disregarded the Spaniards at the mouth and on the west bank. Able to harass any interloper, the Iberians were the original impediment to the realization of the British dream. A solution seemed at hand, however, when Spain and Britain went to war as allies against revolutionary France. British co-operation was even requested by Madrid in supplying client Indians, an opportunity which must have delighted government and merchants alike. With a stout British boot in the door, Spain would presumably be unable to close it again when peace came, should she try; and Hawkesbury, with unshakable faith in his country's economic prowess, said as much to Lord Grenville. The future held many surprises which made British aspirations in the Mississippi Valley impracticable; but this does not belittle the vision of British policy-makers. Events might just have unfolded as they hoped. In any case, it was worth a try.

As happened so monotonously often during the first dozen years of American independence, another prime difficulty for Britain arose from the imperfect treaty of peace. A critical part of the Canadian-American boundary was declared to run due west from the Lake of the Woods, following the 49th parallel until it intersected the Mississippi. By 1794 it was suspected that the river and the parallel did not meet, and that the prescribed line was an impossibility. Jay proposed an article to Grenville on August 6 which called for the establishment of the facts by a geographical survey made under the authority of a joint Anglo-American commission. If the westward line did not intersect the river, Jay said, the commissioners should immediately establish such a line "as shall be adjudged and determined to be most consistent with the true Intent and Meaning of the said Treaty."

It was typical of Jay to desire to submit the dangerous issue to the rational and deliberate process of arbitration. But he must have known, too, that time was the friend of the United States; western settlers might be expected to produce a *de facto* line within a few years. Grenville and his colleagues, as aware as Jay of the implication of postponement, intended to have a new boundary at once. In the "Projet of Heads of Proposals," the British Foreign Secretary countered Jay by demanding that, if the Lake of the Woods line was impossible, a southerly adjustment be made to allow the intersection prescribed in the treaty of peace. Let the line run westward from, say, Lake Superior. It was unfortunate that some thirty to thirty-five thousand square miles of territory (lying in the upper portion of the present state of Minnesota) would have to be repossessed; but the fault within the treaty was attributable to neither party, and the intent was obvious: Britain was to have a territorial connection with the navigable portion of the Mississippi. Otherwise, freedom to navigate the river made no sense.

Jay's rejection of the argument was immediate and absolute. On September 1 he notified Grenville that a cession of American territory was quite beyond his powers and so unacceptable that to insist upon it would "entirely frustrate my hopes." The threat of a rupture in the negotiations was followed up with a long and brilliantly argued memorandum. Jay insisted that Britain could deduce from its freedom to navigate the Mississippi no right to demand a cession of American territory. "A right freely to navigate a bay, a straight, a sound, or a river," he declared, "is perfect without, and does not *necessarily* presuppose the dominion and property of lands *adjacent* to it." In answer, Grenville minced as few words as Jay. The Lake Superior line implied no more of a dereliction of American territory than of Canadian. Britain was assuredly entitled to access to the river without passing through foreign territory. The facts remained to be established. A survey was proper enough; but it involved delay, always a peril when relations between nations were tense and strained.

With the two negotiators at direct issue and a distinct breakdown in negotiations threatening, evidence suddenly, disconcertingly vanishes. Jay's sketchy dispatches, written amidst the heat and dust of battle, are of little help; his list of points to be raised at the meeting with Grenville on September 6 does not directly mention the northwestern boundary. After that lengthy conference, he remarked on the Briton's willingness to listen and to accommodate differences, but added that "we may not finally be able to agree," perhaps an indirect reference to the dispute. Grenville's note to Jay on the seventh affords no light either. A week later, however, fundamental agreement had been reached: "I now have some reason to hope," Jay told Randolph, "that the business of the northwest corner will be so managed as to cease to be an obstacle"—an opinion he repeated four days later when he sent to Philadelphia a draft article incorporating substantially his own proposal to Grenville. He had already conferred with the Foreign Secretary about it, and Grenville had reacted "in his usual temperate and candid manner." A definitive answer was expected within a few days.[48] Optimism was justified. Article IV of Jay's Treaty provided for a survey of the Mississippi under the authority of the two governments. If the need was proved, the boundary was to be settled by amicable negotiation. Grenville had resisted powerfully, but Jay had prevailed.

Did Grenville's retreat make Britain's freedom to navigate the Mississippi "a meaningless form of words," as some scholars have claimed? Did it finally extinguish the political and economic unity of the "empire of the St. Lawrence"?[49] Article IV was not, after all, a final settlement; it merely prescribed a means to the end. The boundary convention of 1818 ultimately established the line of forty-nine degrees north latitude; but in 1794, there was still a chance that a survey might prove the treaty of 1783 capable of literal fulfilment, or that some new line of communication with the great river might be found in the process. Secondly, insistence on the Lake Superior line would have brought a rupture in the negotiations and, quite probably, war. With peace maintained, privileges for British traders were ready at hand, in Article III, to be developed as entering channels into the markets of the backcountry; and the natural forces of supply and demand might be counted on to increase Britain's trade there. When Grenville gave way on the boundary gap, he bowed to Jay's uncompromising refusal to give up American territory; but he was also showing himself the political child of Lord Shelburne, aiming at trade, not dominion. As the great imperial statesman had done before him in 1782, Grenville maintained that Britain's true interests lay in reconstructing a close and amicable Anglo-American economic partnership.[50]

V

The third and last object of Jay's diplomacy was a treaty of commerce. Basically, the goal was the same as that of John Adams and Gouverneur Morris: freedom for American vessels to trade to the British West Indies. Where his predecessors had failed, however, Jay succeeded.

Jay's commercial instructions were contained in nineteen points, virtually all desiderata. They ranged from reciprocity in navigation to the definition of contraband, the establishment of consulates, rules of convoy, and larger participation in the British fisheries. The great *sine qua non* was stated in a subsequent paragraph:

If to the actual footing of our commerce and navigation in the British European dominions could be added the privilege of carrying directly from the United States to the British West Indies, in our own bottoms, generally, or of certain defined burthens, the articles which may be carried thither in British bottoms, and of bringing from thence, directly to the United States, in our own bottoms, of like description, the articles which may be brought from thence to the United States in British bottoms, this would afford an acceptable basis of treaty for a term not exceeding fifteen years.

Failing the concession, Jay was to avoid concluding any commercial accord, referring any agreed articles home and awaiting further instructions. A breakdown in this area, however, should not affect the issue of his earlier labors.

Jay made his opening after a settlement of the pressing spoliation issue had been agreed upon. During one of several informal conversations—"desultory discussions," he called them—with Grenville, the American asked Grenville to acquiesce in "partially opening to us a trade with the West India Islands."[51] The idea, doubtless presented first sometime during July, appeared in more elaborate form in his outline for a convention and treaty of commerce, which was sent to Grenville on August 6: American citizens were to carry, in their own vessels of one hundred tons burthen or under, any goods, ware, and merchandises to Britain's sugar islands which British subjects took thither from the United States. They might also carry off island produce, provided always that cargoes be landed in the United States and in no other place. Jay was ready, too, to declare expressly that West Indian products or manufactures—except, principally, rum made from island molasses in the United States—should not be transported in American vessels from either the British West Indies or the United States to any other part of the world.

The outline included several other important propositions: reciprocity of tonnage and import duties; exclusion of privateers commissioned against either party during war; prevention of the sale of prizes taken by or from one of the contracting powers, being belligerent, in the ports of the other, being neutral; and inviolability of the rights of merchants and of private property at the outbreak of any future hostilities. There is no sign that any of these, mostly standard features of commercial treaties, presented any great problem in negotiation. The West Indian proposal was, however, another matter altogether. Around it there developed one of the sharpest clashes of Jay's mission, although, surprisingly, it did not involve the American. It occurred between Grenville and Hawkesbury.

From the moment Jay arrived in the kingdom, Hawkesbury scented danger to his cherished system, laid down in the great Reports of 1784 and 1791 and implemented in numerous Orders and Acts of Parliament. Within a week, he began quietly to look to his defenses, reviewing the government's official position and requesting again that his First Clerk George Chalmers and former Inspector-General Thomas Irving supply the most recent figures on the American trade. His prudence was timely. In July he learned the unpleasant truth: the West Indians were playing their petition game again, asking for the admission of American vessels to their ports; and the subject had actually been bruited in Grenville's talks with the American envoy. Reaction was almost reflex. To arms! A new battle was in the offing, and its issue was quite simply "whether this Country shall give up the principal advantages which it derives from her Sugar Islands." Hawkesbury's office took on the air of a general headquarters. George Chalmers was the adjutant; and even the Sabbath brought no respite to the First Clerk.[52]

The campaign was patterned after that which Eden and Sheffield had perfected a dozen years earlier: an aroused public and Parliament would force the abandonment of the ill-conceived proposal, much as they had done with the American Intercourse Bill in 1783. Working through Chalmers—Hawkesbury himself was sick during much of the critical period—the President of the Committee for Trade sent warnings to friendly Canadian and West Indian merchants. At his order, Chalmers brought out in pamphlet form William C. Smith's speech of 1791 to the American House of Representatives, opposing Madison's discriminatory resolutions: it would, the First Clerk commented to his chief, "prove out of their own mouth, how favourable Great Britain has been in her regulations, and how little, if any, resentful she has been in her policy." Even Sheffield, aging, but as truculent as ever, was asked to unlimber the battery which had caused such devastation in 1783.

The operation was a gigantic failure. Hawkesbury and his doughty little band soon found themselves not in the van of an aroused and militant nation rallying to the defense of the laws of navigation, but isolated, outflanked, and outmaneuvered. They were not even clear about the identity of the principal enemy—the West Indians, John Jay, or Lord Grenville himself. Even close friends failed to respond to the call to battle. It was summer; and, growled Chalmers, many were at "the Watering places," full of frivolous excuses, but unhelpful. From one came the rather ambiguous remark that while he was "firm on the general question," he was willing "to admit small American vessels." Even Sheffield's condemnation of West Indian "impudence" had something of the perfunctory and mechanical about it. Eden, now Lord Auckland, was distracted by military disasters on the continent, and could only hope "we shall avoid a disagreement with America." Appalled at the prospect before him, Hawkesbury girded himself for a fight to the finish in the only possible arena, the cabinet itself.[53]

Evidence makes perfectly clear the broad outline and many details of the clash. Grenville spent much time in August drafting his counterproposals to Jay's outline of the sixth of that month. His earliest notes prove that he was considering a treaty which would be limited in duration and based upon reciprocal duties and tonnage at the most favored nation level, mutual prohibition of further discriminations against imports, and the "usual Articles" relating to security of debts and persons. There was a significant marginal query: "What may be fit to be proposed, or agreed to, either permanently, or as a temporary measure, with respect to the Commerce between America and the West Indies, so as, if possible, to give America an Interest in Our retaining the newly acquired Colonies?"[54] Presently, the two *projets* which were later sent to Jay on August 30 took shape and were circulated among the members of the cabinet for comment.[55] Hawkesbury's worst fears were realized. The sixth article of the commercial plan included Jay's earlier proposal, even duplicating much of his language. Admittedly, the article was limited to the existing war and the two years after the signing of a preliminary peace treaty, and Jay's proposed limit on burthen had been reduced from a hundred tons to seventy tons; but these were minor considerations. The British Foreign Secretary was actually proposing to His Majesty's ministers that the navigation system be set aside in favor of the alien Americans. Did Grenville wish his comments? He should have them.

Hawkesbury blasted the proposed concession to the United States with all the forceful logic of his earlier reports. Britain already granted the Americans greater advantages in the West Indian trade than any other European power. The only major restriction was the British monopoly of maritime carriage. Perhaps this monopoly diminished American shipping and even raised a little the price of provisions in the islands; but the benefits accruing to the Empire as a whole were too great to be cast away. Using new data to bolster old conclusions, he argued that British exports to the West Indies had risen from the £1.33 million of 1774 to £2.2 million in 1792, an increase directly attributable to the exclusion of the Americans. To abandon the policy would also injure Ireland, whose exports had grown in the two previous years from £3 million to £5.4 million, the result in great part, he said, of new sales of corn and flour to merchants of the sugar islands. The latter had no reason to complain: their own exports to Britain stood at £3.5 million in 1786; in 1792, at £4.25 million. In addition, their dependence on American supplies had been lessened, if not ended, as their easy survival of the recent American embargo clearly indicated.

These were reasons touching opulence. National power was even more fundamental. British navigation, "depressed enough already" by the war, would sustain a double injury: diminution by American competition, and a corresponding increase in American martime resources—this, in "those Seas where We have most Reason to be apprehensive of it." The peroration was dark: enterprising Yankees would certainly re-export West Indian produce to the world at large, their promises to the contrary notwithstanding; the islanders would be debauched by republican principles; and British sailors would desert in great numbers to nearby American vessels during times of war. The ultimate would not be long postponed: if the former colonists were admitted, the agitated mercantilist wrote, "the United States will in a short Time become Masters in Effect of the West India Islands."

Did Hawkesbury believe, as he commented on Grenville's *projets*, that he could carry his point? Or did he already know that the cause was lost? It is impossible to say. A denouement of sorts was expected at the cabinet meeting summoned for August 28 to consider Grenville's proposals. Hawkesbury, ill and troubled, traveled up to London from his country residence, Addiscombe Place, prepared to give battle. He was greeted by a dispiriting anticlimax: the meeting was postponed until the twenty-ninth. Returning to the country, the embattled warrior found himself too unwell to repeat the journey and could but send in his place the paper he would have read to his colleagues. It was a last, desperate effort to counter what he believed to be a deep and dangerous intrigue of the Americans and the West Indians.

Praising the boundary plan and the settlement proposed for other differences outstanding between the two countries, Hawkesbury took mild exception to the wording of the article on reciprocity of duties. His absolute and uncompromising condemnation was reserved for the proposed infraction of the navigation system. By all means, he urged, let Britain conciliate the Americans, but she should—must— stop short of perilous and gratuitous concession. Satisfied on other points, the United States would not go to war for the West Indian carrying trade.[56]

What passed at the cabinet meeting on the twenty-ninth is not clear in any detail, although, presumably, Hawkesbury's paper was read. Dundas, perhaps Pitt's closest ministerial friend, had already told Grenville that his *projets* were "perfectly right."[57] Beyond this, evidence of individual attitudes is slight. The outcome is clear, however: Hawkesbury was absolutely overruled, and Grenville's proposals, sanctioned by the cabinet, went forward unchanged to Jay.

Did Hawkesbury consider resignation? Ministers in the past— most recently, Foreign Secretary Leeds—had given up office for less reason; but there is no indication that the idea occurred to the President of the Committee for Trade. He declined, however, to attend further cabinet meetings on the touchy West Indian question or to give advice on it. When Portland's Home Office received a copy of an address from the General Assembly of Nova Scotia to their lieutenant-governor urging the continued exclusion of the Americans from the West Indian islands to prevent engrossment of the fish trade, it was referred to Hawkesbury and his committee as a matter of course. The response was sullen and tart: "The Lords of this Committee have already reported their opinion on this important Subject." If His Grace of Portland wished to be instructed, let him read the Reports of May 31, 1784, and January 28, 1791. In mid-October,

Grenville circulated a final draft. Hawkesbury refused any communication on the West India article, "irrevocably decided against the Opinion I have always entertained and publicly professed." He must decline the summons to the cabinet council: "My attendance may occasion Discussion, which cannot now be of any Use."[58]

Article XII of Jay's Treaty sealed Hawkesbury's discomfiture and gave the American what he himself considered his major diplomatic triumph: recompense alike for retention of the posts and for the slaves. Americans gained the rights of British subjects in the West Indian trade, except for the limit of seventy tons placed on their vessels, and for the prohibition attached to the re-exportation of a list of island products: molasses, sugar, coffee, cocoa, and cotton. Rum was conspicuously omitted. Jay considered it regrettable that the article was, as Grenville had wished, limited in duration; but if his country met Britain's "good humor and cordiality," he wrote to Randolph, "I am much inclined to believe it will be renewed." Indeed, in the future, even more favorable arrangements were possible, "as the public mind in Britain shall gradually become more reconciled to this, and the other unprecedented departures from their favorite navigation act."[59]

Article XII was, of course, subsequently rejected by the Senate of the United States, angered by the restrictions on re-exportation of island produce; and Britain herself then agreed to the suspension of that portion of the treaty. It is unlikely, however, that either action had much effect. Profit-hungry Yankees and needy West Indians would not be inclined to abide scrupulously by the terms of the amended treaty, and suspension of Article XII would scarcely keep American vessels out of West Indian ports if British authorities were willing to receive them. Furthermore, the ill-tempered and ill-considered suspension cannot conceal the importance of the British concession on reversing a cardinal and long-established point of national policy.

What was the British motive? Why was the concession won so easily, when little more than a decade before, much the same proposition was rejected out of hand?

It is tempting to accept the simplistic explanation that the liberal doctrines associated with the name of Adam Smith were responsible. It is true that both Pitt and Grenville found the redoubtable Scot's views attractive; if the political situation had permitted in

1783, Pitt would have welcomed the passage of the American Intercourse Bill. By 1794, the situation was very different. Pitt, chancellor of the exchequer in an unpopular and disavowed government in 1782, was, in 1794, prime minister, firmly entrenched in power and leading a great national effort in a war of unprecedented danger and gravity. Opposition was weak and divided; a considerable portion of the Whigs actually followed the Duke of Portland into the government while negotiations with Jay were underway. In 1782 and 1783, the voice of the nation roared out against Shelburne. Eleven years later, Pitt spoke for the nation.

It would be grossly inaccurate, however, to explain Article XII solely in terms of the desire of Pitt and Grenville to reverse the defeat of the American Intercourse Bill. The stark truth in 1794 was that Britain simply could ill afford a war with America. William Eden, Lord Auckland, described well the national preoccupation when he wrote of his own gloom and despondency at "the numberless and strange defeats, Treacheries, Retreats, Capitulations, Incapacities, and Disgraces of the last four months."[60] In Europe, the First Coalition against revolutionary France was falling apart. The Duke of York was in full retreat in the Low Countries, which were presently to be abandoned. Prussia intended peace with the enemy; and the Hapsburg was not far behind. A swarm of enemy privateers, storming out of captured channel ports, fell upon British shipping in the narrow seas. Rumblings of revolt were heard in Ireland, ever ready to seize the opportunity offered by Britain's distress. Rumors of imminent French invasion flew the rounds; and accounts, all too true, from the West Indies told of a successful republican counteroffensive. The cankers of internal sedition, treason, and suspicion of disloyalty ate away at national self-confidence. Hawkesbury's efforts to raise the wind against the West India article failed in part because it proved impossible to lecture Britannia on the beauties of the mercantile system while, virtually deserted, she struggled with her would-be murderer.

Britain's acceptance of Article XII also rested on the knowledge that her interests intertwined, in many important ways, with those of the Americans. Balancing American requirements of British goods and capital and supplementing the multitudinous ties of private Anglo-American enterprises was the imperial dependence—in the remaining North American colonies, the European possessions, and the most delicate area of all, the British West Indies—upon the United States as a source of supply. The recent American embargo, Hawkesbury's whistling in the dark notwithstanding, pointed out the danger which it was hoped Article XII would obviate. Furthermore, as Grenville himself observed, a corollary of the article was that America would gain an interest in Britain's retention of the conquered West Indies.

Jay's Treaty, in general, and the West India article, in particular —limited in duration as they were—marked the final passage into oblivion of British bitterness at the American War. The wheel had turned full circle; and Pitt, Grenville, and many of their countrymen caught at least a glimpse of Shelburne's vision: a working, harmonious, and mutually beneficial Anglo-American partnership.[61]

VI

The remaining articles of Jay's Treaty touched a number of subjects, many quite routine in commercial instruments, none violently disputed by either negotiator. A reciprocal right of citizens and subjects to hold and devise land in each other's country was granted. Private debts and investments in public funds or banks were not to be sequestered in the event of war. American vessels were formally granted admission to the British East Indies; and a free peacetime trade thence to the United States was allowed in all legal articles. Commerce and navigation between His Majesty's European dominions and the territories of the United States were to be on terms of reciprocity and perfect liberty. The ships or merchandise of one party were to pay in ports of the other duties no greater than were charged the vessels and goods of other nations. A similar stipulation was made for imports, the native growth or manufacture of the producing nation. The British government reserved the right to match the tonnage and import duties payable by her subjects in American ports, although a more precise balancing of duties was postponed to future negotiations. Consulates were to be established formally. Nationals, particularly commanders of ships of war and privateers, were forbidden to commit any damage or outrage against those of the other contracting power; nor were they to act in a hostile or violent way against each other or to accept commissions from any enemy state. Pirates—and the term included privateers commissioned in the ports of the one by an enemy of the other—were excluded from the ports of each, their captures restored wherever possible. Each country's ships of war were to be hospitably received in ports of the other. The arming of privateers against each other was forbidden. The sale in the ports of one country of prizes taken from the other by her enemies was not to be allowed, although the French liberty to the contrary, granted by the Franco-American treaty of alliance of 1778, was left intact by the stipulation that nothing in Jay's Treaty was to interfere with the operation of earlier agreements. Ships of war and privateers of each power, however, were allowed to bring in and take out prizes from ports of the other; and no shelter was to be given to an enemy of either who might wish a similar liberty. (The French right was, of course, again excepted.) The first ten articles of the treaty—the noncommercial ones—were permanent. The remaining articles—excepting the twelfth, which was limited to the war plus two years—were to run for twelve years from the date of the exchange of ratifications. Impressment was not mentioned.[62]

Jay's Treaty has often been described as the outcome of a contest, with the American hopelessly outmatched and the Briton running off with the prize. Certainly, Grenville scored heavily; he won conditional recognition of provisions as contraband, arrangements for payment of the prewar debts, access on favorable terms to the markets south of the Canadian-American border, compensation for irregular or illegal captures of British vessels, and safeguards against future sequestrations in the event of war with the United States. In addition, there were the important assurances, suggested by Hawkesbury in the great Report of 1791, that no unusual discrimination would be levied against British goods and ships during the treaty's operation. Although these were real and solid advantages, however, they outweighed not a whit those won by John Jay. He got the posts, foiled Grenville on the northwestern boundary issue, settled the spoliation question, and gained direct entry into the British West Indian trade, a concession unparalleled in Britain's imperial history. Access was secured, too, to important markets in Canada, via overland trade routes, and in the Far East. Other articles, enjoining reciprocity and mutual advantages, must be reckoned equally beneficial to both parties.

Could Jay have forced better terms from Grenville by brandishing the "abortive armed neutrality of the north"? The idea is vain.

Secretary Randolph's instructions on the subject told Jay that while he was in London, it should not be difficult to establish contact with the ministers of Russia—a power friendly to Britain—Denmark, and Sweden; and that the "principles of the armed neutrality would abundantly cover our neutral rights." *If*, therefore, the situation in London appeared to make co-operation with foreign powers advisable, *if* accommodation with Britain would not be thwarted by the measure, and *if*, in his view of American political relations as a whole, Jay concluded such a step was conducive to his country's interests, then he was to "sound those ministers upon the probability of an alliance with their nations to support those principles." The conditions were so numerous that the instruction could not reasonably be interpreted as imperative. Furthermore, several very important reasons, obvious to all thoughtful men whose gaze was not too clouded by the passions of partisan politics, made American adherence to a league impracticable and unwise. Britain would have preferred war to acquiescence in a second armed neutrality. If Jay had used the threat, his own mission would in all probability have terminated upon the instant. Without Russia, Sweden and Norway, the ostensible initiators of the revived maritime alliance, were weak and ineffectual; with the active opposition of Russia in 1795, the scheme of an Amercan adherence would have been lunacy. Alexander Hamilton was displaying no ill-timed anglophilia, nor was he committing an unfortunate diplomatic indiscretion, when he almost gratuitously told Hammond, who had been instructed to ascertain the American attitude, that the United States shared no vital interests with Sweden and Denmark. His country's policy in every contingency, "even in that of an open contest with Great Britain," was, he said, to avoid "entangling itself with European connexions, which, could only tend to involve this country in disputes, wherein it might have no possible interests, and commit it in a common cause with allies, from whom, in the moment of danger, it could derive no succour."[63] Thus, Hamilton presaged a fundamental principle of future American foreign policy; in immediate terms, his statement—unknown to Grenville until September 20, after substantial agreement on many important issues had been achieved with Jay—merely enunciated an important reality of political life, as evident as the rise and fall of the tides. The "abortive armed neutrality" has been well named. It never possessed a spark of life.[64]

Was Jay's Treaty to be condemned because America's ally, France, found it offensive? To do so, Fisher Ames pointed out in one of his greatest speeches to the House of Representatives, was to render Americans colonials once more.[65] His colleague Robert Goodloe Harper agreed: to ask if the treaty were disadvantageous to France, he stated in his *Address to His Constituents*, was to assume that the United States government was "not to be guided by the interests of its own citizens, but by those of its allies." France was, furthermore, an ally which had been none too gentle with American interests or susceptibilities since the outbreak of war.[66] That the treaty served American interests without violating honorable commitments to other nations—as Hamilton, in the celebrated guise of "Camillus," pointed out—was in itself a sufficient justification for it.

The stormy reception of the treaty in the United States and the long delay in its ratification reflected no inherent fault in Jay's and Grenville's work. Responsibility for persistent—indeed, mounting—anglophobia and condemnation of the treaty in the United States must rest in other quarters. The publication of the treaty, the strict order of the Senate to the contrary notwithstanding, coincided with a spate of fresh grievances arising from what appeared to be Britain's studied disregard of the new accord. British privateersmen, for example, continued their depredations upon American vessels in West Indian waters, especially around the Bermudas, impudently claiming never to have heard of the revocation of the Order of November, 1793. Further, since the spring of 1794 the French had been making new and mammoth purchases of flour in the country, emptying the stores at Philadelphia, New York, Baltimore, and all the Virginia ports, and driving prices up to record levels. Determined to deprive the enemy of these provisions, Britain issued a secret Order in Council on April 25, 1795, directing the interception of vessels carrying suspect cargoes to French ports. Americans, who learned of the Order in June, but a few days after the Senate had ratified the treaty, generally but inaccurately regarded the new measure as a revival of the Order of June, 1793. Directed specifically against French property and clearly within the provisions of the recent treaty, it coincided, however, with a renewed crisis in the West Indies. British forces, pressed by the resurgent enemy, proclaimed a blockade of Guadaloupe and certain other French islands in the area, interdicting, in accordance with international practice, all neutral trade there.[67]

American hostility increased when, in an outrageous violation of American territorial waters, Captain Home of H.M.S. *Africa* attempted to seize a French vessel carrying Fauchet, the departing minister of France to the United States. Federalists and Republicans alike were furious; and an angry Washington deliberately withheld ratification of the treaty, awaiting, he said, more information on British intentions, and inveighing the while against the "domineering spirit" and "outrageous and insulting conduct" of the officers of the Royal Navy.[68] Anti-British sentiment, building up from many sources, was bound to be exacerbated, too, by the efforts of British offices ordered to intercept and search American vessels for enemy property. The possibility of legitimate error was always great; and extensive Franco-American collusion and co-operation on the private level complicated the British task enormously, while rendering ill-tempered and even violent Anglo-American clashes at sea virtually inevitable.

Britain's anger was also building, as numerous Americans continued to serve aboard French privateers; an exasperated Grenville even threatened to treat them as pirates, if taken. Wrath rose higher when it became known that Americans in considerable number had participated in a particularly infamous French assault upon Sierra Leone, founded as a refuge for freed slaves.[69] Even more infuriating, because more dangerous, was the continual fitting out of French privateers in American ports, a gross violation of the neutral status and directly contrary to the orders of the Philadelphia government. In November, 1794, Hammond sent home a list of seventy-five prizes, worth a quarter of a million pounds sterling. Forty-six were victims of privateers fitted out in and enjoying the sanctuary of American ports. Hammond, Bond, and other British representatives in the country tried repeatedly, but with very limited success, to prevent the sailings of the privateers or, after their return to port, to effect the rescue of their British prizes by appealing to the federal authorities and to the courts. There could be no doubt about the attitude of the government of the United States toward illicit privateers. The establishment of legal proofs of ownership and of intent was, however, a lengthy judicial process under the best of circumstances; in the face of wilful collusion between French and American citizens and bland protestations of innocence of any privateering intent, it became virtually impossible—particularly since many state

officials, upon whom the responsibility rested to establish the facts
and to render judgment, showed themselves ready to connive at any
measure designed to profit fellow citizens and to hurt Britain. When
the *Lovely Lass*, fitted out at Baltimore in the autumn of 1794, took
the British packet carrying the November and December mails, it
must have seemed the last straw in Britain.[70] There was more than a
note of exasperation in Phineas Bond's reply to Secretary of the
Treasury Walcott's complaint that his country's commerce and revenues were being seriously reduced by the British cruisers: the American was bluntly bidden to consider "whether We had not infinitely
more to complain of, from the wanton depredations committed upon
our Commerce, by picaroons fitted out under the Eyes of this government."[71]

A clandestine trade was developed on a grand scale by American
merchants and a desperately needy French Republic, wracked by
harsh winters, poor harvests, and a terrific military effort. Systematically disguising French purchases as American property, the trade
was a profound irritant to worried British leaders. Provisions and
even implements of war bought by French agents in the United
States went to the West Indies under the American flag and contributed directly to France's ability to resist British conquests of her
island possessions. Sir John Jervis commented bitterly on Jay's allegations that Americans had been mistreated by persons under his command in the West Indies: the object of Jay's solicitude had "so blend-
ed with the Republican Frenchmen," he claimed with a touch of
irony, that they had become "One and Indivisible."[72] America was
guilty, an outraged British naval captain wrote home, of "a shameful
Prostitution of neutrality." To distinguish between French and American property, he said of the vessels he had intercepted, was utterly
impossible; and Britain's only recourse was "the strictest legal Inves-
tigations without paying regard to Ships Papers." Phineas Bond expressed almost the same sentiment in the conversation with Walcott
noted earlier: Britain, he told the American, was under "the necessity
of a Strict and almost indiscriminate Search . . . when such frequent
Frauds were practised by the French Agents, favor'd and assisted
by so many American Traders who, departing from the Character of
Neutrality, lend their Names, and their best aid to favor the Enter-
prizes of our Enemies."[73]

While Hammond wrote home of "Tumultous Meetings of the

people" at Portsmouth, Boston, New York, Philadelphia, Norfolk, and Charleston, of petitions against the treaty pouring into the President's office, of copies of the offensive document burned before the doors of his and Bond's residences, in Britain, public reaction to the treaty was mild. The East India Company muttered against the open admission of the Americans to their Far Eastern preserves, and mercantilists greeted Article XII sullenly enough, Sheffield later growling that Grenville had been duped by Jay; but the prevalent reaction was expressed by the king himself. In a speech to Parliament at the end of 1794, he announced the signing of the treaty and praised it for having removed "all grounds of jealousy and misunderstanding" and for opening the way to the increase of "an intercourse beneficial to both countries."[74] Even when reports from the United States turned somber, Britons did not believe that the treaty itself was in serious danger. The outcry in America was the work of "the French and Democratical Party," which would naturally hate any treaty settling differences between the United States and Great Britain and laying the basis of future harmony and friendship between the two countries. Misapprehensions, even when they did arise, did not last long. Federalists, it was soon learned, were strong in support of the treaty; and news that Washington had signed the ratification arrived on the heels of the disturbing reports of popular indignation.[75]

The violent outcry in America against the treaty—arising from a new and highly offended nationalism and whipped on by Jeffersonian Republicans in pursuit of political objectives, both foreign and domestic, has often been allowed to obscure the true character of the Jay-Grenville agreement. *Vox populi*, John Adams observed with both candor and truth, is not always *vox dei*; the emotional condemnations of the treaty should not be accepted as manifestations of divine inspiration. The treaty was a fair, honorable, and reasonable settlement wrought by two fair, honorable, and reasonable men. Grave differences, some of long standing, others more recent, were settled; and substantial and matching advantages accrued to both sides.[76] Britain was saved another declared enemy at a moment of great national peril; and the United States escaped a war which would have put her own existence at hazard. The treaty did not mark Britain's final acceptance of American independence—that was accomplished in the Order of July, 1783—but it was a critical test of the country's "Strength and Firmness," as Grenville himself re-

marked.[77] Had Jay's and Grenville's work been rejected, the authority and prestige of the United States government would have been
so badly damaged at home and abroad that it is impossible to see
how it could have survived.

To dwell on what might have happened, however, is to neglect
the actual course of events. Excepting Article XII, the treaty *was*
ratified, accepted, and enforced. Peace *was* preserved. Arbitration, the
mixed commission, and reasonable compromise became the established
methods of settling future differences between the United States and
Great Britain.

John Quincy Adams, in the essay which figured in the introduction to this book, enunciated a view of British policy destined to become a classic interpretation of national history: Britain was the vil-
lain; America, the virtuous damsel in distress. The evidence presented
in these pages supports a broader view and a different judgment. That
a multitude of important problems vexed Anglo-American relations
is beyond dispute; but responsibility was not the monopoly of either
country. Each bears an equal share.

Some writers, inspired by Jefferson and Jeffersonianism, seek to
justify anti-British sentiments by arguing that the fate of democracy
was somehow at stake in the quarrels between Great Britain and the
United States after the American Revolution. A form of political
and social organization which developed (in Britain as well as America) in the nineteenth and twentieth centuries, modern democracy
was no more at issue between the two countries during the period
under review than it was during the war which preceded it. To condemn Federalist or British policies because they were not democratic
is to indulge in profound anachronism. In any event, it may reasonably be asked if popular acclaim, especially in a time of intense public excitement, is the most reliable test of wise foreign policy.

A more serious omission for the historian of the period is the failure to go beyond the differences, as important as they were, between
Britain and America. The experience of the first critical dozen years
after the Peace of 1783 is significant not only because it shows how
British and American interests clashed, but also because it shows how
greatly they coincided and complemented each other. On balance, it
represents the reappearance of a motif, temporarily disrupted and
altered by the War for Independence, but characteristic of the whole
broad sweep of Anglo-American history: the development and pro-

liferation of a wide and unique community of interests binding the two countries and their people in a close and special way.

When Jefferson and his friends insisted on substituting France for Britain as America's major European correspondent, they inverted the natural order of things and flew in the face of forces quite beyond their power to control or extinguish. Had they carried their point, their country would have suffered grave, perhaps fatal consequences. Similarly, Hawkesbury and his mercantilist friends in Britain would have hazarded vital national interests in 1794 by continuing to draw the line against American vessels in the West Indies. Both groups, left and right, were overruled by men who sensibly sought and built upon the great common ground. In this context, the creative impulse came from Shelburne and Grenville, Hamilton and Jay, not from Sheffield and Hawkesbury, Madison and Jefferson. The anomaly is not Lord Grenville's treaty with Mr. Jay, but the War of 1812.

APPENDIX A: CHAPTER I

Data from the Report of January 28, 1791

I

AVERAGE TONNAGE employed between Great Britain and the United States (N.B.: The figures for 1770-72 are totals, and, therefore, include American vessels):

	1770-72	1787-89
Outward bound		
British		272 ships (55,785 tons)
American		157 ships (25,725 tons)
Total	628 ships (81,951 tons)	429 ships (81,510 tons)
Inward bound		
British		251 ships (49,405 tons)
American		169 ships (27,403 tons)
Total	699 ships (91,540 tons)	420 ships (76,808 tons)
Median		
British		261 ships (52,595 tons)
American		163 ships (26,564 tons)
Total	663 ships (86,745 tons)	425 ships (79,160 tons)

Thus it appears that the number of British vessels directly engaged in trade between the United States and Great Britain decreased in the postwar period by 238 vessels, but only by 7,585 tons. Obviously, larger ships—suitable for the triangular trade involving Great Britain, North America, and the West Indies—were being used.

II

Average tonnage employed between Great Britain and the British West Indies:

	1770-72	1787-89
Outward bound	420 ships (75,143 tons)	531 ships (128,207 tons)
Inward bound	563 ships (85,821 tons)	588 ships (139,265 tons)
Median	491 ships (80,482 tons)	559 ships (133,736 tons)

Thus an increase appears of 68 ships (about 14%), but of 53,254 tons (about 62.5%). The increase was the more dramatic because the earlier figures included American vessels, while the latter, of course, excluded them.

III

Average tonnage employed between the British West Indies and the United States:

	1770-72	1787-89
Outward bound	2,172 ships (103,540 tons)	510 ships (57,904 tons)
Inward bound	2,297 ships (111,939 tons)	579 ships (67,573 tons)
Median	2,234 ships (107,739 tons)	544 ships (62,738 tons)

Apparently, a disastrous decrease had occurred: 1,670 ships, amounting to about 75% of the total number and about 50% of the tonnage. However, almost 62.5% of the vessels employed between the British West Indies and the United States before the war belonged to colonial Americans and the great balance of the remainder to British merchants occasionally resident in America, with only a very few belonging to British merchants living either in Britain or in the islands. In the later period, British merchants resident in the British dominions owned all the vessels listed—a new and valuable acquisition to British navigation, the more to be prized because the triangular trade had formerly been monopolized by the colonial Americans. Thus, British policy operated "to the Increase of British Navigation compared with that of the United States in a double Ratio: It has taken from the Navigation of the United States even more than it has added to that of Great Britain."

Data from the Report of January 28, 1791

THE DATA given below clearly show dramatic gains in the number of vessels engaged in trade with British North America. The advance is the more meaningful when it is remembered that the prewar figures included American vessels, undoubtedly the predominant element in the trade, while the postwar figures excluded them.

I

Average tonnage employed between Great Britain and the remaining British colonies in North America:

	1770-72	1787-89
Outward bound	250 ships (9,582 tons)	486 ships (61,858 tons)
Inward bound	273 ships (12,857 tons)	249 ships (30,355 tons)
Median	261 ships (11,219 tons)	367 ships (46,106 tons)

Thus, there was an increase of about 50% in the number of ships and almost 400% in tonnage.

II

Average tonnage employed between the remaining British colonies in North America and the United States:

	1770-72	1787-89
Outward bound	250 ships (9,582 tons)	208 ships (15,135 tons)
Inward bound	276 ships (12,857 tons)	269 ships (15,524 tons)
Median	263 ships (11,219 tons)	238 ships (15,329 tons)

Thus, the number of vessels decreased about 10%; but the tonnage increased about 33.33%.

There was, finally, a substantial increase in average tonnage em-

ployed between the remaining British colonies in North America
and the British West Indies.

	1770-72	1787-89
Outward bound	15 ships (753 tons)	142 ships (12,696 tons)
Inward bound	23 ships (1,240 tons)	171 ships (16,331 tons)
Median	19 ships (996 tons)	156 ships (14,513 tons)

The increase amounted to about 700% in the number of ships
and 1,300% in tonnage. It was due in large part to the fish trade
between the West Indies and Newfoundland. The numbers of vessels have been corrected to account for multiple voyages.

APPENDIX C: CHAPTER I

American Topsail Vessels

THE REPORT of January 28, 1791, using data furnished by the assiduous Phineas Bond, consul-general at Philadelphia, showed that in 1772 the American colonies built the following topsail vessels:

	Vessels	Tons
New England	123	(18,149)
New York	15	(1,640)
New Jersey	1	(80)
Pennsylvania	18	(2,897)
Maryland	8	(1,626)
Virginia	7	(933)
North Carolina	3	(253)
South Carolina	2	(213)
Georgia	5	(753)
Total	182	(26,544)

By 1789, however, the pattern had altered radically:

	Vessels	Tons
New England	11	(no figures supplied)
New York	0	—
New Jersey	1	(200)
Pennsylvania	14	(2,966)
Maryland	5	(1,200)
Virginia, North and South Carolina, and Georgia built none.		
Total	31	(4,366)

Data Collected by William Eden, 1786

TOTAL BRITISH IMPORTS, from Christmas, 1783, to Christmas, 1784, stood at £14,111,165; total exports were £14,803,946, leaving a comfortable balance in favor of Britain. Of these totals, exports to and imports from the United States (excluding Georgia) amounted to well over £4.25 million as against £700,000, leaving a staggering balance in favor of Britain. The figures (B.M. Add. MSS 45729, no folio) were broken down further:

	Imports from	Exports to
Virginia and Maryland	£352,792	£2,009,782
Pennsylvania, New York, and New Jersey	111,187	1,307,185
New England	49,830	521,743
The Carolinas	163,539	442,464

The British Share of Foreign Shipping at American Ports

CONSUL GEORGE MILLER in Charleston, South Carolina, reported on foreign shipping clearing outward from that port from November, 1785, to November, 1786:

British	168 vessels	(16,855 tons)
Spanish	37 vessels	(1,251 tons)
French	13 vessels	(1,122 tons)

With a scattering of Danish, Dutch, and German vessels, there was a grand total of 234 vessels (21,933 tons). The British share was thus about 73% of the vessels and about 76% of the tonnage.

November, 1786, to November, 1787

British	150 vessels	(17,106 tons)
French	8 vessels	(715 tons)

There were a few vessels of other nationalities, making a total of 212 vessels (20,587 tons). The British share was thus about 71% of the vessels and about 73% of the tonnage.

Miller also provided information on vessels inward bound:

November, 1786, to November, 1787

British	92 vessels	(7,080 tons)
Spanish	41 vessels	(837 tons)
French	7 vessels	(647 tons)
Dutch	1 vessel	(80 tons)

The totals were 141 vessels and 8,644 tons. The British share was thus about 66% of the vessels and about 80% of the tonnage.

November, 1787, to November, 1788

British	158 vessels	(19,199 tons)
French	13 vessels	(1,510 tons)

There were a few vessels from other nations, making a total of 231 vessels (25,063 tons). The British share was thus about 68% of the vessels and about 77% of the tonnage. Miller's reports were made to the Duke of Leeds, formerly Marquis of Carmarthen, and are January 28, 1790, F.O. 4/8, fols. 38-42. Miller submitted two other reports on shipping as consul for the Carolinas and Georgia. They are December 31, 1788, F.O. 4/7, fols. 32-33, and February 9, 1791, F.O. 4/9, fol. 160.

From Phineas Bond, in Philadelphia, came information indicating that in the year beginning September 5, 1787, 23,004 tons of British shipping had entered that port; in the succeeding year, 39,372 tons entered. Bond estimated that Britain held 80% of the foreign carrying trade and was within 20% of the total American tonnage in the port. (His dispatch is dated June 20, 1789, and contains fifty-three enclosures, F.O. 4/7, fols. 238-39. See, too, his dispatch of January 4, 1789, ibid., fol. 1.)

As for the West Indian carrying trade from Philadelphia, Britain was paramount, her tonnage standing at 17,529—4,000 tons more than the total combined tonnage of all others. This splendid performance Bond attributed directly to the exclusion of American vessels by the Order of July 2, 1783. A year later, Bond gave information on vessels entering the port of New York in 1789. (The figures in parentheses are average tonnage. Bond's information is in his dispatch of January 8, 1790, F.O. 4/8, fols. 27-29.)

Nationality	Ships	Brigantines	Schooners	Sloops	Total Tonnage
United States	43 (240)	145 (130)	167 (60)	415 (50)	61,440
Britain	68 (300)	73 (180)	91 (60)	73 (50)	42,750
Portugal	3 (200)	3 (140)	1 (60)	—	1,380
Spain	3 (300)	3 (140)	1 (60)	4 (50)	1,580
Holland	2 (200)	1 (160)	—	—	960
France	1 (200)	5 (160)	—	—	1,000
Sweden	—	2 (200)	—	3 (?)	400
Total	120	233	260	495	109,510

The British share of *total* tonnage was thus about 40%, compared with 56% for the United States herself. Britain's share of *foreign* tonnage was about 98%.

Colonel John Hamilton, consul at Norfolk, Virginia, provided statistics on imports and exports for Anglo-American trade in 1788. (See his dispatch, F.O. 4/7, fol. 3.)

Imports into Great Britain from the United States

New England	£ 67,146- 3-11d.
New York	111,848- 4- 2d.
Pennsylvania	32,807- 7- 8d.
Maryland	142,651-17-10d.
Virginia	362,020- 0-11d.
North Carolina	30,738- 9- 1d.
South Carolina	251,520- 5- 7d.
Georgia	35,057- 3-10d.
Total	£1,023,789-13- 0d.

Exports from Great Britain to the United States

New England	£ 233,689- 6-11d.
New York	330,675- 4- 1d.
Pennsylvania	212,502-18-11d.
Maryland	254,071-10- 6d.
Virginia	512,210-17- 2d.
North Carolina	14,159-13- 5d.
South Carolina	304,487- 7- 0d.
Georgia	24,345- 4-10d.
Total	£2,106,142- 2-10d.

The balance was thus £1,182,352-9-10d. in favor of Britain. It should also be noted that the figures for exports represent American domestic consumption only, there being no longer a direct legal trade between the United States and the British West Indies.

APPENDIX F: CHAPTER VI

General Maunsell's Memorandum

THERE IS EVIDENCE of yet another informal approach from the British to the American government—a curious undated memorandum preserved in the Hamilton Manuscripts (vol. 9) in the Library of Congress. It is in an unknown hand and docketed "Genl. Maunsell with Instructions from Mr. Pitt delivered (?) at London." The assumption is that General John Maunsell traveled to the United States on private business in 1791, and the Prime Minister seized the opportunity to assure the Americans of Britain's desire to treat. Little is known of Maunsell, although the army lists show his date of rank as October 31, 1762. In 1775, he was a half-pay lieutenant colonel, and in 1777 was promoted to colonel (half-pay). On October 19, 1781—an interesting date—Maunsell became major general.

The memorandum reads:

Mr. Pitt has authorized me to acquaint the ministers of the United States of America that Great Britain is anxious to establish and preserve the strikest [sic] Amity and friendship, with the United States and that a person properly Authorized will shortly be sent out for the discussion of matters that may require it, in order to make the necessary arrangement for the above purpose.

Mr. Pitt has likewise Authorized Genl. Maunsell to procure for, and transmit to him, what were the wishes and demands of America.

As the President has in his message to the Senate and Assembly of 14 Feby. 1791 mentioned that 'soon after he was called to the Administration he found it important to come to an understanding with the Court of London—respecting its disposition to enter into commercial arrangements with the United States on the principles of reciprocal advantages' &c. as mentioned in that message for which he authoriz'd 'informal conferences with the British Minister from which he does not infer any disposition on their part to enter into any arrangements merely Commercial.'

General Maunsell tho' not diplomatically employed hopes that the United States will from the message he brings be satisfied of the friendly disposition of the court of London, and that this information will satisfy the Government of the United States that the Disposition of Great Britain is favorable to a friendly Intercourse with the United States.

Data from the Report of January 28, 1791

Duties Paid in Britain on:	*By the United States*	*By Other Foreign Countries*
Potash (per cwt.)	Free	0- 2- 3d.
Pearl Ash	Free	0- 2- 3d.
Bar iron (per ton)	Free	£2-16- 2d.
Pitch (per last)	£0-11- 0d.	0-12- 5d.
Tar (per last)	0-11- 0d.	0-12-4½d.
Beaver skins, each	0- 0- 1d.	0- 0-8¼d.
Tobacco (per lb.)	0- 1- 3d.	0- 3- 6d.
Woods (except masts, yards, bowspirits)	Free	No rate quoted, but existing taxes accounted for annual revenue of £250,000.

A. *Average Annual Value of British Exports:*	*1768-1774*	*1783-1789*	*Annual Increase*	*Annual Decrease*
1. To the United States				
Manufactures	£2,216,970	£2,119,837		£ 97,133
Other articles	515,066	213,806		301,260
			Totals:	£398,394
2. To the remaining British colonies in North America				
Manufactures	£ 310,916	£ 603,928	£293,012	
Other Articles	68,495	225,160	156,665	
			Total:	£449,677

A. *Average Annual Value of British Exports:*	1768-1774	1783-1789	*Annual Increase*	*Annual Decrease*	
3. To the British West Indies					
Manufactures	£1,182,379	£1,297,275	£114,896		
Other Articles	167,240	167,145		£	95

B. *Average Annual Value of British Imports:*

	1768-1774	1783-1789	*Annual Increase*	*Annual Decrease*
1. From the United States	£1,752,142	£ 908,636		£843,506
2. From the remaining British colonies in North America	£ 123,372	£ 220,358	£ 96,986	
3. From the British West Indies	£3,232,119	£3,903,185	£671,066	

"Free Ships, Free Goods" and the Eden Treaty

IT HAS SOMETIMES been supposed, by Thomas Jefferson among others, that Britain's acceptance of "free ships, free goods" in the commercial treaty with France in 1786 constituted a general acceptance of the principle. Britain's negotiator, William Eden, preparing himself for his mission, was quite explicit on the subject: it was "contrary to the Laws and Usage and Right of Nations" to allow neutral shipping to protect enemy property. This had been, and remained, true "in all ages and in all Countries." From time to time, when her interests required it, Great Britain specifically agreed to deviate from established international practice and allowed neutral shipping to protect enemy property. She had done this, for example, in a treaty, no longer subsisting, with the Dutch in 1674. The suspension of the principle by treaty, however, merely demonstrated that without such an agreement it would continue to exist, Eden argued. Reason, justice, and necessity supported it, "for it would be to little purpose to undertake or to prosecute a maritime War, if the Conveyance of the Enemies' property might be secured from Molestation under the Banner of Neutrality and of Friendship."[1]

In the light of Eden's general and unequivocal reasoning on the subject, how is his acceptance of the principle, "free ships, free goods," in the treaty with France to be explained? He accepted it because extending the privilege of the neutral flag to France was, in all probable circumstances, a concession of very little importance. Eden himself told his brother Morton that making the stipulation with France was very different from making the same stipulation with any other power: if Britain were engaged in a general war, France would in all likelihood become a belligerent enemy.[2] The concession helped purchase a highly favorable treaty of commerce, although it did not, as has been seen, escape bitter attack on the ground that it sacrificed a cardinal principle of British maritime policy and tradition.

So far was Britain from accepting the Eden treaty as a general endorsement of "free ships, free goods" that, with the outbreak of war, she invariably insisted in agreements with allies that neutral rights did not comprise the freedom of the neutral flag. Memories of the hurtful League of Armed Neutrality during the American War were very fresh. George III, recovered temporarily from the first terrible attack of insanity, expressed what must have been a joy shared with his ministers that Russia, the wheelhorse of the league in 1780, had disavowed (in a treaty signed March 25, 1793) "the most inimical measure adopted by any Nation." The Russo-British accord, he hoped, would also prevent the Danes and Swedes, cohorts in the earlier league, from carrying supplies to France. The measure was "so essential that I would rather see both those Crowns join France than submit to their adopting a conduct much more disadvantageous towards a Speedy conclusion of the War."[3]

The heart of the League of Armed Neutrality was removed with the Russian treaty and the northern power's involvement in the rape of Poland, as the abortive attempts of Sweden and Denmark to reconstitute it somewhat later clearly showed. Furthermore, there were important Britons—Hawkesbury, for example—who considered the United States potentially the most dangerous of all neutrals because of geographical proximity to the French West Indies and a certain political affinity for the French Republic. Jefferson's bland assumption of a binding consensus must have seemed doubly suspect: if a consensus existed, it was clearly against the American position; and, secondly, insistence upon it appeared, in British eyes, to be an announcement of benevolence toward France just short of war with Britain. There is little doubt that Britain would have preferred war with the United States to an acceptance of the Jeffersonian argument. Her chief weapon against France was her navy. She could not afford to allow one arm to be tied behind her back.

Impressment of American Seamen

ALTHOUGH THE IMPRESSMENT issue was relatively unimportant during the period before the ratification of Jay's Treaty, it undoubtedly made a minor contribution to rising American hostility. For this reason, and more especially because of its very great importance as a cause of the War of 1812, the subject deserves to be examined in some detail.

In times of crisis, Britain habitually manned the Royal Navy by a press of merchant seamen carried out under the authority of an act of Parliament, always passed in haste and in as much secrecy as possible. Press gangs were thus enabled to take their unsuspecting quarry by surprise either ashore or aboard vessels in port. A grim game of hide-and-seek was usual, and brutality was regularly employed to buttress faltering patriotism.

The practice made friction with the United States inevitable. There was a "similarity of manners, language and names," in the words of Canadian merchant Adam Lymburner, which rendered it always difficult and sometimes impossible to distinguish bona fide American tars from decamping British.[1] In both the crisis with France over Dutch affairs in 1787 and that with Spain over Nootka in 1790, impressment of a few American seamen occurred. These were inadvertent accidents, the ministry in London assured American representatives; and steps were quickly taken to meet their complaints.[2] Obviously, some sure method for establishing proof of American citizenship was needed. From time to time, there was desultory talk of certificates of nationality.[3] Jefferson, to whom impressment seemed one more heinous British crime against long-suffering Americans, held forth the idea of a tonnage-nationality ratio cer-

tified by the nation of origin, which would automatically exempt
vessels from interference by press gangs.[4] When war broke out in
Europe in 1793, however, Britain and the United States were as far
as ever from a solution.

The London ministry did refer the question to Phineas Bond,
who was then on the point of returning to Philadelphia as consul-
general. In his report, Bond was sympathetic to the Americans: their
complaint was understandable, and some method for preventing confusion was highly desirable. What it might be, however, he was unable to say. He did not refuse outright the suggestion of nationality
certificates; but, perhaps remembering the brilliance of American
forgers in reproducing British Mediterranean passes to evade the
Barbary pirates, he clearly had no faith in the expedient. His rejection of the idea of a tonnage-nationality ratio was, however, blunt
and explicit. Britain's marine would suffer "most fatally" from allowing American vessels, certifying the nationality of their own
crews, to become virtually unchallenged refuges for deserting British
sailors.[5]

The war with France intensified the impressment issue. Britain
needed to find as many trained seamen as possible for the royal service, and she had to hold those she found. Emigration and desertion
were twin evils to be checked. The question was, how? There was
an informality and simplicity in the process of acquiring American
nationality which British leaders found shocking. Their own assumptions were that British nationality was indelible and that the necessary qualification for American status consisted of birth or residence
in the United States at the time of separation. Americans could not
be expected to acquiesce in British reasoning. "I much fear," Grenville told Jay after they had negotiated their treaty, "that the ideas
prevalent in America on the subject of emigration" would operate
to prevent any mutually satisfactory solution to the impressment
issue.[6] The failure of the federal government to speak clearly and explicitly on the subject of naturalization created confusion, allowed
the British doctrine to go without effective rebuttal, and encouraged
visitation of American vessels and impressment of "Britons" found
aboard, the only means available to Britain to plug the holes in what
often seemed a sieve.

All evidence points to an emigration of British seamen of really
massive proportions. American ship owners and masters, requiring

ever more sailors as neutral trade expanded, made undisguised and successful efforts to entice British mariners into their service. Pay for an able seaman aboard their vessels stood at an unprecedented £6 per month. Although it was virtually useless except as a psychological bolster for the buyer, a deserting tar could easily buy from port authorities a "certificate" of American citizenship; at Norfolk, Virginia, the price was $37.[7] Adam Lymburner told Home Secretary Dundas in the autumn of 1793 that "one half of the Crews which navigate the American merchant ships are British Seamen." During the press which took place in the spring of 1793, he continued, "American ships in the Thames got as many Men as they pleased, as their ships afforded that protection which the seamen desired." His description of American practice must have given British ministers pause: their vessels came to Britain with skeleton crews, "as they are sent to get sailors enough here and they like them better than their own men."[8]

Even French agents in the United States tried to entice British seamen to desert. In August, 1793, Hammond sent home a handbill put out by the French consul at Philadelphia, urging "all able bodied Seamen" to rally to "the Cause of Liberty" and promising a particularly warm welcome for "the generous and intrepid Natives of Ireland."[9] Hammond warned Captain Home, who was destined to win some notoriety in the United States, that he should beware of allowing Americans to visit his ship, the *Africa*, and of permitting his crew ashore without proper precautions, since "every artifice and allurement will be employed to induce them to desert." Already, he added, "a great majority of the crews of all vessels departing from ports to the Southward of Connecticut is composed of natives of his Majesty's European dominions."[10] Fully nine-tenths of the navigation of the middle and southern states, Hammond estimated to Grenville, was carried on by British subjects.[11] Consul John Hamilton wrote from Richmond in the same vein, and asked Grenville's instructions.[12] On April 8, 1795, the British government issued an Order in Council forbidding "Artificers, Manufacturers, Seamen and Seafaring Men, His Majesty's Subjects," to embark aboard foreign ships.[13] It was unquestionably a failure, however; Admiral Nelson, it has been stated, estimated in 1803 that in the first part of the war with France, 42,000 seamen deserted from the fleet. During the same period, some 30,000 to 40,000 entered American service.[14]

It is not surprising that a threat of such magnitude called forth strong measures. Hammond, for example, instructed the commanders of ships of the Royal Navy in American waters to "take such natives of Great Britain as you may find on board of any American vessel you may search at sea, leaving merely a sufficient number of hands to navigate it," explaining that "the navigation of this country has been long carried on by British Seamen to the great detriment of his Majesty's government."[15] In August, 1794, with the emotional temperature in the United States rising for a number of reasons, Hammond consulted hurriedly with Admiral Murray off Sandy Hook. It continued to be "extremely necessary," the envoy told Murray, "to obviate the inconvenience which would arise from the indiscriminate demand and release of all persons stiling themselves American citizens." Murray was therefore to require of pressed seamen who claimed American nationality satisfactory proof of their allegation. The power of deciding to accept or reject evidence of American nationality remained, of course, in British hands.[16] Grenville subsequently transmitted His Majesty's approbation.

With British stakes so high, incidents were bound to occur. Three notable ones took place in American waters in 1794 and 1795. The first, noted in the text, was the fracas in May, 1794, at Newport, Rhode Island, between Captain Baynton of the *Nautilus*, a unit of Murray's squadron, and the General Assembly of Rhode Island. It ended only after a combination of Assembly action and at least the threat of mob action forced the release of six Americans. The second saw another of Murray's captains, Alexander Cochrane of the *Thetis*, collide with the authorities at New York. Imprudently allowing officers and men shore leave in spite of prevailing suspicion in the city that he held several Americans against their will aboard his ship, he was greeted by a mob at the wharf. There was no violence, but enticements were bawled out to sailors manning the captain's own gig: $100 for any deserter from "the British Scoundrels." Three men leapt ashore and accepted the offer on the spot. Cochrane's sense of outrage was the greater because, far from holding Americans forcibly aboard his ship, he was giving some twenty of them transportation to Halifax to attend the Court of Vice-Admiralty, where cases involving vessels in which they were interested were being heard.[17]

The third clash was caused by Home of the *Africa*, who—in

pursuit of the French frigate *Medusa,* which had been assigned to carry Minister Fauchet to Europe—violated American neutrality in almost every way possible short of bombarding the shore. He also had aboard three impressed Americans. The London authorities gave him a very sharp reprimand, mollifying to a degree outraged American sensibilities.[18]

Despite the occasional "incident" perpetrated by overzealous British officers and the readiness of the Jeffersonian Republicans to seize on any issue to whip up anti-British sentiment in the United States, impressment remained subordinate to other matters throughout the period. One reason was the very magnitude of the major differences between the two powers. Another was the willingness of both governments to discuss cases of impressment reasonably and calmly as they arose. The Pitt ministry maintained a generally conciliatory policy—without, to be sure, giving up the practice. When American vessels were sent into British ports under the Orders in Council, impressments from their crews became frequent. Pinckney was indefatigable in their behalf, and he was invariably met with goodwill and co-operation. In the autumn of 1793, he reported home that British authorities "profess a willingness to secure to us all real American seamen, when proved to be such." Generally, the combined oaths of master and mariner were allowed to constitute sufficient proof, although Pinckney conceded that "some irregularities occasionally take place."[19] When Randolph submitted his report on foreign aggressions upon American commerce on March 2, 1794 (transmitted to Congress on the fifth), impressment was mentioned, but only as one of several charges against Britain, all of which were set off against objectionable French practices.[20]

Influential Federalists naturally wished a solution to the problem but were generally understanding of Britain's predicament. Jay, for example, thought Britain ought to agree not to remove any seamen from American vessels on the high seas or in colonial ports because of the difficulty impressment would create for the return voyage. He could not, however, deny Britain the right to seek and take her own seamen aboard vessels in British or Irish ports. A settlement of the issue, he rightly predicted, would nevertheless "continue to prove an arduous task."[21] Hamilton agreed with Jay, believing his suggestion "unexceptionably just, and at the same time safe for Great Britain."[22]

In the period of relative tranquillity after Jay's Treaty, Grenville seems to have been willing to accept the idea of citizenship certificates issued under the authority of the federal government, but matters were allowed to rub along by both nations. The British Foreign Secretary clearly believed the initiative lay with the United States; and he strongly defended British actions: "I do not think one instance can be brought," he wrote to Jay, "where a seaman has not been discharged, who could produce, I do not say proof, but any probable, or even plausible ground for supporting him a native citizen of the United States, or a resident there at the time of the separation from this country."[23]

In 1796, Phineas Bond reported to Grenville that the only causes of complaint against Great Britain in the United States were the capture of American vessels and the impressment of seamen from them. These were only "inconveniences," however, which would have to be borne as long as the Americans forced "prescribed channels of commerce." If only they would devise "some mode" to obviate "those deceptions in respect to our seamen to which a similarity of language and of habits so seriously expose us," their complaints might be settled.[24]

The British practice was the origin of the grievance, although Americans themselves contributed to it by the enticement of British seamen to desert. Granted the cause, however, Bond and Grenville seem correct in having expected an American initiative. The failure of the United States to act decisively in the fields of diplomacy and legislation before the ratification of Jay's Treaty is simply explained, however: the government was involved in a host of more important and vexatious problems in Anglo-American relations, whose solution claimed priority. This was the view, too, of the dominant Federalists, upon whom the "inconveniences" from impressment bore most heavily.

APPENDIX J: CHAPTER XVI

British Complicity in the Indian War

DESPITE FREQUENT ASSURANCES by the British government to the American authorities, there remained in the United States a deep suspicion amounting to conviction that Great Britain was actively stirring up, encouraging, and supporting the Indians in their frontier hostilities. The belief served to render even more suspect than they might ordinarily have been, Britain's persistent efforts in behalf of an Indian barrier territory and a mediated peace between the savages and the Americans.

That the British government itself should have been freed of any charge of complicity is clearly established by the evidence, but American suspicions were not groundless. In his account of travels through the United States and Upper Canada, a British traveler, Isaac Weld, Jr., wrote of St. Clair's defeat: "A great many young Canadians, and in particular many that were born of Indian women, fought on the side of the Indians in this action."[1] As Wayne began his advance northward in 1794, Dorchester and Simcoe must have been tempted to bolster with Indian forces what they considered their perilously inadequate military capacity. An illuminating exchange took place between the two generals. When Dorchester sent urgently to Simcoe asking him to report his "combined powers," the latter responded that he presumed "Your Lordship includes the Indian Nations, altho' I am to observe that you have never expressed these people by name as a means of defence."[2] The temptation, if it existed at all, was quickly put aside. Instructions from the home government were too categorical to be misunderstood, and events were moving rapidly to a climax.

It is very probably true, however, that as the showdown approached, Canadian authorities, particularly those on the lower levels, tended to turn a blind eye to "unofficial" aid; and there are suggestive indications that as Wayne drew nearer Detroit, supplies of guns, rifles, ball, flints, and knives—all ordinary items of trade in ordinary times—were increased.[3] As early as July 7, Wayne himself reported to his principals that he was encountering both "white and red savages" in the backcountry. His dispatches immediately before and after Fallen Timbers explicitly charged that the enemy had been assisted by Canadian militia and volunteers, and that McKee, the Indian agent, was the "principal stimulator" of the war.[4] The charges cannot be dismissed altogether as the imaginings of a worried military commander in the field. Simcoe himself, writing to his old friend Sir Henry Clinton in September, described the battle of the preceding August. Dwelling on the American plundering of the Indian dead, he stated that among the casualties there had been "a few of their [the Americans'] *friends,* our Loyalists." In London, reports circulated that at least "a few renegade whites" had fought at the side of the Indians in the battle.[5]

It seems apparent that white and half-breed combatants did, in fact, fight with the Indians and that others supplied or supported them. It is equally apparent, however, that these were irregulars, acting without the knowledge or the approval of the London authorities. There is every reason to believe that Grenville correctly and candidly described his government's position in his dispatch to Hammond dated November 20, 1794: even if the American complaints should unfortunately be grounded in fact, "the Conduct of a few unauthorized Individuals joining the Indians cannot be considered as affording any Evidence of the Intentions or Instructions of the King's Government here or in America any more than the numerous Acts of Hostility committed by Americans against this Country during the present War would prove the Conduct or Views of the American Government to be hostile towards Us."[6] The same assurances were given to Jay for transmission to Washington, but the treatment commonly accorded the subject by American writers indicates that the explanation was considered inadequate.[7]

APPENDIX K

The Anglo-American Treaty (Jay's Treaty) of 1794

(REPRINTED from Samuel Flagg Bemis, *Jay's Treaty* [New Haven: Yale University Press, 1962], pp. 453-87, who follows the text found in Hunter Miller's *Treaties and other International Acts of the United States of America*, 2:245-67.)

Treaty of Amity Commerce and Navigation, between His Britannick Majesty;—and The United States of America, by Their President, with the advice and consent of Their Senate.

His Brittanick Majesty and the United States of America, being desirous by a Treaty of Amity, Commerce and Navigation to terminate their Differences in such a manner, as without reference to the Merits of Their respective Complaints and Pretensions, may be the best calculated to produce mutual satisfaction and good understanding: And also to regulate the Commerce and Navigation between Their respective Countries, Territories and People, in such a manner as to render the same reciprocally beneficial and satisfactory; They have respectively named their Plenipotentiaries, and given them Full powers to treat of, and conclude, the said Treaty, that is to say; His Brittanick Majesty has named for His Plenipotentiary, The Right Honourable William Wyndham Baron Grenville of Wotton, One of His Majesty's Privy Council, and His Majesty's Principal Secretary of State for Foreign Affairs; and The President of the said United States, by and with the advice and Consent of the Senate thereof, hath appointed for Their Plenipotentiary The Honourable John Jay, Chief Justice of the said United States and Their Envoy Extraordinary to His Majesty, who have agreed on, and concluded the following Articles

ARTICLE 1.

There shall be a firm inviolable and universal Peace, and a true and sincere Friendship between His Britannick Majesty, His Heirs and Successors, and the United States of America; and between their respective Countries, Territories, Cities, Towns and People of every Degree, without Exception of Persons or Places.

ARTICLE 2.

His Majesty will withdraw all His Troops and Garrisons from all Posts and Places within the Boundary Lines assigned by the Treaty of Peace to the United States. This Evacuation shall take place on or before the first Day of June one thousand seven hundred and ninety six, and all the proper Measures shall in the interval be taken by concert between the Government of the United States, and His Majesty's Governor General in America, for settling the previous arrangements which may be necessary respecting the delivery of the said Posts: The United States in the mean Time at Their discretion extending their settlements to any part within the said boundary line, except within the precincts or Jurisdiction of any of the said Posts. All Settlers and Traders, within the Precincts or Jurisdiction of the said Posts, shall continue to enjoy, unmolested, all their property of every kind, and shall be protected therein. They shall be at full liberty to remain there, or to remove with all or any part of their Effects; and it shall also be free to them to sell their Lands, Houses, or Effects, or to retain the property thereof, at their discretion; such of them as shall continue to reside within the said Boundary Lines shall not be compelled to become Citizens of the United States, or to take any Oath of allegiance to the Government thereof, but they shall be at full liberty so to do, if they think proper, and they shall make and declare their Election within one year after the Evacuation aforesaid. And all persons who shall continue there after the expiration of the said year, without having declared their intention of remaining Subjects of His Britannick Majesty, shall be considered as having elected to become Citizens of the United States.

ARTICLE 3.

It is agreed that it shall at all Times be free to His Majesty's Subjects, and to the Citizens of the United States, and also to the

Indians dwelling on either side of the said Boundary Line freely to
pass and repass by Land, or Inland Navigation, into the respective
Territories and Countries of the Two Parties on the Continent of
America (the Country within the Limits of the Hudson's Bay Company only excepted) and to navigate all the Lakes, Rivers, and waters
thereof, and freely to carry on trade and commerce with each other.
But it is understood, that this Article does not extend to the admission of Vessels of the United States into the Sea Ports, Harbours,
Bays, or Creeks of His Majesty's said Territories; nor into such parts
of the Rivers in His Majesty's said Territories as are between the
mouth thereof, and the highest Port of Entry from the Sea, except
in small vessels trading bonâ fide between Montreal and Quebec,
under such regulations as shall be established to prevent the possibility of any Frauds in this respect. Nor to the admission of British
vessels from the Sea into the Rivers of the United States, beyond the
highest Ports of Entry for Foreign Vessels from the Sea. The River
Mississippi, shall however, according to the Treaty of Peace be entirely open to both Parties; And it is further agreed, That all the
ports and places on its Eastern side, to whichsoever of the parties
belonging, may freely be resorted to, and used by both parties, in as
ample a manner as any of the Atlantic Ports or Places of the United
States, or any of the Ports or Places of His Majesty in Great Britain.

All Goods and Merchandize whose Importation into His Majesty's
said Territories in America, shall not be entirely prohibited, may
freely, for the purposes of Commerce, be carried into the same in the
manner aforesaid, by the Citizens of the United States, and such
Goods and Merchandize shall be subject to no higher or other Duties
than would be payable by His Majesty's Subjects on the Importation
of the same from Europe into the said Territories. And in like manner, all Goods and Merchandize whose Importation into the United
States shall not be wholly prohibited, may freely, for the purposes
of Commerce, be carried into the same, in the manner aforesaid, by
His Majesty's Subjects, and such Goods and Merchandize shall be
subject to no higher or other Duties than would be payable by the
Citizens of the United States on the Importation of the same in
American Vessels into the Atlantic Ports of the said States. And all
Goods not prohibited to be exported from the said Territories re-
spectively, may in like manner be carried out of the same by the Two
Parties respectively, paying Duty as aforesaid.

No Duty of Entry shall ever be levied by either Party on Peltries brought by Land, or Inland Navigation into the said Territories respectively, nor shall the Indians passing or repassing with their own proper Goods and Effects of whatever nature, pay for the same any Impost or Duty whatever. But Goods in Bales, or other large Packages unusual among Indians shall not be considered as Goods belonging bonâ fide to Indians.

No higher or other Tolls or Rates of Ferriage than what are, or shall be payable by Natives, shall be demanded on either side; And no Duties shall be payable on any Goods which shall merely be carried over any of the Portages, or carrying Places on either side, for the purpose of being immediately reimbarked, and carried to some other Place or Places. But as by this Stipulation it is only meant to secure to each Party a free passage across the Portages on both sides, it is agreed, that this Exemption from Duty shall extend only to such Goods as are carried in the usual and direct Road across the Portage, and are not attempted to be in any manner sold or exchanged during their passage across the same, and proper Regulations may be established to prevent the possibility of any Frauds in this respect.

As this Article is intended to render in a great Degree the local advantages of each Party common to both, and thereby to promote a disposition favourable to Friendship and good neighbourhood, It is agreed, that the respective Governments will mutually promote this amicable Intercourse, by causing speedy and impartial Justice to be done, and necessary protection to be extended, to all who may be concerned therein.

ARTICLE 4.

Whereas it is uncertain whether the River Mississippi extends so far to the Northward as to be intersected by a Line to be drawn due West from the Lake of the woods in the manner mentioned in the Treaty of Peace between His Majesty and the United States, it is agreed, that measures shall be taken in Concert between His Majesty's Government in America, and the Government of the United States, for making a joint Survey of the said River, from one Degree of Latitude below the falls of St. Anthony to the principal Source or Sources of the said River, and also of the parts adjacent thereto, And that if on the result of such Survey it should appear that the said River would not be intersected by such a Line as is above mentioned; The two Parties will thereupon proceed by amicable negotiation to regulate the Boundary Line in that quarter as well as all other Points to be adjusted between the said Parties, according to Justice and mutual Convenience, and in Conformity, to the Intent of the said Treaty.

Article 5.

Whereas doubts have arisen what River was truly intended under the name of the River St. Croix mentioned in the said Treaty of Peace and forming a part of the boundary therein described, that question shall be referred to the final Decision of Commissioners to be appointed in the following Manner—Viz—

One Commissioner shall be named by His Majesty, and one by the President of the United States, by and with the advice and Consent of the Senate thereof, and the said two Commissioners shall agree on the choice of a third, or, if they cannot so agree, They shall each propose one Person, and of the two names so proposed one shall be drawn by Lot, in the presence of the two original Commissioners. And the three Commissioners so appointed shall be Sworn impartially to examine and decide the said question according to such Evidence as shall respectively be laid before Them on the part of the British Government and of the United States. The said Commissioners shall meet at Halifax and shall have power to adjourn to such other place or places as they shall think fit. They shall have power to appoint a Secretary, and to employ such Surveyors or other Persons as they shall judge necessary. The said Commissioners shall by a Declaration under their Hands and Seals, decide what River is the River St. Croix intended by the Treaty. The said Declaration shall contain a description of the said River, and shall particularize the Latitude and Longitude of its mouth and of its Source. Duplicates of this Declaration and of the Statements of their Accounts, and of the Journal of their proceedings, shall be delivered by them to the Agent of His Majesty, and to the Agent of the United States, who may be respectively appointed and authorized to manage the business on behalf of the respective Governments. And both parties agree to consider such decision as final and conclusive, so as that the same shall never thereafter be called into question, or made the subject of dispute or difference between them.

ARTICLE 6.

Whereas it is alledged by divers British Merchants and others His Majesty's Subjects, that Debts to a considerable amount which were bonâ fide contracted before the Peace, still remain owing to them by Citizens or Inhabitants of the United States, and that by the operation of various lawful Impediments since the Peace, not only the full recovery of the said Debts has been delayed, but also the Value and Security thereof, have been in several instances impaired and lessened, so that by the ordinary course of Judicial proceedings the British Creditors, cannot now obtain and actually have and receive full and adequate Compensation for the losses and damages which they have thereby sustained: It is agreed that in all such Cases where full Compensation for such losses and damages cannot, for whatever reason, be actually obtained had and received by the said Creditors in the ordinary course of Justice, The United States will make full and complete Compensation for the same to the said Creditors; But it is distinctly understood, that this provision is to extend to such losses only, as have been occasioned by the lawful impediments aforesaid, and is not to extend to losses occasioned by such Insolvency of the Debtors or other Causes as would equally have operated to produce such loss, if the said impediments had not existed, nor to such losses or damages as have been occasioned by the manifest delay or negligence, or wilful omission of the Claimant.

For the purpose of ascertaining the amount of any such losses and damages, Five Commissioners shall be appointed and authorized to meet and act in manner following—viz—Two of them shall be appointed by His Majesty, Two of them by the President of the United States by and with the advice and consent of the Senate thereof, and the fifth, by the unanimous voice of the other Four; and if they should not agree in such Choice, then the Commissioners named by the two parties shall respectively propose one person, and of the two names so proposed, one shall be drawn by Lot in the presence of the Four Original Commissioners. When the Five Commissioners thus appointed shall first meet, they shall before they proceed to act respectively, take the following Oath or Affirmation in the presence of each other, which Oath or Affirmation, being so taken, and duly attested, shall be entered on the Record of their Proceedings,—viz.—I. A: B: One of the Commissioners appointed in pursuance of the 6th Article of the Treaty of Amity, Commerce and Navigation between His Britannick Majesty and The United States of America, do solemnly swear (or affirm) that I will honestly, diligently, impartially, and carefully examine, and to the best of my Judgement, according to Justice and Equity decide all such Complaints, as under the said Article shall be preferred to the said Commissioners: and that I will forbear to act as a Commissioner in any Case in which I may be personally interested.

Three of the said Commissioners shall constitute a Board, and shall have power to do any act appertaining to the said Commission, provided that one of the Commissioners named on each side, and the Fifth Commissioner shall be present, and all decisions shall be made by the Majority of the Voices of the Commissioners then present. Eighteen Months from the Day on which the said Commissioners shall form a Board, and be ready to proceed to Business are assigned for receiving Complaints and applications, but they are nevertheless authorized in any particular Cases in which it shall appear to them to be reasonable and just to extend the said Term of Eighteen Months, for any term not exceeding Six Months after the expiration thereof. The said Commissioners shall first meet at Philadelphia, but they shall have power to adjourn from Place to Place as they shall see Cause.

The said Commissioners in examining the Complaints and applications so preferred to them, are impowered and required in pursuance of the true intent and meaning of this article to take into their Consideration all claims whether of principal or interest, or balances of principal and interest, and to determine the same respectively according to the merits of the several Cases, due regard being had to all the Circumstances thereof, and as Equity and Justice shall appear to them to require. And the said Commissioners shall have power to examine all such Persons as shall come before them on Oath or Affirmation touching the premises; and also to receive in Evidence according as they may think most consistent with Equity and Justice all written Depositions, or Books or Papers, or Copies or Extracts thereof. Every such Deposition, Book or Paper or Copy or Extract being duly authenticated either according to the legal Forms now respectively existing in the two Countries, or in such other manner as the said Commissioners shall see cause to require or allow.

The Award of the said Commissioners or of any three of them as aforesaid shall in all Cases be final and conclusive, both as to the

Justice of the Claim, and to the amount of the Sum to be paid to the
Creditor or Claimant.—And the United States undertake to cause
the Sum so awarded to be paid in Specie to such Creditor or Claimant without deduction; and at such Time or Times, and at such Place
or Places, as shall be awarded by the said Commissioners, and on
Condition of such Releases or assignments to be given by the Creditor or Claimant as by the said Commissioners may be directed; Provided always that no such payment shall be fixed by the said Commissioners to take place sooner then twelve months from the Day of
the Exchange of the Ratifications of this Treaty.

ARTICLE 7.

Whereas Complaints have been made by divers Merchants and
others, Citizens of the United States, that during the course of the
War in which His Majesty is now engaged they have sustained considerable losses and damage by reason of irregular or illegal Captures
or Condemnations of their vessels and other property under Colour
of authority or Commissions from His Majesty, and that from
various Circumstances belonging to the said Cases adequate Compensation for the losses and damages so sustained cannot now be
actually obtained, had and received by the ordinary Course of Judicial proceedings; It is agreed that in all such Cases where adequate
Compensation cannot for whatever reason be now actually obtained,
had and received by the said Merchants and others in the ordinary
course of Justice, full and Complete Compensation for the same will
be made by the British Government to the said Complainants. But it
is distinctly understood, that this provision is not to extend to such
losses or damages as have been occasioned by the manifest delay or
negligence, or wilful omission of the Claimant.

That for the purpose of ascertaining the amount of any such
losses and damages Five Commissioners shall be appointed and authorized to act in London exactly in the manner directed with respect to those mentioned in the preceding Article, and after having
taken the same Oath or Affirmation (mutatis mutandis). The same
term of Eighteen Months is also assigned for the reception of Claims,
and they are in like manner authorised to extend the same in particular Cases. They shall receive Testimony, Books, Papers and Evidence in the same latitude, and exercise the like discretion, and powers respecting that subject, and shall decide the Claims in question,

according to the merits of the several Cases, and to Justice Equity and the Laws of Nations. The award of the said Commissioners or any such three of them as aforesaid, shall in all Cases be final and conclusive both as to the Justice of the Claim and the amount of the Sum to be paid to the Claimant; and His Britannick Majesty undertakes to cause the same to be paid to such Claimant in Specie, without any Deduction, at such place or places, and at such Time or Times as shall be awarded by the said Commissioners and on Condition of such releases or assignments to be given by the Claimant, as by the said Commissioners may be directed.

And whereas certain merchants and others, His Majesty's Subjects, complain that in the course of the war they have sustained Loss and Damage by reason of the Capture of their Vessels and Merchandize taken within the Limits and Jurisdiction of the States, and brought into the Ports of the same, or taken by Vessels originally armed in Ports of the said States:

It is agreed that in all such cases where Restitution shall not have been made agreeably to the tenor of the letter from Mr. Jefferson to Mr. Hammond dated at Philadelphia September 5th 1793. A Copy of which is annexed to this Treaty, the Complaints of the parties shall be, and hereby are referred to the Commissioners to be appointed by virtue of this article, who are hereby authorized and required to proceed in the like manner relative to these as to the other Cases committed to them, and the United States undertake to pay to the Complainants or Claimants in specie without deduction the amount of such Sums as shall be awarded to them respectively by the said Commissioners and at the times and places which in such awards shall be specified, and on Condition of such Releases or assignments to be given by the Claimants as in the said awards may be directed: And it is further agreed that not only the now existing Cases of both descriptions, but also all such as shall exist at the Time, of exchanging the Ratifications of this Treaty shall be considered as being within the provisions intent and meaning of this article.

Article 8.

It is further agreed that the Commissioners mentioned in this and in the two preceding articles shall be respectively paid in such manner, as shall be agreed between the two parties, such agreement being to be settled at the Time of the exchange of the Ratifications of this

Treaty. And all other Expences attending the said Commissions shall be defrayed jointly by the Two Parties, the same being previously ascertained and allowed by the Majority of the Commissioners. And in the case of Death, Sickness or necessary absence, the place of every such Commissioner respectively, shall be supplied in the same manner as such Commissioner was first appointed, and the new Commissioners shall take the same Oath, or Affirmation, and do the same Duties.

ARTICLE 9.

It is agreed, that British Subjects who now hold Lands in the Territories of the United States, and American Citizens who now hold Lands in the Dominions of His Majesty, shall continue to hold them according to the nature and Tenure of their respective Estates and Titles therein, and may grant Sell or Devise the same to whom they please, in like manner as if they were Natives; and that neither they nor their Heirs or assigns shall, so far as may respect the said Lands, and the legal remedies incident thereto, be regarded as Aliens.

ARTICLE 10.

Neither the Debts due from Individuals of the one Nation, to Individuals of the other, nor shares nor monies, which they may have in the public Funds, or in the public or private Banks shall ever, in any Event of war, or national differences, be sequestered, or confiscated, it being unjust and impolitick that Debts and Engagements contracted and made by Individuals having confidence in each other, and in their respective Governments, should ever be destroyed or impaired by national authority, on account of national Differences and Discontents.

ARTICLE 11.

It is agreed between His Majesty and the United States of America, that there shall be a reciprocal and entirely perfect Liberty of Navigation and Commerce, between their respective People, in the manner, under the Limitations, and on the Conditions specified in the following Articles.

ARTICLE 12.

His Majesty Consents that it shall and may be lawful, during the time hereinafter Limited, for the Citizens of the United States, to carry to any of His Majesty's Islands and Ports in the West Indies from the United States in their own Vessels, not being above the burthen of Seventy Tons, any Goods or Merchandizes, being of the Growth, Manufacture, or Produce of the said States, which it is, or may be lawful to carry to the said Islands or Ports from the said States in British Vessels, and that the said American Vessels shall be subject there to no other or higher Tonnage Duties or Charges, than shall be payable by British Vessels, in the Ports of the United States; and that the Cargoes of the said American Vessels, shall be subject there to no other or higher Duties or Charges, than shall be payable on the like Articles, if imported there from the said States in British vessels.

And His Majesty also consents that it shall be lawful for the said American Citizens to purchase, load and carry away, in their said vessels to the United States from the said Islands and Ports, all such articles being of the Growth, Manufacture or Produce of the said Islands, as may now by Law be carried from thence to the said States in British Vessels, and subject only to the same Duties and Charges on Exportation to which British Vessels and their Cargoes are or shall be subject in similar circumstances.

Provided always that the said American vessels do carry and land their Cargoes in the United States only, it being expressly agreed and declared that during the Continuance of this article, the United States will prohibit and restrain the carrying any Melasses, Sugar, Coffee, Cocoa or Cotton in American vessels, either from His Majesty's Islands or from the United States, to any part of the World, except the United States, reasonable Sea Stores excepted. Provided also, that it shall and may be lawful during the same period for British vessels to import from the said Islands into the United States, and to export from the United States to the said Islands, all Articles whatever being of the Growth, Produce or Manufacture of the said Islands, or of the United States respectively, which now may, by the Laws of the said States, be so imported and exported. And that the Cargoes of the said British vessels, shall be subject to no other or higher Duties or Charges, then shall be payable on the same articles if so imported or exported in American Vessels.

It is agreed that this Article, and every Matter and Thing therein contained, shall continue to be in Force, during the Continuance of

the war in which His Majesty is now engaged; and also for Two
years from and after the Day of the signature of the Preliminary or
other Articles of Peace by which the same may be terminated.

And it is further agreed that at the expiration of the said Term,
the Two Contracting Parties will endeavor further to regulate their
Commerce in this respect, according to the situation in which His
Majesty may then find Himself with respect to the West Indies, and
with a view to such Arrangements, as may best conduce to the mutual advantage and extension of Commerce. And the said Parties
will then also renew their discussions, and endeavour to agree,
whether in any and what cases Neutral Vessels shall protect Enemy's
property; and in what cases provisions and other articles not generally Contraband may become such. But in the mean time their
Conduct towards each other in these respects, shall be regulated by
the articles hereinafter inserted on those subjects.

ARTICLE 13.

His Majesty consents that the Vessels belonging to the Citizens of
the United States of America, shall be admitted and Hospitably received in all the Sea Ports and Harbours of the British Territories in
the East Indies: and that the Citizens of the said United States, may
freely carry on a Trade between the said Territories and the said
United States, in all articles of which the Importation or Exportation
respectively to or from the said Territories, shall not be entirely prohibited; Provided only, that it shall not be lawful for them in any
time of War between the British Government, and any other Power
or State whatever, to export from the said Territories without the
special Permission of the British Government there, any Military
Stores, or Naval Stores, or Rice. The Citizens of the United States
shall pay for their Vessels when admitted into the said Ports, no
other or higher Tonnage Duty than shall be payable on British Vessels when admitted into the Ports of the United States. And they
shall pay no other or higher Duties or Charges on the importation or
exportation of the Cargoes of the said Vessels, than shall be payable
on the same articles when imported or exported in British Vessels.
But it is expressly agreed, that the Vessels of the United States shall
not carry any of the articles exported by them from the said British
Territories to any port or Place, except to some Port or Place in
America, where the same shall be unladen, and such Regulations shall

be adopted by both Parties, as shall from time to time be found necessary to enforce the due and faithful observance of this Stipulation: It is also understood that the permission granted by this article is not to extend to allow the Vessels of the United States to carry on any part of the Coasting Trade of the said British Territories, but Vessels going with their original Cargoes, or part thereof, from one port of discharge to another, are not to be considered as carrying on the Coasting Trade. Neither is this Article to be construed to allow the Citizens of the said States to settle or reside within the said Territories, or to go into the interior parts thereof, without the permission of the British Government established there; and if any transgression should be attempted against the Regulations of the British Government in this respect, the observance of the same shall and may be enforced against the Citizens of America in the same manner as against British Subjects, or others transgressing the same rule. And the Citizens of the United States, whenever they arrive in any Port or Harbour in the said Territories, or if they should be permitted in manner aforesaid, to go to any other place therein, shall always be subject to the Laws, Government and Jurisdiction, of what nature, established in such Harbour, Port or Place according as the same may be: The Citizens of the United States, may also touch for refreshment, at the Island of St. Helena, but subject in all respects to such regulations, as the British Government may from time to time establish there.

Article 14.

There shall be between all the Dominions of His Majesty in Europe, and the Territories of the United States, a reciprocal and perfect liberty of Commerce and Navigation. The people and Inhabitants of the Two Countries respectively, shall have liberty, freely and securely, and without hindrance and molestation, to come with their Ships and Cargoes to the Lands, Countries, Cities, Ports Places and Rivers within the Dominions and Territories aforesaid, to enter into the same, to resort there, and to remain and reside there, without any limitation of Time: also to hire and possess, Houses and warehouses for the purposes of their Commerce; and generally the Merchants and Traders on each side, shall enjoy the most complete protection and Security for their Commerce; but subject always, as to what respects this article, to the Laws and Statutes of the Two Countries respectively.

ARTICLE 15.

It is agreed, that no other or higher Duties shall be paid by the Ships or Merchandize of the one Party in the Ports of the other, than such as are paid by the like vessels or Merchandize of all other Nations. Nor shall any other or higher Duty be imposed in one Country on the importation of any articles, the growth, produce, or manufacture of the other, than are or shall be payable on the importation of the like articles being of the growth, produce or manufacture of any other Foreign Country. Nor shall any prohibition be imposed, on the exportation or importation of any articles to or from the Territories of the Two Parties respectively which shall not equally extend to all other Nations.

But the British Government reserves to itself the right of imposing on American Vessels entering into the British Ports in Europe a Tonnage Duty, equal to that which shall be payable by British Vessels in the Ports of America: And also such Duty as may be adequate to countervail the difference of Duty now payable on the importation of European and Asiatic Goods when imported into the United States in British or in American Vessels.

The Two Parties agree to treat for the more exact equalization of the Duties on the respective Navigation of their Subjects and People in such manner as may be most beneficial to the two Countries. The arrangements for this purpose shall be made at the same time with those mentioned at the Conclusion of the 12th Article of this Treaty, and are to be considered as a part thereof. In the interval it is agreed, that the United States will not impose any new or additional Tonnage Duties on British Vessels, nor increase the now subsisting difference between the Duties payable on the importation of any articles in British or in American Vessels.

ARTICLE 16.

It shall be free for the Two Contracting Parties respectively, to appoint Consuls for the protection of Trade, to reside in the Dominions and Territories aforesaid; and the said Consuls shall enjoy those Liberties and Rights which belong to them by reason of their Function. But before any Consul shall act as such, he shall be in the usual forms approved and admitted by the party to whom he is sent, and it is hereby declared to be lawful and proper, that in case of illegal or improper Conduct towards the Laws or Government, a Consul may either be punished according to Law, if the Laws will reach the Case, or be dismissed or even sent back, the offended Government assigning to the other, Their reasons for the same.

Either of the Parties may except from the residence of Consuls such particular Places, as such party shall judge proper to be so excepted.

Article 17.

It is agreed that, in all Cases where Vessels shall be captured or detained on just suspicion of having on board Enemy's property or of carrying to the Enemy, any of the articles which are Contraband of war; The said Vessel shall be brought to the nearest or most convenient Port, and if any property of an Enemy, should be found on board such Vessel, that part only which belongs to the Enemy shall be made prize, and the Vessel shall be at liberty to proceed with the remainder without any Impediment. And it is agreed that all proper measures shall be taken to prevent delay, in deciding the Cases of Ships or Cargoes so brought in for adjudication, and in the payment or recovery of any Indemnification adjudged or agreed to be paid to the masters or owners of such Ships.

Article 18.

In order to regulate what is in future to be esteemed Contraband of war, it is agreed that under the said Denomination shall be comprized all Arms and Implements serving for the purposes of war by Land or Sea; such as Cannon, Muskets, Mortars, Petards, Bombs, Grenades Carcasses, Saucisses, Carriages for Cannon, Musket rests, Bandoliers, Gunpowder, Match, Saltpetre, Ball, Pikes, Swords, Headpieces Cuirasses Halberts Lances Javelins, Horsefurniture, Holsters, Belts and, generally all other Implements of war, as also Timber for Ship building, Tar or Rosin, Copper in Sheets, Sails, Hemp, and Cordage, and generally whatever may serve directly to the equipment of Vessels, unwrought Iron and Fir planks only excepted, and all the above articles are hereby declared to be just objects of Confiscation, whenever they are attempted to be carried to an Enemy.

And Whereas the difficulty of agreeing on the precise Cases in which alone Provisions and other articles not generally contraband may be regarded as such, renders it expedient to provide against the inconveniences and misunderstandings which might thence arise: It is further agreed that whenever any such articles so becoming Contraband according to the existing Laws of Nations, shall for that reason be seized, the same shall not be confiscated, but the owners thereof shall be speedily and completely indemnified; and the Captors, or in their default the Government under whose authority they act, shall pay to the Masters or Owners of such Vessels the full value of all such Articles, with a reasonable mercantile Profit thereon, together with the Freight, and also the Demurrage incident to such Detention.

And Whereas it frequently happens that vessels sail for a Port or Place belonging to an Enemy, without knowing that the same is either besieged, blockaded or invested; It is agreed, that every Vessel so circumstanced may be turned away from such Port or Place, but she shall not be detained, nor her Cargo, if not Contraband, be confiscated; unless after notice she shall again attempt to enter; but She shall be permitted to go to any other Port or Place She may think proper: Nor shall any vessel or Goods of either party, that may have entered into such Port or Place before the same was besieged, blockaded or invested by the other, and be found therein after the reduction or surrender of such place, be liable to confiscation, but shall be restored to the Owners or proprietors thereof.

ARTICLE 19.

And that more abundant Care may be taken for the security of the respective Subjects and Citizens of the Contracting Parties, and to prevent their suffering Injuries by the Men of war, or Privateers of either Party, all Commanders of Ships of war and Privateers and all others the said Subjects and Citizens shall forbear doing any Damage to those of the other party, or committing any Outrage against them, and if they act to the contrary, they shall be punished, and shall also be bound in their Persons and Estates to make satisfaction and reparation for all Damages, and the interest thereof, of whatever nature the said Damages may be.

For this cause all Commanders of Privateers before they receive their Commissions shall hereafter be obliged to give before a Competent Judge, sufficient security by at least Two responsible Sureties, who have no interest in the said Privateer, each of whom, together with the said Commander, shall be jointly and severally bound in the Sum of Fifteen hundred pounds Sterling, or if such Ships be provided with above One hundred and fifty Seamen or Soldiers, in the Sum of Three thousand pounds sterling, to satisfy all Damages and Injuries, which the said Privateer or her Officers or Men, or any of them may do or commit during their Cruize contrary to the tenor of this Treaty, or to the Laws and Instructions for regulating their Conduct; and further that in all Cases of Aggressions the said Commissions shall be revoked and annulled.

It is also agreed that whenever a Judge of a Court of Admiralty of either of the Parties, shall pronounce sentence against any Vessel or Goods or Property belonging to the Subjects or Citizens of the other Party a formal and duly authenticated Copy of all the proceedings in the Cause, and of the said Sentence, shall if required be delivered to the Commander of the said Vessel, without the smallest delay, he paying all legal Fees and Demands for the same.

Article 20.

It is further agreed that both the said Contracting Parties, shall not only refuse to receive any Pirates into any of their Ports, Havens, or Towns, or permit any of their Inhabitants to receive, protect, harbour conceal or assist them in any manner, but will bring to condign punishment all such Inhabitants as shall be guilty of such Acts or offences.

And all their Ships with the Goods or Merchandizes taken by them and brought into the port of either of the said Parties, shall be seized, as far as they can be discovered and shall be restored to the owners or their Factors or Agents duly deputed and authorized in writing by them (proper Evidence being first given in the Court of Admiralty for proving the property,) even in case such effects should have passed into other hands by Sale, if it be proved that the Buyers knew or had good reason to believe, or suspect that they had been piratically taken.

Article 21.

It is likewise agreed that Subjects and Citizens of the Two Nations, shall not do any acts of Hostility or Violence against each other, nor accept Commissions or Instructions so to act from any

Foreign Prince or State, Enemies to the other party, nor shall the Enemies of one of the parties be permitted to invite or endeavour to enlist in their military service any of the Subjects or Citizens of the other party; and the Laws against all such Offences and Aggressions shall be punctually executed. And if any Subject or Citizen of the said Parties respectively shall accept any Foreign Commission or Letters of Marque for Arming any Vessel to act as a Privateer against the other party, and be taken by the other party, it is hereby declared to be lawful for the said party to treat and punish the said Subject or Citizen, having such Commission or Letters of Marque as a Pirate.

ARTICLE 22.

It is expressly stipulated that neither of the said Contracting Parties will order or Authorize any Acts of Reprisal against the other on Complaints of Injuries or Damages until the said party shall first have presented to the other a Statement thereof, verified by competent proof and Evidence, and demanded Justice and Satisfaction, and the same shall either have been refused or unreasonably delayed.

ARTICLE 23.

The Ships of war of each of the Contracting Parties, shall at all times be hospitably received in the Ports of the other, their Officers and Crews paying due respect to the Laws and Government of the Country. The officers shall be treated with that respect, which is due to the Commissions which they bear. And if any Insult should be offered to them by any of the Inhabitants, all offenders in this respect shall be punished as Disturbers of the Peace and Amity between the Two Countries.

And His Majesty consents, that in case an American Vessel should by stress of weather, Danger from Enemies, or other misfortune be reduced to the necessity of seeking Shelter in any of His Majesty's Ports, into which such Vessel could not in ordinary cases claim to be admitted; She shall on manifesting that necessity to the satisfaction of the Government of the place, be hospitably received, and be permitted to refit, and to purchase at the market price, such necessaries as she may stand in need of, conformably to such Orders and regulations as the Government of the place, having respect to the circumstances of each case shall prescribe. She shall not be allowed to break bulk or unload her Cargo, unless the same shall be bonâ fide necessary to her being refitted. Nor shall be permitted to sell any part of her Cargo, unless so much only as may be necessary to defray her expences, and then not without the express permission of the Government of the place. Nor shall she be obliged to pay any Duties whatever, except only on such Articles, as she may be permitted to sell for the purpose aforesaid.

ARTICLE 24.

It shall not be lawful for any Foreign Privateers (not being Subjects or Citizens of either of the said Parties) who have Commissions from any other Prince or State in Enmity with either Nation, to arm their Ships in the Ports of either of the said Parties, nor to sell what they have taken, nor in any other manner to exchange the same, nor shall they be allowed to purchase more provisions than shall be necessary for their going to the nearest Port of that Prince or State from whom they obtained their Commissions.

ARTICLE 25.

It shall be lawful for the Ships of war and Privateers belonging to the said Parties respectively to carry whithersoever they please the Ships and Goods taken from their Enemies without being obliged to pay any Fee to the Officers of the Admiralty, or to any Judges whatever; nor shall the said Prizes when they arrive at, and enter the Ports of the said Parties be detained or seized, neither shall the Searchers or other Officers of those Places visit such Prizes (except for the purpose of preventing the Carrying of any part of the Cargo thereof on Shore in any manner contrary to the established Laws of Revenue, Navigation or Commerce) nor shall such Officers take Cognizance of the Validity of such Prizes; but they shall be at liberty to hoist Sail, and depart as speedily as may be, and carry their said Prizes to the place mentioned in their Commissions or Patents, which the Commanders of the said Ships of war or Privateers shall be obliged to shew. No Shelter or Refuge shall be given in their Ports to such as have made a Prize upon the Subjects or Citizens of either of the said Parties; but if forced by stress of weather or the Dangers of the Sea, to enter therein, particular care shall be taken to hasten their departure, and to cause them to retire as soon as possible. Nothing in this Treaty contained shall however be construed or operate contrary to former and existing Public Treaties with other Sovereigns or States. But the Two parties agree, that while they continue in amity neither of them will in future make any Treaty that shall be inconsistent with this or the preceding article.

Neither of the said parties shall permit the Ships or Goods belonging to the Subjects or Citizens of the other to be taken within Cannon Shot of the Coast, nor in any of the Bays, Ports or Rivers of their Territories by Ships of war, or others having Commission from any Prince, Republic or State whatever. But in case it should so happen, the party whose Territorial Rights shall thus have been violated, shall use his utmost endeavours to obtain from the offending Party, full and ample satisfaction for the Vessel or Vessels so taken, whether the same be Vessels of war or Merchant Vessels.

ARTICLE 26.

If at any Time a Rupture should take place (which God forbid) between His Majesty and the United States, the Merchants and others of each of the Two Nations, residing in the Dominions of the other, shall have the privilege of remaining and continuing their Trade so long as they behave peaceably and commit no offence against the Laws, and in case their Conduct should render them suspected, and the respective Governments should think proper to order them to remove, the term of Twelve Months from the publication of the order shall be allowed them for that purpose to remove with their Families, Effects and Property, but this Favor shall not be extended to those who shall act contrary to the established Laws, and for greater certainty it is declared that such Rupture shall not be deemed to exist while negotiations for accommodating Differences shall be depending nor until the respective Ambassadors or Ministers, if such there shall be, shall be recalled, or sent home on account of such differences, and not on account of personal misconduct according to the nature and degrees of which both parties retain their Rights, either to request the recall or immediately to send home the Ambassador or Minister of the other; and that without prejudice to their mutual Friendship and good understanding.

ARTICLE 27.

It is further agreed that His Majesty and the United States on mutual Requisitions by them respectively or by their respective Ministers or Officers authorized to make the same will deliver up to Justice, all Persons who being charged with Murder or Forgery committed within the Jurisdiction of either, shall seek an Asylum within any of the Countries of the other, Provided that this shall only be done on such Evidence of Criminality as according to the Laws of the Place, where the Fugitive or Person so charged shall be found, would justify his apprehension and commitment for Tryal, if the offence had there been committed. The Expence of such apprehension and Delivery shall be borne and defrayed by those who make the Requisition and receive the Fugitive.

ARTICLE 28.

It is agreed that the first Ten Articles of this Treaty shall be permanent and that the subsequent Articles except the Twelfth shall be limited in their duration to Twelve years to be computed from the Day on which the Ratifications of this Treaty shall be exchanged, but subject to this Condition that whereas the said Twelfth Article will expire by the Limitation therein contained at the End of two years from the signing of the Preliminary or other Articles of Peace, which shall terminate the present War, in which His Majesty is engaged; It is agreed that proper Measures shall by Concert be taken for bringing the subject of that article into amicable Treaty and Discussion so early before the Expiration of the said Term, as that new Arrangements on that head may by that Time be perfected and ready to take place. But if it should unfortunately happen that His Majesty and the United States should not be able to agree on such new arrangements, in that Case, all the Articles of this Treaty except the first Ten shall then cease and expire together.

Lastly. This Treaty when the same shall have been ratified by His Majesty, and by The President of the United States, by and with the advice and Consent of Their Senate, and the respective Ratifications mutually exchanged, shall be binding and obligatory on His Majesty and on the said States, and shall be by Them respectively executed and observed with punctuality, and the most sincere regard to good Faith. And Whereas it will be expedient in order the better to facilitate Intercourse and obviate Difficulties that other Articles be proposed and added to this Treaty, which Articles from want of time and other circumstances cannot now be perfected; It is agreed that the said Parties will from Time to Time readily treat of and concerning such Articles, and will sincerely endeavor so to form them, as that they may conduce to mutual convenience, and tend to promote mutual Satisfaction and Friendship; and that the said Articles after having been duly ratified, shall be added to, and make a part of this Treaty.

In Faith whereof We the Undersigned, Ministers Plenipotentiary of His Majesty The King of Great Britain; and the United States of America, have signed this present Treaty, and have caused to be affixed thereto, the Seal of Our Arms.

Done at London, this Nineteenth Day of November, One thousand seven hundred and ninety Four.

GRENVILLE [Seal]   JOHN JAY [Seal]

[Annexed Copy of the Letter Mentioned in Article 7]

PHILADELPHIA *Sept. 5th, 1793.*

SIR, I am honored with yours of August 30th. Mine of the 7th of that Month assured you that measures were taken for excluding from all further Asylum in our Ports Vessels armed in them to Cruize on Nations with which we are at Peace; and for the restoration of the Prizes the Lovely Lass, Prince William Henry, and the Jane of Dublin, and that should the measures for restitution fail in their Effect, The President considered it as incumbent on the United States to make compensation for the Vessels.

We are bound by our Treaties with Three of the Belligerent Nations, by all the means in our Power to protect and defend their Vessels and Effects in our Ports, or waters, or on the Seas near our Shores and to recover and restore the same to the right owners when taken from them. If all the means in our Power are used, and fail in their Effect, we are not bound, by our Treaties with those Nations to make Compensation.

Though we have no similar Treaty with Great Britain, it was the opinion of the President that we should use towards that Nation the same rule, which, under this Article, was to govern us with the other Nations; and even to extend it to Captures made on the High Seas, and brought into our Ports; if done by Vessels, which had been armed within them.

Having for particular reasons, forbore to use all the means in our power for the restitution of the three vessels mentioned in my Letter

of August 7th. The President thought it incumbent on the United
States to make Compensation for them; and though nothing was
said in that Letter of other Vessels taken under like Circumstances
and brought in after the 5th of June, and before the date of that
Letter, yet when the same forbearance had taken place it was and is
his opinion that Compensation would be equally due.

As to Prizes made under the same Circumstances, and brought in
after the date of that Letter the President determined, that all the
means in our power, should be used for their restitution. If these fail
as we should not be bound by our Treaties to make Compensation to
the other Powers, in the analogous Case, he did not mean to give
an opinion that it ought to be done to Great Britain: But still if
any Cases shall arise subsequent to that date, the circumstances of
which shall place them on similar ground with those before it, the
President would think Compensation equally incumbent on the
United States.

Instructions are given to the Governors of the different States to
use all the means in their Power for restoring Prizes of this last description found within their Ports. Though they will of course take
measures to be informed of them, and the General Government has
given them the aid of the Custom-house Officers for this purpose,
yet you will be sensible of the importance of multiplying the Channels of their Information as far as shall depend on yourself, or any
person under your direction, in order that the Governors may use
the means in their power, for making restitution. Without knowledge of the Capture they cannot restore it. It will always be best
to give the notice to them directly: but any information which you
shall be pleased to send to me also, at anytime, shall be forwarded
to them as quickly as distance will permit.

Hence you will perceive Sir, that, The President contemplates
restitution or Compensation in the Case before the 7th August, and
after that date restitution if it can be effected by any means in our
power: And that it will be important that you should substantiate
the fact, that such prizes are in our Ports or waters.

Your List of the Privateers illicitly armed in our ports, is, I
believe Correct.

With respect to losses by detension, waste Spoilation sustained
by vessels taken as before mentioned between the dates of June 5th
and August 7th it is proposed as a provisional measure, that the

Collector of the Customs of the district, and the British Consul, or any other person you please, shall appoint persons to establish the Value of the Vessel and Cargo, at the time of her Capture and of her arrival in the port into which She is brought, according to their value in that Port. If this shall be agreeable to you, and you will be pleased to signify it to me with the Names of the Prizes understood to be of this description Instructions will be given accordingly to the Collector of the Customs where the respective Vessels are.

I have the Honor to be &c

(Signed)   THO. JEFFERSON.

ADDITIONAL ARTICLE

It is further agreed between the said contracting parties, that the operation of so much of the twelfth Article of the said Treaty as respects the trade which his said Majesty thereby consents may be carried on between the United States and his Islands in the West Indies, in the manner and on the terms and conditions therein specified, shall be suspended.

NOTES

INTRODUCTION

1. *American Quarterly Review*, September, 1827, pp. 267-306. For identification of John Quincy Adams as the author, see Vernon G. Setser, *The Commercial Reciprocity Policy of the United States, 1774-1829* (Oxford, 1937), bibliography, p. 269.

2. British historians have generally neglected the subject, although Professor Vincent T. Harlow, *The Founding of the Second British Empire, 1763-1793* (London, 1952) is a considerable exception, at least for the making of the Peace of 1783.

Canadian writers have made great and significant contributions. Among the best of these are Gerald S. Graham, *Sea Power and British North America, 1783-1820* (Cambridge, Mass., 1941); Donald G. Creighton, *The Commercial Empire of the St. Lawrence, 1760-1850* (Toronto, 1937); John Bartlett Brebner, *North Atlantic Triangle* (New York, 1945); and Alfred LeRoy Burt, *The Old Province of Quebec* (Minneapolis, 1933). Generally, however, the flow of Anglo-American relations is interesting only as it touches Canada.

3. John Adams, *The Life and Works of John Adams*, ed. Charles Francis Adams, 10 vols. (Boston, 1850-56), 1:420, 424.

4. Nathan Schachner, *Founding Fathers* (New York, 1954), pp. 134-35.

5. John Fiske, *Critical Period of American History* (Boston, 1888), p. 141.

6. Merrill Jensen, *The New Nation* (New York, 1950), p. 164.

7. Alexander De Conde, *Entangling Alliance* (Durham, N.C., 1958), pp. 82-83.

8. See, for example, John C. Miller, *The Federalist Era* (New York, 1960), pp. 85-87.

9. This is true of the authoritative study by Samuel Flagg Bemis, *Jay's Treaty: A Study in Commerce and Diplomacy* (New York, 1923; rev. ed., New Haven, 1962). Professor Bemis' revision in the new edition does not alter essentially the thesis set out in the earlier work.

CHAPTER I

1. Vincent T. Harlow, *The Founding of the Second British Empire, 1763-1793* (London, 1952), pp. 438-39, shows Shelburne's use of British naval weakness to justify the treaty of peace to Parliament. See also Robert Greenhalgh Albion, *Forests and Sea Power* (Cambridge, Mass., 1926), pp. 135, 282; Bryan Edwards, *The History, Civil and Commercial, of the British Colonies in the West Indies*, 3d ed. in 3 vols. (London, 1801), 2:457-58, n.; Helen T. Manning, *British Colonial Government after the American Revolution* (New Haven, 1933); p. 251; and Christopher John Bartlett, *Great Britain and Sea Power* (Oxford, 1963), *passim*.

2. For the American threat to British seapower, see John Bartlett Brebner, *North Atlantic Triangle* (New York, 1945), p. 68; Robert Livingston Schuyler, *The Fall of the Old Colonial System* (London, 1945), pp. 5-6; Vernon G. Setser, *The Commercial Reciprocity Policy of the United States, 1774-1829* (Oxford, 1937), p. 6; and Harlow, *Second British Empire*, p. 457. Professor Harlow rightly stresses the importance of expanding production

and markets to makers of British maritime policy, but he seems to undervalue the decisive importance at this point of "defence" over "opulence."

3. Shelburne to Richard Oswald, July 27, 1782, Shelburne MSS, Clements Library, vol. 70, fols. 61-69 (hereafter cited as Clem. Lib.); and the instructions to Oswald, July 31, 1782, Public Record Office, Foreign Office Papers 27/2 (hereafter cited as F.O.). Both are used by Harlow, *Second British Empire*, pp. 232-33.

4. May 6, 1782, F.O. 95/511; and Oswald to Shelburne, May 18-20, 1782, ibid. Transcripts of both documents are in the R. G. Adams collection in the Clements.

5. The debate, March 7 and 11, 1783, is in William Cobbett and John Wright, eds., *Parliamentary History*, 36 vols. (London, 1806-20), 24:602-14, 643-45 (hereafter cited as *Parl. Hist.*). The act authorizing regulation by King in Council is 23 George III, c. 39.

6. Sheffield to William Knox, July 3, 1783, *Royal Historical Manuscripts Commission Reports, Knox Papers (Various Collections)*, VI (Dublin, 1909), p. 191. See, too, *Parl. Hist.*, 23:762-64; and Harlow, *Second British Empire*, p. 455, n. 11.

7. Cabinet minute, Apr. 8, 1783, George III, *Correspondence of George III*, ed. Sir John Fortescue, 6 vols. (London, 1927-28), 6:349. Fox's covering letter is in Charles James Fox, *Memorials and Correspondence of Charles James Fox*, ed. Lord John Russell, 2 vols. (London, 1853), 1:122; and Stephen Cottrell, secretary to the Privy Council, to William Eden, May 31, 1783, Additional MSS 34419, British Museum, fol. 214 (hereafter cited as Add. MSS).

8. Hartley to Fox, June 2, 1783, F.O. 4/2. Hartley would have excluded the Americans from trading between the West Indies and Britain, however, presumably by limiting tonnage.

9. Hartley to Fox, June 20, 1783, ibid. The emissary's assertion that before the war Britain received two-thirds of her vessels from the Americans was an exaggeration. See Harlow, *Second British Empire*, p. 475, n. 37; and Gerald S. Graham, *Sea Power and British North America, 1783-1820* (Cambridge, Mass., 1941), p. 44, n. 29.

10. John Adolphus, *History of England from the Accession to the Decease of George III*, 7 vols. (London, 1840), 4:4. For newspaper comment in this vein, see *Morning Chronicle*, July 23, Dec. 27, 1783 (hereafter cited as *Morn. Chron.*); and *London Packet*, Mar. 17, 1784. My article, "The London Press and the First Decade of American Independence," *Journal of British Studies* 2 (May, 1963): 88-109, briefly analyzes the importance of press opinion at this time.

11. Lowell Joseph Ragatz, *The Fall of the Planter Class in the British Caribbean, 1763-1833* (New York, 1928), p. 113.

12. Richard Pennant, created Baron Penrhyn in the peerage of Ireland in 1783, was the grandson of Edward Pennant, chief justice of Jamaica, and of Joseph Hodges, a considerable property-owner in the island. He sat in the House of Commons from 1761 to 1780 and from 1784 to 1790.

13. William Knox, *Extra Official State Papers*, 2 vols. (London, 1789), 2:Appendix 13, pp. 54-59. See, too, Graham, *Sea Power*, p. vii; and Harlow, *Second British Empire*, pp. 478-81.

14. "A West India Planter," *Morn. Chron.*, Nov. 11, 1783; "A West Indian," *Morning Herald*, Dec. 27, 1783 (hereafter cited as *Morn. Her.*); "H. G.," *Morn. Chron.*, Jan. 23, 1784.

15. Bryan Edwards, *Thoughts on the Late Proceedings of Government Respecting the Trade of the West Indian Islands with the United States of America*, 2d ed. (London, 1784). Edwards elaborated his position in his impressive *History, Civil and Commercial, of the British Colonies in the West Indies*. The anonymous pamphlet, *Considerations of the Present State of the Intercourse between His Majesty's Sugar Colonies and the Dominions of the United States of America* (London, 1784), is, in my judgment, undoubtedly from the same author. Prefaced by an appropriate resolution of the West Indian Planters and Merchants meeting in London, May 14, 1784, it was printed for distribution to all members of Parliament and to merchants in the principal trading towns of Great Britain and Ireland.

16. Edwards, *British Colonies in the West Indies*, 2:444-45, 454-55, 455-56. For a similar position, see the *Daily Register*, Jan. 12, 1786.

17. Klaus E. Knorr, *British Colonial Theories, 1570-1850* (Toronto, 1944), p. 218.

18. John Stevenson to Bryan Edwards, *Morn. Her.*, Sept. 24, 1784; and "Commercialis," *ibid.*, Aug. 20, Sept. 24, 1784. Stevenson also wrote a vituperative and violent pamphlet against Edwards, *An Address to Bryan Edwards, Esq.* (London, 1784).

19. *Opinions on Interesting Subjects of Public Law and Commercial Policy Arising from American Independence* (London, 1784), esp. pp. 50, 93. See, too, "A Seaman," *Morn. Her.*, Nov. 11, 1784, for similar views. Ragatz, *Fall of the Planter Class*, has a good, brief survey of the pamphlet literature. His judgment, p. 179, is that "logic lay wholly on the side of the Sheffield group."

20. Manning, *British Colonial Government*, p. 43. John Ehrman's *The British Government and Commercial Negotiations with Europe, 1783-1793* (Cambridge, 1962) is a highly perceptive exploration of Pitt's economic views. The Prime Minister's "liberalism," Ehrman argues, is subject to strict qualification: "He had absorbed the principles of the *Wealth of Nations*; he was able on occasion to refer his domestic policies to them; and, in the matter of foreign trade, he favored low duties where they were possible" (pp. 174 ff.). Still, Pitt and his ministerial colleagues aimed at the national advantage "viewed much as before, although the means to attain it and the methods of reckoning it might sometimes need to be revised." The guiding principle was "to take each case strictly on its merits, and yield nothing from the past without very good cause." Expanding industrial production and the need for new markets might induce "liberal" thoughts about "free trade," but as Mr. Ehrman points out (and Adam Smith before him): "It was one thing . . . to apply such terms to commerce . . . quite another to apply them to the allied problems of navigation" (p. 180).

21. The proceedings of the committee, including testimony from those heard, are in the "Minutes of the Committee for Trade," Public Record Office, Board of Trade Series 5 (hereafter cited as P.R.O., B.T.). Some evidence was presented in written form. See Add. MSS 38345, fols. 136-51, for Thomas Irving's statement. See, too, a second paper, Add. MSS 36388, fols. 147-50.

22. Knox testified that the West Indian carrying trade involved some 700 topsail (112,000 tons). This was an apparent disagreement with the customs house figures, which set the number of 1,500 to 1,600 vessels. Knox explained that the larger set of figures was based on multiple voyages. Tonnage figures were the same.

Thomas Irving, in the paper cited above, also took note of a new trade which had sprung up to fill the gap left by the Americans—the "seekers," who called at West Indian ports searching for cargoes of rum, molasses, and sugar for the American market. There, lumber and provisions were taken aboard and returned to the islands, thence to Britain with West Indian produce or a repeat voyage to the United States. Virtually an American monopoly before the war, this trade was now firmly in British hands and growing, Irving asserted.

23. Apr. 2, 1785, Public Record Office, Privy Council Series 1/61/14 B (hereafter cited as P.R.O., P.C.). For expressions of disapprobation of the West Indians, see George Aust, undersecretary of state, to Lord Hardwicke, June 5, 1784, Add. MSS 35621, fols. 247-48; *Public Advertiser*, July 22, 1786; "Canadiensis," *Morn. Chron.*, Feb. 27, 1786; and, most important, "A Seaman," *Morn. Her.*, Nov. 11, 1784. From the similarity of argument and style, the author could have been George Chalmers. British resentment against the islanders was based, too, on the high price of sugar. See the paper of Thomas Irving, cited above in note 21.

See, too, "A Well-Wisher to Old England," *Diary: Or Woodfall's Register*, June 19, 1789 (hereafter cited as *Diary*). There is some evidence that the West Indian efforts in England were opposed by some islanders at home. Charles Hamilton, writing to George Rose, Jamaica Customs House, Mar. 2, 1785, Add. MSS 38218, speaks of "a respectable number of Planters and Merchants, within my district" who opposed opening their ports to the Americans.

24. The figures stand in an undated statement preserved in the papers of William Wyndham Grenville, Lord Grenville, at Boconnoc House, Lostwithiel, Cornwall (hereafter cited as Gren. Pps., Boc. H.). Schuyler, *Old Colonial System*, p. 65, shows that 932,219

tons of British shipping cleared outward from Britain in 1772. In 1785, for the first time, the total exceeded one million tons.

25. Thomas Irving, "Observations on the Trade Carried on between the W. Indies and America," Gren. Pps., Boc. H.

26. P.R.O., P.C. 1/19/24 A/1791(3), Non-Colonial. A more readable copy is in F.O. 4/9. A résumé of relevant data from the report is to be found in Appendixes A-C.

27. The prohibitory act is 15 Geo. III, c. 31. See also Graham, Sea Power, pp. 97-99.

28. Parl. Hist., 25:271 ff. Begun February 2, 1785, debate continued for several days.

29. "A Letter from a Member of Parliament to One of His Constituents; Giving a Short View of Some Late Laws Respecting Our Trade and Shipping," Add. MSS 38347, fols. 14-22; undated, but in 1786, before August 21. Jenkinson is the hero of the piece, which was possibly written by George Chalmers. See Grace A. Cockroft, Public Life of George Chalmers (New York, 1939), p. 82. For a general treatment, see Graham, Sea Power, pp. 103-4.

30. 26 Geo. III, c. 26.

31. For more detailed figures extending to 1792, see Graham, Sea Power, p. 105 and n. 28; and Harold Adams Innis, The Cod Fisheries (New Haven, 1940), pp. 292-96. The attempts of the French to break into the fisheries are described by D. D. Irving, "The Newfoundland Fishery," Canadian Historical Review 13 (1932): 268-84.

32. 26 Geo. III, c. 6.

33. Margaret Ells, "Settling the Loyalists in Nova Scotia," Report of the Canadian Historical Association (1934), pp. 105-9. For the rising shipbuilding industry in Nova Scotia and New Brunswick, see Graham, Sea Power, p. 47. For more detailed data drawn from the Report of January, 1791, see Appendix B.

34. 26 Geo. III, c. 60.

35. Apr. 11, 1786, Parl. Hist., 26:1373 ff.

36. Adams to Jefferson, July 18, 1785, Thomas Jefferson, Papers of Thomas Jefferson, ed. Julian P. Boyd, 17 vols. to date (Princeton, 1950—), 8:301-2 (hereafter cited as Jefferson, Papers); idem to Jay, July 29, 1785, John Adams, The Life and Works of John Adams, ed. Charles Francis Adams, 10 vols. (Boston, 1850-56), 8:289-90; idem to Jefferson, Aug. 7, 1785, Jefferson, Papers, 8:340-42. American shipbuilding had suffered a disastrous decline. See the data supplied from the Report of January, 1791, in Appendix C. See also, Samuel Eliot Morison, The Maritime History of Massachusetts, 1783-1860 (Boston, 1921), pp. 30-31, 33.

37. Adams to Jay, Aug. 25, 1785, J. Adams, Works, 8:302-10.

38. A View of the Treaty of Commerce with France (London, 1787).

39. Alfred T. Mahan, Sea Power in its Relation to the War of 1812, 2 vols. (Boston, 1905), 1:23-24.

40. Jenkinson's speech is cited in note 35 above.

CHAPTER II

1. Alleyne Fitzherbert to Secretary of State Thomas Townshend, Aug. 8, 1782, Shelburne MSS, Clem. Lib., vol. 87, fol. 185; Lord Grantham to Fitzherbert, Most Secret and Confidential, Sept. 23, 1782, F.O. 27/3. See also Vincent T. Harlow, The Founding of the Second British Empire, 1763-1793 (London, 1952), pp. 263-443, passim.

2. Petition of April 18, 1782, signed by representatives of twenty firms active in the American trade before 1776, Shelburne MSS, Clem. Lib., vol. 87, fol. 177; and Edmund C. Burnett, ed., "Observations of London Merchants on American Trade, 1783," American Historical Review, 18 (1912-13): 769-80. See especially ibid., p. 772, n. 13. American diplomatists, not surprisingly, sought to capitalize on these fears. See John Adams, "Letters to Dr. Calkoen" (London, 1786). The letters were actually written in 1780. In the second, he declared one of the blessings of coming independence to be "a free trade with all the commercial world, instead of that mean monopoly in which they were shackled by Great Britain."

3. Adam Smith, An Inquiry into the Nature and Causes of the Wealth of Nations, ed. Edwin Cannan, 2 vols. (London, 1950), 2:116-17; Smith to William Eden, Dec. 15, 1783, William Eden, The Journal and Correspondence of William, Lord Auckland, ed. G.

Hogge, 4 vols. with preface and introduction by the Bishop of Bath and Wells (London, 1860-62), 1:64-66.

4. James Anderson, *The Interest of Great Britain with Regard to Her American Colonies, Considered* (London, 1782). (The work was passed to Shelburne by Jeremy Bentham.) See, too, Anderson to Shelburne, (1782), Shelburne MSS, Clem. Lib., vol. 67, fols. 247-61. Josiah Tucker, *A Series of Answers to Certain Popular Objections against Separating from the Rebellious Colonies, and Discarding Them Entirely* (Gloucester, 1776), p. 61. Harlow, *Second British Empire*, pp. 207-10, quotes from Tucker extensively.

5. The act is 28 Geo. III, c. 56. See also Cabinet minute, Apr. 8, 1783, George III, *Correspondence of George III*, ed. Sir John Fortescue, 6 vols. (London, 1927-28), 6:349; Fox to George III, Apr. 10, 1783, ibid., pp. 349-50. The Orders are summarized in James Munro and W. L. Grant, eds., *Acts of the Privy Council, Colonial Series*, 6 vols. (London, 1908-12), 5:527-32. As it stood, the Order of May 14 would have admitted American whale oil. At the end of the year, the item was prohibited as competitive with the British whale fisheries. An Order of February 14, 1786, extended to American rice the same privileges of bonding and warehousing enjoyed by tobacco.

6. Add. MSS 38346, fols. 230-35, 282.

7. George Chalmers, *Opinions on Interesting Subjects of Public Law and Commercial Policy Arising from American Independence* (London, 1784), pp. 36, 39-40.

8. Fox to David Hartley, June 10, 1783, F.O. 4/2, quoted extensively by Harlow, *Second British Empire*, pp. 472-74. Henry Martin of Virginia reported a conversation on the subject with Secretary of State Sydney (Thomas Townshend) in a letter to Jefferson, London, Nov. 15, 1784, Jefferson, *Papers*, 7:521-24. See, too, Edmund Burke's and William Eden's remarks during the debate on the American Intercourse Bill, Mar. 7, 1783, *Parl. Hist.*, 23:612-14.

9. The report and the testimony on which it was based have been fully cited in chapter 1, note 26, and in Appendix A-C.

10. Massive data, completely substantiating the committee's judgment, was collected by William Eden, who had access to official sources when preparing for his commercial negotiations with France early in 1786. See his gleeful letter to Lord Sheffield, Jan. 11, 1786, Add. MSS 45729, no folio; Sheffield's delighted response, Jan. 15, 1786, Add. MSS 34420, fols. 345-46; and Eden to Sheffield, Jan. 17, 1786, Add. MSS 45729, no folio, "Communication between the Continent of America and Our Islands in British Vessels, Which Will Shew How Well the Proclamation Operates Notwithstanding the Anger of the United States." For a summary of Eden's data, see Appendix D.

11. "Philodemus," *Morn. Chron.*, Oct. 30, 1783; "A. Z.," ibid., Sept. 1, 1784; ibid., Sept. 11, 1784. On August 27, 1784, the editor of the *Morning Herald* sharply rebuked a correspondent who seemed "to rejoice that we have so far recovered the commerce of America that all the nations of Europe joined together do not equal ourselves." The fact was true, "but if he had been a creditor of one of the three houses which have exported to America above £ 400,000 worth of goods, and have lately stopped payment, he would have had no great reason to triumph. . . . The tradesmen of this great metropolis begin to discover that to send goods abroad without having effects in hand for the payment thereof, is not a reciprocal advantage between nations, but a species of speculative Quixotism and mercantile insanity." American experiments with paper money further exasperated British traders. See, too, "Z. M.," *Morn. Her.*, Aug. 14, 1786; and *Public Advertiser*, June 30, 1786. The last quotation is from the *Morn. Chron.*, Sept. 9, 1786.

12. R. King to D. Kilham, New York, July 25, 1785, Rufus King, *Life and Correspondence of Rufus King*, ed. C. R. King, 6 vols. (New York, 1894-1900), 2:605-6.

13. Abigail Adams to J. Q. Adams, Abigail Adams, *Letters of Mrs. Adams*, ed. Charles Francis Adams (Boston, 1848), pp. 267-69. See, too, Abigail Adams to Mrs. Cranch, Oct. 1, 1785, ibid., pp. 272-75. John Gardiner's Fourth of July speech in Boston, 1785, also contains some interesting animadversions on the loss of the stern wartime virtues and the appearance of a "sudden depravity" and "rapid degeneracy of manners." He took particular exception to the affectation of ostrich plumes by the country girls around Boston. His speech appeared *in extenso* in the *Morn. Chron.*, Oct. 20, 1785.

14. John Adams to Rufus King, London, June 14, 1786, King, *Correspondence*, 1:181-84. For similar statements, see Adams to Arthur Lee, Sept. 6, 1785, John Adams, *The Life and Works of John Adams*, ed. Charles Francis Adams, 10 vols. (Boston, 1850-56), 9:536-37; Jay to Adams, Sept. 6, 1785, William Jay, *Life of John Jay*, 2 vols. (New York, 1833), 2:171-72; and Jefferson to Nathaniel Tracey, Aug. 17, 1785, Jefferson, *Papers*, 8:398-99.

15. The meeting was on October 20, 1785. Adams' account is in his dispatch to Jay, Oct. 21, 1785, J. Adams, *Works*, 8:325-33. Carmarthen's account is in F.O. 4/3, fols. 317-18, and contains the passage quoted. See, too, Ralph Willard Hidy, *The House of Baring in American Trade and Finance* (Cambridge, Mass., 1949), pp. 12 ff.; and Richard Warner Van Alstyne, *The Rising American Empire* (Oxford, 1960), p. 70, who, referring to Hidy, appreciates the importance of the British-American economic connection in destroying the Franco-American understanding.

For a detailed description of standard arrangements for the extension of credit by British merchants to Americans in the southern states, see Jefferson, *Papers*, 16:528-30.

16. Memorial of James Bowdoin of Boston to the French envoy to the United States, de la Luzerne, Jan. 21, 1782, Shelburne MSS, Clem. Lib., vol. 35. See also Vernon G. Setser, *The Commercial Reciprocity Policy of the United States, 1774-1829* (Oxford, 1937), pp. 90-91, who gives a splendid account of the bewildering twists and turns in French policy. Frederick Louis Nussbaum, "The French Colonial Arrêt of 1784," *South Atlantic Quarterly* 27 (1928): 62-78, is also useful. For a firsthand account of the hectic course of Franco-American commercial relations, see Gouverneur Morris to the Marquis de Chastellux, Oct. 7, 1783, Jefferson's abstracts, May, 1784, Jefferson, *Papers*, 7:350-55; idem to de la Luzerne, Oct., 1783, ibid., pp. 351-53; and Stephen Higginson to ?, Apr., 1784, John Franklin Jameson, ed., "Higginson's Letters," *Annual Report of the American Historical Association* (1896), 1:713-19.

17. The first conversation between Jefferson and Vergennes here referred to occurred on December 9, 1785, and is reported in Jefferson to Jay, Jan. 2, 1786, Jefferson, *Papers*, 9:136-46. For congressional reaction to the consular convention, see Monroe to Jefferson, New York, June 16, 1786, ibid., pp. 652-53. Vergennes' second warning, October 30, 1785, is ibid., 8:685-86. Gov. James Bowdoin to John Adams, Boston, Jan. 12, 1786, J. Adams, *Works*, 8:363-65, is also relevant.

18. Dorset's dispatch is Aug. 12, 1784, Add. MSS 28060, fols. 149-50. See, further, Daniel Hailes, Dorset's competent secretary, to Carmarthen, Dec. 8 and 23, 1784, Egerton MSS 3499, British Museum; and Dr. Edward Bancroft, the extraordinary double-spy, "Facts," Oct. 24, 1785, F.O. 4/3, fols. 323-24.

19. Franks to Jefferson, New York, Apr. 23, 1787, Jefferson, *Papers*, 11:305-6. The packet in question left Le Havre on February 17 and arrived in New York on April 9. Useful information is also in John Adams to Jefferson, Feb. 20, 1787, ibid., p. 169; and Otto to idem, New York, Apr. 11, 1787, ibid., pp. 285-86; and John Bannister, Jr., who also made the crossing with Franks, to idem, Apr. 23, 1787, ibid., p. 303.

20. Bowdoin to de la Luzerne, Jan. 21, 1782, cited in note 16 above.

21. Oct. 31, 1787, Jefferson, *Papers*, 12:298-301. Useful information is to be found in Gov. Patrick Henry to Jefferson, Richmond, Sept. 10, 1785, ibid., 8:507-10. Thomas Pleasants, Jr., tobacco merchant in Raleigh, to idem, Oct. 24, 1785, ibid., pp. 666-67, wrote, "Every port of this Country is filled with British Goods and British Factors, which affords every excitement to Luxury and Extravagance, and unless some immediate measures are taken . . . so as to place the Merchant Citizens upon a better footing, there will not be in Virginia a merchant unconnected with G. Britain or a Single ship owned here, so that the whole advantage of the trade will be lost to this country." See Jefferson's despairing reply, May 8, 1786, ibid., 9:473-74; and Stephen Higginson to John Adams, July, 1786, Jameson, ed., "Higginson's Letters," pp. 733-41.

22. Otto to Vergennes, June 30, 1785, Jefferson, *Papers*, 8:272.

23. Jefferson to Samuel House, Aug. 18, 1785, ibid., pp. 402-3. See also Jay to Jefferson, June 16, 1786, ibid., 9:650-51. Jay admitted to "much Wisdom and Knowledge in France,"

but claimed that commerce did not appear to be as "well understood in that Country as in England."

24. Adams to Jay, June 17, 26, Aug. 6, 1785, J. Adams, *Works*, 8:268-73, 273-76, 289-91. See, too, idem to idem, ibid., pp. 286-88.

25. Adams to Jay, Aug. 25, 1785, ibid., pp. 302-10.

26. The interview was on October 20. Adams stated again that America had voluntarily revived "almost the very monopoly which had been established before the war," and threatened that if British policy continued to discriminate against his country, the United States would conclude a permanent agreement (discriminating against Britain) with France. See his dispatch to Jay, Oct. 21, 1785, ibid., pp. 325-33.

27. Adams to Jay, Nov. 4, 1785, ibid., pp. 335-37.

28. John Ehrman, *The British Government and Commercial Negotiations with Europe, 1783-1793* (Cambridge, 1962), pp. 208-9. The author also treats Eden's apparently contradictory positions on Pitt's Irish propositions of 1785 and the French negotiations in his charge in 1786. For Eden's blending of liberal and protectionist sentiment in the French negotiations, see pp. 33-69. Lord Sheffield, too, urged liberal arrangements with France, because "we should greatly have the advantage in an open trade with France." Hence, Eden should speak the "fashionable" language, "viz., liberal arrangement." See Sheffield to Eden, Dec. 28, 1785, Add. MSS 34430, fols. 296-300; Jan. 6, 1785, ibid., fols. 348-50; Feb. 27, 1787, Add. MSS 34423, fols. 114-15; Nov., 1785, Add. MSS 34420, fols. 156-57; and Eden to Sheffield, Dec. 11, 1785, Add. MSS 45729, no folio. Sheffield urged similar "liberal" negotiations with Spain and Russia. William Knox, too, arch-mercantilist, argued for a liberal understanding with France, urging that both economic and political strength would grow from an *entente cordiale* with the entire House of Bourbon. With typical inflation of ego, he wrote that he knew well "how heartily disposed our West India Islands were to assist the revolt of North America to join in it, if they could have had any hope of success; and their late attempts, which I happily defeated, to transfer to the American States the profits of their Commerce and to raise them a marine on the ruins of that of Great Britain are proofs that they have not abandon'd the Idea of being one day Independent." It was only in the West Indies, he continued, that the United States could ever harm Britain; and he would have a treaty with Bourbon promising aid to prevent American conquests in the islands. He had no illusion about the final effect of such a treaty, "yet the *sound*, would help put down the idea among the Americans and the islanders." See his memorandum to Eden, Jan. 7, 1786, Add. MSS 34420, fols. 351-58.

29. Adams to Jay, Oct. 27, 1786, J. Adams, *Works*, 8:415-17.

30. Debate of Feb. 12 and 21, 1787, *Parl. Hist.*, 26:381 ff.

31. Jefferson, *Papers*, 10:474-76, publishes the letter.

32. Adams to Jay, Dec. 3, 1787, J. Adams, *Works*, 8:350-56.

33. For relevant data, see Appendix E.

34. Cited above in note 21.

35. "Draft Report of the Committee for Trade," Mar. 6, 1789, Add. MSS 38224, fols. 30-32. The chief object of the report was the prohibition of American wheat then infected by weevil.

CHAPTER III

1. Sir John Stepney, British envoy to Berlin, to Secretary of State Lord Grantham, Oct. 22, 1782, Shelburne MSS, Clem. Lib., vol. 34. Barbé to Vergennes, Philadelphia, Mar. 21, 1782, copy, ibid., vol. 35. Chatellux to Gouverneur Morris, Dec. 8, 1784, Jared Sparks, *Life of Gouverneur Morris*, 3 vols. (Boston, 1832), 1:271-72.

2. Tucker to Shelburne, May 28, 1782, Shelburne MSS, Clem. Lib., vol. 67. Price to Jefferson, Mar. 21, 1785, Jefferson, *Papers*, 8:52-54. Lansdowne to Jay, Sept. 4, 1785, John Jay, *Correspondence and Public Papers of John Jay*, ed. Henry P. Johnston, 4 vols. (New York, 1890-93), 3:189, n. 1. Morgann to Shelburne, Oct. 4, 1782, Shelburne MSS, Clem. Lib., 68:405-7, 427-30. Morgann took no pleasure in the gloomy prospects before the United States, writing that it was "no Consolation, if so great a Part is to be divided from the Body of the Empire that Such Part will soon afterwards decay." See also idem to idem,

June 12, 1782, ibid., pp. 373-87. Sir Guy Carleton to idem, New York, Dec. 16, 1782, ibid., pp. 277-79. Barbé's dispatch quoted in the text was among those intercepted by the British.

3. Oswald to Shelburne, May 6, 1782, F.O. 95/511; a transcript is in R. G. Adams Transcripts of Documents Relating to the Negotiation of the Treaty of Peace, Clem. Lib., vol. 3 (hereafter cited as R. G. Adams Transcripts). John Adams, *Diary and Autobiography of John Adams*, ed. Lyman H. Butterfield, 4 vols. (Cambridge, Mass., 1961), 3:43-44. The entry in the diary is November 3, 1782.

4. November 4, 1782, J. Adams, *Diary and Autobiography*, 3:46; and ibid., pp. 54-55. The subject of the mistreatment of the loyalists is explored in the context of British grievances in the succeeding chapter.

5. Adams repeated the argument to Benjamin Vaughan, ibid., p. 57, stating his conviction that Parliament should compensate the loyalists. Privately, he ruminated that it would be well to "recollect the Burning of Cities, and the Thefts of Plate, Negroes and Tobacco."

6. Secretary of State Townshend to Henry Strachey, Nov. 19, 1782, Public Records Office, Colonial Office Series 5/8, fol. 141 (hereafter cited as P.R.O., C.O.). Vincent T. Harlow, *The Founding of the Second British Empire, 1763-1793* (London, 1952), p. 295, makes use of the document.

7. J. Adams, *Diary and Autobiography*, 3:81, n. 1. Alfred LeRoy Burt, *The Old Province of Quebec* (Minneapolis, 1933), p. 357; and Harlow, *Second British Empire*, p. 296.

8. William Belsham, *Memoirs of the Reign of George III*, 4 vols. (London, 1795), 3:305; quoted by Harlow, *Second British Empire*, pp. 434-35.

9. See John Jay to R. R. Livingston, Paris, Sept. 12, 1783, William Jay, *Life of John Jay*, 2 vols. (New York, 1833), 2:127-28.

10. "Mens Sibi, Conscia Recti," *Morn. Chron.*, Oct. 4, 1783.

11. Alexander Hamilton to Jay, July 25, 1783, W. Jay, *Life of John Jay*, 2:122-23; also idem to Washington, Mar. 24 and 25, Hamilton MSS, Library of Congress, vol. 4, fols. 544, 547 (hereafter cited as Lib. Cong.); and Washington to Hamilton, April 16, 1783, ibid. Charles Thompson, secretary to Congress, to Jefferson, May 19, 1784, Jefferson, *Papers*, 7:272-73. Also relevant are John Fiske, *Critical Period of American History* (Boston, 1888), pp. 57-58; Edward Channing, *History of the United States*, 6 vols. (New York, 1927-30), 4:8; Robert Balmain Mowat, *Diplomatic Relations of Great Britain and the United States* (New York, 1925), p. 14; and Alfred T. Mahan, *Sea Power in its Relation to the War of 1812*, 2 vols. (Boston, 1905), 1:70-71.

12. *Morn. Chron.*, Aug. 30, 1783. See also Undersecretary of State George Aust to Lord Hardwicke, Aug. 7, 1783, Add. MSS 35621, fols. 15-16.

13. Dr. Edward Bancroft, secretary to Benjamin Franklin in Paris, systematically betrayed the American commissioners to the British. After the war, in the summer of 1783, he went out to America for about a year. Privately employed by British creditors, he nonetheless called on Lord North, then a dominant member of the coalition ministry, and offered his services in "promoting measures and dispositions favourable to the interests of this Country, as well as in giving information of the State of things there." See Bancroft to Carmarthen, Sept. 17, 1784, F.O. 4/3, fol. 92. When the coalition fell, Bancroft, whose treachery knew no party allegiance, renewed from Philadelphia his offers to Pitt's new government. The numerous subsequent dispatches to the Foreign Office indicate his success. See Bancroft to Undersecretary William Fraser, Nov. 8, 1783, May 28, 1784, Aug. 19, 1784, F.O. 4/3, fols. 7-8, 57-58, 88. The memorandum quoted is entitled "Additional Informations," Aug. 26, 1784, ibid., fols. 90-91. By the end of the year, Bancroft was back in Paris, giving friendly advice and counsel to the American commissioners Adams and Jefferson as they prepared for negotiations with the British, who were, of course, kept fully informed of American plans. See Bancroft to Carmarthen, Dec. 8, 1784, ibid., fols. 108-11.

14. The evidence is that of Grey Elliot, clerk of the Privy Council. John Ehrman, *The British Government and Commercial Negotiations with Europe, 1763-1793* (Cambridge, 1962), p. 137, n. 4 is relevant. There is a mass of evidence indicating that many Americans agreed with the report's assumptions about American political weakness. See

Stephen Higginson to John Adams, (about April), 1784, extracts, quoted in Jefferson, *Papers*, 7:463-70, n.; Madison to Jefferson, May 13, 1786, ibid., 9:268-69, among many others. Thomas Irving presented written testimony to the committee. It is in Add. MSS 38345, fols. 136-51, and was delivered on March 30 and April 1, 1784.

15. Eden to Fox, Sept. 24, 1783, Add. MSS 34419, fols. 269-70.

16. Jefferson to Edmund Pendleton, member of the Virginia legislature, Annapolis, Dec. 16, 1783, Jefferson, *Papers*, 6:385-87. See, too, idem to Monroe, Paris, June 17, 1785, ibid., 8:227-34; and idem to Elbridge Gerry, Nov. 11, 1784, ibid., 7:501-2, and to Madison, same date, ibid., 7:503-6.

17. Both Adams and Jay paid private visits to Britain in 1783; but it was not until May, 1784, that Congress finally adopted a report, written chiefly by Jefferson, authorizing treaties of amity and commerce with some sixteen nations, Britain among them. At the same time, Jay was named foreign secretary to succeed Robert R. Livingston (whose resignation was by then a year old), and Jefferson was appointed to succeed Jay as commissioner with Adams and Franklin.

18. J. Adams, *Diary and Autobiography*, 3:177, n. 1. The letters to Dorset are in Jefferson, *Papers*, 7:457-58. Dorset's letter, November 24, 1784, is published ibid., p. 547.

19. Jefferson to Monroe, Dec. 10, 1784, Jefferson, *Papers*, 7:562-65. See, too, Adams to Carmarthen, Sept. 26, 1785, F.O. 4/3, fols. 305-6, recounting the contacts with Dorset. See Adams to Eldridge Gerry, Dec. 12, 1784, Jefferson, *Papers*, 8:56-59, n.

20. J. Adams, *Diary and Autobiography*, 3:174, entry for March 19, 1785. See, too, Jefferson to Madison, Mar. 18, 1785, Jefferson, *Papers*, 8:38-41; and Charles Storer to Adams, undated, but obviously early March, 1785, ibid., pp. 56-59, n. The approach was made through one Petree, a member of the London Committee of American Merchants. Adams' "Air Balloon" remark is in his letter to Storer, Mar. 28, 1785, ibid.

21. Jefferson, *Papers*, 8:55-56. For an American view in general agreement with the implication, see Christopher Gore to Rufus King, Feb. 5, 1786, Rufus King, *Life and Correspondence of Rufus King*, ed. C. R. King, 6 vols. (New York, 1894-1900), 1:155-56. Jefferson to Monroe, Apr. 15, 1785, Jefferson, *Papers*, 8:88-90, is relevant. See, too, Dorset to Carmarthen, Apr. 7, 1785, Oscar Browning, ed., *Despatches from Paris, 1787-90*, 2 vols. (London, 1909-10), 1:49; Jefferson, *Papers*, 8:153, n. Dorset personally believed that the commissioners were fully authorized to treat "notwithstanding any appearance of want of subordination to Congress on the part of the States in other matters." See Dorset to Carmarthen, Apr. 28, 1785, also quoted in the text, F.O. 27/16, France. See, too, Matthew Ridley to Jay, London, May 2, 1785, Jefferson, *Papers*, 8:56-59, n.

22. Commissioners to Dorset, May 17, 1785, Jefferson, *Papers*, 8:153.

23. Adams to Jay, John Adams, *The Life and Works of John Adams*, ed. Charles Francis Adams, 10 vols. (Boston, 1850-56), 8:268-73.

24. Adams to Jay, June 26, 1785, ibid., pp. 273-76. See, too, Jefferson to Adams, Paris, July 7, 1785, Jefferson, *Papers*, 8:265-67; and Adams to Jay, July 19, 1785, J. Adams, *Works*, 8:279-93. To substantiate Adams' view of the popular opinion in Britain, see "Sum Veras," *Morn. Her.*, Sept. 23, 1785: "Why now, Johnny, now will you be so notion simple as to try your Yankey here? We know well that the Congress have no more power to bind any state to the performance of any thing whatever, than they have power to bind the geese to remain in the Lakes of Canada for the whole winter season."

25. Adams' account is to Jay, Aug. 25, 1785, J. Adams, *Works*, 8:302-10. Idem to idem, Aug. 30, 1785, ibid., pp. 310-14, is relevant, as is Matthew Ridley to idem, Sept. 5, 1785, Jefferson, *Papers*, 8:56-59, n., who predicated no commercial treaty "until we place a proper Power somewhere and adopt some legal measures to give weight and Dignity to that Power." See, finally, Abigail Adams to John Q. Adams, Sept. 6, 1785, Abigail Adams, *Letters of Mrs. Adams*, ed. Charles Francis Adams (Boston, 1848), pp. 267-69.

26. For evidence on the threatening trade war among the several states, see Madison to Jefferson, Mar. 18, 1786, Jefferson, *Papers*, 9:332-36; and David Humphreys to idem, Hartford, Conn., Francis Landon Humphreys, ed., *Life and Times of David Humphreys*, 2 vols. (New York, 1917), 1:352-54; and Jay to Washington, June 27, 1786, W. Jay, *Life of John Jay*, 1:244-46. On the evil effects of sectionalism, see R. King to Adams,

Nov. 2, 1785, King, *Correspondence*, 1:112-13; Higginson to idem, Boston, Dec. 30, 1785, John Franklin Jameson, ed., "Higginson's Letters," *Annual Report of the American Historical Association* (1896), 1:725-33; and especially Jay to idem, Nov. 1, 1785, W. Jay, *Life of John Jay*, 2:177-78, who wrote that the diversity of opinion about a strong retaliatory trade policy against Britain lay between the "eastern and middle States," which were generally for strong measures, and the southern states, whose representatives in Congress "throw cold water on all such ideas." Jay explained that the southern states, possessing few ships of their own, were averse to discrimination against foreign vessels because it would raise the price of freight and favor "their neighbours who have ships and wish to have more."

27. Madison to Jefferson, Jan. 22, 1786, Jefferson, *Papers*, 9:194-204. In the same vein, see Benjamin Lincoln to R. King, Hingham, Mass., Feb. 11, 1786, King, *Correspondence*, 1:156-60; Madison to Jefferson, Aug. 20, 1785, Jefferson, *Papers*, 8:413-16; Jay to Adams, Feb. 22, 1786, W. Jay, *Life of John Jay*, 2:181; R. King to idem, New York, May 5, 1786, King, *Correspondence*, 1:172-74.

28. The quotation from Madison is in his letter to Jefferson, Aug. 12, 1786, Jefferson, *Papers*, 10:229-36.

29. Bancroft to Jefferson, London, Nov. 18, 1785, Jefferson, *Papers*, 9:40-41. See also the *Public Advertiser*, July 24, 1786.

30. Undersecretary Frazer to Adams, Apr. 3, 1786, F.O. 4/4, fol. 81; and the commissioners to Carmarthen, Apr. 4, 1786, ibid., fol. 83.

31. Jefferson to John Page, Paris, May 4, 1786, Jefferson, *Papers*, 9:444-46; and Adams to Gov. Bowdoin, May 9, 1786, J. Adams, *Works*, 8:389-90.

32. To Charles Jenkinson (Lord Hawkesbury), May 10, 1786, Add. MSS 38219, fol. 131.

33. Dec. 14, 1786, Jefferson, *Papers*, 10:596-99. British consul Sir John Temple reported from Boston on the Shays Rebellion, which, he said, portended a dissolution of the American Union and at least the possibility that "in this hour of their Confusion and distress, some or all of the States may seek for European friendship, Council, and advice." His dispatch is Oct. 4, 1786, F.O. 4/5, fols. 325-26. See, too, his of Nov. 2, 1786, ibid., fols. 351-52; and Feb. 7, 1787, F.O. 4/6, fols. 31-32. Jefferson characteristically blamed the British for the American tumults and hinted at the former enemy's tacit co-operation with the Algerine pirates' attacks on American vessels. See his letter to William Carmichael, Jefferson, *Papers*, 10:632-34. For Adams' deep pessimism, see his to Jefferson, Oct. 9, 1787, ibid., pp. 220-21; and Abigail Adams to Mrs. Cranch, Feb. 25 and Apr. 28, 1787, A. Adams, *Letters of Mrs. Adams*, pp. 317-20, 320-22.

34. Bond to Carmarthen, May 1, 16, 1787, F.O. 4/5, fols. 110-11, 139-40. See, too, idem to idem, July 2, 1787, ibid., fols. 190-92: "It is plain, my Lord, Things cannot long run as they are." Sir John Temple for once agreed with Bond. His dispatch to Carmarthen, May 3, 1787, from New York is ibid., fols. 119-20.

35. To Jefferson, Philadelphia, May 30, 1787, Jefferson, *Papers*, 11:389-90.

CHAPTER 4

1. Sept. 1, 1784.

2. To Messrs. Bridges and Waller, Nantes, Aug. 10, 1782, Shelburne MSS, Clem. Lib., vol. 35. For more moderate sentiments, see Peter Van Schaack to John Jay, Oct. 15, 1782, William Jay, *Life of John Jay*, 2 vols. (New York, 1833), 1:162-64.

3. Ralph Izard to Jefferson, Apr. 1784, Jefferson, *Papers*, 7:129-31.

4. Defending America from subsequent British charges of violating the treaty of peace by mistreating loyalists, James B. Scott, Introduction, Samuel Flagg Bemis, ed., *American Secretaries of State and Their Diplomacy*, 10 vols. (New York, 1927-29), 1:98-99, argues that the American commissioners had "clear consciences" because they persistently warned the British negotiators of the peace that Congress lacked power to bind the states. This argument from weakness contradicts Bemis' own charge in "John Jay," ibid., p. 227, that Britain was guilty of the first infraction. The first would admit that the commissioners ex-

ceeded their powers, hence did not bind the several states; the second would say that the states were bound, but were justified in refusing to perform.

5. William H. Nelson, *The American Tory* (Oxford, 1961), is a recent and authoritative study of the loyalists' background and mentality; it contains useful generalizations about individual states and regions. There is no estimate of total numbers, however, and it is probably impossible to solve the problem.

6. Loughborough to Eden, Oct. 1, 1782, Add. MSS 34419, fols. 50-51.

7. Eden to Loughborough, Oct. 5, 1782, ibid., fols. 55-56.

8. William Belsham, *Memoirs of the Reign of George III*, 4 vols. (London, 1795), 3:305. See chapter 3 above.

9. Adams to Jefferson, Nov. 1, 1785, Jefferson, *Papers*, 9:3-4; Adams to Jay, July 29, 1785, John Adams, *The Life and Works of John Adams*, ed. Charles Francis Adams, 10 vols. (Boston, 1850-56), 8:288-89; Aug. 6, 1785, ibid., pp. 289-91; Nov. 4, 1785, ibid., pp. 335-37; and Dec. 3, 1785, ibid., pp. 350-56. See, too, Morris to Washington, London, Sept. 18, 1790, Jared Sparks, *Life of Gouverneur Morris*, 3 vols. (Boston, 1832), 1:44.

10. Quoted by Robert Livingston Schuyler, *The Fall of the Old Colonial System* (London, 1945), p. 93.

11. Adams' approximation is in *Works*, 10:87. The second is from Nelson, *American Tory*, p. 92.

12. Claude Halstead Van Tyne, *Loyalists in the American Revolution* (New York, 1902), p. 183, estimates fifty thousand. Edward Channing, *History of the United States*, 6 vols. (New York, 1927-30), 3:216, believes that thirty thousand may be too large. Paul H. Smith, in an excellent recent study, "The American Loyalists: Notes on Their Organization and Numerical Strength," *William and Mary Quarterly* 25 (April 1968): 29-77, concludes that only nineteen thousand loyalists actually fought for the king, and estimates that loyalists comprised about 16 percent (513,000 persons) of the total population, or about 20 percent of white Americans.

13. John Fiske, *Critical Period of American History* (Boston, 1888), p. 130; Arthur Granville Bradley, *Colonial Americans in Exile* (New York, 1932), p. 108.

14. Nelson, *American Tory*, p. 153.

15. Vincent T. Harlow, *The Founding of the Second British Empire, 1763-1793* (London, 1952), p. 468, n. 31.

16. Helen T. Manning, *British Colonial Government after the American Revolution* (New Haven, 1933), p. 44.

17. Simcoe to Undersecretary Evan Nepean, Mar. 16, 1791, in E. A. Cruikshank, ed., *The Correspondence of Lieut. Governor John Graves Simcoe, with Allied Documents*, 5 vols. (Toronto, 1923-31), 1:21.

18. Galloway to Hardwicke, Nov. 19, 1783, Add. MSS 35621, fols. 202-3; Dec. 16, 1783, ibid., fols. 258-59.

19. Quoted in Nelson, *American Tory*, p. 159.

20. *Morn. Her.*, Mar. 20, 1783; "Arion," *Morn. Chron.*, Sept. 6, 1783; and "An Impartial Englishman," ibid., Oct. 25, 1783.

21. Grace A. Cockroft, *Public Life of George Chalmers* (New York, 1939), p. 62. Chalmers himself was receiving £100 per annum at the time.

22. *Parl. Hist.*, 23:1041. There was no debate on the motion made by Lord John Cavendish, chancellor of the exchequer, who spoke in eloquent terms of future Anglo-American friendship, but warned, "this must necessarily be a work of some little time."

23. See Manning, *British Colonial Government*, p. 39; Bradley, *Colonial Americans in Exile*, p. 108; *Parl. Hist.*, 27:1788-89; and John Holland Rose, *William Pitt and National Revival* (London, 1911), pp. 444-45 and n. Loyalist pensions continued beyond 1789, of course. The total outlay would thus be considerably larger than the figure for 1789.

24. Sept. 16, 1783.

25. Gen. Leslie to Gen. Sir Guy Carleton, Charleston, Nov. 18, 1782, Shelburne MSS, Clem. Lib., 69: 203-6. Leslie assembled a considerable convoy: twenty ships, carrying 3,873 persons (including 2,613 Negroes) bound for Jamaica. Two others with refugees aboard made for Halifax. Ten, including two reserved for crown officers and their families, cleared

for England. Nine sailed to St. Augustine. A reasonable estimate for the total number of refugees in this single operation would be about eight thousand.

26. Vaughn to Shelburne, Paris, Nov. 1, 1782, Vaughn MSS, Emmons Transcripts, Clem. Lib.; Morgann to Shelburne, June 12, 1782, Shelburne MSS, Clem. Lib., 68: 373-87.

27. Public Records Office, Treasury Papers, vol. 79 (hereafter cited as P.R.O., T.); Report of Apr. 3, 1790, F.O. 4/8. An interesting recent appraisal of the 58 volumes of the transcripts of the manuscript books and papers of the commission's proceedings is Eugene R. Fingerhut, "Uses and Abuses of the American Loyalists' Claims: A Critique of Quantitative Analyses," *William and Mary Quarterly* 25 (April 1968): 245-58.

28. John Adams to John Jay, London, Apr. 19, 1787, J. Adams, *Works*, 8:438, enclosing a copy of the "very curious bill" which he attributed to Benedict Arnold and which he said "shows the spirit of the present ministry," an obvious misreading in view of the treatment of the bill.

29. Add. MSS 38211, fol. 334.

30. Apr. 28, 1787. See my "The London Press and the First Decade of American Independence," *Journal of British Studies* 2 (May 1963): 105-7.

31. May 30, 1787; and ibid., p. 106, n. 61.

32. Apr. 28, 1783, Abigail Adams, *Letters of Mrs. Adams*, ed. Charles Francis Adams (Boston, 1848), pp. 138-41.

33. Merrill Jensen, *The New Nation* (New York, 1950), pp. 226-29; Nelson, *American Tory*, p. 166; John Randolph to Jefferson, Richmond, Apr. 24, 1784, Jefferson, *Papers*, 7:116-17. See, too, Isaac S. Harrell, *Loyalism in Virginia* (Philadelphia, 1926), pp. 137-38.

34. John Chester Miller, *Alexander Hamilton* (New York, 1959), pp. 103-4; Fiske, *Critical Period of American History*, p. 124.

35. Samuel Eliot Morison, *The Life and Letters of Harrison Gray Otis, Federalist*, 2 vols. (Boston, 1913), 1:38-39.

36. Hamilton to Morris, New York, Feb. 21, 1784, Hamilton MSS, Lib. Cong.; Schuyler to John Jay, Feb. 18, 1784, W. Jay, *Life of John Jay*, 2:148-50.

37. Miller, *Alexander Hamilton*, pp. 105-6.

38. Jay to R. R. Livingston, July 19, 1783, W. Jay, *Life of John Jay*, 1:174-81; and Sept. 12, 1783, ibid., 2:127-28. Jay to Hamilton, Sept. 28, 1783, ibid., 2:132-34; Madison to Jefferson, Sept. 20, 1783, Jefferson, *Papers*, 6:36-39; and Jefferson to Madison, Dec. 11, 1783, ibid., pp. 381-82. Franklin to Hartley, Sept. 7, 1783, F.O. 4/2, fol. 226, enclosing an extract of Boudinot's letter. See, too, Livingston to Jay, Jan. 25, 1784, W. Jay, *Life of John Jay*, 2:139-40, 145-46; Jay to Benjamin Vaughan, New York, Sept. 2, 1784, ibid., p. 158; and Jefferson to Chastellux, Annapolis, Jan. 16, 1784, Jefferson, *Papers*, 6:466-67.

39. Afred Le Roy Burt, *The Old Province of Quebec* (Minneapolis, 1933), pp. 340-42; Andrew C. McLaughlin, "The Western Posts and the British Debts," *Annual Report of the American Historical Association* (1894), pp. 413-44. The subject of the posts is treated in detail in the next chapter. Opinion in the press was bitter against America, and there was no question about which party first broke the treaty. See, for example, "Mens Sibi, Conscia Recti," *Morn. Chron.*, Oct. 4, 1783. Adams' fears notwithstanding, the loyalist issue figured little in his negotiations. See Adams to Carmarthen, Feb. 6, 1786, J. Adams, *Works*, 8:371-72; and idem to Jay, May 25, 1786, ibid., pp. 394-96.

40. Add. MSS 38348, fols. 65-68, a draft report of the Committee for Trade on the question of America's "unjust transactions," undated, but obviously in the summer of 1787. Harrell, *Loyalism in Virginia*, chap. 4, esp. pp. 139-40, has much valuable information on the debts in Virginia.

41. Irving Brant, *James Madison*, 5 vols. (New York, 1941-56), 3:66.

42. Jensen, *New Nation*, p. 279.

43. Charles A. Beard, *Economic Origins of Jeffersonian Democracy* (New York, 1927), pp. 271-72, who quotes extensively from an anonymous British pamphlet, *A Review of the Laws of the United States* (London, 1790).

44. See the statement of Duncan Campbell, John Nutt, and William Molleson, for the merchants interested in the debts issue, Public Record Office, Chatham Papers (including papers of the younger Pitt) 30/8, vol. 343 (hereafter cited as P.R.O. 30/8). Divided

among the individual states, the debts stood thus: Virginia, £2.3 million; South Carolina, £690,000; Maryland, £570,000; North Carolina, £380,000; Massachusetts, £290,000; Georgia, £250,000; Pennsylvania, £230,000; New York, £175,000; Rhode Island, £50,000; Connecticut, £30,000; New Hampshire, £22,000; and New Jersey, £500. The creditors were distributed in this way: Glasgow, 95 houses, holding £2.1 million in debts; London, 67 houses, holding £2.3 million; Liverpool, 6 houses, £120,000; Bristol, 5 houses, £94,000; and Whitehaven, 5 houses, £30,000. There were sixteen other houses scattered among Workington, Kilmarnock, Leeds, Chester, and Greenock, holding relatively small amounts.

45. The memorial is dated May 30, 1782, Shelburne MSS, Clem. Lib., vol. 87.

46. F.O. 4/3, fols. 319-20.

47. Oliver Morton Dickerson, *The Navigation Acts and the American Revolution* (Philadelphia, 1951), p. 34; Beard, *Economic Origins*, pp. 271-72.

48. Brant, *Madison*, 2:307; 3:66, 167, 220. Frank Monaghan, *John Jay* (New York, 1935), p. 253, quotes George Mason's report that everywhere in Virginia he heard, "If we are now to pay the debts . . . what have we been fighting for all this while?" The inhabitants of Caroline County also complained to the legislature of "the impolicy, and oppression of paying British debts." Ames's speech is in Fisher Ames, *The Works of Fisher Ames*, ed. J. T. Kirkland (Boston, 1809), pp. 103 ff., and is used extensively by Beard, *Economic Origins*, pp. 242-44. Walcott's remarks are in his *British Influence on the Affairs of the United States, Proved and Explained* (Boston, 1804); he condemned the "measures of a very extraordinary nature" adopted by the debtor planters during the war to extinguish their debts. The Adolphus reference is *History of England from the Accession to the Decease of George III*, 7 vols. (London, 1840), 3:13. See, too, Robert Hunter, Jr., *Quebec to Carolina in 1785-1786*, ed. Louis B. Wright and Marion Tingling (San Marino, Calif., 1943), p. 237, for the sense of British outrage. See, too, Elsworth to Oliver Walcott, Philadelphia, Apr. 4, 1794, George Gibbs, *Memoirs of the Administrations of Washington and Adams*, 2 vols. (New York, 1846), 1:134; used by Beard, *Economic Origins*, p. 245.

49. Brant, *Madison*, 2:269; and Jefferson to Jay, Philadelphia, Apr. 11, 1783, Jefferson, *Papers*, 6:260-61; Randolph to Jefferson, Richmond, Apr. 24, 1785, ibid., 7:116-17. See also Jensen, *New Nation*, pp. 68-69.

50. James Monroe to Gov. Harrison of Virginia, Annapolis, May 26, 1784, Jefferson, *Papers*, 7:47-49. Monroe, noting the scarcity of specie in the state—he estimated a total of a mere £100,000—declared "the very nature of the affair" made it impossible to comply literally with the debt provisions of the treaty. "What then is the remedy?" he asked. "We must obtain delay at least in the payment till by continued frugality and a succession of crops we can pay it." He wished negotiations, however, to effect a delay, not a unilateral breach of the treaty. Strict observation of the agreement was required, since, he believed, it "very essentially involves the interest of the character of the State." It is significant that Monroe did not suggest using the "abducted" slave issue to force the British to amend the debt articles.

51. See Randolph to Jefferson, Apr. 24, 1785, cited in note 48 above.

52. P.R.O., T. 79/10, American Loyalist Claims. Unbound and very poorly preserved, the series runs to 151 bundles and constitutes the researcher's nightmare. The index is so incomplete that it is useless. There were certain other categories of losses, on personal bonds and interest, amounting to £8,653 in the case of Alexander Donald & Co.

53. The analysis is made in Jackson T. Main, "Sections and Politics in Virginia, 1781-1787," *William and Mary Quarterly*, 3d ser., 12 (1955): 96-112. See, too, Jacob M. Price, "The Rise of Glasgow in the Chesapeake Tobacco Trade, 1705-1775," ibid., 11 (1954): 179-99.

54. Henry "learned" that three hundred Negroes had been shipped recently from New York to Nova Scotia. This scant information was sufficient to give "reluctant debtors a firm feeling that they should not pay what they owed to Glasgow merchants." See Brant, *Madison*, 2:358.

55. See *Public Advertiser*, Aug. 4, 1786. Britons read with grim pleasure Charleston judge Pendleton's charge to the grand jury, delivered in December, 1786, and published in full in the *Morn. Chron.*, Feb. 23, 1787. Pendleton was especially bitter at his fellow citizens

for indifferently bearing "the degrading character of a profligate, dishonest, and faithless people." In an editorial in ibid., Jan. 8, 1787, news that Massachusetts was moving to repeal all legislation violating the treaty was seen as "a trick to get the credulous English to deliver up the forts to them." When this was accomplished, the prediction ran, "they will keep the same good faith as they did with the convention made with General Burgoyne."

There were two fierce controversies in the press in 1787 and 1788 involving, among others, Dr. Richard Price and Benjamin Rush of Philadelphia. See Price's letter introducing Rush's optimistic report on American life in *Morn. Chron.*, Apr. 23, 1787. "Hater of Incendiaries" roasted Price and the Americans in ibid., Apr. 26, May 4 and 18, and June 8 and 15. For a full account of the controversy in the *Morning Chronicle*, see my article cited in note 29 above. The second exchange involved "Revolution," generally considered to be an American lady, who upset the beehive by admonishing Englishmen to celebrate the centennial of the Glorious Revolution with the same civic ardor Americans displayed toward the Fourth of July. She published her undiplomatic, florid, and repetitive effusions in the issues of Sept. 27 and Oct. 1, 7, 14, and 27, 1788. Among her antagonists were "Scourge," Sept. 30, 1788, and "The People of Great Britain and Ireland," Oct. 20, 1788, the source of the last quotation.

56. The British assertion that the posts were retained to compel America to abide by the treaty has been widely questioned, not to say scorned, by the great majority of American writers. Samuel Flagg Bemis, *Jay's Treaty: A Study in Commerce and Diplomacy* (New York: 1923), pp. 6-7, for example, asserts that the fur trade was the real reason for Britain's retention of the posts. The debts and loyalists provided mere "*ex post facto*" excuses. A. L. Burt, in his splendid *Old Province of Quebec*, among other places, asserts the decisiveness of the British fear of an Indian uprising. Donald G. Creighton, *The Commercial Empire of the St. Lawrence, 1760-1850* (Toronto, 1937), pp. 93-95, points to the intimate connection between fur trade and Indians, both vital to "the integrity of the commercial empire of the St. Lawrence" (itself an excellent reason why Britain would wish to keep peace in the backcountry). He asserts that the posts were "officially kept in retaliation" and offered as a *quid pro quo*, accepting this as "partly an explanation . . . partly an excuse."

It is beyond question that Haldimand and the fur traders made frequent representations pointing to the Indian danger and profits from the fur trade; but the London government had before it a much wider range of problems, including the whole of the American commerce, the prewar creditors, and the new situation presently created by the inception of the new, vigorous federal government. The fact remains that British ministers and public repeatedly *said* the posts were retained as retaliation and bargaining counters. The efforts to prove they *meant* something else have yet to succeed. It is a pity that the United States did not put British intentions to the ultimate test, as honest John Adams wished, by herself performing the treaty and demanding that Britain do the same forthwith.

CHAPTER 5

1. Benjamin Quarles, *The Negro in the American Revolution* (Chapel Hill, N.C., 1961), pp. 159-62.

2. Irving Brant, *James Madison*, 5 vols. (New York, 1941-56), 2:255.

3. The figures are from Quarles, *Negro in American Revolution*, pp. 163-64, 166, 170-72. See, too, Leslie to Carleton, Nov. 18, 1782, Shelburne MSS, Clem. Lib., 69: 203-6, informing him that a convoy of twenty vessels was just departing from Jamaica, carrying 3,873 refugees, including 2,612 Negroes. Frederic Austen Ogg, "Jay's Treaty and the Slavery Interests of the United States," *Annual Report of the American Historical Association for 1901*, 1(1902): 275-98, is hopelessly out of date and full of unreliable data, as, for example, David Ramsay's estimate—it could have been nothing else—in his history of South Carolina in the Revolution (which appeared in 1785) that the state lost twenty-five thousand slaves, a wildly inflated figure. Charles A. Beard, *Economic Origins of Jeffersonian Democracy* (New York, 1927), p. 273, accepts Jefferson's statement that Virginia lost thirty thousand slaves during Cornwallis' campaign in 1778. This, too, seems a palpable exaggeration. The fact remains that no official compilation was ever made. Statements made

in 1791 by Patrick Colquhoun of Glasgow and Gouverneur Morris referred to only three thousand slaves. (See below.) Alexander Hamilton in the "Camillus" essays puts the figure at two thousand and the cash value at $400,000. See John Chester Miller, *Alexander Hamilton* (New York, 1959), p. 430. It is noteworthy that when Monroe wrote to Jefferson on August 20, 1784, urging negotiations with Britain to obtain a delay in paying prewar debts, he made not the slightest use of the slave issue (Jefferson, *Papers*, 7:401-8). Jefferson's view seems much sounder when he told Monroe, May 10, 1786, ibid., 9:499-503, that the prewar debts should be paid, although he hoped by instalments, else the national character would be "stained with infamy among all nations and to all times"; as for compensation for slaves, it was "a bagatelle which if not made good before the last instalment becomes due, may be secured out of that." In his negotiations with George Hammond, Jefferson alleged that "near 3000" Negroes had been publicly carried away by the British. See his letter to Hammond, Dec. 15, 1791, *American State Papers*, I. Foreign Relations, p. 19.

4. Aug. 9, 1783, F.O. 4/2, fol. 200.

5. Aug. 13, 1783, ibid., fol. 204.

6. Oct. 28, 1784, Jefferson, *Papers*, 7:456, 457-58.

7. Adams to Jay, Auteuil, May 13, 1785, John Adams, *The Life and Works of John Adams*, ed. Charles Francis Adams, 10 vols. (Boston, 1850-56), 8:248-50.

8. Adams to Jay, June 6, 1785, ibid., pp. 259-61.

9. Adams to Jay, Aug. 25, 1785, ibid., pp. 302-10.

10. Sept. 6, 1785, Abigail Adams, *Letters of Mrs. Adams*, ed. Charles Francis Adams (Boston, 1848), pp. 267-69; and Adams to Jay, May 25, 1786, J. Adams, *Works*, 8:394-96.

11. Merrill Jensen, *The New Nation* (New York, 1950), pp. 16-17, 68-69, 275 ff., and Arthur Burr Darling, *Our Rising Empire* (New Haven, 1940), p. 113, are prominent among American historians who believe Britain's retention of the posts justified the refusal to pay prewar debts. Two authors of major importance in considering the posts are Samuel Flagg Bemis, *Jay's Treaty: A Study in Commerce and Diplomacy* (New York, 1923); and Alfred Le Roy Burt, *The United States, Great Britain, and British North America* (New Haven, 1940). The latter's article, "A New Approach to the Problem of the Western Posts," *Annual Report of the Canadian Historical Association* (1931), pp. 61-75, is included substantially in the book. His *The Old Province of Quebec* (Minneapolis, 1933), also bears upon the subject. A good general treatment is given by John Bartlett Brebner, *North Atlantic Triangle*, 5th printing (New York, 1958), who recognizes the connection between the retention of the posts and the mistreatment of loyalists, as well as the prewar debts. William Renwick Riddell, *Life of John Graves Simcoe* (Toronto, 1926), is not up to the high scholarly standard of the foregoing, but he delivers an effective criticism of Bemis' quotation of the Canadian archivist, Brymner, p. 230. The first "standard" treatment, Andrew C. McLaughlin, "The Western Posts and the British Debts," *Annual Report of the American Historical Association* (1894), pp. 413-44, is highly nationalistic in tone and of little use beyond the antiquarian.

12. Vincent T. Harlow, *The Founding of the Second British Empire, 1763-1793* (London, 1952), pp. 464-65.

13. John Adams, Diary, May 1, 1783, J. Adams, *Works*, 3:367.

14. Burt, *United States, Great Britain, British North America*, p. 83; and *Old Province of Quebec*, pp. 340-41, where it is observed that Haldimand did not even mention the fur traders in his dispatch, although the General's concern for British subjects would clearly include them. Burt rightly points out, in addition, that by accepting the "all convenient speed" stipulation, the Americans themselves bear a measure of responsibility for subsequent events.

15. McLaughlin, "Western Posts and British Debts," and Burt, *Old Province of Quebec*, p. 342. See, too, E. Gerry to Jefferson, Boston, Aug. 24, 1784, Jefferson, *Papers*, 7:411-13. Some have considered it "striking" that Sydney's letter was dated April 8, 1784, the day before Britain's ratification of the definitive treaty of peace, and attribute to the ministry a secret intention to retain the posts indefinitely. This is specious. The preliminaries had long been in force, and Sydney's dispatch was no more secret than other official communications between minister and military commander.

16. Monroe to Jefferson, Nov. 1, 1784, Jefferson, *Papers*, 7:459-62. Darling, *Our Rising Empire*, p. 114, asserts that Britain's retention of the posts reflected a conviction that there was "much that could be done . . . among the pioneers in western Pennsylvania, Kentucky, and the Northwest." There is no positive evidence supporting this view. Bemis, *Jay's Treaty*, p. 10, calls the inability of the weak Confederation government to compel states to remove legal impediments a "convenient excuse" for the British retention. The simplest and most direct explanation—resting on positive evidence, not on speculative and hypothetical reasoning—is that the British held the posts as "rods" over American heads to compel payment of the prewar debts.

17. Abigail Adams to J. Q. Adams, Sept. 6, 1785, A. Adams, *Letters*, pp. 267-69.

18. Adams to Jay, Auteuil, May 13, 1785, J. Adams, *Works*, 8:248-50.

19. Adams to Jay, June 6, 17, 1785, ibid., pp. 259-61, 268-73.

20. F.O. 4/3, fol. 192. See also Adams to Jay, June 26, 1785, J. Adams, *Works*, 8:273-76.

21. The chief of these was the post-armistice capture and condemnation of eight American vessels at New York and one French ship at Jamaica. See Dr. William Wynne, an authority on maritime law, to Carmarthen, Aug. 6, 1785, F.O. 4/3, fols. 273-74; and Lord Camden to idem, Aug. 11, 1785, ibid., fols. 277-78.

22. Adams to Jay, Aug. 25, 1785, J. Adams, *Works*, 8:302-10. On the question of wartime interest, Pitt argued that no war in which Britain had ever engaged had suspended interest in private business transactions. Adams countered by asserting that the American War had been a dissolution of government and law, hence of contracts. The treaty of peace had been necessary to revive them. Rufus King called Adams' reasoning "more artificial than solid." See King to E. Gerry, Apr. 16, 1786, Rufus King, *Life and Correspondence of Rufus King*, ed. C. R. King, 6 vols. (New York, 1894-1900), 1:66-67.

23. Adams to Jay, Oct. 21, 1785, J. Adams, *Works*, 8:325-33, and Carmarthen's notes, F.O. 4/3, fols. 317-18.

24. Carmarthen to the Lords of the Admiralty, draft, Nov. 1, 1785, F.O. 4/3, fols. 327-28; and idem to Adams, Dec. 9, 1785, ibid., fols. 373-74.

25. Oct. 22, 1785, F.O. 4/3, fols. 319-20. The Glaswegians' attitude, fully shared by the second committee mentioned below, directly contradicts W. S. Smith's statement to Jefferson that the "merchants begin to speak plain and to give strong symptoms of returning reason," that is, of a disposition to accept the American position. The letter is Dec. 21, 1785, Jefferson, *Papers*, 9:118-19, and is fairly characteristic of Smith's habitual superficiality.

26. F.O. 4/3, fols. 385-86; and ibid., fols. 439-40.

27. Adams to Jay, Dec. 9, 1785, J. Adams, *Works*, 8:358-60.

28. Egerton MSS 3498, British Museum.

29. Adams to Jay, Jan. 4, 1786, J. Adams, *Works*, 8:360-61; idem to R. King, Dec. 23, 1785, King, *Correspondence*, 1:117-18. He told Jay that the optimistic predictions would prove to be "only a delusion, for, if the ministry really are desirous of an equitable settlement I am well persuaded they cannot yet carry it in parliament." For Colonel Smith's vaporings, see his letter to Jefferson, Feb. 13, 1786, Jefferson, *Papers*, 9:281-83.

30. Adams to King, Jan. 19, 1786, King, *Correspondence*, 1:181-84. See, too, idem to Jay, Jan. 21, 1786, J. Adams, *Works*, 8:368-69.

31. Adams to Jay, Feb. 27, 1786, J. Adams, *Works*, 8:381-82.

32. F.O. 4/4, fols. 39-40, draft. The "State of the Grievances" is ibid., fols. 41-54. Carmarthen instructed Sir John Temple to keep him informed of congressional reaction to his reply to Adams. See his dispatch, June 7, 1786, F.O. 4/4, fols. 203-4.

33. See chapter 3.

34. Jefferson to Jay, London, Apr. 23, 1786, Jefferson, *Papers*, 9:402-3. Jensen, *New Nation*, p. 174, asserts that the Americans induced the merchants to waive wartime interest. I find no evidence to support the statement. Alexander McCaul, one of Jefferson's creditors, said he was convinced wartime interest would be forgiven in return for payment of capital and pre- and postwar interest. See Jefferson to Monroe, May 10, 1786, Jefferson, *Papers*, 9:499-503. This, however, was scarcely an "agreement." The merchants actually intensified

their complaints against the Americans because of paper-money laws in several states, deemed new infractions of Article IV. See the memorial of the Committee of Merchants trading to North America to Carmarthen, June 20, 1786, F.O. 4/4, fols. 209-10. George Miller to Carmarthen, Nov. 30, 1788, ibid., fols. 325-28; and idem to Pinckney, copy, ibid., fols. 295-96 are also relevant.

The second meeting of the Glasgow merchants with Adams meant the complete collapse of confidence in the envoy; they now began to search for other means to settle their debts. Phineas Bond, for example—a favorite with the creditors, who strongly supported his appointment as consul at Philadelphia—was fitted out with a new title "agreeable to the wishes of the merchants." (Carmarthen to Pitt, Apr. 8, 1786, P.R.O. 30/8, vol. 151, fol. 47; idem to Bond, Mar. 4, 1787, F.O. 4/7, fol. 73; and Bond to Carmarthen, Philadelphia, Mar. 30, 1788, F.O. 4/6, fols. 107-10.) Bond consequently went out to Philadelphia not only as consul, but also as "Commissary for Commercial Affairs," with the manifest design of opening negotiations directly with the individual states. Congress declined, however, to accept him as "Commissary." Even so, he appeared before the council of the state of Pennsylvania to argue against proposed laws which would further impede collection of prewar debts. George Miller at Charleston also protested certain measures in South Carolina directly to the governor, Thomas Pinckney. Quite obviously, the London government had written off the Adams mission.

35. Jay to Jefferson, Jan. 19, 1786, Jefferson, *Papers*, 9:185-86. The conference with Vergennes was on May 23. Jefferson's account to Jay is May 23, 1786, ibid., pp. 567-69.

36. Adams to Cotton Tufts, May 26 and June 2, 1786, J. Adams, *Works*, 1:436-37, 549-50. His letter to Jay, May 25, 1786, and to Gov. Bowdoin, June 2, 1786, ibid., 8:394-96 and 397-98, restate these views. See, too, Adams to R. King, June 14, 1786, King, *Correspondence*, 1:184-85.

37. Jay to Adams, Aug. 15, 1786, William Jay, *Life of John Jay*, 2 vols. (New York, 1833), 1:247-49. He expresses similar sentiments in his correspondence with Jefferson and others.

38. Temple to Carmarthen, New York, Dec. 7, 1786, F.O. 4/4, fols. 401-2.

39. The memorial, dated September 24, 1787, is in F.O. 4/5, fols. 264-65.

40. Bond to Carmarthen, ibid., fols. 10-11. Temple to idem, May 3, 1787, ibid., fols. 119-20, is also of interest.

CHAPTER 6

1. Philadelphia, F.O. 4/5, fol. 257.

2. Adams to Jay, Feb. 14, 1788, John Adams, *The Life and Works of John Adams*, ed. Charles Francis Adams, 10 vols. (Boston, 1850-56), 8:475-77. Merchant demands for the government's intervention were rising, however. Great bitterness was felt at South Carolina's extension of instalment payment from three to five years. See the Committee of Merchants trading to North America, memorial of Feb., 1789, F.O. 4/7, fol. 38; and the memorial of the merchants trading to South Carolina, Feb. 24, 1789, ibid., fol. 57. Other requests for government intervention are memorials dated May 21, 1789, Add. MSS 38224; and Jan., 1790, Add. MSS 38225, fol. 27.

3. *Morn. Chron.*, Dec. 8, 1787, July 22 and Oct. 3, 1788; *Public Advertiser*, Dec. 2, 1789. For an expression of doubt about "that boasted *Astrea redux* of American morality," see the *Diary*, June 25, 1789.

4. Consul George Miller to Carmarthen, Charleston, Nov. 17, 1787, F.O. 4/5, fols. 359-60. Isaac S. Harrell, *Loyalism in Virginia* (Philadelphia, 1926), pp. 157-58, is useful. Phineas Bond was more cautious in his appraisal, noting particularly the continuing infringements of the rights of British subjects, especially in the southern states. Virginia was unchanged in her disposition, he noted, and both North Carolina and Maryland continued to invoke very severe doctrines of alienage against British subjects. He strongly urged that Britain should by no means give up the posts until justice was done to British subjects. See his dispatch to Carmarthen, Philadelphia, Mar. 3, 1788, F.O. 4/6, fols. 85-86; idem to Leeds, July 12, 1789, F.O. 5/7, fols. 133-35; and Aug. 15, 1789, ibid., fols. 160-61.

5. The best account of these and related subsequent proceedings in Congress is in Irving

Brant, *James Madison*, 5 vols. (New York, 1941-56), 3:246 ff. See also Vernon G. Setser, *The Commercial Reciprocity Policy of the United States, 1774-1829* (Oxford, 1937), pp. 105-7.

6. Nathan Schachner, *Founding Fathers* (New York, 1954), pp. 38 and 46, asserts the victory in this first great congressional debate was New England's. This neglects the opposition to Madison from southerners who feared giving undue encouragement to eastern shipping and who believed that the burden of discrimination against foreign shipping, especially British, would fall ultimately upon themselves. George Miller made the point in his dispatch of May 20, 1789, F.O. 4/7, fols. 98-99.

7. Bond to Carmarthen, Apr. 29, 1789, F.O. 4/7, fol. 84.

8. Miller to Carmarthen, May 20, 1789, cited in note 6 above; and Temple to idem, May 17, 1789, F.O. 4/7, fol. 96.

9. "Minutes of the Committee for Trade," Add. MSS 38391.

10. Jefferson, *Papers*, 16:513-23. The course of the debate in Congress is not altogether clear. Hawkesbury, particularly, had trouble in learning about it, since at a critical juncture the agent recording proceedings in shorthand for him collapsed "from drunkenness and other Vices." See George Chalmers to Hawkesbury, Oct. 22, 23, 1790, Add. MSS 38225, fols. 278-81, 282-85.

11. See the account of Beckwith's mission below.

12. Washington to Morris, New York, Oct. 13, 1789, Jared Sparks, *Life of Gouverneur Morris*, 3 vols. (Boston, 1832) 2:3-5. A copy is in the British Museum, Add. MSS 28065, fol. 233. On the same day, the President offered Jefferson the office of secretary of state in a letter received on December 11, 1789, after his arrival in Virginia.

13. Paris, Jan. 22, 1790, Sparks, *Gouverneur Morris*, 2:5-6. Morris expressed optimism that the British would agree to form a "connexion" with the United States, but displayed the common American preoccupation with and overestimation of the power of George III.

14. Ibid., 1:323. On Morris' misjudgment, see his opinion of Pitt, the man who had humbled France in the Dutch crisis a few years earlier and who had ended Britain's diplomatic isolation: "engrossed by borough politics and ignorant of continental affairs." The letter is to Washington, and is cited in note 13 above. He also cast Queen Charlotte, the royal *Hausfrau*, in the role of crafty politician and power in Britain. See Morris to Washington, London, Sept. 18, 1790, ibid., 2:46.

15. Morris to Washington, Apr. 7, 1790, ibid., pp. 6-9. From the outset, Morris displayed his *ideé fixe* that the British ministers were intent on concealing their true intentions from him and hence deliberately aimed to mislead him in conversations. See his dispatch to the President, Apr. 13, 1790, ibid., pp. 9-10. Hence, he was preoccupied with attempts to unmask his opponents by analyzing the minutiae of chance remarks and facial expressions. The fact that Carmarthen's atlas was observed to be lying open at the map of Poland sent Morris rushing to his dispatch desk.

16. Morris to Washington, Apr. 7 and May 2, 1790, ibid., pp. 9 and 18-19. Morris said Fox declared that he and Burke were "now almost alone in their opinions, that we should be permitted to trade in our own bottoms" to the British West Indies. Fox did not, however, explain why he and Burke failed to make a more determined fight for the idea in 1783.

17. See Morris to Leeds, Apr. 19, 1790, copy, F.O. 4/8, fol. 234. Morris mistakenly referred to the earlier interview as having occurred on March 28 instead of March 29. See, too, idem to idem, Apr. 29, 1790, Add. MSS 28065, fol. 315, and Leeds's answer, Apr. 28, 1790, copy, F.O. 4/8, fols. 236-37. There is another draft of the Leeds letter, dated merely April, 1790, Add. MSS 28065, fols. 317-18. It is in interesting contrast with the friendly letter Morris received, the tone of the draft being cold and formal. It was bluntly stated that the fulfilment of the treaty of peace would come "whenever the United States may think proper to remove, on their part, the obstacles which hitherto have impeded an Object certainly desirable for both Powers." The final form included the excuse for the delay. The plea of illness was true. See Leeds to the Lord Chancellor, May 2, 1790, ibid., fol. 330.

18. Morris to Leeds, Apr. 30, 1790, F.O. 4/8, fols. 240-41; idem to Washington, May 1, 1790, Sparks, *Gouverneur Morris*, 2:14-18; Washington to Jefferson, June 19, 1790, Jefferson, *Papers*, 16:531 and nn., 531-36.

19. Morris to Washington, May 29, 1790, Sparks, *Gouverneur Morris*, 2:20-28.

20. "Journal Intîme du General Haldimand," May 31, 1790, E. A. Cruikshank, ed., *The Correspondence of Lieut. Governor John Graves Simcoe, with Allied Documents*, 5 vols. (Toronto, 1923-31), 1:12-13. On April 17, Stephen Cottrell, secretary to the Privy Council, wrote to Grenville that there was "reason to suppose, that a commercial Treaty may soon be negociated with the Congress." The letter is P.R.O. 30/8, vol. 343.

Haldimand's response was unequivocal: "That with respect to the trade a part would certainly be lost, but that this loss would perhaps be made up by the goods that our merchants [would sell] to the Americans, and further, that if the Americans insisted upon having the posts, a merit should be made of giving them up; that if they were determined to have them, they were so numerous they could take them when they thought proper; that I did not believe Great Britain would undertake a war to defend them."

21. Morris to Washington, July 3, 1790, Sparks, *Gouverneur Morris*, 2:29-30.

22. New York, Aug. 12, 1790, ibid., pp. 31-32.

23. Ibid., pp. 40-46. Morris also informed the French that he "had good reason to believe it was their [Britain's] wish to form an offensive and defensive alliance with us, and presumed that he [Foreign Minister Montmarin] was acquainted with their intentions." See Morris to Jefferson, Paris, Feb. 26, 1791, ibid., p. 122.

24. Aug. 16 and 30, 1790, ibid., pp. 32-35 and 35-38. The Nootka Convention was signed on October 28, 1790, but the crisis had long since abated. Morris to Leeds, Sept. 10, 1790, is Add. MSS 28066, fols. 257-58, and is printed by Sparks, *Gouverneur Morris*, 2:38-39.

25. Add. MSS 28066, fol. 259, and printed by Sparks, *Gouverneur Morris*, 2:40. The quotation follows the manuscript. Leeds's perfectly straightforward, uncomplicated letter, Morris interpreted to mean that the ministry was in fundamental disagreement about American policy and that the ministers favoring friendship with the Republic were outnumbered by those "whose sour prejudices and hot resentment render them averse to every intercourse, except that which may immediately subserve a selfish policy." See his dispatch to Washington, Sept. 18, 1790, ibid., pp. 40-47.

26. Morris to Washington, Sept. 18, 1790, cited in previous note. Detained briefly by impressment business, Morris finally left London in late November.

27. Morris to Jefferson, Dec. 24 and 28, 1790, ibid., pp. 52-54 and 55-56.

28. Washington referred Morris' correspondence to Jefferson on December 11. For the report, see Thomas Jefferson, *Writings of Thomas Jefferson*, ed. Paul L. Ford, 10 vols. (New York, 1892-99), 6:167-70. Washington's message is in *American State Papers*, I. Foreign Relations (Washington, 1832), pp. 121-22, where much of Morris' official correspondence is also to be found (hereafter cited as *A.S.P.*, For. Rel.).

29. To Leeds, Mar. 19, 1791, F.O. 4/9, fols. 201-2.

30. Major George Beckwith to Grenville, Philadelphia, July 31, 1791, F.O. 4/12, pp. 146-50.

31. John Chester Miller, *Alexander Hamilton* (New York, 1959), pp. 223-24.

32. David Humphreys to Washington, Oct. 31, 1790, Francis Landon Humphreys, *Life and Times of David Humphreys*, 2 vols. (New York, 1917), 2:50-54. For Jefferson's instructions, August 11, 1790, see Jefferson, *Writings*, 6:118-20.

33. The sketch of Beckwith's career is drawn from his memorial to Home Secretary Dundas, London, June 20, 1792, F.O. 4/14, fols. 191-94. See also his letter to Hawkesbury, Mar. 30, 1789, Add. MSS 38224, fol. 67. For Temple's typically petty and jealous reaction to Beckwith's presence in the United States, see his dispatch to Leeds, May 23, 1791, F.O. 4/10, fols. 61-62. Consul John Hamilton was also critical. See the dispatch of April 10, 1791, F.O. 4/9, fols. 224-25.

34. Julian P. Boyd, *Number 7: Alexander Hamilton's Secret Attempts to Control American Foreign Policy* (Princeton, 1964), develops a scathing and uncompromising attack upon Hamilton for his "interference" in matters of foreign policy. My review in *Journal of Southern History* 31 (1965): 202-3, explains why I find Boyd's assumptions, reasoning, and conclusions unacceptable.

35. Beckwith to Grenville, Apr. 7 and Aug. 5, 1790, F.O. 4/12, fols. 1 and 7. He said he detected a disposition to cultivate good relations with Britain.

36. Hamilton's undated memorandum is in Alexander Hamilton, *Works of Alexander Hamilton*, ed. Henry Cabot Lodge, 12 vols. (New York, 1904), 4:30-32. It corresponds closely in most respects with Beckwith's memorandum, July 15, 1790, F.O. 4/12, fols. 9-10, enclosed in his dispatch to Grenville of August 5, 1790. He said Hamilton emphasized "commercial objects."

37. Hamilton to Washington, July 22, 1790, Hamilton, *Works*, 4:299-302. The Anglo-Spanish crisis further deepened the division between Jefferson and Hamilton, and Beckwith and his government were well aware of it. The occasion was Washington's query to his cabinet about the proper American response in the event of a request from Lord Dorchester for leave to traverse American territory to attack the Spaniards along the Mississippi.

38. Hamilton to Washington, Sept. 30, 1790, and Washington's reply, Oct. 10, 1790, ibid., pp. 73-75 and 76. Hamilton reported another visit from "a certain gentleman" in his letter to the President, Oct. 17, 1790, ibid., p. 77. See, too, Beckwith to Grenville, Nov. 30, 1790 and Apr. 6, 1791, F.O. 4/12, fols. 17-22 and 86-87. The federal government was on the point of moving to Philadelphia. Beckwith asked Hamilton if he could correspond with him, but the Secretary replied that this would be "precarious." Obviously, he preferred personal interviews.

39. See especially Bond to Grenville, Philadelphia, Jan. 3, 1791, F.O. 4/9, fols. 19-22, for indications of rising anti-British sentiment in America.

40. Beckwith to Grenville, New York, Jan. 23, 1791, ibid., fol. 23.

41. Beckwith to Grenville, Mar. 3, 1791, ibid., fols. 31-37, with appendixes referring to specific conversations, fols. 39-50. A copy is in F.O. 95/1, docketed as received May 26, 1791. Beckwith reported, too, on a conversation of February 26 with an unidentified senator, who said he did not believe a treaty of alliance with Britain practicable at the moment, although he thought "a majority of the sensible, cool headed Men in this country would prefer it, but Mr. Jefferson's influence and his exertions would defeat it." A commercial accord would "infallibly lead to the other, and completely undermine the French interest."

The dispatches of March 11-14, 1791, F.O. 95/1, provide comments on domestic American politics and a running commentary on the congressional debates.

Bond, also alarmed at the course of events in America, nonetheless saw the timing of Washington's message as an indication of "a Desire to prevent any hasty measures, which might interrupt commercial Intercourse with Great Britain." His dispatch is March 14, 1791, F.O. 4/9, fols. 191-94.

42. The principal documents relating to the Smith-Colquhoun affair are: "Observations on the Proposed Commercial Treaty between Great Britain and America," Boc. H., Gren. Pps., endorsed "March, 1791, from Mr. Colquhoun"; Smith to Colquhoun, London, Apr. 4, 1791, Melville Papers, Clem. Lib., endorsed, "Stating the points likely to promote a closer Connection between Great Britain & America"; Colquhoun to Grenville, Apr. 15, 1791, F.O. 4/9, f. 220, transmitting the "Memo. of Colo. Smith, rec'd 9th April 1791," ibid., fols. 222-23. It was considered important enough to copy (see F.O. 95/1).

Grenville also received reports on congressional proceedings directed against Britain from William Pulteney, who knew both Smith and Colquhoun. In his letter to Grenville, London, May 29, 1791, Gren. Pps., Boc. H., enclosing congressional news, he wrote, "I imagine your Ldp. will think it important that no time should be lost in sending out an Ambassador to that Country." Additional information is to be found in Colquhoun to Grenville, July 29, 1791, enclosing an abstract of a letter from Smith written in America, *Royal Historical Manuscripts Commission Reports, Fortescue Papers*, 10 vols. (London, 1892), 2:145-46 (hereafter cited as *R.H.M.C.R., Fortescue Pps.*); also printed in Cruikshank, *Correspondence of Simcoe*, 1:38-39; and idem to idem, Aug. 5, 1791, *R.H.M.C.R. Fortescue Pps.*, 2:157-58. Colquhoun saw Grenville next day. His letter of August 8, 1791, ibid., p. 160, urged the Foreign Secretary to receive young Nathaniel Cutting, sometime law student in London and friend of Colonel Smith, then on the point of returning to the

United States. By this time, there were unmistakeable signs that Grenville was growing annoyed with Colquhoun's persistence.

43. Home Secretary Dundas to Grenville, Jan. 5, 1792, *R.H.M.C.R., Fortescue Pps.*, 2:249, urging Colquhoun's appointment to the American consular service because he was in financial difficulties and possessed the esteem of his fellow merchants in Glasgow. Grenville, probably reflecting annoyance stemming from the earlier episode, replied crisply that there was no vacancy in America, and even if there were, he doubted circumstances would allow him to nominate Colquhoun.

44. Beckwith to Grenville, July 31, 1791, F.O. 4/12, fols. 139-44. Grenville had expressed the hope to Smith that the Americans would not seek to extirpate the Indians, as Britain could not remain indifferent to such a policy. When Smith replied that the depredations of the savages along the frontier made war against them necessary, Grenville responded that he "hoped the States would consider of it," a remark which, according to Beckwith, Hamilton found liable to a sinister interpretation. It would be a misfortune, Hamilton said to Beckwith, if the fair prospect of an Anglo-American settlement were to be blasted by "this comparatively trivial" matter. (The Hamilton-Beckwith exchange took place on June 15, 1791.) See also Beckwith to Grenville, June 14, 1791, ibid., fols. 132-34. For evidence of yet another informal approach by a British agent, see appendix F.

45. Jefferson's draft memorandum is July (13), 1791, Jefferson MSS, Lib. Cong., vol. 65, fol. 11388.

46. Beckwith claimed some success in countering Jefferson on his tour. See his dispatch, July 31, 1791, F.O. 4/12, fols. 146-50. Jay also pressed Beckwith for American entry into British West Indian ports. The Major's last dispatch was to Dorchester, Dec. 2, 1791, F.O. 4/11, fols. 181-82, after the arrival of Minister George Hammond. It dealt with Indian troubles along the Georgia frontier. Dundas subsequently instructed Dorchester to recall Beckwith to Quebec or to send him to England, as the agent himself might desire. In response to Dundas' request for a recommendation of a proper mark of the royal favor for a successful mission, Dorchester suggested promotion to lieutenant colonel, a rank which was immediately bestowed upon the agent.

47. Bond to Grenville, Mar. 14, 1791, F.O. 4/9, fols. 191-94, written after the end of the session of Congress on March 3.

CHAPTER 7

1. "Minutes of the Committee for Trade," Add. MSS 38391. See also William Fawkener to Leeds, June 18, 1789, F.O. 4/7, fols. 115-16; and Leeds to Temple, Miller, and Bond (draft), June 30, 1789, complying with the committee's request, ibid., fols. 118-22.

2. Hawkesbury to Wilckens, Sept. 23, 1789, Add. MSS 38310, fols. 42-43. He cautioned, however, that "this should arise from themselves, and not from any suggestion of mine. I beg therefore you would not make any mention of what I am now writing to you."

3. Hawkesbury to Wilckens, Jan. 25, 1790, ibid., fol. 47. See, too, Wilckens to Hawkesbury, Feb. 11 and Mar. 24, 1790, Add. MSS 38225, fols. 36-37 and 106-7, urging immediate retaliation against the Americans.

4. Bond to Hawkesbury, Aug. 15, 1789, F.O. 4/7, fols. 164-66.

5. The reference was made on Sept. 30, 1789. See P.R.O., P.C. 1/62/B18. The committee began its deliberations within the week, merging them with those begun on June 9. The minutes are Add. MSS 38391.

6. Wilckens to Hawkesbury, Feb. 11, 1790, Add. MSS 38225, fols. 36-37, and Mar. 24, 1790, ibid., fols. 106-7.

7. Jefferson, *Papers*, 16:513-23.

8. See George Chalmers to Hawkesbury, Oct. 22 and 23, 1790, Add. MSS 38225, fols. 278-81, 282-85.

9. Chalmers to Hawkesbury as cited in previous note, and further, Nov. 8, 1790, ibid., fols. 303-4. See also Undersecretary for Foreign Affairs George Aust to idem, Nov. 1, 1790, ibid., fol. 297, and Hawkesbury's undated notes, Add. MSS 38350, fols. 202-3.

10. An original copy of the Report is P.R.O., P.C. 1/19/24 A/1791 (3) Non-Colonial. A more readable contemporary copy is in F.O. 4/9, fols. 85 ff. A résumé of relevant data is to be found in appendix G.

11. Jefferson MSS, Lib. Cong., vol. 63, fols. 11159-82. It is docketed as "communicated in a Letter dated London 15th June 1791." Security of the report could not have been too great. A copy of it was sent to Bushy for the edification of the blind and ailing Lord Guilford, erstwhile Lord North. See also Jefferson to Joshua Johnson, American consul in London, Aug. 29, 1791, ibid., vol. 65, fols. 11471-73: "The paper indeed which you mention in your letter of April 18 would be worth a good deal." Fifty to a hundred guineas was mentioned as not too much for the whole of the original, but "from what I know already of it, however, I expect it cannot be obtained."

12. Patrick Colquhoun to Grenville, Nov. 15, 1791, enclosing an extract of Morris' letter from Philadelphia of August 27, 1791, *R.H.M.C.R.*, *Fortescue Pps.*, 2:228.

13. Sept. 10, 1791, F.O. 4/12, fols. 182-83.

14. Oct. 8, 1791, F.O. 4/11, fol. 81.

15. See Jefferson to William Short, Mar. 15, 1791, Jefferson MSS, Lib. Cong., vol. 62, enclosing a proposed act which would "deeply strike at that of Gr. Britain," and predicting discrimination by Congress in the autumn. If he thought it worthwhile, Short was authorized to have the proposed act printed at the public expense and circulated among members of the French National Assembly as a hint to pass a similar act. He was instructed, however, not to reveal the source of the act. See also Jefferson to Humphreys, Mar. 15, 1791, ibid., and printed in Thomas Jefferson, *Writings of Thomas Jefferson*, ed. Paul L. Ford, 10 vols. (New York, 1892-99), 6:218-20; and idem to Carmichael, Mar. 17, 1791, ibid., pp. 220-22.

16. "Minutes of the Committee," Add. MSS 38393.

17. See Thomas Walpole to the Duke of Grafton, Paris, July 30, 1784, Grafton MSS, Bury St. Edmunds, Public Record Office, no. 829. I am indebted to Ian Christie for bringing this letter to my attention, as well as Pitt's response to Grafton here quoted, Aug. 28, 1784, ibid., no. 830.

18. A humorous and malicious nomination was forthcoming from Leeds, who told Pitt that William Eden, the scheming and troublesome leader of the Opposition, should be given the mission. He would, the Duke said, "be as well *out* of England as in it," and possessed abilities "just of the nature I think fit for the business of that appointment, consisting chiefly of narrow and illiberal Intrigues." See Leeds to Pitt, Aug. 14, 1784, copy, Egerton MSS, British Museum, 3498. See also Sir James Harris to Carmarthen, Dec. 16, 1785, Add. MSS 28060, f. 512; and idem to idem, Feb. 21, 1786, Add. MSS 28061, fols. 35-36.

19. Adams to Jay, June 16, 1786, John Adams, *The Life and Works of John Adams*, ed. Charles Francis Adams, 10 vols. (Boston, 1850-56), 8:401-3.

20. See, for example, Jay to the president of Congress, Nov. 24, 1785, William Jay, *Life of John Jay*, 2 vols. (New York, 1833), 2:179-80. Joshua Johnson was appointed to London in October, 1790, and William Knox, brother of Washington's secretary of war, became consul at Dublin at about the same time.

21. Carmichael to Jefferson, San Lorenzo, Nov. 15, 1787, Jefferson, *Papers*, 12:361-65.

22. The Portuguese government was pleading the same excuse. See David Humphreys to President Washington, Lisbon, Nov. 30, 1790, Francis Landon Humphreys, *Life and Times of David Humphreys*, 2 vols. (New York, 1917), 2:65-67.

23. Leeds to Morris, Sept. 10, 1790, copy, Add. MSS 28066, fol. 259; printed in Jared Sparks, *Life of Gouverneur Morris*, 3 vols. (Boston, 1832), 2:40. See also Morris to Washington, Sept. 18, 1790, ibid., pp. 40-47; idem to Jefferson, Dec. 24 and 28, 1790, ibid., pp. 52-55 and 55-56.

24. Simcoe to Undersecretary Evan Nepean, Mar. 16, 1791, E. A. Cruikshank, ed., *The Correspondence of Lieut. Governor John Graves Simcoe, with Allied Documents*, 5 vols. (Toronto, 1923-31), 1:21.

25. Leeds to Hammond, Sept. 17, 1790, copy, Add. MSS 28066, fol. 263.

26. Grenville to Hammond, May 24, 1791, *R.H.M.C.R.*, *Fortescue Pps.*, 2:80. The rank was well below the ambassadorial level, taking precedence after that of envoy extraordinary and plenipotentiary. It was commonly reserved for relatively minor posts such as Brussels, Ratisbon, and the court of the Elector Palatine. By making Hammond minister plenipotentiary, the British government was not offering a studied mark of contempt for the

new Republic, but was merely following the precedent already established by France and the United Provinces. For the definitive treatment of British diplomatic ranks, see David Bayne Horn, *The British Diplomatic Service, 1689-1789* (Oxford, 1961).

27. Bernard Mayo, ed., *Instructions to the British Ministers to the United States* (Washington, 1941), pp. 5-8 (hereafter cited as *Instr. Brit. Min.*). Hawkesbury's draft was dated July 4, 1791. The original is in F.O. 4/10, fols. 159-61.

28. *Instr. Brit. Min.*, pp. 8-13. The original is in F.O. 4/10, fols. 149-57.

29. Hammond's "General Instructions" are in *Instr. Brit. Min.*, pp. 2-5. These were cast in the broadest terms and followed a pattern in common use for a century. The "General Instructions" were expanded through periodic additional instructions. See especially, no. 1, dated Sept. 2, 1791, F.O. 115/1, fols. 1-5. The draft is dated September 1, and is in F.O. 4/11, fols. 1-6. See also *Instr. Brit. Min.*, pp. 13-16.

30. Grenville was unable to give Hammond precise instructions on the subject for the moment "because the Expectation of Lord Dorchester's arrival in England in the course of the present Autumn has occasioned His Majesty's Servants to delay for a few weeks longer their ultimate decision on points of so much importance to the Government which has been placed under his care." Hammond was not to have it understood, however, that the delay was due to "any Disinclination to enter into discussion of the Subject, and to form a satisfactory Arrangement respecting it."

31. F.O. 4/11, fols. 7-10; *Instr. Brit. Min.*, pp. 17-19.

CHAPTER 8

1. To Edward Rutledge, Aug. 29, 1791, Thomas Jefferson, *Writings of Thomas Jefferson*, ed. Paul L. Ford, 10 vols. (New York, 1892-99), 6:309.

2. Isaac S. Harrell, *Loyalism in Virginia* (Philadelphia, 1926), pp. 161-62.

3. Ibid., p. 154. From evidence already presented, it has been proved that Harrell's assumption that "the British debts were almost always" above £10 is incorrect. His quotation of Monroe to the effect that "few British debt cases, if any, came in these courts" has another meaning than that he has assigned.

4. Ibid., pp. 162-67.

5. Society of British Merchants trading to North America (John Nutt and William Molleson for the committee) to Henry Dundas, Aug. 31, 1791, Melville MSS, Clem. Lib.; idem (John Nutt, Duncan Campbell, and William Molleson for the committee) to idem, Nov. 30, 1791, copy, ibid. See also Bond to Leeds, Nov. 4, 1790, F.O. 4/8, fol. 373.

6. William Molleson to Dundas, Dec. 1, 1791, enclosing a detailed memorandum from Cunningham, which arrived too late for inclusion in the earlier representation, Melville MSS, Clem. Lib.

7. An additional problem needing settlement was the "Northwest Boundary Gap" between the source of the Mississippi and the northwestern corner of the Lake of the Woods. It was minor, however, and did not figure significantly until the Hammond mission. (See Samuel Flagg Bemis, "Jay's Treaty and the Northwestern Boundary Gap," *American Historical Review*, 27[1921-22]:465-84.) Even then, it was strictly secondary to more important considerations.

8. James Benjamin Wilbur, *Ira Allen, Founder of Vermont*, 2 vols. (Boston, 1928), 1:522.

9. John Bartlett Brebner, *North Atlantic Triangle* (New York, 1958), p. 62.

10. Wilbur, *Ira Allen*, 1:426-33.

11. Ibid., pp. 458-59.

12. Apr. 7, 1785, ibid., p. 459.

13. Dorchester to Sydney, Apr. 10, 1787, ibid., pp. 502-3. See also Levi to Ira Allen, June, 1788, ibid., pp. 506 and 508-9.

14. Ibid., pp. 510-12.

15. Allen's memorial is dated May 3, 1789, and a copy is in F.O. 4/7, fols. 111-13. See also Wilbur, *Ira Allen*, 1:540-41. On two occasions, he asked his brothers to procure a commission for him, but none was ever forthcoming.

16. The figure was a gross exaggeration. A credible estimate for 1784 is 30,000. See

Wilbur, *Ira Allen*, 1:449. See Donald G. Creighton, *The Commercial Empire of the St. Lawrence, 1760-1850* (Toronto, 1937), pp. 104-5, who mentions the number 70,000. The first federal census in 1791 put the figure at 85,533.

17. Stephen Cottrell, secretary to the Committee for Trade, to Secretary Grenville, Apr. 17, 1790, Add. MSS 38225, fols. 162-79; printed by Frederick Jackson Turner, ed., "English Policy toward America in 1790-1791," *American Historical Review* 7 (1901-2): 706-35. Allen's communication was dated June 13, 1789.

18. To the Lords of the Committee, June 10, 1789, F.O. 4/7, fol. 110.

19. Simcoe to Evan Nepean, Dec. 3, 1789, E. A. Cruikshank, ed., *The Correspondence of Lieut. Governor John Graves Simcoe, with Allied Documents*, 5 vols. (Toronto, 1923-31), 1:7-8.

20. Simcoe to Grenville, Mar. 25, 1790, Boc. H., Gren. Pps. Allen's new memorial is Mar. 3, 1790, ibid. In addition to eternal neutrality, Vermont would wish, according to Allen, to "receive" an Anglican bishop and a college. His own candidate for the episcopal office was the much-seeking Reverend Samuel Peters, described by his sponsor as "a uniform Loyalist, and not a Jacobite, nor a Chaplain of Congress." Vermont would bind herself to form no "civil Connections" with the United States.

21. See Evan Nepean to Hawkesbury, Apr. 1, 1790, Add. MSS 38225, fol. 130; and Simcoe to Nepean, same date, ibid., fol. 132. The report is in the form of a letter from Stephen Cottrell to Foreign Secretary Grenville, and is printed by Turner, "English Policy Toward America." It is probable that Grenville himself drafted the letter. In the Grenville Papers at Boconnoc House is a draft in his hand headed "the request of the Vermonters," containing most of the major points, including suspicion of Allen's motives, which later appeared in Cottrell's communication. See also in the same collection a memorandum on Vermont, April 3, 1790, listing pertinent official correspondence relating to the province.

22. My italics.

23. Wilbur, *Ira Allen*, 1:540. Alfred Le Roy Burt, *The United States, Great Britain, and British North America* (New Haven, 1940), pp. 109-10, occupies weak ground on three points: first, by assuming that British policy toward the United States in the Nootka crisis reflected a conviction that the Republic could be disregarded in dealing with Spain in the event of war; secondly, in having the British ministry interpret the Morris mission as betraying an American "leaning toward London"; and, finally, by reading the "central idea" of Grenville's dispatches of May 6, 1790, as "the preservation of the posts." There was bigger game in the woods.

Samuel Flagg Bemis, "The Vermont Separatists and Great Britain, 1789-1791," *American Historical Review* 21(1916): 547-60, sees a deliberate British plot in keeping Allen dangling in London until the issue of war or peace with Spain was decided. Grenville received information from Hamilton, via Beckwith in the United States, "that the United States would not go to war over the question of the posts, even should Spain and Britain come to grips." The Foreign Secretary was thus able to discount Morris' threats and to refuse further favors to Allen and Vermont. Professor Bemis' version needs some correction, particularly in the light of the chronology of relevant events. Cottrell's letter for the committee in April and Grenville's dispatches to Dorchester in May, 1790, were written while the Nootka crisis was building to a denouement. The policy toward Vermont was thus effectually laid down barring *any* favors to Vermont beyond the treatment extended to the United States in the inland trade. It was a bitter blow to Simcoe and Allen, the latter inveighing against "lessening the favour done Vermont by making the same cheap, in bestowing it on undeserving Enemies unmasked." See Allen to Simcoe, Apr. 24, 1790, Gren. Pps., Boc. H., who passed it on to Grenville. See also the bitter letter of Sir Henry Clinton to idem, Apr. 26, 1790, Simcoe MSS, Clem. Lib.: "Oeconomy and Commerce are the Stalking Horses of the Times; to name political connection with V[ermon]t is thought dangerous, and yet it must be named, followed up, and the consequences risked even if it engages us in a war of short duration as of certain success, for by that means we may avoid one (ten years hence) durable and doubtfull." The military mind is at its most dangerous when laying down lines of political policy.

Allen had to be persuaded by Simcoe to remain in London after Cottrell's letter. On the eve of the public explosion of the Nootka crisis, his bitterness was unabated. See Allen to Simcoe, May 1, 1790, Gren. Pps., Boc. H.: "We are commanded to rejoice in the day of Prosperity, and to consider in the day of adversity. I have considered a long time, and am prepared to rejoice in running a course *with the Strong Man*." British policy had no use for a backwoods Sforza. Morris' "veiled threats" were delivered on May 21. Hamilton did not discuss American policy toward Spain with Beckwith until the following July, and the Major's account could not have arrived in Britain until mid-August.

24. The old article by Frederick Jackson Turner, "The Diplomatic Contest for the Mississippi," *Atlantic Monthly* 93 (1904): 676-91, 807-17, remains useful. More recent valuable studies of the American West at this time are Arthur Burr Darling, *Our Rising Empire* (New Haven, 1940), and Richard Warner Van Alstyne, *American Diplomacy in Action* (Stanford, 1947). See also the latter's *The Rising American Empire* (Oxford, 1960), pp. 71-75.

25. The copy is preserved in the Gren. Pps., Boc. H. Watson described the author as "a Gentleman well informed of what passes in the States and capable of Judging what may follow."

26. Turner, "Diplomatic Contest," p. 679. The French memorial in Grenville's possession is in the Gren. Pps., Boc. H., and is attached to the "Desultory Reflections."

27. Van Alstyne, *Rising American Empire*, p. 74; Darling, *Our Rising Empire*, p. 120.

28. To Carmarthen, Nov. 17, 1787, F.O. 4/5, fols. 359-60.

29. The memorandum is dated May 6, 1790, and is in the Gren. Pps., Boc. H.

30. It is dated May 26, 1790, and is in ibid.

31. To Leeds (Carmarthen), Philadelphia, Jan. 3, 1791, F.O. 4/9, fols. 19-22.

32. See Jefferson's "Opinion on War between Great Britain and Spain," July 12, 1790, Jefferson, *Writings*, 6:90-95. James Madison concurred. See also Jefferson's response to Washington's question on the possibility of Dorchester's moving across American territory to attack the Spanish, Jefferson, *Papers*, 17:129-30.

33. Jefferson to William Carmichael, New York, Aug. 2, 1790, Jefferson, *Writings*, 6:111-14. The dispatch was carried by David Humphreys. The even more bellicose draft is the same date, Jefferson MSS, Lib. Cong., vol. 56, fols. 2678-79. See also the dispatch to William Short in Paris, Aug. 10, 1790, Jefferson, *Writings*, 6:114-18. Short was told to be "in some degree on your guard" with the French, as Jefferson was suspicious of that government's intentions in the Louisiana country.

CHAPTER 9

1. See Samuel Eliot Morison's introductory essay in his *Sources and Documents Illustrating the American Revolution* (Oxford, 1929), pp. xxx-xxxii.

2. Quoted by Richard Warner Van Alstyne, *The Rising American Empire* (Oxford, 1960), pp. 72-73.

3. See Alfred Le Roy Burt, *The Old Province of Quebec* (Minneapolis, 1933), pp. 335, 337; Van Alstyne, *Rising American Empire*, p. 72.

4. Burt, *Old Province of Quebec*, pp. 352-53. See also Sydney Papers (Secret Service Payments), Clem. Lib., showing disbursement to Brant of £1,449-14-9d. "in consideration of injuries sustained by him and his Sister from the depredations of the American troops during the late war."

5. Quoted extensively by Burt, *Old Province of Quebec*, p. 342.

6. Ibid., p. 353.

7. Ibid.

8. Adams to Jay, Oct. 21, 1785, John Adams, *The Life and Works of John Adams*, ed. Charles Francis Adams, 10 vols. (Boston, 1850-56), 3:326; ibid., pp. 357-58.

9. Morris to Washington, Sept. 18, 1790, Jared Sparks, *Life of Gouverneur Morris*, 3 vols. (Boston, 1832), 2:43.

10. Hamilton to Washington, memorandum on Beckwith's communication of July 8, 1790, Alexander Hamilton, *Works of Alexander Hamilton*, ed. Henry Cabot Lodge, 12 vols. (New York, 1904), 4:296-99.

11. Hamilton to Washington, July 22, 1790, ibid., p. 301.

12. Quoted by Irving Brant, *James Madison*, 5 vols. (New York, 1941-56), 1:337.

13. Thomas Jefferson, *Writings of Thomas Jefferson*, ed. Paul L. Ford, 10 vols. (New York, 1892-99), 6:143-44.

14. Jan. 3, 1791, F.O. 4/9, ff. 19-20.

15. Jan. 20, 1791, E. A. Cruikshank, ed., *The Correspondence of Lieut. Governor John Graves Simcoe, with Allied Documents*, 5 vols. (Toronto, 1923-31), 1:19.

16. The best account of the course of the Nootka crisis is still Hubert Howe Bancroft, *History of the Northwest Coast*, The Works of H. H. Bancroft, vols. 27 and 28 (San Francisco, 1884). See especially 27:185-359.

17. The standard biography is William S. Robertson, *Life of Miranda*, 2 vols. (Chapel Hill, N.C., 1929).

18. Ibid., 1:110. In his talks with British ministers, Miranda revealed that he counted to a certain degree on American cooperation in the British-sponsored revolution against Spain; but Washington's secretary of war, General Knox, while answering Miranda's letter affably enough, did not encourage him to believe that the United States would give up its neutrality in the Nootka crisis. The collapse of Miranda's scheme saw him cast in the role of impecunious solicitor for ministerial favors. Pitt gave him £500 in July, 1791, and a cold brush-off when he asked a pension of the outrageous amount of £1,200 per annum. After leaving Britain, he "promoted" a commission as major-general in the armies of Girondist France. The rank was obviously far above the level of his military abilities, as the subsequent course of his exploits proved.

19. The standard biography is John W. Caughey, *McGillivray of the Creeks* (Norman, Okla., 1938).

20. Ibid., p. 36. See Frederick Jackson Turner, ed., "English Policy Toward America in 1790-1791," *American Historical Review*, 7(1902):706-35; 8(1902):78-86.

21. Panton to Miro, printed *in extenso*, with many related documents, in Caughey, *McGillivray*, pp. 295-97.

22. Ibid., p. 44; and McGillivray's apologia to Miro, Feb. 26, 1791, ibid., pp. 288-91.

23. Viar to Zespedes' successor as governor of East Florida, Quesada, Apr. 13, 1790, ibid., pp. 276-77; and Carlos Howard to idem, Sept. 24, 1790, ibid., pp. 281-84.

24. The memorial is in the name of the entire "delegation." See F.O. 4/9, fols. 5-6.

25. Jan. 13, 1791, ibid., fols. 69-74.

26. Jan. 14, 1791, copy, private, Boc. H., Gren. Pps.

27. Caughey, *McGillivray*, pp. 277-78, 255.

28. Beckwith to Dorchester, Philadelphia, Dec. 2, 1791, F.O. 4/11, fols. 181-82; and Dec. 8, 1791, ibid., fols. 207-8.

29. Grenville to Hammond, F.O. 4/14, fol. 13.

30. Cruikshank, *Correspondence of Simcoe*, 1:17-19, 21, 27-34. Clinton warned Simcoe of American intentions in his letter of July 24, 1791, Simcoe MSS, Clem. Lib.: "Get you gone, my good friend, to your Government. The present state of Europe gives you a *Lull*. Don't neglect the moment; depend upon it, the instance the[y] dare, America will pick a quarrel with you; the influence which your present situation in that continent gives you over her provinces west of Allegany Mountains and with which she has as little connection while you hold Canada, as Piedmont has with Italy, will render her a restless neighbour."

31. *Instr. Brit. Min.*, pp. 13-17.

32. To Dorchester, Sept. 16, 1791, Cruikshank, *Correspondence of Simcoe*, 1:66-68.

33. On December 9, 1791, the merchants of Montreal memorialized Simcoe, urging a revision of the Canadian-American boundary by establishing it at the Ohio, or, if, as seemed to them inconceivable, the government intended to surrender the posts, then to gain several years for the evacuation. See ibid., pp. 91-94. Simcoe was habitually suspicious and contemptuous of merchant attempts of this sort, however, even when their representations supported policies which he himself favored. See also Charles Stevenson to Evan Nepean, New York, Jan. 11, 1792, ibid., p. 102.

CHAPTER 10

1. *Morn. Chron.*, Apr. 22, Aug. 30, 1785; Dec. 8, 1787; July 22, Oct. 3 and 24, 1788; and *Public Advertiser*, Dec. 2, 1789, Jan. 22, May 23, 1791.

2. Apr. 5, 1791, Hamilton MSS, Lib. Cong., vol. 11.

3. *Public Advertiser*, Dec. 2 and 8, 1789, June 24, 1791; and *Morn. Chron.*, Oct. 15, 1791.

4. *Public Advertiser*, Jan. 14, May 23, Dec. 12, 1791. See also the *Morning Post and Daily Advertiser*, July 15, 1791.

5. See appendixes A and E.

6. Temple to Leeds, Oct. 10, 1789, F.O. 4/7, fols. 222-23.

7. *Public Advertiser*, June 24, 1791. The volume of British trade with the European continent was increasing, too; but it was falling in proportion to Britain's trade with America, Ireland, and other non-European countries. See John Ehrman, *The British Government and Commercial Negotiations with Europe, 1783-1793* (Cambridge, 1962), p. 202.

8. *Morn. Chron.*, July 27, 1791. Compare these figures with Vincent T. Harlow, *The Founding of the Second British Empire, 1763-1793* (London, 1952), p. 486, n. 60; and Samuel Flagg Bemis, *Jay's Treaty: A Study in Commerce and Diplomacy* (New York, 1923), p. 33. Harlow, *Second British Empire*, p. 486, n. 60, gives the figures for American imports in 1790.

9. July 28, 1791.

10. Donald G. Creighton, *The Commercial Empire of the St. Lawrence, 1760-1850* (Toronto, 1937), pp. 104-5; Gerald S. Graham, *Sea Power and British North America, 1783-1820* (Cambridge, Mass., 1941), pp. 87-88.

11. To Sydney, Quebec, June 13, 1787, Howard Adams Innis and A. R. M. Lower, eds., *Select Documents in Canadian Economic History, 1497-1783* (Toronto, 1929), pp. 320-21.

12. Add. MSS 38310, fol. 4. See also "Minutes of the Committee," ibid. 38390. On August 18, 1787, George Rose, secretary of the Treasury, wrote to the committee raising the question of the legal status of American produce imported into Canada and subsequently sent on to Britain. An answer was given on August 21, stating that if any doubts should arise, that is, if a test case were actually brought, the opinion of the law officers would be taken as a preliminary to issuing a new Order in Council on the subject. This actually occurred in 1790, when the law officers reported that no law existed distinguishing between goods which were the growth and produce of foreign states in North America and territories of Great Britain when imported into the mother country. The ruling provision was that such goods should be brought from the ports of the British colony in America in British vessels, navigated according to law.

The Committee for Trade never deviated from the opinion that it was advisable both commercially and politically to permit and even to encourage all produce which was the growth of countries bordering Canada to be brought into the province and exchanged for British manufactures, and exported from Canada in British ships to any European or American ports where Canadian produce could legally be received.

13. Quoted by Graham, *Sea Power*, pp. 88-89.

14. Add. MSS 38347, fols. 350-55, undated, but obviously the "Report of February 5, 1785," mentioned in that of January 14, 1786.

15. See part 1, chapter 1.

16. Minutes of the meeting of Feb. 9, 1788, Add. MSS 38391. Testimony was taken from Canadian merchants, Adam Lymburner, Fraser, Lindsay, and Aldjo, and from London merchants trading to Canada, Dyer, Hunter, Patterson, and Brickwood.

17. Minutes of meetings of Feb. 9 and Mar. 7, 1789, ibid.

18. See Richard Routh to Hawkesbury, Poole, Feb. 28, 1789, Add. MSS 38224, fol. 21; and idem to idem, Feb. 7, 1791, ibid. 38226, fol. 55.

19. Minutes of meeting of Mar. 14, 1789, Add. MSS 38391.

20. Hawkesbury to Dorchester, June 16, 1789, copy, Add. MSS 38224, fols. 163-64.

21. W. W. Grenville to Hawkesbury, July 15, 1789, ibid., fol. 214; July 16, ibid., fol. 215, announcing he had brought in the bill.

22. Minutes of meeting of Jan. 30, 1792, Add. MSS 38392.

23. Creighton, *Commercial Empire*, pp. 120-22.

24. Add. MSS 38349, fols. 92-111, undated, but clearly in the first half of 1788.

25. Because prices were always lower in America and in the Baltic than in Britain, however, the bounty on export of British grain until the price of 44/ was reached and the restriction of the import of foreign grain until the price of 48/ had been reached were to continue in order to allow British grain to compete with the cheaper foreign produce. See Henry Wilckens to Hawkesbury, Mar. 29, May 20, 1789, Add. MSS 38224, fols. 63-64, 135-36.

26. William Fawkener, for the Privy Council, to Carmarthen, June 25, 1788, F.O. 4/6, fol. 191.

27. Jefferson to Benjamin Vaughan, May 17, 1789, Jefferson, *Papers*, 15:133-34. Jefferson's extracts of Paine's letters, Mar. 12 and Apr. 10, 1789, are in Jefferson MSS, Lib. Cong.

28. July 13, 1789, F.O. 4/7, fols. 137-38.

29. To Carmarthen (Leeds), Nov. 3, 1788, F.O. 4/6, fols. 301-2.

30. See the testimony of the London corn factor, Claude Scott, before the Committee for Trade, minutes of meeting of Feb. 9, 1789, Add. MSS 38391.

31. F.O. 4/7, fol. 353.

32. Ibid., fol. 364.

33. Minutes of meeting of Nov. 27, 1789, Add. MSS 38349, fol. 303; Fawkener to Undersecretary Burges, Dec. 3, 1789, F.O. 4/7.

34. Mar. 1, 1790, Philadelphia, F.O. 4/8, fols. 177-79.

35. Jefferson to President Washington, Apr. 17, 1791, Thomas Jefferson, *Writings of Thomas Jefferson*, ed. Paul L. Ford, 10 vols. (New York, 1892-99), 6:243-47. See also idem to McHenry, Mar. 28, 1791, Jefferson MSS, Lib. Cong.

36. *Parl. Hist.*, 29:161-62. See also the *Public Advertiser*, Aug. 26, 1790.

CHAPTER 11

1. Dec. 12, 1791.

2. *Public Advertiser*, Aug. 10 and 12, 1792.

3. Beckwith to Grenville, Philadelphia, Sept. 10, 1791, F.O. 4/11, fols. 46-50. Beckwith reported that the shares in the National Bank had been taken up immediately by the investors, and would have been even though the capital had been twice the amount. See also Sir John Temple to idem, Sept. 2, 1791, ibid., fol. 37.

4. *Public Advertiser*, Oct. 25, 1791.

5. The data upon which I have based my treatment of British investment in the American national debt are derived from the meticulous and voluminous notes compiled by my once and future colleague Paul B. Trescott, professor-designate of economics and history at Southern Methodist University. I express thanks for his generosity. The records which Professor Trescott studied are in the National Archives, Washington, D.C. Material from Pennsylvania's Central Office is missing until 1797. All offices kept individual records; and, unfortunately, there was no central compilation.

The figures are face, not real, value. Face value fluctuated from time to time. Convenient studies comparing real and face values are Joseph Stancliffe Davis, *Essays in the Earlier History of American Corporations*, 2 vols. (Cambridge, Mass., 1917), 1:340; and Walter Buckingham Smith and Arthur Harrison Cole, *Fluctuations in American Business, 1790-1860* (Cambridge, Mass., 1935). The use here of face value does not affect the major contention: that important quantities of British capital were invested in the debt. A measure of comparison is furnished when it is recalled that American exports from August, 1789, to September, 1790, amounted to about $20.5 million.

6. Samuel Eliot Morison, *The Maritime History of Massachusetts, 1783-1860* (Boston, 1921), pp. 44-51. See also Gouverneur Morris to Jay, Nov. 27, 1783, William Jay, *Life of John Jay*, 2 vols. (New York, 1833), 2:138-39; and Temple to Carmarthen, Dec. 7, 1785, F.O. 4/3, fol. 33; and Jan. 5, 1786, F.O. 4/4, fol. 2. See, too, "P. Allaire" (to Sir George Yonge), "Occurances," May 3 to June, 1787, F.O. 4/3, fols. 153-62, enclosed in Yonge to Undersecretary Fraser, July 1, 1787, ibid., fol. 147.

7. Bond to Carmarthen, May 17 and July 2, 1787, F.O. 4/5, fols. 141-42 and 190-92.

8. Bond to Carmarthen, Nov. 20, 1787, ibid., fols. 371-74; Temple to idem, New York, Apr. 3, 1788, F.O. 4/6, fol. 113; Bond to idem (Leeds), June 2 and July 3, 1789, F.O. 4/7, fols. 102 and 127.

9. Carmarthen to Temple, Apr. 5, 1786, F.O. 4/4, fol. 87.

10. Jan. 8, 1785, P.R.O., C.O. 5/272, fols. 466-67. See also Charles Hamilton to George Rose, Jamaica Customs House, Mar. 2, 1785, Add. MSS 38218, suggesting the cancellation of all old registers and issuing of new ones.

11. Boc. H., Gren. Pps., undated.

12. Jan. 19, 1786, Add. MSS 34420, fols. 383-84.

13. Minutes, Jan. 20, 1786, Add. MSS 38349.

14. A copy of the main points of Anderson's testimony is June 13, (1786), Add. MSS 38346, fols. 353-54. Sheffield's warning is in Add. MSS 38347, fols. 203-4. Jenkinson's speech is cited in part 1, chapter 1, note 35.

15. To Carmarthen, Feb. 21 and May 14, 1787, F.O. 4/5, fols. 52-54 and 131-32. In his dispatch of December 29, 1787, ibid., fol. 398, Bond reported the detection of another case of fraudulent papers. He had gained possession of the documents and was forwarding them to the home government. Fearing they would be stolen from the regular post, he traveled personally to New York to put them aboard the British packet. See Bond to Carmarthen, Jan. 2, 1788, F.O. 4/6, fol. 3. For more information on illicit Anglo-American co-operation, see Gilbert Francklyn to Hawkesbury, Customs House, Jamaica, Apr. 11, 1789, Add. MSS 38224, fols. 74-84.

16. To Sir George Yonge, Dec. 6, 1786, F.O. 4/4, fols. 48-49. The owners of the American snow *Experiment* had the audacity to advertise in the Philadelphia *Independent Gazette*, November 12, 1787, that their vessel was available for sale or charter. Much was made of her Mediterranean pass. The clipping is in F.O. 4/5, fol. 377.

17. Minutes of the Committee, Add. MSS 38291.

18. Hawkesbury to Wilckens, Jan. 25, 1790, Add. MSS 38310, fol. 47. Wilckens suggested countervailing duties on American vessels. See his letter to Hawkesbury, Feb. 11, 1790, Add. MSS 38225, fols. 36-37. See, too, Edward Burrow to idem, Add. MSS 38310, fol. 62 b.

19. Bond to Leeds, Sept. 18, 1790, F.O. 4/8, fol. 348.

20. Hawkesbury to Wilckens and Wilckens to Hawkesbury, cited in note 18 above. Wilckens suggested that the practice of jumping ship in American ports—contrary to all contract stipulations, which bound seamen to a round trip— would "remain in its present state" until consuls were empowered to act in American ports, a suggestion Americans would have found very unacceptable.

21. For this and other references to Nelson's experience, see his "Narrative" of late June, 1786, in *Dispatches and Letters of Lord Nelson*, ed. Sir Nicholas H. Nicolas, 7 vols. (London, 1844), 1:171-86.

22. Francklyn to Hawkesbury, cited in note 15 above.

23. Dawson to Hawkesbury, Dec. 8, 1786, Add. MSS 38221, fols. 9-10.
Island governors held a certain discretionary power to admit American vessels to their ports. In cases of hurricane, famine, or other natural disaster, they were allowed to suspend the usual prohibition. It is often asserted that this authority was systematically abused. Thomas Irving, for example, was deeply suspicious of the frequency with which the emergency powers were used to produce an "inundation" of American vessels in the British West Indies. See his report on Hughes's dispatch, cited in note 11 above. In fact, there is little evidence of a frivolous use of the emergency powers. London kept a close eye on the islands and resolutely declined to enlarge the area of discretion. See the "Committee for Trade Report of February 14, 1786," Add. MSS 38389, reaffirming the principles of the Report of 1784 and rejecting the request from John Brathwaite, agent for the Barbadoes Assembly, "especially as the experience of Two Years has clearly shewn that the Commerce and supply of His Majesty's Islands in the West Indies have not suffered from the Regulations subsisting." Occasionally, the London government felt compelled to remind island governors of their emergency powers. See minutes of the Committee for Trade, ibid., meeting of Jan. 20, 1786; and Add. MSS 38390, meeting of May 21, 1787.

24. Meeting of Jan. 20, 1786, cited in previous note; and Elliot to Hawkesbury, July 23, 1786, Add. MSS 38119, fols. 281-82.

25. Dawson to Hawkesbury, cited in note 23. In December, 1787, a customs house was

established at Turks Island. See Add. MSS 38390, Minutes, meetings of Dec. 18 and 21, 1787.

26. Ibid., Meetings of Jan. 29 and Mar. 8, 1787. At the later meeting, the committee considered a letter from the governor of St. Vincents. See also a detailed, though anonymous, paper on the trade between North America and the West Indies, Add. MSS 38348, fols. 19-22, received from Evan Nepean on March 20, 1787. The author, obviously a West Indian with an ax to grind, argued that Jenkinson's Act had put an end to direct illicit trade. The result, he maintained, was to force the growth of indirect trade, which had delivered the islands' carrying trade into American hands. He recommended a free trade.

27. Minutes of meeting of May 21, 1787, cited in note 23.

28. Feb. 6, 1788, F.O. 4/6, fols. 44-46.

29. Gren. Pps., Boc. H., undated, but at the same time as the report on Hughes's dispatch cited in note 11 above.

30. Add. MSS 38291, Minutes, meeting of Mar. 14, 1787; Add. MSS 38390, Minutes, meeting of Aug. 29, 1787; Add. MSS 38389, Minutes, meeting of May 1, 1786; and King to Hawkesbury, Nov. 24, 1792, Add. MSS 38311, fols. 283-84.

31. There was a small illicit traffic in cotton. Rum was more important, though not as much so as tobacco. See Add. MSS 38390, meetings in April, 1787, considering a memorial from merchants trading to Africa, complaining against the introduction of American rum into British settlements there. See also Stephen Higginson of Massachusetts to John Adams, Boston, July 4, 1789, John Franklin Jameson, ed. "Higginson's Letters," *Annual Report of the American Historical Association* (1896), 1:765-67: "The British are coming fast into their old practice, of taking from hence the rum necessary for their Factories upon the Coast of Guinea." He hoped Congress would free the beverage from duty, thereby encouraging greater British consumption. See also Adams to Jefferson, July 24, 1785, Jefferson, *Papers*, 8:310-11. Hawkesbury's notes are in Add. MSS 38350, fols. 202-3, undated, but after February 2, 1790. See, finally, Bond to Carmarthen, May 17, 1787, F.O. 4/5, fols. 141-42; and idem to Fraser, June 10, 1787, ibid., fol. 175.

32. Hawkesbury to Eden, Apr. 30, 1787, Add. MSS 34423, fols. 361-62.

33. King to Hawkesbury, cited in note 31 above.

34. In July, 1787, Thomas Orde, secretary to the lord lieutenant of Ireland, forwarded to Evan Nepean a copy of a letter from Thomas Winder, secretary to the Irish commissioners of the customs, recounting the adventures of the *Penelope*. See Orde's letter of July 23, 1787, F.O. 4/5, fols. 229, 231-32. Carmarthen subsequently transmitted to Bond the thanks of the ministry. See his letter of Feb. 6, 1788, F.O. 4/6, fols. 55-56.

35. Edward Burrows to Hawkesbury, undated (1791), cited above in note 18.

36. Jan. 31, 1792, F.O. 115/1, fol. 63.

37. Hammond to Grenville, Apr. 14, 1792, F.O. 4/14, fols. 381-91; idem to Jefferson, Aug. 3, 1792, copy, F.O. 4/16, fol. 100; and idem to Grenville, New York, Aug. 2, 1792, ibid., fol. 94.

CHAPTER 12

1. Jefferson to Consul Joshua Johnson, Philadelphia, Dec. 17, 23, 1790, Thomas Jefferson, *Writings of Thomas Jefferson*, ed. Paul L. Ford, 10 vols. (New York, 1892-99), 6:170-73, 173-74; William Knox, U. S. consul at Dublin, to Pitt, Apr. 11, 1791, F.O. 4/9, fol. 232; and Undersecretary George Aust to Knox, May 16, 1791, F.O. 4/10, fol. 40. For Hamilton's actions, see Bond to Grenville, Sept. 1, 1791, F.O. 4/11, fol. 32.

2. Hammond to Grenville, Nov. 1, 1791, private, *R.H.M.C.R., Fortescue Pps.*, 2:233; idem to idem, Nov. 16, 1791, F.O. 4/11, fols. 148-50 (printed in *R.H.M.C.R., Fortescue Pps.*, 2:534-36). See, however, his private letter to Aust, same date, ibid.: "My situation has been, in many points of view, new, critical, and rather embarrasing."

3. Hammond to Grenville, Dec. 19, 1791, F.O. 4/11, fols. 255-81.

4. Jefferson, *Writings*, 6:338-39; *A.S.P.*, For. Rel., pp. 188-89.

5. *A.S.P.*, For. Rel., p. 189.

6. Dec. 5, 1791, Jefferson, *Writings*, 6:341-42. The letter is omitted from *A.S.P.*, For. Rel.

7. Dec. 6, 1791, *A.S.P.*, For. Rel., p. 189; a copy was transmitted in a dispatch to Grenville, same date, F.O. 4/11, fols. 183-93.

8. Dec. 13, 1791, *A.S.P.*, For. Rel., p. 189. See also Jefferson's notes, Dec. 12, 1791, Jefferson, *Writings*, 6:343-44.

9. Dec. 14, 1791, F.O. 4/11, fols. 183-93; Dumas Malone, *Jefferson and the Rights of Man*, vol. 2 of Jefferson and His Time (Boston, 1951), p. 412, writes that Jefferson forced Hammond "to admit that he had no authority to negotiate a treaty of commerce." This is precisely what Jefferson did *not* do, and what Hammond did *not* admit.

10. Malone, *Jefferson and the Rights of Man*, p. 398, states that the American Secretary of State "assumed that commercial negotiations with Hammond would have been entirely futile," a judgment which makes Jefferson's persistence on the point more interesting. It may be relevant, too, to note that Jefferson had had fairly recent and unpleasant dealings with his own British creditors. See ibid., p. 393.

For Jefferson's French hopes, see his "Questions to be Considered Of," Nov. 26, 1791, Jefferson, *Writings*, 6:337-38. For the impact of the Hammond negotiations on domestic American politics, see Hammond to Grenville, Dec. 19, 1791, cited in note 3 above; and Stephen Higginson to Congressman George Cabot, Boston, Jan. 2, 1792, Hamilton MSS, Lib. Cong., vol. 15, fols. 2012-15: "I expect there will be much management and much party spirit exhibited in adjusting our commercial intercourse with Britain and France." Cabot, Hamilton, and their friends would "have only right objects in view . . . but others again will enter upon it replete with prejudice and with all the zeal of party men or interested agents."

11. Hammond to Grenville, Dec. 19, 1791, cited in note 3 above. Hammond sadly underestimated Jefferson, telling Grenville: "Whatever may be that gentleman's predelictions in favor of one nation, or his prejudices against another, there seems little reason to apprehend they will materially influence his countrymen in their final decision."

12. *A.S.P.*, For. Rel., pp. 190-93, with enclosures.

13. Hammond to Grenville, November 16, 1791, cited in note 2. Letters had been sent to all British consuls in the country and to many private agents as well.

14. Malone, *Jefferson and Rights of Man*, p. 412, criticizes Hammond for taking more than three months to reply to Jefferson. From December 15, 1791, to March 5, 1792, is actually considerably less than three months—not as long, indeed, as it took Jefferson to prepare and transmit *his* reply to Hammond on May 29, 1792. Malone's judgment that "procrastination was the approved method" of Hammond's mission seems unjustified.

15. Hammond to Grenville, Jan. 9, 1792, F.O. 4/4, fols. 38-40. For early indication that Hammond was aware of the American desire to gain entry into the British West Indian ports, see idem to idem, Nov. 17, 1791, F.O. 4/11, fols. 164, 167. Perhaps at the request of Hamilton himself, Phineas Bond prepared at this time his "remarks concerning the Commercial Policy of G. Britain towards this country," Hamilton MSS, vol. 15, fols. 2021-23. The information it contained would have made an excellent rebuttal to Jefferson's expected onslaught against British commercial policy. Britain, it was pointed out, allowed importation of any unprohibited goods of American growth or manufacture, directly from the United States, in British or American bottoms navigated according to law. In addition, any American raw material, excepting fish oil, blubber, whale fins, spermaceti, pig iron, and a few other enumerated articles, could be imported into Britain on the same footing enjoyed by Britain's American colonies. All else was placed on the footing of most favored nation, except where Britain was bound to the contrary in treaties with other powers. American goods were free of Alien's Duty in Great Britain, "peculiar advantages" detrimental to foreign competitors and the British revenue. (On the single item of wood, for example, Britain derived a revenue of £300,000 on imports from nations other than the United States.) It was, in short, quite clear that Britain, "so far from being considered as the commercial Enemy of these States, has extended benefits and privileges to the Commerce of this Country which originated in colonial indulgences; nor will it be going too far to aver that Great Britain has granted America greater advantages, in point of Commerce than any other Nation in Europe can grant."

Ultimately, of course, Jefferson could not argue from the standpoint of economic interest, which was too obviously in favor of the Hamiltonian position. Hence, he was driven back upon what he considered more fundamental ground, questioning the importance of commerce itself. By the end of March, both Jefferson and Hamilton had prepared reports on American commerce with foreign powers, Hamilton warily awaiting Jefferson's publication. See Hammond to Grenville, Apr. 5, 1792, F.O. 4/14, fols. 253-55.

16. *A.S.P.*, For. Rel., pp. 193-200. Hammond is occasionally taken to task for merely listing (by title) the American Acts contravening the peace. See Malone, *Jefferson and Rights of Man*, p. 412. Jefferson himself did not object, having readily at hand or easily available eighty-one of the ninety-four items specified. See Jefferson to Hammond, Mar. 30, 1792, *A.S.P.*, For. Rel., p. 200. Malone, *Jefferson and Rights of Man*, p. 412, writes that Hammond's specifications "were not tied closely" to his charge of American infraction. It is difficult to understand the statement.

The power of Hammond's argument was implicitly recognized by Washington himself, who wrote to Jefferson almost naïvely after reading the document: "May not our loss of the Indian trade—the participation of it I mean—and the expense and losses sustain'd by the Indian War—be set against Mr. H[ammond's] list of grievances in behalf of the B. Merchants—as well as by taking our Slaves away depriving us of the means of paying debts." See Washington to Jefferson, Mar. 6, 1792, Jefferson MSS, Lib. Cong., vol. 71, fol. 12392. It is clear that the President had no thought of denying British grievances altogether.

17. *A.S.P.*, For. Rel., pp. 201-37, with sixty supporting documents. Jefferson's treatment of Hammond may well have reflected his resentment of the free and easy relationship of the Briton with Alexander Hamilton. He knew, too, precisely what Hammond thought of him. Late in March, 1792, there was a dinner, arranged with Jefferson's knowledge, at which both Hammond and Jefferson's friend, General Philemon Dickinson, the New Jersey senator, were present. Under fairly rough treatment, Hammond finally gave way to the temptation to be candid: he liked Hamilton because he was "more a man of the world than J. and I like his manners better, and can speak more freely to him. J. is in the Virginia [i.e., the debtors'] interest and that of the French. And it is his fault that we are at a distance; he prefers writing to conversing and thus it is that we are apart." The whole conversation was reported to Jefferson by the host, Senator Benjamin Hawkins, Mar. 26, 1792, Jefferson MSS, Lib. Cong., vol. 73, fols. 12575-76.

18. June 2, 1792, *A.S.P.*, For. Rel., p. 237.

19. Hammond to Grenville, June 8, 1792, F.O. 4/15, fols. 84-88.

20. Malone, *Jefferson and Rights of Man*, p. 412.

21. At the very moment Jefferson was writing, it seemed far from clear that the federal courts would give justice to British creditors. An important and precedent-setting decision in Virginia had just been postponed for the second time, although it had been solemnly promised. See Consul John Hamilton to Grenville, Norfolk, Va., July 24, 1792, Melville Papers, Clem. Lib. (hereafter cited as Melville Pps.). Hamilton feared the case "will not soon be decided without the interference of the British government."

22. Malone, *Jefferson and Rights of Man*, p. 414.

23. Hammond to Grenville, June 8, 1792, cited in note 19 above.

24. For Hamilton's attempts to moderate Jefferson's position, see Jefferson, *Writings*, 7:3-7, note. See, too, Alexander Hamilton, *Works of Alexander Hamilton*, ed. Henry Cabot Lodge, 12 vols. (New York, 1904), 6:144-45, 345-48, 354-58. For Jefferson's opinion of Hamilton's suggestion, see Jefferson, *Writings*, 7:3-8.

Alfred Le Roy Burt, *The United States, Great Britain, and British North America* (New Haven, 1940), p. 123, says that Hammond "had no power to negotiate," and that the American government "knew from the beginning" that this was so. This seems a misreading of the facts and rests ultimately on the assumption that Grenville and his colleagues were insincere in the instructions to Hammond of September 2, 1791. When he wrote his memorial, Hammond was, of course, unaware of the new instructions of March 17, 1792.

25. Jefferson to Madison, June 4, 1792, Jefferson, *Writings*, 7:100-102.

26. Hammond to Grenville, June 8, 1792, cited in note 19 above. Hammond also raised questions about the Canadian-American boundary at the St. Croix and on the Upper Mississippi. (The knowledge of the Northwestern "boundary gap" had begun to dawn.) Jefferson

assured him the United States would readily concur in "any reasonable settlement of all those subjects." Hammond wished to secure British overland access to the Mississippi, and Jefferson was not of a mind to admit a dereliction of American territory. See Burt, *United States, Great Britain*, pp. 121-22. The problem was a subordinate one, however, touching only incidentally the major point of contention: the violated treaty of peace.

27. Hammond was aware, for example, that his information about the unpaid debts was not altogether accurate, although, he told Simcoe, the total "far exceeds my expectations." See Hammond to Simcoe, Mar. 3, 1792, copy, F.O. 116/2, pp. 13-15. The original is in the Clements Library. Early in 1792, Home Secretary Dundas sent material furnished by the merchants. See Dundas to Grenville, Jan. 3, 1792, F.O. 4/14, fol. 1. With the new data before him, Hammond wrote to Grenville on April 5, 1792 (F.O. 4/14, fols. 333-34), after he had presented his memorial (which made no mention of a specific sum of unpaid debts), saying that "the amount . . . stated to be due . . . does not correspond with the information which I have been able to collect in this country, and appears to me to be somewhat exaggerated." He suggested the discrepancy was due to the calculation of interest upon interest and to the failure to deduct debts recently paid.

28. For merchant reaction to Jefferson's communication, see Dundas to Grenville, July 7, 1792, *R.H.M.C.R., Fortescue Pps.*, 2:289; Grenville to Dundas, same date, ibid., pp. 289-90; idem to idem, Aug. 4, 1792, ibid., p. 297; William Molleson to idem, Aug. 8, 1792, Melville Pps., Clem. Lib.; James Ritchie to Molleson, Glasgow, Aug. 2, 1792, enclosing a letter from his Richmond agent, all forwarded to Dundas in Molleson's letter of August 8. See, finally, Consul John Hamilton to Dundas, Apr. 4, 1792, Melville Pps., Clem. Lib., enclosing a copy of his petition, dated December 10, 1791, to the North Carolina legislature against the wartime confiscation laws which were still in effect. The legislature responded sharply: the Acts "were not only consistent with wisdom & sound policy, but with the dignity of a sovereign & independent nation laboring under the yoke of the most galling tyranny & oppression." This was as late as December 29, 1792. Hamilton also included a copy of a judgment handed down in a flagrantly collusive suit before an inferior court at Wilkes, Georgia, in the autumn of 1792, between one of his debtors and the man's son-in-law. The object was for Hamilton's debtor to divest himself of some £5,000 worth of property to avoid a judgment of execution.

29. Grenville to Hammond, Aug. 4, 1792, F.O. 4/16; printed in *Instr. Brit. Min.*, pp. 30-31.

30. To Dundas, Aug. 14, 1792, Melville Pps., Clem. Lib. See also, Bond to Grenville, Oct. 12, 1792, F.O. 4/16, fols. 194-206; printed in *Annual Report of the American Historical Association*, 1897, pp. 500-523. For some reason, Bond's final report was not presented to Grenville until November 23.

31. Hammond to Grenville, Oct. 3, 1792, F.O. 4/16, fols. 167-68.

32. Hammond to Grenville, Jan. 1, 1793, F.O. 5/1, fol. 29.

33. Jefferson sent circular letters to foreign ministers accredited to the United States in February, 1793, announcing that he had compiled the report requested of him by Congress, but requesting, too, comments, private and informal, on the extract pertaining to the recipient's own nation. See Jefferson, *Writings*, 7:234-39. The extract on Britain was by far the longest and dwelt in detail on that country's duties and burdens on the trade of the United States. British favors were slighted. Much was made of the failure to secure British trade relations with the United States "by standing Laws" and of a dependence on royal proclamation "subject every moment to be withdrawn on that single will."

34. Hammond to Grenville, Mar. 7, 1793, F.O. 5/1, ff. 100-117, with enclosures. See, too, Jefferson to Washington, Feb. 16, 1793, Jefferson, *Writings*, 7:239-40.

35. Grenville informed Hammond in a dispatch of August 21, 1792, *Instr. Brit. Min.*, p. 32, that the British ambassador had been ordered home from Paris. Early in the following January, he wrote that the continuation of peace with France was very doubtful. The French declaration came on February 1, and Grenville transmitted the information to Hammond on the 8th, the day the news arrived in Britain. Intelligence reached the United States in the following April.

CHAPTER 13

1. Alfred Le Roy Burt, *The United States, Great Britain, and British North America* (New Haven, 1940), pp. 117-18. The second standard account is "The Frontier Crisis," chap. 8 in Samuel Flagg Bemis, *Jay's Treaty: A Study in Commerce and Diplomacy* (New York, 1923).

2. F.O. 116/2.

3. Hammond to Grenville, Jan. 9, 1792, F.O. 4/14, fols. 38-40.

4. Instructions of Mar. 17, 1792, *Instr. Brit. Min.*, pp. 25-27. The draft is F.O. 4/14, fols. 258-62. See also Dorchester to Grenville, Mar. 14, 1792, ibid., fol. 243, who read the draft and called it "perfectly proper." See idem to Dundas, Mar. 23, 1792, ibid., fols. 266-70, in which he wrote that there could be no stronger proof of the King's "disinterested Liberality" toward both Indians and Americans than the willingness to give up the posts to facilitate the creation of a barrier state. See Burt, *United States, Great Britain*, p. 119, and Bemis, *Jay's Treaty*, p. 117. Dundas was solicitous that territory assigned to the Indians should be "most considerable in such points of His Majesty's frontier as from their situation are most obvious to attack or interruption from any Quarter belonging to the American States." See Dundas to Dorchester, Mar. 15, 1792, quoted by Bemis, ibid., p. 118.

5. It is printed in Bemis, *Jay's Treaty*, opposite p. 119.

6. Hammond to Grenville, June 8, 1792, F.O. 4/15, fols. 288-95; and idem to Simcoe, Apr. 21, 1792, Simcoe Papers, Clem. Lib., F.O. 116/2, p. 32.

7. Quoted by Bemis, *Jay's Treaty*, p. 114.

8. Hammond to Grenville, June 8, 1792, cited in note 6 above.

9. See Burt, *United States, Great Britain*, pp. 130-31.

10. Quoted by Bemis, *Jay's Treaty*, p. 116.

11. Hammond to Grenville, Feb. 2, 1792, F.O. 4/14, fol. 153; idem to Simcoe, Mar. 3, 1792, Simcoe Pps., Clem. Lib. A copy is F.O. 116/2, pp. 13-15. Hammond added: "I do not imagine that England will ever consent to gratify their wishes to the extent which they expect, but I presume that some modification may be practicable."

12. Ironically, American suspicions were fed by loose talk from Dorchester's subordinates. Washington to Jefferson (Mar. 7, 1792), Jefferson MSS, Lib. Cong., vol. 71, fol. 12398, enclosing the extract of a letter dated Kanandaique, February 25, 1792. Washington noted the report (from the neighborhood of Niagara) that the British at Kanandaique "hold out this idea, that the U.S. will not be able to refund the confiscated tory estates— therefore a new boundary line must be made," and that Hammond was in Philadelphia for the purpose.

13. Hammond to Grenville, Feb. 2, 1792, F.O. 4/14, fol. 153; printed in *R.H.M.C.R., Fortescue Pps.*, 2:254.

14. Jefferson to Hammond, Feb. 2, 1792, F.O. 4/14, fol. 131.

15. Mar. 16, 1792, F.O. 116/2, pp. 19-22. Hammond mentioned in particular one Peter Pond at Niagara. Two weeks later, the envoy made another disclaimer, to which Jefferson replied suavely and insincerely that his government felt "perfect satisfaction" with the British role. See Hammond to Jefferson, Mar. 30, 1792, Jefferson MSS, Lib. Cong., vol. 73, fols. 12585-86; and Jefferson's reply Mar. 31, 1792, copy, ibid., fol. 12590.

16. Burt, *United States, Great Britain*, p. 118; Bemis, *Jay's Treaty*, pp. 113-14.

17. Hammond to Grenville, June 8, 1792, cited in note 6 above.

18. Hammond to Grenville, June 12, 1792, F.O. 4/15, fols. 306-9. See also Bemis, *Jay's Treaty*, p. 121.

19. Hammond to Grenville, June 8, 1792, cited in note 6 above.

20. Hammond to Simcoe, Apr. 21, 1792, cited in note 6 above.

21. Instructions of Apr. 25, 1792, *Instr. Brit. Min.*, pp. 27-29. Grenville included instructions dealing with revisions of the frontier on Lake Champlain and the river St. Croix. It was also "an object of the greatest Importance" to secure, "if possible," free and uninterrupted communication between the Lakes and the Mississippi. He concluded with a reference to loyalists and debts somewhat firmer than in the preceding instructions, although he claimed to be merely restating the earlier set. In his negotiations, Hammond would "advert to the necessity . . . of including in any agreement . . . a Stipulation for the Execution

of those articles of the Treaty which relate to the Loyalists and British Creditors, as far as the Circumstances of the present Time render it practicable." It is very doubtful that even the sanguine British government, urged on in its euphoria by Dorchester, could have considered it a serious possibility that the United States would admit British mediation, agree to a cession of territory, *and* compensate loyalists and creditors. Grenville was setting up a bargaining position. The concluding clause provided the means for a graceful retreat.

22. To Grenville, June 8, 1792, cited in note 6 above.

23. To Grenville, July 3, 1792, F.O. 4/16. See Bemis, *Jay's Treaty*, p. 122. Toward the end of April, a group of Montreal merchants memorialized Simcoe, stating anew their opinion that Canadian security and their own commerce would be forwarded by a retention of the posts. The measure would constitute a commutation of American indemnification to the pre-war creditors (and, presumably, the British government would undertake to provide payment). If it were impossible to retain the posts permanently, however, the merchants wished "a proposal of neutrality or reciprocity of Trade with the Indians" on both sides of the boundary line. See E. A. Cruikshank, ed., *The Correspondence of Lieut. Governor John Simcoe, with Allied Documents*, 5 vols. (Toronto, 1923-31), 1:133-37. Hammond, to whom Simcoe sent the memorial, called the proposal "somewhat remarkable" in view of a recent comment from Hamilton that the United States government would consent to grant the very liberty now requested by the Montreal merchants.

Obviously, neither Hamilton nor the merchants were thinking in terms of an Indian barrier; and both expected a cession of the posts.

24. He informed Simcoe and Clarke of his decision in a dispatch of July 11, 1792, F.O. 116/2, pp. 43-51.

25. Ibid.

26. *Instr. Brit. Min.*, pp. 30-31. As late as July 12, Dundas was still assuming that there was a serious chance of success for the Indian barrier state. See his dispatch to Simcoe, Cruikshank, *Correspondence of Simcoe*, 1:178-79.

27. Hammond to Clarke and Simcoe, July 11, 1792, cited in note 24 above.

28. Hammond to Clarke, Apr. 21, 1792, F.O. 116/2, pp. 26-31; Simcoe Pps., Clem. Lib.

29. Clarke to Simcoe, Montreal, June 17, 1792, Cruikshank, *Correspondence of Simcoe*, 1:166-67. See also Simcoe to Dundas, June 21, 1792, ibid., pp. 171-73; and Clarke to Simcoe, Aug. 7, 1792, ibid., pp. 188-89.

30. Simcoe to McKee, Aug. 30, 1792, quoted at length by Bemis, *Jay's Treaty*, pp. 130-31, and by Burt, *United States, Great Britain*, pp. 124-25.

31. Oct. 19, 1792, F.O. 116/2, pp. 64-69; printed in Cruikshank, *Correspondence of Simcoe*, 1:233-34.

32. Nov. 17, 1792, Cruikshank, *Correspondence of Simcoe*, 1:262.

33. Nov. 27, 1792, F.O. 116/2, pp. 71-79.

34. Dec. 4, 1792, F.O. 4/16, fols. 272-75.

35. Hammond to Grenville, Jan. 1, 1793, F.O. 5/1, fols. 50-56. Jefferson asked permission for his government to buy provisions in Canada to feed the coming council, a traditional Indian perquisite, because the Lakes would furnish the best transportation in the spring. Hammond stated his opinion that the request would be granted. He was wrong; but it is equally wrong to see Simcoe's refusal of Jefferson's request as a violation of Hammond's "assurance." See Bemis, *Jay's Treaty*, p. 132, n. 56. Simcoe's action was the direct result of advice from Joseph Brant, who told him that if the United States were allowed to provision the council, the Indians would feel their bargaining position compromised. Simcoe also suspected that the American request was related to more sinister intentions in the Old Northwest. The governor of Upper Canada decided to supply provisions himself. See Simcoe to Hammond, Jan. 21, 1793, copy, F.O. 116/3, pp. 113-18. Hammond subsequently explained to Hamilton that Simcoe was not seeking to impede the Sandusky negotiations; but the latter brusquely replied that while he personally might understand, it would be difficult to explain to the American people. See Hammond to Grenville, Mar. 7, 1793, F.O. 5/1, fol. 118.

36. Jan. 5, 1793, F.O. 116/2, pp. 80-84.

37. May 2, 1793, Cruikshank, *Correspondence of Simcoe*, 1:326-27.

38. Aug. 24, 1793, ibid., 2:40-44.

39. See Burt, *United States, Great Britain*, pp. 126-27. The territorial limits laid down in the Treaty of Fort Harmar were along the shore of Lake Erie between the Cuyahoga and Maumee Rivers, and southward to include approximately the northwestern third of the modern state of Ohio. See Bemis, *Jay's Treaty*, p. 163.

40. Dundas to Simcoe, May 2, 1793, cited in note 37. Colonel McKee's presence at Sandusky was approved "provided no circumstances should be stated to you by Mr. Hammond or should otherwise occur to render, in your own Judgment such a step improper."

41. Cited in note 36 above. See also Burt, *United States, Great Britain*, p. 129. The deputy superintendents were also ordered to guard to the utmost the personal safety of the American commissioners. Clarke was worried about untoward incidents. See his dispatch to Simcoe, Quebec, June 6, 1793, Cruikshank, *Correspondence of Simcoe*, 1:349. See also Burt, *United States, Great Britain*, p. 131 and n. 71, who explains the refusal of the British captain commanding the vessel Simcoe made available to the commissioners to carry the Americans to the mouth of the Maumee on August 12, on the ground of concern for their safety at the hands of the Indians.

42. The word is Bemis'. See his *Jay's Treaty*, pp. 163-64, where he writes that the commissioners "reluctantly" accepted Simcoe's hospitality, that they were "beguiled" by it, and that this pleasant captivity somehow interfered with the discharge of their duties. Burt, *United States, Great Britain*, p. 128, holds another view. To say that three responsible American officials, charged with a commission of importance from their government, could be diverted from their purpose by even the most abundant British hospitality is a curious reflection upon the competence of the commissioners. The Americans also asked Simcoe's safe conduct to the West, a military escort, and the presence of British officers at the council. See the commissioners' labored explanation for their action, quoted at length by Bemis, *Jay's Treaty*, p. 164, n. 9.

43. For a biographical study of Brant, see William Leete Stone, *Life of Joseph Brant*, 2 vols. (Albany, N.Y., 1865).

44. Burt, *United States, Great Britain*, pp. 131-32.

45. Quoted at length by Bemis, *Jay's Treaty*, pp. 116-17. McKee was clearly wrong, however, in concluding that the Indians would in the future enjoy their lands without dispute, and that their territory would "form an extensive Barrier between the British and American territory."

46. Professor Burt, whose account of the "Sandusky council," *United States, Great Britain*, pp. 126-32, I have generally followed, has exculpated the British from Professor Bemis' charges in *Jay's Treaty*, chap. 8.

47. Hammond to Grenville, Nov. 6, 1792, Hammond MSS, Clem. Lib.

48. To Jefferson, Aug. 23, 1792, Jefferson MSS, Lib. Cong., vol. 77, fols. 13331-34.

49. Sept. 25, 1793, Clinton MSS, Clem. Lib.

50. Burt, *United States, Great Britain*, p. 117.

51. Hammond to Simcoe, Apr. 21, 1792, Hammond MSS, Clem. Lib., F.O. 116/2, p. 32.

52. To Simcoe, same date, Hammond MSS, Clem. Lib.; F.O. 116/2, pp. 26-31.

53. To Secretary at War Sir George Yonge, June 17, 1792, Cruikshank, *Correspondence of Simcoe*, 1:166-67; and to Dundas, June 21, 1792, ibid., pp. 171-73.

54. Stevenson to Hammond, New York, Mar. 7, 1792, ibid., pp. 116-17; idem to Simcoe, Montreal, Mar. 27 and May 8, 1792, ibid., pp. 123-24 and 155.

55. Clinton MSS, Clem. Lib.

56. July 12, 1792, Cruikshank, *Correspondence of Simcoe*, 1:178-79. Simcoe's plan to build up the population of Upper Canada by enticing Americans to settle there was brushed aside with the brisk remark that "nothing could be more justly offensive to other Nations, especially Neighbouring States."

57. Simcoe to Clarke, Niagara, Aug. 20, 1792, ibid., pp. 199-204. Simcoe concluded in an even more impracticable vein: "Should Congress adopt a Prince of the House of Brunswick for their future President or King, the happiness of the two Nations would be interwoven and united, all jealousies removed, and the most desirable affections cemented that perhaps ever were formed between two Nations."

58. Simcoe to Hammond, replying to the latter's dispatch of July 11, 1792, ibid. A part of his argument was economic. Referring to the Report of the Board of Trade, March 7, 1768, which described the purpose of American colonization as the extension of commerce, navigation, and manufactures of the mother country, and deduced the principle that it should therefore be confined as much as possible to the seaboard, the founder of Upper Canada took issue: "But, Sir, it must be obvious to you that sooner or later, this great tract of Country will be settled, and that Power which shall command the Lakes will as inevitably possess its Commerce." It would thus be folly, he believed, to limit naval forces on the Lakes.

59. Hammond to Grenville, Nov. 6, 1792, Hammond MSS, Clem. Lib.

60. Dec. 6, 1792, Cruikshank, Correspondence of Simcoe, 1:269. Clarke, too, was urging caution, answering Simcoe's question about possible American naval armaments in the Lakes with the reminder of "the earnest desire of His Majesty and His Ministers to avoid war, and the consequence it is of to the ease and prosperity of the Canadas to cultivate peace and good understanding with our Neighbours." Dorchester's standing orders seemed sufficient answer to Simcoe's question. He relied on his colleague, however, to maintain "a decided Superiority of naval Force upon the Lakes" should the Americans begin to build. As Simcoe's letter contained "much useful information," he transmitted it to London. See Clarke to Simcoe, Quebec, Jan. 21, 1793, ibid., p. 276. To Dundas, he reported that while he felt his orders did not allow him to interrupt American naval building which "did not molest the territory or Possessions" of the king, he thought the matter sufficiently important to merit consideration by the ministry and specific orders both to himself and to Simcoe. See his dispatch of Feb. 2, 1793, enclosing Simcoe's dispatch of Nov. 25, 1792, ibid., p. 284. See also Clarke to Simcoe, June 24, 1793, ibid., pp.. 367-68, showing a distinct increase of alarm at American intentions and reiterating that force should be repelled by force.

61. To Clarke, Apr. 5, 1793, ibid., pp. 309-10.

62. To Simcoe, Quebec, May 19, 1793, ibid., pp. 331-32.

63. Burt, United States, Great Britain, p. 134, n. 74, has corrected Bemis' version in Jay's Treaty, p. 169, of Stevenson's and Simcoe's relations.

64. Stevenson to Simcoe, London, Apr. 27, June 18, and July 12, 1793, Cruikshank, Correspondence of Simcoe, 1:326-27, 358-59, and 384-85; Buckingham to Grenville, July 17, 1793, ibid., p. 391; the "Requisitions," ibid., pp. 409-13; Stevenson to Simcoe, ibid., pp. 413-14.

65. Sept. 8, 1793, draft, Simcoe MSS, Clem. Lib.; printed in Cruikshank, Correspondence of Simcoe, 3:49-50. See also Simcoe to Dundas, Sept. 20, 1793, ibid., pp. 56-65, stating the necessity of fitting out a naval port safe from American attack at Toronto.

66. Sept. 25, 1793, Clinton MSS, Clem. Lib.

67. Aug. 31, 1793, Cruikshank, Correspondence of Simcoe, 3:46.

68. Ibid., pp. 2-3.

69. Oct. 2, 1793, ibid., pp. 79-83.

70. To Dundas, Feb. 28, 1793, ibid., p. 166. He had earlier disavowed Stevenson in his letter to Clinton, cited in note 66 above.

71. Simcoe to Dorchester, Nov. 10, 1793, ibid., pp. 101-4; idem to Dundas, Dec. 15, 1793, ibid., pp. 122-23; and Dorchester to Simcoe, Feb. 17, 1794, ibid., p. 154.

CHAPTER 14

1. The subject figures in one form or another in Adams' and Morris' missions. See also William Carmichael to Jefferson, San Lorenzo, Nov. 15, 1787, Jefferson, Papers, 12:361-65, recounting a long "informal" conversation with Robert Liston, British chargé at Madrid at the time. William Eden, passing through Paris, called on Jefferson, then American minister there, to inquire about the extent of the American guarantee. He received the dash of cold water the Virginian commonly reserved for British officials. Hammond, in both the General Instructions and the first set of Additional Instructions in September, 1791, was told to inform himself of America's foreign relations, especially those with France and Spain. News that William Short had gone to Madrid to join Carmichael in conversations with the Spanish government about the navigation of the Mississippi brought instructions on the subject and

an "accidental" conversation between Hammond and Hamilton, who gave assurances that any agreement would not militate against British rights. See further, Grenville to Hammond, Jan. 5, 1792, *Instr. Brit. Min.*, pp. 21-23, enclosing Lord St. Helens' dispatch to Grenville, Nov. 25, 1791, F.O. 115/1, fols. 10-11; and Hammond to Grenville, Apr. 5, 1792, F.O. 4/14, fols. 341-42.

2. Burgess to Hammond, Jan. 4, 1793 (in cipher, most secret), *Instr. Brit. Min.*, pp. 33-34. See also John Hamilton to Grenville, Feb. 27, 1793, F.O. 4/1, fol. 511; and the *Morn. Chron.*, Aug. 16, 1793. For another view, see the *Diary*, May 21, 1793, declaring it "not a very probable circumstance" that the United States would enter the war against Britain. She would thereby expose herself to attack from the Spanish North American colonies, at the same time that she was hotly engaged with the Indians. She was also "very different from the Republic of France," with a government formed to "answer the ends of good government." She could never "give sanction to the doctrines of sedition without equally endangering its existence."

3. Grenville to Hammond, Jan. 5, 1792, cited in note 1 above; and Feb. 8, 1793, *Instr. Brit. Min.*, pp. 34-35.

4. See Hammond's two dispatches, both dated Mar. 7, 1793, F.O. 5/1, fols. 93-98. Phineas Bond, who was well aware of the magnitude of private British investment in the American funds and lands since he was often asked to act as agent in the receipt of dividends, also delivered a warning against the investment of British capital in the United States. It did not merely benefit that country, he said, but was also subject to the whims and vagaries of American politics. See Bond to Grenville, Philadelphia, July 7, 1793, F.O. 5/2, fol. 124.

5. Grenville to Hammond, Mar. 12, 1793, *Instr. Brit. Min.*, p. 39; and Hammond to Grenville, Apr. 2, 1793, F.O. 5/1, fols. 127-30.

6. Pinckney formally transmitted a copy of the proclamation to Grenville on June 21, 1793; it is in F.O. 5/3. It is published in *A.S.P., For. Rel.*, p. 140. See also Secretary Jefferson to Gouverneur Morris, minister at Paris, Apr. 20, 1793, Thomas Jefferson, *Writings of Thomas Jefferson*, ed. Paul L. Ford, 10 vols. (New York, 1892-99), 7:281.

7. Jefferson, *Writings*, 7:281. Cf. Rufus King's sentiments, King to Hamilton, Apr. 24, 1793, Rufus King, *Life and Correspondence of Rufus King*, ed. C. R. King, 6 vols. (New York, 1894-1900), 1:439-40. See Grenville to Hammond, Feb. 8, 1793, *Instr. Brit. Min.*, p. 35. It is obvious that Jefferson aimed to make American neutrality favor France to the maximum. See his letter to the Girondist leader, Brissot de Warville, May 8, 1793, Jefferson, *Writings*, 7:322-23, professing himself "eternally attached to the principles of your revolution," and inveighing against "the zealous apostles of English despotism here." See also his violent letter, attacking Hamilton, Knox, and Randolph, to Madison, May 12, 1793, ibid., pp. 323-24. Pinckney wrote home on March 13, the day after Grenville's instructions to Hammond on the subject were sent, indicating that the "idea" that some of the belligerents intended to stop American grain vessels was, in fact, well founded.

8. Add. MSS 38352, fols. 130-32, minutes of Jan. 21, 1793. By the end of February, the British government was offering 7/ bushel for American wheat. The prevailing price for the domestic grain was only 5/10d. See Robert Crew to Jefferson, London, Feb. 22, 1793, Jefferson MSS, Lib. Cong., vol. 81, fol. 14184.

9. Hammond to Grenville, Apr. 2, 1793, F.O. 5/1, fols. 132-34. Washington's cabinet considered Ternant's request on February 25, 1793. See Jefferson to the President, Feb. 25, 1793, Jefferson MSS, Lib. Cong., vol. 81, fol. 14194. The arrearage was actually $318,000. Jefferson, Randolph, and Knox apparently favored a more extensive arrangement to meet French needs. Hamilton opposed, and because financial considerations were the special concern of the Secretary of the Treasury, his view was allowed to prevail. See also Jefferson to Ternant, Feb. 25 (probably a mistake for Feb. 26), 1793, Jefferson MSS, Lib. Cong., vol. 81, fol. 14915, in which he mentions an earlier promise, apparently made on his own initiative, to make $100,000 available at once to allow Ternant to begin his "operations." Jefferson expressed pleasure "in shewing on every possible occasion our earnest desire to serve your nation, and the interest we take in its present situation." See also Jefferson, *Writings*, 7:252, a cabinet opinion of March 2, 1793, unanimously in favor of Hamilton's informing Smith,

who had renewed Ternant's application, "that the government of the United States have made engaged payments to France to the extent which is at present consistent with their arrangements; and do not judge it advisable to take any measures on the subject of his application." The British intercepted Ternant's dispatches describing his dealings with the Americans and his subsequent purchases and shipments of supplies to France. See, *Instr. Brit. Min.*, p. 40, n. 18. See also Jefferson to Gouverneur Morris, Mar. 12, 1793, Jefferson, *Writings*, 7:258-62. Genêt, Ternant's successor, renewed the request for anticipation of debt payment, but received from Hamilton—according to Hammond—"a direct negative." See his dispatches, June 10, 1793, F.O. 5/1, fols. 175-82; and July 7, 1793, ibid., fols. 193-204. For subsequent and successful French efforts to use the United States as a source of supply, see Howard C. Rice, "James Swan, Agent of the French Republic, 1794-1796," *New England Quarterly* 10 (Sept. 1937): 464-86, an article demonstrating the grounds for British suspicions of Franco-American collusion and of widespread fraud in passing off French property as American.

10. The relevant Orders in Council, from the reign of Anne, were dated April 28 and May 19, 1709. Significantly enough, copies are to be found in Hawkesbury's papers. See Add. MSS 38353, fols. 196-97.

11. Grenville to Hammond, Mar. 12, 1793, *Instr. Brit. Min.*, pp. 36-40. The dispatch was carried by Phineas Bond, then returning to Philadelphia with the new rank of consul-general for the southern and middle states, a promotion which gave great offense to Sir John Temple.

Had the American government granted the French request to liquidate the entire debt, thereby changing its peacetime arrangements to meet the convenience of a belligerent, Britain would rightly have made an issue of it.

12. F.O. 5/1, fol. 21. The case was referred to Advocate-General William Scott, who reported on April 29 that a question of law did in fact exist, and that its determination lay properly within the jurisdiction of the admiralty courts. See also the *Public Advertiser*, Nov. 15, 1793, for a sample "anecdote" describing the boarding of an American vessel out of Bordeaux. The cargo consisted of wine and brandy, and the ship's papers represented it as American-owned. An informing American sailor led the visitors to the real papers, proving, of course, French ownership. They were found sealed in a liquid-proof container in a cask of claret.

13. Grenville to Hammond, May 2 and July 5, 1793, *Instr. Brit. Min.*, pp. 40 and 40-42.

14. Pinckney to Jefferson, July 5, 1793, *A.S.P.*, For. Rel., p. 241; and *Instr. Brit. Min.*, p. 42, n. 22.

15. To Madison, Mar. 1793, Jefferson, *Writings*, 7:250-52.

16. May 7, 1793, ibid., pp. 312-15. For an examination of the implications of Britain's treaty with France, see appendix H.

17. Aug. 31, 1793, Jefferson, *Writings*, 8:8-10, and Jefferson to Pinckney, Sept. 7, 1793, ibid., pp. 24-31; *A.S.P.*, For. Rel., pp. 239-40. Jefferson also took exception to a second provision of the Order calling for the seizure and condemnation of ships, except those belonging to Swedes or Danes, attempting to enter a blockaded port. Swedish or Danish-owned ships were to be turned back on the first attempt to enter and seized only on subsequent efforts to run the blockade. The special treatment was the result of treaties between Britain and the Scandinavian powers. Jefferson saw it as an additional attempt to hurt the United States. He told Pinckney to argue that Britain could not be bound by treaty to withhold the same favor from the United States. If it should be withheld "merely because not established with us by treaty, what might not we, on the same ground, have withheld from Great Britain, during the short course of the present war, as well as the peace which has preceded it." The position is a variation of that he took in arguing that free ships made free goods because the principle stood in several international treaties. Hamilton, too, took exception to the favored treatment of the Scandinavians, however, telling Hammond that it "appeared to be peculiarly directed against the commerce and navigation of the United States." See Hammond to Grenville, Sept. 17, 1793, F.O. 5/1, fols. 290-99.

18. Hammond to Jefferson, Sept. 12, 1793 *A.S.P.*, For. Rel., p. 240; and Jefferson to

Hammond, Sept. 22, 1793, ibid., pp. 240-41. See also Hammond to Grenville, Sept. 17, 1793, cited in note 17.

19. Pinckney's memorandum, dated July 22, 1783, and Grenville's response, July 31, 1793, are in *A.S.P.*, For. Rel., p. 242. A copy of the former is in F.O. 5/3, fols. 157-58; the latter memorial is in F.O. 5/3, fols. 159-61, and is printed (without date) in *A.S.P.*, For. Rel., pp. 242-43.

20. Grenville to Pinckney, Aug. 1, 1793, F.O. 5/7, fols. 212-17; Pinckney to Jefferson, Aug. 12, 1793, *A.S.P.*, For. Rel., p. 315. The editor of the latter doubts the date of Pinckney's dispatch, but it is probably correct.

21. Aug. 22, 1793, Charles James Fox, *Memorials and Correspondence of Charles James Fox*, ed. Lord John Russell, 2 vols. (London, 1853), 2:44-48.

22. Aug. 20, 1793. See also the *Public Advertiser*, Aug. 22, 24; *Diary*, Aug. 22, 23, and 24. The *Public Advertiser* of August 27 trumpeted that "the Jacobin scribblers" had given up their effort to convince Britons that America intended to pick a quarrel. The last quotation is from the *Public Advertiser*, Sept. 2, 1793. See also ibid., Sept. 3 and 4, 1793. In the latter, "A British Merchant" maintained that the United States could not stand by while France was crushed. Britain would then hold the posts in the Old Northwest; and Spain would hold the Mississippi. See also ibid., Sept. 10 and 27, 1793. In the latter, it was admitted that a majority in Congress favored neutrality, but they would be overborne by the "popular clamour" if Britain did not end her war with France by January 1, 1794.

23. Anna C. Clauder, *American Commerce as Affected by the Wars of the French Revolution and Napoleon, 1793-1812* (Philadelphia, 1932), pp. 28-29. It is somewhat surprising that Grenville did not adduce the earlier official action by the French as justification for the British Order of June 8, 1793. His failure to do so may be read to imply that British action would not have been changed materially even if the French had chosen to leave neutral grain carriers in peace. He may also have felt that to have taken refuge behind the French precedent would have been to weaken Britain's argument from right, especially if France had performed one of her frequent and unpredictable *voltes faces*.

24. See appendix A.

25. Memorandum by Lord Hawkesbury (1790?), Add. MSS 38345, fols. 277-81.

26. [Charles Jenkinson], *Discourse on the Conduct of Great Britain in Respect to Neutral Nations* (London, 1757). Jenkinson also laid down the "Rule of '56," holding that there was no neutral right to take advantage of a war "to constitute a new species of traffic, which in peace you never enjoyed, and which the necessity of one party is obliged to grant you, to the detriment, perhaps destruction of the other." See also the anonymous pamphlet, *A Complete Investigation of Mr. Eden's Treaty* (London, 1787), a bitter attack upon the commercial treaty with France for its supposed infringement of traditional British policy. Eden was savagely criticized and Jenkinson was quoted with approbation.

27. Hawkesbury to Pitt, Oct. 12, 1791, Add. MSS 38351, fols. 3-93.

28. Pinckney to Jefferson, Aug. 15, 28, 1793, *A.S.P.*, For. Rel., p. 241; Hammond to Grenville, July 7, 1793, F.O. 5/1, fols. 193-204.

29. A convenient and brief account of Genêt in the United States is in Edward Channing, *History of the United States*, 6 vols. (New York, 1927-30), 4:130-34.

30. Mar. 12, 1793, cited in note 5 above.

31. Hamilton's attack upon Genêt was especially strong and effective. See his "No Jacobin, No. III," Alexander Hamilton, *Works of Alexander Hamilton*, ed. Henry Cabot Lodge, 12 vols. (New York, 1904), 5:36-40: "While by the treaty between the United States and France the goods of her enemies on board our ships are exempt from capture, the goods of France on board our ships are subject to the depredations of her enemies." He was quite explicit in stating that the "general law of nations" made enemy goods lawful prize wherever found, except within the territorial jurisdiction of a neutral state. He rejected Jefferson's favorite contention without qualification: "An established rule of the law of nations can only be altered by agreements between all the civilized powers, or a new usage generally adopted and sanctioned by time." The United States might appeal to a few treaties between herself and foreign powers; but none existed with Britain, Russia, Spain, Portugal, Austria, or Savoy. An appeal to a consensus could not possibly support Jefferson's position.

Hammond's gleeful dispatch is that of March 12, 1793, cited in note 5 above. If any doubts remained in the minds of the London authorities about the stormy course of the Genêt affair, they were dissipated when the French minister's correspondence with Jefferson and dispatches to his superiors in Paris, dating from May to August, 1793, were captured by the British. They are in F.O. 97/1. Other pertinent correspondence is Hammond to Grenville, June 10, 1793, F.O. 5/1, fols. 175-82; idem to Jefferson, June 19, 1793, copy, ibid., fol. 218; idem to Grenville, July 7, 1793, ibid., fols. 193-204.

32. Jefferson to Genêt, July 24, 1793, Jefferson, *Writings*, 7:456-59. The Franco-American treaty allowed a grace period of two months after the outbreak of war during which a plea of ignorance of hostilities would be allowed. The time had, of course, expired; and Genêt refused to extend it in this instance. For an elaboration of Jefferson's reasoning on the general principle, see ibid., 8:120-24.

33. Hammond to Grenville, Aug. 10, 1793, F.O. 5/1, fols. 239-51; idem to Gov. Hamilton of the Bahamas, Aug. 27, 1793, F.O. 116-2, pp. 124-28; idem to Grenville, Sept. 17, Oct. 12, and Nov. 10, 1793, F.O. 5/1, fols. 290-99, 329-32, 353. Thornton's private letter to Undersecretary Burgess, Sept. 1, 1793, is quoted by J. A. Carroll and M. W. Ashworth, *George Washington*, vol. 7: *First in Peace* (New York, 1957) [vols. 1-6 by Douglas Southall Freeman (1948-52)], p. 117, n. 122.

34. The relevant Admiralty Order of September 3, 1793, is printed in *A.S.P.*, For. Rel., p. 315.

35. Pinckney to Grenville, July 5, 1794, F.O. 5/7, fols. 161-62.

36. Charles Long, secretary to the Lords of the Treasury, to Grenville, July 19, 1794, ibid., fol. 191.

37. Pinckney to Jefferson, Aug. 28 and Sept. 25, 1793, *A.S.P.*, For. Rel., pp. 241 and 243.

38. Hamilton to Randolph, Apr. 24, 1794, Hamilton, *Works*, 6:119-21.

39. Hammond to Grenville, Aug. 10, 1793, cited in note 33 above.

CHAPTER 15

1. See J. A. Carroll and M. W. Ashworth, *George Washington*, vol. 7: *First in Peace* (New York, 1957) [vols. 1-6 by Douglas Southall Freeman (1948-52)], p. 142. The message and correspondence are printed in *A.S.P.*, For. Rel., pp. 141 ff. Randolph's subsequent report on spoliations, dated March 2, 1794, was sent to Congress on March 5. See ibid., pp. 423-24.

2. Only the day before Washington's message of December 5, Congress was given the documents relating to the unsuccessful negotiations with the Indians. See Samuel Flagg Bemis, *Jay's Treaty: A Study in Commerce and Diplomacy* (New Haven, 1962), pp. 254-55, 257-59, and n. 7.

3. Hammond to Grenville, Feb. 22, 1794, F.O. 5/4, fols. 43-57. Hammond, unknowingly, had the support of Vice-President Adams on at least one point. See Adams to Mrs. Adams, Dec. 5, 1793, John Adams, *The Life and Works of John Adams*, ed. Charles Francis Adams, 10 vols. (Boston, 1850-56), 1:461: "How a government can go on publishing all their negotiations with foreign nations, I know not. To me it appears as dangerous and pernicious as it is novel." In the same letter, he expressed wry pleasure that recent press attacks on Washington had relieved him, at least temporarily, of "the office of libelee-general." It was only right, he believed, that its burden should be "participated and equalized, according to modern republican principles."

4. *A.S.P.*, For. Rel., pp. 300-304. The comparison between France and Britain became even more unfavorable to the latter when the former's decree of March 26, 1793, opening the colonial trade to American vessels on the footing of French, was laid before the House of Representatives on December 30. See ibid., pp. 306-7.

5. Hammond to Grenville, Feb. 22, 1794, cited in note 3 above. Hammond was angry, too, at the imputation of unwillingness to negotiate a commercial treaty. Fisher Ames in his speech to the House of Representatives on January 27, 1794 (see below), also took exception, asserting that both Pitt and Hammond had made it quite clear that Britain was willing to negotiate a commercial accord.

6. *A.S.P.*, For. Rel., pp. 288-99.

7. Humphreys to Jefferson, Gibraltar, Oct. 8, 1793, ibid., p. 295; and idem to Washington, Oct. 7, 1793, Francis Landon Humphreys, *Life and Times of David Humphreys*, 2 vols. (New York, 1917), 2:187. By November, some ten vessels and 105 American citizens were reported taken. See Capt. O'Brien to Washington, Nov. 7, 1793, ibid., p. 417.

8. The documents dealing with the Algerian depredations are in *A.S.P.*, For. Rel., pp. 413-24. See also ibid., pp. 530-32; Grenville to Hammond, Jan., 1794, *Instr. Brit. Min.*, pp. 49-50; Jefferson to Martha Randolph, Dec. 22, 1793, Thomas Jefferson, *Writings of Thomas Jefferson*, ed. Paul L. Ford, 10 vols. (New York, 1892-99), 8:124-25. Joel Barlow to Jefferson, Paris, Dec. 2, 1793, Jefferson MSS, Lib. Cong., vol. 95, fols. 16299-300; and Rufus King, *Life and Correspondence of Rufus King*, ed. C. R. King, 6 vols. (New York, 1894-1900), 1:503, 508, 510-11.

9. Ames's speech is in Fisher Ames, *The Works of Fisher Ames*, ed. J. T. Kirkland (Boston, 1809), pp. 26-57. See further, Hamilton's two essays, signed "Americanus," which appeared in the *American Daily Advertiser* on February 1 and 8, 1794, Alexander Hamilton, *Works of Alexander Hamilton*, ed. Henry Cabot Lodge, 12 vols. (New York, 1904), 5:74-96, arguing that either France was able to save herself, or American aid as a belligerent would be to no avail. By engaging in the war, he continued, America would blast her own prosperity by losing the neutral trade and suffering annihilation of her seaborne commerce. Ninety per cent of the federal government's revenues would disappear and a substitute was not to be found, without new and heavy burdens for all Americans.

10. Philadelphia, Mar. 2, 1794, F.O. 5/6, fols. 32-35, copy. A second copy is in Melville MSS, Clem. Lib. The crisis produced several similar letters from anxious Federalists to British correspondents.

11. *A.S.P.*, For. Rel., pp. 327-28.

12. *Instr. Brit. Min.*, pp. 49-50, cited in note 8 above. On April 15, 1794, Hammond wrote to Grenville stating that he had given Randolph *"informally* and *orally"* (since Portuguese-British business could not become an object of official notice on the part of a third party) the explanation outlined in Grenville's earlier instructions. Randolph exp. ssed his pleasure, and promised to inform Washington. See F.O. 5/4, fol. 169.

13. My italics.

14. Despite the agreement that negotiations on the posts should be allowed to continue in Philadelphia, Pinckney, alarmed at Grenville's "extraordinary hint," pressed the Briton to say "whether, in case we should comply with what they conceived to be the full execution of the treaty . . . they would relinquish the posts to us?" Grenville answered that "in case one party to a treaty had deferred the accomplishment of their part of the obligation for nine years, *whereby the complete execution could not afterwards be had, neither reason nor the law of nations would exact a strict compliance from the other party."* The phrase in italics (which are mine) should be understood strictly in the conditional sense; and it must not be forgotten that Grenville's reply was deliberately brief, the negotiations on the subject being relegated to Philadelphia. The British foreign secretary was not rejecting the idea of "compliance" with the treaty, but he was laying a groundwork for questioning "strict compliance."

15. Pinckney's dispatch, transmitted to Congress on February 24, 1794, must have been especially useful in countering the bad impression made by an exchange of notes between Randolph and Hammond on the twenty-first (also communicated on the twenty-fourth); the former inquiring if Hammond were prepared to resume negotiations on the unfulfilled treaty of peace, the latter responding that he had not yet received the expected instructions from London. See *A.S.P.*, For. Rel., p. 328. Formal exchanges over the Order of June 8, 1793, did not occur until its importance had been overshadowed by newer and grimmer events. Pinckney's written memorial to Grenville of January, 1794, which added nothing new to his earlier argument, was laid before Congress on May 12, 1794. Grenville instructed Hammond to reply to Pinckney's memorial in Philadelphia. (Jan., 1794, *Instr. Brit. Min.*, pp. 45-47.) He reasoned that the envoy was familiar with the points at issue and would be able to direct his communication, which was to be conciliatory, at the existing state of American public opinion. Hammond accordingly memorialized Randolph on April 11. Only

one new point was made: to controvert Pinckney's argument to Grenville that American acquiescence to British treatment of her provisions vessels would give France a right to do the same, Hammond pointed out that France had actually initiated the policy. Randolph's blistering but discursive rejoinder came on May 1, 1794. See *A.S.P., For. Rel.*, pp. 448-54. Undoubtedly, much of Randolph's heat came from the seizures under the November order. See also Hammond to Grenville, Boston, Feb. 26, 1794, F.O. 5/6, fols. 278-79.

16. Hammond to Grenville, Mar. 12, 1794, F.O. 5/4, fols. 136-37.

17. *Instr. Brit. Min.*, p. 47, n. 10; and *A.S.P., For. Rel.*, pp. 430-31.

18. P.R.O., P.C. 1/64/B28 (Colonial), Secretary to the Treasury Charles Long to J. King, Clerk of the Council, June 28, 1793, enclosing an extract of Home's letter to Dundas, May 2, 1793. It was considered on July 3, and Hawkesbury's reply was dated July 6. Both Long and Hawkesbury spoke of the inexpedience and danger of allowing American vessels into British island ports in time of war.

19. Skipwith to Randolph, Mar. 1, 1794, transmitted to Congress on Mar. 25, *A.S.P., For. Rel.*, pp. 428-29. For Dutch collaboration with Britain, see the journal of James Bland Burgess, Dec. 30, 1793, *R.H.M.C.R., Fortescue Pps.*, 2:488-89. The "Account of Proceedings in February, 1794," is in F.O. 5/7, fols. 94-95, and may have been carried to Britain by Jay. See Grenville to Hammond, Aug. 8, 1794, *Instr. Brit. Min.*, p. 65 and n. 53.

20. See Grenville to Hammond, June 5, 1794, *Instr. Brit. Min.*, pp. 57-58, and also n. 37. Hammond's dispatches from February 22 to April 18, 1794, dealing with the steadily mounting crisis in the United States including the embargo, did not arrive in London until June 10, after John Jay was already on the scene. The entire August mail from London to the United States was lost at sea by enemy action.

21. See William Edward Hall, *A Treatise on International Law* (Oxford, 1890), pp. 641-42; and Frederick Louis Nussbaum, "The French Colonial Arrêt of 1784," *South Atlantic Quarterly* 27 (1928): 62-78; and the same author's "American Tobacco and French Politics, 1783-89," *Political Science Quarterly* 40 (Dec. 1925): 497-516. See further, Anna C. Clauder, *American Commerce as Affected by the Wars of the French Revolution and Napoleon, 1793-1812* (Philadelphia, 1932), p. 28. The French measure applied also to the East Indies and to the Isles de France and Bourbon. In March, the gum trade of Senegal was opened. See also Alfred T. Mahan, *Sea Power in its Relation to the War of 1812*, 2 vols. (Boston, 1905), 1:90-91.

22. For a general treatment of the West Indian situation at the time and of British policy there, see John Holland Rose, *William Pitt and the Great War* (London, 1911), pp. 219 ff. See, too, the *Morn. Chron.*, Aug. 16, 1793; and Hawkesbury to Grenville, Aug. 10, 1793, F.O. 5/1, fols. 239-51.

23. Hawkesbury to Nepean, Aug. 19, 1793, F.O. 4/1, fols. 545-46. An American vessel with both native and French papers had recently been brought into Guernsey. The rules on the transfer of nationality for vessels were far from clear and uniform. Britain herself allowed prizes to become British.

See further Consul John Hamilton to [Grenville], June 20, 1793, F.O. 95/1, enclosing a copy of a letter from Jefferson to a friend, June 4, 1793, suggesting that a vessel had only to be American-owned (not American-built) to enjoy the protection of the flag: "Were we to depend on *Home built* vessels only," the American secretary of state said, "much of our Production must remain in our Hands."

Grenville's dispatch to Hammond is Jan. 10, 1794, *Instr. Brit. Min.*, pp. 47-49.

24. Pinckney's dispatch was given to Congress on April 4, 1794. See *A.S.P., For. Rel.*, pp. 429-31. Pinckney wrote that Grenville told him the November order had *two* purposes: "to prevent the abuses which might take place in consequence of the whole of the St. Domingo fleet having gone to the United States"; and "on account of the attack designed upon the French West India Islands by the armament under Sir John Jervis and Sir Charles Grey." The latter reason was not included in the dispatch to Hammond here quoted.

25. See Hall, *Treatise*, pp. 641-42, cited in note 21 above. The *Morn. Chron.* dates are Dec. 28, 1793, and Jan. 7, 1794. The *Public Advertiser* responded with a strong defense of the ministry and its measures.

26. *Parl. Hist.*, 30:1391-1422.

27. Grenville to Hammond, Jan. 10, 1794, *Instr. Brit. Min.*, p. 47. The copy in F.O. 5/4, fols. 11-15, is dated the eleventh. See, too, Rufus King's diary, King, *Correspondence*, 1:523-24. At the end of March, reports were being circulated by correspondents of the London trading house of Bird, Savage, and Bird that a committee of merchants interested in the American trade had seen Pitt, and had been told that the intent of the November Order had clearly been exceeded and that sufferers would receive "most ample" compensation. See H. LeRoy to King, Mar. 30 and Apr. 10, 1794, ibid., pp. 557 and 560.

28. Hammond to Grenville, Mar. 12, 1794, F.O. 5/4, fols. 136-37. See also Rufus King to Christopher Gore, Mar. 10, 1794, King, *Correspondence*, 1:550.

The Federalist's letter, dated March 22, 1794, is anonymous. A copy is in the Melville MSS, Clem. Lib. See also John Jay to Rufus King, New York, Mar. 22, 1794, King, *Correspondence*, 1:555-56; and J. Lawrence to idem, Mar. 23, (1794), ibid., p. 556. Jay favored a complete embargo. Lawrence, however, said that those "who were very pacific are now differently disposed, and I really believe should you make use of the last reason, great unanimity would prevail." See also John Adams to Abigail Adams, Philadelphia, Mar. 27, 1794, J. Adams, *Works*, 1:469, written the day after the embargo passed Congress. He expressed a characteristic worry: "If the French has a better government and better morals, I should feel easier."

Hammond's fear for peace was stated in a dispatch to Dorchester (by special messenger), Mar. 16, 1794, F.O. 116/2, pp. 195-207.

29. The anonymous letter of March 22, 1794, cited in note 28 above.

30. King, *Correspondence*, 1:517-18, King's diary on the origin of the Jay mission.

31. Hammond to Grenville, Mar. 23, 1794, F.O. 116/2, pp. 259-66.

32. King, *Correspondence*, 1:562. King's memorandum is dated April 16, 1794.

33. Hammond to Grenville, Apr. 17, 1794, F.O. 5/4, fols. 173-85.

34. See Washington's message in *A.S.P.*, For. Rel., p. 447.

35. Randolph's letter is dated May 20, 1794, and Hammond's response is May 22. Both were laid before Congress on the twenty-third. The more alarming event was Simcoe's southward movement to occupy the post at the Maumee Rapids, "private" news of which was given by the President to Congress on the twenty-first. All are printed in ibid., p. 461.

36. The source is cited in note 32 above.

37. Apr. 15, 1794, J. Adams, *Works*, 1:471.

38. Bond to Grenville, Apr. 17, 1794, F.O. 5/6, fols. 44-45.

39. Relevant papers were laid before Congress on June 4, 1794. See *A.S.P.*, For Rel., pp. 466-68.

40. To James Bland Burgess, Apr. 28, 1794, E. A. Cruikshank, ed., *The Correspondence of Lieut. Governor John Graves Simcoe, with Allied Documents*, 5 vols. (Toronto, 1923-31), 2:220.

41. Dorchester's orders, Feb. 17, 1794, are in Cruikshank, *Correspondence of Simcoe*, 2:154. See also Simcoe to Dundas, Feb. 28, 1794, ibid., pp. 164-65; Dorchester to idem, Feb. 24, 1794, ibid., pp. 163-64; and Simcoe to Hammond, July 5, 1794, draft, Hammond-Simcoe Correspondence, Clem. Lib., printed in ibid., 2:323-25, under date of July 18, probably the date it was dispatched.

42. Consul John Hamilton to Simcoe, Norfolk, Mar. 14, 1794, Cruikshank, *Correspondence of Simcoe*, 3:177; Hammond to Dorchester, Mar. 16, 1794, F.O. 116/2, pp. 195-205.

43. Carondelet to Simcoe, New Orleans, Jan. 2, 1794, enclosed in Dorchester to Dundas, June 7, 1794, Cruikshank, *Correspondence of Simcoe*, 3:129-30; and Simcoe to Carondelet, "At the Rapids of the Miamis River of Lake Erie," April 11, 1794, ibid., pp. 200-201.

44. The exchange is cited in note 35 above.

45. May 25, 1794, F.O. 5/4, fols. 293-99.

46. May 26, 1794, F.O. 116/2, pp. 221-24. A copy is in the Hammond-Simcoe Corr., Clem. Lib.

47. It is dated June 2, 1794, and is in *A.S.P.*, For. Rel., pp. 464-66. Washington laid it before Congress two days later.

48. July 11, 1794, Cruikshank, *Correspondence of Simcoe*, 2:317-18.

CHAPTER 16

1. F.O. 95/1. The dispatches had been received on August 6, 1793.

2. F.O. 5/7, (America/Domestic Communications, Jan.-Dec., 1794), fols. 72-73. See Samuel Flagg Bemis, *Jay's Treaty: A Study in Commerce and Diplomacy* (New Haven, 1962), pp. 301-2, n. 8, who attributes the notation first quoted to Grenville. The handwriting matches that of Dundas, however, and it is initialed by the Home Secretary.

3. See the *Public Advertiser*, Feb. 17, 1794, printing a letter from Norfolk, Virginia, describing the situation in the country as "very critical." For the Opposition's somewhat languid efforts, see W. Pitt to Grenville, (Feb. 23, 1794), *R.H.M.C.R., Fortescue Pps.*, 2:511-12; and Grenville to Pitt, Feb. 24, 1794, ibid., p. 512. See, too, Dundas to Hammond, Mar. 16, 1794, E. A. Cruikshank, ed., *The Correspondence of Lieut. Governor John Graves Simcoe, with Allied Documents*, 5 vols. (Toronto, 1923-31), 2:184-87.

4. *Morn. Chron.*, Apr. 29, 1794. The paper held the Order of November 6 responsible and demanded satisfaction be given to America by "paying all expences incurred upon the captures made under that order." Even so, the preservation of peace and the salvation of the country from "the rashness of our ministers" would be due to "the wisdom of General Washington." See also the *Oracle and Public Advertiser*, May 6, 1794, publishing the account here referred to in a letter from Niagara dated more than a week before Dorchester's speech to the Indians, and a fortnight before the orders to reoccupy the Miamis post. Dundas' admonition is in his dispatch to Simcoe, May 11, 1794, Cruikshank, *Correspondence of Simcoe*, 2:235-36.

5. Grenville to Hammond, June 5, 1794, *Instr. Brit. Min.*, pp. 57-58.

6. *Morn. Chron.*, June 20, 1794. Very nearly the same words were used in Canadian merchant C. T. A. Schoede to E. B. Littlehales, Ft. Ontario, Sept. 13, 1794, Cruikshank, *Correspondence of Simcoe*, 3:89-90. See also the *Times*, June 13, 1794, reporting the defeat of the Virginia senators' motion to suspend the debt article of the peace treaty; and James Ackers to Dundas, June 3, 1794, transmitting a worried letter of inquiry from the merchants and manufacturers of Manchester, F.O. 4/1, fol. 590. The *Oracle and Public Advertiser* published reassuring reports, emanating from the Committee of American Merchants in London and supposedly based on a ministerial letter of June 26, 1794. On June 28, the same newspaper reported several vessels newly fitting out for America because of prevailing optimism among London merchants.

7. See Hammond to Grenville, Aug. 16, 1794, F.O. 5/5, fols. 249-52; idem to idem, Apr. 28, 1794, F.O. 5/4, fols. 238-42; Bond to idem, Apr. 28, 1794, F.O. 5/6, fol. 72. Bond strongly recommended that the islands be required to cultivate their own provisions. No dependence upon American "candour" was tolerable. Britain had to guard against "the evil Effects of their Inveteracy." Hammond was worried as early as the summer of 1793, writing to Dorchester that he ought to stockpile grain and provisions for the West Indies if American supplies were suddenly stopped. Commanders in chief and governors in the Caribbean were also put on their guard. By the end of April, 1794, the embargo already a month old and renewed for another month, Jamaica and occupied Santo Domingo were severely pinched for supplies, according to Hammond. Phineas Bond also wrote of "the critical Situation" throughout the islands, mentioning especially St. Kitts and Antigua, as well as the garrisons on Santo Domingo. The end of the embargo on May 27 brought an immediate and great outpouring of American produce in American bottoms. Even so, warnings continued to be circulated of the evil consequences to be feared from dependence on the United States. Edward Thornton was especially forceful in a letter to Burgess, May 27, 1794, Cruikshank, *Correspondence of Simcoe*, 2:250-51. See also Bond to Grenville, May 27, 1794, F.O. 5/6, fol. 76. Thornton declared that British merchants had to accept the constant danger of debt confiscation in America, just as West Indian planters had to face sporadic and unpredictable hurricanes. See Hammond to Grenville, May 25, 1794, F.O. 5/4, fols. 293-99. The dispatch was received July 1. See finally, idem to Governor Hamilton of the Bermudas, May 28, 1794, F.O. 116/2, pp. 225-26, urging him to prepare for fresh embargoes.

8. Dundas to Simcoe, July 4, 1794, Cruikshank, *Correspondence of Simcoe*, 2:300; and idem to Dorchester, July 5, 1794, summarized in Bemis, *Jay's Treaty*, p. 321, n. 5. See also Randolph to Jay, May 27, 1794, *A.S.P., For. Rel.*, p. 474; Jay to Randolph, July 16, 1794,

ibid., p. 479. See, further, the *Morn. Chron.*, July 7, 1794, bitterly attacking Dorchester's "extraordinary Speech," which they had treated at first as fiction "because of its extreme absurdity." They feared the Canadian governors' provocations would ruin "Mr. Jay's pacific mission."

9. Jay to Randolph, July 5, 1794, A.S.P., For. Rel., p. 478; Grenville to Hammond, July 15, 1794, *Instr. Brit. Min.*, pp. 58-60; and Jay to Randolph, July 12 and 16, 1794, A.S.P., For. Rel., p. 479.

10. See Simcoe to Dorchester, Niagara, Aug. 18, 1794, Cruikshank, *Correspondence of Simcoe*, 2:391; idem to Hammond, Aug. 30, 1794, ibid., 3:15-16; and idem to Dorchester, Sept. 5, 1794, ibid., 3:41-43. It was not until September 28, 1794, that Hammond was able to forward copies of Grenville's instructions to Dorchester and Simcoe. He could only hope that they would "arrive in time, if not to prevent the commencement at least to arrest the progress of hostilities." His dispatch is in F.O. 5/5, fol. 317. See *Instr. Brit. Min.*, p. 60, n. 44. Simcoe wrote a very full explanation of his fears and motives to Sir Henry Clinton. It is dated September 18, 1794, and is in the Clinton MSS, Clem. Lib. See, too, Randolph to Jay, Aug. 30, 1794, A.S.P., For. Rel., p. 484. For a note on alleged British complicity in the Indian war, see appendix J.

11. See the *Courier*, Oct. 15, 17, 18, 25, 1794; *Morn. Chron.*, Oct. 17, 21, 1794; *Oracle and Public Advertiser*, Oct. 20, 1794. See Jay to Grenville, Oct. 13, 1794, the representation on the Sodus affair, Gren. Pps., Boc. H.; and John King, secretary to the Duke of Portland, the new home secretary, to Undersecretary James B. Burgess, Oct. 17, 1794, F.O. 5/7, fol. 372. See, too, *Morn. Chron.*, Oct. 17, 1794.

12. Hammond to Simcoe, Aug. 10, 1794, Cruikshank, *Correspondence of Simcoe*, 5:101-2; and Grenville to Hammond, Aug. 8, 1794, (nos. 15, 17), *Instr. Brit. Min.*, pp. 60, 65.

13. A convenient summary is Frank Monaghan, *John Jay* (New York, 1935), p. 372.

14. For a discussion of Grenville as foreign secretary, see Ephraim D. Adams, *The Influence of Grenville on Pitt's Foreign Policy, 1787-1798* (Washington, 1904).

15. Hawkesbury to Grenville, Addiscombe Place, June 19, 1794, Gren. Pps., Boc. H.; Grenville to Hawkesbury, June 20, 1794, Add. MSS 38229, fol. 231; and Jay to Washington, June 23, 1794, William Jay, *Life of Jay*, 2 vols. (New York, 1833), 2:216-17. To the anticipated British argument that justice should first be sought and refused in the royal courts before an official complaint on spoliations was made, Jay was instructed to answer that "peculiarities distinguish the present from past cases." The issue was not misapplication of law. The law itself was wrong, and could be corrected only by the lawmaker, or compensation made by him. Depredations upon American shipping were continuing, moreover, especially at Martinique, where prison ships for "multitudes" of American seamen and systematic "plunder, persecution, and cruelty" moved Randolph to write to Jay that if immediate remedy were not found in London, he did not know "how the general irritation can be checked." See Randolph's dispatch, May 27, 1794, A.S.P., For. Rel., pp. 474-75.

16. Much valuable material on the spoliation and compensation issues is to be found in A.S.P., For Rel., pp. 470. ff.

In London, Jay learned of the case of the American ship *Charlotte*, which had been condemned at Antigua, but apparently declined to bring it to Grenville's attention. It was not, Jay told Randolph, "among the strongest examples." The owner, one Crafts, then in London, had sought legal counsel and had been advised that his cargo, French island produce brought directly from there to Europe, was "considered as liable to confiscation, although it should be the property of Americans." Jay's reluctance was based on an unwillingness to challenge the Rule of '56. He subsequently brought to Grenville's attention the case of the *Amsterdam Packet*, bound from New York for Havre-de-Grace with a cargo of sugar, cotton, coffee, pot and pearl ash, oil, and tobacco. She was taken by a British privateer and carried into Liverpool. There she remained some seven months awaiting adjudication. Jay's complaint was directed solely to the delay. See, too, Jay to Grenville, July 3, 1794, transmitted to Randolph in a dispatch of July 6, 1794, ibid., p. 477.

17. See Jay to Randolph, Nov. 19, 1794, ibid., p. 503; and Bemis, *Jay's Treaty*, p. 298.

18. Both Hamiltonians and the British ministry reserved a special respect for the

Swiss jurist, Emeric de Vattel (1714-67), whose *Droit des gens* was published in Neuchâtel in 1758.

19. See W. Jay, *Life of John Jay*, 1:327; Jay to Randolph, July 30, 1794, John Jay, *Correspondence and Public Papers of John Jay*, ed. Henry P. Johnston, 4 vols. (New York, 1890-93), 4:36-38; and *A.S.P., For. Rel.*, p. 480. The two ministerial communications are in ibid., pp. 481-82. Jay also referred to "unusual personal severities" and impressments in the course of the "irregularities." Pressed Americans should be released, he said, and orders issued to prevent similar violence in the future. Grenville's reply was conciliatory. See, too, Jay to Washington, Aug. 5, 1794, W. Jay, *Life of John Jay*, 2:220-22.

20. A report on reorganization of vice admiralty courts, signed by Advocate-General William Scott and Attorney- and Solicitor-General John Scott and John Mitford, is dated August 9, 1794; and a copy is in Wedderburn MSS, Clem. Lib., vol. 2. See Lord Buckingham to Grenville, August 6, 1794, *R.H.M.C.R., Fortescue Pps.*, 2:610-12. At the request of his brother, Buckingham made inquiries of Major Finch Mason, aide-de-camp to Sir Charles Grey, commander of British troops during the Martinique campaign. He was asked "what were the severities or the grounds of them" inflicted by Sir John Jervis, the naval commander, on American seamen. Finch replied that "Sir J. Jervis's construction of the proclamation respecting American Ships had given very great offense and, as far as I understand it, with reason, but that he was not aware of any *severity*, which is your [Grenville's] word, unless by confining and afterwards impressing many American seamen who had been personally very active on the French batteries and army." See also Grenville to Hammond, Aug. 8, 1794, *Instr. Brit. Min.*, pp. 65-66.

The first Order of August 6 is printed in *A.S.P., For. Rel.*, p. 482. See Jay to Randolph, Aug. 21, 1794, ibid., p. 483. The Order was printed with approbation by the *Morning Chronicle* on August 11. For the second Order, see Josiah T. Newcomb, "New Light on Jay's Treaty," *American Journal of International Law* 28 (1934): 686 and n.; and *Instr. Brit. Min.*, p. 66, n. 54.

21. The paper, in Grenville's hand, is in the Gren. Pps., Boc. H.

22. The document is in ibid. Bemis has published it in *Jay's Treaty*, pp. 381-90. On provisions and contraband, Grenville would have spoken in generalities; but he posed a query to himself (and Hawkesbury) in the margin: "A more particular enumeration of these? What should in that case be said about Provisions?" Hawkesbury's reply, as has been seen, was unequivocal. Hawkesbury's notes are in Add. MSS 38354, fols. 38-55. Bradford Perkins has published the document in his "Lord Hawkesbury and the Jay-Grenville Negotiations," *Mississippi Valley Historical Review*, 40 (1953-54): 291-304.

23. *Morn. Chron.*, Aug. 11, 1794. Further proof of Britain's conciliatory disposition is seen in the treatment accorded Pinckney's request of August 11 to be allowed to purchase copper sheathing for the six frigates fitting out in the United States. The request was speedily granted, although it involved consultation of Hawkesbury and Portland and an application to and decision by the Privy Council. Grenville informed Pinckney of the favorable action on August 26. See Pinckney to Grenville, Aug. 11, 1794, F.O. 5/7, fol. 263; Stephen Cottrell, Secretary to the Council, to Hawkesbury, Aug. 16, 1794, Add. MSS 38230, fols. 3, 10; and idem to J. B. Burgess, Aug. 22, 1794, F.O. 5/7, fol. 277.

Jay's "Outline," discussed below, is in Add. MSS 38229, fols. 340-46, and is endorsed, "In Mr. Jay's August 6, 1794." See ibid., fols. 348-52, a proposed commercial treaty in the same unknown hand as the "Outline," from whence it is concluded that Jay was also responsible for the second document. See Jay to Randolph, Sept. 13, 1794, *A.S.P., For. Rel.*, p. 487, in which the envoy wrote: "From the 6th to the 30th of August nothing of importance occurred." Jay also pressed Grenville to conclude their treaty in time for it to arrive in the United States for the meeting of Congress in early November, a gentle reminder of the state of American public opinion.

24. *A.S.P., For. Rel.*, pp. 487-90, enclosed in Jay to Randolph, Sept. 13, 1794. One of Grenville's notes circulating his *projets* among his cabinet colleagues is dated August 25, 1794, and is in Add. MSS 38353, fol. 110. Jay, in a letter of August 16, 1794, Grenville's Letter Book, "Amer., 1793, R.," Gren. Pps., Boc. H., urged Grenville to hurry up negotiations in order to have definite news when Congress met, a point about which he expressed anxiety more than once.

25. Hawkesbury to Grenville, Aug. 29, 1794, Add. MSS 38310, fol. 113. He objected, however, to the admission of American vessels to British West Indian ports, a provision in the second *projet*.

The spoliation commission had a long and stormy career. By 1804, the members—three Americans and two Britons—had awarded $10,345,200 to citizens of the United States, and $143,428 to British subjects. See John Bassett Moore, *History and Digest of the International Arbitrations to which the United States Has Been a Party*, 6 vols. (Washington, 1898), 1:270-349. Bemis' criticism of the settlement is in *Jay's Treaty*, pp. 439-41. For an excellent, brief treatment of the appointment and working of the commission, see Bradford Perkins, *The First Rapprochement* (Philadelphia, 1955), pp. 53-56, 116-17, 142-43.

26. The communication of September 1 is in *A.S.P., For. Rel.*, p. 490. A lengthy memorandum on the cession of territory in the Old Northwest, Sept. 4, 1794, is ibid., pp. 490-92. A copy of Jay's list is to be found in Grenville's letterbook, "Amer., 1794, R.," Gren. Pps., Boc. H.

On the subject of the neutral flag and enemy goods, Jay was impressed by the opinion of two experts in maritime law, Sir William Scott and Dr. Nicholl, whom he retained to advise Americans wishing to prosecute the appeals allowed under the first Order of August 6, 1794. The lengthy opinion, dated September 10, 1794, is in *A.S.P., For. Rel.*, pp. 494-96, and states flatly as the law of nations that "the goods of an enemy, on board the ship of a friend may be taken." Goods of a friend aboard an enemy, however, were free. (Jay subsequently attempted—unsuccessfully—to incorporate the provision in the treaty.) The legality of any prizes taken at Martinique, they added, had to be established in the high court of admiralty in Britain, there being no legal court of admiralty on the conquered island. Jay recommended to Randolph that the lengthy opinion be published as a pamphlet in the United States for the guidance of interested Americans.

27. Grenville to Jay, Sept. 7, 1794, ibid., pp. 493-96; a copy is in Grenville's Letterbook, "Amer., 1794, S.," Gren. Pps., Boc. H.

28. The counter-*projet* is in F.O. 95/512, and is printed with a comparison of the final treaty by Bemis, *Jay's Treaty*, pp. 391-433. There is a second copy, used here, in the Gren. Pps., Boc. H. Grenville has made notes on it. There is also an introduction to a treaty of amity and commerce in Jay's own hand. Jay's cover letter, Sept. 30, 1794, is in ibid., and is unprinted as far as I know. See also Bemis, *Jay's Treaty*, p. 420, n. 44.

29. A copy of the unpublished letter is in the Gren. Pps., Boc. H.

30. Jay to Grenville, Oct. 13, 1794, ibid.

31. The phrase and the charge are Bemis'. See *Jay's Treaty*, p. 336. There were certain other propositions in the draft, untreated here, relating to the technical problems of ships' identification, the amenability of foreign naval officers to local law, and similar matters. They can scarcely be thought to constitute "an avalanche," however, even when added to the points raised in the text. Jay, one of the most conscientious of men, did not transmit his counter-*projet* home—a failure which has called forth some criticism from Professor Bemis—simply because it was a set of working notes.

32. Jay to Randolph, Nov. 19, 1794, cited in note 17 above.

33. *R.H.M.C.R., Fortescue Pps.*, 3:520-28. The *Morning Chronicle* on October 25, 1794, published a letter, "Conciliator No. 1," on American affairs, charging Britain with prior infraction because of both the posts and the slaves. The author promised a continuation of his treatment of the subject, but none was forthcoming.

Grenville to Jay, Aug. 5, 1794 (private), Letter Book, "Amer., 1791, S.," Gren. Pps., Boc. H. In his "Notes respecting the Posts," Grenville argued that the provisional articles of the treaty of peace signed at Paris on November 30, 1782, were to come into force only when terms of peace were settled with France. The preliminaries were ratified in America on April 15, 1783. The definitive treaty was signed September 3, 1783, and was ratified in America on January 14, 1784. Ratifications were exchanged in Europe on May 28, 1784. Until that time, the Foreign Secretary maintained, no order for evacuating the forts would properly have been sent. In the meantime, America herself had already committed incontestible infractions, "measures not merely resulting from the continuance of a status quo, agreeably to reason and to the practice of all Nations."

See Grenville to Jay, Sept. 7, 1794, quoted in note 27 above. Jay's treaty account is in his dispatch to Randolph, Sept. 13, 1794, *A.S.P.*, For. Rel., pp. 485-86.

34. Bemis, *Jay's Treaty*, pp. 356-57.

35. John Hamilton to Grenville, June 20, 1793, F.O. 95/1. See also Hammond to idem, June 10, 1793, F.O. 5/1, fols. 175-82. The consul praised Jay, who "stood boldly forward" in rendering his decision, but noted, too, that the Chief Justice had been insulted by the Richmond mob.

36. Hamilton and Findlay to Grenville, July 21, 1794, F.O. 5/7, fol. 302, enclosing a copy of a letter from Richmond, Dec. 10, 1793; and idem to Pitt, July 21, 1794, ibid., fols. 304-5, copy, from which it is seen that these and copies of other representations were forwarded to Home Secretary Portland by James Ritchie, Alexander Oswald, Gilbert Hamilton, and Robert Findlay, a committee representing the Glasgow merchants.

37. June 24, 1794, Melville MSS, Clem. Lib.

38. Jay to Randolph, July 30, 1794, J. Jay, *Correspondence*, 4:36-38. In addition to Glassford's letter to Dundas, cited in note 37 above, see the provost of Glasgow and Mr. Findlay, chairman of the Chamber of Commerce, to Grenville, July 4, 1794, Gren. Pps., Boc. H.; and Hamilton and Findlay to Dundas, July 14, 1794, Melville MSS, Clem. Lib., a mere sample of numerous similar papers in that collection. See also Pitt to Grenville, (July, 1794), *R.H.M.C.R.*, *Fortescue Pps.*, 2:607 and 607-8. John Nutt and William Molleson, leaders of the Glasgow committee, wrote to Grenville on October 24, 1794, of "our just expectations which involve the welfare of thousands." See ibid., p. 530.

39. Grenville to Ritchie, Sept. 7, 1794, Letter Book, "Amer., 1794, S.," Gren. Pps., Boc. H. John Nutt and William Molleson wrote on the thirteenth, expressing concern on behalf of their Glasgow committee. See P.R.O. 30/8, vol. 344 (America). A detailed statement of the principle upon which the Glaswegians were willing to compromise is in Grenville's Letter Book, noted above, and is dated August 26, 1794. A second similar statement, August 27, 1794, is in the Melville MSS, Clem. Lib. The most convenient and representative selection of relevant material, including copies of earlier letters, is in the Ritchie, Oswald, Hamilton, and Findlay letter to Portland, Sept. 17, 1794, cited in note 36 above.

The £2 million figure was accepted by the Addington ministry after the turn of the century in the negotiations with the American minister, Rufus King.

The debt commission, which began to function only in 1797, had an even stormier career than the commission on spoliations. It was 1800 before Rufus King and Lord Grenville returned to the idea rejected in 1794: a lump sum paid by the American government. After many delays, a convention was signed in 1802, whereby £600,000 (about $2,750,000) was paid to extinguish the creditors' claims. Britons complained at the low sum, while Federalists made much of the low cunning of the Virginians. See Perkins, *First Rapprochement*, pp. 116-20, 138-41.

40. Jay's sentiments about the slave issue are in his letter, Feb. 6, 1795, *A.S.P.*, For. Rel., p. 518. Robert Goodloe Harper, a Federalist member of the House of Representatives, published a defense of Jay's Treaty in 1796, *An Address to His Constituents* (Philadelphia, 1796). In one passage, he estimated the number of "abducted" slaves at two thousand, and their value at $400,000. "Is this a sum for two countries to quarrel about?" he asked. "A war of three months would cost five times as much." Harper did not reveal the source of his evidence.

See also Jay to James Duane, Sept. 16, 1795, J. Jay, *Correspondence*, 4:191-94. Hawkesbury, curiously enough, expressed ignorance about both posts and Negroes early in the negotiations. See his letter to Grenville, June 19, 1794, Gren. Pps., Boc. H. After his customary and painstaking study, however, he commented on Grenville's "Projet of Heads of Proposals to be made to Mr. Jay": "These Posts are certainly retained contrary to the express stipulation of the 2d Article of the Treaty of 3d Sept. 1783. They were retained because the Americans had not made good their Engagements with respect to the Payment of British Debts."

41. There were two cogently argued and authoritative memoranda submitted to the ministry at this time by unknown advisers. One was a "Memorandum on the Canadian trade to the Indian country," P.R.O. 30/8, vol. 344 (America), and was probably the paper given

to Hawkesbury by Brickwood, a Canadian merchant, and passed on to Grenville. In this connection, see Hawkesbury's comments on Grenville's "Projet of Heads of Proposals," Add. MSS 38354, fols. 38-55. The second was "Considerations on the propriety of Great Britain abandoning the Indians Posts and coming to a good understanding with America," July, 1794, P.R.O. 30/8, vol. 344.

42. The memorandum and Hawkesbury's comments are Oct. 17, 1794, F.O. 116/2, fol. 123. A copy is in P.R.O. 30/8, vol. 152. Jay's response to Grenville is F.O. 5/5, fols. 39-43.

43. Freedom for British subjects to continue trading as usual with the Indians in the northwestern territory of the United States was the result of a "decided ultimatum" from Grenville to Jay, and a considerable triumph for British diplomacy. It was balanced, however, by Jay's refusal to agree to the abolition of all duties on the traffic. Obviously apprehensive at "the inconveniences which we should experience from such a measure"—a backhanded tribute to British industry and commerce—Jay forced a critical compromise which was incorporated in Article III of the final treaty. All goods not prohibited by law might be carried freely into Canada by Americans or into the United States by Canadians subject to duties laid on goods brought into either country by native importers. See Jay to Randolph, Nov. 19, 1794, cited in note 17 above. The treaty is printed *in toto* as the final appendix to this book.

The exception of the Hudson Bay Company's trading preserve, extending over an enormous and ill-defined portion of Canada, was based on the ministry's belief that it could not legally infringe upon charter rights. Bemis, *Jay's Treaty*, p. 352, considers the provision to have "emasculated" the reciprocal American right to "pass and repass" the Canadian boundary; but this is much too pessimistic a view.

44. Nov. 19, 1794, F.O. 5/7, fols. 432-34. See also Portland to Simcoe, Jan. 8, 1795, Cruikshank, *Correspondence of Simcoe*, 3:255-56, repeating the instructions to tell the Indians that the treaty secured and guaranteed trade and intercourse, placing both on "a more unrestrained and general footing than they could rest upon under the present circumstances." He also urged Simcoe to use all his influence to procure British mediation of the Indian war.

45. Grenville's dispatch to Hammond is Nov. 20, 1794 (no. 21), *Instr. Brit. Min.*, pp. 71-73.

46. Bemis, *Jay's Treaty*, pp. 360-62, believes that the British purpose at this time was still the erection of the Indian barrier state. He also looks askance at the instructions to avoid communicating the plan to Randolph. A fair reading of the evidence does not support his first assumption. As for the second, it is certainly true that the British government experienced "the greatest dissatisfaction" with Randolph, "particularly as with respect to the Indian War," a reference to his assertions of British complicity. Great umbrage was also taken at the style and tenor of his communications and his capricious and unilateral publication of official correspondence in the middle of negotiations. See Grenville to Hammond, Nov. 20, 1794, F.O. 5/5, fols. 44-48. Jay himself expressed disapproval of premature publication. See his letter to Grenville, Nov. 22, 1794, W. Jay, *Life of John Jay*, 1:340-42.

47. See Hawkesbury to Grenville, Aug. 29, 1794, Add. MSS 38310, fol. 113; and Dundas to idem (same date?), Gren. Pps., Boc. H. Bemis, *Jay's Treaty*, pp. 329-32, argues that the establishment of the Superior line "would have placed the starting point of the boundary to be drawn westward in the future to the Pacific much farther to the south." The hypothesis is too extended. In 1794, it was by no means inevitable that the western line would be a Canadian-American one. Conceivably, it could have been a Canadian-Spanish boundary, or even a Canadian-French one. An Anglo-American agreement would scarcely have dictated the western line under such circumstances. In any event, it is just as reasonable to assume that the southerly rectification to close the northwestern gap would have been viewed as a small and necessary deviation from the terms of the treaty of peace of 1783, and that in any future boundary settlements with the United States west of the Mississippi, Britain would have returned to the intent expressed in 1783, namely, the 49th parallel.

The northeastern boundary was also in dispute, the specific question concerning the identity of the true St. Croix River designated by the peace as the line between Canada and Maine. It was of secondary importance, however, and was quickly resolved by Jay and

Grenville. Article V of their treaty referred the matter to the final decision of a mixed commission.

See, too, Jay to Grenville, Sept. 1, 1794, A.S.P., For. Rel., pp. 490-92. Grenville's answer, Sept. 5, 1794, is ibid., p. 492. In view of the latter, I am unable to understand Bemis' assertion, Jay's Treaty, pp. 351-52, that there is "no indication" that Grenville pressed his demands vigorously.

48. Jay to Randolph, Oct. 29, 1794, A.S.P., For. Rel., p. 500.

49. Donald G. Creighton, The Commercial Empire of the St. Lawrence, 1760-1850 (Toronto, 1937), pp. 136-37, has made the suggestion.

50. Governor Simcoe's long and interesting memorandum to the Committee for Trade, Sept. 1, 1794, Cruikshank, Correspondence of Simcoe, 3:52-69, shows that he, too, was caught up in the great dream of Britain's economic future in the American Midwest.

51. Jay to Randolph, Sept. 13, 1794, A.S.P., For. Rel., p. 486.

52. Chalmers to Hawkesbury, June 21, 1794, Add. MSS 38229, fol. 233; (no date), Add. MSS 38230, fols. 126-27; (July 27, 1794), ibid., fols. 307-8; and July 28, 1794, ibid.

53. Chalmers to Hawkesbury (no date), Add. MSS 38230, fol. 327; Aug. 2, 5, ibid., fols. 331-34, 335; and Aug. 9, 1794, Add. MSS 38229, fol. 359. See, too, Sheffield to Auckland, Aug. 17, 1794, Add. MSS 34453, fols. 8-9; and Auckland to Sheffield, Aug. 19, (1794), Add. MSS 45730 (supplementary Auckland MSS; no folio number).

54. The document, entitled merely "Projet," is in the Gren. Pps., Boc. H.

55. Dundas to Grenville, no date, but obviously from this period, ibid.

56. The paper is dated August 29, 1794, and is in Add. MSS 38310, fol. 113. In addition to the arguments presented earlier in his comments on the projets, Hawkesbury now urged that the seventy-ton limit on American vessels would actually increase the number of seamen more than larger vessels would, since the smaller craft would require proportionally larger crews. The continued prohibition of fish and salted provisions, a sop to Ireland and Newfoundland, would not prevent America from seizing the lion's share of the carrying trade, he continued; and the prohibition itself would be systematically evaded through smuggling. Finally, the proposed arrangement was directly contrary to a policy a century and a half old. Parliament ought therefore to be consulted before it was cast aside.

57. The letter is cited in note 55 above.

58. The Nova Scotia address is dated July 8, 1794, and is in Add. MSS 38353, fols. 101-4. See also William Fawkener, secretary to the Privy Council, to Portland's undersecretary, John King, Oct. 13, 1794, Add. MSS 38230, fols. 64-65. Sheffield, too, grumbled that ministers paid him no attention. See his letter to Auckland, Sept. 5, 1794, Add. MSS 34453, fols. 21-22.

See, too, Hawkesbury to Grenville, Oct. 17, 1794, F.O. 116/2, fol. 123. A copy was also given to Pitt. It is in P.R.O. 30/8, vol. 152. A copy for his personal files is in Hawkesbury's papers, Add. MSS 38230, fol. 68. A final bitter reference to the lost cause is in Chalmers to Hawkesbury, Nov. 8, 1794, ibid., fols. 109-10.

59. Jay to Randolph, June 1, 1795, A.S.P., For. Rel., pp. 519-20. He suggested further that if the article were deemed "ineligible" at home, the necessary legislation forbidding re-exportation of enumerated articles might be withheld and the British government requested to allow the article to lie dormant.

60. To Lord Herbert Spencer, Oct. 6, 1794, Add. MSS 34453, fol. 45.

61. See, for example, the Morn. Chron., Mar. 4 and 12, 1795, for unqualified praise of the American Constitution and people. The Republic possessed "present importance, progressive prosperity, and approaching greatness." The 6%'s stood at 98½ to 99.

In parliamentary debate on the Opposition's motion for a committee on the state of the nation in March, 1795, both sides seemed to vie with each other to compliment the United States. This was the occasion of Grenville's graceful encomium on Jay. He would, he told the peers, "always consider the conduct of the gentleman who carried on the negociation on the part of America as highly honourable to them, marked as it was by temper, moderation, and good sense." See Parl. Hist., 31:1345 ff. for the debates.

62. For Jay's explanation of the omission, see his letter to Washington, Sept. 3, 1795, W. Jay, Life of John Jay, 2:257-59. See, further, Jay to Grenville, May 1, 1796, and Gren-

ville's reply, July 9, 1796, ibid., pp. 268-77. Grenville was hoping that Congress would adopt a system of citizenship certificates, a step which would remove "the greatest part of our difficulties on the subject." It was also argued by some Federalists that the prohibition of outrages by citizens of one power upon those of the other reached to impressment.

63. On the subject in general, see Bemis, *Jay's Treaty*, pp. 295-96, chap. 9, pp. 337-45. See, further, Grenville to Hammond, May 10, 1794, *Instr. Brit. Min.*, pp. 54-56. The Scandinavians also made an approach through David Humphreys at Lisbon. See Humphreys to Washington, June 28, 1794, Francis Landon Humphreys, *Life and Times of David Humphreys*, 2 vols. (New York, 1917), 2:121-23. Even Randolph concluded that the Danish-Swedish proposition had little to offer the United States. See his letter to Humphreys, Philadelphia, Nov. 8, 1794, ibid., pp. 226-29.

64. Grenville did urge Hammond to remain watchful, however, since he had reason to believe that Sweden had not dropped the idea. See Grenville to Hammond, Oct. 2, 1794, F.O. 5/5, fols. 30-32; *Instr. Brit. Min.*, pp. 67-68.

65. Fisher Ames, *The Works of Fisher Ames*, ed. J. T. Kirkland (Boston, 1809), pp. 58-93. The speech was delivered on April 28, 1796.

66. The speech was published as a pamphlet in Philadelphia, 1796.

67. See Hammond to the governor of the Bermudas, New York, Oct. 4, 1794, F.O. 116/2, p. 284: "As I understand you have not received his Majesty's Order . . . of the 8th of January 1794 . . . I take the liberty of forwarding to your Excellency an authentic copy of it." See also, Bridger Goodrich—described in Randolph's dispatch to Jay, Oct. 11, 1794, *A.S.P.*, *For. Rel.*, pp. 498-99, as the "Prince of Privateers"—to Pitt, Nov. 10, 1794, F.O. 5/7, fols. 427-28, pathetically complaining at the injury done his friends and himself by the revocation of the Order of November 6, 1793. His own privateer had taken twenty-two American vessels, and he was obviously perturbed at the prospect of having to disgorge his spoils. See also, Jay to Grenville, Feb. 24, 1795, F.O. 5/12, enclosing an extract from a letter from Russel Sturges of Boston, dated January 1, 1795, and complaining that the Bermudians were continuing to take and condemn American vessels indiscriminately. Hammond wrote again to the governor of the Bermudas, Apr. 9, 1795, F.O. 116/5, pp. 198-200, transmitting Secretary Randolph's complaint on the subject and expressing the fear that there was legitimate ground for it. He mentioned again that he had heard the Order of January 8, 1794, had not yet arrived; and he enclosed an authenticated copy, remarking rather pointedly that it was extremely desirable to restrain the privateers to legitimate objects of capture. See also Hammond to Grenville, Apr. 28, 1795, ibid., p. 186, reporting on the matter. For further information, see F.O. 5/9, passim. See also, William Allen Deas, American chargé in London, to Grenville, July 6, 1795, F.O. 5/12, complaining that the "Outrages . . . are daily and hourly repeated." For an even more violent and impertinent effusion from the young American to Grenville, see his note of July 27, 1795, ibid. See further, Evan Nepean to J. B. Burgess, Aug. 21, 1795, ibid., promising to transmit fresh instructions to the Bermudian authorities on the revocation of the Order of November, 1793. For Washington's personal sense of outrage at the continuing depredations, see his letter to Jay, Aug. 31, 1795, W. Jay, *Life of Jay*, 2:256-57, telling him of the long-delayed ratification of the treaty, but inveighing against "the domineering spirit of Great Britain."

68. Bond to Grenville, Jan. 5, 21, and Aug. 24, 1795, F.O. 5/10, fols. 25, 35, and 106. Grenville's response, sympathetic to the Americans in the Home affair, is Nov. 4, 1795, ibid., fol. 17; *Instr. Brit. Min.*, pp. 99-100. See also, Washington to Jay, private, Aug. 31, 1795, W. Jay, *Life of John Jay*, 2:256-57. Finally, see Bond to Grenville, Sept. 29, 1795, F.O. 5/10, fols. 200-205, representing that "in the present uncertain Situation of all Commercial Engagements in France, most of the Merchants whose vessels with Cargoes of Provisions, have been carried into England, prefer that mode of Disposal to precarious Sales in the ports of their original Destination—and that, whatever clamor has been made upon the subject, originated with heated partisans, or with Traders, who under the Masque of Neutrality, are furnishing supplies to the French rulers."

It was years before the relatively limited nature of the November Order was generally recognized in the United States—long after the damage had been done.

Josiah T. Newcomb, "New Light on Jay's Treaty," explores this subject in detail. He does not seem convinced that Jay acknowledged pre-emption, at least for the duration of the war. Anna C. Clauder, *American Commerce as Affected by the War of the French Revolution and Napoleon, 1793-1812* (Philadelphia, 1932), p. 37, apparently believes the new Order restored pre-emption.

69. Grenville to Hammond, July 1, 1795, F.O. 5/9, fols. 41-45. See, too, Grenville to Jay, Feb. 10, 1795; Jay to Grenville, Feb. 15, 1795; and Grenville to Hammond, Apr. 15, 1795, ibid., fols. 11-16. The settlement of former slaves was destroyed on September 26, 1794. News was published in the *London Oracle* on February 9, 1795.

70. Hammond to Grenville, Nov. 5, 1794, F.O. 5/5, fols. 345-50. Bond agreed. See his dispatch, Nov. 23, 1794, F.O. 5/6, fols. 112-16. See too, Hammond to Murray, Jan. 18, 1795, F.O. 116/2, pp. 303-6: "The spirit of privateering continues to operate with great activity and to an increasing extent." See Hammond to Grenville, Apr. 28, 1795, F.O. 116/5, p. 186; and idem to idem, same date, F.O. 5/9, fols. 146-55. In the latter, Hammond castigated Charleston, "whence projects of plunder and depredations are perpetually prosecuted that would disgrace the most piratical state of Barbary." Governor Wentworth of Nova Scotia described to Home Secretary Portland, July 5, 1795, F.O. 5/12, the burning of a British coastal vessel, which put in at Boston in distress, by "an outrageous Assembly" including many Frenchmen. See, finally, Bond to Grenville, Sept. 29, 1795, F.O. 5/10, fols. 200-205.

71. Bond to Grenville, Oct. 13, 1795, F.O. 5/10, fols. 218-21.

72. British representatives in America worked ceaselessly to learn about French purchases in the United States, as well as shipments, often in American bottoms and disguised as American property, to Europe. See Hammond to Capt. Rupert George, R.N., Aug. 23, 1794, F.O. 116/2, pp. 259-66. He reported the purchase of 400,000 barrels of flour by emissaries of the French government at Norfolk and Baltimore. It was intended, he said, to ship it in American bottoms ostensibly to Britain, but in reality to France. Similar accounts from Hammond are in F.O. 5/5, passim. See too, Bond to Grenville, Dec. 16, 1794, F.O. 5/6, fol. 124; Hammond to Rear Admiral Murray, Jan. 18, 1795, F.O. 116/2, pp. 303-6, urging the interception of vessels loading produce at Norfolk, "that sink of villainy"; idem to commanders in West Indian waters, Mar. 21, 1795, ibid.; and idem to Grenville, Apr. 3, 1795, F.O. 5/9, fol. 137. For indications that France was "in a state of starvation for the want of bread and all the necessaries of life," see Thomas Eldred to R. Pittman, Brest, Jan. 29, 1795, intercepted by the British, *R.H.M.C.R., Fortescue Pps.*, 3:13-14; and the *Oracle and Public Advertiser*, May 20, 1795, admitting that Britain, too, in common with Europe generally, was feeling the pinch. On this point, see also Add. MSS 38230, passim.

The British found additional proof of French purchases in the United States and collusion with the Americans when they captured Minister Fauchet's official correspondence. The dispatches, covering the period from September to December, 1794, were sent to Hammond for confidential communication to Jay and others. See Grenville's dispatch, June 5, 1795, F.O. 115/4, fols. 71 ff.

See, too, Lords of the Admiralty to Grenville, Nov. 10, 1794, F.O. 5/7, fol. 425. See especially Undersecretary John King in the Home Office to George Aust in the Foreign Office, July 3, 1795, F.O. 5/12, transmitting the observations on the neutrals' conduct in the West Indies by the attorney-general on British-conquered Guadeloupe.

73. The naval officer was Captain Robinson of the *Arethusa*, who intercepted the American schooner *Isis* off the French coast in June, 1795. The discovery of a cache of concealed letters from the New York firm, Cheriot and Richard, to their French correspondents clearly revealed the systematic and mammoth clandestine trade protecting French property as American. See the Lords of the Admiralty to Grenville, June 10, 1795, enclosing a copy of Capt. Robinson's report, June 2, 1795, F.O. 5/12; and Grenville to Hammond, July 1, 1795, F.O. 5/9, fol. 48, directing him to communicate an enclosed précis of the Cheriot and Richard correspondence to his American friends.

74. See Hammond to Grenville, July 27, 1795, F.O. 5/9, fol. 378. The King's speech is *Parl. Hist.*, 31:960-61. The *Morning Chronicle*, Apr. 4, 1795, seems to have been the first to publish reports of American complaints about infringement of the treaty by the new instructions.

75. Hammond to Grenville, June 25 and 28, 1795, F.O. 5/9, fols. 290-92, 293, 295, and 306. For Gouverneur Morris' reassurances to British correspondents, see Burgess to Grenville, June 28, 1795, *R.H.M.C.R.*, *Fortescue Pps.*, 3:87-89.

76. The *Oracle and Public Advertiser*, August 14, 1795, was high in praise of the treaty, mentioning particularly the West Indian article.

The prohibition of the export of cotton from the United States has been adduced as a special disadvantage for the United States: however, the crop's importance in the American economy lay in the future; and, in any event, the whole West Indian article was due for review two years after the war ended.

77. Grenville to Hammond, Aug. 31, 1795, F.O. 5/9, fols. 58-62; *Instr. Brit. Min.*, pp. 92-93.

APPENDIX H

1. Eden's memorandum is British Museum Additional MSS 34421, fols. 287-88.

2. To Morton Eden, Paris, Feb. 1, 1787, ibid., 34434, fols. 5-6.

3. The king to Grenville, Mar. 19, 1793, Boconnoc Papers. For the stipulations with Russia and Sardinia, see *A.S.P.*, For. Rel., p. 243.

APPENDIX I

1. To Home Secretary Dundas, Sept. 18, 1793, "Loose hints on the present situation of America," Melville MSS, Clem. Lib.

2. See John Adams to Foreign Secretary Jay, Sept. 22, 1787, John Adams, *The Life and Works of John Adams*, ed. Charles Francis Adams, 10 vols. (Boston, 1850-56), 8:450-51; and John Rutledge, Jr. to Jefferson, London, May 6, 12, 1790, Jefferson MSS, Lib. Cong., vol. 54, fols. 9306-7.

3. See Pinckney to Grenville, Dec. 5, 1792, F.O. 4/16, fol. 286.

4. Jefferson to Joshua Johnson, consul in the port of London, Dec. 17, 1790, Thomas Jefferson, *Writings of Thomas Jefferson*, ed. Paul L. Ford, 10 vols. (New York, 1892-99), 6:170-73. See idem to idem, Dec. 23, 1790, ibid., pp. 173-74, a private letter covering the foregoing which was written for Foreign Secretary Leeds's benefit. Jefferson was particularly exercised about the case of Hugh Purdie of Williamsburg, seized in London in July and discharged only in September, and then after being put in irons and bound and scourged in the presence of his involuntary shipmates.

Jefferson instructed Pinckney to express the tonnage-nationality ratio idea as the American position in his dispatch of May 7, 1793.

5. Bond to Grenville, Feb. 1, 1793, F.O. 5/2 fols. 90-91.

6. July 9, 1796, William Jay, *Life of John Jay*, 2 vols. (New York, 1833), 2:274-77.

7. See F.O. 5/12, passim.

8. Cited in note 1 above.

9. F.O. 5/2.

10. July 20, 1794, F.O. 116/2, pp. 234-37.

11. Aug. 1, 1793, F.O. 5/2, fols. 233-34.

12. Aug. 29, 1794, F.O. 5/5, fols. 264-69.

13. The Order was transmitted to Hammond in a dispatch of April 15, 1795, *Instr. Brit. Min.*, p. 81.

14. Edward Channing, *History of the United States*, 6 vols. (New York, 1927-30), 4:366, n. 2.

15. To Captain Rupert George, New York, Aug. 23, 1794, F.O. 116/2, pp. 259-66.

16. New York, Aug. 3, 1794, F.O. 5/5, fols. 181-91. See also *Instr. Brit. Min.*, p. 68, n. 62.

17. See Governor Clinton to Cochrane, copy, July 17, 1794, F.O. 5/7, fol. 328; Cochrane to Clinton, copy, July 18, 1794, ibid., fol. 330; and *Instr. Brit. Min.*, p. 68, no. 61.

18. See Grenville to Bond, Nov. 4, 1795, F.O. 5/10, fol. 17; printed in *Instr. Brit. Min.*, pp. 99-100, n. 77; Deas, the American chargé d'affaires in London, to Grenville, Nov. 5, 1795, F.O. 5/12; and Bond to idem, Nov. 15, 1795, F.O. 5/10, fols. 232-35. For

further information on Home's outrageous conduct, and on the revenge exacted by angry Rhode Islanders, see Hammond to Randolph, copy, July 30, 1794, F.O. 5/7, fols. 346-47; Home to Hammond, copy, Aug. 3, 1795, ibid., fols. 350-51; and Murray to idem, same date, ibid., fol. 352.

19. To Jefferson, Sept. 25, 1793, A.S.P., For Rel., p. 243. See also Pinckney to Grenville, July 5, 1794, F.O. 5/7, fols. 161-62 and passim, for Pinckney's efforts in specific cases of impressment. See idem to idem, July 25, 1794, ibid., fols. 195-96, enclosing a list of six Americans impressed in the West Indies and brought to Britain. See, for example, Undersecretary George Aust to American Consul William Knox, May 16, 1791, F.O. 4/10, fol. 50, stating that Pitt himself had directed him to take measures for the release of impressed Americans and to take steps to see that similar events did not recur in the future.

20. Randolph's report is in A.S.P., For Rel., p. 424.

21. Jay to Washington, Sept. 3, 1795, W. Jay, Life of John Jay, 2:257-59.

22. Sept. 4, 1795, Alexander Hamilton, Works of Alexander Hamilton, ed. Henry Cabot Lodge, 12 vols. (New York, 1904), 6:201-5. See also, Robert Goodloe Harper's masterful defense of Jay's Treaty, An Address to His Constituents (Philadelphia, 1796), claiming that Article XIX, forbidding outrages to citizens of one nation by those of the other, extended to impressment. He urged Congress, however, to adopt by law a system of federal citizenship certification.

23. Grenville to Jay, July 9, 1796, W. Jay, Life of John Jay, 2:274-77.

24. Philadelphia, Apr. 5, 1796, R.H.M.C.R., Fortescue Pps., 2:163-64.

APPENDIX J

1. Extract, E. A. Cruikshank, ed., The Correspondence of Lieut. Governor John Graves Simcoe, with Allied Documents, 5 vols. (Toronto, 1923-31), 3:9-12.

2. Aug. 16, 1794, ibid., 2:382-84.

3. McKee to Simcoe, July 26, 1794, enclosed in Simcoe to Dundas, Aug. 5, 1794. See also J. King to Burgess, Oct. 25, 1794, F.O. 5/7, fol. 397.

4. Wayne's dispatches are in American State Papers, IV. Indian Affairs (Washington, 1832), pp. 477 ff.

5. Simcoe to Clinton, Sept. 18, 1794, Clinton MSS, Clem. Lib. See also Morn. Chron., Oct. 22, 1794.

6. Instr. Brit. Min., pp. 73-75.

7. Jay to Washington, Nov. 19, 1794, William Jay, Life of John Jay, 2 vols. (New York, 1833), 2:236-37; but see Jay to Grenville, Feb. 24, 1795, F.O. 5/12, no folio, communicating "informally" new American complaints on the subject.

BIBLIOGRAPHY

BIBLIOGRAPHIES AND GUIDES

ALLEN, H. C. *Great Britain and the United States: A History of Anglo-American Relations (1783-1952)*. New York: St. Martin's Press, 1955.

ANDREWS, CHARLES MCLEAN. *Guide to the Materials for American History, to 1783, in the Public Records Offices of Great Britain*. 2 vols. Washington: Carnegie Institution of Washington, 1912-14.

BEERS, HENRY PUTNEY. *Bibliographies in American History*. New York: H. W. Wilson Co., 1938.

BEMIS, SAMUEL FLAGG, and GRIFFIN, G. G. *Guide to the Diplomatic History of the United States*. Washington: Government Printing Office, 1935.

FAY, BERNARD. *Bibliographie Critique des Ouvrages Français Relatifs aux États-Unis, (1770-1800)*. Bibliothèque de la Revue de Littérature Comparés dirigée par F. Baldensperger et Paul Hazard, vol. 7, pt. 2. Paris: Champion, 1925.

GREENE, EVARTS BOUTELL, and MORRIS, RICHARD BRANDON. *Guide to the Principal Sources for Early American History in the City of New York*. New York: Columbia University Press, 1953.

Harvard Guide to American History. Cambridge, Mass.: Harvard University Press, 1954.

MATTHEWS, M. ALICE. "Neutrality and American Policy on Neutrality." Carnegie Endowment for International Peace Library, Brief Reading List nos. 4 and 5. Washington, 1935.

PARGELLIS, STANLEY, and MEDLEY, D. J. *Bibliography of British History, 1714-89*. Oxford: Clarendon Press, 1951.

RAGATZ, LOWELL JOSEPH. *A Guide for the Study of British Caribbean History, 1763-1834*. Washington: Government Printing Office, 1932.

ORIGINAL SOURCES AND TRANSCRIPTS

Ann Arbor. Clements Library. Clinton Manuscripts.

————. Hammond Manuscripts.

————. Hammond-Simcoe Correspondence.

————. Melville Manuscripts.

————. The R. G. Adams Transcripts of Documents Relating to the Negotiation of the Treaty of Peace.

————. Secret Service Papers.

————. Shelburne Manuscripts.

————. Simcoe Manuscripts.

————. Vaughan Manuscripts, Emmons Transcripts.

————. Wedderburn Manuscripts.

Bury St. Edmonds. Public Records Office. Grafton Manuscripts. London.

British Museum. Additional Manuscripts. Auckland Manuscripts.

————. Additional Manuscripts. Hardwicke Papers.

————. Additional Manuscripts. Leeds Papers.

————. Additional Manuscripts. Liverpool Papers.

————. Additional Manuscripts. Wedderburn Papers.

————. Egerton Manuscripts.

London. Public Record Office. Board of Trade Series.

————. Chatham Papers (including papers of the younger Pitt).

————. Colonial Office Series.

————. Foreign Office Series.

————. Privy Council Series.

————. Treasury Papers.

Lostwithiel, Cornwall. Boconnoc House. Grenville Papers.

Washington. Library of Congress. Hamilton Manuscripts.

————. Jefferson Manuscripts.

LONDON NEWSPAPERS

London. British Museum. Burney Collection.

Courier.

Daily Register.

Diary, or Woodfall's Register.

London Packet.

Morning Chronicle.

Morning Herald.

Morning Post and Daily Advertiser.

Oracle.

Oracle and Public Advertiser.

Public Advertiser.

Times.

PRINTED SOURCES

ADAMS, ABIGAIL. *Letters of Mrs. Adams.* Edited by Charles Francis Adams. Boston: Wilkins, Carter, and Co., 1848.

————. *New Letters.* Edited by Stewart Mitchell. Boston: Houghton Mifflin, 1947.

ADAMS, JOHN. *Diary and Autobiography of John Adams.* Edited by Lyman H. Butterfield. 4 vols. Cambridge, Mass.: Harvard University Press, 1961.

————. *Familiar Letters of John Adams and His Wife Abigail Adams, During the Revolution.* Edited by Charles Francis Adams. New York, 1876.

————. *Letters to Dr. Calkoen.* London, 1786.

————. *The Life and Works of John Adams.* Edited by Charles Francis Adams. 10 vols. Boston: Little, Brown and Co., 1850-56.

————, and ADAMS, JOHN QUINCY. *Selected Writings.* Edited by Adrienne Koch and William Peden. New York: Alfred A. Knopf, 1946.

[ADAMS, JOHN QUINCY.] "British Colonial and Navigation System." *American Quarterly Review,* September 1827, pp. 267-306.

ALLEN, JOSEPH. *The Navigation Laws of Great Britain, Historically and Practically Considered.* London, 1849.

American State Papers. I. Foreign Relations. Washington: Gales and Seaton, 1832.

American State Papers. II. Indian Affairs. Washington: Gales and Seaton, 1832.

AMES, FISHER. *The Works of Fisher Ames.* Edited by J. T. Kirkland. Boston: T. B. Wait and Co., 1809.

ANDERSON, JAMES. *The Interest of Great Britain with Regard to Her American Colonies, Considered.* London: T. Cadell, 1782.

BARING, ALEXANDER. *An Inquiry into the Causes and Consequences of the Orders in Council and an Examination of the Conduct of Great Britain towards the Neutral Commerce of America.* 2d ed. New York, 1808.

BELSHAM, WILLIAM. *Memoirs of the Reign of George III.* 4 vols. London, 1795.

BEMIS, SAMUEL FLAGG, ed. "The Vermont Separatists and Great Britain, 1789-91." *American Historical Review* 21 (1915-16): 547-60.

BENTON, THOMAS HART, ed. *Abridgement of the Debates of Congress from 1789-1865.* Vols. 1-4. New York: D. Appleton and Co., 1858-61.

BISSET, ROBERT. *Reign of George III to Termination of the Late War.* 6 vols. London, 1803.

BOURNE, HENRY E., ed. "Correspondence of the Comte de Moustier with the Comte de Montmorin, 1787-1789." *American Historical Review* 8 (1902-3): 709-33.

BRISSOT DE WARVILLE, JACQUES PIERRE. *Nouveau Voyage dans les États-Unis de l'Amérique Septentrionale, fait en 1788.* Paris, 1791.

British Diplomatic Instructions, 1689-1789. 7 vols. Camden Society Publication, 3d ser., vol. 49. London: Royal Historical Society, 1922-34.

BROWNING, OSCAR, ed. *Despatches from Paris, 1787-90*. 2 vols. Camden Society Publication, 3d ser., vols. 16 and 19. London: Royal Historical Society, 1909-10.

BRYMNER, DOUGLAS. *Report on Canadian Archives, 1890*. Ottawa, 1891.

BUCKINGHAM AND CHANDOS, 2D DUKE OF. *Memoirs of the Courts and Cabinets of George III*. London: Hurst and Blackett, 1856.

BURGES, SIR JAMES BLAND. *Selections from Letters and Correspondence*. Edited by James Hutton. London, 1885.

BURNETT, EDMUND C., ed. *Letters of Members of the Continental Congress*. Washington: Carnegie Institution of Washington, 1921.

————, ed. "Observations of London Merchants on American Trade, 1783." *American Historical Review* 18 (1912-13): 769-80.

CHALMERS, GEORGE. *An Estimate of the Comparative Strength of Great Britain*. London, 1794.

————. *Opinions on Interesting Subjects of Public Law and Commercial Policy Arising from American Independence*. London, 1784.

COBBETT, WILLIAM, and WRIGHT, JOHN, eds. *Parliamentary History*. 36 vols. Vols. 1-12, London: R. Bagshaw, 1806-12; vols. 13-36, London: Longman and Co., 1812-20.

A Complete Investigation of Mr. Eden's Treaty. London, 1787.

Considerations of the Present State of the Intercourse between His Majesty's Sugar Colonies and the Dominions of the United States of America. London, 1784.

COXE, TENCH. *Brief Examination of Lord Sheffield's "Observations."* Philadelphia, 1791.

CRUIKSHANK, E. A., ed. *The Correspondence of Lieut. Governor John Graves Simcoe, with Allied Documents*. 5 vols. Toronto: Ontario Historical Society, 1923-31.

————, ed. *The Settlement of the United Empire Loyalists on the Upper St. Lawrence and Bay of Quinte in 1784*. Toronto: Ontario Historical Society, 1934.

DAVENPORT, FRANCES G., and PAULLIN, CHARLES OSCAR, eds. *European Treaties Bearing on the History of the United States, 1455-1815*. Washington: Carnegie Institution of Washington, 1917-37.

EDEN, WILLIAM. *The Journal and Correspondence of William, Lord Auckland*. Edited by G. Hogge. Preface and introduction by the Bishop of Bath and Wells. 4 vols. London, 1860-62.

EDWARDS, BRYAN. *The History, Civil and Commercial, of the British Colonies in the West Indies*. 3 vols. 3d ed. London, 1801.

————. *Thoughts on the Late Proceedings of Government Respecting the Trade of the West Indian Islands with the United States of America*. 2d ed. London, 1784.

FORD, WORTHINGTON CHAUNCEY, ed. *Abstract of the Report of the Lords of the Privy Council.* Washington, 1888.

———, et al, eds. *Journals of the Continental Congress, 1774-1789.* 34 vols. Washington, 1904-37.

FOX, CHARLES JAMES. *Memorials and Correspondence of Charles James Fox.* Edited by Lord John Russell. 2 vols. London, 1853.

GEORGE III. *Correspondence of George III.* Edited by Sir John Fortescue. 6 vols. London: Macmillan and Co., 1927-28.

GIBBS, GEORGE. *Memoirs of the Administrations of Washington and Adams.* 2 vols. New York: W. Van Norden, 1846.

HADFIELD, JOSEPH. *An Englishman in America, 1785.* Edited by Douglas S. Robertson. Toronto: Hunter-Rose Co., 1933.

HAMILTON, ALEXANDER. *Works.* Edited by John C. Hamilton. 7 vols. New York, 1850-51.

———. *Works of Alexander Hamilton.* Edited by Henry Cabot Lodge. 12 vols. New York: G. P. Putnam's Sons, 1904.

HARPER, ROBERT GOODLOE. *An Address to His Constituents.* Philadelphia, 1796.

HUNTER, ROBERT, JR. *Quebec to Carolina in 1785-1786.* Edited by Louis B. Wright and Marion Tingling. San Marino, Calif.: Huntington Library, 1943.

INNIS, HAROLD ADAMS, and LOWER, A. R. M., eds. *Select Documents in Canadian Economic History, 1497-1783.* Toronto: University of Toronto Press, 1929.

JAMESON, JOHN FRANKLIN, ed. "Higginson's Letters." *Annual Report of the American Historical Association* (1896): 1:713-19, 725-33, 733-41.

———, ed. "Letters of Phineas Bond to the Foreign Office, 1787-89." *Annual Report of the American Historical Association* (1897):513-659; (1898):454-568.

JAY, JOHN. *Correspondence and Public Papers of John Jay.* Edited by Harry P. Johnston. 4 vols. New York: G. P. Putnam's Sons, 1890-93.

———. *Diary during the Peace Negotiations of 1782.* Edited by Frank Monaghan. New Haven: Yale University Press, 1934.

JEFFERSON, THOMAS. *Jefferson Papers.* Edited by Julian P. Boyd. 17 vols. to date. Princeton: Princeton University Press, 1950—.

———. *Writings of Thomas Jefferson.* Edited by Paul L. Ford. 10 vols. New York: G. P. Putnam's Sons, 1892-99.

[JENKINSON, CHARLES.] *Discourse on the Conduct of Great Britain in Respect to Neutral Nations.* London, 1757.

KING, RUFUS. *Life and Correspondence of Rufus King.* Edited by C. R. King. 6 vols. New York: G. P. Putnam's Sons, 1894-1900.

KNOX, WILLIAM. *Extra Official State Papers.* 2 vols. London, 1789.

LEEDS, FRANCIS, 5th DUKE OF. *Political Memoranda.* Edited by Oscar Browning. London: Camden Society, 1884.

MADISON, JAMES. "Autobiography." Edited by Douglass Adair. *William and Mary Quarterly,* 3d ser. 2 (1945): 191-209.

―――. *Writings.* Edited by Gaillard Hunt. 9 vols. New York: G. P. Putnam, 1900-10.

Massachusetts Historical Society Collections. Vol. 9. Letters of the Marquis of Buckingham to Sir John Temple. Boston, 1867.

―――. 7th ser. Vol. 6. The Letters of Governor Bowdoin and Sir John Temple. Boston, 1907.

MAYO, BERNARD, ed. *Instructions to the British Ministers to the United States.* Washington: Government Printing Office, 1941.

MONROE, JAMES. *Writings.* Edited by Stanislaus Murray Hamilton. 7 vols. New York: G. P. Putnam, 1898-1903.

MOORE, JOHN BASSETT. *History and Digest of the International Arbitrations to Which the United States Has Been a Party.* 6 vols. Washington, 1898.

―――, ed. *International Adjudications.* New York: Oxford University Press, 1929.

MORRIS, GOUVERNEUR. *Diary and Letters of Gouverneur Morris.* Edited by Anne Cary Morris. 2 vols. New York, 1888.

MUNRO, JAMES, and GRANT, W. L., eds. *Acts of the Privy Council, Colonial Series.* 6 vols. London: By the authority of His Majesty's Treasury, 1908-12.

NELSON, HORATIO. *Dispatches and Letters of Lord Nelson.* Edited by Sir Nicholas H. Nicolas. 7 vols. London, 1844.

PALLAIN, GEORGES, ed. *Correspondence Diplomatique de Talleyrand. La Mission de Talleyrand à Londres en 1792. Ses Lettres de l'Amérique à Lord Lansdowne.* Paris, 1889.

REEVES, JOHN. *The Law of Shipping and Navigation.* 2d ed. London: W. Clarke & Sons, 1807.

A Review of the Laws of the United States. London, 1790.

ROSE, GEORGE. *Diaries and Correspondence.* Edited by L. V. Harcourt. 2 vols. London, 1860.

Royal Historical Manuscripts Commission Reports, Fortescue Papers. 10 vols. London, 1892.

―――. *Knox Papers (Various Collections),* VI. Dublin, 1909.

RUSH, BENJAMIN. *Letters of Benjamin Rush.* Edited by Lyman H. Butterfield. 2 vols. Princeton: Princeton University Press, 1951.

RUSSELL, PETER. *Correspondence with Allied Documents.* Edited by E. A. Cruikshank and A. F. Hunter. 3 vols. Toronto: Ontario Historical Society, 1932.

SHEFFIELD, JOHN BAKER HOLROYD, 1st EARL OF. *Observations on the*

Commerce of the American States with Europe and the West Indies. London, 1783.

SHELBURNE, WILLIAM, EARL OF. *Life of William Earl of Shelburne.* Edited by Lord Fitzmaurice. 2 vols. London: Macmillan and Co., 1912.

SHORTT, ADAM, and DOUGHTY, A. G., eds. *Documents Relating to the Constitutional History of Canada, 1759-1791.* Ottawa, 1907.

SMITH, ADAM. *An Inquiry into the Nature and Causes of the Wealth of Nations.* Edited by Edwin Cannan. 2 vols. London: Methuen, 1950.

SMITH, CHARLES CARD, ed. "Letters of Benjamin Vaughan to Shelburne." *Proceedings of the Massachusetts Historical Society,* 2d ser. 17 (1903): 406-38.

SMYTH, JOHN FERDINAND DALZIEL. *A Tour in the United States of America.* 2 vols. Dublin, 1784.

STEINER, BERNARD C. "Correspondence of William Smith." *Sewanee Review* 14 (1906): 76-104.

STEVENSON, JOHN. *An Address to Bryan Edwards, Esq.* London, 1784.

TALLEYRAND-PÉRIGORD, CHARLES MAURICE DE. *Memoir Concerning Commercial Relations of the United States with England.* Boston, 1809.

Treaties and Conventions Concluded between the United States of America and Other Powers. Compiled by William Malloy. Vols. 1 and 2. Washington: Government Printing Office, 1910.

TUCKER, JOSIAH. *A Series of Answers to Certain Popular Objections against Separating from the Rebellious Colonies, and Discarding Them Entirely.* Gloucester, 1776.

TURNER, FREDERICK JACKSON, ed. "Correspondence of the French Ministers to the United States, 1791-97." Introduction to *Annual Report of the American Historical Association* (1903), vol. 2.

————, ed. "English Policy toward America in 1790-1791." *American Historical Review* 7 (1901): 706-35; 8 (1902): 78-86.

U.S. *Embargo Laws.* Boston, 1809.

U.S. Congress. *Debates and Proceedings in the Congress of the United States, 1789-1824.* 42 vols. Washington, 1834-56.

A View of the Treaty of Commerce with France. London, 1787.

WALCOTT, OLIVER. *British Influence on the Affairs of the United States, Proved and Explained.* Boston, 1804.

WASHINGTON, GEORGE. *Diaries of George Washington, 1748-99.* Edited by John Clement Fitzpatrick. 4 vols. Boston and New York: Houghton Mifflin Co., 1925.

WHARTON, FRANCIS, ed. *The Revolutionary Diplomatic Correspondence of the United States.* 6 vols. Washington, 1889.

WINDHAM, WILLIAM, ed. *Windham Papers.* Introduction by the Earl of Roseberry. 2 vols. London, 1913.

SECONDARY WORKS

ADAMS, CHARLES FRANCIS. *Life of John Adams.* 2 vols. Philadelphia: Lippincott & Co., 1871.

ADAMS, EPHRAIM D. *The Influence of Grenville on Pitt's Foreign Policy, 1787-1798.* Washington: Carnegie Institution of Washington, 1904.

ADAMS, RANDOLPH G. *Political Ideas of the American Revolution.* Durham, N.C.: Trinity College Press, 1922.

ADOLPHUS, JOHN. *History of England from the Accession to the Decease of George III.* 7 vols. London, 1840.

ALBION, ROBERT GREENHALGH. *Forests and Sea Power.* Cambridge, Mass.: Harvard University Press, 1926.

ALVORD, CLARENCE WALWORTH. *The Illinois Country, 1673-1818.* Springfield: Illinois Centennial Commission, 1920.

———. *Lord Shelburne and the Founding of British-American Good Will.* London: Oxford University Press, 1926.

ANDREWS, CHARLES MCLEAN. *Colonial Period of American History.* 4 vols. New Haven: Yale University Press, 1934-38.

ANGELL, JAMES BURRILL. "The Diplomacy of the United States, 1789-1850." In *Narrative and Critical History of America,* edited by Justin Winsor, 7:461-525. Boston and New York: Houghton Mifflin Co., 1884-89.

BANCROFT, H. H. *History of the Northwest Coast.* The Works of H. H. Bancroft, vols. 27 and 28. San Francisco: A. L. Bancroft and Co., 1884.

BARNES, DONALD GROVE. *George III and William Pitt.* Stanford, Calif.: Stanford University Press, 1939.

BARTLETT, CHRISTOPHER JOHN. *Great Britain and Sea Power.* Oxford: Clarendon Press, 1963.

BEARD, CHARLES A. *Economic Interpretation of the Constitution of the United States.* New York: Macmillan Co., 1913.

———. *Economic Origins of Jeffersonian Democracy.* New York: Macmillan Co., 1927.

———. *The Idea of National Interest.* New York: Macmillan Co., 1934.

BECKER, CARL. *Benjamin Franklin.* Ithaca, N.Y.: Cornell University Press, 1946.

BEMIS, SAMUEL FLAGG. *Jay's Treaty: A Study in Commerce and Diplomacy.* New York: Macmillan Co., 1923; rev. ed., New Haven and London: Yale University Press, 1962.

———. "John Jay." In *American Secretaries of State and Their Diplomacy,* edited by Samuel Flagg Bemis, vol. 1. New York: Knopf, 1927.

———. *Pinckney's Treaty: A Study of America's Advantage from Europe's Distress, 1783-1800.* Baltimore: Johns Hopkins Press, 1926.

BENNS, F. LEE. "The American Struggle for the British West Indies Carrying Trade, 1815-1830." Ph.D. dissertation, Indiana University, 1923.

BEVERIDGE, ALBERT JEREMIAH. *Life of John Marshall.* 4 vols. Boston and New York: Houghton Mifflin Co., 1916-19.

BOURNE, HENRY ELDRIDGE. *The Revolutionary Period in Europe, 1768-1810.* New York: Century Co., 1914.

BOWDEN, WITT. *Industrial Society in England towards the End of the Eighteenth Century.* New York: Macmillan Co., 1925.

———. *The Rise of the Great Manufacturers in England, 1760-1790.* Allentown, Pa.: H. R. Haas and Co., 1919.

BOYD, JULIAN P. *Anglo-American Union: Joseph Galloway's Plans to Preserve the British Empire, 1774-1788.* Philadelphia: University of Pennsylvania Press, 1941.

———. *Number 7: Alexander Hamilton's Secret Attempts to Control American Foreign Policy.* Princeton: Princeton University Press, 1964.

BRADLEY, ARTHUR GRANVILLE. *Colonial Americans in Exile.* New York: E. P. Dutton & Co., 1932.

———. *Lord Dorchester.* London and Toronto: Morang Co., 1907.

BRANT, IRVING. *James Madison: Father of the Constitution. James Madison,* vol. 1. Indianapolis: Bobbs-Merrill Co., 1941.

BREBNER, JOHN BARTLETT. *North Atlantic Triangle.* New York: Columbia University Press, 1945.

BROWN, ALICE. *Mercy Warren.* New York: Charles Scribner's Sons, 1896.

BROWNING, OSCAR. "The Treaty of Commerce between England and France." In *Transactions of the Royal Historical Society,* 3d ser. 3:349-64. London, 1885.

BRUNHOUSE, ROBERT L. *The Counter-Revolution in Pennsylvania, 1776-1790.* Harrisburg: University of Pennsylvania Press, 1942.

BRYMNER, DOUGLAS. "Vermont Negotiations." In *Report on Canadian Archives,* pp. 53-58. Ottawa, 1890.

BUCK, NORMAN S. *Development of Anglo-American Trade.* New Haven: Yale University Press, 1925.

BUCK, PHILIP W. *Politics of Mercantilism.* New York: Henry Holt Co., 1942.

BUCK, SOLON JUSTUS. *The Story of the Grand Portage.* Minneapolis: Cook County Historical Society, 1931.

BURNETT, EDMUND C. *The Continental Congress.* New York: Macmillan Co., 1941.

BURT, ALFRED LE ROY. *The Old Province of Quebec.* Minneapolis: University of Minnesota Press, 1933.

———. *The United States, Great Britain, and British North America.* New Haven: Yale University Press, 1940.

CAIRNS, WILLIAM B. *British Criticism of American Writing, 1783-1833.* Madison: University of Wisconsin Press, 1918.

CARROLL, JOHN A., and ASHWORTH, M. W. *George Washington: First in Peace. George Washington: A Biography,* vol. 7. New York: Scribner, 1957. Vols. 1-6, Douglas S. Freeman, *George Washington: A Biography,* 1948-55.

CAUGHEY, JOHN W. *McGillivray of the Creeks.* Norman: Oklahoma University Press, 1938.

CHANNING, EDWARD. *History of the United States.* 6 vols. New York: Macmillan Co., 1927-30.

CHINARD, GILBERT. *Honest John Adams.* Boston: Little, Brown & Co., 1932.

CLARK, DORA M. *British Opinion and the American Revolution.* New Haven: Yale University Press, 1930.

CLARK, MARY E. *Peter Porcupine in America.* Philadelphia: Times and News Publishing Co., 1939.

CLAUDER, ANNA C. *American Commerce as Affected by the Wars of the French Revolution and Napoleon, 1793-1812.* Philadelphia: University of Pennsylvania Press, 1932.

COCKROFT, GRACE A. *Public Life of George Chalmers.* New York: Columbia University Press, 1939.

CORWIN, EDWARD SAMUEL. *French Policy and the American Alliance of 1778.* Princeton: Princeton University Press, 1916.

COUPLAND, REGINALD. *The American Revolution and the British Empire.* London: Longmans, Green & Co., 1930.

CRANE, VERNER WINSLOW. *Benjamin Franklin: Englishman and American.* Baltimore: Williams and Walkins Co., 1936.

CREIGHTON, DONALD G. *The Commercial Empire of the St. Lawrence, 1760-1850.* Toronto: Ryerson Press, 1937.

CRESSON, WILLIAM PENN. *James Monroe.* Chapel Hill: University of North Carolina Press, 1946.

CRITTENDEN, CHARLES CHRISTOPHER. *The Commerce of North Carolina, 1763-1789.* New Haven: Yale University Press, 1936.

DARLING, ARTHUR BURR. *Our Rising Empire.* New Haven: Yale University Press, 1940.

DAVIDSON, PHILIP. *Propaganda and the American Revolution, 1763-1783.* Chapel Hill: University of North Carolina Press, 1941.

DAVIS, JOSEPH STANCLIFFE. *Essays in the Earlier History of American Corporations.* 2 vols. Cambridge, Mass.: Harvard University Press, 1917.

DE CONDE, ALEXANDER. *Entangling Alliance.* Durham, N.C.: Duke University Press, 1958.

DEMOND, ROBERT O. *The Loyalists in North Carolina,* Garden City, N.Y.: Anchor Books, 1964.

DICKERSON, OLIVER MORTON. *The Navigation Acts and the American Revolution.* Philadelphia: University of Pennsylvania Press, 1951.

DUNBAR, LOUISE BURNHAM. *A Study of "Monarchial" Tendencies in the United States, from 1776 to 1801.* Urbana: University of Illinois Press, 1922.

EDWARDS, NINIAN WIRT. *History of Illinois from 1778 to 1833.* Springfield: Illinois State Journal Co., 1870.

EHRMAN, JOHN. *The British Government and Commercial Negotiations with Europe, 1783-1793.* Cambridge: Cambridge University Press, 1962.

FEE, WALTER RAY. *Transition from Aristocracy to Democracy in New Jersey.* Somerville, N.J.: Somerset Press, 1933.

FEILING, KEITH G. *History of the Second Tory Party.* London: Macmillan Co., 1938.

FISH, CARL RUSSELL. *The Development of American Nationality.* New York: American Book Co., 1940.

————. *Foundations of American Neutrality.* Madison: University of Wisconsin Press, 1932.

————. *United States and Great Britain.* Chicago: University of Chicago Press, 1932.

FISKE, JOHN. *The Critical Period of American History.* Boston and New York: Houghton Mifflin and Co., 1888.

FITZPATRICK, JOHN CLEMENT, ed. *George Washington Himself.* Indianapolis: Bobbs-Merrill Co., 1933.

FORD, WORTHINGTON CHAUNCEY. *The United States and Spain in 1790.* Brookline, Mass.: Historical Printing Club, 1890.

FURBER, HOLDEN. *Henry Dundas, First Viscount Melville.* London: Oxford University Press, 1931.

GEWEHR, WESLEY M. *The Great Awakening in Virginia, 1740-1790.* Durham, N.C.: Duke University Press, 1930.

GOOCH, GEORGE PEABODY, and WARD, ADOLPHUS WILLIAM, eds. *Cambridge History of British Foreign Policy.* Cambridge: Cambridge University Press, 1922.

GOODMAN, NATHAN GERSON. *Benjamin Rush, Physician and Citizen.* Philadelphia: University of Pennsylvania Press, 1934.

GOTTSCHALK, LOUIS R. *Lafayette between the American and the French Revolutions.* Chicago: University of Chicago Press, 1950.

————. *Lafayette Comes to America, 1783-1789.* Chicago: University of Chicago Press, 1935.

————. *The Place of the American Revolution in the Causal Pattern of the French Revolution.* Easton, Pa.: American Friends of Lafayette, 1948.

GRAHAM, GERALD S. *British Policy and Canada, 1774-91.* London and New York: Longmans, Green & Co., 1930.

————. *Empire of the North Atlantic*. Toronto: University of Toronto Press, 1950.

————. *Sea Power and British North America, 1783-1820*. Cambridge, Mass.: Harvard University Press, 1941.

GUTTRIDGE, GEORGE HERBERT. *David Hartley, M.P.: An Advocate of Conciliation, 1774-1783*. University of California Publications in History, vol. 14, no. 3. Berkeley: University of California Press, 1926.

————. *English Whiggism and the American Revolution*. University of California Publications in History, vol. 28. Berkeley: University of California Press, 1942.

HACKER, LOUIS M. *The Triumph of American Capitalism*. New York: Simon and Schuster, 1940.

HALL, WALTER P. *British Radicalism, 1791-97*. New York: Columbia University, Longmans, Greene & Co., Agents, 1912.

HALL, WILLIAM EDWARD. *A Treatise on International Law*. Oxford: Clarendon Press, 1890.

HARASZTI, ZOLTAN. *John Adams and the Prophets of Progress*. Cambridge: Harvard University Press, 1952.

HARLOW, VINCENT T. *The Founding of the Second British Empire, 1763-1793*. 2 vols. London: Longmans, Green & Co., 1952-64.

HARRELL, ISAAC S. *Loyalism in Virginia*. Philadelphia: University of Pennsylvania Press, 1926.

HAYDEN, JOSEPH R. *Senate and Treaties, 1789-1817*. New York: Macmillan Co., 1920.

HAZEN, CHARLES D. *Contemporary American Opinion of the French Revolution*. Gloucester, Mass.: P. Smith, 1964.

HECKSHER, ELI. *Mercantilism*, 2 vols. London: G. Allen and Unwin, 1935.

HENDRICK, BURTON JESSE. *The Lees of Virginia*. Boston: Little, Brown & Co., 1935.

HIDY, RALPH WILLARD. *The House of Baring in American Trade and Finance*. Cambridge, Mass.: Harvard University Press, 1949.

HODGINS, THOMAS. *British and American Diplomacy Affecting Canada*. Toronto: Publishers' Syndicate, 1900.

HOLT, ANNE. *Life of Joseph Priestly*. London: Oxford Press, 1931.

HORN, DAVID BAYNE. *The British Diplomatic Service, 1689-1789*. Oxford: Clarendon Press, 1961.

HORTON, JOHN T. *James Kent: A Study in Conservatism*. New York: Appleton-Century Co., 1939.

HUMPHREYS, FRANCIS LANDON. *Life and Times of David Humphreys*. 2 vols. New York: G. P. Putnam's Sons, 1917.

HUNT, GAILLARD. *Life of James Madison*. New York: Doubleday, Page & Co., 1902.

HUNT, WILLIAM. *History of England from the Accession of George III to the Close of Pitt's First Administration.* London: Longmans, Green & Co., 1905.

HUTCHESON, HAROLD. *Tench Coxe: A Study in American Economic Development.* Baltimore: Johns Hopkins Press, 1938.

HYNEMAN, CHARLES SHANG. *The First American Neutrality.* Urbana: University of Illinois Press, 1934.

INNIS, HAROLD ADAMS. *The Cod Fisheries.* New Haven and Toronto: Ryerson Press, 1940.

———. *The Fur Trade in Canada.* New Haven: Yale University Press, 1930.

JAY, WILLIAM. *Life of John Jay.* 2 vols. New York, 1833.

JENSEN, MERRILL. *The New Nation.* New York: Alfred A. Knopf, 1950.

JOHNSON, EMORY RICHARD. *History of Domestic and Foreign Commerce of the United States.* 2 vols. Washington: Carnegie Institution of Washington, 1915.

KNORR, KLAUS E. *British Colonial Theories, 1570-1850.* Toronto: University of Toronto Press, 1944.

KOCH, ADRIENNE. *Jefferson and Madison.* New York: Knopf, 1950.

———. *The Philosophy of Thomas Jefferson.* New York: Columbia University Press, 1943.

KROUT, JOHN ALLEN. *The Completion of Independence, 1790-1830.* New York: Macmillan Co., 1940.

KROUT, JOHN ALLEN, and FOX, DIXON R. *Completion of Independence.* New York: Macmillan Co., 1944.

LEWIS, GEORGE E. *The Indiana Company.* Glendale, Calif.: Arthur H. Clark Co., 1941.

LIPSON, EPHRAIM. *Economic History of England.* 3 vols. London: A. C. Black, 1915-31.

LODGE, HENRY CABOT. *Alexander Hamilton.* Boston: Houghton Mifflin Co., 1882.

McILWRAITH, JEAN N. *Sir Frederick Haldimand.* London and Toronto: Oxford University Press, 1904; 2d ed., 1926.

McMASTER, JOHN BACH. *History of the People of the United States.* 8 vols. New York: D. Appleton Co., 1883-1913.

MAHAN, ALFRED THAYER. *Sea Power in Its Relation to the War of 1812.* 2 vols. Boston: Little, Brown and Co., 1905.

———. *The Influence of Sea Power upon the French Revolution and Empire.* Boston: Little, Brown and Co., 1892.

MALCOLM-SMITH, ELIZABETH FRANCES. *British Diplomacy in the Eighteenth Century.* London: Williams and Norgate Ltd., 1937.

———, et al. *British Diplomatic Representatives, 1789-1852.* London: Offices of the Royal Historical Society, 1934.

MALONE, DUMAS. *Jefferson and the Rights of Man. Jefferson and His Time,* vol. 2. Boston: Little, Brown and Co., 1951.

MANNING, HELEN T. *British Colonial Government after the American Revolution.* New Haven: Yale University Press, 1933.

MASSEY, WILLIAM N. *History of England during the Reign of George III.* 4 vols. London: J. W. Parker & Son, 1855-63; 2d ed., 1865.

MATHESON, CYRIL. *Life of Henry Dundas.* London: Constable and Co., 1933.

MAXWELL, LLOYD W. *Discriminating Duties and the American Merchant Marine.* New York: H. W. Wilson Co., 1926.

MESICK, JANE LOUISE. *The English Traveler in America, 1785-1835.* New York: Columbia University Press, 1922.

MILLER, JOHN CHESTER. *Alexander Hamilton.* New York: Harper, 1959.

————. *The Federalist Era.* New York: Harper, 1960.

MONAGHAN, FRANK. *John Jay.* New York and Indianapolis: Bobbs-Merrill Co., 1935.

MOORE, JOHN BASSETT. *History and Digest of the International Arbitrations to Which the United States Has Been a Party.* 6 vols. Washington: Government Printing Office, 1898.

MOREY, WILLIAM CAREY. *Diplomatic Episodes.* New York and London: Longmans, Green & Co., 1926.

MORISON, SAMUEL ELIOT. *The Life and Letters of Harrison Gray Otis, Federalist.* 2 vols. Boston: Houghton Mifflin Co., 1913.

————. *The Maritime History of Massachusetts, 1783-1860.* Boston: Houghton Mifflin Co., 1921.

————. Introduction to *Sources and Documents Illustrating the American Revolution,* edited by Samuel Eliot Morison. Oxford: Clarendon Press, 1929.

MORRIS, RICHARD B. *The Peacemakers.* New York: Harper & Row, 1965.

MORSE, A. E. *Federalist Party in Massachusetts.* Princeton: Princeton University Press, 1909.

MOWAT, ROBERT BALMAIN. *Diplomatic Relations of Great Britain and the United States.* New York: Longmans, Green and Co., 1925.

NELSON, WILLIAM H. *The American Tory.* Oxford: Clarendon Press, 1961.

NEVINS, ALLAN. *American Social History as Recorded by British Travellers.* New York: Holt and Co., 1923.

————. *American States during and after the Revolution.* New York: Macmillan Co., 1924.

O'DONNELL, WILLIAM E. *The Chevalier de la Luzerne.* Louvain: Descleé de Brouwer, 1938.

PARRINGTON, VERNON L. *Main Currents in American Thought.* 3 vols. New York: Harcourt, Brace & Co., 1927-30.

PARTON, JAMES. *Life and Times of Benjamin Franklin.* 2 vols. New York: Mason Bros., 1864.

PAYNE, GEORGE HENRY. *England: Her Treatment of America.* New York: Sears Publishing Co., 1931.

PELL, JOHN. *Ethan Allen.* Boston and New York: Houghton Mifflin Co., 1929.

PELLEW, GEORGE. *John Jay.* Boston and New York: Houghton Mifflin Co., 1909.

PERKINS, BRADFORD. *The First Rapprochement.* Philadelphia: University of Pennsylvania Press, 1955.

PHILIPPI, GERTRUDE. *Imperialistische und pazisfizistische Strömungen in der Politik der Vereinigten Staaten von Amerika während der ersten Jahrzehnte ihres Bestehens.* Heidelberg: C. Winter, 1914.

PHILLIPS, PAUL C. *The West in the Diplomacy of the American Revolution.* Urbana: University of Illinois Press, 1913.

POWER, EILEEN. *The Industrial Revolution, 1750-1850.* London: Economic History Society, 1927.

QUARLES, BENJAMIN. *The Negro in the American Revolution.* Chapel Hill: University of North Carolina Press, 1961.

RAGATZ, LOWELL JOSEPH. *The Fall of the Planter Class in the British Caribbean, 1763-1833.* New York: Century Co., 1928.

READ, CONYERS, ed. *The Constitution Reconsidered.* New York: Columbia University Press, 1938.

RIDDELL, WILLIAM RENWICK. *Life of John Graves Simcoe.* Toronto: McClelland and Stewart Ltd., 1926.

RIPPY, JAMES FRED, and DEBO, ANGIE. *The Historical Background of the American Policy of Isolation.* Smith College Studies in History, vol. 9. Northampton, Mass.: Smith College Press, 1924.

ROBERTSON, WILLIAM S. *Life of Miranda.* 2 vols. Chapel Hill: University of North Carolina Press, 1929.

ROOSEVELT, THEODORE. *Gouverneur Morris.* Boston and New York: Houghton Mifflin Co., 1888.

ROSE, JOHN HOLLAND. *William Pitt and the Great War.* London: G. Bell and Sons, 1911.

————. *William Pitt and National Revival.* London: G. Bell and Sons, 1911.

————, NEWTON, A. P., and BEMANS, E. A. *Cambridge History of the British Empire.* Vols. 1 and 2. Cambridge: Cambridge University Press, 1929-40.

ROWLAND, KATE M. *Life of George Mason,' 1725-1792.* 2 vols. New York: G. P. Putnam's Sons, 1892.

RUSSELL, LORD JOHN. *The Life and Times of Charles James Fox.* 3 vols. London: R. Bentley Co., 1859-66.

SCHACHNER, NATHAN. *Alexander Hamilton*. New York: D. Appleton-Century Co., 1946.

———. *Founding Fathers*. New York: G. P. Putnam's Sons, 1954.

———. *Thomas Jefferson*. 2 vols. New York: Appleton-Century-Crofts, 1951.

SCHUYLER, ROBERT LIVINGSTON. *The Fall of the Old Colonial System*. London: Oxford University Press, 1945.

SCOTT, JAMES BROWN. *The Armed Neutralities of 1788-1800*. New York: Oxford Press, 1918.

———. *The United States and France: Some Opinions on International Gratitude*. New York: Oxford University Press, 1926.

SETSER, VERNON G. *The Commercial Reciprocity Policy of the United States, 1774-1829*. Oxford: Oxford University Press, 1937.

SLOCUM, CHARLES ELIHU. *Ohio Country between 1783 and 1815*. New York and London: G. P. Putnam's Sons, 1910.

SMITH, EDGAR F. *Priestly in America, 1794-1804*. Philadelphia: P. Blackiston's Sons, 1920.

SMITH, EDWARD. *England and America after Independence: A Short Examination of Their International Intercourse, 1783-1872*. Westminster: A. Constable & Co., 1900.

SMITH, WALTER BUCKINGHAM, and COLE, ARTHUR HARRISON. *Fluctuations in American Business, 1790-1860*. Cambridge, Mass.: Harvard University Press, 1935.

SPARKS, JARED. *Life of Gouverneur Morris*. 3 vols. Boston: Gray and Bowen, 1832.

SPECTOR, MARGARET MARION. *The American Department of the British Government, 1768-1782*. New York: Columbia University Press, 1940.

STANHOPE, PHILIP HENRY, 5TH EARL OF. *History of Europe, 1713-1783*. 7 vols. London: J. Murray Co., 1853.

———. *The Life of William Pitt*. 4 vols. London: J. Murray Co., 1861-62.

STEVENS, WAYNE EDSON. *Northwestern Fur Trade*. Urbana: University of Illinois Press, 1928.

STONE, WILLIAM LEETE. *Life of Joseph Brant*. 2 vols. Albany, N.Y.: J. Munsell, 1865.

STOURZH, GERALD. *Benjamin Franklin and American Foreign Policy*. Chicago: University of Chicago Press, 1954.

THOMAS, CHARLES MARION. *American Neutrality in 1793: A Study in Cabinet Government*. New York: Columbia University Press, 1931.

THOMAS, ROLAND. *Richard Price*. Oxford and London: Oxford University Press, 1924.

THOMPSON, CHARLES MINER. *Independent Vermont*. Boston: Houghton Mifflin Co., 1942.

TRESCOT, WILLIAM HENRY. *Diplomatic History of the Administrations of Washington and John Adams*. Boston: Little, Brown & Co., 1857.

TURNER, FREDERICK JACKSON. *The Significance of Sections in American History*. New York: H. Holt & Co., 1932.

VAN ALSTYNE, RICHARD WARNER. *American Diplomacy in Action*. Stanford, Calif.: Stanford University Press, 1947.

————. *The Rising American Empire*. Oxford: Oxford University Press, 1960.

VAN DOREN, CARL. *Benjamin Franklin*. New York: Viking Press, 1938.

VAN TYNE, CLAUDE HALSTEAD. *Loyalists in the American Revolution*. New York: Macmillan Co., 1902.

VEITCH, GEORGE STEAD. *The Genesis of Parliamentary Reform*. London: Constable & Co., 1913.

WEEDEN, WILLIAM BABCOCK. *Economic and Social History of New England, 1620-1789*. Boston and New York: Houghton Mifflin and Co., 1890.

WEINBERG, ALBERT K. *Manifest Destiny*. Baltimore: Johns Hopkins Press, 1935.

WHITAKER, ARTHUR P. *The Mississippi Question, 1795-1803*. New York and London: D. Appleton-Century Co., 1934.

————. *Spanish-American Frontier, 1783-1803*. New York: Houghton Mifflin Co., 1934.

WHITE, LEONARD. *The Federalists*. New York: Macmillan Co., 1948.

WILBUR, JAMES BENJAMIN. *Ira Allen, Founder of Vermont*. 2 vols. Boston and New York: Houghton Mifflin Co., 1928.

WILLIAMSON, CHILTON. *Vermont in Quandary*. Montpelier: Vermont Historical Society, 1949.

WILLSON, BECKLES. *America's Ambassadors to England*. London: J. Murray, 1928.

WILSON, PHILLIP WHITWELL. *William Pitt the Younger*. Garden City, New York: Doubleday, Doran & Co., 1932.

WOODBURY, MARGARET. *Public Opinion in Philadelphia, 1789-1801*. Durham, N.C.: Seaman Printery, 1919.

WOOLERY, WILLIAM KIRK. *The Relations of Thomas Jefferson to American Foreign Policy, 1783-93*. Johns Hopkins Studies in History and Political Science, ser. 45, no. 2. Baltimore: Johns Hopkins Press, 1927.

YOSHPE, HENRY B. *The Disposition of Loyalist Estates in the Southern District of the State of New York*. New York: Columbia University Press, 1939.

PERIODICAL LITERATURE

BALDWIN, SIMEON E. "Franklin and the Rule of Free Ships, Free Goods." *Proceedings of the American Antiquarian Society*, vol. 25, pt. 2 (1915), pp. 345-57.

BAMFORD, PAUL WALDEN. "France and the American Market in Naval Timber and Masts, 1776-86." *Journal of Economic History* 12 (1952): 21-34.

BASSET, JOHN S. "The Relation between the Virginian Planter and the London Merchant." *Annual Report of the American Historical Association* 1 (1902): 553-75.

BAXTER, JAMES PHINNEY. "Our First National Shipping Policy." *Proceedings of the United States Naval Institute* 46 (1920): 1251-64.

BELL, HERBERT CLIFFORD. "British Commercial Policy in the West Indies." *English Historical Review* 31 (1916): 429-41.

――――. "The West Indian Trade Before the American Revolution." *American Historical Review* 22 (1917): 272-87.

BEMIS, SAMUEL FLAGG. "Alexander Hamilton and the Limitation of Armaments." *Pacific Review* 2 (1922): 587-602.

――――. "Canada and the Peace Settlement of 1783." *Canadian Historical Review* 14 (1933): 265-84.

――――. "Jay's Treaty and the Northwestern Boundary Gap." *American Historical Review* 27 (1921-22): 465-84.

――――. "The London Mission of Thomas Pinckney, 1792-96." *American Historical Review* 28 (1923): 228-47.

――――. "The United States and the Abortive Armed Neutrality of 1794." *American Historical Review* 24 (1918): 26-47.

BERTRAND, A. "Les États-Unis et la Révolution Française." *Revue des Deux Mondes* 33 (1906): 392-430.

BOWDEN, WITT. "The English Manufacturers and the Commercial Treaty of 1786 with France." *American Historical Review* 25 (1919-20): 18-35.

BOYD, JULIAN P. "The Remarkable Adventures of Stephen Sayre." *Princeton University Library Chronicle* 2 (1941): 51-64.

BRANT, IRVING. "Edmund Randolph, Not Guilty." *William and Mary Quarterly*, 3d ser. 7 (1950): 179-98.

BROWN, GEORGE W. "The Opening of the St. Lawrence to American Shipping." *Canadian Historical Review* 7 (1926): 4-12.

BROWNING, OSCAR. "The Triple Alliance of 1788." *Transactions of the Royal Historical Society* 2 (1885): 77-96.

BURNETT, EDMUND C. "Note on the American Negotiations for Commercial Treaties, 1776-1786." *American Historical Review* 16 (1910-11): 579-87.

BURON, EDMOND. "Statistics on Franco-American Trade, 1778-1806." *Journal of Economic and Business History* 4 (1931-32): 571-80.

BURT, ALFRED LE ROY. "A New Approach to the Problem of the Western Posts." *Annual Report of the Canadian Historical Association*, 1931, pp. 61-75.

COMETTI, ELIZABETH. "John Rutledge, Jr., Federalist." *Journal of Southern History* 13 (1947): 186-219.

COULTER, ELLIS MERTON. "The Efforts of the Democratic Societies of the West to Open the Navigation of the Mississippi." *Mississippi Valley Historical Review* 11 (1924): 376-89.

———. "Elijah Clarke's Foreign Intrigues and the Trans-Oconee Republic." Supplement to the *Mississippi Valley Historical Review*, November 1921, pp. 260-79.

COX, I. J. "The Indians as a Diplomatic Factor in the History of the Old Northwest." *Ohio Archaeological and Historical Quarterly* 18 (1909): 542-65.

DAVIDSON, JOHN. "England's Commercial Policy towards Her Colonies since the Treaty of Paris." *Political Science Quarterly* 14 (1899): 39-68.

DAVIES, WALLACE E. "The Society of the Cincinnati in New England, 1783-1800." *William and Mary Quarterly*, 3d ser. 5 (1948): 3-25.

DUNIWAY, CLYDE A. "French Influence on the Adoption of the Federal Constitution." *American Historical Review* 9 (1904): 304-9.

ELLS, MARGARET. "Settling the Loyalists in Nova Scotia." *Report of the Canadian Historical Association*, 1934, pp. 105-9.

FARRAND, MAX. "The Indian Boundary Line." *American Historical Review* 10 (1904-5): 782-91.

FINGERHUT, EUGENE R. "Uses and Abuses of the American Loyalists' Claims: A Critique of Quantitative Analyses." *William and Mary Quarterly*, 3d ser. 25 (1968): 245-58.

FLETCHER, MILDRED STAHL. "Louisiana as a Factor in French Diplomacy, 1763-1800." *Mississippi Valley Historical Review* 17 (1930): 367-76.

FORD, WORTHINGTON CHAUNCEY. "Edmund Randolph on the British Treaty, 1795." *American Historical Review* 12 (1906-7): 587-99.

GILBERT, FELIX. "The English Background of American Isolationism in the Eighteenth Century." *William and Mary Quarterly*, 3d ser. 1 (1944): 138-60.

———. "The New Diplomacy of the Eighteenth Century." *World Politics* 4 (1951-52): 1-38.

GIPSON, LAWRENCE HENRY. "The American Revolution as an Aftermath of the Great War for the Empire." *Political Science Quarterly* 65 (1950): 86-104.

———. Review of *The Fall of the Old Colonial System*, by Robert Livingston Schuyler. *William and Mary Quarterly*, 3d ser. 2 (1945): 407.

GOTTSCHALK, LOUIS R. "Lafayette as Commercial Expert." *American Historical Review* 36 (1931): 561-70.

GRAHAM, GERALD S. "Maritime Foundations of Imperial History." *Canadian Historical Review* 31 (1950): 113-24.

————. "Migrations of the Nantucket Whale Fishery: An Episode in British Colonial Policy." *New England Quarterly* 8 (1935): 179-202.

GRANT, WILLIAM L. "Pitt's Theory of Empire." *Queen's Quarterly* 16 (1908): 32-43.

HAMER, PHILIP MAY. "The British in Canada and the Southern Indians, 1790-94." *East Tennessee Historical Society Publication* 2 (1930): 107-34.

HANDLIN, OSCAR. "Radicals and Conservatives in Massachusetts." *New England Quarterly* 17 (1944): 343-55.

HENDERSON, ARCHIBALD. "Isaac Shelby and the Genêt Mission." *Mississippi Valley Historical Review* 6 (1920): 451-69.

IRVING, D. D. "The Newfoundland Fishery." *Canadian Historical Review* 13 (1932): 268-84.

JAMES, JAMES ALTON. "French Diplomacy and American Politics, 1794-5." *Annual Report of the American Historical Association* 1 (1913): 151-63.

JENSEN, MERRILL. "Cession of the Old Northwest." *Mississippi Valley Historical Review* 23 (1936-37): 27-48.

KEITH, ALICE B. "Relaxations in the British Restrictions on the American Trade with the British West Indies, 1783-1802." *Journal of Modern History* 20 (1948): 1-18.

KIRKLAND, FREDERICK. "Jefferson and Franklin." *Pennsylvania Magazine of History and Biography* 71 (1947): 218-22.

LAMBERT, ROBERT STANSBURY. "Confiscation of Loyalist Property in Georgia, 1782-1786." *William and Mary Quarterly*, 3d ser. 20 (1963): 80-94.

LATANÉ, JOHN HOLLADY. "Jefferson's Influence on American Foreign Policy." *University of Virginia Alumni Bulletin*, 3d ser. 17 (1924): 245-68.

LEAVITT, ORPHAE. "British Policy on the Canadian Frontier, 1782-92." *Proceedings of the Wisconsin Historical Society*, 1915, pp. 151-85.

LINDSAY, ARNETT G. "Diplomatic Relations between the United States and Great Britain Bearing on the Return of the Negro Slaves, 1793-1828." *Journal of Negro History* 5 (1920): 391-419.

LINGELBACH, ANNA L. "The Inception of the British Board of Trade." *American Historical Review* 30 (1925): 701-27.

LOW, WILLIAM A. "Merchants and Planter Relations in Post-Revolutionary Virginia, 1783-1789." *Virginia Magazine of History and Biography* 61 (1953): 308-19.

MACKINTOSH, W. A. "Canada and Vermont." *Canadian Historical Review* 8 (1927): 9-30.

MCLAUGHLIN, ANDREW C. "The Western Posts and the British Debts."

Annual Report of the American Historical Association, 1894, pp. 413-44.

MAIN, JACKSON T. "Sections and Politics in Virginia, 1781-1787." *William and Mary Quarterly*, 3d ser. 12 (1955): 96-112.

MANNING, WILLIAM RAY. "The Nootka Sound Controversy." *Annual Report of the American Historical Association*, 1904, pp. 363-87.

MASON, ALPHEUS THOMAS. "The Federalists—A Split Personality." *American Historical Review* 57 (1951-52): 625-43.

MILLER, WILLIAM. "First Fruits of Republican Organization." *Pennsylvania Magazine of History and Biography* 63 (1939): 118-43.

MORISON, SAMUEL ELIOT. "Elbridge Gerry, Gentleman-Democrat." *New England Quarterly* 2 (1929): 6-33.

NASATIR, ABRAHAM P. "Anglo-Spanish Rivalry on the Upper Mississippi." *Mississippi Valley Historical Review* 16 (1929-30): 359-82, 507-28.

NEWCOMB, JOSIAH T. "New Light on Jay's Treaty." *American Journal of International Law* 28 (1934): 685-92.

NUSSBAUM, FREDERICK LOUIS. "American Tobacco and French Politics, 1783-89." *Political Science Quarterly* 40 (1925): 497-516.

———. "The French Colonial Arrêt of 1784." *South Atlantic Quarterly* 27 (1928): 62-78.

———. "The Revolutionary Vergennes and Lafayette vs. the Farmers General." *Journal of Modern History* 3 (1931): 592-604.

OGG, FREDERIC AUSTEN. "Jay's Treaty and the Slavery Interests of the United States." *Annual Report of the American Historical Association* 1 (1902): 275-98.

OSGOOD, HOWARD LAWRENCE. "British Evacuation of the United States." *Rochester Historical Society Publication* 6 (1927): 55-63.

PALMER, ROBERT ROSWELL. "A Neglected Work: Otto Vossler on Jefferson and the Revolutionary Era." *William and Mary Quarterly*, 3d ser. 12 (1955): 462-71.

PENSON, LILLIAN MARGERY. "The London West Indies Interest in the Eighteenth Century." *English Historical Review* 36 (1921): 373-92.

PERKINS, BRADFORD. "Lord Hawkesbury and the Jay-Grenville Negotiations." *Mississippi Valley Historical Review* 40 (1953-54): 291-304.

PHILLIPS, ULRICH B. "The South Carolina Federalists." *American Historical Review* 14 (1908-9): 529-43.

PRICE, JACOB M. "The Rise of Glasgow in the Chesapeake Tobacco Trade, 1705-1775." *William and Mary Quarterly*, 3d ser. 11 (1954): 179-99.

RANKIN, ROBERT REAM. "The Treaty of Amity . . . between the United States and Great Britain, 1794." Supplement to *University of California Chronicle* 9, no. 2 (1907): 1-100.

READ, CONYERS. "The English Elements in Benjamin Franklin." *Pennsylvania Magazine of History and Biography* 64 (1940): 314-30.

REES, JAMES F. "The Phases of British Commercial Policy in the Eighteenth Century." *Economica* 14 (1925): 130-50.

REID, DAVID S. "An Analysis of British Parliamentary Opinion on American Affairs at the Close of the War of Independence." *Journal of Modern History* 18 (1946): 202-21.

RICE, HOWARD C. "James Swan, Agent of the French Republic, 1794-1796." *New England Quarterly* 10 (1937): 464-86.

RIDDELL, WILLIAM RENWICK. "Interesting Notes on Great Britain and Canada with Respect to the Negro." *Journal of Negro History* 13 (1928): 185-98.

———. "Settlements of International Disputes by and between English Speaking Nations." *Yale Law Journal* 22 (1913): 845-53, 583-89.

———. "When International Arbitration Failed," *Canadian Law Times* 40 (1920): 351-60.

RITCHESON, CHARLES R. Review of *Number 7: Alexander Hamilton's Secret Attempts to Control American Foreign Policy*, by Julian P. Boyd. *Journal of Southern History* 31 (1965): 202-3.

———. "The London Press and the First Decade of American Independence." *Journal of British Studies* 2 (1963): 88-109.

ROBBINS, CAROLINE. "Thomas Brand Hollis, 1719-1804." *American Philosophical Society Proceedings* 97 (1953): 239-47.

ROSE, J. HOLLAND. "The Franco-British Commercial Treaty of 1786." *English Historical Review* 23 (1908): 709-24.

SAVELLE, MAXWELL. "The Appearance of an American Attitude toward External Affairs, 1750-1775." *American Historical Review* 52 (1946-47): 655-66.

———. "Colonial Origins of American Diplomatic Principles." *Pacific Historical Review* 3 (1934): 334-50.

SCHAPER, WILLIAM A. "Sectionalism in South Carolina." *Report of the American Historical Association*, 1900, pp. 237-463.

SCOTT, JAMES BROWN. "America and the New Diplomacy." *International Conciliation*, no. 16 (1909), pp. 1-12.

SEARS, LOUIS MARTIN. "Thomas Jefferson and the Law of Nations." *American Political Science Review* 13 (1919): 379-99.

SÉE, HENRI. "Commerce Between France and the United States, 1783-84." *American Historical Review* 31 (1926): 732-52.

SMITH, PAUL H. "The American Loyalists: Notes on Their Organization and Numerical Strength." *William and Mary Quarterly*, 3d ser. 25 (1968): 259-77.

TURNER, FREDERICK JACKSON. "Origins of Genêt's Projected Attack on Louisiana and the Floridas." *American Historical Review* 3 (1898): 650-71.

————. "The Diplomatic Contest for the Mississippi." *Atlantic Monthly* 93 (1904): 676-91, 807-17.

————. "The Policy of France Toward the Mississippi Valley in the Period of Washington and Adams," *American Historical Review* 10 (1905): 249-79.

VAN ALSTYNE, RICHARD. "The Significance of the Mississippi Valley in American Diplomatic History, 1686-1890." *Mississippi Valley Historical Review* 36 (1949): 215-38.

VINER, JACOB. "English Theories of Foreign Trade before Adam Smith." *Journal of Political Economy* 38 (1930): 404-57.

WAGNER, DONALD O. "British Economists and the Empire." *Political Science Quarterly* 46 (1931): 248-76.

WARDNER, HENRY STEELE. "The Haldimand Negotiations." *Proceedings of the Vermont Historical Society* 2 (1931): 3-29.

WEAD, EUNICE. "British Public Opinion of the Peace with America, 1782." *American Historical Review* 34 (1929): 513-31.

WEINBERG, ALBERT K. "The Historical Meaning of the American Doctrine of Isolation." *American Political Science Review* 34 (1940): 539-47.

WERNER, RAYMOND C. "War Scare and Politics in 1794." *New York State Historical Association Quarterly Journal* 11 (1930): 324-35.

WILSON, JAMES GRANT. "Judge Bayard and His London Diary, 1795-96." *Proceedings of the New Jersey Historical Society*, 2d ser. 8 (1884): 204-16.

WRIGHT, BENJAMIN FLETCHER, JR. "The *Federalist* on the Nature of Political Man." *Ethics*, vol. 59, no. 2 (1948-49), pt. 2, pp. 1-31.

WRIGHT, LOUIS B. "The Founding Fathers and 'Splendid Isolation.'" *Huntington Library Quarterly* 6 (1942-43): 173-96.

ZOOK, GEORGE F. "Proposals for a New Commercial Treaty between France and the United States, 1778-93." *South Atlantic Quarterly* 8 (1909): 267-83.

INDEX